ANNUAL REVIEW OF PSYCHOLOGY

ANNUAL REVIEW OF PSYCHOLOGY

VOLUME 42, 1991

MARK R. ROSENZWEIG, *Editor*

University of California, Berkeley

LYMAN W. PORTER, *Editor*

University of California, Irvine

ANNUAL REVIEWS INC.   4139 EL CAMINO WAY   P.O. BOX 10139   PALO ALTO, CALIFORNIA 94303-0897

ANNUAL REVIEWS INC.
Palo Alto, California, USA

International Standard Serial Number: 0066–4308
International Standard Book Number: 0–8243–0242-7
Library of Congress Catalog Card Number: 50-13143

∞ The paper used in this publication meets the minimum requirements of American National Standard for Information Sciences—Permanence of Paper for Printed Library Materials, ANSI Z39.48-1984.

Typesetting by Kachina Typesetting Inc., Tempe, Arizona; John Olson, President Typesetting Coordinator, Janis Hoffman

PRINTED AND BOUND IN THE UNITED STATES OF AMERICA

PREFACE

In recent years, each volume of the *Annual Review of Psychology* has featured a combination of chapters that are scheduled on a regular cycle in accordance with the editorial Master Plan and chapters that represent special "timely topics" or are otherwise not directly related to Master Plan categories. Examples of chapters relating to "regularly scheduled" topics this year include "Diagnosis and Assessment" (by Thomas A. Widiger and Timothy J. Trull). "Perception" (by William P. Banks), and "Social Motivation" (by Russell G. Geen). Current chapters that are not a product of the Master Plan include "Behavioral Functioning in Individuals with Mental Retardation" (by Edward Zigler and Robert M. Hodapp), "History of Psychology" (by Ernest R. Hilgard and colleagues), "Motor Skill Acquisition" (by K. M. Newell), "Psychological Perspectives on Nuclear Deterrence" (by Philip E. Tetlock et al), and Music Psychology" (by Carol L. Krumhansl). The Editorial Committee believes that this mix of regular and special topics illustrates the wide breadth of interests and research of scholars in psychology.

Again this year, the prefatory chapter is written by a distinguished senior member of our field: William K. Estes. He focuses on "Cognitive Architectures from the Standpoint of an Experimental Psychologist."

Three members of the Editorial Committee are scheduled to complete their five-year terms in 1991: Albert Bandura, Frances Horowitz, and Auke Tellegen. All have served with distinction and with dedication to the goals of the *Annual Review*. The Committee welcomes its newest member, Don C. Fowles.

Annual Review of Psychology
Volume 42 (1991)

CONTENTS

RELATED ARTICLES OF INTEREST TO READERS

From the *Annual Review of Anthropology*, Volume 19 (1990)

Language and Affect, N. Besnier
The Built Environment and Spatial Form, D. L. Lawrence and S. M. Low

From the *Annual Review of Medicine*, Volume 42 (1991)

Epidemiology and Outcome of Child Abuse, D. A. Rosenberg and R. D. Krugman
Organic Bases of Depression in the Elderly, K. R. R. Krishnan
Hypothalamic-Pituitary-Adrenal Axis in Psychiatric Disorders, P. E. Stokes and
  C. R. Sikes
Genetics of Major Affective Disorders, R. D. Ciaranello and A. L. Ciaranello
Management of the Alcohol Withdrawal Syndrome, M. K. Romach and
  E. M. Sellers

From the *Annual Review of Neuroscience*, Volume 13 (1990)

*Perceptual Neural Organization: Some Approaches Based on Network Models and
  Information Theory*, R. Linsker
Biological Foundations of Language: Clues from Sign Language, H. Posner,
  U. Bellugi, and E. S. Klima
Neurotransmitters in the Mammalian Circadian System, B. Rusak, K. G. Bina
Do Insects Have Cognitive Maps?, R. Wehner, R. Menzel
The Attention System of the Human Brain, M. I. Posner and S. E. Petersen

From the *Annual Review of Public Health*, Volume 12 (1991)

Recent Developments in Mental Health Perspectives and Services, D. Mechanic

From the *Annual Review of Sociology*, Volume 16 (1990)

*Concepts of the Life Cycle: Their History, Meanings, and Uses in the Social
  Sciences*, A. O'Rand and M. L. Krecker
Deinstitutionalization: An Appraisal of Reform, D. Mechanic and D. A. Rochefort

ANNUAL REVIEWS INC. is a nonprofit scientific publisher established to promote the advancement of the sciences. Beginning in 1932 with the *Annual Review of Biochemistry,* the Company has pursued as its principal function the publication of high quality, reasonably priced *Annual Review* volumes. The volumes are organized by Editors and Editorial Committees who invite qualified authors to contribute critical articles reviewing significant developments within each major discipline. The Editor-in-Chief invites those interested in serving as future Editorial Committee members to communicate directly with him. Annual Reviews Inc. is administered by a Board of Directors, whose members serve without compensation.

For the convenience of readers, a detachable order form/envelope is bound into the back of this volume.

Annu. Rev. Psychol. 1991. 42:1–28

COGNITIVE ARCHITECTURES FROM THE STANDPOINT OF AN EXPERIMENTAL PSYCHOLOGIST

W. K. Estes

Department of Psychology, Harvard University, Cambridge, Massachusetts 02138

KEY WORDS: connectionist models, distributed memory, category learning, memory format, memory traces and associations

CONTENTS

INTRODUCTION

At times the concept of an architecture seems to me entirely too grand for psychology at the present stage of theory development. But at other times, it seems that I have been seeking an appropriate architecture for cognition

1

0066-4308/91/0201-0001$02.00

during the whole half century of my professional life. When I entered research in psychology in the 1940s, the term architecture was not in use, but there was much concern with the problem of establishing a suitable framework for theories in the broad area now termed cognition. The nature of the proper framework seemed obvious.

> Since propositions concerning psychological events are verifiable only to the extent that they are reducible to predictions of behavior under specified environmental conditions, it appears likely that greatest economy and consistency in theoretical structure will result from statement of all fundamental laws in the form R = f(S), where R and S represent behavioral and environmental variables, respectively. (Estes 1950:94)

My, such confidence. Could any future turn of events overturn the insight that the stimulus-response architecture is basic to, and indeed sufficient for, psychological theory? Such a turn of events was, in fact, not far in the future. During the next decade and a half, the focus of my research moved from animal learning and conditioning to human visual processing and short-term memory, and it is remarkable what a shift of research interest can do for one's theoretical outlook.

> [T]he type of theory to which we are evidently being led by a wide range of current experimental developments differs in a number of major respects from classical association and stimulus-response theories. There is now a large amount of detailed and extensive evidence which indicates that theoretical interpretations will gain more than they will lose in the way of parsimony by accentuating and sharpening the distinction between the processes of learning and response selection. A striking simplification in the interpretation of many learning phenomena is achieved at a stroke if we conceive the result of an organism's experiencing a sequence of events to be, not simply the strengthening or weakening of the constituent stimulus-response connections, but rather the establishment in memory storage of a *representation* of the entire sequence . . . (Estes 1969:185–86, Ital. added)

That passage appeared at a time when I had one hand still in conditioning research while the other was working in information processing. But it wasn't long before both hands were at work together in the new framework.

> Just as the physical sciences can be conceived as the study of energy in its many aspects, the behavioral and social sciences can be characterized in terms of their concern with the processing and transformation of information. The adaptation of living organisms to an ever-changing environment depends upon the ability to acquire information about environmental regularities and to use this information as the basis of adaptive response. (Estes 1975b:1)

From that time on, although learning continued to be one of my central research interests, I viewed it, not as a simple mechanism for strengthening and weakening response tendencies, but as a collection of processes responsible for the building and elaborating of memory structures. I and others who bridged the gap between the old and newer paradigms faced the task of discovering how to replace the comfortable but now clearly inadequate stimulus-response framework with a framework, or architecture, capable of accommodating the variety of models flourishing in the broad domain of information processing.

TOWARD A COGNITIVE ARCHITECTURE

The concept of cognitive architecture has at present no generally accepted definition and can only be understood by observing it in use. The concept was imported into the cognitive literature from computer science, and not only its meaning but also its applicability in the new context is unsettled.

In computer science, architecture refers to the general characteristics of a computer that make programming possible. By far the most familiar version is the von Neumann architecture, the basis of virtually all digital computers. In this architecture, informational units, the physical embodiments of strings of binary digits, are stored in locations that can be accessed either by their addresses or their contents. The machine carries out its computations by sequencing through the stored items and, in effect, applying operators such as comparison or logical combination. The informational units take on meaning by virtue of their correspondence to familiar symbols like numbers, letters, or mathematical operators. Thus, in artificial intelligence, the programming languages that enable computers to manifest human-like cognitive functions can be characterized as symbol processors.

In view of the many similarities between the computer and the human being, viewed as information processing systems, which have done much to spark the development first of artificial intelligence and then of cognitive science, it has seemed to many investigators that the symbol-processing architecture should carry over from one realm to the other. For cognitive science, the architecture would characterize the set of informational (as distinguished from neural) structures and symbol-manipulating processing that underlies all of the specific cognitive models and theories. This expectation has in fact been realized for some subdomains of cognition—for example, problem solving (Newell & Simon 1972). In other subdomains, however, popular lines of research of the 1970s demanded concepts like spreading activation (Collins & Loftus 1975) and automatization (Schneider & Shiffrin 1977) that seemed quite out of the spirit of the symbol-processing architecture.

How, then, are we to arrive at a satisfactory characterization of a general cognitive architecture? I can see two possible routes, one direct and the other indirect. The direct route is for some individual investigator, or possibly group of investigators, to develop and present a proposed architecture, just as is routinely done for more limited theories. Recently there have been several major proposals of this sort. One of these is the Adaptive Control of Thought (ACT*) architecture of Anderson (1983), another the State, Operator, and Result (SOAR) architecture of Newell and his associates (Laird et al 1987; Newell 1990). Perhaps prematurely, some would include in this category a new contender, the parallel, distributed processing (PDP) or "connectionist" architecture (McClelland & Rumelhart 1986; Rumelhart & McClelland 1986a).

A difficulty with the direct approach is that formulating a whole architecture is an enterprise of such complexity that the large number of decisions about details must reflect the preferences and biases of the formulator, and the product is very difficult to evaluate. Unlike the situation with experimental investigation and limited theory construction, we have no stock of tested methods for the construction of whole architectures, nor generally accepted standards for accessing their merits. As pertinent evidence, consider that Anderson's deservedly influential architecture has run through some half dozen versions in a short period of years (Anderson 1976, 1983), the shifts often unaccompanied by any empirical developments that appear compelling to an outside observer.

The alternative I see to the direct approach is an indirect one based on the idea that if cognitive theory has any general architecture, it must have evolved over the last century of research on cognition. If so, then the architecture should be discoverable by adapting the standard methods of scientific investigation, that is, by tracing the development of the lines of theory that have been influential over the century, examining their similarities and differences, and discovering whether there are commonalities of structure general enough to qualify as the basis of an architecture. Whether this inductive approach will work is an open question, of course, and I expect this essay to accomplish no more than to provide an illustration that may set the stage for discussion.

In this chapter, I sketch the evolution of the notion of a cognitive architecture over the last half century from my own standpoint as an observer and participant; I conclude with a discussion of current issues and prospects. My interest in what may seem to be an esoteric concept derives from its relevance to my longtime concern with the problem of comparing and testing mathematical and computer models in psychology (Estes 1975a, 1986a). Verbally formulated theories are notoriously difficult to test because of the inadequacy of verbal arguments for deriving their implications or even for ascertaining when the implications of two such theories differ. But the problem does not automatically vanish when theories are cast as mathematical or computer simulation models, for superficial differences can mask basic commonalities. The task of determining when apparent differences between theories are testable requires their examination within a common framework, and for theories of cognition this common framework would be the cognitive architecture.

A salient aspect of my personal history is the corresponding of shifts in ideas about architecture with shifts in loci of research activity. If we regard a research domain—for example, cognition—as a collection of different kinds of experimental subdomains, theory construction is relatively straightforward. We choose for any given subdomain the concepts that prove most serviceable for its interpretation, thus generating what may be termed local architectures (see Table 1).

However, suppose we take our task to be, not interpreting various clusters of experiments, but interpreting the cognizing organism? Then the experimental clusters are just the results of looking at the organism from different perspectives, and we need some way to fit the interpretations of them together in a more comprehensive structure. The question then arises whether as ambitious a goal as Newell's "general cognitive architecture" (Newell 1990) is a feasible target. We cannot foresee whether achieving such a goal is possible, but continuing pursuit of that goal may nonetheless be the best way to ensure that cognitive science will achieve some generality of theory in spite of the enormous complexities of its subject matter and the pressures to settle for heuristic principles and local models.

MEMORY FORMAT: ASSOCIATION OR TRACE

One essential constituent of a cognitive architecture is a specification of the form of information storage in memory. Two more or less parallel approaches to this problem have run through the history of memory theory, one centered in the tradition of association theory and the other in the concept of a memory trace. Though its roots are traceable to the British associationists James Mill and David Hume, the concept of association was given its first formulation as a theoretical principle with experimental interpretations by Ebbinghaus (1964

Table 1 Local architectures for subdomains of cognitive research

Subdomain	Local architecture
conditioning	stimulus-response
language	rules, semantic nets
classification	array structures
short-term memory	list structures
perception	multidimensional space
knowledge acquisition	propositional networks
problem solving	problem spaces, production systems

[1885]); its continuing elaboration over the next several decades was thoroughly reviewed by Robinson (1932). The central idea was that any form of memorization results in the laying down of associations between units, with the property that if an association is formed between units A and B, then later activation of A tends to lead to reactivation of B. For the earlier associationists, the units were vaguely defined ideas; for Ebbinghaus, they were mental representations of the elements, usually words or nonsense syllables, of the lists he so laboriously studied. Learning consists, not in modifying the units, but only of establishing associations between units.

Almost coextensive with association theory has been the development of models of memory based on the concept of a memory trace, or engram, the modern version dating from the work of Hollingworth (1913, 1928) and Semon (1921). In this tradition, it is assumed that any learning experience results in the deposit of a trace in the memory system. Whatever is perceived may enter into the trace, which typically takes the form of a sensory image. Perceived or learned relationships among objects or events are embodied in the trace itself, rather than in associations among units. Memory traces give rise to reconstruction or recall of an experience by virtue of the process of *redintegration*, whereby later perception of some portion of the stimulus pattern comprising a trace leads to reactivation of the entire pattern, as when a glimpse of some portion of a familiar face or scene gives rise to an image of the whole.

As a preliminary to examining architectural properties of current models, I give a brief sketch of each of these lines of theory, organized in terms of some salient theoretical attributes.

Association Theory

On the whole, there has been remarkably little change in the structural assumptions of association theory over the last century. Ebbinghaus's formulation was based on a single layer of interconnected associative units. Following study of a list of items, A, B, C, D, and E, in order (the capital letters denoting any type of item), direct pairwise associations would be established between a starting signal and A, between A and B, between B and C, and so on, providing the basis for subsequent recall of the whole list on presentation of the starting signal. This structure would be fragile, however, for if the connection between A and B were impaired, the remainder of the list would be unrecallable. For this reason and others, Ebbinghaus admitted also indirect associations between items such as A and C or A and D that were not contiguous during study. The indirect associations are typically weaker than the direct ones, but they produce a structure that is less fragile in the face of possible interfering factors.

As research on simple learning, both human and animal, progressed over several decades, it became apparent that the simple association model could not explain why learning sometimes occurs on an all-or-none basis but sometimes requires many repetitions of an experience or why temporal spacing of learning experiences is a critical factor in retention. The remedy I proposed in my first contribution to learning theory was to introduce a layer of abstract units (originally termed "stimulus elements," later "memory elements") that were interposed between stimuli and responses; on a learning trial, a sample of these units, corresponding to the stimulus aspects attended to by the learner, could become associated with the correct ("reinforced") response category (Estes 1950). Also, the units were assumed to fluctuate in level of availability over time, providing a mechanism to account for temporal aspects of learning and retention (Estes 1955).

The minimal structural assumptions of classical association and stimulus sampling models seemed satisfactory in an age of high concern for parsimony and operationism but offered few resources for addressing problems of organization in memory. This limitation came to be felt acutely when list and paired-associate memorization were replaced by free recall as the experimental paradigm of choice for studies of verbal learning in the 1950s. In a standard free recall study, a subject hears or reads a list of words, presented singly, then attempts to recall the words in any order. Typically there proves to be little correlation between presentation order and recall order; rather, words tend to be clustered in recall, with semantically related words tending to occur adjacently in recall regardless of their input positions (Bousfield 1953). This observation gave rise to the idea that associative links may fan out from a studied word to a number of others semantically related to it, allowing growth of a hierarchical structure of the kind illustrated in Figure 1 (Mandler 1967); then recall can be effected by proceeding from the topmost node of the hierarchy downward, reading out the cluster of words associated with each lower-order node as it is encountered. The topmost node may be viewed as corresponding to a representation of the list as a unit (hence the common designation *list marker*), the next level of nodes to category labels, especially if category labels are supplied by the experimenter prior to recall, and the nodes at lower levels to members of categories. However, these identifications are not essential to the concept of a hierarchical structure, and the upper level nodes may be regarded as abstract constituents of the structure, *control elements* in the general hierarchical model of Estes (1972a), that serve an organizational function but have no specific empirical referents.

This notion of a hierarchical memory structure has been widely extended simply by redefining the types of units that correspond to the nodes at various levels. Thus, for the purpose of representing the mental lexicon—that is, an individual's long-term memory for vocabulary—the nodes are taken to correspond to words and semantic categories (Collins & Quillian 1972); for the

INPUT LIST   **HIERARCHICAL ORGANIZATION**

iron
animal
bird
pike
helium
wren
gold
metal
element
fish
canary
gas

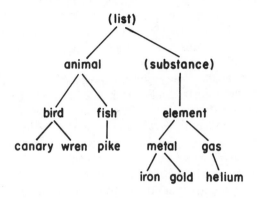

SAM NETWORK

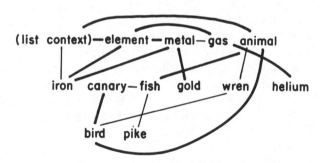

Figure 1 Memory for a list of words presented in a hypothetical free-recall experiment is represented in hierarchical and nonhierarchical network structures. Widths of lines in the SAM diagram signify strengths of associative connections (presumably deriving from different degrees of familiarity in the learner's experience).

interpretation of factual memory, the nodes are taken to correspond to concepts (Anderson & Bower 1973) or to propositions (Anderson 1976, 1983).

The Search of Associative Memory (SAM) model of Raaijmakers & Shiffrin (1981) is perhaps the most general current representative of association theory and has certainly yielded the most detailed interpretations of a wide variety of phenomena of recall and recognition (Clark & Shiffrin 1987; Gillund & Shiffrin 1984; Gronlund & Shiffrin 1986); Shiffrin et al 1989). On first encounter, the SAM model seems much more elaborate than any of its predecessors. The elaboration has, however, occurred largely through the augmentation of the classical scheme by a variety of control processes, with little actual change in the basic structure. In the free recall example, each word studied is represented by a node in a memory network, with connections between those representing words that were adjacent in the input list or that were rehearsed together during study. As shown in the lower part of Figure 1, the network resembles the hierarchical structure except that superordinate-subordinate relationships are not immediately apparent. However, in the SAM network, associations differ in strength (shown by light and heavy lines in the figures), and the stronger associations would be expected to be generally the same as those represented in the hierarchy. Thus, it appears that the differences between the hierarchical model and SAM are at the level of process other than at the level of structure.

This analysis suggests a distinction between the features common to all associative models, which may reasonably be taken to comprise the architecture, and the features that distinguish among them. All associative models are based on networks of nodes and associative links, the products of learning being the establishment of links or the strengthening of already established ones. The nodes are units whose function is to enter into associations; they may be classified according to the kinds of objects they correspond to in empirical interpretations, but they are opaque in that there is no direct access to their internal structures. In SAM, the units are referred to as images and described as containing clusters of information. In actual implementations of the model, however, the information contained in an image is manifest only in the probabilities of evocation of the responses, usually words, associated with it.

Trace Theory

TRACE MODELS FOR MEMORIZATION   In the second main type of memory theory, the product of a learning experience is the laying down of a memory trace, the information accrued being represented in the trace itself rather than in connections among traces. The beginnings of formalization of the concept appeared when Hollingworth (1913) added the notions of a threshold and of strength, or degree of familiarity, of a trace, which varied with repetition and recency of activation. In Hollingworth's version, a percept that activated a stored trace with a strength falling above the threshold would be recognized as "old"—that is, as representing a previously experienced pattern of objects or events—whereas a strength falling below the threshold would yield nonrecognition. Except for some refinements contributed by the importation of signal detectability theory (Murdock 1974), the threshold model has served as the canonical interpretation of recognition down to the present.

The concept of a memory trace was important in gestalt psychology (Koffka 1935), the main new assumption being that a trace is not a static representation but rather one that changes autonomously over time in the direction of better conformity to gestalt laws of symmetry, "good figure," and the like. Attempts to adduce experimental support for autonomous processes yielded mixed results, however, and the concept has remained a bypath in the evolution of present-day memory theory.

The next major development in trace theory was the introduction of the idea that information is stored in a trace in the form of values on a set of attributes or dimensions. This concept was formalized by Bower (1967) in his model based on a multicomponent memory trace; with a strong boost from an influential article by Underwood (1969), it quickly became the standard interpretation. Now a memory trace was conceived as a vector, or list, of features, each representing a value on an attribute or dimension (usually, but not necessarily, binary). Important assumptions in Bower's version were that features could fluctuate in level of availability over time in the manner of stimulus sampling theory (Estes 1955) and could be independently lost as a consequence of factors responsible for forgetting. Bower showed that trace theory, so elaborated, could yield quantitative accounts of numerous phenomena of recognition and simple verbal learning and forgetting.

RELATIONAL INFORMATION IN TRACE MODELS   An important limitation of the multicomponent trace model, as of stimulus sampling models, was the lack of any principled way of handling relational information. An adequate theory must be able to account for the fact that both human learners and higher animals readily discriminate between patterns and their components. It is trivial, for example, to remember that the number of the hotel room one has checked into is 49 even though there are rooms 4 and 9 on the same floor assigned to other people, but an unelaborated multitrace model would have to predict interference. This problem was a focus of interest for members of my Mathematical Psychology Laboratory at Rockefeller University in the 1970s. It was one of our group, Douglas Medin, who came up with the insight that sensitivity to relations among elements of a pattern need not be based on the storage of some kind of special relational information (as relational features) in the memory trace but may, rather, emerge in the computations performed when perceived patterns are compared to stored representations. In the discrimination model he formulated, features, or attributes, of a stimulus are stored in a multicomponent trace, and the process for accessing stored representations is a computation of a multiplicative measure of the similarity of a perceived stimulus pattern to each member of the relevant memory array (Medin 1975). Any decision called for on the part of the learner is based on these similarity measures, and because of the multiplicative character of the similarity function, discrimination of patterns from their components can occur automatically. The simple but powerful idea that access to stored memories is achieved by a computation based on similarity between perceived and stored patterns is embodied in many contemporary theories, among them the "resonance" model of Ratcliff (1978) and the "Minerva II" simulation model of Hintzman (1986). The outcome of many decades of evolution of trace theory seems, then, to be a schema based on the storage of multi-component memory vectors in partitioned arrays accessible via similarity computations—evidently as deserving of the appellation "architecture" as the general schema of association theory.

A Common Architecture for Trace and Association

Have we at this point arrived at two architectures, one for association and one for trace theory? I surmise that actually they are homologous, the familiar networks and hierarchical structures of current association theory being just graphical depictions of relationships among percepts and memories that are common to both kinds of theory. For a simple illustration of the correspondence, consider the memorization of a list of words W1, W2, W3, . . . Wn. In an associative model the memory structure formed could be depicted as

$$S' - W1' - W2' - W3' - \ldots -Wn',$$

the units corresponding to the starting context, S, and the words of the list. In a trace model the corresponding structure would be a list of vectors whose elements are the units of the associative structure.

(S' W1')
(W1' W2')
(W2' W3')
.
.
.
(Wn−1' Wn').

Now the starting context, S, being most similar to the first trace, would have the highest probability of reactivating it when presented, and therefore of producing recall of W1; the result of recalling W1 would similarly be most likely to activate the trace including W1', and so on. A similar analysis has been presented by Greeno et al (1978). If the associative scheme were interpreted as a particular application of the SAM model and the trace structure as a particular application of the exemplar-memory model, even the formulas for response probability would be identical in form, one entering sums and ratios of associative strengths and the other sums and ratios of similarities, both in the manner of Luce's (1963) choice model. The exemplar trace model may be viewed as a special case of the SAM model in which associative strengths are constrained to be values on a similarity dimension. The set of structural properties common to association and trace models I henceforth refer to, for brevity, as the *array* architecture.

Some psychological models that appear very different in form from those reviewed above may nonetheless be shown to share the same architecture. An important case is the class of geometric models of memory (Cunningham & Shepard 1974; Hutchinson & Lockhead 1977). These first appeared in the semantic memory literature just when hierarchical network models were approaching their peak of popularity. The geometric models did not receive wide attention, perhaps in part because their applications were largely limited to studies of similarity judgments in the tradition of psychophysical scaling. Following the scaling approach, Hutchinson & Lockhead (1977) showed that words could be assigned to positions in a multidimensional space, consistently across different methods of collecting similarity data, and that reaction times for discriminations between words were directly related to distances between them. Their results suggested that priming effects, a cornerstone of the network models, were readily interpretable in the metric framework.

The geometric model is useful in bringing out relationships between phenomena of semantic memory and psychophysics that would not otherwise be apparent, whether or not it exemplifies a unique architecture. Hutchinson & Lockhead offered, without a proof, the conjecture that it is actually isomorphic to feature and network models. It is not obvious that these classes of models are well enough defined to make a general proof possible, but Nosofsky (1984) has shown that the isomorphism does hold for models of categorization and identification formulated in the array framework. Building on earlier work of Shepard (1958), Nosofsky showed that with similarity between memory vectors in an array related to distance between corresponding points in a cognitive space by an exponential function, an exemplar-memory model is equivalent to a geometric model. The correspondence is not unique, for a particular array model can be mapped onto different geometric models based on different metrics, but it does seem clear that geometric models need not be considered to assume a different architecture from that of array models.

Summary of the Array Architecture

What is common to all of the models that I have subsumed under the array architecture? A central assumption is that memory of any experience with objects or events can be stored in the form of a multicomponent trace, the components being features or values on attributes or dimensions. (I use the latter two terms interchangeably.) These traces can be viewed as vectors or lists, as nodes in a network, or as points in a multidimensional space. When any one trace is activated, most commonly by occurrence of an appropriate percept (i.e. one with the same feature values or a subset of them), it may in turn activate others. The tendency for this activation to occur is interpretable as a similarity relation between traces, as strength of an associative link, or as distance in a cognitive space. A measure of strength of activation in any one of these interpretations can be converted into any of the others by a simple transformation, so they are not empirically distinguishable. Again, a memory array can be partitioned into subarrays corresponding to categories; a network or cognitive space can be similarly divided into regions.

Nearly all cognitive theories now make a distinction between long-term memory and short-term, or working, memory. The former is conceived to be of indefinitely large capacity but slow access, the latter of sharply limited capacity and rapid access, and also subject to cognitive operations like comparison and counting. It does not seem that this distinction need be built into the architecture, however. In the array framework, for example, we need only assume that the temporal-spatial context of a learning experience is represented in the memory trace but decays in availability as a function of time following the experience.

COMPOSITE DISTRIBUTED MEMORY

In array models, an encoded memory trace is conceived to be stored in a distinct, content-addressable location and to preserve its identity, so that it is meaningful to speak of carrying out cognitive operations on individual traces. In contrast, distributed memory models, which began to appear in the early 1970s, are based on an architecture in which the individual identity of a trace is lost. Typically, a percept is encoded as a vector of feature values, as in an array model; however, the vector is not stored in a memory location, but is, rather, added into a composite trace that represents cumulative memory. In the model of Anderson (1973), successively encoded vectors are literally added (by matrix addition). Thus, if two successive learning experiences were encoded as $(1,-1,-1,1)$ and $(1,1,-1,-1)$, the composite memory for these experiences would be $(2,0,-2,0)$. If the vectors are orthogonal (roughly speaking, if their components are uncorrelated), the evocation of a percept corresponding to any one of the traces on a later test will revive that trace, providing a basis for recognition. Technically, a test vector, say $(1,1,-1,-1)$, is applied to the composite memory vector by a form of matrix multiplication, and the product, multiplied by a scalar if appropriate, is the same as the test vector. If the vectors are large, then this result may be obtained to a good approximation even if there are departures from orthogonality. Thus, in general, the result of a recognition test is not revival of a particular stored trace, but, rather, generation of a vector similar to one or more stored traces. A model with a very similar mathematical structure has been formulated and applied to recall as well as recognition by Pike (1984).

A distributed memory model that has been progressively elaborated and applied to many different types of situations is the theory of distributed associative memory (TODAM) of Murdock and his associates (Murdock 1979, 1982; Murdock & Hockley 1989) and a closely related composite holographic associative recall model, CHARM (Eich 1982; Metcalfe & Fisher 1986). These models differ from those of Anderson (1973) and Pike (1984) in using some different mathematical operations. To enter new vectors into the composite memory, they employ *convolution,* a combination of addition and multiplication, and to obtain information from the composite memory, *correlation,* the inverse of convolution.

Two questions immediately come to mind regarding a proposed architecture requiring a mathematical formalism and methods so different from those familiar to psychologists in the tradition of trace and association theory: What suggested this novel architecture, and how is it faring in current memory theory? The prime answer to the first question appears to lie in the intuition of some investigators that a distributed, composite memory has properties much more congenial to what is known about the brain than those of traditional theories (Anderson 1973; Anderson et al 1977). Brain function is conspicuous for redundancy, tolerance of noise, and resistance to disturbance from localized damage—all properties that seem out of keeping with localized storage of discrete memory traces. Also, trace and association theories that had appeared prior to about 1970 had been so austerely simple in structure that they seemed to offer little prospect of helping to interrelate and integrate research in different paradigms, such as recognition, recall, and classification. In its continuing development, the family of composite memory models has shown enough promise in this respect to present an interesting alternative to the quite different lines of elaboration of classical association theory by Anderson & Bower (1973), Estes (1972a), and Raaijmakers & Shiffrin (1981).

The typically impatient psychologist is likely to ask at this point why, in the course of a decade or so of research, no one has carried out an experimental test to determine which type of model is superior. Such tests have been attempted, but none has yielded a decision, and I suspect that none is likely to. Still, it is possible to say something about evaluation. In the hands of their proponents, the composite models appear to be serving about as well as array models for instigating instructive experiments and bringing out theoretically interesting relationships among different empirical domains (Eich 1982; Metcalfe & Fisher 1986; Murdock & Lamon 1988; Murdock 1989). The latter function is illustrated by the fact that Murdock's convolution model has been shown to imply a formal relationship between recall and recognition (Murdock 1989; Murdock & Hockley 1989) comparable in parsimony and elegance to those that have been derived by Gillund & Shiffrin (1984), for example, for the SAM model and by Nosofsky (1986, 1988) for the exemplar-memory model.

THE CONNECTIONIST ARCHITECTURE

Perhaps the only reason why the composite models developed by Metcalfe-Eich and Murdock are not more widely influential than they currently appear to be is that they have been overshadowed somewhat by the sudden flowering of what are termed *connectionist,* or *parallel-distributed-processing* (PDP) models, a family sharing some architectural features with the convolution models but stemming from quite different origins. The basic elements of connectionist models are nodes and links, as in association models. The nodes are, however, simple, homogeneous units that do not, individually, correspond to external referents; their only properties are levels of activity and the capability of transmitting activation over the links between nodes. A connectionist network comprises two or more layers of nodes, typically a lowest level, in which nodes are activated by inputs from perceptual channels, a highest level, in which nodes receive activation from lower levels and in turn activate response mechanisms, and one or more intermediate levels of "hidden units," which receive input from lower levels and transmit it upward. Each link between nodes has an associated weight, which determines the strength of transmission over it, and memory resides wholly in the pattern of weights, which is modified ("updated") by the inputs to the network on each learning experience. The richness of the architecture is greatly amplified by the hidden units, which have no direct correspondence to input or output nodes but in the course of learning may come to act as feature detectors or classifiers.

Immediate precursors of the current wave of connectionist activity in cognitive science include PDP network models of visual processing (Ballard et al 1983; Marr 1982), mathematical investigations of feature detection and classification in adaptive networks (Grossberg 1976), and development of an "interactive activation" network model of processes in reading (McClelland & Rumelhart 1981). Some unity was brought to a heterogeneous collection of theoretical developments by the imagination and initiative of two leaders of the movement within psychology in assembling a two-volume handbook, including both summary and tutorial presentations of the formal concepts and methods of connectionism and a sampling of applications of PDP models to several cognitive domains (McClelland & Rumelhart 1986; Rumelhart & McClelland 1986a).

The special relevance of connectionist models to my long-term research interests and to this essay is that they have offered the promise of rescuing learning theory from its near eclipse during several decades in which cognitive research has been dominated by concern with problems of information-processing, representation in memory, and cognitive operations. Whether we look at research and theory on short-term memory, semantic memory, propositional networks, or even the earlier distributed memory models, we see almost no efforts to interpret in any detail the processes whereby information comes to be stored in memory. The connectionist movement, in contrast, brings a new emphasis on learning. In traditional information-processing models, mechanisms like feature detectors are laid down as part of the architecture; items of information from input channels are deposited in memory buffers or stores to await retrieval; motives and goals may be important in the minds of the investigators, but they receive no explicit representation in the models. In connectionist models, feature detectors are generated from initially "blind and dumb" nodes and links; items of input information gain memorial representation by a process of weight adjustment; the capacity to recognize and classify perceptual patterns develops by means of a learning process that is driven by an overall tendency toward error correction. An "error," in this context, is a discrepancy between the current output ("response") of a network and a target, or goal, specified by a *teaching signal,* which may be either supplied by the environment or (a critically important property) internally generated. Thus, in the connectionist approach, learning is not viewed as a subsidiary problem to be left for consideration after the big problems are taken care of, but, rather, is a major aspect of the cognitive system from the start. For an investigator who grew up scientifically in the golden age of learning theory, this renewed emphasis on learning is a welcome development.

We have recently seen an abundance of discussions of general properties of learning in connectionist networks and similar architectures (Grossberg 1987; Hinton & Sejnowski 1986; Rumelhart & Zipser 1986; Rumelhart et al 1986; Stone 1986). As a complement to these, I wish to compare detailed properties of representatives of the network and array model families as developed and applied in a particular line of research, namely human category learning.

A COMPARISON OF MODELS FOR CATEGORY LEARNING

Category Learning in Array Models

Research on the learning of categories has followed two main strands. Historically prior was what Smith & Medin (1981) called the "classical approach," dealing with learning of categories that are sharply delimited by necessary and sufficient properties and definable in terms of simple verbal rules, like those of formal school subjects like geometry and grammar. In the information-processing approach dating from Hovland (1952), the standard experimental task is classifying multidimensional stimulus patterns into categories defined in terms of logical combinations of attributes, the prime research question being how task difficulty is related to complexity of the logical rules (Bourne 1970; Hunt 1962; Shepard et al 1961). The body of theory generated in this tradition took the form of hypothesis-testing models (Hunt 1962; Trabasso & Bower 1968). Thus the main focus was on performance, perhaps the reason why work in this tradition dwindled as the center of interest for cognitive psychologists shifted during the 1970s from problems of performance to problems of representation in memory.

In the other principal strand of research on concept learning, research is addressed to acquisition and representation of what may be termed "fuzzy sets," that is, categories that do not have sharp boundaries and are best definable in terms of family resemblance or probability distributions. This approach was a center of attention for me and my associates from the mid 1950s because it provided an ideal research context for the testing and development of models based on stimulus sampling theory (Estes 1950). The favorite experimental paradigm of that period is very similar to some that are popular today, though the connection has generally been missed by writers of introductions to research articles, perhaps largely because the vocabulary used to describe it has changed. Studies that would now be characterized in terms of classification or categorization were reported in the earlier period under the label "discrimination learning," a term now almost wholly confined to the animal learning literature.

In a typical study of that period (Estes et al 1957), subjects viewed a display panel containing a row of 12 light bulbs. They were instructed, in effect, that on each of a series of trials some subset of the lights would be illuminated and that they should try to assign it to one of two alternative categories. Correct assignment would be indicated by a feedback signal. Different probability distributions defined over the display positions determined the samples of lights drawn for the two categories. The collections of samples that occurred on the two types of trials would be termed fuzzy sets in modern parlance. The stimulus sampling model that the study was intended to test predicted quite accurately the asymptotic proportions of correct responses for groups that learned with different category base rates as well as transfer performance on tests given at the end of the learning series with subsets of lights not previously seen.

The conditions of the 1957 study differed from those characteristic of related current work in that the populations of stimulus patterns associated with the categories were very large, so that individual patterns would rarely have recurred even during a learning series of several hundred trials. It occurred to me that the success of the stimulus sampling model might have been peculiar to that constraint, so I carried out several followups with similar designs but much smaller population sizes (and, in tune with the changing tenor of the times, a change from meaningless signal lights to symbols for medical symptoms, or the like, as the component features of category ex-amplars). The result was that the model in its original form broke down and could be brought into accord with the new data only with the added assump-tion that repeated experience with individual subsets of features led to the patterns' being encoded as units (Atkinson & Estes 1963; Estes 1972b; Estes & Hopkins 1961). It was apparent that the stimulus sampling model was not rich enough in structure to provide a satisfactory linkage between the two distinct versions needed to handle learning with large and small categories. It was not so apparent how to mend matters.

The next step forward needed a fresh viewpoint, and one was finally supplied by the extension of the discrimination model of Medin (1975) to the interpretation of human category learning (Medin & Schaffer 1978).

Although preserving some of the basic ideas of stimulus sampling theory, Medin & Schaffer's model presented a distinctly new look. The subject in a category learning experiment was assumed, not to associate individual cues with responses, but rather to store in memory on each learning trial a featural representation of the perceived exemplar together with its category tag. When asked to assign a pattern to a category, the learner was conceived to compare it to each of the stored representations, compute the similarity by the multi-plicative rule, and then generate a choice probability for each category proportional to its summed similarity to the test exemplar. This model im-mediately aroused much interest because it not only yielded predictions of transfer effects under some novel experimental routines but also accounted for phenomena that had been taken to support prototype models, as, for example, the fact that a stimulus pattern corresponding to a category prototype pre-sented for the first time on a test at the end of learning is likely to be correctly categorized with higher probability than patterns that have actually occurred during learning (Medin & Schaffer 1978). Numerous applications of various special cases of this exemplar-memory model (for which some investigators prefer the less mnemonic designation *context model*) during the next several years yielded consistently good accounts of asymptotic learning data and transfer to new patterns following learning, and tended to support the ex-emplar-memory model over prototype models (Busemeyer et al 1984; Estes 1986b; Nosofsky 1984, 1986). My own related work went further in demon-strating similarly good accounts of the detailed course of category learning over hundreds of trials and brought out the close parallelism between categorization and recognition that is implied by the exemplar-memory model (Estes 1986b).

When treading any primrose path, one is likely to run eventually into brambles, and this one proved no exception. It would be expected on theoreti-cal grounds that such closely related processes as identification and classifica-tion of the same set of stimulus patterns should be predictable by an adequate model without changes in paramater values from one task to the other, but a direct test by Nosofsky (1984) yielded an apparent negative result for the exemplar-memory model. I say "apparently" because, although the model provided good fits to both identification and categorization, it was at the cost of a drastic change from one situation to the other in the attentional weights associated with stimulus dimensions in Medin & Schaffer's formulation of the model (to reflect a direct relationship between selective attention and feature validity). This finding was not unanticipated by Nosofsky, and he accomplished a partial rescue of the model by showing that during categorization learning, the values of the attentional weights (estimated from performance data) moved systematically in the direction of the values that would be optimal for efficient categorization. Thus, it seemed that the exemplar-memory model plus an auxiliary model for attentional learning might be able to account for both identification and categorization. Since no such auxiliary model has been formulated, the issue remains open. However, it will be seen in the next section that a more elegant solution to the problem than grafting mechanisms onto the exemplar-memory model may be forthcoming.

In my own studies related to the exemplar-memory model, I have employed only a special case that does not include parameters for dimensional weights, in order to simplify the problem of testing hypotheses about storage and retrieval processes. This version fared well enough at accounting for the details of learning in situations where selective attention would not be expected to play a significant role (Estes 1986a,b); but, even with this qualification met, the model has run into difficulties when called on to predict across a change in conditions. In a recent study, for example, I set out to test a particular aspect of the model having to do with hysteresis. Subjects were given the task of learning to classify artificial words into grammatical categories, the set of stimulus patterns having different probability distributions in each of three categories. For one category, conditions were constant throughout a 240-trial learning series, but the probability distributions for the other two categories were switched after trial 60 for an early-shift group and after trial 180 for a late-shift group. According to the exemplar-memory model, many more patterns, with their category tags, would be stored in the memory array by the point of the shift for the late-shift than for the early shift group; and therefore performance would be impaired after the shift until enough patterns could be correctly stored to outweigh the ones now incorrectly stored in the two shifted categories. The quantitative predictions of the model were exactly as advertised, but the predicted post-shift impairment for the late-shift group was much greater than that observed (Estes 1989).

Again, the setback for the model is not fatal, of course. In further analyses (not yet published), I have found that, as one might expect, the model can be brought into line with the shift data by adding the assumption of a decay-like process whereby a stored pattern declines in availability as an exponential function of trials following storage, so that, in effect, the retrieval and similarity-comparisons of the model only operated on a limited set of recently stored patterns. This assumption seems a quite natural one, and I now regard it as part of the "standard equipment" of an updated exemplar-memory model. Nonetheless, as in the case of predicting from identification to categorization, would it not be fine if the model under test proved able to handle the new results without requiring elaboration? The continuing elusiveness of that goal for models of the array family prepared me to be immediately much interested in the potentialities of connectionist models when they were introduced into categorization research.

Category Learning in PDP Network Models

A stripped-down PDP model, based on a connectionist architecture but lacking hidden units, was developed and applied to categorization learning by Gluck & Bower (1988b). Their model, denoted an "adaptive network," includes an input node for each member of the feature set used to generate category exemplars in an experiment, an output node for each category, and a link, with an associated weight, from each input to each output node. The probability of a categorization response is based on the summed output of the system to each of the category nodes in response to an input pattern. It is assumed that each learning trial comprises presentation of a stimulus pattern, which activates a set of feature nodes, computation of the system's categorization response, and presentation of a feedback, or "teaching," signal indicating the correct category. Learning is accomplished by a set of functions that update the associative weights for each node active on a trial in such a way that the weights move toward the target value specified by the teaching signal. The functions are similar to the learning functions of stimulus sampling models except that they embody a competitive property in that the increment to a weight on any trial is reduced to the degree that other active nodes already predict the correct category. Formally, the increment, or decrement, is proportional to the difference between the current output of the network for the given input pattern and the target output, a property deriving from the conditioning model of Rescorla & Wagner (1972) and the "delta rule" familiar in adaptive network theory (Stone 1986; Widrow & Hoff 1960).

Gluck & Bower noted that even a very simple categorization problem of suitable design could yield an interesting test of differing predictions by exemplar ("pattern-matching," in their terms) models and their network model. In their study (Gluck & Bower 1988b, Exp 1), subjects were given a task simulating that of a diagnostician. Stimulus patterns were generated from a set of four features, labelled as medical symptoms, and subjects were to assign each pattern presented (interpreted as the symptom chart of a hypothetical patient) to one of two disease categories. The two categories, A and B occurred with probabilities .25 and .75, respectively; on each type of trial, the features occurred with the probabilities shown in Table 2. Prime interest is in the subjects' response to Feature 1 when it was tested alone at the end of the learning series and they were asked to estimate the probability of either category in its presence. It will be seen that, owing to the unequal category probabilities, Feature 1 will be expected to occur equally often in both categories over the learning series. Consequently, the prediction of the exemplar-memory model (or a stimulus sampling model) is that the subjects' probability estimates for categories A and B should each be equal to .5 on the test. In contrast, the network model predicts a large bias for Category A—the result observed in Gluck & Bower's study. Shortly after this demonstration, Estes et al (1989) replicated this finding and went on to show that the network model yielded an account of the detailed course of learning considerably superior to that of the exemplar-memory model.

A major limitation of the simple network model is that it can only learn categorizations for situations in which the features of category exemplars combine independently—that is, the features are uncorrelated within categories. Thus the network could not, for example, exhibit learning in Experiment 2 of Estes (1986b), where all members of the feature set were invalid (that is, occurred equally often in each category) but some pairs of cues were partially valid (that is, occurred with different frequencies in the two categories)— although both the subjects and the exemplar-memory model did exhibit significant learning.

The minimal elaboration of the network needed to get around this difficulty is to allow for three levels of nodes, the first level representing individual features and the second level patterns of features, with both levels being connected to the category nodes at the third level (Estes 1988). In a realization of this elaborated network that might be termed the feature/pattern (F/P) model, learning of a new categorization begins with the model having only the simple network structure, but as each presented exemplar activates its feature nodes, a pattern node is added to the network. Henceforth, the pattern

Table 2 Feature probabilities on trials assigned to each category (Gluck & Bower 1988b)

Feature	Category	
	A	B
1	.6	.2
2	.4	.3
3	.3	.4
4	.2	.6

node is activated whenever its set of feature nodes is active, thus acting as an AND gate in network parlance, and it is linked to nodes at the category level just as are the feature nodes. The system is still linear, since the outputs are assumed to be summed activations just as in the simple model, but the additional structure enables the network to learn problems like that of Estes (1986b, Exp. 2). In fact, on the data of that experiment, the F/P model (with one free parameter added to allow for different learning rates on features and patterns) closely matches the performance of the neo–exemplar memory model, and the same has been true for several sets of unpublished data. An important property of the F/P model is that, in a categorization task, the network can concurrently learn quite different things about exemplars and their features (for example, that presence of a particular pattern points strongly to one category whereas each of its features points to other categories). Consequently, the network model may prove significantly more powerful than exemplar-memory models for the prediction of transfer phenomena.

An experiment well designed to tax the capabilities of both the exemplar-memory and F/P models was conducted by J. B. Hurwitz as part of his Harvard dissertation study. The task for his subjects was learning to classify a set of strings of four binary features into two categories A or B. The category structure was a bit complex. Two of the string positions were filled with an exclusive-OR problem (denoted XOR1); the features in those positions were the same (11 or 22 in binary coding) on Category A and different (12 or 21) on Category B trials throughout learning. The other two positions were filled with a different problem, XOR2, for which the contingencies were reversed for some strings after the second 60-trial training block. By "reversed," I mean that if feature pairs 11 and 22 originally occurred in these positions only on A trials, after reversal they occurred only on B trials. Programming of exemplar and category occurrences was such that optimally efficient learners who attended only to the XOR1 letter positions would move quickly to 100% correct responding and remain at that level throughout the series; if they attended only to the XOR2 positions, they would approach 100% correct during the first two blocks but would revert to chance responding in the third block. This scheme sounds complex, but those of Hurwitz's subjects who learned at all moved steadily from chance to a level near 100% correct responding with very little disturbance from the reversal of the XOR2 problem. The picture was as though the subjects were able to do quite well at screening out the XOR2 letter positions and attending only to the XOR1 positions. Exemplar-memory models have no mechanism for producing this apparent selective attention, so it is not surprising that the neo–exemplar memory model gave only a poor account of the data, predicting much too large a drop in performance at the point of partial reversal. The network model, even in the F/P version, did little better [and the same is true of the "configural-cue" model of Gluck & Bower (1988a)].

The reason for special interest in Hurwitz's result is not just that it is the first massive failure recorded in this line of research for the models considered, but that Hurwitz went on to show that the data could be well handled by an elaboration of the F/P network model that included learning on the weights from input to pattern nodes by back-propagation of error signals from the output nodes (Rumelhart et al 1986). Thus, at this stage of the current wave of research on category learning, an adaptive network model with an architecture closer to that of typical connectionist models has proved able to cope with a novel and complex learning regime in a way well beyond the capabilities of the array models or simpler, linear networks that have been applied in this line of research to date.

PROBLEMS FOR CONNECTIONIST MODELS

Despite this and other successes, all is not smooth going for connectionist models. A disturbing note is sounded by reports that as soon as they are extended beyond the task of accounting for the concurrent learning of a set of materials, as a single categorization task or a single to-be-memorized list, they may prove unable to maintain several clusters of successively acquired memories simultaneously and therefore exhibit massive interference effects on recognition or recall tests (McCloskey & Cohen 1989; Ratcliff 1990). In the study of McCloskey & Cohen, for example, simulations of classical paired-associate list learning experiments like that of Barnes & Underwood (1959) yielded interference effects in recall much larger than those shown by human subjects, and this interference was not alleviated by any of the obvious remedial tactics, such as varying the number of hidden units, giving overtraining on the first of two successive lists, or including representation of list contexts. Further, the ambitious, and in many respects impressive, effort by Rumelhart & McClelland (1986b) to produce a connectionist model of the way children acquire certain linguistic competences has run into heavy criticism (Prince & Pinker 1988), including a claim that connectionist networks cannot, in principle, learn rules of the kind that are basic to language. Thus we have a curious situation: Connectionist models are built to learn, but there are reasons to question whether they can be made to learn like human beings.

Of course, these failures of connectionist networks have attracted wide attention, and there have already been reports of some results that limit somewhat the generality of the massive interference findings. Hetherington & Seidenberg (1989) have shown that the extremely large interference effects manifest when lists of items are learned successively are mitigated to some degree under a learning routine intended to be closer to that of vocabulary learning by children in a natural environment. Following a somewhat different approach, Brousse & Smolensky (1989) have found that once a hidden-unit network has learned a subset of items from a large combinatorial do-main, as, for example, strings of six letters, additional items can be learned rapidly and the increasingly large memory can be maintained without in-terference.

Returning to the more restricted successive list paradigm, which remains at the least an annoying pebble in the connectionist shoe, I can add that I have run my F/P network model on tasks very similar to those studied by McClos-key & Cohen (1989), including the Barnes & Underwood (1959) experiment, and have found interference only of the level seen in human subject data. There are too many differences between the specific models simulated to make interpretation of the different results feasible until the analyses are carried further. My model is a linear system, which should not be a critical difference in itself; and it has more a priori structure, in that the nodes at the second level are mapped onto particular input patterns, rather than having stimulus patterns correspond to patterns of activity across a layer of un-differentiated nodes. A stray thought that comes to mind is that the situation is a bit reminiscent of a segment of the history of learning theory. In the learning theories of the period 1930–1960, it was assumed that learning processes are basically the same at least for all of the higher animals and that learning in the individual organism starts from a *tabula rasa,* the counterpart of a network of homogeneous and mutually interconnected nodes. During the next decade, however, under the impact of ethology and the beginnings of modern neuroscience, the prevalent view shifted to one that recognized biological constraints on learning (Estes 1988; Hinde 1973; Shettleworth 1972); and it is now quite generally assumed that learning in any organism, human or subhu-man, builds on a substrate of species-specific predispositions and products of previous learning. Implementing this more biologically founded orientation in connectionist learning models is a tall order; but the effort will surely have to be made sooner or later, and the results may cast some of the current problems in a new light.

REFLECTIONS

Is memory distributed? I find it hard to doubt that at the neural level the answer is yes, at least within the components of modular structures. The implication for constructors of cognitive models is not obvious, however, for models that differ only in their assumptions about distributed versus localized storage may not be differentiable at the behavioral level. The latter comment is relevant also to questions about composite memories. Convolution models and associative network models appear very different when diagrammed or described in words, but it is possible that one type can be mapped onto the other. For example, following a given learning experience, the set of informational patterns recoverable from a composite memory by members of a set of recall cues might correspond one-to-one to the set of images stored at the nodes of an associative network. Much theoretical work is needed to assess the possibilities of such equivalences.

Are there built-in memory structures? The notion of a cognitive architecture may seem to connote a set of permanent memory structures, waiting to receive information and constraining the form of storage, as in the models of Anderson & Bower (1973), Atkinson & Shiffrin (1968), or Norman & Rumelhart (1970). But, alternatively, it may be assumed that the cognitive system has only very general built-in capabilities and creates memory structures on-line in response to task demands (Newell 1973). There may well be a peripheral-central gradient, with the more peripheral, or modality-specific, subsystems, like primary visual and auditory memory, tending to have more fixed structures. Examples of reasonably direct evidence for on-line formation of memory structures tailored to particular task demands can be found in research on ordered recall (Lee & Estes 1981) and memory for dates of events (Huttenlocher et al 1988).

Architecture or architectures? I think pluralism gets the nod, certainly for the present and quite possibly for a long way into the future. The complexity of the human cognitive system demands approaches from differing perspectives, and these must be expected to give rise to successions of limited models and restricted architectures. The idea that the connectionist and the symbol-processing architecture might fit neatly into the different levels of an overall theory (Smolensky 1988) is attractive, but in my view not ready for evaluation.

Parallel cultivation of symbol-processing and connectionist architectures need not imply anything like equality of effort or rate of progress, however. The former seems to be lagging in new theoretical development, but remains influential because concepts of symbol processing and array representation fit the intuitions of the majority of investigators in cognitive science. The connectionist approach has the enormous advantage of resonating more strongly with the current groundswell of interest in cognitive neuroscience, and brings a variety of new concepts, metaphors, and formal tools into cognitive theory. Intuitions can change, and they may have to do so if the connectionist movement, broadly conceived, continues to gain momentum at the rate that now seems likely from my perspective.

ACKNOWLEDGMENT

Preparation of this chapter was supported in part by Grant BNS 86-09232 from the National Science Foundation.

Literature Cited

Anderson, J. A. 1973. A theory for the recognition of items from short memorized lists. *Psychol. Rev.* 80:417–38

Anderson, J. R. 1976. *Language, Memory, and Thought.* Hillsdale, NJ: Erlbaum

Anderson, J. R. 1983. *The Architecture of Cognition.* Cambridge, MA: Harvard Univ. Press

Anderson, J. R., Bower, G. H. 1973. *Human Associative Memory.* Washington, DC: Winston

Anderson, J. A., Silverstein, J. W., Ritz, S. A., Jones, R. S. 1977. Distinctive features, categorical perceptions, and probability learning: some applications of a neural model. *Psychol. Rev.* 84:413–51

Atkinson, R. C., Estes, W. K. 1963. Stimulus sampling theory. In *Handbook of Mathematical Psychology,* ed. R. D. Luce, R. R. Bush, E. Galanter 2:121–268. New York: Wiley

Atkinson, R. C., Shiffrin, R. M. 1968. Human memory: a proposed system and its control processes. In *The Psychology of Learning and Motivation: Advances in Research and Theory,* ed. K. W. Spence, J. T. Spence, pp. 89–105. New York: Academic

Ballard, D. H., Hinton, G. E., Sejnowski, T. J. 1983. Parallel visual computation. *Nature* 306:21–26

Barnes, J. M., Underwood, B. J. 1959. "Fate" of first-list associations in transfer theory. *J. Exp. Psychol.* 58:97–105

Bourne, L. E. Jr. 1970. Knowing and using concepts. *Psychol. Rev.* 77:546–56

Bousfield, W. A. 1953. The occurrence of clustering in the recall of randomly arranged associates. *J. Gen. Psychol.* 49:229–40

Bower, G. H. 1967. A multicomponent theory of the memory trace. In *The Psychology of Learning and Motivation: Advances in Research and Theory,* ed. K. W. Spence, J. T. Spence, pp. 230–327. New York: Academic

Brousse, O., Smolensky, P. 1989. *Virtual memories and massive generalization in connectionist combinatorial learning.* Presented at Annu. Meet. Cognit. Sci. Soc., 11th, Ann Arbor

Busemeyer, J. R., Dewey, G. I., Medin, D. L. 1984. Evaluation of exemplar-based generalization and the abstraction of categorical information. *J. Exp. Psychol.: Learn. Mem. Cogn.* 10:638–48

Clark, S. E., Shiffrin, R. M. 1987. Recognition of multiple item probes. *Mem. Cog.* 15:367–78

Collins, A. M., Loftus, E. F. 1975. A spreading activation theory of semantic processing. *Psychol. Rev.* 82:407–28

Collins, A. M., Quillian, M. R. 1972. How to make a language user. In *Organization of Memory,* ed. E. Tulving, W. Donaldson, pp. 310–51. New York: Academic

Cunningham, J. P., Shepard, R. N. 1974. Monotone mapping of similarities into a general metric space. *J. Math. Psychol.* 11:335–65

Ebbinghaus, H. 1964. [1885]. *Memory.* Ed. transl. H. A. Ruger, C. E. Bussenius. New York: Dover

Eich, J. M. 1982. A composite holographic associative recall model. *Psychol. Rev.* 89:627–61

Estes, W. K. 1950. Toward a statistical theory of learning. *Psychol. Rev.* 57:94–107

Estes, W. K. 1955. Statistical theory of spontaneous recovery and regression. *Psychol. Rev.* 62:145–54

Estes, W. K. 1969. New perspectives on some old issues in association theory. In *Fundamental Issues in Associative Learning,* ed. N. J. Macintosh, W. K. Honig, pp. 162–89. Halifax: Dalhousie Univ. Press

Estes, W. K. 1972a. An associative basis for coding and organization in memory. In *Coding Processes in Human Memory,* ed. A. W. Melton, E. Martin, pp. 161–90. Washington, DC: Winston

Estes, W. K. 1972b. Elements and patterns in diagnostic discrimination learning. *Trans. NY Acad. Sci.* 34:84–95

Estes, W. K. 1975a. Some targets for mathematical psychology. *J. Math. Psychol.* 12:263–82

Estes, W. K. 1975b. The state of the field: general problems and issues of theory and metatheory. In *Handbook of Learning and Cognitive Processes.* Volume 1. *Introduction to Concepts and Issues,* ed. W. K. Estes, pp. 1–24. Hillsdale, NJ: Erlbaum

Estes, W. K. 1986a. Array models for category learning. *Cogn. Psychol.* 18:500–49

Estes, W. K. 1986b. Storage and retrieval processes in category learning. *J. Exp. Psychol.: Gen.* 115:155–74

Estes, W. K. 1988. Toward a framework for combining connectionist and symbol-processing models. *J. Mem. Lang.* 27:196–212

Estes, W. K. 1989. Early and late memory processing in models for category learning. In *Current Issues in Cognitive Processes: The Tulane Symposium on Cognition,* ed. C. Izawa, pp. 11–24. Hillsdale, NJ: Erlbaum

Estes, W. K., Burke, C. J., Atkinson, R. C., Frankmann, J. P. 1957. Probabilistic discrimination learning. *J. Exp. Psychol.* 54:233–39

Estes, W. K., Campbell, J. A., Hatsopoulos, N., Hurwitz, J. B. 1989. Base-rate effects in category learning: a comparison of parallel network and memory storage-retrieval models. *J. Exp. Psychol.: Learn. Mem. Cognit.* 15:556–71

Estes, W. K., Hopkins, B. L. 1961. Acquisition and transfer in pattern-vs.-component discrimination learning. *J. Exp. Psychol.* 61:322–28

Gillund, G., Shiffrin, R. M. 1984. A retrieval model for both recognition and recall. *Psychol. Rev.* 91:1–67

Gluck, M. A., Bower, G. H. 1988a. Evaluating an adaptive network model for human learning. *J. Mem. Lang.* 27:166–95

Gluck, M. A., Bower, G. H. 1988b. From conditioning to category learning: an adaptive network model. *J. Exp. Psychol.: Gen.* 117:225–44

Greeno, J. G., James, C. T., DaPolito, F., Polson, P. G. 1978. *Associative Learning: A Cognitive Analysis.* Englewood Cliffs, NJ: Prentice-Hall

Gronlund, S. D., Shiffrin, R. M. 1986. Retrieval strategies in recall of natural categories and categorized lists. *J. Exp. Psychol.: Learn. Mem. Cognit.* 12:550–56

Grossberg, S. 1976. Adaptive pattern classification and universal recoding: I. Parallel development and coding of neural feature detectors. *Biol. Cybern.* 23:121–34

Grossberg, S. 1987. Competitive learning: from interactive activation resonance. *Cognit. Sci.* 11:23–63

Hetherington, P. A., Seidenberg, M. S. 1989. *Is there "catastrophic interference" in connectionist networks?* Presented at Annu. Meet. Cognit. Sci. Soc., 11th, Ann Arbor

Hinde, R. A. 1973. Constraints on learning: an introduction to the problems. In *Constraints on Learning,* ed. R. A. Hinde, J. Hinde, pp. 1–19. New York: Academic

Hinton, G. E., Sejnowski, T. J. 1986. Learning and relearning in Boltzmann machines. See Reumelhart & McClelland 1986, pp. 282–317

Hintzman, D. 1986. "Schema abstraction" in a multiple-trace memory model. *Psychol. Rev.* 93:411–28

Hollingworth, H. L. 1913. Characteristic differences between recall and recognition. *Am. J. Psychol.* 24:532–44

Hollingworth, H. L. 1928. General laws of redintegration. *J. Gen. Psychol.* 1:79–90

Hovland, C. I. 1952. A "communication analysis" of concept learning. *Psychol. Rev.* 59:461–72

Hunt, E. B. 1962. *Concept Learning: An Information Processing Problem.* New York: Wiley

Hutchinson, J. W., Lockhead, G. R. 1977.

Similarity as distance: a structural principle for semantic memory. *J. Exp. Psychol.: Hum. Learn. Mem.* 3:660–78

Huttenlocher, J., Hedges, L., Prohaska, V. 1988. Hierarchical organization in ordered domains: estimating dates of events. *Psychol. Rev.* 95:471–84

Koffka, K. 1935. *Principles of Gestalt Psychology.* New York: Harcourt Brace

Laird, J. E., Newell, A., Rosenbloom, P. S. 1987. SOAR: An architecture for general intelligence. *Artif. Intell.* 33:1–64

Lee, C. L., Estes, W. K. 1981. Item and order information in short-term memory: evidence for multilevel perturbation processes. *J. Exp. Psychol.* 7:149–69

Luce, R. D. 1963. Detection and recognition. In *Handbook of Mathematical Psychology,* ed. R. D. Luce, R. R. Bush, E. Galanter, 1:103–90. New York: Wiley

Mandler, G. 1967. Organization and memory. In *The Psychology of Learning and Motivation: Advances in Research and Theory,* ed. K. W. Spence, J. T. Spence, pp. 328–72. New York: Academic

Marr, D. 1982. *Vision: A Computational Investigation into the Human Representation and Processing of Visual Information.* San Francisco: Freeman

McClelland, J. L. Rumelhart, D. E. 1981. An interactive interaction model of context effects in letter perception. *Psychol. Rev.* 88:375–407

McClelland, J. L., Rumelhart, D. E. 1986. *Parallel Distributed Processing: Explorations in the Microstructure of Cognition,* Vol. 2. Cambridge, MA: MIT Press

McCloskey, M., Cohen, N. J. 1989. Catastrophic interference in connectionist networks: the sequential learning problem. *Psychol. Learn. Motiv.: Adv. Res. Theory* 24:109–65

Medin, D. L. 1975. A theory of context in discrimination learning. In *The Psychology of Learning and Motivation,* ed. G. H. Bower, 9:263–314. New York: Academic

Medin, D. L., Schaffer, M. M. 1978. Context theory of classification learning. *Psychol. Rev.* 85:207–38

Metcalfe, J., Fisher, R. P. 1986. The relation between recognition memory and classification learning. *J. Exp. Psychol.: Learn. Mem. Cogn.* 14:164–73

Murdock, B. B. Jr. 1974. *Human Memory: Theory and Data.* Potomac, MD: Erlbaum

Murdock, B. B. Jr. 1979. Convolution and correlation in perception and memory. In *Perspectives on Memory Research,* ed. L.-G. Nilsson, pp. 105–19. Hillsdale, NJ: Erlbaum

Murdock, B. B. Jr. 1982. A theory for the storage and retrieval of item and associative information. *Psychol. Rev.* 89:609–26

Murdock, B. B. Jr. 1989. Learning in a distributed memory model. See Izawa, pp. 70–106

Murdock, B. B. Jr., Hockley, W. E. 1989. Short-term memory for associations. *Psychol. Learn. Motiv. Res. Theory* 24:71–108

Murdock, B. B. Jr., Lamon, M. 1988. The replacement effect: repeating some items while replacing others. *Mem. Cogn.* 16:91–101

Newell, A. 1973. Production systems: models of control structures. In *Visual Information Processing*, ed. W. G. Chase, pp., 463–526. New York: Academic

Newell, A. 1990. *Unified Theories of Cognition.* Cambridge, MA: Harvard Univ. Press. In press

Newell, A., Simon, H. A. 1972. *Human Problem Solving.* Englewood Cliffs, NJ: Prentice-Hall

Norman, D. A., Rumelhart, D. E. 1970. A system for perception and memory. In *Models of Human Memory*, ed. D. A. Norman, pp. 21–64. New York: Academic

Nosofsky, R. M. 1984. Choice, similarity, and the context theory of classification. *J. Exp. Psychol.: Learn, Mem. Cognit.* 10:104–14

Nosofsky, R. M. 1986. Attention, similarity, and the identification-categorization relationship. *J. Exp. Psychol.: Gen.* 115:39–57

Nosofsky, R. M. 1988. Similarity, frequency, and category representations. *J. Exp. Psychol.: Learn. Mem. Cognit.* 14:54–65

Pike, R. 1984. A comparison of convolution and matrix distributed memory systems. *Psychol. Rev.* 91:281–94

Prince, A., Pinker, S. 1988. On language and connectionism: analysis of a parallel distributed processing model of language acquisition. *Cognition* 28:73–194

Raaijmakers, J. G. W., Shiffrin, R. M. 1981. Search of associative memory. *Psychol. Rev.* 88:93–134

Ratcliff, R. 1978. A theory of memory retrieval. *Psychol. Rev.* 85:59–108

Ratcliff, R. 1990. Connectionist models of recognition memory: constraints imposed by learning and forgetting functions. *Psychol. Rev.* 98:285:308

Rescorla, R. A., Wagner, A. R. 1972. A theory of Pavlovian conditioning: variations in the effectiveness of reinforcement and non-reinforcement. In *Classical Conditioning II: Current Research and Theory*, ed. A. H. Black, W. F. Prokasy, pp. New York: Appleton-Century-Crofts

Robinson, E. S. 1932. *Association Theory Today.* New York: Century

Rumelhart, D. E., Hinton, G. E., Williams, R. J. 1986. Learning internal representations by error propagation. See McClelland & Rumelhart 1986, pp. 318–62

Rumelhart, D. E., McClelland, J. L., eds. 1986a. *Parallel Distributed Processing: Explorations in the Microstructure of Cognition.* Cambridge, MA: MIT Press/Bradford Books

Rumelhart, D. E., McClelland, J. L. 1986b. On learning the past tense of English verbs. See McClelland & Rumelhart 1986, pp. 216–71

Rumelhart, D. E., Zipser, D. 1986. Feature discovery by competitive learning. See Rumelhart & McClelland 1986b, pp. 151–93

Schneider, W., Shiffrin, R. M. 1977. Controlled and automatic human information processing: 1. Detection, search, and attention. *Psychol. Rev.* 84:1–66

Semon, R. 1921. *The Mneme.* London: George Allen & Unwin

Shepard, R. N. 1958. Stimulus and response generalization: deduction of the generalization gradient from a trace model. *Psychol. Rev.* 65:242–56

Shepard, R. N., Hovland, C. I., Jenkins, H. M. 1961. Learning and memorization of classifications. *Psychol. Monogr.* 75:1–41

Shettleworth, S. J. 1972. Constraints on learning. *Adv. Study Behav.*, 4:1–68

Shiffrin, R. M., Murnane, K., Gronlund, S., Roth, M. 1989. On units of storage and retrieval. In *Current Issues in Cognitive Processes: The Tulane Floweree Symposium on Cognition*, ed. C. Izawa, pp. 25–68. Hillsdale, NJ: Erlbaum

Smith, E. E., Medin, D. L. 1981. *Categories and concepts.* Cambridge, MA: Harvard Univ. Press

Smolensky, P. 1988. On the proper treatment of connectionism. *Behav. Brain Sci.* 11:1–59

Stone, G. O. 1986. An analysis of the delta rule and the learning of statistical associations. See Rumelhart & McClelland 1986b, pp. 423–43

Trabasso, T., Bower, G. H. 1968. *Attention in Learning: Theory and Research.* New York: Wiley

Underwood, B. J. 1969. Attributes of memory. *Psychol. Rev.* 76:559–73

Widrow, B., Hoff, M. E. 1960. Adaptive switching circuits. *Inst. Radio Eng., West. Electron. Show & Convent. Rec.* Pt. IV, pp. 96–104

Annu. Rev. Psychol. 1991. 42:29–50

BEHAVIORAL FUNCTIONING IN INDIVIDUALS WITH MENTAL RETARDATION

Edward Zigler and Robert M. Hodapp

Yale University Department of Psychology, New Haven, Connecticut 06520

KEY WORDS: two-group approach, Down syndrome, fragile X syndrome, developmental approach to mental retardation, mainstreaming and group homes

CONTENTS

INTRODUCTION

Only 30 years ago little was known about mental retardation. We now possess a significant amount of information about the condition's etiologies, and about the functioning and care of many different types of retarded individuals. Despite the tightening of research funding and opportunities in the 1980s, progress continues in the mental retardation field.

The most obvious advances have occurred in genetics and biomedicine. As recently as 1959, for example, researchers discovered that Down Syndrome, the most common genetic form of mental retardation, was caused by a trisomy

0066-4308/91/0201-0029$02.00

on the 21st chromosome. New types of mental retardation have also been discovered. Fragile X syndrome, discovered in the late 1960s and early 1970s, is thought to be the second most common genetic, and the most common hereditary, cause of mental retardation (Bregman et al 1987) (see below). Other recent advances include the discovery and successful treatment of phenylketonuria (PKU) and other inborn errors of metabolism; the ability to save infants born many weeks prematurely and at very low birth weights; and the successful treatment of heart defects and other associated health problems in retarded persons.

Here we selectively review new research on behavioral functioning in retarded individuals. We begin with an overview of the two-group approach to mental retardation and of new information about Down Syndrome and fragile X syndrome. We then discuss issues in the developmental approach to mental retardation, examining how knowledge of nonretarded development informs us about retarded functioning and vice versa. This section concludes with a discussion of psychopathology in retarded populations, an area that links retardation with other, broader psychological issues.

In addition to research advances, recent years have also seen great strides in the care of retarded individuals. We therefore end the chapter with a brief overview of issues involving appropriate educational placements and de-institutionalization–community living for retarded persons. Although these are but two of many policy issues, they help to illuminate both the advances and the remaining problems in service delivery to the mentally retarded population.

PSYCHOLOGICAL RESEARCH IN MENTAL RETARDATION

The Two-Group Approach and Beyond

In attempting to describe the behavior of mentally retarded individuals, workers have been faced with the problem that retarded persons differ one from another in a variety of ways. The question becomes how best to subdivide retarded persons into meaningful groups for research or intervention purposes.

To date, two contrasting solutions have been offered. The first involves differentiating by level of functioning, such that the behaviors of persons with mild (IQs 55–69), moderate (IQs 40–54), severe (IQs 25–39), or profound (IQ below 25) levels of mental retardation are compared to behaviors of persons of the same mental or chronological age. Using this strategy, retarded subjects are grouped by level of impairment, even though these groups are comprised of individuals with different etiologies of retardation. This practice is followed in most studies in the mental retardation field.

A second approach differentiates retarded groups based on etiology. The starting point for such a strategy is the so-called "two-group approach" to mental retardation (Zigler 1967, 1969). According to this view, there are two distinct types of retarded individual—those whose retardation has no clear organic cause (familial or cultural-familial retarded persons) and organically retarded persons (those whose retardation has one of a number of clear organic causes). Although exact prevalence estimates are difficult to obtain, it appears that from one half to three quarters of all retarded persons are of the familial type, whereas the remaining one quarter to one half suffer organic retardation (Zigler & Hodapp 1986).

At present, the cause of mental retardation in the first group, the familial retarded group, remains unclear. These persons may be retarded owing to polygenic factors (i.e. receiving fewer genes for high intelligence from their parents), to growing up in poor environments, or to some combination of polygenic and environmental factors. Familial retarded individuals generally have IQs in the 50–70 range and exhibit few biological or behavioral characteristics that distinguish them from nonretarded individuals.

The second group is comprised of persons whose retardation has a clear organic cause, whether of prenatal, perinatal, or postnatal origin. Prenatal factors include all of the genetic syndromes (Down Syndrome, fragile X syndrome), rubella, thalidomide, and other conditions causing damage to the developing fetus. Perinatal factors include anoxia, prematurity, and other birth-related events; the after-effects of meningitis, head trauma, or other insults in the childhood years constitute the postnatal causes of organic mental retardation. Grossman (1983) estimates that there are over 200 types of organic mental retardation.

Although this method is an advance over grouping by level of impairment, the characterization of retarded persons into familial versus organic retardation may itself require further differentiation. Burack et al (1988) have noted that organically retarded individuals demonstrate behavioral differences specific to one or another organic etiology. They further argue that these etiology-specific patterns occur despite wide heterogeneity within any particular etiological group. Thus, children with Down Syndrome behave very differently from those with fragile X syndrome or cerebral palsy. These etiology-specific behavioral profiles would seem useful for both research and intervention purposes (Burack et al 1990; Gibson 1991; Hodapp & Dykens 1991).

This interest in specific etiology has so far focused mainly on the genetic, epidemiologic, and biomedical aspects of individual etiological groups; but we are rapidly accumulating information about the behavior and development of individuals with Down Syndrome (e.g. Cicchetti & Beeghly 1990), fragile X syndrome (Dykens & Leckman 1990), autism (Cohen & Donnellan 1987), and Prader-Willi Syndrome (Taylor & Caldwell 1988). Below we focus on two prevalent disorders, Down Syndrome and fragile X syndrome.

Down Syndrome

Down Syndrome, the most common genetic form of mental retardation, is usually diagnosed at birth. It has a prevalence rate between 1.0 and 1.5 per 1000 live births and is much more likely to occur in infants born of older mothers. Levels of impairment range widely, with most Down Syndrome children functioning in the moderately retarded range (IQs 40–54) (Pueschel 1983). As the most common and longest studied genetic cause of mental retardation, it has by far the most extensive behavioral literature.

LANGUAGE   Almost all researchers have found Down Syndrome children deficient in language compared to their overall levels of cognitive ability. After reviewing numerous studies of the language of Down Syndrome individuals, Gibson (1978) concluded that "the manipulation of symbols and images [i.e. language] provides something of a developmental wall for the syndrome" (p. 33).

It appears, however, that not all aspects of language are equally impaired in the Down Syndrome population. For example, when matched to nonretarded children on the average length of their sentences (Mean Length of Utterance), Down Syndrome children perform better than nonretarded children on pragmatics, or the uses of language (Beeghly & Cicchetti 1987). These children are fairly adept at taking their turn within a conversation, maintaining the topic of conversation, and in other ways holding up their end of a conversation with another. A second area of strength in Down Syndrome language is vocabulary, which is often several years more advanced than are levels of grammar (Fowler 1990).

In contrast to pragmatics and vocabulary, grammatical abilities seem particularly impaired in children with Down Syndrome. These children begin speaking at older ages and move particularly slowly (with spurts and lags) through the early stages of grammar (Fowler 1990). It is common for Down Syndrome children aged 5 or older to speak in two- and three-word sentences (Beeghly & Cicchetti 1987), well below what one would predict given their overall levels of mental age. The difference between levels of grammar and nonverbal intelligence may also increase as children reach older ages (Miller 1991). In short, it appears that while linguistic abilities are deficient in this population, the area of linguistic grammar—the manipulation of [linguistic] symbols—presents by far the greatest difficulties.

SOCIAL SKILLS   Consistent with the findings about language pragmatics, social skills of Down Syndrome children seem relatively high. Social quotients of these children exceed IQs throughout the 4–17 year old period (Cornwell & Birch 1969). There may, however, be a limit upon the degree to which social skills can be advanced over intellectual abilities, as most higher-level social and adaptive behaviors require linguistic abilities (Cornwell & Birch 1969).

As in the area of language, the abilities of Down Syndrome children may not be uniform across all social or adaptive tasks. Recent findings suggest that these children are particularly good in adaptive tasks requiring the ability to get along with others and to follow rules, the so-called socialization domain of adaptive behavior (Sparrow et al 1984). Conversely, these individuals show a relative weakness in tasks involving personal (washing, grooming), domestic (cleaning, cooking), and community (managing money, attending work) daily living skills (Sparrow 1989).

AFFECT   Most studies have found the affect of Down Syndrome children to be muted as compared to nonretarded children of the same mental age. For example, the Down Syndrome infant smiles to stimuli evoking laughter in nonretarded infants, or wimpers when the nonretarded child cries vigorously (Cicchetti & Stroufe 1976). Mothers of infants with Down Syndrome begin to adapt themselves to the lowered arousal levels of their infants. Sorce & Emde (1982) note that when shown pictures of infants who are smiling, mothers of Down Syndrome babies (as opposed to mothers of nonretarded infants) rate the baby as laughing; when shown babies with frowns, mothers of Down Syndrome infants consider the child to be crying, etc.

This muted affect of infants with Down Syndrome may be tied to the lower muscle tone, or hypotonicity, of children with this disorder. In addition, across individual Down Syndrome children, the greater the child's degree of hypotonicity, the lower the level of functioning on cognitive (Cicchetti & Sroufe 1976) and adaptive (Cullen et al 1981) tasks.

ATTENTION   Down Syndrome children seem to have particular difficulty in regulating their gaze to gather information. They are less likely to scan the environment visually during play, instead looking longer at a single stimulus (Krakow & Kopp 1982). This relative inability to glance quickly to new and interesting visual information (or to take longer to consider information "old") may be related to a slower speed of habituation in the Down Syndrome population, one of the few measures of infant intelligence that shows moderate correlations from infancy into the childhood years (Bornstein 1989).

In addition to a gaze pattern that is more immobile than that of nonretarded infants, young Down Syndrome children are less likely to engage in what have been called "referential glances"—the use of eye contact as a communication signal about an object or event (Jones 1980). This finding is surprising in that Down Syndrome infants are relatively social, looking to their mothers often; they seem less able, however, to coordinate their glances toward the mother with those toward a desired object. The rarity of both visual scanning of the environment and referential eye contact with other persons makes less rich their nonsocial and social contacts with the environment, lessening the ability of these children to extract environmental information (Kopp 1983).

RATE OF DEVELOPMENT   Down Syndrome children are thought to decrease in their rates of intellectual development over time. Such decreases do not mean that these children fail to develop, but rather that the rate at which they develop new skills becomes increasingly slower. Some researchers (e.g. Reed et al 1980) question this slowing of development, but most studies do reveal decreases in the IQ scores of Down Syndrome children as they get older (e.g. Morgan 1979; Gibson 1978).

Such decreases in rates of intellectual development may be related to the difficulties Down Syndrome children have in mastering qualitatively new and difficult intellectual tasks. For example, Dunst (1988, 1990) has found that Down Syndrome children decline in IQ as they attempt to develop from one Piagetian sensorimotor stage to another. Similarly, Fowler (1990) has found that the transition into language (especially grammar) is particularly difficult for these children. We say more about this issue when we discuss the developmental implications of slowed developmental rates over the childhood years.

Fragile X Syndrome

Although the presence of X-linked mental retardation had long been suspected (Martin & Bell 1943), it was only in 1969 that Yale University's Herbert Lubs correlated retardation with a "fragile site" on the long arm of the X chromosome. Lubs's discovery could not be replicated until in the mid-1970s it was noted that the fragile site in fragile X syndrome only appears when karyotypes are performed in the absence of folate. Since that time, researchers have discovered that fragile X syndrome, while it can also occur in females, is particularly prevalent in males, accounting for from 5–7% of all retarded males. Males with the disorder characteristically have long faces, big ears, and, as adults, large testes. The genetic transmission of the disorder also differs from customary patterns in that both males and females can be either affected or unaffected carriers (Bregman et al 1987; Opitz & Sutherland 1984).

Fragile X syndrome has been a subject of much behavioral work over the past decade. As males are more often affected and most work has focused on them, the review below focuses on males with the disorder. (For a review of the psychological functioning of girls with this disorder, see Kemper et al 1986).

COGNITIVE FUNCTIONING   Males with fragile X syndrome have particular difficulty performing tasks involving sequential processing, or tasks requiring short-term memory in the recall or reproduction of items in serial or temporal order (Dykens et al 1987a; Kemper et al 1988). For example, they are impaired on tasks involving the recall of a series of digits or object words and even more impaired on tasks that require the imitation of a series of motor movements. This inability to perform tasks of sequential processing in the fragile X population is notable in that a particular, specific impairment in sequential tasks does not appear to be present in other retarded groups, such as those of mixed etiology (Kaufman & Kaufman 1983) or those with Down Syndrome (Pueschel et al 1987).

In contrast to their inability to perform sequential tasks, fragile X males are relatively strong in simultaneous processing, or on those tasks that require integrative (i.e. gestalt), frequently spatial approaches to problem solving. These children perform fairly well on block design tests of the Wechsler series and can decipher a picture from examining only partial lines. With the exception of arithmetic, achievement tests such as those tapping vocabulary or basic information are also relatively less impaired in fragile X males.

LANGUAGE   The language of males with fragile X syndrome has been called "jocular," "litany-like," "perseverative," and "defective." Recent work reveals that many of the linguistic problems experienced by fragile X males may relate to their difficulties in sequential processing (Dykens & Leckman 1990). Even in areas seemingly distinguishable from sequential processing, such as the ability to articulate words correctly, fragile X males manifest their sequential deficits: When the task involves pronouncing a single word, they perform adequately (Klasner & Hagerman 1987), but when asked to imitate several words, a sentence, or a series of syllables, these children perform poorly (Marans et al 1987).

ADAPTIVE BEHAVIOR   Although difficulties with "social adaptability" have long been postulated for fragile X males (Herbst 1980), only recently has a particular adaptive profile been identified in males with this disorder. In samples of fragile X males who were either institutionalized (Dykens et al 1989a) or living in the community (Dykens et al 1987b), daily living skills were found superior to communication and socialization abilities. Within the domain of daily living skills, personal (e.g. grooming, toileting) and domestic (e.g. cooking, cleaning) skills are better developed than community skills (e.g. managing money, using a phone).

RATES OF DEVELOPMENT   Males with fragile X syndrome decrease in their rates of intellectual development, or IQ, over time (e.g. Lachiewicz et al 1987). In contrast to the case of children with Down Syndrome, however, IQ declines in fragile X males do not occur consistently from infancy onward, but are most noticeable during the pubertal period, roughly from 10 to 15 years (Dykens et al 1989). Most such children show declines in IQ during the pubertal period, although the exact mechanisms causing such widespread declines have not yet been identified. Certain boys, especially those with higher initial IQs, also show declines in the pre-10 year old period, but younger fragile X boys as a group show only slight and nonsignificant declines in IQ when repeatedly tested in the years before age 10 (Hodapp et al 1990b).

Overview of Work Examining Different Etiological Groups

Data on cognition, language, adaptive behavior, and rates of development in Down Syndrome and fragile X syndrome lead to the tentative conclusion that particular etiological groups display different behavioral profiles. If so, better research and intervention practices will arise from separating retarded groups by etiology, not by level of functioning (Burack et al 1988).

Although few studies simultaneously compare several etiological groups, those that have done so also show differences across different etiologies of mental retardation. For example, in a study of linguistic pragmatics (the uses of language) in Down Syndrome vs fragile X males, Wolf-Schein et al (1987) found that jargon, perseveration, echolalia, and inappropriate and tangential language were more apparent in the fragile X group. Ferrier (1987) also found that the language of fragile X boys could be distinguished from that of both Down Syndrome and autistic children. Similar differences between Down Syndrome and fragile X syndrome children may also be present in tests of intellectual abilities (R. M. Hodapp et al, unpublished).

This etiology-specific approach is not without its problems. Many etiologies of mental retardation are low in prevalence, making it difficult to obtain sufficiently large subject groups. Some etiologies have different subgroups that may differ among themselves (e.g. trisomy 21, mosaicism, and translocation types of Down Syndrome). Finally, there are often vast differences in level of functioning among individuals with identical disorders. Even granting such difficulties, however, there do appear to be profiles of ability specific to different etiological groups.

In addition, as noted above, between one half and three quarters of all retarded individuals show the so-called familial or nonspecific form of retardation (Zigler & Hodapp 1986). Some of these individuals may have genetic and other problems undetectable by present means, as was the case with fragile X syndrome only a few decades ago. Others form the lower end of the normal distribution of intelligence (although see Akesson 1987 for the view that mild mental retardation does not involve polygenic factors). We discuss this group's functioning in the next section.

The Developmental Approach to Mental Retardation

Originally proposed by Zigler (1969) in the late 1960s, the developmental approach to mental retardation is predicated on the idea that retarded children, while they develop at a slower rate and stop developing at lower levels, otherwise develop in the same way nonretarded children do. These children are hypothesized to follow universal sequences of development (the *similar sequence hypothesis*) and to perform identically to nonretarded children of the same mental age on cognitive-linguistic tasks (the *similar structure hypothesis*). These hypotheses were originally meant to apply only to those children whose retardation shows no clear organic cause, although recent work has applied developmental principles to a variety of different etiological groups (Cicchetti & Beeghly 1990; Hodapp et al 1990a).

The developmental approach has also benefited from a larger definition of development. In line with work on the transactional model of development, mother-child interaction, and families and family systems theory, the field of developmental psychology now encompasses both the child and the surrounding environment as each changes over time. Many of these expansions have found expression in work with retarded children and their families. The review below thus summarizes new findings about such traditional topics as developmental sequences, rates, and cross-domain relationships, but also includes work on personality-motivational functioning in retarded individuals, mother-child interactions, and families of retarded children.

SEQUENCES AND RATES OF DEVELOPMENT   Zigler (1967, 1969) originally proposed that retarded children traverse the same universal sequences of development as nonretarded children. Thus these children are expected to progress in order through Piaget's four major stages of cognitive development, just as they are expected to develop sequentially in the smaller substages within each larger stage.

Although originally applied only to familial retarded children, the similar sequence hypothesis has generally held for all retarded children. With the possible exception of children with severe seizure disorders, all familial retarded and organically retarded children appear to traverse Piagetian and other universal sequences in the same, invariant order as shown by nonretarded children (Weisz et al 1982).

With a renewed interest in the contexts of development, however, many developmental psychologists are currently focusing not on universal sequences that apply to all children in all cultures but on individual paths of development (Bronfenbrenner et al 1986). In general, the degree of sequential similarity seems related to the type of development studied and to the point when that development occurs during childhood: Earlier developments in areas that may be more biologically influenced (e.g. cognition) seem more sequential (McCall 1981; Scarr-Salapatek 1975) than do social, cultural, or moral achievements, especially in older children (Miller 1986).

Such findings seem well illustrated by development in many types of retarded child. In areas such as infant cognitive development, most etiological groups acquire abilities in universal stages (Cicchetti & Mans-Wagener 1987; Dunst 1990). In social areas, retarded children, like nonretarded children, generally but not always follow similar sequences in their development (Hodapp 1990). A good example is the way autistic children develop in linguistic pragmatics. In contrast to nonretarded children, who generally engage in both social and object uses of language at the earliest ages, autistic children always use language first to express object-related needs, and only engage in language for its social functions (greetings, showing off, etc) at a much later period, if at all. As Wetherby (1986) notes, "the function of directing another's attention to an object or event for a social end appears to be a 'later emerging' function for autistic children" (p. 305). This pattern illustrates how a social skill—the use of language—can develop in different (in this case, etiology-specific) sequences.

In a similar way, information about various groups of retarded individuals demonstrates the types of factors that can affect developmental rate. McCall et al (1977) have identified 2, 8, 13, and 21 months as the ages during infancy at which the nature of intelligence changes qualititively, when complex new tasks face the developing infant. Down Syndrome children may lose ground at each of these points, as they have particular difficulties in comprehending the new tasks that constitute intelligence (Dunst 1988, 1990; Kopp & McCall 1982). The inability to master easily each new qualitative task of intelligence may be one reason for the progressive slowing of rate of intellectual progress (IQ) in the Down Syndrome population, particularly during the preschool years (Hodapp & Zigler 1990).

In contrast, lowered IQs in boys with fragile X syndrome may be more based on changes tied to the child's chronological age. Thus males with fragile X syndrome seem to decline in IQ during the pubertal years, roughly from ages 10 to 15 (Dykens et al 1989b; Hodapp et al 1990b). Just as data from Down Syndrome children help elucidate the presence and nature of task-related changes, so might the IQ decreases found in fragile X syndrome boys help clarify the relationship between age-related neurobiologic changes and rates of intellectual development.

CROSS-DOMAIN RELATIONSHIPS   In the original formulations of the developmental approach to mental retardation (Zigler 1967; 1969), it was hypothesized that functioning from one domain to another for retarded children showing no clear organic retardation (i.e. familial retarded individuals) would resemble that of nonretarded children. Specifically, because the retardation of these individuals was presumably not caused by organic deficit, they should show no group-wide intellectual weaknesses or strengths different from those of the nonretarded population.

To date, research has supported this hypothesized similarity of domain strengths and weaknesses between familial retarded groups and nonretarded groups, at least for Piagetian tasks. Weisz et al (1982) found that, when matched on mental age (MA) with nonretarded children, familial retarded children perform identically on a variety of Piagetian tasks throughout the childhood years. These studies cover the entire spectrum of Piagetian tasks, including tests of conservation, role taking, sex identity, relative thinking, moral judgments, and color identity. Similarly, Groff & Linden (1982) and Achenbach (1970) found that familial retarded children and nonretarded children exhibit the same relationships among intellectual abilities across subtests of IQ tests.

However, the functioning of familial retarded children may be lower than that of MA-matched nonretarded children on tasks that measure information processing. At present, approximately half of the relevant studies show that children with familial or nonspecific mental retardation perform about the same as MA-matched peers on tasks of selective attention, concept usage, and discrimination and incidental learning, whereas half show decreased performance by the mentally retarded group (Weiss et al 1986). Two reasons have been advanced for the possibly deficient performance of familial retarded children on information processing (but not Piagetian) tasks: (a) Information processing tasks may be less intrinsically interesting to retarded children than more real-life Piagetian tasks (Weiss et al 1986), or (b) there may be a distinction between information processing and Piagetian tasks that evinces a deficit in the familial retarded population (Mundy & Kasari 1990).

In contrast to familial retarded children, organically retarded children differ widely in their functioning across domains. As discussed above, fragile X males show particular deficits in sequential processing, whereas language is a particular weakness for individuals with Down Syndrome. Indeed, several organically retarded groups show particular, etiology-specific patterns of intellectual strengths and weaknesses.

Several cross-domain relationships appear to hold for nonretarded and various retarded populations. Such relationships involve small areas of functioning that are usually the result of two seemingly disparate behaviors reflecting a similar underlying structure (so-called "local homologies of shared origin"; Bates et al 1979). Thus, McCune-Nicholich & Bruskin (1982) have found that levels of symbolic play and early language skills develop in tandem for nonretarded children. Prelinguistic children mouth or handle objects, children in the one-word stage engage in single-schemed play (e.g.

using a toy cup to "drink"), and children beginning two-word sentences (early stage I language) combine simple schemes such as feeding a doll, then grooming it. Identical relationships between levels of symbolic play and early language have also been found in children with Down Syndrome (Hill & McCune-Nicholich 1981) and with autism (Mundy et al 1987), leading to speculation that such relationships hold true for all types of children.

There may be constraints on the degree to which one individual's abilities in one area can differ from abilities in a different area. This idea of limits to cross-domain variability is best shown in Down Syndrome children, whose social abilities can only exceed their linguistic abilities by a certain amount because higher-level social abilities require language (Cornwell & Birch 1969). As in the case of homologies, even though levels of development may not be even across domains, there may be some degree of "organization" across developments in different areas. In addition, the ways cross-domain organization is manifested in retarded and in nonretarded populations can be informed by studies of different types of retarded individuals (Cicchetti & Ganiban 1990).

INTERACTIONS BETWEEN MOTHERS AND THEIR RETARDED CHILDREN   Beginning with Bell's (1968) article in the late 1960s, workers in child development have come to appreciate that caregivers and children influence each other, that the behaviors of the child affect the parent just as the behaviors of the parent affect the child. This view of adult-child interaction is an elaboration and completion of the prior view of socialization, which focused on how parents affect their children (Zigler et al 1982).

Studies performed during the 1970s and 1980s showed that mothers simplify their speech and in many ways modulate their behaviors in response to the child's level of functioning. At the same time, mothers help children to perform by structuring the environment, getting the child's attention, breaking difficult tasks into component parts, and in other ways providing what has been called a "social scaffold" for the developing child (Bruner 1978). Such maternal behavior might thus be characterized as "interaction with a pull": A mother matches her behavior to the child's level of development but at the same time attempts to elicit higher-level behaviors from the developing child. For their part, children are "apprentices" in their own development through their interactions with their mothers (Kaye 1982).

Subsequent studies have shown that interactions between mothers and their retarded children both resemble and differ from those between mothers and nonretarded children. Mothers of Down Syndrome children provide their children with language of the same grammatical complexity as that provided by mothers of nonretarded children of the same levels of language (Rondal 1977); they also behave similarly on other aspects of "motherese"—repeating and emphasizing key words, speaking in a higher-pitched voice, etc.

However, mothers of retarded children differ greatly from mothers of nonretarded children in their styles of interaction. Mothers of several types of handicapped child are more didactic, more often initiate interactions, and in other ways are more controlling in their interactions (Cardoso-Martins & Mervis 1985; Jones 1980). Such differences in interactive style may result from the emotional reactions experienced by mothers of retarded children (Blacher 1984), from different maternal perceptions of the needs of the retarded child (Mahoney et al 1990), or from actual differences in the best ways to interact with less active, often more lethargic, handicapped children (Tannock 1988). In any event, mothers of retarded children match their behavior to their child's level of functioning but are at the same time more didactic and intrusive.

FAMILY SYSTEMS   Related to this interest in mother-child relations is the burgeoning interest in families and how families change as children develop. This interest in families can be traced to Bronfenbrenner's (1979) descriptions of the so-called ecology of childhood, and many studies have recently been performed on children's development within the family and other social systems (cf Kaye & Furstenberg 1985).

In much of both the earlier work on families of retarded children, (e.g. Farber 1959; Grossman 1972) and the recent (Krauss et al 1989) work on families of retarded children, the retarded child is thought of as a stressor in the family system, one buffered by the financial and emotional resources the family possesses (Crnic et al 1983). It is not surprising, therefore, that economically disadvantaged families are less able to handle the stress of a retarded child than families that are more well-off (Farber 1959), that one-parent families cope worse than two-parent families (Beckman 1983), and that mothers in less-successful marriages have more difficulty coping than those in better marriages (Friedrich 1979).

The most recent work attempts to conceptualize both the positive and negative aspects of families with handicapped children. Thus, Frey et al (1989) have found that the presence of a supportive social network leads to better coping on the part of mothers of handicapped children (see also Suelzle & Keenan 1981), whereas fathers cope better when there are minimal amounts of criticism from extended families. For both mothers and fathers, belief systems were the single most important factor in coping: If parents feel that they can cope with raising a handicapped child, that their spouse can also cope, and that they have a strong measure of personal control in raising their child, they in turn experience less psychological distress. While such a finding may not be surprising, it does show the change in emphasis from pathology to coping in studies of families of children with handicaps.

In addition, each member of such a family is differentially affected. Most interesting in this regard is the recent work on sibling relationships. Although most workers feel that nonhandicapped siblings of retarded or otherwise handicapped children are at greater risk for psychiatric disorders, such has not been shown for siblings as a group (Lobato 1983). Certain members, however, such as the oldest female child, may be more at risk (Cleveland & Miller 1977). In addition, nonhandicapped siblings may be more at risk in certain specific situations: when parents have difficulty accepting the handicapped child's condition; when the nonhandicapped child is of the same gender as the handicapped child; when the handicapped child's condition is not clearly diagnosed; and when the condition is serious, requiring a great deal of parental care and attention (McHale et al 1984).

Growing up as a handicapped child's sibling may also lead to beneficial outcomes. Some children clearly benefit from growing up with a retarded sibling: They become more empathetic toward persons with problems, are more altruistic and idealistic, and show a greater tolerance toward others (Grossman 1972; Wilson et al 1989). As adults, on the other hand, some are resentful, feeling that their parents gave too much time and attention to the retarded child (Grossman 1972). A similar bimodal distribution of effects applies to the family as a whole. Note once again that researchers are gaining a more balanced and realistic view of families of retarded children.

PERSONALITY-MOTIVATION FUNCTIONING IN RETARDED INDIVID-UALS   Another expansion of work in developmental psychology involves what has been termed the "whole child" approach (Zigler 1971). In this view, the child is seen as more than a thinking or language-using being. Aspects of development such as personality and motivational variables are included, allowing for a more complete picture of development.

The following five constructs are among those examined:

1. *Positive reaction tendency* is the tendency of retarded children to be more dependent on and aware of surrounding adults. The positive reaction tendency has been examined in a variety of settings, but the general thrust of this work is that retarded children often demonstrate a desire to interact with supportive adults greater than that shown by nonretarded children (e.g. Balla & Zigler 1975; Zigler et al 1968).

2. *Negative reaction tendency* involves the initial wariness of retarded individuals when interacting with strange adults. This initial wariness toward adults is later overcome by the positive reaction tendency, providing that subsequent interactions from adults are not perceived as negative or harmful (Harter & Zigler 1968; Zigler et al 1968).

3. *Expectancy of success* is the degree to which one expects to succeed or fail when presented with a new task. Retarded children have a lower expectancy of success than nonretarded children at intellectual tasks (e.g. Gruen & Zigler 1968; MacMillan & Keough 1971).

4. *Outer-directedness* is the tendency of retarded persons to look to cues in the external world for solutions to difficult problems. Like a lowered expectancy of success, an outer-directed style of problem solving is thought to be due to a history of failure for retarded children (e.g. Lustman & Zigler 1982).

5. *Effectance motivation* is the pleasure derived from tackling and solving difficult problems. Harter & Zigler (1974) have found that retarded children have less effectance motivation than do nonretarded children.

These constructs constitute only a few of the personality-motivational variables affecting performance in retarded children. However, these are powerful factors that seem to have real-world consequences. For example, Bybee & Zigler (unpublished) have found that the degree of outer-directedness shown can be directly manipulated by the order in which tasks are presented to retarded children. Those retarded children who began by receiving easier tasks became less outer-directed on later, more difficult tasks.

Retarded children of different types may vary systematically on these personality-motivational factors. Yando et al (1989), for example, have found that the etiology of the child's retardation determines the degree to which children exhibit outer-directed behavior (in this case, imitate the behaviors of an adult in a problem-solving situation). Organically retarded children imitated a greater percentage of the experimenter's acts that they remembered (i.e. they were more imitative); organically retarded children were also less likely to distinguish between the adult's relevant vs irrelevant acts when imitating. In addition, unlike nonretarded children and children with familial retardation, organically retarded children do not become less imitative with increasing age. Like the findings of the Bybee & Zigler (unpublished) study, these results have important implications for intervening with different types of retarded children.

PSYCHOPATHOLOGY   Until fairly recently, mental retardation and mental illness were considered as separate entities. Now, however, there is considerable interest in dual diagnosis, the co-occurrence of mental retardation and emotional disorder. Many retarded persons suffer from psychiatric disturbance; some studies have shown that 30% or more of retarded persons suffer from one or another type of behavioral or emotional disorder (e.g. Gillberg et al 1986). Moreover, emotional and behavioral problems—manifested either in trouble getting along with others or in fulfilling societal norms—are among the most important determinants of the life success of retarded individuals, especially those who are mildly retarded (Granat & Granat 1978).

The study of psychopathology in the retarded population is beset with several problems. First, there is a tendency on the part of clinicians not to diagnose emotional problems in mentally retarded samples; it is as if the person's mental retardation "overshadows" any psychiatric disorders that might also be present (Reiss et al 1982). Second, the self-reports of individuals with retardation are often unreliable. As Matson et al (1984) note, "Mentally retarded individuals may have difficulty discriminating the particular type of psychopathology they are experiencing" (p. 88).

Given these limitations, researchers are nonetheless documenting several interesting aspects of psychopathology in retarded populations. Retarded persons may show patterns of psychiatric disorders different from those of nonretarded populations. Psychoses and conduct disorder–antisocial behavior are more prevalent in psychiatrically impaired mentally retarded populations, whereas afffective disorders such as depression are less prevalent than in nonretarded in- or out-patient groups (e.g. Lund 1985; Meyers 1986). Retarded individuals may also show depressed affect indirectly, such that aggression against others, withdrawal, or somatic complaints may occur instead of classic depressive complaints such as feelings of hopelessness (Sovner & Hurley 1983). Although more work is needed in this area, such differences in the type and/or symptomatology of psychopathology might ultimately allow for more targeted clinical interventions with retarded persons suffering from behavioral and emotional problems.

There may also be a connection between different etiologies of mental retardation and types of psychopathology. Although recent studies question the previously reported association between fragile X syndrome and autism, 10–20% of fragile X males present with prominent autistic features (Bregman et al 1987). Anxiety and hyperactivity may be even more prevalent in the fragile X population (Bregman et al 1988). In three different samples of fragile X males, the symptom constellation of distractability, impulsivity, and motoric hyperactivity was reported in 41 of 50 fragile X boys (82%) (cf Bregman et al 1987).

Overview of Research on the Behavior of Retarded Individuals

An explosion in research interest has enabled us to distinguish different etiological groups and to study aspects of retarded functioning (e.g. psychopathology) about which little was known 10 or 15 years ago. Much of the most interesting research on the behavior of retarded persons comes at the intersection of two or more scholarly enterprises. Thus the phenomenon of dual diagnosis encompasses retardation as well as clinical psychology and psychiatry, just as the work on the developmental approach to mental retardation takes as its starting point the theories, findings, and approaches generated in the field of child development. In a similar way, genetics, neuropsychology, child psychiatry, and speech and language pathology all play a role in the growing understanding of behavior in retarded individuals.

SERVICE DELIVERY TO RETARDED INDIVIDUALS

Related to research advances and to societal shifts have come changes in how we treat our retarded citizens. These changes have been staggering, with many new educational and residential initiatives occurring over the past several decades. In education, PL 94-142, the Education for All Handicapped Children Act, was made federal law in 1975. Until that time, school systems were not legally responsible for providing a "free, appropriate education" for all retarded and otherwise impaired children. As a result of similar initiatives, most retarded persons now live successfully in group homes or in other community-living settings (a situation far different from that in the 1960s and 1970s); the remaining large institutions have become much smaller and more humane.

At the same time, however, there remain many difficult issues in both education and residential services. While PL 94-142 has ensured education for all handicapped children, it has been widely interpreted to mean that most retarded children should be mainstreamed into classes with nonhandicapped children. The rationale for such a policy is that retarded children perform equally in educational achievement in special education and mainstreamed classes, that social interaction will be enhanced and stigmatization decreased when retarded children are in contact with nonhandicapped age-mates, that segregation will be decreased, and that costs can be kept down while the degree of individualized instruction remains the same (Dunn 1968). Not surprisingly, given such an optimistic agenda, the results of mainstreaming have generally been mixed (Gottlieb 1981; Zigler & Hodapp 1986). As Meyers et al (1980:201) note, "there appears to be no unambiguous answer to the primitive question of whether segregated or integrated placement is superior" for retarded children.

Two recent trends are noteworthy, however. The first is the movement by schools to tailor mainstreaming to the needs of their handicapped students. In a survey of teachers throughout a medium-sized northeastern state, Yando et al (submitted) found that schools mainstream handicapped children based on a combination of the child's level of ability and the degree to which the activity requires higher-level student participation. Almost all children participate in assembly and lunch with nonhandicapped children, but only the highest-functioning special-needs children are mainstreamed into industrial arts or academic classes. This tailoring of mainstreaming practices would seem a useful compromise to the mainstreaming–special class dilemma for most public schools.

A second and more troubling change involves stigmatization. Partly in order to minimize stigmatization, fewer children are being diagnosed as mentally retarded. From 1976–1977 to 1985–1986, the US Department of

Education reported that the percentage of school children served as mentally retarded dropped from 2.16% to 1.68% (MacMillan 1988). At the same time, the number of children diagnosed as learning disabled increased by 142%, and many children "fell through the cracks" because they have IQs slightly too high to meet diagnostic criteria for learning disablities. MacMillan (1989) notes that this "virtual refusal to identify mildly mentally retarded children in some states" is denying many children the special services they require.

Related issues and problems occur in residential services. In the late 1960s and early 1970s, the desire to make more normal the lives of mentally retarded persons, together with public objection to widespread abuses at several large institutions, caused most large institutions to be depopulated. Group homes and community living settings arose throughout the country (see Vitello & Soskin 1985; Zigler & Hodapp 1986 for reviews).

Although this movement has generally been beneficial, several caveats are in order. First, in many cases, mental retardation workers may be creating "institutions in the community." Not all group homes, for example, promote greater involvement in the community for retarded persons than do some residential institutions, and smaller group homes do not always promote more friendships among retarded residents than do slightly larger group homes (Landesman & Butterfield 1987). In addition, specialized group homes or small institutional settings are sometimes necessary, as in the management of eating disorders associated with Prader-Willi syndrome (Walsh & McCallion 1987). There is also a need to monitor carefully the provision of services by group-home providers, as abuses are beginning to be documented (Hurst 1989).

At the same time, there may always be a need for some types of institutional settings for at least some retarded persons. Many retarded persons, especially those at the lowest levels of functioning, who have associated handicaps and/or behavioral disorders, may have difficulty with community living and need either short- or long-term institutional care. Of course this continued role for the mental retardation institution does not mean that larger institutions should not be improved (Crissey & Rosen 1986).

Finally, the field of mental retardation must realize that *where* a person receives services—be it in special vs mainstreamed classes or group home vs institutional settings—is probably less important than *what* services the person receives (Zigler et al 1990). This simple idea that the environment does not equal one's "social address," originally promulgated by Bronfenbrenner (1979) for the environments of nonretarded children, is no less true for retarded children and adults. The provision of better services, in all settings for all retarded persons, is the major challenge in service delivery as we enter the 1990s.

Literature Cited

Achenbach, T. 1970. Comparison of Stanford-Binet performance of nonretarded and retarded persons matched for MA and sex. *Am. J. Ment. Defic.* 74:488–99

Akesson, H. O. 1987. Traditional views and new perspectives on the genetics of mild mental retardation. *Upsala J. Med. Sci. Suppl.* 44:30–33

Balla, D., Zigler, E. 1975. Preinstitutional social deprivation, responsiveness to social reinforcement, and IQ change in institutionalized retarded individuals: a five-year follow-up study. *Am. J. Ment. Defic.* 80:228–30

Bates, E., Benigni, L., Bretherton, I., Camaioni, L., Volterra, V. 1979. *The Emergence of Symbols.* New York: Academic

Beckman, P. 1983. Influence of selected child characteristics on stress in families of handicapped infants. *Am. J. Ment. Defic.* 88:150–56

Beeghly, M., Cicchetti, D. 1987. An organizational approach to symbolic development in children with Down Syndrome. In *Symbolic Development in Atypical Children. New Directions for Child Development*, ed. D. Cicchetti and M. Beeghly No. 36, pp. 5–29. San Francisco: Jossey-Bass

Bell, R. Q. 1968. A reinterpretation of the direction of effects in studies of socialization. *Psychol. Rev.* 75:81–95

Blacher, J. 1984. Sequential stages of parental adjustment to the birth of a child with handicaps: fact or artifact? *Ment. Retard.* 22:55–68

Bornstein, M. 1989. Information processing (habituation) in infancy and stability in cognitive development. *Hum. Dev.* 32:129–36

Bregman, J., Dykens, E., Watson, M., Ort, S., Leckman, J. 1987. Fragile X syndrome: variability in phenotypic expression. *J. Am. Acad. Child Adolesc. Psychiatr.* 26:463–71

Bregman, J., Leckman, J., Ort, S. 1988. Fragile X syndrome: genetic predisposition to psychopathology. *J. Autism Dev. Disor.* 18:343–54

Bronfenbrenner, U. 1979. *The Ecology of Human Development.* Cambridge, MA: Harvard Univ. Press

Bronfenbrenner, U., Kessel, F., Kessen, W., White, S. 1986. Toward a critical social history of developmental psychology: a propadeutic discussion. *Am. Psychol.* 41:1218–30

Bruner, J. 1978. Learning to do things with words. In *Human Growth and Development*, ed J. Bruner and A. Garton, pp. 62–84. Oxford: Oxford Univ. Press

Burack, J. A., Hodapp, R. M., Zigler, E. 1988. Issues in the classification of mental retardation: differentiating among organic etiologies. *J. Child Psychol. Psychiatr.* 29:765–79

Burack, J. A., Hodapp, R. M., Zigler, E. 1990. Toward a more precise understanding of mental retardation: a rejoinder to Goodman. *J. Child Psychol. Psychiatr.* 31:471–75

Cardoso-Martins, C., Mervis, C. 1985. Maternal speech to prelinguistic children with Down Syndrome. *Am. J. Ment. Defic.* 89:451–58

Cicchetti, D., Beeghly, M., eds. 1990. *Children with Down Syndrome: A Developmental Perspective.* New York: Cambridge Univ. Press

Cicchetti, D., Ganiban, J. 1990. The organization and coherence of developmental processes in infants and children with Down syndrome. See Hodapp et al 1990, pp. 169–225

Cicchetti, D., Mans-Wagener, L. 1987. Sequences, stages, and structures in the organization of cognitive development in infants with Down syndrome. In *Infant Performance and Experience: New Findings with the Ordinal Scales*, ed. I. Uzgiris and J. McV. Hunt. Urbana: Univ. Illinois Press

Cicchetti, D. Sroufe, L. A. 1976. The relationship between affective and cognitive development in Down's Syndrome children. *Child Dev.* 47:920–29

Cleveland, D., Miller, N. 1977. Attitudes and life commitments of older siblings of mentally retarded adults: An exploratory study. *Ment. Retard.* 3:38–41

Cohen, D., Donnellan, A., eds. 1987. *Autism and Pervasive Developmental Disabilities.* New York: John Wiley & Sons

Cornwell, A., Birch, H. 1969. Psychological and social development in home-reared children with Down's Syndrome (mongolism). *Am. J. Ment. Defic.* 74:341–50.

Crissey, M. S., Rosen, M., eds. 1986. *Institutions for the Mentally Retarded: A Changing Role in Changing Times.* Austin: Pro-Ed Press

Crnic, K., Friedrich, W., Greenberg, M. 1983. Adaptation of families with mentally retarded children: a model of stress, coping, and family ecology. *Am. J. Ment. Defic.* 88:125–38

Cullen, S., Cronk, C., Pueschel, S., Schnell, R., Reed, R. 1981. Social development and feeding milestones of young Down Syndrome children. *Am. J. Ment. Defic.* 85:410–15

Dunn, L. M. 1968. Special education for the mildly retarded—Is much of it justifiable? *Except. Children* 35:5–22

Dunst, C. J. 1988. Stage transitioning in the sensorimotor development of Down's syndrome infants. *J. Ment. Defic. Res.* 32:405–10

Dunst, C. J. 1990. Sensorimotor development of infants with Down Syndrome. See Cicchetti & Beeghly, pp. 180–230

Dykens, E. M., Hodapp, R. M., Leckman, J. F. 1987a. Strengths and weaknesses in the intellectual functioning of males with fragile X syndrome. *Am. J. Ment. Defic.* 92:234–36

Dykens, E. M., Hodapp, R. M., Leckman, J. F. 1989a. Adaptive and maladaptive functioning in institutionalized and noninstitutionalized fragile X males. *J. Am. Acad. Child Adolesc. Psychiatr.* 28:427–30

Dykens, E. M., Hodapp, R. M., Ort, S., Finucane, B., Shapiro, L., Leckman, J. F. 1989b. The trajectory of cognitive development in males with fragile X syndrome. *J. Am. Acad. Child Adolesc. Psychiatr.* 28:422–26

Dykens, E. M., Leckman, J. F. 1990. Developmental issues in fragile X syndrome. See Hodapp et al 1990a, pp. 226–45

Dykens, E. M., Leckman, J. F., Paul, R., Watson, M. 1987b. The cognitive, behavioral, and adaptive functioning of fragile X and non-fragile X retarded men. *J. Autism Dev. Disord.* 18:41–52

Farber, B. 1959. The effects of a severely retarded child in family systems. *Monogr. Soc. Res. Child Dev.* 24:(2)

Ferrier, L. 1987. *A comparative study of the conversational skills of fragile X, autistic, and Down Snydrome individuals.* PhD thesis. Boston Univ. (Abstr. Int. #DA8715419)

Fowler, A. 1990. The development of language structure in children with Down Syndrome. See Cicchetti & Beeghly, pp. 302–28

Frey, K., Greenberg, M., Fewell, R. 1989. Stress and coping among parents of handicapped children: a multidimensional approach. *Am. J. Ment. Retard.* 94:240–49

Friedrich, W. 1979. Predictors of coping behavior of mothers of handicapped children. *J. Consult. Clin. Psychol.* 47:1140–41

Gibson, D. 1978. *Down's Syndrome: The Psychology of Mongolism.* Cambridge: Cambridge Univ. Press

Gibson, D. 1991. Down Syndrome and cognitive enhancement: Not like the others. In *Early Intervention in Transition: Current Perspectives on Programs for Handicapped Children,* ed. K. Marfo. New York: Praeger Publishers. In press

Gillberg, C., Persson, E., Grufman, M., Themner, U. 1986. Psychiatric disorders in mildly and severely mentally retarded urban children and adolescents: epidemiologic aspects. *Br. J. Psychiatr.* 149:68–74

Gottlieb, J. 1981. Mainstreaming: fulfilling the promise? *Am. J. Ment. Defic.* 86:115–26

Granat, K., Granat, S. 1978. Adjustment of intellectually below-average men not identified as mentally retarded. *Scand. J. Psychol.* 19:41–51

Groff, M. G., Linden, K. W. 1982. The WISC-R factor score profiles of cultural-familial retarded and nonretarded youth. *Am. J. Ment. Defic.* 87:147–52

Grossman, F. 1972. *Brothers and Sister of Retarded Children.* Syracuse, NY: Syracuse Univ. Press

Grossman, H., ed. 1983. *Classification in Mental Retardation.* Washington, DC: Am. Assoc. Ment. Retard. 3rd ed.

Gruen, G., Zigler, E. 1968. Expectancy of success and the probability learning of middle-class, lower-class, and retarded children. *J. Abnorm. Psychol.* 73:343–52

Harter, S., Zigler, E. 1968. The effectiveness of adult and peer reinforcement on the performance of institutionalized and noninstitutionalized retardates. *J. Abnorm. Psychol.* 73:144–49

Harter, S., Zigler, E. 1974. The assessment of effectance motivation in normal and retarded children. *Dev. Psychol.* 10:169–80

Herbst, D. 1980. Nonspecific X-linked mental retardation. I: A review with information from 24 families. *Am. J. Med. Genet.* 7:443–60

Hill, P., McCune-Nicholich, L. 1981. Pretend play and patterns of cognition in Down's syndrome infants. *Child Dev.* 23:43–60

Hodapp, R. M. 1990. One road or many? Issues in the similar sequence hypothesis. See Hodapp et al 1990a, pp. 49–70

Hodapp, R. M., Burack, J. A., Zigler, E., eds. 1990a. *Issues in the Developmental Approach to Mental Retardation.* New York: Cambridge Univ. Press

Hodapp, R. M., Dykens, E. M. 1991. Toward an etiology-specific strategy of early intervention with handicapped children. See Gibson 1991. In press

Hodapp, R. M., Dykens, E. M., Hagerman, R., Shreiner, R., Lachiewisc, A., Leckman, J. F. 1990b. Developmental implications of changing trajectories of IQ in males with fragile X syndrome. *J. Am. Acad. Child Adolesc. Psychiatr.* 29:214–19

Hodapp, R. M., Zigler, E. 1990. Applying the developmental perspective to individuals with Down syndrome. See Cicchetti & Beeghly 1990, pp. 1–28

Hurst, J. 1989. Private care for retarded—a gamble. *Los Angeles Times,* January 8–10

Jones, O. 1980. Prelinguistic communication skills in Down's syndrome and normal infants. In *High-Risk Infants and Children: Adult and Peer Interactions,* ed. T. Field, S. Soldberg, D. Stern, and A. Sostek, New York: Academic

Kaufman, A., Kaufman, S. 1983. *Kaufman Assessment Battery for Children*. Circle Pines, MN: Am. Guid. Serv.

Kaye, K. 1982. *The Mental and Social Life of Babies*. Chicago, IL: Univ. Chicago Press

Kaye, K., Furstenberg, F., eds. 1985. Special issue: family development and the child. *Child Dev.* 56 (Whole No. 2)

Kemper, M. B., Hagerman, R., Ahmad, R., Mariner, S. 1986. Cognitive profiles and the spectrum of clinical manifestations in heterozygous fra(X) females. *Am. J. Med. Genet.* 23:139–56

Kemper, M. B., Hagerman, R., Altshul-Stark, D. 1988. Cognitive profiles of boys with fragile X syndrome. *Am. J. Med. Genet.* 30:191–200

Klasner, E., Hagerman, R. 1987. *Speech and language characteristics and intervention strategies with fragile X patients*. Presentation to the 1st Nat. Fragile X Conf., Denver, Colorado

Kopp, C. 1983. Risk factors in development. In *Handbook of Child Psychology. Infancy and Developmental Psychobiology*, ed. P. Mussen, Vol. 2. New York: John Wiley and Sons

Kopp, C., McCall, R. 1982. Predicting later mental performance for normal, at risk, and handicapped infants. In *Lifespan Development and Behavior*, ed. P. Baltes & O. Brim, vol. 4. New York: Academic

Krakow, J., Kopp, C. 1982. Sustained attention in young Down syndrome children. *Top. Early Child. Spec. Educ.* 2:32–42

Krauss, M., Simeonsson, R., Landesman-Ramey, S., eds. 1989. Special issue on research on families. *Am. J. Ment. Retard.* 94 (Whole No. 3)

Lachiewicz, A., Gullion, C., Spiridigliozzi, G., Aylsworth, A. 1987. Declining IQs of young males with fragile X syndrome. *Am. J. Ment. Defic.* 92:272–78

Landesman, S., Butterfield, E. 1987. Normalization and deinstitutionalization of mentally retarded persons: controversy and facts. *Am. Psychol.* 42:809–16

Lobato, D. 1983. Siblings of handicapped children: a review. *J. Autism Dev. Disord.* 13:347–64

Lubs, H. A. 1969. A marker X chromosome. *Am. J. Hum. Genet.* 21:231–44

Lund, J. 1985. The presence of psychiatric morbidity in mentally retarded adults. *Acta Psychiatr. Scand.* 72:563–70

Lustman, N., Zigler, E. 1982. Imitation by institutionalized and noninstitutionalized mentally retarded and nonretarded children. *Am. J. Ment. Defic.* 87:252–58

McCall, R. B. 1981. Nature-nurture and the two realms of development: a proposed integration with respect to mental development. *Child Dev.* 52:1–12

McCall, R. B., Eichorn, D., Hogarty, P.

1977. Transitions in early mental development. *Mongr. Soc. Res. Child Dev.* 38.

McCune-Nicholich, L., Bruskin, C. 1982. Combinatorial competency in symbolic play and language. In *The Play of Children*, ed. D. Pepler and K. Rubin. New York: Karger

McHale, S., Simeonnson, R., Sloan, J. 1984. Children with handicapped brothers and sisters. In *The Effects of Autism on the Family*, ed. E. Shopler and G. Mesibov. New York: Plenum

MacMillan, D. 1989. Equality, excellence, and the EMR populations: 1970–1989. *Psychol. Ment. Retard. Dev. Disabil.* 15 (2):1–10

MacMillan, D. 1988. Issues in mild mental retardation. *Educ. Train. Ment. Retard.* 23:273–83

MacMillan, D., Keough, B. 1971. Normal and retarded children's expectancy for failure. *Dev. Psychol.* 4:343–48

Mahoney, G., Fors, S., Wood, S. 1990. Maternal directive behavior revisited. *Am. J. Ment. Retard.* 94:398–406

Marans, W., Paul, R., Leckman, J. 1987. *Speech and language profiles in males with fragile X syndrome*. Paper presented to the Am. Speech and Hearing Assoc. Conf. New Orleans

Martin, J., Bell, S. 1943. A pedigree of mental defect showing sex linkage. *J. Neurol. Psychol.* 6:154–57

Matson, J., Kazdin, A., Senatore, V. 1984. Psychometric properties of the Psychopathology Instrument for Mentally Retarded Adults. *Appl. Res. Ment. Retard.* 5:81–89

Meyers, B. 1986. Psychopathology in hospitalized developmentally disabled individuals. *Comprehens. Psychiatr.* 27:115–26

Meyers, C. E., MacMillan, D., Yoshida, R. 1980. Regular class education of EMR students, from efficacy to mainstreaming: a review of issues and research. In *Educating Mentally Retarded Persons in the Mainstream*, ed. J. Gottlieb. Baltimore: University Park Press

Miller, J. 1986. Early cross-cultural commonalities in social explanation. *Dev. Psychol.* 22:514–20

Miller, J. F. 1991. Language and communication characteristics of children with Down syndrome. In *Down Syndrome: State of the Art*, ed. A. Crocker, S. Pueschel, J. Rynders, and C. Tingley. Baltimore: Brooks. In press

Morgan, S. 1979. Development and distribution of intellectual and adaptive skills in Down syndrome children: implications for early intervention. *Ment. Retard.* 17:247–49

Mundy, P., Kasari, C. 1990. The similar structure hypothesis and differential rate hypothesis in mental retardation. See Hodapp et al 1990a, pp. 71–92

Mundy, P., Sigman, M., Ungerer, J., Sherman, T. 1987. Nonverbal communication and play correlates of language development in autistic children. *J. Autism Dev. Disord.* 17:349–64

Opitz, J., Sutherland, G. 1984. History, nosology, and bibliography of X-linked retardation. Conference report: International workshop on the fragile X and X-linked mental retardation. *Am. J. Med. Genet.* 17:19–33

Pueschel, S. M. 1983. The child with Down Syndrome. In *Developmental Pediatrics,* ed. M. Levine, W. Carey, A. Crocker, and R. Gross. Philadelphia: Saunders

Pueschel, S. M., Gallagher, P., Zartler, A., Pezzullo, J. 1987. Cognitive and learning profiles in children with Down Syndrome. *Res. Dev. Disabil.* 8:21–37

Reed, R., Pueschel, S., Schnell, R., Cronk, C. 1980. Interrelationships of biological, environmental, and competency variables in young children with Down syndrome. *Appl. Res. Ment. Retard.* 1:161–74

Reiss, S., Levitan, G., Szyszko, J. 1982. Emotional disturbance and mental retardation: diagnostic overshadowing. *Am. J. Ment. Defic.* 86:567–74

Rondal, J. 1977. Maternal speech in normal and Down's Syndrome children. In *Research to Practice in Mental Retardation,* ed. P. Mittler, 2:320–28. Baltimore: University Park Press

Scarr-Salapatek, S. 1975. An evolutionary perspective on infant intelligence: species patterns and individual variations. In *Origins of Intelligence,* ed. M. Lewis, pp. 165–97. New York: Plenum

Sorce, J., Emde, R. 1982. The meaning of infant emotional expressions: regularities in caregiving responses in normal and Down's Syndrome infants. *J. Child Psychol. Psychiatr.* 23:145–58

Sovner, R., Hurley, A. 1983. Do the mentally retarded suffer from affective illness? *Arch. Gen. Psychiatr.* 40:61–67

Sparrow, S., Balla, D., Cicchetti, D. 1984. *Vineland Adaptive Behavior Scales.* Circle Pines, MN: Am. Guid. Serv

Suelzle, M., Keenan, V. 1981. Changes in family support networks over the life cycle of mentally retarded persons. *Am. J. Ment. Defic.* 86:267–74

Tannock, M. 1988. Control and reciprocity in mothers' interactions with Down Syndrome and normal children. In *Parent-Child Interaction and Developmental Disabilities,* ed. K. Marfo, pp. 163–80. New York: Praeger

Taylor, R., Caldwell, M., eds. 1988. *Prader-Willi Syndrome: Selected Research and Management Issues.* New York: Springer-Verlag

Vitello, S., Soskin, R. 1985. *Mental Retardation: Its Social and Legal Context.* Englewood Cliffs, NJ: Prentice-Hall

Yando, R., Seitz, V., Zigler, E. 1989. Imitation, recall, and imitativeness in children with low intelligence of organic and familial etiology. *Res. Dev. Disabil.* 10:383–97

Walsh, K., McCallion, P. 1987. The role of the small institution in the community services continuum. In *Transitions in Mental Retardation. The Community Imperative Revisited,* ed. R. Antonak and J. Mulick, 3:218–36. Norwood, NJ: Ablex

Weiss, B., Weisz, J., Bromfield, R. 1986. Performance of retarded and nonretarded persons on information-processing tasks: further tests of the similar structure hypothesis. *Psychol. Bull.* 100:157–75

Weisz, J., Yeates, K., Zigler, E. 1982. Piagetian evidence and the developmental-difference controversy. In *Mental Retardation: The Developmental-Difference Controversy,* ed. E. Zigler and D. Balla. Hillsdale, NJ: Erlbaum

Wetherby, A. 1986. Ontogeny of communicative functions in autism. *J. Autism Dev. Disord.* 16:295–316

Wilson, J., Blacher, J., Baker, B. 1989. Siblings of children with severe handicaps. *Ment. Retard.* 27:167–73

Wolf-Schein, E., Sudhalter, V., Cohen, I., Fish, G., Hanson, D., Pfadt, A., et al. 1987. Speech-language and fragile X syndrome: initial findings. *J. Am. Speech-Lang. Hearing Assoc.* 29:35–38

Zigler, E. 1967. Familial mental retardation: a continuing dilemma. *Science* 155:292–98

Zigler, E. 1969. Developmental versus difference theories of mental retardation and the problem of motivation. *Am. J. Ment. Defic.* 73:536–66

Zigler, E. 1971. The retarded child as a whole person. In *Advances in Experimental Child Psychology,* ed. H. E. Adams and W. K. Boardman, Vol. 1 New York: Pergamon

Zigler, E., Balla, D., Butterfield, E. 1968. A longitudinal investigation of the relationship between preinstitutional social deprivation and social motivation in institutionalized retardates. *J. Pers. Soc. Psychol.* 10:437–45

Zigler, E., Hodapp, R. M. 1986. *Understanding Mental Retardation.* New York: Cambridge Univ. Press

Zigler, E., Hodapp, R., Edison, M. 1990. From theory to practice in the care and education of mentally retarded individuals. *Am. J. Ment. Retard.* 95:1–12

Zigler, E., Lamb, M., Child, I., eds. 1982. *Socialization and Personality Development* New York: Oxford Univ. Press 2nd ed.

Annu. Rev. Psychol. 1991. 42:51–78

ORGANIZATION DEVELOPMENT AND TRANSFORMATION

Jerry I. Porras and Robert C. Silvers

Graduate School of Business, Stanford University, Stanford, California 94305

KEY WORDS: planned change, applied behavioral science, organizational change

CONTENTS

INTRODUCTION

Rapidly changing environments demand that organizations generate equally fast responses in order to survive and prosper. Planned change that makes organizations more responsive to environmental shifts should be guided by generally accepted and unified theories of organizations and organizational change—neither of which currently exists. Yet despite this absence of clear conceptual underpinnings, the field continues to evolve and grow.

In this chapter, we review recent research that improves our understanding of planned change theory and practice. We begin by proposing a new model

51

0066-4308/91/0201-0051$02.00

of the change process rooted in a conception of organizations presented by Porras (1987) and Porras et al (1990). This change model organizes our understanding of the field and guides the discussion of research presented in the second half of the chapter.[1]

A MODEL OF PLANNED CHANGE

Organizational change is typically triggered by a relevant environmental shift that, once sensed by the organization, leads to an intentionally generated response. This intentional response is "planned organizational change" and consists of four identifiable, interrelated components: (a) a change intervention that alters (b) key organizational target variables that then impact (c) individual organizational members and their on-the-job behaviors resulting in changes in (d) organizational outcomes. These broad components of planned change are shown at the top of Figure 1. The lower part of the figure adds more detail to each component and graphically summarizes our Planned Process Model;[2] we discuss each component below.

Change Interventions

Planned change interventions can be divided into two general types. The first comprises the more traditional approach, Organization Development (OD), which until recently was synonymous with the term *planned change*. The second, Organization Transformation (OT), is the cutting edge of planned change and may be called "second-generation OD." At present, OD is relatively well defined and circumscribed in terms of its technologies, theory, and research. OT, on the other hand, is emerging, ill-defined, highly experimental, and itself rapidly changing.[3]

---

[1]The six previous major reviews of the field (Friedlander & Brown 1974; Beer 1976; Alderfer 1977; Faucheux et al 1982; Beer & Walton 1987; Porras et al 1990) each used different frameworks to organize their discussions—frameworks based on change targets, strategies, functions, or theories. None, however, was based on a model of the change process itself. We hope our attempt to model the change process will interest others in doing the same. The field sorely needs a clear model of change to guide research and action.

[2]This perspective is rooted in the Stream Organization Model, a model of organizations proposed by Porras (1987) and Porras et al (1990) as a conceptual base for planned change work. Its key assumptions include these: that individual behavior is central to producing organizational outcomes; that individual work behavior is mostly driven by the context (work setting) of individual employees; that organizational vision provides the basic rationale for the design of the work setting; and that two major outcomes, organizational performance and individual development, derive from collective behaviors.

[3]Each of these two intervention approaches will be defined in terms of subsequent sections of the Change Process Model. As such, these definitions may not be completely clear to the reader at this point. We ask the reader to bear with us until all components are discussed.

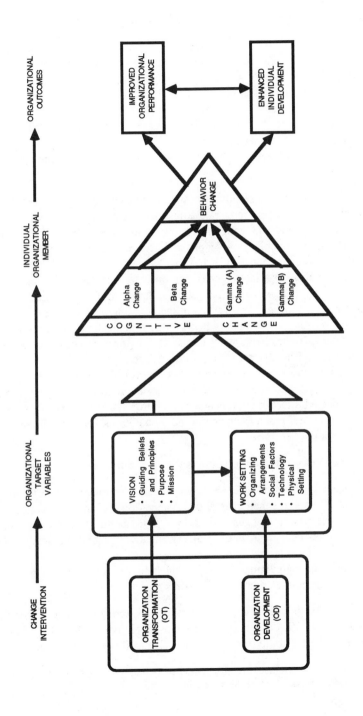

ORGANIZATION DEVELOPMENT   Organization Development is defined as:

1. a set of behavioral science theories, values, strategies, and techniques
2. aimed at the planned change of organizational work settings
3. with the intention of generating alpha, beta, and/or gamma (A) cognition change in individual organizational members, leading to behavioral change and thus
4. creating a better fit between the organization's capabilities and its current environmental demands, or
5. promoting changes that help the organization to better fit predicted future environments.

OD often occurs in response to modest mismatches with the environment and produces relatively moderate adjustments in those segments of the organization not congruent with the environment. This form of OD results in individuals' experiencing only alpha and beta cognition change, with a correspondingly limited change in behaviors.

Additionally, OD is triggered not only by current environmental mismatches but also by an organization's desire to fit into future desirable environmental niches. This results in the creation of new modes of functioning and impacts substantial segments of the organization. This second type of OD leads to alpha, beta, and gamma(A) cognition change in organizational members, and behavioral changes are broader.[4]

In summary, then, OD concentrates on work-setting changes that either help an organization better adapt to its current environment or improve its fit into expected future environments. This approach to planned change produces appreciable, not radical, change in individual employees' cognitions as well as behaviors.

ORGANIZATION TRANSFORMATION   Organization Transformation is:

1. a set of behavioral science theories, values, strategies, and techniques
2. aimed at the planned change of organizational vision and work settings.
3. with the intention of generating alpha, beta, gamma (A) and/or gamma (B) cognition change in individual organizational members, leading to behavioral change and thus
4. promoting paradigmatic change that helps the organization better fit or create desirable future environments.

OT is also planned and primarily directed at creating a new vision for the organization. Vision change occurs most effectively when an organization develops the capability for continuous self-diagnosis and change; a "learning

---

[4]While this type of change is primarily caused by OD, some OT interventions focus on the work setting and also produce this pattern of change.

organization" evolves—one that is constantly changing to more appropriately fit the present organizational state and better anticipate desired futures. This set of interventions leads to alpha, beta, gamma(A), and gamma(B) cognition change in organizational members, and concomitant radical change in their behaviors.

Organizational Target Variables

Planned change interventions impact two major types of organizational variables: organizational vision and the work setting. Taken together, these create the internal organizational environment in which individual employees function.

Vision consists of three main factors: (a) the guiding beliefs and principles of the organization; (b) the enduring organizational purpose that grows out of these beliefs; and (c) a catalyzing mission that is consistent with organizational purpose and, at the same time, moves the organization toward the achievement of that purpose (Collins & Porras 1989).

The work setting consists of many dimensions and, as such, requires a parsimonious framework to organize our understanding of it. From our perspective, the organizational work setting can be subdivided into four major streams of variables: (a) organizing arrangements, (b) social factors, (c) technology, and (d) physical setting (Porras 1987). Table 1 lists the subvariables that constitute each of these streams. These four streams of variables are themselves shaped by the organization's vision, which gives them coherence and direction.

Individual Organizational Members

Individual organizational members must change their on-the-job behaviors in order for the organization to change over a longer term. The complex environment surrounding individuals at work is the primary catalyst for behaviors on the job (moderated, as discussed below, by cognitive change). Organizational behaviors are generated by individuals behaving in response to the signals received directly from their work setting and indirectly from organizational vision. Therefore, successful planned change efforts must alter these two components of the internal organizational environment such that new signals influence individuals to produce new behaviors. Employees consciously process work setting cues and modify their behavior as a result.

INDIVIDUAL COGNITION AND PLANNED CHANGE   The types of individual cognitive change that occur as a result of planned change activities have been discussed in the management and organization literature for over four decades (e.g. Lindblom 1959; Vickers 1965; Greiner 1972; Sheldon 1980). For our purposes, the most useful conceptualization appeared in the OD literature 15 years ago when Golembiewski and his colleagues proposed alpha, beta, and

Table 1 Organizational components in the stream organizational model[a]

Organizing Arrangements (OA)	Social Factors (SF)	Technology (T)	Physical Setting (PS)
A. goals	A. culture	A. tools, equipment,	A. space configuration
B. strategies	1. basic assumptions	& machinery	1. size
C. formal structure	2. values	B. technical expertise	2. shape
D. administrative	3. norms	C. job design	3. relative locations
policies & procedures	4. language & jargon	D. work flow design	B. physical ambiance
E. administrative	5. rituals	E. technical policies	1. light
systems	6. history	& procedures	2. heat
F. formal reward	7. stories	F. technical systems	3. noise
systems	8. myths		4. air quality
1. evaluation system	9. symbols		5. cleanliness
2. pay systems	B. interaction processes		C. interior design
3. benefits packages	1. interpersonal		1. decorations
G. ownership	2. group		2. furniture
	3. intergroup		3. window coverings
	C. social patterns &		4. floor coverings
	networks		5. colors
	1. communication		a. floors
	2. problem solving/		b. walls
	decision making		c. ceilings
	3. influence		D. architectural design
	4. status		
	D. individual attributes		
	1. attitudes & beliefs		
	2. behavioral skills		
	3. feelings		
	E. management style		

[a] Source: Adapted from Porras, J. I. 1987. *Stream Analysis*. Reading, MA: Addison-Wesley; p. 52, Table 3-1

gamma change as the three possible measurable outcomes of OD interventions (Golembiewski et al 1976):

1. "Alpha change involves a variation in the level of some existential state, given a constantly calibrated measuring instrument related to a constant conceptual domain" (p. 134).
2. "Beta change involves a variation in the level of some existential state complicated by the fact that some intervals of the measurement continuum associated with a constant conceptual domain have been recalibrated" (p. 135).
3. "Gamma change involves a redefinition or reconceptualization of some domain, a major change in the perspective or frame of reference within which phenomena are perceived and classified, in what is taken to be some relevant slice of reality" (p. 135).

This perspective is primarily oriented toward framing change in the context of measurement issues, but it highlights some important principles. Alpha change is a perceived change in objective circumstances, while beta change is that type of change coupled with changing standards of individual interpretation. Gamma change is a radical shift in an individual's assumptions about causal relationships, the values attached to various dimensions of reality, and the interpretive frameworks that describe reality. In other words, gamma change describes a "paradigm shift" in organizational members' mental constructs (Kuhn 1970).

The notion of paradigm is useful for conceptualizing the change process. An organizational paradigm may be defined as:

> a prevailing worldview or collective belief system. The fundamental set of beliefs or organizing principles which are unquestioned and unexamined assumptions about the nature of reality (Adams 1984:278).[5]

Integrating the construct of organizational paradigm with the notions of alpha, beta, and gamma change is a useful way to develop a new typology that conceptualizes individual cognitive change processes. The focus here is not on measurement but on broad categories of individual cognitive change. This leads to the following four types:

1. Alpha change: change in the perceived levels of variables within a paradigm without altering their configuration (e.g. a perceived improvement in skills).
2. Beta change: change in people's view about the meaning of the value of any variable within an existing paradigm without altering their configuration (e.g. change in standards).
3. Gamma(A) change: change in the configuration of an existing paradigm without the addition of new variables (e.g. changing the central value of a "production-driven" paradigm from "cost containment" to "total quality focus"; this results in the reconfiguration of all variables within this paradigm).
4. Gamma(B) change: the replacement of one paradigm with another that contains some or all new variables (e.g. replacing a "production-driven" paradigm with a "customer-responsive" paradigm).

[5]Kuhn (1970) defined a knowledge paradigm as "the collection of ideas within the confines of which scientific inquiry takes place, the assumed definition of what are legitimate problems and methods, the accepted practice and point of view with which the student prepares for membership in the scientific community, the criteria for choosing problems to attack, the rules and standards of scientific practice" (p. 11). This definition of paradigm, which is widely cited in both the natural and social sciences, is consistent with Adams's definition, which focuses specifically on organizations.

Each of these cognitive changes leads to corresponding changes in behavior. As an illustration, a change in standards (the example given above for beta change) causes behavior to change in order to meet these new standards. As another example, a paradigm shift from "production-driven" to "customer-responsive" alters existing behaviors, creates new behaviors, and gives individual employees a totally new way of viewing their work. The level and depth of behavior change will therefore correspond to the shift in individual cognitions.

Organizational Outcomes

Two kinds of organizational outcomes are central to our model. The first is organizational performance, captured in factors such as productivity, profitability, efficiency, effectiveness, quality, etc. The second is individual development, an actualization of the self that occurs as individuals alter their world views, expand their repertoire of behaviors, and/or improve their skills and abilities.

Summary

The Change Process Model identifies the key components of a change process and organizes them in a way that improves one's understanding of the field as a whole. We use this model to categorize our review of recent research by analyzing articles according to the intervention approach used, the variables targeted for change, the type of individual cognitive change that occurs, and the organizational outcomes derived from the intervention activity. Unfortunately, much of the research does not give enough detail to fully analyze work by the last two above-mentioned categories, so we categorize articles primarily by intervention approach and target variables.

RESEARCH FINDINGS

This review examines articles concerning OD and OT that were published between 1985 and 1989 in journals with an organizational behavior and/or organization development focus (e.g. the *Journal of Applied Behavioral Science, Human Relations, Group and Organizational Studies, Journal of Applied Psychology, Academy of Management Journal, Academy of Management Review, Organizational Dynamics*, etc). Because little literature on OT was found in these sources, we reviewed books and other journals that do contain work on OT (e.g. Levy & Merry 1986; Adams 1984).

Organization Development

We first focus our discussion on OD research and structure our comments using the change targets (i.e. organizing arrangements, social factors, technology, physical space) as subcategories in our review. Articles that do not fit these categories are reviewed at the end of this section.

ORGANIZING ARRANGEMENTS   Research on a variety of interventions focuses on this stream of target variables. Quality circles (QCs), gainsharing interventions, and other forms of employee involvement are the topics most prevalent in the period reviewed. Some research also focused on other OA dimensions such as alternative work schedules, new design tools, and new design options. We review the key articles that further our understanding of these various interventions and/or discuss innovative practices and ideas.[6]

Quality circles   Generally, the literature on QCs lacks empirical and statistical rigor. One important cause of this appears to be the absence of a clear theoretical foundation to guide research. Initial attempts at theory have been made that primarily classified QCs as focusing on work technology, with productivity as its end target (Steel & Shane 1986). Later attempts to strengthen QC theory provided a more detailed model of the QC process, focusing on both structural and processual variables. However, the empirical evidence supporting these models has been mixed (Steel & Lloyd 1988).

Other additions to QC theory emphasize the conditions leading to failure in QC implementation. One approach views disappointments with QCs as due to flawed assumptions (e.g. that groups always outperform individuals) and a lack of understanding regarding the cultural differences between the United States and Japan (Ferris & Wagner 1985). Another proposes that a myriad of organizational factors hamper QC success, such as supervisory resistance, lack of volunteers, departmental transfer of employees (leading to less QC continuity), unskilled meeting facilitation, etc (Meyer & Stott 1985). A third suggests that QCs are an employee-involvement strategy leading to minimal changes in organizational power and should be used primarily when conditions are not favorable for more extensive employee involvement (Lawler & Mohrman 1987; Lawler 1988). These perspectives all imply that changes in both structure and process are necessary to improve QC success rates.

Additional empirical research investigating QC efficacy has focused on assessing the impact of QC interventions on a variety of attitudinal and perceptual variables. QC membership significantly affects attitudes specific to QC functioning such as communication, participation (Marks et al 1986), and influence (Rafaeli 1985); changes in more general attitudes such as satisfaction and commitment have also been found (Griffin 1988).[7]

---

[6]This same criteria will be applied to each of the following sections.

[7]It should be noted, however, that these findings were reported for the second and third years of a longitudinal study. By the fourth year, the measures of these indicators did not differ from the first year.

Findings on the effects of QCs on task perceptions have been contradictory. Rafaeli (1985) showed significant effects from QC membership on task perceptions while, in a similar study, Head et al (1986) did not. Overall, the evidence regarding QCs is most positive for attitudinal and behavioral impacts directly related to QC functioning; the evidence is contradictory about QC impact on task perceptions.

Gainsharing   Theory and research on gainsharing has emphasized its motivational effects on performance. Although the theory base for this approach is relatively weak, there have been recent attempts at strengthening it. For example, Florkowski (1987) proposed a theoretical model explaining the connection between profit sharing and behavioral and attitudinal outcomes. Drawing on expectancy theory and labor relations theory, he hypothesizes that profit sharing is a motivator for individual employees to the extent that it is a salient and important part of earnings and/or based on subunit performance.

Empirical investigations of this motivation dimension have not yielded highly positive findings. For example, Pearce et al (1985) found that merit pay for federal agency managers had no effect on improved performance in the manager's units. Jordan (1986) examined the effects of performance-contingent rewards and found that this type of pay for social service workers decreased intrinsic motivation and did not affect satisfaction with pay. However, positive effects were reported in a study of a manufacturing firm that had employed the Scanlon Plan for approximately a decade. Miller & Schuster (1987) found that the Plan had statistically significant effects on employment stability along with positive effects on productivity and labor-management cooperation.

The negative empirical findings regarding gainsharing theory appear to be derived from change projects of more limited scope and duration. On the other hand, much more positive findings seem to obtain when gainsharing is part of a long-term, broad-based program (i.e. the Scanlon Plan study). It appears that gainsharing has the greatest effect when it is part of a larger-scale and more extensive change process.

Employee ownership   Research on employee ownership is expanding and developing a stronger theory base. Some of the most substantial work in this arena was done by Klein (1987), who tested three competing models relating employee stock ownership to employee attitudes. She found that the financial benefits and influence opportunities of ownership most strongly impacted attitudes. This evidence supported extrinsic and instrumental models of ownership, but not an intrinsic model where ownership is satisfying in and of itself.

Regarding the influence effects of employee ownership, some research contradicts the "expected" link between employee ownership and desire for influence in organizational policies. For example, French (1987) characterized employees as investors who only seek influence when it is in their best financial interests to do so. As a consequence, he concludes that ownership may not be a solution for increasing power equalization within the firm.

In summary, research on employee ownership has grown and illustrates a promising and innovative approach to organizing in this country. However, it still lacks a strong theory base, one that is much needed to guide both practice and research.

Alternative work schedules   Researchers here have primarily investigated the impact of alternative work schedules on attitudes and productivity. Attitude changes about the schedule and free time have been found to be a primary effect of work schedule changes, with smaller impacts on general attitudes and effectiveness (Dunham et al 1987). The process used to implement alternative work schedules is also important. As would be expected, the greater the participation in the implementation process, the more favorable the attitudes toward the change (Latack & Foster 1985).[8] Regarding only the relationship between alternative work schedules and productivity, positive effects of flextime on productivity occur when resources are scarce and productivity is measured at the group level (Ralston et al 1985).

In summary, although this approach to organizational improvement has existed for over a decade, there has been little research on it. Alternative schedules appear to improve attitudes and performance, but more research is needed to determine the conditions under which these effects extend beyond variables specific to the intervention.

Organizational structure   Changes in organizational structure have been discussed in the literature from a variety of perspectives. One approach has foused on the development of new structural options. Ackoff (1989) proposed the "circular organization," where each manager reports to a "board of directors" consisting of his/her immediate superiors, subordinates, and important peers or outsiders. These boards are responsible for planning and coordination with other units, and, in some cases, for evaluating managerial performance. This approach to organization structure highlights one way that democracy and responsiveness need not conflict in modern organizations.

---

[8]Latack & Foster (1985) also propose an interesting unanticipated consequence of altering work schedules—that if they are compressed schedules they will tend to lead to job enrichment, since workers on duty at any one time will have to perform more tasks.

A second perspective focuses on new tools for design, rather than the final design itself. Two such tools have been proposed by McDaniel et al (1987) and Nelson (1988). The former examined the usefulness of decision analysis for interventions involving organizational design. They found this tool helped participants to identify problems and resolve them productively. The latter discussed the uses of "blockmodeling" (a form of network analysis found primarily in sociology) for structural diagnosis, coalition identification, and intergroup relations analysis. Network analysis uncovers groupings and patterns not easily identified by traditional OD diagnostic methods. These two approaches to the problem of organization design are creative and should set the stage for additional (and much needed) development in this area.[9]

Summary   While it is encouraging to see more theory related to organization-level issues and structural interventions, most of the above research consists of "little studies." Although these further knowledge of a specific intervention and its particular effects, no attempt is made to explore multifaceted interventions and systemic outcomes. Intervention research in this and other areas would be more profitable if it explored broader and more complex system change and its outcomes (e.g. the effects of gainsharing on social factors variables such as culture). In addition, research needs to expand its focus from direct effects to more pervasive and indirect impacts in order to assess the overall effectiveness of organizing arrangement interventions.

SOCIAL FACTORS   The social factors (SF) variables have historically been the most frequent targets of OD in organizations, but research in this area has decreased somewhat in recent years. In addition, the particular dimensions of interest have shifted; team interventions and group variables (which used to be the primary focus of this area) do not dominate the more current literature.

We begin our discussion with interventions oriented toward the alteration of individual attributes, next review research on group change, and then treat work focusing on culture change.

Personality theory   An exciting development in the SF area is the increased integration of personality theory with OD. Personality theory research reported in the period reviewed has been applied to all levels of analysis: to the

---

[9]It is useful to note that, irrespective of the technique used to design organizational structures, their implementation is strongly enhanced through the use of employee involvement and process consultation work. Stebbins & Shani (1989) reviewed four major approaches to organizational design (Galbraith's Information Processing Model; MacKenzie's ABCE model and OA&A process; Kilmann's MAPS technology; and Sociotechnical Systems consulting) and found that while all four methods varied in their foci and key variables, they all incorporated process consultation and employee involvement principles in their implementation process.

individual employee, the manager, the small group, and the overall organization.

At the individual level, personality theory has been applied to identifying traits that might moderate the acceptance and effects of planned change. One that has been identified is the employee's "focus of attention" (Gardner et al 1987). Employees may either focus on the job, the work unit, or off-the job; each focus leads to different effects from various interventions. It was hypothesized that job design interventions would positively affect individuals focused on their jobs, with similar types of predictions made for the other foci. Empirical evidence indicated that job focus and job change impacted hard measures, whereas work unit focus and job change impacted soft measures. Off-the-job focus impacted both types of measures negatively.

An important application of personality theory to the understanding of manager behavior has been made by Fisher et al (1987), who drew on developmental psychology to create a four-stage model of the managerial life cycle. Their research showed that few managers have reached the final two stages (which emphasize a tolerance for ambiguity and "transformational" leadership); therefore, problems in the organization may indicate a mismatch between organizational needs and managers' development. This framework could be useful as a diagnostic tool to identify dysfunctional matches.

Krantz (1985) used a Tavistock Institute approach to explore how unconscious group processes, such as defenses against anxiety, serve to create a specific organizational structure and culture. Examples of organizational decline were used to elucidate this process. This analysis provides an innovative method for understanding resistance to change and implementing more effective organizational designs.

These three articles further our understanding of the impact of individual differences on intervention efficacy. They also highlight the link between organizational form and individual personality. However, this area (like many others) needs substantially more attention than it has been given. Other personality factors should be explored, and a more comprehensive model of personality related to OD should be developed.

Team building   We found relatively few studies of team building. Those we identified were clustered into three broad groups: one that investigated the effects of team building on group process variables, a second that explored the impact of team building on the productivity or performance of the group, and a third that presented new perspectives on team building dynamics and appropriate research methods.

The impact of team building interventions on process measures was explored in two studies by Eden (1985, 1986a). Working with Israel Defense Forces (IDF) officers, Eden found that team building significantly affected self-perceptions of the efficacy of the intervention but did not effect actual changes (as rated by subordinates). A follow-up study (Eden 1986a) showed significant effects on teamwork, conflict handling, and information about plans but not on other variables less directly related to the intervention itself (such as challenge, officer support, etc). These studies provide only mixed evidence for the efficacy of the team building intervention.

The impact of team building on performance measures was examined in three different investigations. Bottger & Yetton (1987) studied the impact of individual training in problem solving on group performance and found significantly positive effects. Mitchell (1986) showed that revealing one's "internal frame of reference" leads to improved task accomplishment. However, these results were not significantly better than a traditional team building intervention. Research by Buller & Bell (1986) examined a team building/goal setting intervention with miners and found only marginally significant effects on outcomes such as productivity. It appears that narrowly focused team building interventions have a positive effect on performance. This suggests that the creative combination of some of these more narrowly focused intervention techniques could produce a substantially greater impact.

Contributions to the theory base of team building were made by Buller (1986), who utilized concepts from force-field analysis and participative decision making to develop a more precise definition of team building. He proposed that the effect of "team building-problem solving" on task performance occurs due to a variety of individual, group, task, and organizational factors. Finally, Buller suggests that team building research can be substantially improved through the development of clear operational definitions of variables, clear conceptualization of causal mechanisms, increased use of experimental designs, and the development of objective performance measures. We agree with these recommendations except for the use of experimental designs. The reality of field research often precludes the use of true experiments; in addition, there are strong arguments against the use of these types of designs in OD (Bullock & Svyantek 1987).

Multilevel issues   Social factor interventions that attempt to affect more complex organizational problems or arenas were reported in two studies. The first (Evans 1989) dealt with multinational corporate development, where there has been a shift from structural to processual approaches. This is because the major challenge faced today by multinational corporations is to couple global integration with local responsiveness. For OD to be relevant in this arena, it must focus more on macro/substantive issues and become more culturally sensitive.

In contrast to the multinational setting, Golembiewski et al (1987) discussed an intervention within a large company where the human resources staff was experiencing high levels of burnout. Both the sources and solutions to the situation were multilevel and required that a complex set of actions be undertaken. Active intervention into the culture, processes, and structure of the unit not only reduced the incidence of burnout but also improved working conditions.

New tools   An interesting new tool in OD demonstrates the time-honored principle that the sounder the theory base, the more potent any tool derived from it will be. Bernstein & Burke (1989) began with a theory of meaning systems in organizations; an implication of this theory is that belief systems must change in order to produce behavioral change in organizations. The authors used survey data and multivariate methods to uncover basic belief structures held by individuals and groups within organizations, and stated that making beliefs explicit allows for their conscious change. We encourage the use of new tools in OD, especially when these tools are derived from a sound theoretical base.

TECHNOLOGY   Research focusing on interventions in the technology area has utilized primarily sociotechnical systems (STS) and quality of work life (QWL) approaches. These approaches have, over time, been more broadly applied to change of entire organizations or major subsystems. A more recent variant of these two approaches uses parallel organizations (POs) as a key mechanism to implement change. We begin our discussion by focusing on studies where POs were used.

Parallel organizations   Research on POs focuses on the contingencies and outcomes associated with their success or failure. Scholars such as Herrick (1985) view POs as a "metapractice" of STS theory. If successful, POs serve as models leading to the implementation of STS concepts across the whole organization. Bushe (1987) studied a QWL intervention involving POs and found that they were more effective when a permanent middle-management problem-solving group was also created; these groups led to greater feelings of empowerment and security for the managers, who were then less threatened by changes in employees' power. Shani & Eberhardt (1987) examined the implementation of the PO in a hospital, and employees who were a part of the PO became highly involved with organizational issues and suggestions for change. Ironically, this very interest proved threatening to top management, and this aspect of POs must be carefully managed in order to ensure their effective use. Bushe (1988), in a later study, examined the implementation of five QWL projects within a large organization and showed that QWL projects utilizing POs outperformed projects involving QCs.[10]

---

[10]Bushe also found the evidence mixed regarding the usefulness of traditional QWL theory and proposed intergroup theory as a better way to understand QWL.

Quality of work life   Bocialetti (1987) examined a QWL intervention in a unionized metals processing plant and found younger workers more satisfied with the intervention because it allowed them to circumvent both the seniority system and the adversarial relations between management and older workers. Ondrack & Evans (1987) examined the effects of QWL in both greenfield and redesigned plants in the petrochemical industry in Canada. No differences were found in either job enrichment or satisfaction between traditional and QWL plants. Sorenson et al (1985) examined the effects of QWL on a small organization and found positive changes in attitudes and performance over a four-year period. These results suggest that QWL interventions frequently have positive effects on attitudes but that performance effects are somewhat more mixed.

Sociotechnical systems   Two studies explored theoretical issues about STS interventions. Kolody & Stjernberg (1986) drew upon case studies to develop a model of the STS process that highlights specific organizational subsystems as important to design efforts in plant settings. Susman & Chase (1986) explored the technical and social challenges that computer-integrated manufacturing poses for traditional STS plant design. The authors suggest changes in the STS process that will result in more successful implementation. Unfortunately, no subsequent research appears to be guided by either approach.

Other research explored STS interventions in a variety of settings. Pasmore et al (1986) found that negative results from an STS intervention in a health care setting were due to the consultants' lack of sensitivity to the unique dynamics of this setting. Wall et al (1986) instituted an autonomous workgroup design in a greenfield plant site and found positive effects only for intrinsic job satisfaction. Other individual-level measures showed no positive and/or lasting effects. Conversely, Taylor (1986) created an STS intervention in a computer operations department that did not involve semi-autonomous work groups (a mainstay of typical STS interventions). Positive effects on turnover and production were demonstrated.

Reviewing the technology interventions as a whole, we are heartened that, by and large, they increasingly focus on whole-system issues and change. At the same time, the mixed success of these interventions means that their theoretical base still needs more refinement. Questions regarding the appropriateness of STS to different settings as well as the efficacy of QWL arrangements in creating both satisfaction and productivity are prime targets for further examination.

PHYSICAL SETTING   Although planned change interventions focusing on physical settings have been part of the OD literature for over 15 years (e.g. Steele 1973), we located only two more recent studies that focused on this intervention strategy. Oldham, one of the more active researchers in this area, investigated the effects of changing from a normal open office plan to either a more spacious open office plan or partitioned cubicles (Oldham 1988). Both approaches resulted in positive effects on variables specific to the change (such as privacy satisfaction); individual differences in privacy needs and stimulus screening were significant moderators of these relations. In a somewhat similar study, Zalesny & Farace (1987) examined the effects of moving from closed offices to an open office plan for governmental employees. Symbolic theory (i.e. that work environments communicate information symbolically) best explained the results because those with higher positions were less satisfied (i.e. managers felt losing their offices indicated a loss of position).

OTHER AREAS OF INTEREST   A substantial amount of theory and research in OD focuses on general processes and issues.

New settings for OD   Gray & Hay (1986) extended political analysis to interorganizational domains to explicate the necessary conditions and actions for successful interventions in this arena. For interventions to be successful, powerful and legitimate stakeholders must participate in domain definition and action. Key environmental forces must also be successfully managed. Some have focused on how well OD might fit with other cultures. Boss & Mariono (1987) examined the history and practice of OD in Italy and showed that it has primarily occurred in large organizations that train their own professionals. Italian work culture appears to be oriented more toward role-oriented and structural interventions than does the United States. Jaeger (1986) drew upon Hofstede's work (1980) on national values to determine the fit of OD with various cultures. He concluded that some areas, such as Scandinavia, have values very consonant with OD; while others, such as Latin America, do not.[11] The author suggests that the success of OD in other nations will be determined by its adaptation to the dominant local values.

The applicability of OD to settings other than traditional corporate ones has also been examined. Leitko & Szczerbacki (1987) found that applying traditional OD strategies in professional bureaucracies (such as found in human service organizations) often fails. Traditional OD typically uses interpersonal interventions that loosen the constraints imposed by the "machine" bureaucracies found in industry. However, as the authors note, professional bureaucracies are often loosely integrated, and interventions that create more bounded systems are more appropriate here. Shamir & Salomon (1985) investigated telecommuting (i.e. work at home employing computer technolo-

---

[11]Faucheux et al (1982), in their review of OD, also emphasized the substantial differences in change approaches between Latin and Anglo-Saxon countries.

gy) and concluded that home work is not a panacea for the problems of modern organization. Thus, research needs to consider carefully both the problems and benefits of home work before it is suggested as a desirable alternative. These studies explore the role of OD in situations that require the development of new concepts and new techniques for intervention.

Research methods   Methodology issues in OD have also been researched. One controversy in this area concerns the appropriateness of different measurement approaches. Bullock & Svyantek (1987) argued persuasively that evaluating OD interventions using random strategies fundamentally contradicts the need for collaboration and participation found in effective OD. Therefore, the authors suggest the use of more appropriate research methods such as case meta-analysis (discussed below). Eden (1986b) suggested that rigorous research designed to eliminate "expectation effects" associated with interventions is misguided. He argues that these effects are an important part of OD's success, and should be studied and clarified rather than removed from research. Woodman (1989) takes the position that research should be useful to both practitioners and academics, and therefore should require both "thick" description and generalizable propositions. He proposes a "combined paradigm" approach (using both qualitative and quantitative methods), with stream analysis (Porras 1987) and appreciative inquiry (Cooperrider & Srivasta 1987) as possible examples for this.

Appreciative inquiry is an exciting new method of inquiry that deserves mention. Cooperrider & Srivasta view action research as impotent in generating alternative forms for organizing that can lead to social betterment. They propose appreciative inquiry as a revitalization of action research that both improves practice and generates theory. It does this by highlighting areas where an organization "works" and, using collaborative inquiry processes, determines directions for growth and renewal. This approach is distinct from the organizational pathology model implicit in most OD.

Stream analysis is also an important new intervention method. Porras (1987) has developed a graphical tool that maps organizational problems into the four streams (OA, SF, T, and PS), and then diagrams the links between them. By doing this, core problems are identified and targeted for change. A stream diagram is then developed mapping out the intervention's time-line and targets. This approach is a simple yet powerful way to diagnose and intervene in organizational issues.

Research in this period has also focused on better measurement of the Golembiewski et al (1976) typology. Millsap & Hartog (1988) propose a methodology based on factorial structures within a structural equation framework to determine whether either gamma or beta change has occurred. Van de Vliert et al (1985) propose a method to distinguish between alpha and beta change in which, once gamma change is ruled out (by examining the construct validity of pre- and post-test measures), dynamic correlations are used to separate alpha and beta change.

An exciting innovation in OD research is the use of both quantitative and case meta-analysis to combine results across many different studies. Case meta-analysis (Bullock & Tubbs 1987) integrates OD case studies (still the most prevalent form of OD research) by coding study variables and then performing correlational analysis on them. Quantitative meta-analysis uses the statistics provided in more quantitative research and determines "effect sizes" due to interventions on outcome variables.

Guzzo et al (1985) performed a meta-analysis that examined the effects of psychologically based interventions on "hard" measures. Interventions such as team building showed strong effects on productivity (in contrast to the team building research cited above) but not on withdrawal or disruption (e.g. absenteeism, grievances, etc). Beekun (1989) conducted a meta-analysis of STS interventions and demonstrated generally positive effects on productivity and withdrawal behaviors. Several moderator variables were also important to STS success but, interestingly enough, workgroup autonomy was not one of them. This again indicates the need for some rethinking of STS theory. Finally, Neuman et al (1989) conducted a meta-analysis of OD interventions on attitudinal outcomes. The authors find the primary effects on attitudes to be due to human processual, not techno-structural interventions.

Some authors have investigated measures to improve OD research. Porras & Hoffer (1986) conducted a survey of leading OD professionals and found substantial agreement among them on a set of nine behaviors that correlate with successful interventions. Hoffer (1986) operationalized the behaviors into a questionnaire that she then used to explore the relationship between them and hard measures of organizational performance. Her results showed a highly significant relationship between an index representing the entire set of behaviors and various hard measures of organizational performance such as sales levels, market share, costs, profits, etc. This indicates that these behaviors hold promise for providing a common base upon which to aggregate findings from disparate change studies.

Nicholas & Katz (1985) also focused on the same "aggregation" issue. They reviewed OD research from 1948 to 1982 and suggested a set of reporting standards to make cross-study comparison much more effective. It is clear that one of the challenges facing OD research is to find ways to aggregate the research findings of the field. In turn, this aggregation process will help to improve the quality of theory found in OD.

The generation of theory and new methodology in OD should be encouraged. At the same time, much of this research is fragmented and does not build on work done by other authors laboring in a similar arena. More effort should be directed at the development of a paradigm for OD, and thus researchers must build more consciously on each other's work.

Organization Transformation

OT has emerged over the last decade as a distinct form of planned change. It is an advancement over OD owing to its focus on precipitating more profound change in organizations. This occurs because the variables targeted by OT approaches (organizational beliefs, purpose, and mission, the components of organizational vision) affect a "deeper" level in the organization than those traditionally targeted for change by OD (i.e. work setting variables).

First we examine interventions focused on organizational vision. We then discuss the practice of industrial democracy in Norway. This type of intervention has not usually been considered part of OT, but recent developments indicate that the types of change pursued here are transformational. Finally, we survey other areas of interest in the OT field. The literature on OT was quite limited, reflecting the newness of this area.

ORGANIZATIONAL VISION   Organizational-level views of vision examine the processes through which organizations are able to change and learn. Individual-level perspectives assume that organizational transformation is dependent upon individual workers radically shifting their typical ways of thinking and doing.

Levy & Merry (1986) identify two distinct approaches to individual consciousness change: reframing (which draws from theory in family therapy—e.g. Watzlawick et al 1974) and consciousness raising (which has many roots—e.g. Harrison 1984). Reframing consists of organizational interventions that change an organization member's perceptions of reality. Reframing does not change current organizational reality; instead, it alters the way individuals view the world. This new worldview leads to corresponding changes in attitudes and behaviors, and organizational transformation follows.

Consciousness raising, on the other hand, makes the processes of transformation visible to organization members. Thought is viewed as the source of both existing circumstances and potential change; therefore, individuals with more awareness of transformative processes are better able to guide them. Theory here has been primarily adapted from transpersonal psychology (e.g. Walsh & Vaughan 1980). Techniques such as meditation and creativity exercises are suggested as practice interventions in this approach.

Other work on organizational transformation focuses on creating organizations that understand how (and when) to initiate radical change and have strategies and structures in place to produce this change. Beer (1987) examined three cases of organizational transformation where successful change included the concurrent development of a vision of the future and a heightened dissatisfaction with the status quo throughout the whole organization. These factors, coupled with a well-managed change process, led to successful transformation. Nadler & Tushman (1989) developed a model of the transformation process similar to Beer's; however, these authors also stressed diagnosis and provided more detail regarding implementation steps. For example, they stress the need for a "magic leader" who serves as a focus for the change effort, followed by a diffusion of energy for change throughout the organization.

Bartunek & Moch (1987) and Levy & Merry (1986) examined transformation caused by changing the organizational "paradigm." Transformation is accomplished here by increasing the system's ability to analyze and change current paradigms, as well as to envision desirable future paradigms. Lundberg (1989) discussed organizational learning in OD and proposed a cyclical process of learning occurring at three successively deeper levels: organizational change, development, and transformation. His model provides a useful set of analytical tools for implementing transformative processes.

The differences between the micro and macro approaches to organizational vision reflect a "top-down" versus "bottom-up" orientation. Organizational-level approaches typically view top management as the catalyst for changes in organizational vision: these changes then spread throughout the whole organization. Individual-level approaches view vision change as decentralized; when enough organizational members change their consiousness, organizational change occurs. We believe that whether an intervention focuses on the macro or micro level matters less than how effective it is at producing change; it is also likely that interventions combining both strategies will have the greatest impact.

INDUSTRIAL DEMOCRACY   The theory and practice of industrial democracy developed outside the United States and has not been generally considered part of either OD or OT. However, the change processes initiated by this approach result in paradigm shifts. The techiques that constitute the industrial democracy change strategy all relate to the shifting of power in the organization toward the end goal of democratizing the work setting. The intervention techniques used in this approach have their roots in STS and QWL concepts and technology but have evolved to the point where they focus primarily on gamma(A) and gamma(B) change.

Perhaps the most interesting and innovative work in this area has occurred in Norway and increasingly centers on "local theory" (Gustavsen & Engelstad 1986). Local theory evolved when change projects based on general OD, STS, and QWL theory were not successful. This led to the realization that theories of democracy not generated by employees themselves are, in some sense, not democratic. Thus, generative capacity (i.e. the ability of people to develop solutions to their own organizational problems) is most important, and interventions should be designed to increase this capacity. Gustavsen & Engelstad view "the conference" (an off-site meeting involving managers and employees from several companies) as an ideal setting for the practice of industrial democracy. Successes at such conferences can then be translated into practices appropriate for individuals' home organizations.

Elden (1986), in a very insightful piece, discussed how these ideas have become a part of public policy in Norway. Empowering participation is the key phrase in the Norwegian efforts; workers shape the actual conditions of their work through participatory STS activity. Participation is seen as second-order [gamma (A) and gamma (B)] change in this new framework. In this way, the change thrust has moved from empowerment through structure (e. g. instituting autonomous work groups) to empowerment through process (workers making local-level decisions about appropriate work practices). Some necessary conditions for empowering participation include: institutional and political support at higher levels, participatory research, researchers as co-learners, empowering the less powerful, and rejecting conventional OD and STS.

OTHER AREAS OF INTEREST   An interesting area of OT research examines disequilibrium models, where transformation is the rule rather than the exception. Gemmill & Smith (1985) developed a dissipative structure model of transformation, where turbulent conditions prevent organizations from damping change and reaching equilibrium. When this happens, old forms of organizing break down and experimentation with many new forms occurs. Eventually, the most successful experiment reorganizes the system at a higher functional level. Leifer (1989) also proposed a dissipative structure model but stressed that a vision of the future is needed to mobilize the energy for experimentation. The premise of these articles is that organizations move from transformation to transformation, with only brief periods of stability (characterized by efficiency concerns) in between.

Several other authors have proposed intervention methods appropriate for OT work. Argyris et al (1985) described "action science," an approach that attempts to catalyze double-loop learning [roughly equivalent to gamma(B) change] in individuals and organizations. The theoretical underpinning of this work parallels work discussed above on individual consciousness change and paradigm shifts. Pava (1986) proposed the concept of "normative incrementalism," an intervention method appropriate when both high complexity and high conflict exist in organizations (a condition ripe for transformation). These conditions only allow for interventions that are incremental and not threatening to current interests. This intervention therefore introduces some general theme (such as "quality of working life") without specifying how this translates into day-to-day organizational practice. However, this theme triggers employees to engage in activities that begin to clarify it retrospectively. This is a dialectic process that leads to the reformulation of values and ultimately to major organizational change.

After reviewing the breadth of ideas in OT, it is apparent how much vitality exists in this emerging approach to planned change. Although the broad outlines of the field may be sketched (e.g. a focus on vision, consciousness change, etc), there is still considerable diversity in this area and consequently many different directions for future development. It is therefore difficult to predict where the field will be in ten years, but we are certain that it will still be generating excitement and interest for both scholars and practitioners.

Summary

There was much research on OD in the period reviewed, while relatively little published literature exists in the area of OT. OD is still vigorous, as judged by the number of publications in this area, but the field has moved (since the late 1960s) from an energetic adolescence to a somewhat sedate maturity. In categorizing OD intervention approaches and target variables, we noticed two interesting patterns (noted only regarding the OA and SF streams). First of all, SF interventions dominated OD in the 1960s and early 1970s. However, in the period reviewed there had been a definite shift in emphasis from interventions emphasizing individual and group processes to interventions focusing on structural arrangements and reward systems (i.e. a shift from SF to OA research). OD research has, over time, increasingly emphasized organizational-level factors, and this is reflected by the increased volume of work on OA interventions.

The second pattern we noted concerned the target variables of research. OA research, although examining newer types of interventions in OD, typically focuses on "traditional" variables. These include participation (e.g. Marks et al 1986), motivation (e.g. Jordan 1986), task perceptions (e.g. Rafaeli 1985), etc. In addition, OA research typically investigates the connection between these variables and outcomes such as productivity (e.g. Ralston et al 1985). In contrast, SF research has focused on a more innovative set of variables. These include internal frames or reference (Mitchell 1986), managerial life cycles (Fisher et al 1987), organizational embodiments of ego defenses (Krantz 1985), etc. OA research seems to "lag" SF research in its choice of variables, and we suggest more integration of organizational-level intervention research with newer variables. At the same time, SF research can be criticized for not more explicitly theorizing and researching the link between innovative target variables and organizational outcomes (Buller's 1986 study was an exception).

Although there are some innovative areas of OD research in the period reviewed, no fundamental new paradigms have been developed and embraced by the field, and major new insights are rare. OT, on the other hand, is exciting precisely because it involves dramatically new premises for planned change. OT draws on more recent developments in psychology, transpersonal psychology, and systems theory, and often challenges traditional concepts in OD regarding models and methods. However, since this area is so underdeveloped, it is our hope that an increasing amount of rigorous theory development and research will appear in the near future.

FUTURE DIRECTIONS IN PLANNED CHANGE

Our analysis of the last five years of organizational change research has led us to a series of conclusions about where the field should head.

An important arena for future research concerns organizational paradigms. Paradigms are a key concept in OT work, but no clear conceptualization or research strategy for them has been developed. Specifying the mechanisms and boundaries of paradigm change is also important.

Organizational vision is another crucial area where research could improve OT theory and practice. Collins & Porras (1989) discuss vision and its component parts (guiding beliefs, purpose, mission) in detail, but more work needs to be done. The role of vision in maintaining organizational coherence should be explored, as should the dynamics of vision change in organizational change.

Concepts from Asian philosophy underlie some types of OT practice (e.g. the use of meditation as a tool for consciousness change). However, these concepts are not rigorously integrated into OT theory, and more theory development exploring Eastern conceptions of individual and group change should be done.

Planned change theory in general also needs much more development. The Change Process Model is one attempt to improve this area, but we encourage other attempts at developing theoretical models of change. In addition to general models of change, research should focus on how interventions impact important organizational variables and how change in these variables cascades throughout the organizational system.

The dynamics and effects of new organizational forms need much more research. Exploring Ackoff's (1989) circular organization, parallel organizations, and other innovations will increase the knowledge bases of both OD and OT. Another important area of research concerns changes in ownership rather than in governance. More employee ownership research on ESOPs and their outcomes is needed, as well as research on organizations that are fully employee owned.

Finally, as mentioned above, more research is needed on the direct effects of physical-setting change. Beyond that, exploring the interrelationship of physical setting and other organizational factors (such as structure and culture) has important implications for change theory and practice. Research should investigate the contingencies that make different types of physical setting optimal under different conditions.

There are also some important directions in which research methods and measures should head. Of course theory building that results in testable models is a key to improving research. Such models are the best guides for research, and can lead to more productive exploration of OD and OT issues.

In addition to better theory, developing a common set of variables upon which to aggregate findings is important. Meta-analysis provides the analytical tools for cross-study comparison, but meaningful comparisons can only be made when common measures are employed. We believe that the behaviors of individual organizational members are a useful and easily measured set of variables that could serve this function. The set of behaviors proposed by Porras & Hoffer (1986) are an example of this.

The Golembiewski et al (1976) typology of alpha, beta, and gamma change would be another way to develop a common set of measures. Given the amount of interest generated by this typology in the last 15 years, it was shocking to find no studies in our review that used these measures. One reason may be that methodologists are still exploring the optimal way to measure these types of change (e.g. Millsap & Hartog 1988); however, several such measures already exist, and this typology provides another common metric for more integration of research. Better reporting standards (Nicholas & Katz 1985) also would aid in promoting cross-study comparison. All in all, better theory coupled with more integration of findings would immeasurably improve the effectiveness of planned change interventions.

Literature Cited

Ackoff, R. L. 1989. The circular organization: an update. *Acad. Manage. Exec.* 3:11–16

Adams, J. D., ed. 1984. *Transforming Work: A Collection of Organizational Transformation Readings.* Alexandria, VA: Miles River Press

Alderfer, C. P. 1977. Organization development. *Annu. Rev. Psychol.* 28:197–223

Argyris, C., Putnam, R., Smith, D. M. 1985. *Action Science.* San Francisco: Jossey-Bass

Bartunek, J. M., Moch, M. K. 1987. First-order, second-order, and third-order change and organization development interventions: a cognitive approach. *J. Appl. Behav. Sci.* 23:483–500

Beekun, R. I. 1989. Assessing the effectiveness of sociotechnical intervention: antidote or fad? *Hum. Relat.* 42:877–97

Beer, M. 1976. The technology of Organization Development. In *Handbook of Industrial and Organizational Psychology,* ed. M. Dunnette. Chicago: Rand McNally College Publishing

Beer, M. 1987. Revitalizing organizations: change process and emergent model. *Acad. Manage. Exec.* 1:51–55

Beer, M., Walton, A. E. 1987. Organization change and development. *Annu. Rev. Psychol.* 38:339–67

Bernstein, W. M., Burke, W. W. 1989. Modeling organizational meaning systems. See Woodman & Pasmore 1989, pp. 117–59

Bocialetti, G. 1987. Quality of work life: some unintended effects on the seniority tradition of an industrial union. *Group Organ. Stud.* 12:386–410

Boss, R. W., Mariono, M. V. 1987. Organization development in Italy. *Group Organ. Stud.* 12:245–56

Bottger, P. C., Yetton, P. W. 1987. Improving group performance by training in individual problem solving. *J. Appl. Psychol.* 72:651–57

Buller, P. F. 1986. The team building-task performance relation: some conceptual and methodological refinements. *Group Organ. Stud.* 11:147–68

Buller, P. F., Bell, C. H. Jr. 1986. Effects of team building and goal setting on productivity: a field experiment. *Acad. Manage. J.* 29:305–28

Bullock, R. J., Svyantek, D. J. 1987. The impossibility of using random strategies to study the organization development process. *J. Appl. Behav. Sci.* 23:255–62

Bullock, R. J., Tubbs, M. E. 1987. The case meta-analysis method for OD. See Woodman & Pasmore 1987, pp. 171–228

Bushe, G. R. 1987. Temporary or permanent middle-management groups? Correlates with attitudes in QWL change projects. *Group Organ. Stud.* 12:23–37

Bushe, G. R. 1988. Developing cooperative labor-management relations in unionized factories: a multiple case study of quality circles and parallel organizations within joint quality of work life projects. *J. Appl. Behav. Sci.* 24:129–50

Collins, J. C., Porras, J. I. 1989. Making impossible dreams come true. *Stanford Bus. Sch. Mag.* 57:12–19

Cooperrider, D. L., Srivasta, S. 1987. Appreciative inquiry in organizational life. See Woodman & Pasmore 1987, pp. 129–69

Dunham, R. B., Pierce, J. L., Castaneda, M. B. 1987. Alternative work schedules: two field experiments. *Personnel Psychol.* 40:215–41

Eden, D. 1985. Team development: a true field experiment at three levels of rigor. *J. Appl. Psychol.* 70:94–100

Eden, D. 1986a. Team development: quasi-experimental confirmation among combat companies. *Group Organ. Stud.* 11:133–46

Eden, D. 1986b. OD and self-fulfilling prophecy: boosting productivity by raising expectations. *J. Appl. Behav. Sci.* 22:1–13

Elden, M. 1986. Sociotechnical systems ideas as public policy in Norway: empowering participation through worker-managed change. *J. Appl. Behav. Sci.* 22:239–55

Evans, P. A. L. 1989. Organizational development in the transnational enterprise. See Woodman & Pasmore 1989, pp. 1–39

Faucheux, C., Amado, G., Laurent, A. 1982. Organizational development and change. *Annu. Rev. Psychol.* 33:343–70

Ferris, G. R., Wagner, J. A. III. 1985. Quality circles in the United States: a conceptual reevaluation. *J. Appl. Behav. Sci.* 21:155–67

Fisher, D., Merron, K., Torbert, W. R. 1987. Human development and managerial effectiveness. *Group Organ. Stud.* 12:257–73

Florkowski, G. W. 1987. The organizational impact of profit sharing. *Acad. Manage. Rev.* 12:622–36

French, J. L. 1987. Employee perspectives on stock ownership: financial investment or mechanism of control? *Acad. Manage. Rev.* 12:427–35

Friedlander, F., Brown, L. D. 1974. Organization Development. *Annu. Rev. Psychol.* 25:313–41

Gardner, D. G., Dunham, R. B., Cummings, L. L., Pierce, J. L. 1987. Employee focus of attention and reactions to organizational change. *J. Appl. Behav. Sci.* 23:351–70

Gemmill, G., Smith, C. 1985. A dissipative structure model of organizational transformation. *Hum. Relat.* 38:751–66

Golembiewski, R. T., Billingsley, K., Yeager, S. 1976. Measuring change and persistence in human affairs: types of change generated by OD designs. *J. Appl. Behav. Sci.* 12:133–57

Golembiewski, R. T., Hilles, R., Daly, R. 1987. Some effects of multiple OD interventions on burnout and work site features. *J. Appl. Behav. Sci.* 23:295–313

Gray, B., Hay, T. M. 1986. Political limits to interorganizational consensus and change. *J. Appl. Behav. Sci.* 22:95–112

Greiner, L. 1972. Evolution and revolution as organizations grow. *Harv. Bus. Rev.* 50:39–46

Griffin, R. W. 1988. Consequences of quality circles in an industrial setting: a longitudinal assessment. *Acad. Manage. J.* 31:338–58

Gustavsen, B., Engelstad, P. H. 1986. The design of conferences and the evolving role of democratic dialogue in changing work life. *Hum. Relat.* 39:101–16

Guzzo, R. A., Jette, R. D., Katzell, R. A. 1985. The effects of psychologically based intervention programs on worker productivity: a meta-analysis. *Personnel Psychol.* 38:275–91

Harrison, R. 1984. Leadership and strategy for a New Age. In *Transforming Work*, ed. J. Adams. Alexandria, VA: Miles River Press

Head, T. C., Molleston, J. L., Sorenson, P. F. Jr., Gargano, J. 1986. The impact of implementing a quality circle intervention on employee task perceptions. *Group Organ. Stud.* 11:360–73

Herrick, N. Q. 1985. Parallel organizations in unionized settings: implications for organizational research. *Hum. Relat.* 38:963–81

Hoffer, S. J. 1986. *Behavior and organizational performance: an empirical study.*

PhD thesis. Stanford Univ. Grad. Sch. Educ.

Hofstede, G. 1980. *Culture's Consequences: International Differences in Work Related Values.* Beverly Hills, CA: Sage

Jaeger, A. M. 1986. Organization development and national culture: where's the fit? *Acad. Manage. Rev.* 11:178–90

Jordan, P. C. 1986. Effects of an extrinsic reward on intrinsic motivation: a field experiment. *Acad. Manage. J.* 29:405–12

Klein, K. J. 1987. Employee stock ownership and employee attitudes: a test of three models. *J. Appl. Psychol.* 72:319–32

Kolodny, H., Stjernberg, T. 1986. The change process of innovative work designs: new design and redesign in Sweden, Canada, and the U.S. *J. Appl. Behav. Sci.* 22:287–301

Krantz, J. 1985. Group processes under conditions of organizational decline. *J. Appl. Behav. Sci.* 21:1–17

Kuhn, T. 1970. *The Structure of Scientific Revolution.* Chicago: Univ. Chicago Press. 2nd ed.

Latack, J. C., Foster, L. W. 1985. Implementation of compressed work schedules: participation and job redesign as critical factors for employee acceptance. *Personnel Psychol.* 38:75–92

Lawler, E. E. III. 1988. Choosing an involvement strategy. *Acad. Manage. Exec.* 2:197–204

Lawler, E.E. III, Mohrman, S. A. 1987. Quality circles: after the honeymoon. *Organ. Dyn.* 15:42–54

Leifer, R. 1989. Understanding organizational transformation using a dissipative structure model. *Hum. Relat.* 42:899–916

Leitko, T. A., Szczerbacki, D. 1987. Why traditional OD strategies fail in professional bureaucracies. *Organ. Dyn.* 15:52–65

Levy, A., Merry, U. 1986. *Organizational Transformation.* New York: Praeger

Lindblom, C. 1959. The science of muddling through. *Public Admin. Rev.* 21:78–88

Lundberg, C. C. 1989. On organizational learning: implications and opportunities for expanding organizational development. See Woodman & Pasmore 1989, pp. 61–82

Marks, M. L., Mirvis, P. H., Hackett, E. J., Grady, J. F. Jr. 1986. Employee participation in a quality circle program: impact on quality of work life, productivity, and absenteeism. *J. Appl. Psychol.* 71:61–69

McDaniel, R. R. Jr., Thomas, J. B., Ashmos, D. P., Smith, J. P. 1987. The use of decision analysis for organizational design: reorganizing a community hospital. *J. Appl. Behav. Sci.* 23:337–50

Meyer, G. W., Stott, R. G. 1985. Quality circles: panacea or Pandora's box? *Organ. Dyn.* 13:34–50

Miller, C. S., Schuster, M. 1987. A decade's experience with the Scanlon plan: a case study. *J. Occup. Behav.* 8:167–74

Millsap, R. E., Hartog, S. B. 1988. Alpha, beta, and gamma change in evaluation research: a structural equation approach. *J. Appl. Psychol.* 73:574–84

Mitchell, R. 1986. Team building by disclosure of internal frame of reference. *J. Appl. Behav. Sci.* 22:15–28

Nadler, D. A., Tushman, M. L. 1989. Organizational frame bending: principles for managing reorientation. *Acad. Manage. Exec.* 3:194–204

Nelson, R. E. 1988. Social network analysis as an intervention tool: examples from the field. *Group Organ. Stud.* 13:39–58

Neuman, G. A. Edwards, J. E., Raju, N. S. 1989. Organization development interventions: a meta-analysis of their effects on satisfaction and other attitudes. *Personnel Psychol.* 42:461–89

Nicholas, J. M., Katz, M. 1985. Research methods and reporting practices in organization development: a review and some guidelines. *Acad. Manage. Rev.* 10:737–49

Oldham, G. R. 1988. Effects of changes in workspace partitions and spatial density on employee reactions: a quasi-experiment. *J. Appl. Psychol.* 73:253–58

Ondrack, D. A., Evans, M. G. 1987. Job enrichment and job satisfaction in greenfield and redesign QWL sites. *Group Organ. Stud.* 12:5–22

Pasmore, W., Petee, J., Bastian, R. 1986. Sociotechnical systems in health care: a field experiment. *J. Appl. Behav. Sci.* 22:329–39

Pava, C. 1986. New strategies of systems change: reclaiming nonsynoptic methods. *Hum. Relat.* 39:615–33

Pearce, J. L., Stevenson, W. B., Perry, J. L. 1985. Managerial compensation based on organizational performance: a time series analysis of the effects of merit pay. *Acad. Manage. J.* 28:261–78

Porras, J. I., 1987. *Stream Analysis: A Powerful New Way to Diagnose and Manage Change.* Reading, MA: Addison Wesley

Porras, J. I., Hoffer, S. J. 1986. Common behavior changes in successful organization development efforts. *J. Appl. Behav. Sci.* 22:477–94

Porras, J. I., Robertson, P., Goldman, L. 1990. Organization development. In *Handbook of Industrial and Organizational Psychology,* ed. M. Dunnette. Palo Alto, CA: Psychological Press

Rafaeli, A. 1985. Quality circles and employee attitudes. *Personnel Psychol.* 38:603–15

Ralston, D. A., Anthony, W. P., Gustafson, D. J. 1985. Employees may love flextime, but what does it do to the organization's productivity? *J. Appl. Psychol.* 70:272–79

Shamir, B., Salomon, I. 1985. Work-at-home and the quality of working life. *Acad. Manage. Rev.* 10:455-64

Shani, A. B., Eberhardt, B. J. 1987. Parallel organization in a health care institution. *Group Organ. Stud.* 12:147–73

Sheldon, A. 1980. Organizational paradigms: a theory of organizational change. *Organ. Dyn.* 8:61–80

Sorenson, P. F. Jr., Head, T. C., Stotz, D. 1985. Quality of work life and the small organization: a four-year case study. *Group Organ. Stud.* 10:320–39

Stebbins, M. W., Shani, A. B. 1989. Organization design: beyond the Mafia model. *Organ. Dyn.* 17:18–30

Steel, R. P., Lloyd, R. F. 1988. Cognitive, affective, and behavioral outcomes of participation in quality circles: conceptual and empirical findings. *J. Appl. Behav. Sci.* 24:1–17

Steel, R. P., Shane, G. S. 1986. Evaluation research on quality circles: technical and analytical implications. *Hum. Relat.* 39: 449–68

Steele, F. I. 1973. *Physical Settings and Organization Development.* Reading, MA: Addison-Wesley

Susman, G. I., Chase, R. B. 1986. A sociotechnical analysis of the integrated factory. *J. Appl. Behav. Sci.* 22:257–70

Taylor, J. C. 1986. Long-term sociotechnical systems change in a computer operations department. *J. Appl. Behav. Sci.* 22:303–13

Van de Vliert, E., Huismans, S. E., Stok, J. J. L. 1985. The criterion approach to unraveling beta and alpha change. *Acad. Manage. Rev.* 10:269–74

Vickers, G. 1965. *The Art of Judgement.* New York: Basic Books

Wall, T. D., Kemp, N. J., Jackson, P. R., Clegg, C. W. 1986. Outcomes of autonomous workgroups: a long-term field experiment. *Acad. Manage. J.* 29:280–304

Walsh, R. N., Vaughan, F. 1980. *Beyond Ego: Transpersonal Dimensions in Psycology.* Los Angeles: J. P. Tarcher

Watzlawick, P., Weakland, J., Fisch, R. 1974. *Change.* New York: W. W. Norton

Woodman, R. W. 1989. Evaluation research on organizational change: arguments for a 'combined paradigm' approach. See Woodman & Pasmore 1989, pp. 161–80

Woodman, R. W., Pasmore, W. A., eds. 1987. *Research in Organizational Change and Development,* Vol. 1. Greenwich, CT: JAI Press

Woodman, R. W., Pasmore, W. A., eds. 1989. *Research in Organizational Change and Development,* Vol. 3. Greenwich, CT: JAI Press

Zalesny, M. D., Farace, R. V. 1987. Traditional versus open offices: a comparison of sociotechnical, social relations, and symbolic meaning perspectives. *Acad. Manage. J.* 30:240–59

Annu. Rev. Psychol. 1991. 42:79–107

THE HISTORY OF PSYCHOLOGY:
A Survey and Critical Assessment

Ernest R. Hilgard

Stanford University, Stanford, California 94305–2130

David E. Leary

University of Richmond, Richmond, Virginia 23173

Gregory R. McGuire

St. Francis Xavier University, Antigonish, Nova Scotia, Canada B2G 1CO

KEY WORDS: Psychology, History, Historiography, Teaching of History

CONTENTS

0066-4308/91/0201-0079$02.00

INTRODUCTION

Over the past three decades the discipline of psychology has undergone intense self-scrutiny. Simultaneously the history of science, as a field of scholarly research, has broadened its domain to include the history of the social and behavioral sciences. Both trends have contributed to the development of the history of psychology as a field of considerable interest and vitality. Because modern scientific psychology is about 100 years old, several departments in America have in the past few years celebrated their centennials (e.g. Capshew (1988) on Indiana University) and others are about to do so. The American Psychological Association, now in the midst of celebrations of its own centennial, to culminate in 1992, has been encouraging departments (and regional societies—e.g. Bartlett et al 1988) to publish their own histories in forms that may become part of the permanent record of psychology's history.

Besides its evolution as an area of scholarly research, the history of psychology has continued to be a topic widely represented in the typical psychology curriculum. Although more up-to-date information is needed, Riedel (1974) has documented the prevalence of courses on the history of psychology and/or the history and systems of psychology in the undergraduate curriculum. More recently, accreditation stipulations (American Psychological Association 1979) have assured that the history of psychology will remain a feature of graduate training in psychology for some time to come.

Paralleling and supporting the development of the history of psychology has been the establishment of institutional structures that provide the resources, training, means of communication, encouragement, and direction necessary to the maturation of the field. These structures, with the dates of their establishment, include the American Psychological Association's Division of the History of Psychology (1965), the Archives of the History of American Psychology in Akron, Ohio (1965), the *Journal of the History of the Behavioral and Social Sciences* (1965), the graduate program in the History and Theory of Psychology at the University of New Hampshire (1967), the Cheiron Society for the History of the Behavioral Sciences (1968), and more recently the Italian *Storia e Critica della Psicologia* (established in 1979), the Spanish *Revista de Historia de la Psicologia* (1980), the graduate program in the history and theory of psychology at York University in Canada (1981), the European Cheiron Society (1982), the historical sections of the British, Canadian, and German psychological associations (1984, 1988, 1989, respectively), the British *History of the Human Sciences* (1988), the German *Psychologie und Geschichte* (1989), and the History of Science Society's Forum for the History of the Human Sciences (1989).

Perhaps the most tangible sign of the emergence of the history of psychology as a field of academic interest has been the publication of textbooks in the field: More than half of the history-of-psychology textbooks written in or translated into English in this century have been published in the past three decades. Just as tangible and even more important for the field as a professional area of scholarship has been the explosion of the nontextbook secondary literature on the history of psychology. Since the classic "call to arms" issued by Watson (1960) and reinforced by Stocking (1965) and Young (1966), there has been an astonishing increase in well-grounded scholarship on delimited historical topics. This scholarship has become more and more self-conscious and deliberate as scholars, whether trained as psychologists or historians, have responded to the distinctive opportunities and challenges in this domain of research. The development of what has been called the "critical history" of psychology—historical scholarship whose probing questions and demanding methodology evince little interest in affirming or legitimating the assumptions of contemporary psychology—has been the seemingly natural result of this increasing historical sophistication as well as of the particular psychological concerns that have motivated many scholars in the field.

Given the expansion and maturation of the field over the past three decades and its continued—and perhaps increased—relevance to the teaching of undergraduates and graduates, it is reasonable for the *Annual Review of Psychology* to offer its first review on the history and historiography of psychology [except for an earlier historical chapter by Mueller (1979)]. The treatment of the topic, which we hope will be particularly useful to teachers and students of the history of psychology, is rather straightforward. After a discussion of authors and texts on the general history of psychology, we highlight some of the important issues and developments in the historiography of psychology and then review some of the resources that will aid students, teachers, and scholars of the history of psychology.

REPRESENTATIVE AUTHORS AND BOOKS ON THE GENERAL HISTORY OF PSYCHOLOGY

For the teacher about to teach a course on history for the first time, or the student who is refreshing himself or herself on the history of psychology, the initial step in orientation is often to find out something about the available comprehensive history books. Later on we give a little more information useful to the teacher, for too much dependence on a single textbook is not a practice to be preferred.

Numerous histories of psychology have appeared right along. Early in the 20th century the American sources began with three significant books. One of these brought together selections from classical psychologists from Anaxagoras to Wundt (Rand 1912). Another, by Hall (1912), presented in book form six lectures he had given on six eminent German scholars with whom he had studied. In the same year a Canadian philosopher-psychologist published the first volume of a massive 3-volume history (Brett 1912; later volumes 1921). Brett's large books were too massive to be used conveniently as ordinary textbooks, but they served as excellent sources for the history of psychology from the earliest times, particularly for psychology in its philosophical and ecclesiastical contexts. More convenient access was provided by a one-volume abridgment by Peters (1953; revised 1962), who edited and added to the original while condensing it, at the same time also updating it by adding a chapter on 20th-century psychology. Baldwin (1913) published in two small volumes the first textbook history by an American writer in the 20th century.

A great many textbooks on the history of psychology appeared in English and in other languages over the years. A bibliography prepared by one of us lists 180 textbook titles in English through 1988, provided that edited books of readings on history and systems are counted (McGuire 1990). Limitations of space forbid our characterization of many of these except to note that of those books that appeared before 1935, the only strictly general histories to be kept alive through revised editions were those of Boring (1929, revised 1950), Brett, as revised by Peters (1953), Flugel (1933, 1947, 1964), and Murphy (1929, revised 1949; Murphy & Kovach 1972).

The Role of Edwin G. Boring (1886–1968)

Edwin G. Boring, already a prominent psychology professor at Harvard, established himself as a historian with the appearance of his history of experimental psychology (Boring 1929). Through this book, his later historical writings and a revision of the original book in 1950, he began to occupy a special role in the development of the history of psychology in America. He derived satisfaction as he began to feel himself responsible for continuing to call attention to psychology's past. For many years his book did indeed stand as the principal text in the history of psychology. A survey published in 1962 indicated his special influence by finding that 75% of the undergraduate psychology curricula that presented a course in the history of psychology used his book as the principal text (Nance 1962).

In his first edition Boring stated clearly where he stood in relation to experimental psychology: "Naturally the words 'experimental psychology' must mean, in my title, what they meant to Wundt and what they meant to all psychologists for 50 or 60 years—that is to say, the psychology of the generalized, human, normal, adult mind as revealed in the psychological laboratory" (Boring 1929:viii). He went on to say that this was no doctrinaire position and acknowledged that animal psychology and mental tests are in a way experimental, and he had included some treatment of them in his exposition. There were many changes in the second edition including the incorporation of dynamic psychology—foreshadowing a treatment of learning and motivation that he contemplated writing as a separate volume but never completed.

In the preface to a later book on sensation and perception (Boring 1942), written between the two editions of the other book, he remarked that the title of his first book was somewhat inapt, since he had not treated the experimentation in experimental psychology. This second book dealt directly with the experiments in their theoretical contexts in the areas of sensation and perception, and proved to be a masterful exposition. In his preface he also announced the possibility of another book, referred to above, in which he might recount the experimentation in other fields—feeling, emotion, learning, attention, action, and thought.

We note that Boring himself recognized limitations in his historical books, softening somewhat the criticisms that later were offered against his conception of history. The later objections tended to be directed at several targets. One target was the limitations posed by the narrow definition of experimental psychology, derived from Titchener's misinterpretation of Wundt (Blumenthal 1975; Danziger 1979a). Another target was the interpretation of the past as simply a cause of the present. Conversely, the tendency to use the present as a framework for understanding the past, now characterized by historians as "presentism," came to be looked upon unfavorably (Stocking 1965; Young 1966). Two other issues entered into these later critical discussions. One was the "great man" theory, shown by the prominence in his text of the biographies of the influential psychologists; the other was the importance given to the Zeitgeist or "spirit of the times," as allowing little room for the inventiveness, creativity, and initiative of those who advanced psychological knowledge and theory (Rosenzweig 1970; Ross 1969). While the Zeitgeist was more prominent in the second edition, it had been somewhat implicit before, and had been explicitly supported in a paper that appeared before the first edition of the history (Boring 1927). Various other discussions have attempted to explain why some of the difficulties occurred (e.g. Friedmann 1967; O'Donnell 1979; Samelson 1980). Cerullo (1988) has argued that the criticisms of Boring as a historian fail to do justice to his role as a discipline builder and have been overdrawn. His analysis suggests that Boring still merits further objective consideration.

Boring did not confine his historical writing to books. His major historical papers were republished in a book edited by Watson & Campbell (Boring 1963).

The Role of Robert I. Watson, Sr. (1909–1980)

The years of World War II and the early postwar years saw a slackening in the publishing of new history textbooks, but a new surge of interest and publication began in the 1960s. One of the first books to become prominent in the years after 1960, and to reappear in four editions prior to its author's death, was Watson's *The Great Psychologists* (1963, 4th ed. 1978). The book was dedicated "To E. G. B., my teacher, under whom I have never studied." Boring had assisted in its preparation, and in some sense he saw Watson as his successor.

In a symposium held at the 1981 annual meeting of the American Psychological Association, eight contributors paid tribute to Watson's role in making the history of psychology a profession in its own right. The symposium was published in the *Journal of the History of the Behavioral Sciences* that Watson had founded and of which he served as editor from its first issue in 1965 to 1974. The account of the symposium was introduced by Eugene S. Mills, who had been the president of the University of New Hampshire while Watson taught there (Mills 1982).

Watson's interest in history had developed by 1960, while he was still Professor of Psychology and Director of the Graduate Training Program in Clinical Psychology at Northwestern University in Evanston (Watson 1960). From that date he became an initiator, organizer, and promoter, as well as an active contributor through his many books and journal articles. He left Northwestern in 1967 to accept a professorship in psychology at the University of New Hampshire, where, upon invitation, he took a leading role in developing a special PhD program in the History and Theory of Psychology, said to be the first of its kind (Evans 1982). His initiative was also apparent in his promotion of three organized programs that have furthered the development of the history of psychology as an area of scholarship. One of these was the establishment of Division 26: History of Psychology, of the American Psychological Association, of which he became the first president in 1966, after Boring had deferred to him by accepting the designation as Honorary President to indicate his support of the new division (Hilgard 1982). The second was his strong interest in the founding and continuation of the Archives of the History of American Psychology at the University of Akron in Akron, Ohio. While the on-site founding was the work of John Popplestone as Director and his wife, Marion White McPherson, as Associate Director, Watson played a role in convincing the administration at Akron that it was a good idea. He was considered to be a co-founder, and served as the chairman of the Advisory Committee from the founding in 1965 until August 1975 (Popplestone & McPherson 1982). A third promotional activity had to do with the founding of an international society for the history of the behavioral and social sciences, which took the name of Cheiron, the wise centaur in Greek mythology who was knowledgeable in arts and science and liked to share his knowledge. It took form in 1968, after a summer institute on the teaching of the history of psychology co-directed by Josef Brozek and Watson at the University of New Hampshire (Goodman 1982).

While these promotional steps deserve recognition, in the long run Watson will be remembered especially for his scholarly books and articles. After the history book already mentioned, he published his major opus, a massive two-volume work. In the 470 pages of the first volume (Watson 1974), he gathered as primary source material the major writings of 538 individuals, previously identified as eminent by a panel of nine raters (Annin et al 1968). The only other source at all comparable had been the *Psychological Register* (Murchison 1932a), which listed nearly complete bibliographies for some 2400 living psychologists from all over the world. (These were not selected for eminence, although the editor had sought advice on whether or not they were psychologists rather than "just interested in psychology.") Watson's second volume (Watson 1976), in some ways more unique and more ambitious, brought together in 1158 pages the "secondary sources"—that this, the references by others to the works of those in Volume 1. These volumes deserve the praise reviewers (e.g. Brozek 1978) have given them, as resources that should remain valuable over the years (e.g. Brozek 1982).

Watson published two additional volumes to serve as scholarly resources for those interested in the history of the behavioral sciences—a bibliographical guide (Watson 1978) and a source book on the history of psychology (Watson 1979). In the latter he reproduced selections from the writings of 50 psychologists from Galileo to B. F. Skinner. He also participated in editing a volume of Boring's collected papers, as previously mentioned (Boring 1963), and a selection of his own journal papers was published by Brozek & Evans (1977).

It may be noted that Watson was influenced by Boring in choosing to base his history text on great men, which led to a chronological treatment. This does not mean that he did not attend to problems of theory. The nearest thing to a theory of his own was his proposal that psychological orientations could be judged according to 18 "prescriptions" consisting of polarities: determinism-indeterminism, empiricism-rationalism, monism-dualism, and so on, Watson 1971. A psychologist's system could be understood according to his or her position on these prescriptions. Watson's own position was somewhat elaborated in the fourth edition of his textbook, but not sufficiently to clarify how prescriptions could be used to organize a system of psychology.

Other Contributors and Books

There have, of course, been careful reviews of individual books on the history of psychology and at least two collective reviews, both of which are informative.

The first of these, by Erickson (1955), considered 28 books appearing between 1912 and 1953, plus five relevant journal articles that appeared between 1941 and 1953. He discussed in some detail histories written by

Americans—Boring (1950), Murphy (1949), and Roback (1952). Roback's book supplemented the others by treating the history of American psychology prior to William James (in this connection, note also Fay 1966).

As books by British historians, Erickson selected Peters' (1953) abbreviated version of Brett, Flugel (1933), and Spearman (1937). For the German contributions, although he noted the earlier prominence of the translated histories of Dessoir (1912) and Klemm (1914), he relied more on Mueller-Freienfels (1935), which, although originating in Germany, was published in English in America, and never appeared in a German version at home. From the French there was one book on contemporary psychology in French by Foulquié & Deledalle (1951). Erickson also gave some attention to books on psychological systems, such as Heidbreder (1933) and Woodworth (1948), later revised as Woodworth & Sheehan (1964). He also reviewed the edited volumes on systems by Murchison (1926, 1930a), and the initial three volumes in the series on autobiographies of psychologists (Murchison 1930b–1932). The autobiographical volumes of this series have continued to be published intermittently, with other editors and publishers. The latest is Volume 8, edited by Lindzey (1989). These were supplemented by three autobiographical volumes in another series (Krawiec 1972, 1974, and 1978).

The second review mentioned was a collective review of a selected number of recent books that appeared a quarter of a century later (Littman 1981). He featured six American books, although earlier ones entered into his treatment. The six given special attention were: Chaplin & Krawiec (1979), the fourth edition of a book that appeared first in 1960; Leahey (1980), a new book that was subsequently revised in 1987; Lowry (1971), a first edition; and Lundin (1979), a second edition that followed the first of 1972 and preceded the third of 1985. Robinson (1979b) and Watson (1979) were also reviewed. Littman's paper was listed as a Special Review and called An Essay Review in its title. It is indeed a very scholarly and thoughtful interpretative and evaluative review. Other books were appearing during the same period, and while he mentioned some "as histories students are likely to be studying" and lists them in his references, he did not review them, perhaps because they were not included in his assignment. We note the lack, for example, of some others that had appeared but were not listed, or appeared too near in time to the review: Lawry (1981), Misiak & Sexton (1966), Robinson (1976, rev. ed. 1981), and Schulz (1969, 4th ed. 1987). Schulz's 3rd edition of 1981 was buttressed by an associated handbook for teachers of psychology geared to it (Benjamin 1981). There was no review of Wertheimer (1970, 3rd ed. 1987), another of those books the student was "likely to have been studying." Robinson (1977/1978) had also completed the mammoth task of republishing with commentary 28 volumes of historical significance that had appeared between 1750 and 1920. In the meantime an edited book by Hilgard (1978) gave such perspective as might be gained from republishing, in context, a number of the addresses of the presidents of the American Psychological Association, 1892–1977; and a book edited by Hearst (1979) had chapters by many authors recounting the 100 years since the founding of Wundt's laboratory. The topics were selected as those conventionally associated with experimental psychology, but coverage was extended to include developmental psychology, social psychology, and psychopathology.

Several substantial new books appeared in the next few years.

Three major books appeared in the same year: Buxton (1985), Kimble & Schlesinger (1985), and Koch & Leary (1985). Buxton contributed the introductory and concluding chapters to his book, as well as two other chapters. There are 12 topical chapters by various authors; two critical chapters on Wundt and the shaping of the experimental tradition, followed by two on functionalism, then two on behaviorism, two on psychoanalysis, and chapters on cognitive psychology. Gestalt, biological contributions, and the relations between psychology and philosophy.

The Kimble & Schlesinger book appeared in two volumes. After an introductory chapter, the first volume contains seven chapters on standard substantive topics or subfields in psychology, each by an expert or teams of experts in the specific field. The second volume also begins with an orienting chapter, and continues with ten more subfields. While some attention is given to subfields with an applied flavor (psychological testing, psychotherapy) there is nothing specific about such applied areas as educational and industrial–organizational psychology.

The Koch & Leary volume is a massive book of 42 chapters divided into four major subsections: the systematic framework of psychology; the special fields of psychology; psychology and intersecting disciplines; and psychology in relation to society, culture, and sensibility. Each chapter seeks to take a serious look at the present state of psychological theory with due regard to what has happened over the past century.

The next, in order of publication date, is Hilgard's (1987). It differs from the books mentioned just above in that it is a single-author book and insofar as it focuses on American psychology in the modern period. Furthermore, the coverage of substantive topics is very broad, including applied topics such as clinical, educational, and industrial-organizational psychology; it also gives attention to professional problems such as the organization of psychology nationally and internationally. The attention to American psychology is not parochial, and due attention is given to British and European influences. The organization is topical: the number of topics treated in its 21 chapters makes it more like Chaplin & Krawiec (1979) and Kimble & Schlesinger (1985), rather than the other books mentioned. Kendler (1987) also published a single-author book, with its 13 chapters devoted largely to major systematic viewpoints. After an introductory chapter, there are chapters on the influence of Wundt and James, on the major schools, including, along with Watsonian behaviorism, two neo-behaviorisms (Tolman vs Hull; Skinner and Hebb), and on the more recent developments of cognitive psychology and humanistic psychology. The final chapter treats of legacies of the past and projections into the future.

Hilgard (1988) also edited a small multi-author historical book on the last 50 years of psychology, with each of the ten topical fields that were covered represented by contributions from a recognized authority in that area. Hilgard contributed an introductory chapter reflecting on the recurrent themes within psychology during that period.

In addition to books such as these, there are many specialized books that space restraints prevent our listing. Mention should be made particularly of the source books and books of readings that continue to find their places. Illustrative examples are those of Dennis (1948), Diamond (1974), Herrnstein & Boring (1966), and Sahakian (1968). One that was revised during the 1980s is that of Marx & Cronan-Hillix (1987), now in its fourth edition, having first appeared in 1963. Benjamin (1988) published a history of psychology that is essentially a source book in a new style that combines primary and secondary sources. There are 13 selections from significant primary contributors, from Descartes to Skinner, and 37 secondary articles in which the contributions of each primary author have been discussed by others. Benjamin himself writes introductory sections of three to five printed pages for each of the sections, including references that supplement the primary and secondary selected passages, so that the book is designed to be used as a text in the history of psychology.

There are many more specialized histories by topic or subfield of psychology, of which Boring (1942) produced a good example for sensation and perception. Then there are histories of psychology for applied areas, as, for example, the multi-author volume by Glover & Ronning (1987) on educational psychology. There are histories of psychology in different countries of which Joravsky's (1989) history of Russian psychology is a recent example. Watson (1978) and Viney et al (1979) provided useful bibliographic sources for earlier specialized histories, categorized in several ways. The source materials for teachers and others interested in the history of psychology are discussed further in a later section of this chapter.

That the interpretation of psychology in history remains a source of controversy is illustrated by two feature reviews on transitions in psychological theory by Bolles (1990) and Kendler (1990), each dealing with the same two books from his own perspective: Amsel (1989) and Marx & Cronan-Hillix (1987).

Kendler views Amsel's book as a complaint by "an angry young senior citizen" against the distorted attacks on neo-behaviorism by the cognitivists, and suggests that the vigor of the attack might help the cognitivists put their house in order. He notes how Amsel reflects his training at Iowa under Spence and Bergmann, and, similarly, how Marx & Cronan-Hillix reflect a functionalist orientation that derives from Harvey Carr by way of Marx's study with Carr's student, Marion Bunch, and Cronan-Hillix's training under Marx. By contrast with Amsel, Marx & Cronan-Hillix are more tolerant, less harshly critical, and more willing to emphasize similarities than differences among the theories they treat.

Bolles entitles his review of the same two books "Where did everybody go?" He begins with Marx & Cronan-Hillix, whose 4th edition is "nicely polished, a good new edition." It is a good treatment of the early spring days of the schools and systems, but what Bolles misses is an adequate treatment of their autumn days and decline. As an illustration, there is much about Freud and the neo-Freudians, but the reader is left without a feeling for what has happened to psychoanalysis. The issues raised during the height of the controversy over S-R theories, as by Tolman & Hull, remain frozen where they stood about 20 years ago. Amsel, according to Bolles, attributes the decline of the S-R theory to the attacks by the cognitivists, but Bolles believes the trouble was with the reductionism of the S-R unit as revealed by attacks on reinforcement theory, an inheritance from the golden age of learning theory, not the influence of the cognitive interpretations.

THE HISTORIOGRAPHY OF PSYCHOLOGY

As useful as general texts are for the student, teacher, and scholar of the history of psychology, the professional advancement of the field over the past three decades—as predicted by Stocking (1965) and Young (1966)—has been associated in important ways with an increase in attention paid to historical methodology and to more narrowly defined topics of research. Guided by previous discussions on the theories and methods of historical research (e.g. Beringer 1978; Carr 1961; Fischer 1970; Hughes 1964; Kuhn 1968), historians of psychology have produced their own reflections upon the ways their craft should be plied (e.g. Ash 1983; Danziger 1984; Furumoto 1989; Morawski 1984; Woodward 1980). The central issues raised by these discussions, as well as examples of historical research resulting from their implementation over the past three decades, are the major topics of this section. Here we hope to convey some of the intellectual excitement and identify the scholarly contributions that have been generated by this field of research.

Of the many historiographical issues that have preoccupied historians of psychology over the past decades, perhaps the most pressing and useful have revolved around (a) continuity vs discontinuity; (b) presentism vs historicism; (c) internalism vs externalism; (d) "great men" vs "the Zeitgeist"; and (e) ceremonial legitimation vs critical history. These general issues are far from independent of one another, but for the sake of clarity we treat them separately.

Continuity vs Discontinuity

Certainly one of the great inspirations of interest in the history of science over the past three decades has been Kuhn's *The Structure of Scientific Revolutions* (1962). Not surprisingly, its treatment of preparadigmatic science, "normal science," and the role of theory and method in the emergence of paradigmatic science stimulated a great deal of reflection and research on the history of the social and behavioral sciences (e.g. Barnes 1982; Buss 1978; Palermo 1971; Peterson 1981); and these applications of "Kuhnian analysis" elicited a corresponding set of critical responses (e.g. Briskman 1972; Koch 1976; Lipsey 1974; Suppe 1984).

Of the many facets of Kuhn's influence on the field, the question of the continuity vs discontinuity of historical development has been central. Have there been scientific revolutions—truly radical ruptures—in the history of psychology, as Kuhn's theory would suggest to some, or has psychology evolved over time in a more or less consecutive fashion?

The salience of this question has been reinforced by Michael Foucault (1965, 1970, 1975), whose work has challenged historians to look for disjunctures that may have occurred as one historical period, with its distinctive conceptual framework and associated patterns of behavior, yielding to another. Although historiographical practice must presume some sort of continuity between past and present (Leary 1976), Foucault (along with Kuhn) has made historians more aware of the possibility of discontinuities in the history of psychology.

The most radical implication of this issue is conveyed by Roger Smith's recent query, "Does the history of psychology have a subject?" In an article that bears careful reading and consideration by anyone who is serious about the history of psychology, Smith (1988) concludes that "*the* history of psychology should be abandoned. It does not seem possible to conceptualize a continuous and unitary subject" for such a history (p. 162). What is needed, Smith suggests, are multiple studies that reveal the variety of ways "psychology" and its kindred theories and practices have been constituted over time. In a similar vein, Danziger (1990b) has questioned the assumption that psychological terms (sensation, association, motivation, stimulation, and so forth) have meant the same thing in different historical periods. Such cautions deserve the attention and comprehension of teachers, students, and scholars alike, even if some (e.g. Brush 1974) may wonder about their possibly negative impact on potential recruits to the field. Although these cautions suggest limits on what historians (and psychologists) may realistically hope to accomplish, they also point toward exciting new possibilities for historical research and writing. How was the past different from the present and different from how we are accustoned to representing it? What new aspects of the past might we see if we were to shine a new light or take a new perspective on it?

Presentism vs Historicism

The major contention at the heart of discussions about presentism and historicism is that historical research should strive to portray the past in its own terms, through the categories and concerns of *those* times and places rather than of *our* time and place. Building on Butterfield's (1959) work, Stocking (1965) directed the attention of historians of the social and behavioral sciences to the need for more richly and accurately modulated historical analyses, written from the vantage point of the actors involved and with minimal reliance upon the knowledge we have as citizens of a later time.

On the other hand, Stocking and others (e.g. Buss 1977; Marx 1977) have pointed out the opportunity and need for historians to address issues of present concern. This suggests the estimable challenge of pursuing a finely balanced approach to history that is both honest to the past and useful, in some way, in the present. The tensions generated by such a balancing act are well known to historians of psychology sensitive to the role historical research can play in legitimating and/or in critically assessing the past and present status of the discipline and profession. As noted above, some of these historians have been critical of apparent failures of balance in the past—for example, in Boring's (1950) analysis of Wundtian psychology (Blumenthal 1975; Danziger 1979a). Many of the chapters in such edited volumes as Morawski's (1988) and Sokal's (1987) attempt to walk the fine line between historicist objectivity and presentist concerns.

Internalism vs Externalism

Traditional history of science focused primarily on the so-called internal development of scientific thought and procedure—how one idea and method led to other ideas and methods in a more or less progressive fashion, with relatively little influence from "nonscientific' factors (see Kuhn 1968). The initial calls for a more externalist approach (e.g. Hessen 1971, 1st ed., 1931; Merton 1970, 1st ed., 1938) emphasized the need for historians of science to attend the nonideational and nonprocedural factors pertaining to the social, cultural, economic, and political foundations and dimensions of science. Although such calls generated considerable controversy up to fairly recent times, their general point has now been made, and most historians grant that the boundaries of scientific work are more difficult to define than once seemed the case (see Buss 1979). Even historians who attend primarily to the intellectual history of science now routinely grant that scientific theories and method draw upon and influence other social and cultural realms.

Relatedly, the intellectual history of psychology is now typically approached with greater sensitivity to the "external" (extra-disciplinary) origins and significance of scientific ideas. Hence, over the past decade, much of the interesting and innovative work in the history of psychology has been on "the social history of ideas" (Ash 1982). Exemplary works include those of Ash (1987), Leary (1982), and Smith (1986). Although the latter two works provide an almost exclusively intellectual (rather than social) account of their different subject matters, they clearly convey the linkage between psychology and "external" fields of scholarship. Burnham (1987), Fuller (1982), and Young (1985) persuasively illustrate the vital connection between psychology and other domains of society and culture.

"Great Men" vs the Zeitgeist

As noted earlier, Boring (1950) posed a distinction between "great men" and the Zeitgeist. Both concepts are now problematic—in ways worthy of review. "Great men" are no longer considered to "stand alone" in the history of science, either as "great" or as "men." To historians now alerted to the dangers of assuming continuity of influence insulated from external factors, eminence is a concept to be ascribed and understood with care. Furthermore, recent social and intellectual developments, coupled with groundbreaking research on the role of women (Furumoto 1989) and minorities (Guthrie 1976) in psychology, have somewhat relieved the exclusive focus upon the role and contributions of white, middle-class male psychologists. The demographic characteristics of effective and/or historically noticed psychologists have become important topics of research, and the elucidation of the contexts within which career advancement and other rewards have been allocated in the history of psychology has opened up new and significant areas of scholarship, in which historicist approaches are unearthing information and giving rise to interpretations that are of considerable interest and value.

It is not that individuals are now thought to be less significant as historical actors. Rather, the understanding of what constitutes and shapes individual lives and careers has grown in recent years, so that our understanding of eminence in science has been considerably enriched. Recent biographical studies have become much more subtle as a result, and the scholarly literature—even on such "male greats" as Freud (Sulloway 1979), James (Feinstein 1984), Hall (Ross 1972), Thorndike (Joncich 1968), and Watson (Buckley 1989)—has clearly surpassed earlier work. At the same time, as suggested above, studies of female psychologists (e.g. O'Connell & Russo 1983, 1988;

Scarborough & Furumoto 1987; Stevens & Gardner 1982) have made it clear that we have yet to realize fully the historical significance of women and other neglected populations within psychology.

As for the Zeitgeist or spirit of the time, Ross (1969), Rosenzweig (1970), and others have vigorously and successfully attacked simplistic notions about the existence of a rigidly coherent and unified culture that can supposedly override individual variations and efficacy. Although so-called "strong programs" for the sociology of science are still being proposed, more permeable and variable approaches to the social as well as cultural dimensions of science seem by and large to be in the ascendancy. Such works as those of Danziger (1979b), O'Donnell (1985), and Sokal (1981) have attempted to integrate respect for both individual and social factors into a more dynamic and multifaceted approach to history. Leary has tried to highlight the larger rhetorical context within which American psychologists have operated. This context, as more amply illustrated in a recent volume edited by him (Leary 1990), extends well beyond psychology into the broader social and cultural realm.

Ceremonial Legitimation vs Critical History

It is probably obvious, even to the relatively uninitiated that all of the foregoing issues—continuity vs discontinuity, presentism vs historicism, internalism vs externalism, and "great men" vs the Zeitgeist—overlap in significant ways. Furthermore, although our brief discussions have repeatedly suggested that historical practice should be subtle and complex, avoiding simplistic commitments to either of the bipolar extremes that define each of these issues, it may not surprise many readers that the lefthand poles in these historiographical dilemmas—which is to say, an assumption of continuity between past and present, a reading of the past through present categories of analysis, a focus on the internal logic of historical developments, and an emphasis upon the more eminent contributors to psychology—have often been associated with attempts to construct historical accounts that serve in one manner or another to underscore and legitimate aspects of contemporary psychology.

One way of marking historical figures and events as related to current interests is to create an "origin myth," a story that purports to clarify how these persons and events served as founders and precedents of some current theory, practice, or field (Samelson 1974). Harris (1980) has characterized such historical accounts as "ceremonial," and he has contrasted them with accounts that are more "critical" in nature. Ceremonial histories have also been called "monumental" (Nietzsche 1949) and "justificationist" (Weimer 1974), and as the latter term implies, they serve as a sort of apologetics for current theory and practice. Examples typically take the form of accounts that trace contemporary developments back to their "predecessors" and even further back to "anticipations" and "foreshadowings." Most historians have become suspicious of such ventures, not because they are without any value, but because they reduce historical scholarship to a kind of point-to-point linedrawing that ignores more significant and interesting details that surround and contextualize these points.

Critical history, on the other hand, although it can be equally "committed" (Woodward 1985), is more analytic and less apologetic in orientation. It seeks to cut through illusions and myths in order to reveal the practical factors involved in psychology's history. Despite its apparent disengagement, however, critical history can "take a stance," not just *against* the taken-for-granted aspects of psychology's history, but *for* the notion that history is created and constituted in the dynamic interaction between human actors and social situations. Although there is no necessary connection (see Woodward 1980), it has become common for "critical historians" to be committed to one or another form of social constructionism (Danziger 1984). To this extent, critical historians have a good deal in common with some of their psychologist colleagues (e.g. Gergen 1985; Sampson 1983). Works in this mode include those of Danziger (1990a), Finison (1976), Harris (1979b), Lewin (1984), Morawski (1985), Rose (1985), and Samelson (1985).

Models and Methods

Having reviewed five central issues in the historiography of psychology, we conclude this section by noting that, in addition to being reflective about these issues, many active historians are also self-conscious about the model of science and the mode of historical interpretation and narration they use (see Richards 1981). In addition, we want to underscore that historians have access to many different methods—archival, quantitative, biographical, textual/analytical, psychohistorical, and so on (see Brozek & Pongratz 1980; McAdams & Ochberg 1988). In view of these many methods, it is important to emphasize that, from our perspective, the historian's subject, question, or concern should come first, dictating which methods are most appropriate at any given time, not vice versa: method should not dictate the topics of research. A decade or two ago, as historians of psychology passed a milestone of self-reflectiveness, this was not always the case.

For the nonhistorian, we would also like to conclude this section by emphasizing what should now be obvious: Historians do not simply read texts and write history. Decisions about topical or thematic focus, the nature of relevant data, the means of gathering this information, the appropriate mode of analysis and interpretation, and the construction of narrative or other genres of presentation are all at issue, each and every time an historical project is undertaken. For many contemporary historians of psychology, it is exciting to face these intellectual and methodological challenges.

TEACHING THE HISTORY OF PSYCHOLOGY

The history and systems of psychology course has become a standard component of most undergraduate psychology programs (Brozek 1966; Nance 1961, 1971; Raphelson 1982; Riedel 1974; Watson 1966). Lyman (1970) has detailed an example of what might prove to be the next logical progression in this overall trend, a program in which the standard introductory psychology course is taught from an historical perspective. Although the number of publications on the history of psychology has increased dramatically over the last 25 years, a parallel development in the number of publications concerned with the effective teaching of the history of psychology has, until more recently, been rather modest.

New sources to aid the teacher include Benjamin's handbook (1981), which contains an extremely useful yet abbreviated bibliography of pre-1980 publications. McGuire (1990) compiled an annotated bibliography of various approaches to teaching the history of psychology. It covers a wide range of historiographic approaches to psychology, including archival sources, bibliographic sources, biography and psychobiography, content and/or discourse analysis, international perspectives in the historiography of psychology, the application of Kuhn's history of science model to psychology, oral history, the role of origin myths in the history of psychology, philosophy of science influences, psychoanalytic approaches to historiography, psychological interpretations of historical developments, the importance of social factors and the sociology of knowledge tradition, quantifiable measures originating within the sociology of science, the social organization of science, and textbook histories (McGuire 1990).

On a more specific level, several authors recently attempted to examine the teaching of the history of psychology from a single historiographic approach: see, for example, the books and the recent collections of articles devoted to psychohistorical methodology and the teaching of the history and systems course (Adams 1988; Eicholz 1988; Elovitz 1988; McAdams & Ochberg 1988; Runyan 1982, 1988; Shneidman 1988).

The intent of the following section therefore is to survey published resources specifically devoted to the teaching of the history of psychology.

Reflecting the rather slow initial development and acceptance of the history of psychology as an autonomous area of research within psychology, publication outlets for articles and advice on teaching the history of psychology have been limited. Prior to 1977, only an occasional letter or short report referring to teaching the history of psychology appeared in the *Journal of the History of the Behavioral Sciences* or *American Psychologist*. Almost without exception, these brief notes detail one individual's experiences with one particular approach to teaching historical research in psychology. After this date, these brief notes are complemented by occasional articles in the journal *Teaching of*

Psychology. This is typified by the inclusion in 1979 of an entire symposium on teaching the history of psychology. Unfortunately, there have been very few published attempts to integrate the various short reports and articles. As well, the nature of these short reports and correspondence notes has meant that individual authors have seldom had the opportunity to discuss the implications of different approaches to teaching the history of psychology in the kind of detail these questions deserve.

Fostering Student Interest in Historical Research

Yet, for the patient and persistent scholar, there is an abundance of published resources, suggestions, experiences, and criticisms of potential use in introducing historical material into everyday classroom activities. A fair number of these articles have been conceived in response to the oft-stated contention that it is difficult to maintain student interest and enthusiasm regarding the history of psychology course. For example, Weigl & Gottfurcht (1972, 1976) presented innovative approaches to teaching history through participatory projects specifically designed to maintain the interest of students. Similarly, Coffield (1973: 624) briefly discussed the need to address the "dread . . . apathy, boredom, etc" of the typical student in the history of psychology course. This perception of the inherently uninteresting nature of the history and systems of psychology course has been refuted by several authors, including Raphelson (1979) and Benjamin (1979). Most interstingly, Nance (1961, 1971) has twice published surveys of history of psychology students that would appear to contradict this pessimistic outlook, and instead indicates a relatively high level of student interest in this course.

A Reference Shelf as a Resource for Students

If students are to learn how to use historical materials, the course in the history of psychology can have this as one of its objectives. The availability of sources supplementary to the textbook is essential. To be sure, a secondary book of readings based on original sources has its place, and good ones are available; but the additional resources to be found in the library should be accessible. For general reference purposes, including guides to other books and the journal literature, the following books are to be recommended as a representative shelf of books for the history class. Note that the usual textbook histories and texts on systems and theories are not included, for they do not serve the same purposes. Here is a suggested shelf list, arranged alphabetically by author and date, with full citations included in the literature cited section at the end of this chapter: Baldwin (1913), Benjamin (1981, 1988), Boring (1963), Brett (1912, 1921) (but see also Peters 1953), Krawiec (1972, 1974, 1978), McGuire (1990), Murchison (1930b–1932) (and the successive volumes of the *History of Psychology in Autobiography* with other editors;

see Lindzey 1989), Murchison (1932a), Peters (1962), Rand (1912), Viney et al (1979), Watson (1974, 1976, 1978), and Zusne (1975, 1984). These may not all be available locally, but the serious history student should nevertheless be aware of them all. An effective history of psychology course might be one that is evenly divided between basic textbook material and additional readings on different approaches to historical research.

Evaluating Existing Textbooks and Planning New Ones

Looking specifically at the textbooks themselves, several authors offer suggestions and/or frameworks for analyzing various characteristics of history of psychology texts. These comments and suggestions are of potential use both for the evaluation of existing texts and for the planning of future textbooks in the history of psychology. On the level of specific detail, the studies by Buys (1976), Finison (1983), and Harris (1979b) surveyed the wide range of interpretations of a specific historical event as portrayed in a variety of different textbooks. The degree to which these events are differentially recounted and evaluated can only emphasize the importance of considered evaluation in choosing a suitable text.

A particularly important argument was set forth by Ash (1983), who argued that history of psychology texts have played a deliberate and vital role in the self-presentation of psychology as a discipline, provided they have been designed to serve this purpose. Ash traced historical research in psychology in terms of attempts to deal with specific problems of progress, such as writing scientific history, moving away from linear continuity, and the development of historical research as an area of specialization. More recently, several authors have moved beyond the question of choosing the best history of psychology text to considering how most effectively to write and organize a textbook that addresses some of the above concerns (Cherry 1989; Danziger 1989; Dunbar 1989; Langlotz & Lubek 1989; Lubek 1989; McGuire 1989). Sullivan (1973), in addition to providing a framework for evaluating the history text, pointed to the necessity of an increased emphasis on cross-disciplinary research and comparison, a suggestion supported by others (e.g. Carlson & Simpson 1970; Statt 1976; Woodward 1982).

Raphelson (1979) described the necessity of highlighting historical context in understanding the history of psychology. Epstein (1981) has suggested that one of the most efficient means of accomplishing this goal is to focus on one narrowly defined historical period to be explored in some detail, as opposed to a comprehensive overview of a wide-ranging historical period.

Origin Myths as a Point of Reference

One of the most vital considerations in any attempt to teach the history of psychology is the necessity of highlighting and fostering a critical approach to historical research among students (Harris 1984). One way of accomplishing this goal is through an examination of what Samelson (1974) has called "origin myths" in the history of psychology, as discussed above. Students are often fascinated and surprised to learn that celebrated events in the history of psychology are not always accurately portrayed by historians, and that distortions or inaccuracies in historical narrative may reflect a hidden agenda. Watson & Rayner's (1920) Little Albert study has become a classic case study for this sort of revisionist approach to history, with Harris (1979b), LeUnes (1983), and Prytula et al (1977) all exploring the varied historical depictions of "the rat-rabbit" problem in emotional conditioning and the implications of this diversity for teaching the history of psychology.

Winton (1987) performed a similar analysis of the differing historical portrayals of the Yerkes-Dodson Law in various psychology textbooks, and Samelson (1974) developed the term "origin myth" in his examination of Allport's possible misattributions of various comments and accomplishments to Comte. Other illustrations include Misceo & Samelson's (1983:447) demonstration of "how the conditioned reflex discovered Witmer," and descriptions by Furumoto (1985), Scarborough & Furumoto (1987), and Bernstein & Russo (1974) of the role accorded female psychologists in various aspects of the history of psychology. Guthrie (1976) made a similar analysis of the role accorded to black psychologists in the history of psychology. Haines & Vaughan (1979) reexamined Allport's designation of Triplett's dynamogenesis research as the first example of experimental social psychology.

Two lesser known examples of possible origin myths offer similar instructional possibilities: Littman's (1971) criticism of French claims that Piéron was the true founder of behaviorism, and the short note by Wertheimer & Meserow (1980) refuting the often-mentioned claim that Piaget could have worked directly with Binet. A somewhat disappointing impact of this origin-myth research has been pointed out by Finison (1983), who examined introductory psychology texts in the years immediately following the publication of the report by Haines & Vaughan (1979) mentioned above. Finison concludes that the demonstration by Haines & Vaughan of the possible errors or qualifications of Allport's original historical research had little or no impact on the way the foundation of modern social psychology was subsequently depicted in textbooks.

Varied Approaches to Substantive Issues

Several authors have recounted personal experiences with specific approaches to addressing substantive issues in the history of psychology. Many instructors of the history and systems of psychology course have discussed the use of individual and/or group exercises, such as term papers (Capretta 1976;

Furumoto 1985; Harris 1979a) and research projects (Grigg 1974). Caudle (1979) proposed the importance of individual research efforts in helping to foster and demonstrate continuity between earlier and present-day psychology. Benjamin (1976, 1979) emphasized the need to develop research projects and programs that put the accent on sources of historical information and where this information is located, as opposed to limiting consideration to the research topic itself.

One of the best means of encouraging student interest in the history of psychology, while at the same time helping to put historical developments into context, is the employment of realistic demonstrations of classical experiments and research projects drawn from the past. Cogan & Cogan (1984), for example, outlined an inexpensive and easy-to-run demonstration of classical conditioning, and Caudle (1979) provided several striking but relatively simple reproductions of classic experiments from psychology's early history.

Biographical Approaches

Benjamin (1979) suggested that most students find it much more difficult to perform comprehensive historical research on a specific individual than on a particular topic area. Many instructors nevertheless adopt the "great psychologist" approach when assigning research projects for the history and systems of psychology course. Over the past few years, Boice (1975), Furumoto (1984), Kellogg (1981), and Smith (1982) have emphasized what might best be called the biographical approach to the student term paper or project. (For an extensive overview of biographical approaches to the history of psychology, see McGuire 1990.)

Raphelson (1979) and Smith (1982) discussed applying the biographical approach to all aspects of the history of psychology course, including lectures and reading material. A more specific attempt to introduce students to active, participatory biographical research is set forth in faculty genealogy research projects. Each project is a limited exercise examining the personal and theoretical influences on individual psychologists (McGuire 1988; Mindness 1988; Terry 1980; Weigl & Gottfurcht 1972, 1976).

Several authors have emphatically argued for the effectiveness of role-playing debates between prominent individuals in the history of psychology course (Benjamin 1981; Brooks 1985; Shaklee 1957). Similarly, Coffield (1973) described an exercise in which students adopt the perspective of a particular school of psychology and debate as representatives of that school throughout the course. More specifically, Cole (1983) outlined a similar program in which students recreate the potential debates of a specific APA convention. From the other extreme, Vande Kemp (1980) argued for the effectiveness of teaching historical and biographical material through an in-depth examination of specific case studies.

History Teachers as Historians

The individual research and writing of many present-day historians of psychology are often motivated by a reevaluation of earlier historical accounts, yet many teach history in the way they first encountered it. Most historians of psychology today were not trained as historians but have instead moved into the field through a combination of personal interest and professional considerations. Yet the individual moving into historical research and instruction has until recently had access to little information that might serve to orient initial research and teaching strategies. A more consistent effort on the part of the historian of psychology to discuss teaching resources and approaches will not only improve the general level of historical instruction in psychology, but it may also lead to a greater historical sensibility throughout the field of psychology.

FINAL COMMENTS

We hope that this introductory review, the first of its kind on the topic in the *Annual Review of Psychology* will assist the teacher, student, and scholar of the history of psychology. We also hope that it conveys some of the intellectual excitement and potential relevance of this field of scholarship.

While the reasons for studying the history of psychology are varied (Bernstein & Russo 1974; Henle 1976; Milar 1987; Raphelson 1982; Robinson 1979a; Watson 1966; Wertheimer 1980; Woodward 1980), the history of psychology occupies a distinctive position in relation to the discipline and profession it attempts to scrutinize. Perhaps more than any other science or profession, psychology has become reflective about its history. Unlike most other professional scientific organizations, many regional and national psychological societies sponsor divisions and programs devoted to historical self-scrutiny and interpretation. In addition, psychology curricula, particularly in the United States, reserve a larger place for historically oriented courses than do the curricula of other scientific disciplines.

We believe that this is no mere happenstance. Although its full comprehension will require careful historical study, it seems likely that this unique situation is due in large part to a sense of crisis and challenge that has characterized the field over the past three decades. This sense of crisis, now abating, stemmed from the downfall of behaviorism and positivism as the dominating influences on the ethos of the discipline; the sense of challenge, now growing, is focused upon the need to understand the fractionating tendencies within the discipline and profession.

As the diversity and specialization within psychology continue to increase, the historical perspective may be even more important, as the only vantage point from which we might maintain some sense of coherence in the field.

The plethora of current developments are linked temporally, if in no other single way. At the same time, a broader historical perspective that reaches beyond the narrow confines of psychology may prove particularly helpful in clarifying how the seemingly centrifugal tendencies within psychology are part of a larger transdisciplinary set of ongoing developments.

Literature Cited

✓Adams, K. 1988 Teaching psychohistory as "common sense" sociology *J. Psychohist.* 15:445–48

American Psychological Association, 1979 *Criteria for Accreditation: Doctoral Training Programs and Internships in Professional Psychology.* Washington, DC: Am Psychol. Assoc.

Amsel, A. 1989. *Behaviorism, Neobehaviorism and Cognitivism in Learning Theory: Historical and Contemporary Perspectives.* Hillsdale, NJ: Erlbaum

Annin, E. L., Boring, E. G., Watson, R. I. 1968. Important psychologists, 1600–1967. *J. Hist. Behav. Sci.* 4:303–15

✓Ash, M. G. 1982. Reflections on psychology in history. In *The Problematic Science: Psychology in Nineteenth-Century Thought,* ed. W. R. Woodward, M. G. Ash, pp. 347–67. New York: Praeger

✓Ash, M. G. 1983. The self-presentation of a discipline: History of psychology in the United States between pedagogy and scholarship. In *Functions and Uses of Disciplinary Histories,* ed. L. Graham, W. Lepenies, P. Weingart, 7:143–89. Dordrecht: D. Reidel

Ash, M. G. 1987. Psychology and politics in interwar Vienna: the Vienna Psychological Institute, 1922–1942. In *Psychology in Twentieth-Century Thought and Society,* ed. M. G. Ash, W. R. Woodward, pp. 143–64. New York: Cambridge Univ. Press

Baldwin, J. M. 1913, *History of Psychology: A Sketch and an Interpretation,* Vols. 1, 2. New York: Putnam

Barnes, B. 1982. *T. S. Kuhn and Social Science.* New York: Columbia Univ. Press

Bartlett, N. R., Spilka, B., Wertheimer, M., eds. 1988. History of psychology in the Rocky Mountain region. *J. Hist. Behav. Sci.* (Special Issue). 24:1–117

✓ Benjamin, L. T., Jr. 1976. Research orientation in an undergraduate history and systems of psychology course. In *Directory of Teaching Innovations in Psychology.* ed. J. B. Maas, D. A. Kleiber, pp. 543–44. Washington, DC: Am. Psychol. Assoc.

Benjamin, L. T. Jr. 1979. Instructional strategies in the history of psychology. *Teach. Psychol.* 6:15–17

Benjamin, L. T. Jr. 1981. *Teaching History of Psychology: A Handbook.* New York: Academic

Benjamin, L. T. Jr. 1988. *A History of Psychology: Original Sources and Contemporary Research.* New York: McGraw-Hill

Beringer, R. E. 1978. *Historical Analysis:* ✓ *Contemporary Approaches to Clio's Craft.* New York: Wiley

Bernstein, M. D., Russo, N. F. 1974. The ✓ history of psychology revisited or, up with our foremothers. *Am. Psychol.* 29:130–34

Blumenthal, A. L. 1975. A reappraisal of Wilhelm Wundt. *Am. Psychol.* 30:1081–88

Boice, R. 1977. Heroes and teachers. *Teach. Psychol.* 4:55–58

Bolles, R. C. 1990. Where did everybody go? *Psychol. Sci.* 1:107, 112–3

Boring, E. G. 1927. The problem of originality in science. *Am. J. Psychol.* 39:70–90

Boring, E. G. 1929. *A History of Experimental Psychology.* New York: Century

Boring, E. G. 1942. *Sensation and Perception in the History of Psychology.* New York: Appleton-Century

Boring, E. G. 1950. *A History of Experimental Psychology.* New York: Appleton-Century-Crofts. 2nd ed.

Boring, E. G. 1963. *History, Psychology, and* ✓ *Science: Selected Papers,* ed. R. I. Watson, D. T. Campbell. New York: Wiley

Brett, G. S. 1912–21. *A History of Psychology.* Vols. 1, 2, 3. London: Allen

Briskman, L. B. 1972. Is a Kuhnian analysis applicable to psychology? *Sci Stud.* 2:87–97

Brooks, C. I. 1985. A role-playing exercise for the history of psychology. *Teach. Psychol.* 12:84–85

Brozek, J. 1966. Breadth and depth in teaching history. *Am. Psychol.* 21:1075–76

Brozek, J. 1978. Summa psychologiae: a special review. Review of R. I. Watson (1974, 1976). *Eminent Contributors to Psychology* Vols. 1, 2. *J. Hist. Behav. Sci.* 14:74–83

Brozek, J. 1982. Contributions of Robert I. Watson (1909–1980) to the literature on the history of psychology. *J. Hist. Behav. Sci.* 18:326–31

Brozek, J. Evans, R. B., ed. 1977. *R. I. Watson's Selected Papers on the History of Psy-*

chology. Hanover, NH: University Press of New England

Brozek, J., Pongratz, L. J., eds. 1980. *Historiography of Modern Psychology*. Toronto: C. J. Hogrefe

Brush, S. G. 1974. Should the history of science be rated X? *Science* 183:1164–72

Buckley, K. W. 1989. *Mechanical Man: John Broadus Watson and the Beginnings of Behaviorism*. New York: Guilford Press

Burnham, J. C. 1987. *How Superstition Won and Science Lost: Popularizing Science and Health in the United States*. pp. 85–116. New Brunswick, NJ: Rutgers Univ. Press

Buss, A. R. 1977. In defense of a critical-presentist historiography: the fact-theory relationship and Marx's epistemology. *J. Hist. Behav. Sci.* 13:252–60

Buss, A. R. 1978. The structure of psychological revolutions. *J. Hist. Behav. Sci.* 14:57–64

Buss, A. R., ed. 1979 *Psychology in Social Context*. New York: Irvington

Butterfield, H. 1959. *The Whig Interpretation of History*. London: G. Bell Sons. 1st ed. 1931

Buxton, C. E., ed. 1985. *Points of View in the Modern History of Psychology*. Orlando/San Diego: Academic

Buys, C. 1976. Freud in introductory psychology texts. *Teach. Psychol.* 3:160–67

Capretta, P. 1976. Paper-tutorial in conjunction with standard lecture format in a history of psychology course. In *Directory of Teaching Innovations in Psychology*, ed. J. B. Maas, D. A. Kleiber, pp. 543–46. Washington, DC: Am. Psychol. Assoc.

Capshew, J. H. 1988. The legacy of the laboratory (1888–1988): A history of the Department of Psychology at Indiana University. In *Psychology at Indiana University: A Centennial Review and Compendium*, ed. E. Hearst, J. H. Capshew, pp. 1–83. Bloomington, IN: Indiana Univ. Dept. Psychol.

Carlson, E. T., Simpson, M. M. 1970. Interdisciplinary approach to the history of American psychiatry. In Psychiatry and Its History, ed. G. Mora, J. L. Brand. pp. 119–48. Springfield, IL: Thomas

Carr, E. H. 1961. *What is History?* New York: Random House

Caudle, F. M. 1979. Using demonstrations, class experiments, and the projection lantern in the history of psychology course. *Teach. Psychol.* 6:7–11

Cerullo, J. J. 1988. E. G. Boring: reflections on a discipline builder. *Am. J. Psychol.* 101:361–75

Chaplin, J. P., Krawiec, T. S. 1960. *Systems and Theories of Psychology*. New York: Holt, Rinehart, & Winston

Chaplin, J. P., Krawiec, T. S. 1979. *Systems and Theories of Psychology*. New York: Holt, Rinehart, & Winston. 4th ed.

Cherry, F. 1989. *The textbook genre: an overview of its place in the knowledge industry*. Presented at 50th Annu. Meet. Can. Psychol Assoc. Halifax, June 8–10

Coffield, K. E. 1973. Additional stimulation for students in history and systems. *Am. Psychol.* 28:624–25

Cogan, D., Cogan, R. 1984. Classical salivary conditioning: an easy demonstration *Teach. Psychol.* 11:170–71

Cole, D. L. 1983. The way we were: teaching the history of psychology through mock APA conventions. *Teach. Psychol.* 10:234–36

Danziger, K. 1979a. The positivist repudiation of Wundt. *J. Hist. Behav. Sci.* 15:205–30

Danziger, K. 1979b. The social origins of modern psychology. In *Psychology in Social Context*. ed. A. R. Buss, pp. 27–45. New York: Irvington

Danziger, K. 1984. Toward a critical historiography of psychology. *Rev. Hist. Psicol.* 5:99–108

Danziger, K. 1989. *Textbook history and the problem of historical continuity*. Presented at 50th Annu. Meet. Can. Psychol. Assoc., Halifax, June 8–10

Danziger, K. 1990a, *Constructing the Subject: Historical Origins of Psychological Research*. New York: Cambridge Univ. Press

Danziger, K. 1990b. Generative metaphor and the history of psychological discourse. In *Metaphors in the History of Psychology*, ed. D. E. Leary, pp. 331–56. New York: Cambridge Univ. Press

Dennis, W., ed. 1948. *Readings in the History of Psychology*. New York: Appleton-Century-Crofts

Dessoir, M. 1912. *Outlines of the History of Psychology*. Transl. D. Fisher. New York: Macmillan

Diamond, S., ed. 1974. *The Roots of Psychology: A Sourcebook in the History of Ideas*. New York: Basic Books

Dunbar, J. N. 1989. *Textbook accounts of structural and functional psychologies*. Presented at 50th Annu. Meet. Can. Psychol. Assoc. Halifax, June 8–10

Eicholz, A. 1988. Psychohistory as common sense. *J. Psychohist.* 15:413–26

Elovitz, P. H. 1988. Psychohistorical teaching. *J. Psychohist.* 15:435–45

Epstein, R. 1981. A convenient model for the evolution of early psychology as a discipline. *Teach. Psychol.* 8:42–44

Erickson, R. W. 1955. Contemporary histories of psychology. In *Present Day Psychology*. ed. A. A. Roback, pp. 487–506. New York: Philosophical Library

Evans, R. B. 1982. Robert I. Watson and the

history of psychology program at the University of New Hampshire. *J. Hist. Behav. Sci.* 18:312–16

Fay, J. W. 1966. *American Psychology before William James.* New York: Octagon Books

Feinstein, H. M. 1984. *Becoming William James.* Ithaca, NY: Cornell Univ. Press

Finison, L. J. 1976. Unemployment, politics, and the history of organized psychology. *Am. Psychol.* 31:747–55

Finison, L. J. 1983. Origin myths and the teaching of social psychology. *Teach. Psychol.* 10:29–30

Fischer, D. H. 1970. *Historians' Fallacies; Toward a Logic of Historical Thought.* New York: Harper & Row

Flugel, J. C. 1933. *A Hundred Years of Psychology; 1833–1933.* New York: Macmillan

Flugel, J. C. 1947. *A Hundred Years of Psychology: 1964.* New York: Basic Books. 2nd ed. (incl. 1933–47 suppl.)

Flugel, J. C. 1964. *A Hundred Years of Psychology: 1964.* New York: International Univ. Press. 3rd ed. (incl. 1947–63 suppl. by D. J. West)

Foucault, M. 1965. *Madness and Civilization: A History of Insanity in the Age of Reason.* Transl. R. Howard. New York: Random House

Foucault, M. 1970. *The Order of Things: An Archaeology of the Human Sciences.* Transl. not listed. New York: Random House

Foucault, M. 1975. *The Birth of the Clinic: An Archaeology of Medical Perception.* Transl. A. M. Sheridan Smith. New York: Random House

Foulquié, P., Deledalle, G. 1951. *La Psychologie Contemporaine.* Paris: Presses Universitaire

Friedman, R. A. 1967. Edwin G. Boring's mature views of the science of science in relation to a deterministic personal and intellectual motif. *J. Hist. Behav. Sci.* 3:17–26

Fuller, R. C. 1982. *Mesmerism and the Cure of American Souls.* Philadelphia: Univ. Penn. Press

Furumoto, L. 1985. Placing women in history of psychology courses. *Teach. Psychol.* 12:203–6

Furumoto, L. 1989. The new history of psychology. In *G. Stanley Hall Lecture Series.* ed. I. S. Cohen, 9:5–34. Washington, DC: Am. Psychol. Assoc.

Gergen, K. J. 1985. The social constructionist movement in modern psychology. *Am. Psychol.* 40:266–75

Glover, J. A., Ronning, R.R., eds. 1987. *Historical Foundations of Educational Psychology.* New York: Plenum

Goodman, E. S. 1982. Robert I. Watson and the Cheiron Society. *J. Hist. Behav. Sci.* 18:322–25

Grigg, A. E. 1974. Research projects for a history of psychology. *Teach. Psychol.* 1:84–85

Guthrie, R. V. 1976. *Even the Rat Was White: A Historical View of Psychology.* New York: Harper & Row.

Haines, H., Vaughan, G. M. 1979. Was 1898 a "great date" in the history of experimental social psychology? *J. Hist. Behav. Sci.* 15:323–32

Hall, G. S. 1912. *The Founders of Modern Psychology.* New York: Appleton

Harris, B. 1979a. Professional seminar in clinical psychology taught from a historical perspective. *Teach. Psychol.* 6:17–19

Harris, B. 1979b. Whatever happened to Little Albert? *Am. Psychol.* 34:151–60

Harris, B. 1980. Ceremonial versus critical history of psychology. *Am. Psychol.* 35:218–19

Harris, B. 1984. Telling students about the history of social psychology. *Teach. Psychol.* 11:26–29

Hearst, E., ed. 1979. *The First Century of Experimental Psychology.* Hillsdale, NJ: Erlbaum

Heidbreder, E. 1933. *Seven Psychologies.* New York: Appleton-Century-Crofts

Henle, M. 1976. Why study the history of psychology? *Ann. Acad. NY Sci.* 270:14–20

Herrnstein, R. J., Boring, E. G., eds. 1966. *A Sourcebook in the History of Psychology.* Cambridge, MA: Harvard Univ. Press

Hessen, B. 1971. *The Social and Economic Roots of Newton's "Principia."* New York: H. Fertig, 1st ed., 1931

Hilgard, E. R., ed. 1978. *American Psychology in Historical Perspective: Addresses of the Presidents of the American Psychological Association. 1892–1977.* Washington, DC: Am. Psychol. Assoc.

Hilgard, E. R. 1982. Robert I. Watson and the founding of Division 26 of the American Psychological Association. *J. Hist. Behav. Sci.* 18:308–11

Hilgard, E. R. 1987. *Psychology in America: A Historical Survey.* San Diego: Harcourt Brace Jovanovich

Hilgard, E. R., ed. 1988. *Fifty Years of Psychology: Essays in Honor of Floyd Ruch.* Glenview, IL: Scott, Foresman

Hughes, H. S. 1964. *History as Art and as Science.* Chicago: Univ. Chicago Press

Joncich, G. 1968. *The Sane Positivist: A Biography of Edward L. Thorndike.* Middletown, CT: Wesleyan Univ. Press

Joravsky, D. 1989. *Russian Psychology.* Cambridge, MA: Blackwell

Kellogg, R. L. 1981. The mini-biographical approach to psychological instruction. *Teach. Psychol.* 8:178–79

HSU

150.9
F 762

901.9
F 762c

362.11
F 962b

Kendler, H. H. 1987. *Historical Foundations of Modern Psychology*. Philadelphia: Temple Univ. Press

Kimble, G. E. Schlesinger, K., eds. 1985. *Topics in the History of Psychology*. Vols. 1, 2. Hillsdale, NJ: Erlbaum

Klemm, O, 1914. *A History of Psychology*. Transl. E. C. Wilm, R. Pinter. New York: Scribner

Koch, S. 1976. Language communities, search cells, and the psychological studies. In *Nebraska Symposium on Motivation. 1975*. ed. W. J. Arnold, J. K. Cole, pp. 477–559 Lincoln: Univ. Nebraska Press

Koch, S., Leary, D. E., eds. 1985. *A Century of Psychology as Science*. New York: McGraw-Hill

Krawiec, T. S., ed. 1972, 1974, 1978. *The Psychologists: Autobiographies of Distinguished Living Psychologists*, Vol. 1, 2, 3. Brandon, VT: Clin. Psychol. Publ.

Kuhn, T. S. 1962. *The Structure of Scientific Revolutions*. Chicago: Chicago Univ. Press. 2nd rev. ed., 1970

Kuhn, T. S. 1968. The history of science. In *The International Encyclopedia of the Social Sciences*. ed. D. Sills, 14:74–83. New York: Macmillan & Free Press

Kushner, R. L. 1980. The prescriptive approach to the teaching of the history of psychology course. *Teach. Psychol.* 7:184–85

√ Langlotz, D., Lubek, I. 1989. *Paradigmatic consensus in social psychology textbooks and journals: aggression revisited*. Presented at 50th Annu. Meet. Can. Psychol. Assoc. Halifax, June 8–10

Lawry, J. D. 1981. *Guide to the History of Psychology*. Totowa, NJ: Littlefield, Adams

Leahey, T. H. 1980. *A History of Psychology: Main Currents in Psychological Thought*. Englewood Cliffs, NJ: Prentice-Hall. 2nd ed.

Leary, D. E. 1976. Michel Foucault, an historian of the *Sciences Humaines*. *J. Hist. Behav. Sci.* 12:286–93

Leary, D. E. 1982. Immanuel Kant and the development of modern psychology. In *The Problematic Science: Psychology in Nineteenth-Century Thought*. ed. W. R. Woodward, M. G. Ash, pp. 17–42. New York: Praeger Science

Leary, D. E. 1987. Telling likely stories: the rhetoric of the New Psychology. 1880–1920. *J. Hist. Behav. Sci.* 23:315–31

Leary, D. E., ed. 1990. *Metaphors in the History of Psychology*. Cambridge: Cambridge Univ. Press

LeUnes, A. D. 1983. Little Albert from the viewpoint of abnormal textbook authors. *Teach. Psychol.* 10:230–31

Lewin, M., ed. 1984. *In the Shadow of the Past: Psychology Portrays the Sexes*. New York: Columbia Univ. Press

Lindzey, G., ed. 1989. *A History of Psychology in Autobiography*, Vol. 8. Stanford, CA: Stanford Univ. Press.

Lipsey, M. 1974. Psychology: preparadigmatic, postparadigmatic, or misparadigmatic? *Sci. Stud.* 4:406–10

Littman, R. A. 1971. Henri Pieron and French psychology. a comment on Professor Fraisse's note. *J. Hist. Behav. Sci.* 7:261–68

√ Littman, R. A. 1981. Psychology's histories: some new ones and a bit about their predecessors: an essay review. *J. Hist. Behav. Sci.* 17:516–32

Lowry, R. 1971. *The Evolution of Psychological Theory: 1650 to the Present*. Chicago: Aldine

Lubek, I. 1989. *Thoughts on social consensus and textbooks*. Presented at 50th Annu. Meet. Can. Psychol. Assoc., Halifax, June 8–10

Lundin, R. W. 1972. *Theories and Systems of Psychology*. Lexington, MA: Heath.

Lundin, R. W. 1979. *Theories and Systems of Psychology*. Lexington, MA: Heath. 2nd ed.; 3rd ed. 1985.

Lyman, B. 1970. Performance of introductory psychology students. *J. Hist. Behav. Sci.* 6:354–57

Marx, M. H., Cronan-Hillix, W. A. 1987. *Systems and Theories in Psychology*. New York: McGraw-Hill, 4th ed.

Marx, M. H., Hillix, W. 1963. *Systems and Theories in Psychology*. New York: McGraw-Hill

Marx, O. M. 1977. History of psychology; a review of the last decade. *J. Hist. Behav. Sci.* 13:41–47

McAdams, D. P., Ochberg, R. L., eds. 1988. *Psychobiography and Life Narratives*. Durham, NC: Duke Univ, Press

McGuire, G. R., 1988. *The faculty genealogy of York University's psychology department*. Presented at 49th Annu. Meet. Can. Psychol. Assoc., Montreal, June 9–11

McGuire, G. R. 1989. *The responsivity of psychology textbooks to contemporary historical research*. Presented at 50th Annu. Meet. Can. Psychol. Assoc., Halifax, June 8–10

√ McGuire, G. R. 1990. *The Historiography of Psychology: A Critical Annotated Bibliography*. White Plains, NY: Kraus Int. Publ. In press

Merton, R. K. 1970. *Science, Technology & Society in Seventeenth Century England*. New York: Harper

Milar, K. S. 1987. History of psychology: cornerstone instead of capstone. *Teach. Psychol.* 14:236–38

Mills, E. S. 1982. A symposium on Robert I.

Watson and the development of the history of psychology. *J. Hist. Behav. Sci.* 18:307

Mindess, H. 1988. *Makers of Psychology: The Personal Factor.* New York: Sciences Press

Misceo, G., Samelson, F. 1983. History of psychology. XXXIII. On textbook lessons from history, or how the conditioned reflex discovered Twitmyer. *Psychol. Rep.* 52:447–54

Misiak, H., Sexton, V. S. 1966. *History of Psychology: An Overview.* New York: Grune & Stratton

Morawski, J. G. 1984. Historiography as a metatheoretical text for social psychology. In *Historical Social Psychology.* ed. K. J. Gergen, M. Gergen, pp. 37–60. Hillsdale, NJ: Erlbaum

Morawski, J. G. 1985. Organizing knowledge and behavior at Yale's Institute of Human Relations. *Isis* 77:219–42

Morawski, J. G., ed. 1988. *The Rise of Experimentation in American Psychology.* New Haven, CT: Yale Univ. Press

✓Mueller, C. G. 1979. Some origins of psychology as science. *Annu. Rev. Psychol.* 30:9–29

✓Mueller-Freienfels, R. 1935. *The Evolution of Modern Psychology.* Trans. W. B. Wolfe. New Haven, CT: Yale Univ. Press

Murchison, C., ed. 1926. *Psychologies of 1925.* Worcester, MA: Clark Univ. Press

Murchison, C., ed. 1930a. *Psychologies of 1930.* Worcester, MA: Clark Univ. Press

Murchison, C., ed. 1930b–1932. *A History of Psychology in Autobiography.* Vols. 1, 2, 3. Worcester, MA: Clark Univ. Press

Murchison, C., ed. 1932a. *The Psychological Register,* Vol. 3. Worcester, MA: Clark Univ. Press

Murphy, G. 1929. *Historical Introduction to Modern Psychology.* New York: Harcourt Brace.

Murphy, G. 1949. *Historical Introduction to Modern Psychology.* New York: Harcourt Brace. 2nd ed.

Murphy, G., Kovach, J. K. 1972. *Historical Introduction to Modern Psychology.* New York: Harcourt Brace Jovanovich, 3rd ed.

Nance, R. D. 1961. Student reactions to the history of psychology. *Am. Psychol.* 16:189–91

Nance, R. D. 1962. Current practices in teaching the history of psychology. *Am. Psychol.* 17:250–52

Nance, R. D. 1971. Undergraduate students and the history of psychology. *Am. Psychol.* 26:316

Nietzsche, F. 1949. *The Use and Abuse of History.* Transl. A. Collins. Indianapolis, IN: Bobbs-Merrill

✓O'Connell, A. N., Russo, N. F., eds. 1983. *Models of Achievement: Reflections of Emi-*

nent Women in Psychology. New York: Columbia Univ. Press

O'Connell, A. N., Russo, N. F., eds. 1988. ✓ *Models of Achievement: Eminent Women in Psychology.* Vol. 2. Hillsdale, NJ: Erlbaum

O'Donnell, J. M. 1979. The crisis of experimentation in the 1920's: E. G. Boring and his uses of history. *Am. Psychol.* 34:289–95

O'Donnell, J. M. 1985. *The Origins of Behaviorism: American Psychology. 1870–1920.* New York: New York Univ. Press

Palermo, D. S. 1971. Is a scientific revolution taking place in psychology? *Sci. Stud.* 1:135–55

Peters, R. S., ed. 1953. *Brett's History of Psychology* London: Allen & Unwin. Rev. ed., 1962; paperback ed., 1965. Cambridge, MA: MIT Press

Peterson, G. L. 1981. Historical self-understanding in the social sciences: the use of Thomas Kuhn in psychology. *J. Theory Soc. Behav.* 11:1–30

Popplestone, J., McPherson, M. W. 1982. Robert I. Watson: eminent contributor and co-founder of the Archives of the History of American Psychology. *J. Hist. Behav. Sci.* 18:317–19

Prytula, R. E., Oster, G. D., Davis, S. F. 1977. The "rat-rabbit" problem: What did John B. Watson really do? *Teach. Psychol.* 4:44–46

Rand, B., ed. 1912. *Classical Psychologists: Selections Illustrating Psychology from Anaxagoras to Wundt.* Boston: Houghton Mifflin

Raphelson, A. C. 1979. The unique role of the history of psychology in undergraduate education. *Teach. Psychol.* 6:12–14

Raphelson, A. C. 1982. The history course as the capstone of the psychology curriculum. *J. Hist. Behav. Sci.* 18:279–85

Richards, R. J. 1981. Natural selection and other models in the historiography of science. In *Scientific Inquiry and the Social Sciences.* ed. M. Brewer, B. Collins, pp. 37–76. San Francisco: Jossey-Bass

Riedel, R. G. 1974. The current status of the history and systems of psychology course in American colleges and universities. *J. Hist. Behav. Sci.* 10:410–12

Roback, A. A. 1952. *A History of American Psychology.* New York: Philosophical Library

Robinson, D. N. 1976. *An Intellectual History of Psychology.* New York: Macmillan. Rev. 1981

Robinson, D. N., ed. 1977/1978. *Significant Contributions to the History of Psychology. 1750–1920.* Vols. 1–28. Washington, DC: University Publications of America

Robinson, D. N. 1979a. The history of psychology and the ends of instruction. *Teach. Psychol.* 6:4–6

Robinson, D. N. 1979b. *Systems of Modern Psychology: A Critical Sketch.* New York: Columbia Univ. Press

Rose, N. 1985. *The Psychological Complex: Psychology, Politics and Society in England, 1869–1939.* London: Routledge & Kagan Paul

Rosenzweig, S. 1970. E. G. Boring and the Zeitgeist: eruditione gesta beavit. *J. Psychol.* 75:59–71

Ross, D. 1969. The "Zeitgeist" and American psychology. *J. Hist. Behav. Sci.* 5:256–62

Ross, D. 1972. *G. Stanley Hall: The Psychologist as Prophet.* Chicago: Univ. Chicago Press

Runyan, W. M. 1982. *Life Histories and Psychobiography: Explorations in Theory and Method.* New York: Oxford Univ. Press

Runyan, W. M., ed. 1988. *Psychology and Historical Interpretation.* New York: Oxford Univ. Press

Sahakian, W. S., ed. 1968. *History of Psychology: A Source Book in Systematic Psychology.* Itasca, IL: Peacock

Samelson, F. 1974. History, origin myth, and ideaology: Comte's discovery of social psychology. *J. Theory Soc. Behav.* 4:217–31

Samelson, F. 1980. E. G. Boring and his *History of Experimental Psychology. Am. Psychol.* 35:467–70

Samelson, F. 1985. Organizing for the kingdom of behavior: Academic battles and organizational policies in the twenties. *J. Hist. Behav. Sci.* 21:33–47

Sampson, E. E. 1983. Deconstructing psychology's subject. *J. Mind & Behav.* 4:135–64

Scarborough, E., Furumoto, L. 1987. *Untold Lives: The First Generation of American Women Psychologists.* New York: Columbia Univ. Press

Schulz, D. P. 1969. *A History of Modern Psychology.* San Antonio: Academic. 4th ed. 1987

Shaklee, A. B. 1957. Autobiography in teaching history of psychology. *Am. Psychol.* 12:282–83

Shneidman, J. L. 1988. On the teaching of psychohistory to Adelphi University undergraduates. *J. Psychohist.* 15:456–59

Smith, A. H. 1982. Different approaches for teaching the history of psychology course. *Teach. Psychol.* 9:180–82

Smith, L. D. 1986. *Behaviorism and Logical Positivism: A Reassessment of the Alliance.* Stanford, CA: Stanford Univ. Press

Smith, R. 1988. Does the history of psychology have a subject? *History Human Sci.* 1:147–77

Sokal, M. M., ed. 1981. *An Education in Psychology: James McKeen Cattell's Journal and Letters from Germany and England, 1880–1888.* Cambridge, MA: MIT Press

Sokal, M. M., ed. 1987. *Psychological Testing and American Society, 1890–1930.* New Brunswick, NJ: Rutgers Univ. Press

Spearman, C. 1973. *Psychology Down the Ages.* Vols. 1, 2. London: Macmillan

Statt, D. 1976. Undergraduate seminar in psychology history. In *Directory of Teaching Innovations in Psychology,* ed. J. B. Maas, D. A. Kleiber, pp. 547–48. Washington, DC: Am. Psychol. Assoc.

Stevens, G., Gardner, S. 1982. *The Women of Psychology.* Vols. 1, 2. Cambridge, MA: Schenkman

Stocking, G. W. Jr. 1965. On the limits of "presentism" and "historicism" in the historiography of the behavioral sciences. *J. Hist. Behav. Sci.* 1:211–17

Sullivan, J. J. 1973. Prolegomena to a textbook history of psychology. In *Historical Conceptions of Psychology,* ed. M. Henle, J. Jaynes, J. J. Sullivan, pp. 29–46. New York: Springer

Sulloway, F. J. 1979. *Freud, Biologist of Mind: Beyond the Psychoanalytic Legend.* New York: Basic Books

Suppe, F. 1984. Beyond Skinner and Kuhn. *New Ideas Psychol.* 2:89–104

Terry, W. S. 1980. Tracing psychology's roots: a project for the History and Systems course. *Teach. Psychol.* 7:176–77

Vande Kemp, H. 1980. Teaching psychology through the case study method. *Teach. Psychol.* 7:38–41

Viney, W., Wertheimer, M., Wertheimer, M. L. 1979. *History of Psychology: A Guide to Information Sources.* Detroit: Gale Research

Watson, J. B., Rayner, R. 1920. Conditioned emotional reactions. *J. Exp. Psychol.* 3:1–14

Watson, R. I. 1960. The history of psychology: a neglected area. *Am. Psychol.* 15:251–55

Watson, R. I. 1963. *The Great Psychologists: Aristotle to Freud.* Philadelphia: Lippincott. 4th ed. 1978

Watson, R. I. 1966. The role and use of history in the psychology curriculum. *J. Hist. Behav. Sci.* 2:64–69

Watson, R. I. 1971. Prescriptions as operative in the history of psychology. *J. Hist. Behav. Sci.* 2:311–22

Watson, R. I., ed. 1974. *Eminent Contributors to Psychology,* Vol. 1: *A Bibliography of Primary Sources.* New York: Springer

Watson, R. I., ed. 1976. *Eminent Contributors to Psychology,* Vol. 2: *A Bibliography of Secondary Sources.* New York: Springer

Watson, R. I. 1978. *The History of Psycholo-*

gy and the Behavioral Sciences: A Bibliographic Guide. New York: Springer

Watson, R. I., ed. 1979. Basic Writings in the History of Psychology. New York: Oxford Univ. Press

Weigl, R. G., Gottfurcht, J. W. 1972. Faculty genealogies: a stimulus for student involvement in history and systems. Am. Psychol. 27:981–83

Weigl, R. G., Gottfurcht, J. W. 1976. Faculty genealogies: a stimulus for student involvement in history and systems. In Directory of Teaching Innovations in Psychology, ed. J. B. Maas, D. A. Kleiber, pp. 549–50. Washington, DC: Am. Psychol. Assoc.

Weimer, W. B. 1974. The history of psychology and its retrieval from historiography. I. The problematic nature of history. II. Some lessons for the methodology of scientific research. Sci. Stud. 4:235–58, 367–96

Wertheimer, M. 1970. A Brief History of Psychology. New York: Holt, Rinehart & Winston, 3rd ed. 1987.

Wertheimer, M. 1980. Historical research—why? In Historiography of Modern Psychology, ed. J. Brozek, L. J. Pongratz, pp. 3–23. Gottingen/Toronto: Hogrefe

Wertheimer, M., Meserow, S. 1980. Did Piaget work with Binet? A note. J. Hist. Behav. Sci. 16:280

Winton, W. M. 1987. Do introductory text-books present the Yerkes-Dodson law correctly? Am. Psychol. 42:202–4

Woodward, W. R. 1980. Toward a critical historiography of psychology. In Historiography of Modern Psychology, ed. J. Brozek, L. J. Pongratz, pp. 29–67. Gottingen/Toronto: Hogrefe

Woodward, W. R. 1982. A commentary on the symposium "The use of history in the social science curriculum." J. Hist. Behav. Sci. 18:286–89

Woodward, W. R. 1985. Committed history and philosophy of the social sciences in the two Germanies. Hist. Sci. 54:25–72

Woodworth, R. S. 1948. Contemporary Schools of Psychology. New York: Ronald Press. 1st ed. 1931

Woodworth, R. S., Sheehan, M. R. 1964. Contemporary Schools of Psychology. New York: Ronald Press, 3rd ed.

Young, R. M. 1966. Scholarship and the history of the behavioral sciences. Hist. Sci. 5:1–51

Young, R. M. 1985. Darwin's Metaphor, pp. 56–78. Cambridge: Cambridge Univ. Press

Zusne, L. 1975. Names in the History of Psychology: A Biographical Source Book. Washington: Hemisphere Publications

Zusne, L. 1984. Biographical Dictionary of Psychology. Westport, CT: Greenwood Press

Annu. Rev. Psychol. 1991. 42:109–33

DIAGNOSIS AND CLINICAL ASSESSMENT

Thomas A. Widiger

Department of Psychology, University of Kentucky, Lexington, Kentucky 40506-0044

Timothy J. Trull

Department of Psychology, University of Missouri, Columbia, Missouri 65211

KEY WORDS: DSM, classification, mental disorders, psychopathology

CONTENTS

INTRODUCTION

Our review concerns issues that cut across most mental disorders, emphasizing in each case the more recent literature.

We note at the outset a few recent texts of particular interest. Skodol & Spitzer (1987) have edited an annotated bibliography that includes a com-

0066-4308/91/0201-0109$02.00

prehensive list of articles concerning DSM-III published from 1980 through 1986. Not only a useful reference source, it also contains brief overviews. Skodol (1989) has also written an informative text on the transition from DSM-III to DSM-III-R. It is primarily for the clinician, but it also provides a good commentary on the major scientific issues. Tischler (1987) edited a text providing incisive critiques of DSM-III. L. Robins & Barrett (1989) have edited an expensive but stimulating proceedings from a 1988 conference on the validation of psychiatric diagnoses held at the annual meeting of the American Psychopathological Association. International perspectives are the focus of excellent texts edited by Mezzich & Cranach (1988), Rutter et al (1988), and Sartorius et al (1990). Last, but not least, the American Psychiatric Press, the financial offspring of DSM-III, publishes the *Review of Psychiatry*, which often provides excellent overviews of diagnostic issues.

DEFINITION OF MENTAL DISORDER

One of the most basic, controversial, and recurrent issues is which behavior patterns belong in the DSM. The DSM is a manual for the diagnosis of mental disorders, but the concept has been difficult to define precisely. The absence of an explicit definition complicates the effort to assess the validity of controversial constructs, such as the self-defeating personality disorder (Kass et al 1989; Ritchie 1989), late luteal phase dysphoric disorder (Gallant & Hamilton 1988; Spitzer et al 1989a), and homosexuality. Recent discussions of the concept are provided by Frances et al (1991), Gorenstein (1984), Hafner (1989), Kendell (1986), Mezzich (1989), Roth & Kroll (1986), Spitzer & Williams (1982), and Szasz (1987).

The DSM-III-R provides a relatively explicit definition that attempts to account for all of the conditions included in the manual and to exclude all others (APA 1987:xxii). The attempt is commendable but flawed by a number of tenuous assumptions that have been problematic to any effort to construct an internally consistent and precise definition. One assumption is that mental disorders involve relatively distinct syndromes (Guze & Helzer 1987), despite the fact that there are many physical disorders that have an arbitrary and imprecise boundary with normal functioning. Another assumption is that mental disorders are those conditions treated by mental health professionals (Kendell 1986), despite the fact that it is not realistic to assume that all mental disorders are currently being treated or that clinicians confine their activities to the treatment of mental disorders. Many physical disorders are not treated by physicians. Some are treated by mom (or dad), and some are simply accepted as a regrettable aspect of life. The same is true for mental disorders (e.g. sexual dysfunctions, phobias, and personality disorders).

There is also the assumption that mental disorders are invariably associated with significant distress, disadvantage, and/or disability (Spitzer & Williams 1982), despite the fact that there are many physical disorders that are minor and inconsequential. Distress, disability, and disadvantage, along with statistical deviancy, inflexibility, irrationality, violation of social norms, and family history, are valid but quite fallible indicators of disorder. Mental disorder is a hypothetical construct identified and validated by these fallible indicators, but it is not equivalent to them (Meehl 1986).

Some assume that mental disorders are fundamentally physical disorders (Guze & Helzer 1987; Szasz 1987), whereas others attempt to demarcate a distinct boundary with physical disorders. Neither position is realistic. All references to "organic" and "physical" disorders will likely be deleted in DSM-IV to avoid the implication that mental disorders are not at least in part physical (Popkin et al 1989). The proposals would rename "organic" mood disorders as "secondary" mood disorders; place dementia, delirium, and amnesia within a new class of "cognitive" disorders; include physical disorders on Axis I when they are the cause for the psychopathology; and provide Axis III with a title that does not suggest that mental disorders are not physical. However, designating a mental disorder as being secondary to a physical disorder requires a judgment of causality that is beyond current understanding and will likely have to be based on an arbitrary and debatable definition of causality. In addition, there is unlikely to be any term for mental or physical disorders that is fully satisfactory because there is no clear boundary between them. One proposal is to rename "mental" disorders as "psychiatric" disorders (Frances et al 1990a), but this only avoids the conceptual issue and exacerbates a professional issue since there is also no clear boundary between the activities and expertise of psychiatrists, neurologists, psychologists, and other mental health professionals.

DSM-III-R is not a scientific document that provides an extensional definition of mental disorder by listing all possible cases, in a manner comparable to a periodic table of elements. It is a social document that wears many conflicting hats and must be sensitive to a variety of clinical, forensic, professional, international, and public health issues (Frances et al 1990a). It emphasizes for inclusion those conditions that are often seen by clinicians and researchers. For example, caffeine dependence is a mental disorder in that it shares with other substance dependencies the development of tolerance, unsuccessful efforts to control or diminish usage, withdrawal symptoms, and continued usage despite adverse consequences, but it is not included in DSM-III-R because the consequences are usually minimal and the condition is easily treated without professional assistance (Spitzer & Williams 1982). Similarly, persons with a fear of heights who are unable to look out the window of a tall building or fly in airplanes would not be diagnosed by DSM-III-R as having a simple phobia if they lived in a small town and had no interest in or need for flying (Mannuzza et al 1989). To be classified as phobia, fear must interfere significantly with normal activities or result in marked distress. However, it would be appropriate to consider such people as having a mental disorder, analogous to a silent disease that requires additional (potentiating) conditions to manifest the overt symptomatology (Meehl 1986).

The debate over homosexuality confuses the issue of what is a mental disorder with that of what should be in a diagnostic manual. Homosexuality is not considered to be a mental disorder in part because the associated distress is often secondary to social condemnation and discrimination; but a variety of mental disorders are not characterized by subjective distress (e.g. antisocial personality), and others involve distress that is secondary to moral condemnation (e.g. fetishism and pedophilia). It is also argued that homosexuality does not involve an impairment in an important area of functioning (Spitzer & Williams 1982); but then it is just as arbitrary to consider fetishism a disorder as it is not to consider homosexuality one. The major reason for not including homosexuality in the DSM may be the social repercussions. To the extent that homosexuality is a mental disorder it is often relatively minor (at best no worse than obligate heterosexuality), and there are likely to be more costs than benefits to homosexuals by its inclusion in the DSM.

A mental disorder is essentially an involuntary, organismic impairment in psychological functioning (i.e. cognitive, affective, and/or behavioral). Persons who are hindered in their ability to adapt flexibly to stress, to make optimal life decisions, to fulfill desired potentials, or to sustain meaningful or satisfying relationships as a result of an impairment in cognitive, affective, and/or behavioral functioning over which they have insufficient control, have a mental disorder. This definition includes many conditions considered by others to represent simply problems in living (Szasz 1987). Many mental disorders are minor and inconsequential (e.g. inhibitions and anxieties), just as many physical disorders (e.g. colds, cuts, and hay fever). Everyone goes through life suffering from and/or tolerating a variety of mental disorders, some of which are chronic (e.g. personality disorders), just as everyone suffers and/or tolerates a variety of physical disorders, some of which are chronic (e.g. myopia). The extent to which any particular person is mentally ill is only a matter of degree, type, and time of life.

The definition of mental disorder provided above does not include relational or systems disorders. Mental disorders are disorders of the organism. Disorder does occur at all levels of functioning, from the cell (and below) to the social (and beyond), but our definition does not attempt to define cellular or relational pathology. However, dysfunction at one level also interacts with the (dys)function at another, and clinicians are therefore actively involved in neurochemical and interpersonal dysfunction whether this is their intention or not. Many, of course, focus at the neurochemical or the interpersonal level. A major limitation of the DSM-III-R is its confinement to organismic/mental disorders and its failure to recognize social, relational pathology (Group for the Advancement of Psychiatry Committee on the Family [GAPCA] 1989).

DSM-III, DSM-III-R, AND DSM-IV

DSM-III was a productive catalyst for research (Skodol & Spitzer 1987). DSM-III-R, however, may have been more disruptive than facilitating (Fenton et al 1988; Rey 1988). DSM-III-R was intended to be a fine tuning that would be completed by 1984 and published in 1985 (Spitzer & Williams 1987), but the duration of the review and the extent of the revisions were more substantial (e.g. Kendler et al 1989). Proceeding on DSM-IV within a year of the publication of DSM-III-R has therefore been particularly problematic. A cynical suspicion is that the motivation is financial (Zimmerman 1988). The American Psychiatric Association did reap substantial profits from DSM-III, including the development of its own successful publishing company (Spitzer 1985).

DSM-IV, however, was necessitated by the development of the tenth edition of the World Health Organization's International Classification of Diseases (ICD-10), also to be implemented in 1993 (Frances et al 1989; Sartorius 1988). Not proceeding would have hindered international communication and collaboration, and contributed to a diagnostic jingoism (Kendell 1988). The process by which DSM-IV is being constructed, however, is intended to be more explicit, empirically based, and open to critical review, thereby providing some safeguards against arbitrary and whimsical revisions (Frances et al 1989, 1990a; Widiger et al 1990a).

The threshold for revision is also likely to be higher in DSM-IV than was the case for DSM-III(-R) (Frances et al 1990a). Diagnoses proposed for DSM-IV include (but are not limited to) victimization sequelae, post-extreme stress not otherwise specified, paraphilia coercion, serial murderer, atypical depression, bipolar II, seasonal affective (Blehar & Rosenthal 1989; Pichot & Jensen 1989), late luteal phase dysphoria (Spitzer et al 1989a), organic solvent, aphasia, apraxia, apathy, disinhibited, paroxysmal, movement secondary to neuroleptics, mild neurocognitive, age associated cognitive impairment, steroid abuse (Kashkin & Kleber 1989), caffeine dependence, sexual compulsivity, low intensity orgasm, telephone scatalogia, telephone abuse of adolescence, sibling rivalry, failure to thrive, suicidality of childhood and adolescence, childhood (Smoller 1985), conflictual relationship, extramarital affair, codependency, sexual boundary, Munchausen by proxy, delusional dominating personality, depressive personality (Phillips et al 1991), sadistic personality, self-defeating personality (Kass et al 1989), authoritarian personality, pleonectic personality, brief reactive dissociation, minor depression, mixed anxiety-depression, blood-injury (injection) phobia, choking phobia, fear of death, simple schizophrenia (D. Block & Boffeli 1989), adjustment with sleep disturbance, adjustment with denial of physical illness, adjustment with bulimia, adjustment with paranoia, inadequate sleep hygiene, sleep state misperception, bruxism, ideopathic insomnia, psychophysiological insomnia, restless legs syndrome, periodic limb movement, altitude insomnia, narcolepsy, jet lag, shift work, REM sleep behavior, impaired sleep-related penile erections, sleep-related painful erections, pathological spending, pathological overeating, pathological mourning, pathological self-mutilation, and pathological nomen-calator disorder. It might be evident that some of the above are figments of our own imaginations, but it might also be difficult to identify the seven phony proposals. The pseudo-proposals are not presented to make light of the real proposals. A compelling argument could in fact be made for all but one or two of them. Each involves a distinguishable pattern of behavior that is associated with impairment in social and/or occupational functioning, clinicians are likely to be involved in their treatment, and communication would be facilitated by a set of diagnostic criteria and formal recognition.[1] The minimal criteria for including a new diagnosis in DSM-III-R were apparently face validity and a compelling rationale for clinical utility (Kass et al 1989), but it is evident that literally hundreds of such behavior patterns could be identified.

Blashfield et al (1990) suggested that a diagnosis should not be added to the nomenclature until at least 50 journal articles have appeared, half of which would be empirical. These criteria are perhaps too stringent and arbitrary, but it is difficult to argue that there is much need for or interest in a diagnosis for which few to no clinical or empirical articles have appeared. In addition, the impact of a diagnosis on clinical practice is difficult to anticipate without prior critical review and empirical research.

VALIDATION

E. Robins & Guze (1970) outlined five phases for the validation of a diagnosis, including clinical description, laboratory data, delimitation from other disorders, follow-up, and family history. The goal was to develop a set of mutually exclusive, discrete syndromes with established empirical validity. The model for the first phase of clinical description was provided by Feighner et al (1972), who emphasized explicit and specific diagnostic criteria. The paper by E. Robins & Guze is said to represent a landmark in the history of psychiatry (Cloninger 1989). Its importance to the conceptualization and

---

[1]The seven phony diagnosis proposals are serial murderer, telephone abuse of adolescence, childhood, extramarital affair, authoritarian personality, adjustment disorder with bulimia, and pathological nomen-calator.

validation of diagnoses is analogous to the impact of Cronbach & Meehl (1955) on assessment. The Feighner et al and Robins & Guze publications provided the foundation for what has since been referred to as the Neo-Kraepelinian movement, some of whose principles are said to be: psychiatry is a branch of medicine, a boundary exists between the normal and the sick, psychiatric practice should be based on the results of scientific knowledge derived from rigorous empirical study, research and teaching should emphasize diagnosis and classification, and research should use modern scientific methodologies, especially from biology (Klerman 1983).

The development of specific and explicit criteria has contributed to the productive explosion of construct validation research. This format for diagnosis also allows the application of psychometric principles and techniques to the criteria sets themselves, including structural validity and internal consistency (e.g. Grant 1989; Kosten et al 1987; Morey 1988; Trull et al 1987; Zimmerman et al 1989). Most of the research has concerned the reliability and validity of the diagnoses, but it would also be of interest to assess the reliability and validity of the criteria sets' individual items (e.g. which melancholic, schizophrenic, and personality disorder items contribute to the overlap with near neighbor diagnoses, which has the strongest familial history, and which has the weakest reliability). This research might also facilitate the extension of research beyond the DSM-III-(-R) criteria sets through the inclusion of alternative items.

The E. Robins & Guze (1970) model, however, is not without limitations. Notable among them is an implicit bias favoring biogenetic models of pathology. It was the intention of DSM-III(-R) to be atheoretical with respect to etiology (APA 1987; Spitzer 1987), but no diagnostic system can be theory neutral (Faust & Miner 1986; Schwartz & Wiggins 1986). An emphasis on specific and explicit criteria is inherently biased against models of pathology that emphasize inference and clinical judgment (Shapiro 1989). That these models have less empirical support may not extenuate the theoretical bias of an emphasis on specific and explicit criteria. The validation of interpersonal and systems models of pathology are likewise hindered by a taxonomy that recognizes only organismic dysfunction (Denton 1989; GAPCA 1989).

Kendler (1990) in fact questions the purported reliance on empirical validation. He indicates that because data are typically insufficient, nosologic decisions must consider other factors. He suggests that value judgments are inherent in many nosologic decisions, including decisions about the sufficiency of the available data and the relative emphasis to be given to different validators (e.g. family history, course, or descriptive validity). Logical empiricism is an insufficient model for how science does or should proceed (Faust & Miner 1986). Progress is due as well to a variety of other factors, strategies, and events (Feyerabend 1987), at times for the better but perhaps as well at times for the worse (Schacht 1985; Spitzer 1985).

Cloninger (1989) has suggested a number of specific limitations to E. Robins & Guze's model of validation (1970). One is that alternative criteria sets have proliferated in the absence of a gold standard to which they can be compared. However, it is frankly desirable for there to be alternatives (Meehl 1986). We know too little about the diagnosis of mental disorders to rely exclusively on one system. Current research tends to be confined to the DSM-III(-R), limiting the ability to provide data relevant to its revision. In addition, the singular importance of the DSM to clinical, forensic, insurance, and other important social decisions contributes to the pressures and controversies that impede dispassionate and objective research and discussion (Schacht 1985; Spitzer 1985). The absence of external validators does, however, hinder the resolution of a number of controversies (Widiger & Spitzer 1990). An alternative lead standard has been suggested (Spitzer & Williams 1988), but this criterion is largely a euphemism for an informed but overly fallible clinician (Zimmerman et al 1988).

Cloninger (1989) also laments the frequency with which cases must be placed in atypical, residual, and other wastebasket diagnoses. Many purportedly "real" diagnoses serve a similar purpose, such as the adjustment, generalized anxiety, dysthymia, borderline, substance abuse, and schizoaffective diagnoses. These diagnoses are perhaps a necessary fallout of the effort to demarcate homogeneous, discrete categories. Cloninger suggests that a categorical system will only be fully satisfactory if disorders are truly discrete and mutually exclusive, which appears unlikely.

Blashfield (1989), Cantor & Genero (1986), and others propose the prototypal model of classification as an alternative. Diagnoses are categories constructed by clinicians to clarify and distinguish among the patients they have seen. They are not abstractions defined through intensional definitions of necessary and sufficient features. They are instead prototypic exemplars of cases with respect to which patients will vary. From this perspective, it can be as fruitful to assess the cognitive activity of clinicians and the content validity of criteria sets as it is to assess the symptomatology in patients. Recent examples of the application of the prototypal model include work by Blashfield & Breen (1989), Blashfield et al (1989), Livesley et al (1987), Mezzich (1989), and Sprock (1988).

The relative advantages of the prototypal and traditional models of validation are comparable to the advantages of the rational and empirical models of test construction, respectively. A potential limitation of the prototypal methodology is that it could be inadequate for identifying new disorders. New discoveries could be known to only a few researchers or clinicians, and they will not be adequately represented in opinion surveys. The prototypal methodology is also prone to reifying the "implicit diagnostic theories" (i.e. the illusions and misconceptions) of clinicians. It is perhaps more important to know the sensitivity and specificity of the symptoms in persons suspected of having the disorders, and these symptoms' correlations with external validators, than their face validity. On the other hand, to the extent that a taxonomy attempts to represent the concepts used by clinicians, the prototypal methodology is informative. The missassignments of symptoms by the subjects in Blashfield & Breen's study (1989) clearly suggest an overlap in meaning and a confusion of symptomatology.

CLINICAL UTILITY

Absent from E. Robins & Guze's paper (1970) is a consideration of clinical utility. The importance of utility in the construction and validation of a diagnosis is controversial (Meehl 1986). Surveys have suggested that the DSM-III(-R) lacks clinical utility and is not adhered to by clinicians (e.g. Jampala et al 1988; Kutchins & Kirk 1988; Morey & Ochoa 1989; Smith & Kraft 1989). Some of the criticisms cited in these surveys would occur with any nomenclature and reflect a dissatisfaction with diagnosis in general; but a manual that is not being used would appear to lack clinical utility (Burke 1988). The DSM-III-R does at times appear to be more suitable for researchers than for clinicians. For example, the 35 criteria for somatization and the 30 criteria for antisocial personality disorder were based on research protocols that have substantial empirical support but are too impractical for everyday clinical use.

Cantor & Genero (1986) suggest that diagnosis is a process of matching a given case to prototypic exemplars. Clinical utility might then be improved by implementing an exemplar-matching approach that is more consistent with natural cognitive activity. However, exemplar matching was essentially the procedure used in DSM-II, in which a narrative description of the prototypic case was provided and the clinician determined the "family resemblance." The structured format of DSM-III-R is more systematic and reliable, and is in fact consistent with a prototypal matching in that one determines how many of the features of the prototype are possessed by an individual case and then assigns members to the category on the basis of a fixed rule with respect to their resemblance to the prototype.

The difficulty lies in getting clinicians to use the manual. The ICD-10 will address this problem by providing separate manuals for clinicians and researchers (Sartorius 1988). The latter will be comparable to DSM-III-R/IV in providing specific and relatively explicit criteria; the former will be comparable to DSM-II in providing only general guidelines and narrative descriptions. This approach is appealing because it recognizes the different needs of the clinician and the researcher. However, it could also suggest that clinical diagnoses need not be reliable, and it could diminish the relevance of research to clinical practice (and vice versa). Simplifying complex and cumbersome criteria sets is useful only to the extent that validity is not compromised. The manual should indicate how an accurate diagnosis would be made, not how a busy clinician would like to diagnose.

One could, however, extend the proposal of constructing alternative criteria sets to other domains. The DSM-III-R is used for a variety of purposes (e.g. treatment decisions, public health statistics, scientific research, forensic decisions, disability claims, and insurance reimbursements), in a variety of clinical settings (e.g. inpatient hospital, private practice, and primary care), and by a variety of theoretical orientations (e.g. analytic, systems, behavioral, and biogenetic). It is unrealistic to expect that one set of diagnostic criteria could be optimal for all of these needs (Grant 1989). For example, the thresholds for establishing criminal responsibility, for determining when there should be insurance coverage, and for choosing which treatment to use will often conflict. Rather than attempt to find a compromise among all of these needs that would be problematic to most of them, perhaps there should be a different manual for each purpose.

For example, the DSM-III-R criteria for posttraumatic stress disorder require the presence of a stressor that is outside the range of usual experience and markedly distressing to almost anyone (Brett et al 1988). Aversive experiences that are common to most people, however, can result in a posttraumatic stress disorder since the experience of stress is subjective (Breslau & Davis 1987; March 1990). On the other hand, this diagnosis is already prone to substantial misuse in forensic and liability deliberations. Broadening the criteria to allow subjective perceptions and common events would increase the potential for misuse.

Consideration is being given in DSM-IV to developing a separate version for primary care physicians and a set of optional axes that would be available depending upon the needs of the clinician (e.g. an axis for defense mechanisms, familial functioning, and psychosocial stressors). The development of the Diagnosis-Related Groups taxonomy, although controversial, will perhaps contribute to an eventual separation of scientific and financial needs (Feinstein 1988).

DEFINITIONS VS DIAGNOSES

An implicit issue is the distinction between a definition and a diagnosis (Morey & McNamara 1987; Widiger & Frances 1987). The definition of a disorder is the delineation of its pathology, which in the case of mental disorders is typically a description of the phenomenology. Diagnosis concerns the signs and symptoms that indicate that the disorder is likely to be present (or absent). The phenomenology that is optimal in identifying the presence of a disorder is often the same phenomenology that is optimal in describing (or defining) the disorder, but this will not always be the case. The criteria sets provided in DSM-III-R attempt to serve both purposes, and this is at times problematic.

To the extent that the criteria sets provide (operational) definitions they are infallible in diagnosis. From this perspective, persons who meet the DSM-III-R criteria for schizophrenia have schizophrenia because the criteria define what is meant by schizophrenia. However, one might also consider the criteria to be fallible indicators for the presence of schizophrenia (Fenton & McGlashan 1989). From this perspective, there are persons with schizophrenia who lack some or even all of the criteria, and there are persons with the criteria who are not schizophrenic.

DSM-III-R ostensibly provides the optimal set of criteria for identifying the presence of disorders. The items are those that have been shown empirically to decrease false positive and false negative rates. However, if the purpose of the manual is to diagnose, the criteria and cutoff points should then vary across clinical settings and differential diagnoses since the diagnostic efficiency of an indicator varies across settings, comparison groups, and differential diagnoses (Hsu 1988). The optimal criteria for diagnosis would also vary across the source of information (e.g. patient, relative, or teacher), time (adolescence, young adulthood, middle age, and old age), and gender, since the most pertinent and relevant symptoms will vary across these variables (Goldstein & Link 1988; Milich et al 1987; Zimmerman et al 1988). There are precedents already for time (e.g. separate criteria for childhood variants of the mood, anxiety, psychotic, and antisocial personality disorders) and gender (e.g. separate criteria for male and female inhibited orgasm). The manual should also give as much attention to exclusion as it does to inclusion criteria (Meehl 1986). DSM-III-R currently emphasizes indicators that are optimal in identifying the presence of disorders and gives little attention to indicators that would be optimal in ruling out the presence of a disorder (the exclusion criteria that are provided concern arbitrary exclusions of comorbid diagnoses). In addition, emphasis is currently given to sensitivity and specificity rates when the likelihood of a disorder's presence or absence is in fact given by its positive and negative predictive power (Fenton & McGlashan 1989; Hiller et al 1989; Milich et al 1987; Millon et al 1989). Diagnosis is a probabilistic judgment modeled best by such Bayesian statistical approaches as signal-detection and receiver-operating-characteristic methods (Hsiao et al 1989; Kraemer 1988; Siegel et al 1989) and actuarial decision theory (Dawes et al 1989).

On the other hand, DSM-III-R is also said to provide operational definitions (e.g. Farmer & McGuffin 1989; Grant 1989; Zimmerman et al 1989), and this interpretation would not be served well by having the criteria sets vary across settings. In addition, the cutoff points are currently set to maximize the hit rate within clinical settings, as in the case of three of nine items for the diagnosis of substance dependence (Rounsaville et al 1987), eight of 16 for autism (Spitzer & Williams 1988), and five of eight for self-defeating personality disorder (Spitzer et al 1989b). But a cutoff point that maximizes the hit rate within clinical settings does not provide the minimal threshold for defining when the person has the disorder. The result is that there are many subthreshold, atypical cases. The cutoff points would perhaps be less problematic if their purpose was to specify (define) at what point a person manifests a clinically significant level of pathology.

An emphasis on diagnosis over definition can also result in distorted descriptions of disorders. For example, the DSM-III-R antisocial criteria emphasize overt, criminal, delinquent, and irresponsible acts that can be reliably assessed; they deemphasize trait concepts such as lack of empathy, lack of guilt, callousness, lack of sincerity, egocentricity, and glibness, which are central to the concept of psychopathy (Gerstley et al 1990; Harpur et al 1989). Harpur et al in fact argue that the less reliably assessed trait constructs are necessary for a valid diagnosis, but this would again depend on the situation in which the diagnosis occurs. Lack of empathy is useful in differentiating the psychopath from the criminal within a prison setting but perhaps not in differentiating the psychopath from the narcissist or schizoid within a clinical setting.

SPECIFICITY AND INFERENCE

One of the major achievements of DSM-III was the development of specific and explicit diagnostic criteria that substantially improved the reliability of clinical and empirical diagnoses (McReynolds 1989). This specificity was thought to be necessary to obtain replicable findings. However, it is also apparent that increased specificity does not necessarily result in increased validity (Frances et al 1990a). Overly specific criteria tend to lose the construct that is being assessed since there are typically a multitude of acts that will exemplify a particular disposition, and these acts will often vary across ages, ethnic groups, and situations. Representing the disorder by a subset of these acts will then provide a narrow representation of the construct, but a comprehensive list is impractical in clinical diagnosis. Prototypic acts are informative with respect to exploring the meaning of the construct and developing multiple act indexes (Buss & Craik 1986; Livesley et al 1987), but even this approach has limitations in diagnosis (J. Block 1989; Widiger et al 1990b).

On the other hand, one could also argue that the DSM-III-R criteria sets are not specific enough, as they still require a substantial amount of judgment and inference (McReynolds 1989). Research programs have been successful in obtaining acceptable levels of interrater reliability for even the most difficult diagnoses, but this success is often the result of developing criteria for each item at a local research site that do not agree well with the interpretations that are used elsewhere (Grant 1989). The substantial levels of interrater reliability that are reported for semistructured interviews are then somewhat misleading, since they do not necessarily suggest that there will be sufficient intersite reliability. Self-report inventories have an advantage over semistructured interviews in this respect, since it is likely that intersite reliability (e.g. replication of research findings) will be better for an inventory than for a semistructured interview.

These issues are most pertinent to the personality disorders (APA 1987; Widiger et al 1988); but they also apply to many other disorders, as evidenced by the difficulty in specifying what is meant by "bizzare" delusions in the diagnosis of schizophrenia (Kendler et al 1989), the terms "persistent," "great deal of time," "important," and "marked" in the diagnosis of substance dependence (Grant 1989), "senselessness" in the diagnosis of obsessive-compulsive anxiety disorder, and "impairment" in the diagnosis of anxiety disorders (Mannuzza et al 1989). An apparent solution to these ambiguities would be to specify each term further, but such specificity is likely to result in arbitrary distinctions that will compromise validity. Any operational definition will usually fail to represent the construct adequately.

COMORBIDITY

One of the differences between the ICD-9 and DSM-III-R is that the international system places more emphasis on identifying a single, primary disorder while the DSM-III-R encourages a coding of all disorders that apply. To prevent the occurrence of meaningless multiple diagnoses (e.g. schizophrenia and brief reactive psychosis), 60% of the DSM-III criteria sets included exclusion criteria to rule out other disorders. For example, panic disorder could not be diagnosed if it was due to major depression since the panic disorder symptomatology could be simply an associated feature. Providing both diagnoses would suggest the presence of two different disorders when in fact the person was suffering from only one.

The exclusion criteria, however, were problematic (Spitzer & Williams 1987). Determining that one disorder is due to another is an etiological judgment inconsistent with the principle of being atheoretical. Such judgments can also be debatable and unreliable. The exclusionary rules are useful in constructing homogeneous groups for research purposes, but the homogeneity is by fiat and does not accurately reflect the actual heterogeneity of the psychopathology that is present within patient populations. A variety of family history, epidemiology, and comorbidity studies have indicated that an important source of heterogeneity in major depression and other disorders was being obscured by failing to identify concomitant anxiety disorders (Barlow 1987; Weissman 1988).

Many of the exclusionary rules were therefore deleted in DSM-III-R. A few, however, remain. One reason for their retention was again that a diagnosis should not be given if its essential features are typically associated features of another disorder (Spitzer & Williams 1987). For example, generalized anxiety disorder would not be given if the focus of the worrying concerns another Axis I disorder; separation anxiety would not be given in the context of a pervasive developmental disorder; social phobia would not be given if the fear is related to the public occurrence of another Axis I syndrome; and simple phobia would not be given if the phobia is related to the content of an obsessive-compulsive anxiety disorder (APA 1987).

It is perhaps evident that many of the problems that beset DSM-III remain for DSM-III-R. For example, it is not clear why a disorder that is the result of another disorder is not diagnosed. The social phobia that results from experiences with anorexia, stuttering, or other mental disorders can be as real as the phobia that results from other experiences in life. A contrary argument is that the secondary disorder need not be the focus of treatment because it would likely remit with the successful treatment of the primary disorder. However, it need not remit and, in any case, its presence might require additional or at least altered treatment. If the secondary disorder is not always present when the primary disorder occurs, then recording its presence provides additional information that is not indicated by the diagnosis of the primary condition. The presence of a secondary social phobia, for example, could complicate the treatment of and research on anorexia nervosa. Perhaps the only time in which both diagnoses should not be given is when one disorder includes the criteria set for another, as in the case of bipolar affective disorder and major depression.

Comorbidity is particularly difficult to interpret when the constructs and/or criteria sets overlap, as in the case of many sleep and mood disorders, dream anxiety and post-traumatic stress disorder, depression and stroke, substance withdrawal/intoxication and mood/anxiety disorders, bulimia and anorexia, late luteal phase dysphoric disorder and depression, bulimia and depression, mental retardation and dementia, avoidant personality and generalized social phobia, obsessive-compulsive anxiety and schizotypal personality, substance use and antisocial personality, and multiple and borderline personality disorders. There are numerous examples within the anxiety disorders (Barlow 1987; Spitzer & Williams 1987; Weissman 1988), such as hypochondriasis and obsessive-compulsive anxiety (e.g. obsession with the fear that one is developing a major illness), social phobia and obsessive-compulsive anxiety (e.g. obsession with the thought that one smells), and simple phobia and panic (e.g. fear of choking in the context of a panic disorder). It's not clear in these boundary cases whether one has two comorbid disorders or one disorder that meets the criteria for two diagnoses.

Pope & Hudson (1989) suggest that much of the research on the comorbidity of bulimia and borderline personality disorder is an artifact of overlapping criteria sets. Persons with bulimia automatically earn two of the borderline criteria (impulsivity and affective instability). Pope & Hudson therefore suggest deleting the bulimic symptomatology from the diagnosis of borderline when assessing their comorbidity, but one would then artifactually decrease their comorbidity. Bulimia can be a manifestation of a borderline personality disorder, just as a phobia can be a manifestation of an obsessive-compulsive anxiety disorder and substance abuse can be a manifestation of an antisocial personality disorder.

Four of the eight DSM-III-R criteria for borderline personality disorder involve affective symptomatology (Widiger 1989). It is then similarly tautological to obtain correlates of a mood disorder and substantial comorbidity (Kroll 1988). One could delete affective symptomatology from the diagnosis to prevent artifactual comorbidity, but is a person without affective instability, intense anger, and physically self-damaging acts really a borderline? Borderline personality and mood disorder are overlapping constructs, and in the case of their comorbidity it is not clear if one is observing two disorders or one disorder being given two diagnoses (Widiger 1989).

Coding all syndromes that are present without regard to exclusion criteria could result in a confusing set of multiple diagnoses. However, this is a problem with categorical distinctions that is not resolved well by artifactual exclusion criteria. Multiple diagnoses will increase as new diagnoses are created, and given the emphasis on demarcating more and more "homogeneous" syndromes, multiple diagnosis will become increasingly problematic (Frances et al 1990b), particularly for the boundary and residual diagnoses such as generalized anxiety disorder, adjustment disorder, and borderline personality disorder. Further informative discussions of the complexities involved in comorbidity are provided in Maser & Cloninger (1990).

DIMENSIONAL VS CATEGORICAL CLASSIFICATION

Mental disorders are diagnosed categorically, as the clinical judgment is not the extent to which a person has a particular disorder but whether the person has the disorder. The relative advantages and disadvantages of the dimensional (quantitative) versus categorical (qualitative) models have been debated for some time (McReynolds 1989; Grove & Andreasen 1989). Categorical diagnoses do have certain advantages. It is simpler to consider and communicate the presence of one or more distinct disorders than a profile along a set of dimensions. The categorical format is also more familiar to clinicians and consistent with clinical decisions. Most clinical decisions are black and white, and clinicians would likely convert a dimensional rating to categorical distinctions by imposing cutoff points (as is currently done through the DSM-III-R polythetic algorithms). Even though the dimensional model is said to be preferred in psychology, many psychologists convert self-report dimensional profiles to more simplistic categorical code types.

These advantages, however, could pale in comparison to those of the dimensional. The ease in conceptualization is advantageous only if it is accurate. Otherwise, it is misleading, stereotyping, and contributory to many unnecessary classificatory dilemmas (Cantor & Genero 1986; Schacht 1985). The current diagnostic system contains numerous categorical distinctions that have conceptual meaning and utility with respect to prototypic cases but become arbitrary and artifactual at the boundaries. The specific thresholds for the DSM-III-R diagnoses have little empirical support, such as the requirement of four panic attacks within a four week period or one attack followed by at least one month of persistent fear for the diagnosis of a panic disorder; six months duration for the diagnosis of schizophrenia; four of seven items for the diagnosis of avoidant personality disorder; and six months duration of the recurrent intense sexual urges and fantasies involving a prepubescent child, with the person being at least 16 years old and at least five years older than the child for the diagnosis of pedophilia. The empirical data that are available for some cutoff points (e.g. Rounsaville et al 1987; Spitzer et al 1989b) are usually relative to particular base rates or external validators. Different cutoff points would be optimal for different base rates and validators. There is unlikely to be a nonarbitrary boundary between normal variation and abnormality for most disorders (e.g. late luteal phase dysphoric disorder, dependent personality disorder, enuresis, mental retardation, insomnia, alcohol abuse, bulimia nervosa, and premature ejaculation). Many of the inadequacies and controversies surrounding the DSM-III-R are due to the arbitrary categorical distinctions that result in problematic boundary diagnoses (e.g. borderline personality and schizoaffective), wastebasket diagnoses (adjustment disorder), multiple diagnoses, and numerous subthreshold (not otherwise specified) cases (Aronson 1987; Cloninger 1989; Klerman 1989; Widiger 1989). Rather than wrestle with the arbitrary distinctions between schizophrenia, simple schizophrenia, schizophreniform, schizoaffective, schizotypal, and schizoid, for example, it might be preferable to assess patients along the dimensions that underly these distinctions (e.g. severity, course, content, and pattern of schizophrenic symptomatology).

The dimensional model also has the advantage of retaining more information. It is apparent that members of each diagnostic category fail to be homogeneous with respect to the defining features. This was the major impetus for the DSM-III-R conversion from a monothetic to a polythetic format for the disruptive behavior, psychoactive substance use, and personality disorders (Spitzer 1987). Studies that have coded the data both categorically and dimensionally tend to find better results with the dimensional coding (e.g. Zimmerman et al 1988), indicating that reliable and valid information is being lost by the categorical distinctions. Kendler (1990) indicates as well that any single categorical distinction tends to represent an arbitrary compromise with respect to discrepant findings among a variety of external validators. The DSM-III-R threshold for diagnosing schizophrenia is perhaps optimal for predicting outcome but is probably too high for familial history.

Another advantage of the dimensional model is its flexibility. Clinicians will often convert a quantitative score to a categorical distinction but it is the flexibility of the dimensional format that allows this conversion. The dimensional format would in fact allow the use of different cutoff points for different purposes (e.g. predicting course vs family history).

There are a variety of empirical techniques to assess which model is more valid, including the reproducibility of factor analytic solutions across purportedly distinct groups (Eysenck 1987), the incremental validity of the respective models with respect to internal and external validators (Miller & Thayer 1989), discontinuous regression, multimodality (Moldin et al 1987), admixture analysis (Cloninger et al 1985), latent class analysis (Eaton et al 1989), maximum covariance analysis and related methods (MAXCOV; Erlenmeyer-Kimling et al 1989; Golden 1990; Trull et al 1990). For example, MAXCOV capitalizes on the fact that two independent indicators of a latent class taxon will increase in correlation as the sample becomes evenly mixed with respect to class membership. No such peak in the distribution of correlations would occur for a dimensional variable. All of these techniques have limitations, owing in large part to the fallibility of the measurement instruments and the unknown effects of item and sampling characteristics (Grayson 1987; Grove & Andreasen 1989; Tsuang et al 1990), but each is informative with respect to contrasting the assumptions of the respective models. It is then surprising that their application has been so infrequent. It would be of interest, for example, to apply MAXCOV to the criteria sets of such a purportedly latent class taxon as melancholia.

The major resistance to the dimensional model may arise from the tradition of considering mental disorders to involve qualitatively distinct diseases (Guze & Helzer 1987; Smith & Kraft 1989). The categorical model contributes to one's professional identity as a clinician, and it is then difficult to reject. Nevertheless, numerous trends indicate a gradual softening of the categorical boundaries, including the conversion from the monothetic to polythetic format (Spitzer 1987); the inclusion of severity ratings for the conduct, oppositional defiant, paraphilias, psychoactive substance use, and other disorders (APA 1987, p. 23); and the development of categories that add shades of grey to the previous black/white distinctions, such as (a) "mainly affective" vs "mainly schizophrenic" schizoaffectives (Levinson & Levitt 1987), (b) mixed anxiety-depression (Blazer et al 1988; Kendler et al 1987; Klerman 1989), (c) bulimiarexia, and (d) the various configurations and degrees of panic disorder and agoraphobia (Aronson 1987; Barlow 1987; Jacob & Turner 1988). Viable dimensional perspectives are being developed for most of the categories, including (but not limited to) the personality disorders (Cloninger 1987; Costa & McCrae 1990; Eysenck 1987; Wiggins & Pincus 1989), childhood disorders (Achenbach 1988), psychotic disorders (Crow 1986; Gottesman 1987; Strik et al 1989), dissociative disorders (Franklin 1990), substance use disorders (Edwards 1986), and the anxiety and mood disorders (Alarcon et al 1987; Akiskal 1989; Barlow 1987; Tellegen 1985; Watson et al 1988). Even staunch Neo-Kraepelinian clinicians are acknowledging the fuzziness of traditional categorical distinctions (Klein 1989).

LABORATORY FINDINGS

An issue of increasing importance is the proper role of laboratory findings in clinical diagnosis. There is little dispute that laboratory data can increase the validity of a diagnosis, but it is controversial whether the diagnostic criteria should include these tests (Carroll 1989). For example, the dexamethasone suppression test (DST) is likely to be as useful to the diagnosis of melancholia as any of the individual DSM-III-R items, such as psychomotor retardation/ agitation (Zimmerman & Spitzer 1989). To the extent that the purpose of the criteria sets is to provide valid diagnoses, it is reasonable to suggest that the DST be given as much weight and importance to the diagnosis as one of the current, fallible criteria.

The DSM-III-R melancholia criteria already include previous good response to somatic antidepressant therapy (APA 1987). Pharmacologic responsivity is comparable to a laboratory finding and perhaps has even less justification. Including somatic treatment response within the diagnosis imposes a tautological validation, converting an external validator to an internal (consistency) validator and eliminating by fiat cases that would be inconsistent with the theoretical model. This issue has, of course, been raised previously with respect to other criteria, such as the six months duration for the diagnosis of schizophrenia to maximize the likelihood that the diagnosis would in fact predict chronicity.

The case for the inclusion of laboratory tests is perhaps strongest for sleep disorders. Polysomnographic data, including an electroencephalogram, electrocardiogram, electromyogram, electro-oculogram, and measures of leg muscle activity, expired gases, blood oxygen saturation, and body temperature are essential to the diagnosis of some sleep disorders (e.g. narcolepsy, sleep apnea, and restless legs syndrome) and in the differential diagnosis of many others (Jacobs et al 1988; Thorpy 1988). Their importance, however, is not without controversy (Kales et al 1987). One of the arguments against their inclusion is the unavailability of sleep lab instrumentation to many practicing clinicians. A criterion that could not be used by many clinicians is obviously of little use. The inability to diagnose narcolepsy without a sleep lab is in fact one of the arguments against including it in DSM-IV. One could hardly argue that a disorder does not exist because most clinicians lack the facilities to make the diagnosis but, as we indicated earlier, it is not the purpose of the DSM to provide a list of all mental disorders.

A more compelling issue is the variability of laboratory test results and the lack of certainty regarding the nature of their relationship to the disorder. The history of laboratory tests is replete with unrealistic optimism and overzealous clinical application (Kupfer & Thase 1989). A laboratory test has the risk of being given undue importance owing to its apparent (but fallible) objectivity and empirical support. The difficulties in establishing a uniform algorithm for scoring a laboratory test are also substantial (Kupfer & Thase 1989; Potter & Linnoila 1989). In addition, once included within a criteria set any laboratory test algorithm would be frozen for some time and could become quickly antiquated in the face of new research. This is especially problematic when the relationship of the test result to the disorder's pathology is ambiguous (APA Task Force on Laboratory Tests in Psychiatry 1987). To the extent that a criteria set is thought to define the disorder, alterations in the laboratory technology (and pharmacologic treatment) could arbitrarily alter the concept and boundaries of the disorder. If melancholia is that which is responsive to somatic therapies (Zimmerman & Spitzer 1989), then any change in the effectiveness and focus of somatic therapies would arbitrarily alter the concept of melancholia.

The number of laboratory test results that could be incorporated into diagnostic criteria is large. A brief sample of possible tests includes nocturnal penile tumescence for male erectile disorder (Mohr & Beutler 1990), toxicology for substance use disorders (APA 1987:125), smooth pursuit eye tracking for the schizophrenia spectrum, lactate infusion for panic disorder (Cowley & Arana 1990), blunting of thyroid-stimulating hormone for depression, platelet monamine oxidase levels for a variety of disorders, intelligence testing for mental retardation, hypnotizability for dissociative disorders, amytal interview for multiple personality disorder, phallometric testing for paraphilias (Freund & Blanchard 1990), electroencephalogram for delirium, neuropsychological tests for dementia, and computed tomography, magnetic resonance imaging, and positron emission tomography for schizophrenia. There are also many self-report inventories that would be of substantial use in the diagnosis of personality, mood, anxiety, eating, and other mental disorders. Many clinicians in fact prefer the diagnoses generated by these instruments over the DSM-III-R (e.g. MMPI code types). The DSM-III-R criteria for the academic skills disorders already require psychological testing. For example, the diagnosis of developmental receptive language disorder requires that "the score obtained from a standardized measure of receptive language is substantially below that obtained from a standardized measure of nonverbal intellectual capacity (as determined by an individually administered IQ test)" (APA 1987:48). Once one has incorporated one validator, the basis for excluding others becomes increasingly debatable.

ADDENDUM

Because of space limitations, issues that are specific to particular disorders could not be covered, such as the weight that should be given to negative symptoms in the diagnosis of schizophrenia; the distinction among dependence, abuse, and harmful substance use; the importance of panic disorder in the diagnosis of agoraphobia; the role of aggression in the differentiation of conduct and oppositional defiant disorder; the inclusion of psychotic symptoms in the borderline personality diagnosis; the role of mood-incongruent delusions in the diagnosis of schizophrenia; sex bias in the diagnosis of personality disorders; and subtyping attention deficient disorder, anorexia nervosa, and schizophrenia. The reader is referred to past and future reviews of the specific disorders, published in the *Annual Review of Psychology, Review of Psychiatry,* or elsewhere.

ACKNOWLEDGMENTS

The authors express their appreciation to Allen Frances, Harold Pincus, David Berry, Richard Milich, Wendy Davis, Kenneth Walker, Samuel Bowie, and Derrick Miller for their support, suggestions, and/or assistance. Our review has also benefited from the deliberations of the many participants in the DSM-IV design process. The opinions expressed herein, however, are solely those of the authors.

Literature Cited

Achenbach, T. 1988. Integrating assessment and taxonomy. See Rutter et al 1988, pp. 300–43

Akiskal, H. 1989. Validating affective personality types. See L. Robins & Barrett 1989, pp. 217–27

Alarcon, R., Walter-Ryan, W., Rippetoe, P. 1987. Affective spectrum disorders. *Comp. Psychiatry* 28:292–308

American Psychiatric Association. 1987. *Diagnostic and Statistical Manual of Mental Disorders.* Washington, DC: Author. 567 pp. rev. ed.

American Psychiatric Association Task Force on Laboratory Tests in Psychiatry. 1987.

The dexamethasone suppression test: an overview of its current status in psychiatry. *Am. J. Psychiatry* 144:1253–62

Aronson, T. 1987. Is panic disorder a distinct diagnostic entity? *Comp. Psychiatry* 175:584–94

Barlow, D. 1987. The classification of anxiety disorders. See Tischler 1987, pp. 223–42

Blashfield, R. 1989. Alternative taxonomic models of psychiatric classification. See L. Robins & Barrett 1989, pp. 19–31

Blashfield, R., Breen, M. 1989. Face validity of the DSM-III-R personality disorders. *Am. J. Psychiatry* 146:1575–79

Blashfield, R., Sprock, J., Fuller, A. 1990.

Suggested guidelines for including/ excluding categories in the DSM-IV. *Comp. Psychiatry* 31:15–19

Blashfield, R., Sprock, J., Haymaker, D., Hodgin, J. 1989. The family resemblance hypothesis applied to psychiatric classification. *J. Nerv. Ment. Disord.* 177:492–97

Blazer, D., Swartz, M., Woodbury, M., Manton, K., Hughes, D., et al. 1988. Depressive symptoms and depressive diagnoses in a community population. *Arch. Gen. Psychiatry* 45:1078–84

Blehar, M., Rosenthal, N. 1989. Seasonal affective disorders and phototherapy. *Arch. Gen. Psychiatry* 46:469–74

Block, D., Boffeli, T. 1989. Simple schizophrenia: past, present, and future. *Am. J. Psychiatry* 146:1267–73

Block, J. 1989. Critique of the act frequency approach to personality. *J. Pers. Soc. Psychol.* 56:234–45

Breslau, N., Davis, C. 1987. Posttraumatic stress disorder: the stressor criterion. *J. Nerv. Ment. Disord.* 175:255–64

Brett, E., Spitzer, R., Williams, J. 1988. DSM-III-R criteria for posttraumatic stress disorder. *Am. J. Psychiatry* 145:1232–36

Burke, J. 1988. Field trials of the 1987 draft of chapter V (F) of ICD-10. *Br. J. Psychiatry* 152(Suppl.1):33–37

Buss, D., Craik, K. 1986. Acts, dispositions, and clinical assessment: the psychopathology of everyday conduct. *Clin. Psychol. Rev.* 6:387–406

Cantor, N., Genero, N. 1986. Psychiatric diagnosis and natural categorization: a close analogy. In *Contemporary Directions in Psychopathology*, ed. T. Millon, G. Klerman, pp. 233–56. New York: Guilford. 737 pp.

Carroll, B. 1989. Diagnostic validity and laboratory studies: rules of the game. See L. Robins & Barrett 1989, pp. 229–44

Cloninger, C. 1987. A systematic method for clinical description and classification of personality variants: a proposal. *Arch. Gen. Psychiatry* 44:573–88

Cloninger, C. 1989. Establishment of diagnostic validity in psychiatric illness: Robins and Guze's method revisited. See L. Robins & Barrett 1989, pp. 9–16

Cloninger, C., Martin, R., Guze, S., Clayton, P. 1985. Diagnosis and prognosis in schizophrenia. *Arch. Gen. Psychiatry* 42:15–25

Costa, P., McCrae, R. 1990. Personality disorders and the five-factor model of personality. *J. Pers. Disord.* In press

Cowley, D., Arana, G. 1990. The diagnostic utility of lactate sensitivity in panic disorder. *Arch. Gen. Psychiatry* 47:277–84

Cronbach, L., Meehl, P. 1955. Construct validity in psychological tests. *Psychol. Bull.* 52:281–302

Crow, T. 1986. The continuum of psychosis and its implication for the structure of the gene. *Br. J. Psychiatry* 149:419–29

Dawes, R., Faust, D., Meehl, P. 1989. Clinical versus actuarial judgment. *Science* 243:1668–74

Denton, W. 1989. DSM-III-R and the family therapist: ethical considerations. *J. Marital Fam. Ther.* 15:367–77

Eaton, W., Dryman, A., Sorenson, A., McCutcheon, A. 1989. DSM-III major depressive disorder in the community: a latent class analysis of data from the NIMH epidemiologic catchment area program. *Br. J. Psychiatry* 155:48–54

Edwards, G. 1986. The alcohol dependence syndrome: a concept as stimulus to inquiry. *Br. J. Addict.* 81:171–83

Erlenmeyer-Kimling, L., Golden, R., Cornblatt, B. 1989. A taxometric analysis of cognitive and neuromotor variables in children at risk for schizophrenia. *J. Abnorm. Psychol.* 98:203–8

Eysenck, H. 1987. The definition of personality disorders and the criteria appropriate to their description. *J. Pers. Disord.* 1:211–19

Farmer, A., McGuffin, P. 1989. The classification of the depressions. *Br. J. Psychiatry* 155:437–43

Faust, D., Miner, R. 1986. The empiricist and his new clothes: DSM-III in perspective. 1986. *Am. J. Psychiatry* 143:962–67

Feighner, J., Robins, E., Guze, S., Winokur, G., Woodruff, R., et al. 1972. Diagnostic criteria for use in psychiatric research. *Arch. Gen. Psychiatry* 26:168–71

Feinstein, A. 1988. ICD, POR, and DRG. Unsolved scientific problems in the nosology of clinical medicine. *Arch. Intern. Med.* 148:2269–74

Fenton, W., McGlashan, T. 1989. Diagnostic efficiency of DSM-III schizophrenia. *J. Nerv. Ment. Disord.* 177:690–94

Fenton, W., McGlashan, T., Heinssen, R. 1988. A comparison of DSM-III and DSM-III-R schizophrenia. *Am. J. Psychiatry* 145:1446–49

Feyerabend, P. 1987. *Farewell to Reason.* New York: Verso. 327 pp.

Frances, A., Pincus, H., Widiger, T., Davis, W. 1990a. DSM-IV: work in progress. *Am. J. Psychiatry.* In press

Frances, A., Widiger, T., Pincus, H. 1989. The development of DSM-IV. *Arch. Gen. Psychiatry* 46:373–75

Frances, A., Widiger, T., Sabshin, M. 1991. Psychiatric diagnosis and normality. In *Normality: Context and Theory*, ed. D. Offer, M. Sabshin. New York: Basic Books. In press

Frances, A., Widiger, T., Fyer, A. 1990b. The influence of classification methods on comorbidity. See Maser & Cloninger 1990, pp. 41–59

Franklin, J. 1990. The diagnosis of multiple personality disorder based on subtle dissociative signs. *J. Nerv. Ment. Disord.* 178:4–14

Freund, K., Blanchard, R. 1990. Phallometric diagnosis of pedophilia. *J. Consult. Clin. Psychol.* 57:100–5

Gallant, S., Hamilton, J. 1988. On a premenstrual psychiatric diagnosis: what's in a name? *Prof. Psychol.: Res. Pract.* 19:271–78

Gerstley, L., Alterman, A., McLellan, A., Woody, G. 1990. Antisocial personality disorder in patients with substance abuse disorders: a problematic diagnosis? *Am. J. Psychiatry* 147:173–78

Golden, R. 1990. Bootstrapping taxometrics: on the development of a method for detection of a single major gene. In *Thinking Clearly about Psychology,* ed. D. Cicchetti, W. Grove. Minneapolis, MN: Univ. Minnesota Press. In press

Goldstein, J., Link, B. 1988. Gender and the expression of schizophrenia. *J. Psychiatr. Res.* 22:141–55

Gorenstein, E. 1984. Debating mental illness. *Am. Psychol.* 39:50–56

Gottesman, I. 1987. The psychotic hinterland or, the fringes of lunacy. *Br. Med. Bull.* 43:1–13

Grant, B. 1989. DSM III-R and ICD 10 classifications of alcohol use disorders and associated disabilities: a structural analysis. *Int. Rev. Psychiatry* 1:21–39

Grayson, D. 1987. Can categorical and dimensional views of psychiatric illness be distinguished? *Br. J. Psychiatry* 151:355–61

Group for the Advancement of Psychiatry Committee on the Family. 1989. The challenge of relational diagnoses: applying the biopsychosocial model in DSM-IV. *Am. J. Psychiatry* 146:1492–94

Grove, W., Andreasen, N. 1989. Quantitative and qualitative distinctions between psychiatric disorders. See L. Robins & Barrett, pp. 127–39

Guze, S., Helzer, J. 1987. The medical model and psychiatric disorders. In *Psychiatry,* Vol. 1, Ch. 51, ed. J. Cavenar, R. Michels, A. Cooper. Philadelphia, PA: J. B. Lippincott

Hafner, H. 1989. The concept of mental illness. *Psychiatr Dev.* 2:159–70

Harpur, T., Hare, R., Hakstian, R. 1989. Two-factor conceptualization of psychopathy: construct validity and assessment implications. *Psychol. Assess.: J. Consult. Clin. Psychol.* 1:6–17

Hiller, W., Mombour, W., Mittelhammer, J. 1989. A systematic evaluation of the DSM-III-R criteria for alcohol dependence. *Comp. Psychiatry* 30:403–15

Hsiao, J., Bartko, J., Potter, W. 1989. Diagnosing diagnoses. Receiver operating characteristic methods and psychiatry. *Arch. Gen. Psychiatry* 46:664–67

Hsu, L. 1988. Fixed versus flexible MMPI diagnostic rules. *J. Consult. Clin. Psychol.* 56:458–62

Jacob, R., Turner, S. 1988. Panic disorder: diagnosis and assessment. In *Review of Psychiatry,* Vol. 7, ed. A. Frances, R. Hales, pp. 67–87. Washington, DC: Am. Psychiatric Press. 697 pp.

Jacobs, E., Reynolds, C., Kupfer, D., Lovin, P., Ehrenpreis, A. 1988. The role of polysomnography in the differential diagnosis of chronic insomnia. *Am. J. Psychiatry* 145:346–49

Jampala, V., Sierles, F., Taylor, M. 1988. The use of DSM-III in the United States: a case of not going by the book. *Comp. Psychiatry* 29:39–47

Kales, A., Soldatos, C., Kales, J. 1987. Sleep disorders: insomnia, sleepwalking, night terrors, nightmares, and enuresis. *Ann. Int. Med.* 106:582–92

Kashkin, K., Kleber, H. 1989. Hooked on hormones? An anabolic steroid addiction hypothesis. *J. Am. Med. Assoc.* 262:3166–70

Kass, F., Spitzer, R., Williams, J., Widiger, T. 1989. Self-defeating personality disorder and DSM-III-R: development of the diagnostic criteria. *Am. J. Psychiatry* 146:1022–26

Kendell, R. 1986. What are mental disorders? In *Issues in Psychiatric Classification,* ed. A. Freedman, R. Brotman, I. Silverman, D. Hutson, pp. 23–45. New York: Human Sciences Press. 250 pp.

Kendell, R. 1988. Priorities for the next decade. See Mezzich & von Cranach 1988, pp. 332–40

Kendler, K. 1990. Towards a scientific psychiatric nosology: strengths and limitations. *Arch. Gen. Psychiatry.* In press

Kendler, K., Heath, A., Martin, N., Eaves, L. 1987. Symptoms of anxiety and symptoms of depression. *Arch. Gen. Psychiatry* 44:451–57

Kendler, K., Spitzer, R., Williams, J. 1989. Psychotic disorders in DSM-III-R. *Am. J. Psychiatry* 146:953–62

Klein, D. 1989. Schizophrenia and bipolar affective disorders: likeness and differences. *Hillside J. Clin. Psychiatry* 11:3–15

Klerman, G. 1983. The significance of DSM-III in American psychiatry. In *International Perspectives on DSM-III,* ed. R. Spitzer, J. Williams, A. Skodol, pp. 3–25. Washington, DC: Am. Psychiatric Press. 413 pp.

Klerman, G. 1989. Depressive disorders: further evidence for increased medical morbidity and impairment of social functioning. *Arch. Gen. Psychiatry* 46:856–58

Kosten, T., Rounsaville, B., Babor, T., Spitzer, R., Williams, J. 1987. Substance-use disorders in DSM-III-R. *Br. J. Psychiatry* 151:834–43

Kraemer, H. 1988. Assessment of 2 × 2 associations: generalizations of signal-detection methodology. *Am. Stat.* 42:37–49

Kroll, J. 1988. *The Challenge of the Borderline Patient.* NY: W. W. Norton. 337 pp.

Kupfer, D., Thase, M. 1989. Laboratory studies and validity of psychiatric diagnosis: has there been progress? See L. Robins & Barrett 1989, pp. 177–200

Kutchins, H., Kirk, S. 1988. The business of diagnosis: DSM-III and clinical social work. *Soc. Work* 33:215–20

Levinson, D., Levitt, M. 1987. Schizoaffective mania reconsidered. *Am. J. Psychiatry* 144:415–25

Livesley, W., Rieffer, L., Sheldon, A., West, M. 1987. Prototypicality rating of DSM-III personality disorder criteria. *J. Nerv. Ment. Dis.* 175:395–401

Mannuzza, S., Fyer, A., Martin, L., Gallops, M., Endicott, J., et al. 1989. Reliability of anxiety assessment. I. Diagnostic agreement. *Arch. Gen. Psychiatry* 46:1093–101

March, J. 1990. The nosology of post-traumatic stress disorder. *J. Anx. Disord.* 4:61–82

Maser, J., Cloninger, C., eds. 1990. *Comorbidity in Anxiety and Mood Disorders.* Washington, DC: Am. Psychiatric Press. 869 pp.

McReynolds, P. 1989. Diagnosis and clinical assessment: current status and major issues. *Annu. Rev. Psychol.* 40:83–108

Meehl, P. 1986. Diagnostic taxa as open concepts: metatheoretical and statistical questions about reliability and construct validity in the grand strategy of nosological revision. In *Contemporary Directions in Psychopathology,* ed. T. Millon, G. Klerman, pp. 215–31. New York: Guilford. 737 pp.

Mezzich, J. 1989. An empirical prototypical approach to the definition of psychiatric illness. *Br. J. Psychiatry* 154(Suppl.4):42–46

Mezzich, J., von Cranach, M., eds. 1988. *International Classification in Psychiatry.* New York: Cambridge University Press. 390 pp.

Milich, R., Widiger, T., Landau, S. 1987. Diagnosis of attention deficit and conduct disorders using conditional probabilities. *J. Consult. Clin. Psychol.* 55:762–67

Miller, M., Thayer, J. 1989. On the existence of discrete classes in personality: is self-monitoring the correct joint to carve? *J. Pers. Soc. Psychol.* 57:143–55

Millon, T., Bockian, N., Tringone, T., An-

toni, M., Green, C. 1989. New diagnostic efficiency statistics: comparative sensitivity and predictive/prevalence ratio. *J. Pers. Disord.* 3:163–73

Mohr, D., Beutler, L. 1990. Erectile dysfunction: a review of diagnostic and treatment procedures. *Clin. Psychol. Rev.* 10:123–50

Moldin, S., Gottesman, I., Erlenmeyer-Kimling, L. 1987. Searching for the psychometric boundaries of schizophrenia: evidence from the New York High-Risk Study. *J. Abnorm. Psychol.* 96:354–63

Morey, L. 1988. Personality disorders under DSM-III and DSM-III-R: an examination of convergence, coverage, and internal consistency. *Am. J. Psychiatry* 145:573–77

Morey, L., McNamara, T. 1987. On definitions, diagnosis, and DSM-III. *J. Abnorm. Psychol.* 96:283–85

Morey, L., Ochoa, E. 1989. An investigation of adherence to diagnostic criteria: clinical diagnosis of the DSM-III personality disorders. *J. Pers. Disord.* 3:180–92

Phillips, K., Gunderson, J., Hirschfeld, R., Smith, L. 1991. The depressive personality: a review. *Am. J. Psychiatry.* In Press

Pichot, J., Jensen, P. 1989. Seasonal affective disorder: SAD or FAD? *Jefferson J. Psychiatry* 12:41–50

Pope, H., Hudson, J. 1989. Are eating disorders associated with borderline personality disorder? A critical review. *Int. J. Eating Disord.* 8:1–9

Popkin, M., Tucker, G., Caine, E., Folstein, M., Grant, I. 1989. The fate of organic mental disorders in DSM-IV: a progress report. *Psychosomatics* 30:438–41

Potter, W., Linnoila, M. 1989. Biochemical classifications of diagnostic subgroups and D-type scores. *Arch. Gen. Psychiatry* 46:269–71

Rey, J. 1988. DSM-III-R: too much too soon? *Aust. NZ J. Psychiatry* 22:173–82

Ritchie, K. 1989. The little woman meets son of DSM-III. *J. Med. Philos.* 14:695–708

Robins, E., Guze, S. 1970. Establishment of diagnostic validity in psychiatric illness: its application to schizophrenia. *Am. J. Psychiatry* 126:107–11

Robins, L., Barrett, J., eds. 1989. *The Validity of Psychiatric Diagnosis.* New York: Raven Press. 338 pp.

Roth, M., Kroll, J. 1986. *The Reality of Mental Illness.* New York: Cambridge Univ. Press. 128 pp.

Rounsaville, B., Kosten, T., Williams, J., Spitzer, R. 1987. A field trial of DSM-III-R psychoactive substance dependence disorders. *Am. J. Psychiatry* 144:351–55

Rounsaville, B., Kranzler, H. 1989. The DSM-III-R diagnosis of alcoholism. In *Review of Psychiatry,* ed. A. Tasman, R.

Hales, A. Frances, pp. 323–40. Washington, DC: Am. Psychiatric Press. 641 pp.

Rutter, M., Tuma, A., Lann, I., eds. 1988. *Assessment and Diagnosis in Child Psychopathology.* New York: Guilford Press. 477 pp.

Sartorius, N. 1988. International perspectives of psychiatric classification. *Br. J. Psychiatry* 152(Suppl.1):9–14

Sartorius, N., Jablensky, A., Regier, D., Burke, J., Hirschfeld, R., eds. 1990. *Sources and Traditions of Classification in Psychiatry.* Lewiston, NY: Hogrefe & Huber

Schacht, T. 1985. DSM-III and the politics of truth. *Am. Psychol.* 40:513–21

Schwartz, M., Wiggins, O. 1986. Logical empiricism and psychiatric classification. *Comp. Psychiatry* 27:101–14

Shapiro, T. 1989. Psychoanalytic classification and empiricism with borderline personality disorder as a model. *J. Consult. Clin. Psychol.* 57:187–94

Siegel, B., Vukicevic, J., Elliott, G., Kraemer, H. 1989. The use of signal detection theory to assess DSM-III-R criteria for autistic disorder. *J. Am. Acad. Child Adolesc. Psychiatry* 28:542–48

Skodol, A. 1989. *Problems in Differential Diagnosis: From DSM-III to DSM-III-R.* Washington, DC: Am. Psychiatric Press. 535 pp.

Skodol, A., Spitzer, R., eds. 1987. *An Annotated Bibliography of DSM-III.* Washington, DC: Am. Psychiatric Press. 649 pp.

Smith, D., Kraft, W. 1989. Attitudes of psychiatrists toward diagnostic options and issues. *Psychiatry* 52:66–77

Smoller, J. 1985. The etiology and treatment of childhood. *J. Polymorphous Perversity* 1:7–9

Spitzer, R. 1985. DSM-III and the politics-science dichotomy syndrome. *Am. Psychol.* 40:522–26

Spitzer, R. 1987. Nosology. See Skodol & Spitzer 1987, pp. 3–11

Spitzer, R., Severino, S., Williams, J., Parry, B. 1989a. Late luteal phase dysphoric disorder and DSM-III-R. *Am. J. Psychiatry* 146:892–97

Spitzer, R., Williams, J. 1982. The definition and diagnosis of mental disorder. In *Deviance and Mental Illness*, ed. W. Gove, pp. 15–31. Beverly Hills, CA: Sage. 303 pp.

Spitzer, R., Williams, J. 1987. Revising DSM-III. The process and major issues. See Tischler 1987, pp. 425–34

Spitzer, R, Williams, J. 1988. Having a dream. A research strategy for DSM-IV. *Arch. Gen. Psychiatry* 45:871–74

Spitzer, R., Williams, J., Kass, F., Davies,

M. 1989b. National field trial of the DSM-III-R diagnostic criteria for self-defeating personality disorder. *Am. J. Psychiatry* 146:1561–67

Sprock, J. 1988. Classification of schizoaffective disorder. *Comp. Psychiatry* 29:55–71

Strik, W., La Malfa, G., Cabras, P. 1989. A bidimensional model for diagnosis and classification of functional psychoses. *Comp. Psychiatry* 30:313–19

Szasz, T. 1987. *Insanity.* New York: John Wiley & Sons. 414 pp.

Tellegen A. 1985. Structures of mood and personality and their relevance to assessing anxiety, with an emphasis on self-report. In *Anxiety and the Anxiety Disorders*, ed. A. Tuma, J. Maser, pp. 681–706. Hillsdale, NJ: Erlbaum. 1020 pp.

Thorpy, M. 1988. Diagnosis, evaluation, and classification of sleep disorders. In *Sleep Disorders*, ed. R. Williams, I. Karacan, C. Moore, 9–25. New York: John Wiley & Sons. 413 pp.

Tischler, G., ed. 1987. *Diagnosis and Classification in Psychiatry.* New York: Cambridge Univ. Press. 546 pp.

Trull, T., Widiger, T., Frances, A. 1987. Covariation of criteria sets for avoidant, schizoid, and dependent personality disorders. *Am. J. Psychiatry* 144:767–71

Trull, T., Widiger, T., Guthrie, P. 1990. Categorical versus dimensional status of borderline personality disorder. *J. Abnorm. Psychol.* 91:40–48

Tsuang, M., Lyons, M., Faraone, S. 1990. Heterogeneity of schizophrenia: conceptual models and analytic strategies. *Br. J. Psychiatry* 156:17–26

Watson, D., Clark, L., Carey, G. 1988. Positive and negative affectivity and their relation to anxiety and depressive disorders. *J. Abnorm. Psychol.* 97:346–53

Weissman, M. 1988. The epidemiology of panic disorder and agoraphobia. In *Review of Psychiatry*, ed. A. Frances, R. Hales, 7:54–66. Washington, DC: Am. Psychiatric Press. 697 pp.

Widiger, T. 1989. The categorical distinction between personality and affective disorders. *J. Pers. Disord.* 3:77–91

Widiger, T., Frances, A. 1987. Definitions and diagnoses: a brief response to Morey and McNamara. *J. Abnorm. Psychol.* 96:286–87

Widiger, T., Frances, A., Pincus, H., Davis, W. 1990a. DSM-IV literature reviews: rationale, process, and limitations. *J. Psychopathol. Behav. Assess.* In press

Widiger, T., Frances, A., Spitzer, R., Williams, J. 1988. The DSM-III-R personality disorders: an overview. *Am. J. Psychiatry* 145:786–95

Widiger, T., Freiman, K., Bailey, B. 1990b. Convergent and discriminant validity of personality disorder prototypic acts. *Psychol. Assess.: J. Consult. Clin. Psychol.* In press

Widiger, T., Spitzer, R. 1990. Sex bias in the diagnosis of personality disorders: conceptual and methodological issues. *Clin. Psychol. Rev.* In press

Wiggins, J., Pincus, A. 1989. Conceptions of personality disorders and dimensions of personality. *Psychol. Assess.: J. Consult. Clin. Psychol.* 1:305–16

Zimmerman, M. 1988. Why are we rushing to publish DSM-IV? *Arch. Gen. Psychiatry* 45:1135–38

Zimmerman, M., Black, D., Coryell, W. 1989. Diagnostic criteria for melancholia. *Arch. Gen. Psychiatry* 46:361–68

Zimmerman, M., Pfohl, B., Coryell, W., Stangl, D., Corenthal, C. 1988. Diagnosing personality disorder in depressed patients. *Arch. Gen. Psychiatry* 45:733–37

Zimmerman, M., Spitzer, R. 1989. Melancholia: from DSM-III to DSM-III-R. *Am. J. Psychiatry* 146:20–28

Annu. Rev. Psychol. 1991. 42:135–59

SOUND LOCALIZATION BY HUMAN LISTENERS

John C. Middlebrooks

Departments of Neuroscience and Surgery (ENT), University of Florida, Gainesville, Florida 32610

David M. Green

Psychoacoustics Laboratory, Department of Psychology, University of Florida, Gainesville, Florida 32611

KEY WORDS: sound localization, directional hearing, binaural hearing, monaural localization, directional transfer function

CONTENTS

INTRODUCTION

The task of localizing a sound source presents a challenge to the integrative capabilities of the nervous system. In the visual system, locations of objects in the visual world are focused by the optics of the eye directly onto the retina,

0066-4308/91/0201-0135$02.00

and maps of visual space are found in structures of the central nervous system that preserve the intrinsic topography of the retina. Inasmuch as the wavelength of sound is six orders of magnitude greater than that of light, an acoustical focusing mechanism analogous to the optics of the eye is not feasible, and a different mechanism must be employed. The sound wave generated by an external source is diffracted by its interaction with the head and external ears. The resulting changes in the temporal and intensive characteristics of the acoustical stimulus provide cues about the locus of a sound relative to the head. The goal of this chapter is to characterize the acoustical cues for sound localization and to assess the strategies by which subjects utilize these cues to determine the location of a sound source.

Before beginning the review, we must comment on some general features of practically all studies of sound localization. A common objective of many studies is to test the efficacy of some stimulus aspect (interaural level difference, interaural temporal difference, spectral shape, etc) in revealing the locus of the source. With all scientific studies, a degree of abstraction occurs. An important restriction in most behavioral experiments on sound localization is that the potential responses are restricted to a few locations (e.g. a subject must select from a small number of loudspeakers located on a particular plane). Another common restriction is a limitation in the bandwidth or duration of the acoustic stimulus. Although a result might clearly establish the effectiveness of a particular cue in a certain experimental setting, there often is no evidence to indicate the importance of that cue in a more realistic setting. For example, listeners might correctly localize source A 2° to the right of source B, given only an interaural intensity difference at 4720 Hz. That same cue might be totally ignored in determining the site of a broadband sound source that is unrestricted in its possible location. The restricted experiment provides information about the *sensitivity* of the listener to a particular cue. It does not provide information about the larger, and more interesting, issue concerning the synthesis of a central image corresponding to the external sound source. In reviewing studies of sound localization, then, one must be aware that different researchers will champion different cues as most important in localizing sound sources. Each claim is demonstrably valid in some restricted setting. As the set of potential cues becomes better understood, the next item on the agenda is to determine how these different cues are weighted and integrated in a setting in which multiple cues are present. To the extent that it is possible, we try to address this larger issue here.

Sound localization has traditionally received considerable attention in behavioral and physiological studies in animals, and those areas have been the topics of recent reviews (Masterton & Imig 1984; Phillips 1985). Moreover, physiologists and anatomists have made great progress in understanding the mechanisms by which the nervous system detects specific cues for sound localization (Rose et al 1966; Boudreau & Tsuchitani 1968; Goldberg & Brown 1969). In recent years, increasing attention has been focused on localization by human listeners. Evidence of this interest is provided by the recent publication of a book edited by Yost & Gourevitch (1987) that contains chapters by the participants in a symposium on directional hearing held earlier by the Acoustical Society of America. Additional interest has been stimulated by a meeting in 1988 of the National Research Council's Committee on Bioacoustics and Biomechanics (CHABA), the topic of which was sound localization by humans. Part of this renewed interest undoubtedly stems from the 1983 translation of Blauert's classic work on *Spatial Hearing* (Blauert 1974). This review attempts to integrate some of the more recent experimental results with the classic studies. We give only passing attention to experiments using stimuli presented over headphones (e.g. studies of masking level difference and lateralization) in order to focus on issues of localization in a free sound field. Furthermore, since most of the results to be discussed were obtained in anechoic environments, we pay little attention to issues such as localization in reverberant rooms (Blauert 1983; Hartmann 1983) and the precedence effect (Zurek 1980; Gaskell 1983; Clifton 1987).

For convenience in presentation, we draw a somewhat arbitrary distinction between localization in the horizontal and vertical dimensions. To some extent, this distinction is dictated by the design of most previous localization studies. That is, in most studies, the sound sources have been restricted to one of two cardinal planes, either the horizontal plane, defined roughly by the two ear canals and the tip of the nose, or the median (mid-sagittal) plane. The distinction between horizontal and vertical localization also appears to be justified by differences in the principal spatial cues for horizontal and vertical localization (i.e. interaural difference cues vs spectral cues). One can influence these cues differentially by plugging one ear or by filling the convolutions of the pinnae. We begin by reviewing recent studies of localization in which stimulus locations were varied freely in both horizontal and vertical dimensions; we then consider the available spatial cues and behavioral performance specifically in the horizontal compared to the vertical dimension. We pay separate attention to the perception of sound source distance, to the perception of stimulus motion, and to dynamic spatial cues provided by movements of the head.

TWO-DIMENSIONAL SOUND LOCALIZATION

When a subject is presented with a source that can appear at any position about the subject's head, and that source presents the full complement of acoustical spatial cues, how effectively does the listener use that information to synthesize the locus of a sound source? The two dimensions in this localization task are *azimuth* and *elevation*. In this review, localizations are given in a double-pole coordinate system (see Knudsen 1982) in which azimuth is defined as the angle given by the sound source, the center of the listener's head, and the median plane; this is the angle in the horizontal dimension. Elevation is defined as the angle given by the sound source, the center of the head, and the horizontal plane. The origin (0°, 0°) is straight in front of the subject.

Information about sound localization in the two-dimensional space about the listener is available in the recent studies by Oldfield & Parker (1984a), Wightman & Kistler (1989b), and Makous & Middlebrooks (1990). These studies had two basic methodological features in common. First, the stimuli had broadband spectra. The broad bandwidth provided the subjects with means to resolve the spatial ambiguities that are present within any narrow frequency band. Second, the locations of sound sources were varied freely in both the horizontal and vertical dimensions. This avoided a limitation of most previous localization studies in which much of the spatial ambiguity inherent in the localization task was removed by constraining the possible source locations to a single plane. Absolute levels of localization performance varied substantially among these three studies, owing largely to differences in the stimulus bandwidths and durations, differences in the amount of variability in spectra between trials, and differences in the methods by which subjects were required to report the apparent locations of sound sources. Despite the variation in absolute levels of performance, the three studies convey a consistent picture of the general spatial dependence of localization performance.

Figure 1 shows localization data from one subject in the study by Makous & Middlebrooks (1990). Stimulus locations and the subject's responses are drawn on the surface of an imaginary sphere, 1.2 m in radius, centered on the subject's head. Asterisks indicate the locations of stimuli, and open circles indicate the response locations. Sizes of errors and response variability were smallest for stimuli directly in front of the subject and increased at more peripheral stimulus locations. The smallest errors in that study, averaged across trials and across subjects, were about 2° and 3.5° in azimuth and elevation, respectively, increasing to average errors of as much as 20° for some rear locations. Across elevation, the variability in the judgments of azimuth was relatively constant for any given azimuth and, similarly, across azimuth, the variability in the judgments of elevations was relatively constant for any given elevation. The scatter of responses in azimuth was smaller than that in elevation for stimuli near the frontal midline, but the opposite was true for more peripheral locations.

Most sound localization studies have noted the occurrence of front/back confusions, in which a stimulus in front of the subject is localized to the rear, or vice versa. When front/back confusions occur, the azimuthal component of

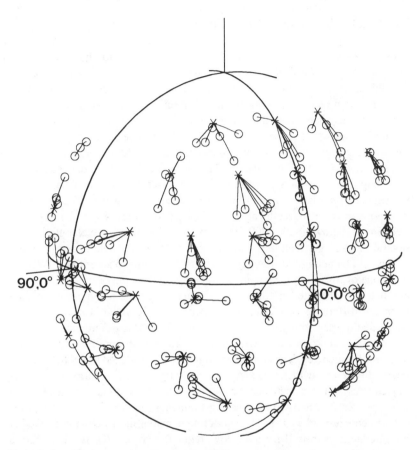

Figure 1   Localization of a broadband sound. Stimulus and response locations are drawn on the surface of an imaginary sphere as if looking in toward the subject from point 30° to the subject's right and elevated 10°. Asterisks indicate the stimulus location and open circles indicate five responses to that stimulus given by a single subject. For clarity, stimulus locations are shown in 20° steps of azimuth and elevation, although data were collected in 10° steps. The data are from the study by Makous & Middlebrooks (1990).

the stimulus and response locations tend to lie in mirror symmetry with respect to the interaural axis. The pattern of elevation errors is less regular (Makous & Middlebrooks 1990). The frequency of occurrence of front/back confusions tends to increase as the bandwidth of the stimulus is decreased (Butler 1986). For example, Makous & Middlebrooks (1990) encountered front/back confusions in 2–10% of localizations of broadband stimuli, depending on the subject, whereas subjects made front/back confusions in more than 20% of the trials when localizing one-octave noise bands (Burger 1958).

HORIZONTAL LOCALIZATION

No study of sound localization in the horizontal dimension has escaped the influence of a series of observations made by Lord Rayleigh near the end of the 19th century and reported in his Segwick lecture in 1906 (Rayleigh 1907). Rayleigh attempted to account for localization in terms of interaural difference cues. He appreciated that when a sound was presented from the side, a listener's head would interrupt the path from the source to the far ear. The far ear would be effectively shadowed and an interaural difference in sound pressure level (ILD) would result. The amount of shadowing depends on the wavelength of the sound compared with the dimensions of the head. At high frequencies, the shadow amounts to a difference of as much as 35 dB between the two ears for a source located at the side (Middlebrooks et al 1989). For frequencies below about 1000 Hz, however, the sound wavelength can be several times larger than the head and, as Rayleigh was able to compute, the ILD would be negligible. Rayleigh "reluctantly" came to accept that "When a pure tone of low pitch is recognized as being on the right or the left, the only alternative to the intensity theory is to suppose that the judgment is founded upon the difference of *phases* at the two ears" (Rayleigh 1907). Rayleigh confirmed the sensitivity of listeners to interaural phase differences (IPDs) by presenting to the two ears a pair of tuning forks that were tuned to slightly different frequencies. The slightly mistuned forks produced a steadily varying phase difference, which produced the sensation of an auditory image that moved back and forth between the two ears. Rayleigh found that the sensitivity to phases declined with increasing frequency, with an upper limit in his experiments around 770 Hz. The notion that spatial information is derived at high frequencies from ILDs and at low frequencies from IPDs is often referred to as the "duplex" theory of sound localization.

Studies of localization in the horizontal plane have produced results consistent with the duplex theory. In an experiment by Stevens & Newman (1936), sounds were presented from a loudspeaker mounted on a boom 12 feet long, and subjects attempted to report the angular location of the sound source. Although broadband stimuli (i.e. clicks and noise bursts) could be localized with reasonable accuracy, subjects often made front/back confusions when attempting to localize sinusoidal stimuli. Discounting the front/back confusions, there was a clear frequency dependence to the localization performance. Specifically, the magnitudes of errors peaked around 3000 Hz and declined at higher and lower frequencies. A similar frequency dependence in localization errors was observed by Sandel and colleagues (1955), who required subjects to adjust the position of a broadband noise source to correspond to the apparent source of a sinusoid: Performance was worst for sinusoids around 1500–3000 Hz. Interpreted with reference to the duplex theory, the accuracy of localization of low frequencies would be attributed to IPDs and that at high frequencies to ILDs. In the range around 1500 to 3000 Hz, stimuli are too high in frequency to provide usable phase cues and too long in wavelength to provide adequate ILDs.

Mills (1958) measured spatial acuity by asking subjects to distinguish between two loudspeakers separated in the horizontal dimension. Consistent with measurements of localization accuracy, the "minimum audible angle" measured in this way was maximal around 3000 Hz. Mills noted that, when the loudspeakers were placed symmetrically around 90° to the side, the minimum audible angle exceeded the largest angle that Mills could test; in this configuration, he noted that the minimum audible angle task is equivalent to a front/back discrimination.

Accuracy in sound localization in the horizontal dimension can be accounted for largely in terms of the spatial dependence of interaural difference cues and the sensitivity of subjects to those cues. The minimum thresholds for ILDs in tones are less than 1 dB (Mills 1960). Hafter and colleagues (1977) have shown that the threshold for changing ILD varies by no more than a factor of two over a broad range of ILDs. The spatial dependence of ILDs has been measured directly by recording from the two ear canals with miniature microphones while presenting sounds at varying locations around the head (Searle et al 1975; Middlebrooks et al 1989); ILD values can also be estimated from other studies that used monaural recordings by assuming that the head is bilaterally symmetrical (e.g. Shaw 1974; Mehrgardt & Mellert 1977). In the results of Middlebrooks and colleagues (1989), maximum ILDs measured near 90° azimuth were around 20 dB at the lowest frequency tested, 4 kHz, and rose to as high as around 35 dB at 10 kHz. When averaged across any perceptually relevant bandwidth, ILDs are roughly proportional to the sine of the azimuthal angle and are roughly constant across elevation at any constant azimuth. Thus, one might expect the sizes of errors in localization and the sizes of minimum audible angles to increase monotonically with increasing azimuth. The ILD produced by a tone (or a single component of a complex sound), however, can show substantial local variation with source location (Middlebrooks et al 1989). Consistent with that view, Mills (1958) found that minimum audible angles for tonal stimuli failed to show an orderly dependence on azimuth for frequencies greater than 4 kHz and for azimuths greater than 30°.

The spatial dependence of IPDs has been estimated by treating the ears as two points on the surface of a rigid sphere and determining, geometrically, the difference in the paths from a sound source to the two points (Woodworth 1938). This analysis gives:

$$\tau = (r/c) \, [\theta + \sin(\theta)]$$

1.

where τ is the interaural delay, c is the speed of sound in air, r is the radius of the sphere, and θ is the azimuthal angle of the sound source in radians. Kuhn (1977, 1987) made a more acoustically based analysis of the delay between two points on a rigid sphere and measured the interaural delays on a mannequin. At frequencies above about 2 kHz, the interaural delay given by Equation 1 corresponds well to measured values. At lower frequencies (below 500 Hz), the acoustical prediction and the measured values are larger than those predicted by this equation by a factor of 3/2.

When tonal stimuli are presented over headphones, human listeners show sensitivity to interaural differences in the ongoing phase of the stimulus for frequencies up to about 1000 to 1300 Hz (Licklider et al 1950; Zwislocki & Feldman 1956). The minimum audible angle for low-frequency tones, predicted from sensitivity to phase differences and the spatial dependence of phase differences, corresponds well with measured minimum audible angles and localization performance (Mills 1958). It is somewhat surprising that humans fail to detect interaural phase differences at higher frequencies, given that significant phase coding has been shown in the auditory nerve of other primates at frequencies up to 5 kHz (Rose et al 1967). The maximum interaural delay for an average human is around 700 μsec, which is equal to the period of a 1400 Hz tone. At higher frequencies, interaural phase would be ambiguous by steps of 360°, and phase leads and lags would be ambiguous even at frequencies as low as 700 Hz, at which the maximum interaural delay corresponds to 180° of phase. Thus, one possibility is that the human auditory system simply rejects phase information at frequencies at which that information would be ambiguous. That explanation does not seem to apply to the barn owl, however, which exhibits both neurophysiological and behavioral sensitivity to interaural phase differences at frequencies greater than 7 kHz (Moiseff & Konishi 1981). At those high frequencies, phase ambiguity is apparent in both neurophysiological and behavioral data, but the phase difference continues to be a salient localization cue. When an owl is presented with a stimulus that contains two or more frequency components, sufficient delay information is available to resolve the phase ambiguity, thus enabling accurate localization in azimuth based on interaural time differences (Knudsen 1984).

Despite the insensitivity of humans to ongoing phase differences in tones above 1000 to 1300 Hz, listeners can detect interaural delays in the *envelopes* of high-frequency sounds. Sensitivity to envelope delays has been demonstrated for highpass and high-frequency bandpass transients (Yost et al 1971; Hafter & Dye 1983), for bandpass noise (Klumpp & Eady 1956; Trahiotis & Bernstein 1986; Amenta et al 1987), for sinusoidally amplitude-modulated (SAM) tones (Henning 1980; Nuetzel & Hafter 1981), and for two-tone complexes (McFadden & Pasanen 1976; McFadden & Moffitt 1977). There is some indication that envelope delay sensitivity declines for carrier frequencies above about 4 kHz or for modulation frequencies above about 500 Hz. The detection of an interaural delay in a two-tone complex probably entails a different mechanism from that used by the barn owl, since the owl is sensitive to phase differences in each of the components of the complex, whereas the human listener can detect a delay only when two or more components are present. There is some question about whether envelope delays in high-frequency sounds provide humans with usable localization cues. The directional dependence of envelope delays suggests that the physical difference would provide a reliable cue to horizontal location (Middlebrooks & Green 1990). When carriers greater than about 1.6 kHz are presented over headphones, however, the extent of laterality provided by an interaural delay is small (Blauert 1982; Bernstein & Trahiotis 1985; Trahiotis & Bernstein 1986). Moreover, the modulation depth of a signal processed through a filter as wide as a critical band might be too small to permit detection of envelope delays (discussed by Middlebrooks & Green 1990).

VERTICAL LOCALIZATION

To the extent that the head and ears are symmetrical, a stimulus presented at any location on the median plane should produce no interaural differences and, thus, interaural differences should provide no cue to the vertical locations of sounds on the median plane. Similarly, any point off this median plane falls on a "cone of confusion," as Woodworth (1938) called it, upon which the interaural differences, either ILD or IPD, are constant. Although an actual set of spatially ambiguous points might differ from an idealized cone, it is clear that the spatial information provided by an interaural difference cue within a restricted band of frequency is spatially ambiguous, particularly along a roughly vertical and front/back dimension.

Batteau (1967, 1968) was one of the first to emphasize that the external ear, specifically the pinna, could be a source of spatial cues that might account for localization. He suggested that sound reflections within the convolutions of the pinna might produce spatial cues that could be used to disambiguate the potential locations of the source. That these cues could rival in importance the interaural difference cues was supported by behavioral data from an experiment reported by Fisher & Freedman (1968). They had subjects discriminate the locations of eight loudspeakers located at 45° angles about the listener in the horizontal plane. Given the paucity of potential source locations, they found that the accuracy of the localization judgments was about the same with one ear occluded as with both ears open. Localization suffered only when a 10-cm tube inserted in the ear canal effectively bypassed the pinna and deprived the listeners of its sound reflections.

Although Batteau's model was formulated in the *time* domain, the convolutions of the pinna would create echoes lasting only a few microseconds, so most current theories interpret the pinna as producing changes in the *spectrum* of the sound source that reaches the tympanic membrane. The influence of the pinna is to produce multiple paths to the ear canal, among them a direct path and a reflection from the *cavum concha* of the pinna. The addition of a direct signal with a delayed (reflected) version of the same signal produces a "comb-filtered" spectrum containing a characteristic pattern of peaks and notches. The length of the reflected path varies with the elevation of the sound source, so particular spectral features tend to vary in frequency according to elevation. We refer to patterns of spectral features associated with particular locations as "spectral shape cues." Because these cues are a product of the acoustics of the pinna, they often are referred to as "pinna cues." Finally, since spectral shape cues do not require an interaural comparison, they often are referred to as "monaural cues," although, at least for a sound source on the median plane, essentially equivalent information is available from each ear.

Several lines of evidence indicate that spectral shape cues are the major cues for vertical localization. For example, accurate vertical localization is observed only when the stimulus has a broad bandwidth (Roffler & Butler 1968; Gardner & Gardner 1973; Butler & Helwig 1983) and contains energy at high frequencies. The cutoff frequency for the high frequency requirement is subject to some debate (Roffler & Butler 1968; Hebrank & Wright 1974b), but it seems that frequencies above 4 kHz are important. Vertical localization is prevented when the convolutions of the pinnae are occluded (Roffler & Butler 1968; Gardner & Gardner 1973; Oldfield & Parker 1984b), thus altering the ear's directional transfer function. Horizontal localization is relatively unimpaired by such a manipulation, but the pinna does aid in resolving front/back ambiguity (Musicant & Butler 1984a; Oldfield & Parker 1984b). Vertical localization is almost as good when listening with a single ear as with binaural listening (Hebrank & Wright, 1974a; Oldfield and Parker, 1986). Finally, as discussed below, vertical localization is sensitive to manipulations of the source spectrum.

Measurements of the transfer function of the external ear have revealed particular spectral features that vary systematically with source location (Butler 1987; Humanski & Butler 1988; Hebrank & Wright 1974b; Watkins 1978). Blauert (1969/1970) has emphasized the presence of "boosted bands," which are peaks in the transfer function associated with front, overhead, or rear source locations. Butler (1987) defines a roughly equivalent concept as the "covert peak"—a band of frequency that produces the greatest level when presented from a particular source location. He has compiled a "spatial referent map" in which particular covert peaks correspond to specific locations on the median or horizontal plane. Among the most prominent features of the external ear transfer functions, at least on visual inspection of the spectra, are relatively narrowband notches that shift systematically in elevation with sound source elevation (Hebrank & Wright 1974b; Bloom 1977a; Watkins 1978; Butler 1987; Humanski & Butler 1988). Transfer functions generally are similar across different subjects, although the spectra tend to show a downward shift in frequency associated with increasing physical size of subjects (Middlebrooks et al 1989).

The apparent elevation of a sound source can be influenced by modifying the source spectrum. In a widely quoted experiment, Blauert (1969/1970) recorded from a subject's ear canals while presenting a noise from two source locations, either directly in back or directly in front of the listener. He then electronically modified both sources, so that each mimicked the spectrum associated with the opposite source position. The listener's judgments of the source's locus were solely determined by the source spectrum and not influenced by its actual location. Thus, the listener localized the source as behind if it had the "back" spectrum, even if played from the front speaker. In a separate experiment, Blauert presented one-third-octave noise bands from the median plane and showed that the probability of a subject's responding that a sound source was in front, overhead, or behind was determined more by the center frequency of the stimulus than by actual source locations. A similar result was reported by Butler & Helwig (1983).

Bloom (1977b) examined the spatial character of spectral notches. He presented stimuli from a fixed location and asked listeners to adjust the center frequency of a band-reject filter so that the perceived elevation most closely matched one of a set of sources located at various elevations in the median plane. The center frequencies selected by the listeners tended to correlate with the frequencies of the notches in the external ear transfer functions measured for stimuli located at corresponding elevations. Similarly, Hebrank & Wright (1974b) found that certain band-reject, band-pass, and high-pass filter characteristics tended to correlate with particular perceived elevations in the median plane. Watkins (1978) processed noise with a delay-and-add system that was intended to mimic the acoustical reflections within the external ear. These signals were presented to listeners over headphones, and the listeners adjusted a mechanical pointer to indicate the perceived source elevation. The reported elevations corresponded well with those predicted by mechanisms proposed by Batteau (1967).

Any model of localization based on spectral cues must acknowledge the importance of a priori information regarding the source spectrum. That is, the presence of a particular spectral feature at the tympanic membrane could be the result of the transfer characteristic of the ear, or it could be a feature that was present in the source spectrum. The experiments described above indicate that the auditory system cannot effectively distinguish the two. Blauert states that his model of vertical localization applies "for nearly all usual signals, as long as their power density curve is to some extent smooth." It remains to be tested how "smooth" a signal must be to permit accurate vertical localization.

This section on vertical localization began with an assumption that the two ears are essentially bilaterally symmetrical and that interaural differences provide no cue to elevation. This assumption may not be strictly valid. Measurements by Searle and colleagues (1975) and by Middlebrooks and colleagues (1989) have demonstrated that, at least within narrow bands of frequency, ILDs along the median plane can be as large as about 10 dB and that ILDs can vary with source elevation at a constant source azimuth. There is some controversy over whether or not ILD cues actually contribute to localization in elevation, particularly on the median plane. For example, Searle and colleagues (1976) devised a model based on statistical decision theory to account for results of published localization trials. Their model predicts that interaural difference ("interaural pinna") cues actually contribute more than monaural spectral shape cues to localization in the median plane. Moreover, several groups have found that plugging one ear can produce a substantial decrement in performance in a median-plane localization task (Butler 1969; Gardner 1973; Ivarsson et al 1980). One must be cautious in interpreting such a result, since the presence of an earplug would cause normal, spectral shape cues to occur in association with unfamiliar interaural difference cues, thus impairing localization. Hebrank & Wright (1974a) found that, initially following the placement of an earplug, subjects showed impaired localization in the median plane. After a short period of training, however, the ability to localize a source in the median plane was nearly the same for monaural or binaural listening. Currently, the evidence for a major contribution of ILDs to vertical localization, at least in the median plane, is not compelling.

MONAURAL LOCALIZATION

Although most investigators agree that two ears are better than one in localizing sounds in space, there is considerable evidence showing that some localization can be achieved with a single ear. Evidence on this issue comes from as early a study as that of Angell & Fite (1901) and from a more recent study by Fisher & Freedman (1968). Since most studies have produced the "monaural" listener by occluding the entrance to one ear canal, we should comment briefly on the controls that must be employed in these studies. A high-quality earplug can produce 30–40 dB attenuation at low frequencies and somewhat greater attenuation at higher frequencies. If the sound level is greater than 40 dB sensation level at the occluded ear, then, although ILDs are severely altered, interaural temporal comparison might be relatively unaffected. Thus, it is critical to conduct the localization tests with the source at a low sensation level, so that the occluded ear will be completely nonfunctional. In the studies we review, this control was exercised.

Oldfield & Parker (1986) measured two-dimensional localization under monaural conditions. Subjects localized a white-noise source that was positioned in 10° intervals ranging from −40° to +40° in elevation and 0° to 180° in azimuth on the left side. In the monaural condition, the absolute error in elevation (12°) was only slightly greater than in the binaural condition (9°). The absolute error in azimuth, however, was barely on the same scale: 30–40° for monaural listening compared to 5°–10° for binaural listening.

The Oldfield & Parker results suggest that binaural cues are primarily responsible for determining the source's azimuth and that monaural, presumable spectral shape, cues are primarily responsible for resolving the source's elevation. On the other hand, Butler and colleagues (Butler 1986; Butler & Flannery 1980; Belendiuk & Butler 1975; Musicant & Butler 1984b) have emphasized that monaural cues also contribute to localization in azimuth. Belendiuk & Butler (1975) established that when a source contains energy above 4 kHz, subjects wearing a plug in one ear can achieve better than chance localization of one of five loudspeakers located in 15° intervals on a horizontal plane in the quadrant between the unoccluded ear and straight ahead. Musicant & Butler (1984a) also showed that monaural spectral cues help resolve front/back confusions in the horizontal plane of the unoccluded ear. Butler & Flannery (1980) and Musicant & Butler (1984b, 1985) showed that narrow bands of noise (1 kHz wide) appear to move back to front in azimuth as the center frequency of the band is varied. Although responses varied among subjects, some subjects showed the following trends. As center frequencies shift from 4 to 10 kHz, the reported azimuth moves from front to back, repeating that trend for frequencies centered between 10 to 14 kHz. In those experiments, the sound was presented from only a few of the many potential loudspeaker locations. The speaker locations were visible to the listener. Whether such constraints were necessary to achieve these localization judgments is unknown.

Again, we remind the reader of the caveat expressed at the beginning of this review. There is little doubt that some of these cues can operate in certain restricted listening situations. Strong biases may develop, however, if the responses are restricted to a limited number of speaker locations. For example, Butler & Planert (1976) show an almost identical distribution of choices among five loudspeakers located in the median plane when the spacing between successive loudspeakers was 15° and when it was 7.5°. The central issue is not whether these cues play some role in certain experiments but whether they contribute significantly to sound localization under more realistic conditions.

A recent experiment tested the relative salience of ILD cues and spectral shape cues for localization in azimuth (Middlebrooks 1990). Subjects localized 1/6-octave bandpass sound sources that were varied simultaneously in azimuth and elevation. Center frequencies range between 6 and 14 kHz. Subjects made substantial and reproducible errors in localization that were largely confined to the vertical dimension. Accuracy of localization in azimuth was near that observed with broadband stimuli. Moreover, the ILDs associated with the response location were roughly the same as those produced by the stimulus. These results suggest that the bandpass filtering operation introduced erroneous spectral shape cues to elevation. The filter probably also influenced spectral cues for azimuth, but the ILD cues for azimuth, unaffected by the filter, were sufficient to support near-normal accuracy in azimuth. That is, the auditory system appears to favor binaural cues over spectral shape cues for azimuth, but must rely on spectral shape cues for elevation.

DISTANCE PERCEPTION

The listener's ability to localize the distance of a sound source is certainly not very good and has been the subject of minimal research. The scholarly review article by Coleman (1963) still provides the best summary of the potential distance cues. Little is known about the effectiveness of any of these cues. If the source intensity is known, then distance can be judged on the basis of sound intensity at the listener's ear. Gardner (1969) showed that the distance of a person speaking in a conversational tone of voice in an anechoic chamber can be judged with some accuracy. The apparent distance of the same speech delivered from a speaker is almost entirely determined by the sound level of the loudspeaker. Thus, familiarity with the signal source is clearly an important variable. In an anechoic environment, the intensity of a source diminishes 6 dB for each doubling of distance. If a change in loudness is the cue for distance, then the just-discriminable change in distance should be predictable from the just-noticeable difference in intensity. Strybel & Perrott (1984) have confirmed that expectation for sources beyond 3 m. For closer distances, much greater changes in distances must be made before the listener can achieve a successful discrimination. Simpson & Stanton (1973) have shown that head motion does not facilitate better distance judgments. Butler et al (1980) listened to sounds over headphones and judged their apparent distance. The apparent distance of the source increased as the low-frequency part of the spectrum increased. Finally, Holt & Thurlow (1969) judged sources located outdoors in a grassy park. The sources ranged in distance from 32 to 64 feet. Noise bursts, 0.5 sec in duration and presented once per second for 10 sec, were adjusted for equal level at the listeners' ears. The estimates of distance, when averaged across listeners and trials, correlated significantly with the actual source distances when the sources were located at one side, but not when placed in front of the listeners.

There is some evidence to suggest that the listener can better estimate the distance of a sound source if the surrounding environment is not anechoic. In an ordinary room, a distant source produces sound energy that reaches the listener's ears via direct and indirect paths. Differences in the ratio of these two energies might produce perceptible differences in the quality of the source as a function of distance. This cue to source distance, however, is strongly influenced by the specific reflections of the particular listening environment. For example, Mershon & Bowers (1979) have demonstrated that estimates of the distance of a wideband noise source (sounded only once for 5 sec) are significantly different from chance in a reverberant room. Apparently these effects are not robust. In an earlier experiment (Mershon & King 1975), the judgments of distance were significantly different from chance for the higher intensity levels but not for the lower intensity level. There are no systematic studies of how the ratio of direct to indirect sound energy influences the judgments of source distance.

MOTION DETECTION

The bulk of the data discussed in this review concerns the ability to identify the location of a stationary sound source or to resolve the locations of two stationary sources. An additional stimulus attribute to be considered is the change of location—that is, the motion of a sound source. We refer here to change in the azimuth and/or elevation of the source, not the change in source distance, which can be cued by a change in sound pressure or by a Doppler shift in the stimulus frequency. In the visual system, there is good evidence for neural systems specialized for the detection of motion (Hubel & Wiesel 1962; Newsome et al 1986). As yet there is no compelling evidence for motion-sensitive systems in the auditory system. The problem is that there are two intepretations for any observation of sensitivity to source motion. One interpretation is that the auditory system is sensitive to dynamic aspects of localization cues—for example, changing ILDs or IPDs. That is, source velocity might be a "directly perceived attribute of moving stimuli" (Lappin et al 1975). A second, more parsimonious interpretation is that the nervous system simply measures the sound source location at two distinct times and interprets a change in location as motion; this has been called the "snapshot theory." The difficulty in resolving these alternatives stems from the fact that most studies of motion detection tend to confound the attributes of duration, velocity, and net change in location. For example, an increase in sound source velocity will result in an increase in the total distance traversed by a stimulus of a given duration.

In studies of motion perception, listeners have typically been asked to discriminate between directions of motion (Harris & Sergeant 1971; Perrott & Tucker 1988) or to discriminate between a stationary and a moving sound source (Perrott & Musicant 1977). Although most studies have used sound sources in actual motion, some have simulated motion by systematically varying the levels of sinusoids presented from two loudspeakers (Grantham 1986; Saberi & Perrott 1990). Thresholds have been measured for duration, velocity, and change in location. All these thresholds, however, can be expressed in terms of a minimum audible movement angle (MAMA), which is the smallest net change in location of a moving stimulus that can be detected under some specified set of conditions. The MAMA shares several properties with the minimum audible angle for static sources. Specifically (*a*) MAMAs in azimuth are smallest for stimuli around 0° azimuth and increase with increasing azimuth (Harris & Sergeant 1971; Grantham 1986). A MAMA often cannot be measured for tonal stimuli around 90° azimuth, since the task is confounded by front/back confusions. (*b*) MAMAs are smaller for broadband than for tonal stimuli (Harris & Sergeant 1971; Saberi & Perrott 1990). (*c*) When measured with tonal stimuli, MAMAs are largest (i.e. performance is worst) for a range of frequencies around 1300–2000 kHz (Perrott & Tucker 1988), the range over which minimum audible angles are largest, owing to the lack of effective spatial cues (Mills 1958).

It has been a common observation that MAMAs are as much as several times larger than static minimum audible angles measured under comparable conditions. For example, Perrott & Musicant (1977) measured a MAMA of 8.3° near 0° azimuth for a 500-Hz tone, whereas the minimum audible angle measured by Mills at 800 Hz was closer to 1°. Perrott & Musicant (1977) showed that, over a range of sound source velocities from 2.8–360°/sec, the MAMA increases linearly with increasing velocity; Saberi & Perrott (1990), looking with finer resolution in the frequency dimension, recently showed that the MAMA actually only begins to grow at velocities around 10°/sec. The finding that MAMAs increase with source velocity is consistent with Grantham's (1986) observation that discrimination deteriorates for stimulus durations less than a minimum "integration time" of about 150–300 msec. That is, the angle traversed by a sound source within the time required for an accurate localization judgment increases with increasing source velocity. At the low end of the frequency range, Saberi & Perrott (1990) also reported that MAMAs can show an increase when source velocities *decrease* below about 1.8°/sec. This decrease in performance probably occurs because, at such low velocities, the duration of the stimulus (5–10 sec) exceeds the storage time of the auditory system. Perrott & Musicant (1977), in a separate experiment, asked listeners to indicate the apparent position of a moving source at stimulus onset and offset. The onset judgments were consistently displaced toward the direction of movement, and the displacement increased with increasing source velocity. This result might also be explained by the presence of a minimum integration time.

None of the results reviewed above distinguishes between a "snapshot" theory and a theory invoking specialized motion-sensitive systems. Perrott & Marlborough (1989) recently tried to test the snapshot theory directly. They presented a noise burst from a source that moved in azimuth in front of the subject at a velocity of 20°/sec, and the subject was required to discriminate the direction of the movement. In one condition, the stimulus was presented continuously. The MAMA was about 1°, corresponding to a stimulus duration of 50 msec. In a second condition, the source sounded in two discrete 10-msec bursts—that is, marking the beginning and end of the loudspeaker traverse. The silent interval between bursts was adjusted to find a threshold for discrimination of movement direction. According to the authors' interpretation, the snapshot theory would predict equal angles measured under the two conditions. The observation was that thresholds measured in the second condition were about 50% larger. Perrott & Marlborough (1989) conclude that "the information arriving after the onset and before the offset of the signal does contribute to the resolution of motion"; that is, the listener uses spatial information collected throughout the traverse of the sound source. Alternative explanations are possible. Pollack & Rose (1967) showed that the average error in localization of a stationary target increases about 60% when the duration of a noise source is shortened from 50 to 20 msec. Thus, one can argue that two 10-msec sounds do not provide sufficient information to localize reliably the beginning and end of the sound source traverse. That is, longer "snapshots" must be provided to equal the 50-msec continuous condition.

In vision, it is common to claim that a motion detector exists, since prolonged exposure to one direction of motion results in an increased threshold for motion in the same direction and no change in the threshold for motion in the opposite direction (Sekuler & Pantle 1967; Pantle & Sekuler 1968). No similar effect has been observed in audition, although Grantham & Wightman (1979), using earphones, have reported a "motion aftereffect" similar in form to the visual "waterfall effect." Grantham (1989) has repeated this experiment using an actual moving source in an anechoic room. He shows that part of the effect is a simple response bias, but there is also a small component showing loss of sensitivity to motion in the adapted direction. Because the auditory sense, as a whole, shows considerably less adaptation than vision, a more appropriate test might be borrowed from Lappin and colleagues (1975). One could construct four distinct moving stimuli by selecting two distances of travel, say 2° and 4°, and two stimulus durations, say 100 msec and 200 msec. Discriminations between two pairs of stimuli

(4°/100 msec vs 2°/200 msec and 2°/100 msec vs 4°/200 msec) involve identical distance and duration cues. One of the pairs (4°/100 msec vs 2°/200 msec) exhibits a maximal velocity difference, whereas the latter pair (2°/100 msec vs 4°/200 msec) has no velocity difference. If sound source velocity is a distinct cue, then performance on the latter discrimination should be substantially worse than on the former.

DYNAMIC CUES FOR LOCALIZATION

Sustained sounds are localized best when the head is turned to face the direction of the source. Head turning occurs spontaneously on the part of practically all subjects seeking to determine the locus of the sound source (Thurlow & Runge 1967). Such scanning is also effective with monaural listening (Perrott et al 1987). Less clear is the contribution of head motion to the localization of brief sounds that permit only a slight change in head orientation. Is the information gained from the two or more head positions integrated, and does it greatly improve the process of disambiguating the source's location? Two views exist.

The earlier view was nicely summarized by Wallach (1939, 1940) nearly five decades ago. He begins the description of his classic experiments by observing that a given interaural time or intensity difference can originate from "a geometrical locus which has the shape of a cone" (Wallach 1939). Wallach is very clear on how this ambiguous information is resolved. "One obtains the cues for a number of lateral angles for the same sound direction by turning one's head while the sound is being given. Geometrically, a sequence of lateral angles obtained in this manner completely determines a given direction, . . . and the experiments to be reported indicate that the perception of sound direction actually works on this principle" (Wallach 1939).

Wallach's experiments demonstrated that certain confusions in localization can be created by moving the locus of the source with the head. For example, if the source is held in the subject's median plane as the subject turns his/her head, then the subject's only reasonable conclusion is that the source is directly overhead. In fact, Wallach found that of the subjects who could localize over their heads (an appreciable proportion of subjects cannot localize an overhead source), all reported the impression that the source was directly overhead (90° elevation) when the actual source was located straight ahead of the subject on the horizontal plane (0° elevation).

Wallach realized that the geometric assumptions are simplistic in nature. In particular, they ignore the fact that the pinnae are asymmetric and respond differently to sources presented in the front and back of the head. He observed that front/back ambiguities are generally resolved under ordinary conditions

"on the basis of the pinna factor alone, i.e., without head movement. . . ."
But he maintains that the systematic confusions generated in his experiments
demonstrate that head motions are the primary means of disambiguating
potential confusions. His experiments demonstrate that the "pinna factor" is
invariably overcome by head motions, and this "indicates quite clearly its [the
pinna's] subordinate role."

Experiments designed to test directly the importance of head motion have
shown this cue to be remarkably weak. Thurlow & Runge (1967) studied the
effect of induced (nonvoluntary) head motions. Although in some conditions
the errors in localization were smaller by a statistically significant amount, the
reduction in error was often less than 30%. Fisher & Freedman (1968) show
no significant influence of head motion in localizing eight loudspeakers
located at 45° angles about the listener on the horizon. Modifying the pinna
had a more profound influence on the errors in localization than did restricting
head motion.

Pollack & Rose (1967) carried out a series of five studies to investigate the
role of head motion in the localization of sounds presented on the equatorial
plane. Only one condition demonstrated a clear improvement in localization
with head motion—when the sound was initially to the side and the stimulus
was present until the head was turned to face the source. One of the more
interesting results was from a condition in which the duration of the sound
was systematically varied. Localization accuracy improved slightly if we
compare conditions where head motion was allowed or restricted. The average error was 10–15% less with head motion. But when no head motion was
allowed, changing the duration from 0.03 sec to 1 sec reduced the average
error from 10° to 2°, an improvement of 500%!

The exact status of head motion and its effects on localization are far from
clear. In light of all the evidence, a defensible argument is that unless the
sound duration is sufficient to allow the listener to turn to face the source,
thereby obtaining the optimum static localization cues, moving one's head
may indeed be a poor strategy for improving the accuracy of localizing
short-duration sources. If a source does not allow such extensive search time,
then there is essentially no evidence to suggest that the information gained
from two head locations (and the information gained from two cones of
confusion) is substantially better than the information gained from a single
head position.

Blauert provides the most diplomatic, if somewhat tautological, means of
resolving the conflicting evidence. He maintains that there is a hierarchy of
cues, and head motion can be superordinate if such information is available.
"If information obtained by means of head movements is evaluated, it over-
rides information derived from monaural signal characteristics" (Blauert
1983).

SIMULATING EXTERNAL SOURCES OVER HEADPHONES

If one really understood all the cues responsible for locating external sound sources, then one should be able to simulate that same set of cues using headphones. This simple, but surprisingly daunting, challenge is the essential premise of the research program initiated by Wightman & Kistler at the University of Wisconsin. In their papers (Wightman & Kistler 1989a,b; Wightman et al 1987), they outline a program of research to compare sound localization in the free field and under headphone listening. The first step in this process is to measure directional transfer functions for multiple sound source locations around the listener. Six loudspeakers face the listener on a circular arc that is rotated about the subject in 15° steps of azimuth. Speakers are spaced from −36° to +54° elevation, in 18° steps. A broadband stimulus (200–14,000 Hz) is presented from each of 144 different sound locations, and recordings are made with miniature microphones located at fixed positions near both tympanic membranes. Dividing the recorded directional spectra by the source spectrum produces the directional transfer function of the ear. Directional spectra can then be reproduced over headphones, after compensating for the transfer functions of the headphones located on the subject's head. As they show in their first article (Wightman & Kistler 1989a), these simulated spectra, measured at the tympanic membrane, are the same as those produced by the free field source to within a few decibels in magnitude and a few degrees in phase over the frequency range measured. The measurements also tend to agree, on average, with previous measurements made by Shaw (1974) and by Mehrgardt & Mellert (1977) under similar circumstances.

Given the catalog of directional transfer functions established for each listener, Wightman & Kistler next compared the localization judgments given by the same subject, in free-field and under headphone listening. The subject indicated the apparent locus of the loudspeaker by simply calling out its location in degrees of elevation and azimuth. The general conclusion is that "The data . . . from the headphone condition are nearly identical to the data from the free-field condition" (Wightman & Kistler 1989b). Thus, to within the error of measurement associated with these experiments, the transfer functions contain all the information needed to simulate the localization of sound sources in the free field.

The enormous power of this technique is that the transfer functions can now be modified in various ways to determine the relative importance of different cue classes. For example, the level or phase cues can be set to point in one direction, while allowing the other cues to retain their natural values, thus placing different cues in opposition. How will localization change in such altered situations? So far the results are still somewhat incomplete and have only been presented at professional meetings (Wightman et al 1989). One consistent finding is that in situations in which interaural time cues point to a lateral location and interaural level cues point straight ahead, the time cues appear to dominate the localization judgment. The priority given to the time cues is mildly surprising, since duplex theory would say that time cues are effective in this experiment only from 200 Hz to about 1000 Hz (i.e. 2.3 octaves), whereas interaural level cues are available from about 2000 Hz up to 14,000 Hz (2.8 octaves).

In addition to their theoretical work, Wightman & Kistler are also involved in investigating whether this basic technique can be used to produce a practical auditory display device. The object of this system is to provide an acoustic signal under headphone listening that maintains an apparently stable location even if the head is moved. The system, being developed in collaboration with Wenzel and Foster, uses a head position indicator (ISOTRAK) to determine the roll, pitch, and yaw angles of the listener's head. The head position information is used to determine which transfer function should be used in the headphone presentation to maintain an apparently stable source location. A prototype of the system has been built and was demonstrated at the annual meeting (1988) of the National Research Council's Committee on Bioacoustics and Biomechanics (CHABA) and at the fall, 1988 meeting of the Acoustical Society of America (Wenzel et al 1988). A similar device has been shown to materially reduce errors associated with judgments of source azimuth in a simulation of an operational setting (Sorkin et al 1989).

SUMMARY

In keeping with our promise earlier in this review, we summarize here the process by which we believe spatial cues are used for localizing a sound source in a free-field listening situation. We believe it entails two parallel processes:

1. The azimuth of the source is determined using differences in interaural time or interaural intensity, whichever is present. Wightman and colleagues (1989) believe the low-frequency temporal information is dominant if both are present.
2. The elevation of the source is determined from spectral shape cues. The received sound spectrum, as modified by the pinna, is in effect compared with a stored set of directional transfer functions. These are actually the spectra of a nearly flat source heard at various elevations. The elevation that corresponds to the best-matching transfer function is selected as the locus of the sound. Pinnae are similar enough between people that certain

general rules (e.g. Blauert's boosted bands or Butler's covert peaks) can describe this process.

Head motion is probably not a critical part of the localization process, except in cases where time permits a very detailed assessment of location, in which case one tries to localize the source by turning the head toward the putative location. Sound localization is only moderately more precise when the listener points directly toward the source. The process is not analogous to localizing a visual source on the fovea of the retina. Thus, head motion provides only a moderate increase in localization accuracy.

Finally, current evidence does not support the view that auditory motion perception is anything more than detection of changes in static location over time.

ACKNOWLEDGMENTS

We wish to acknowledge the support of the National Institutes of Health, the Office of Naval Research, and the A. P. Sloan Foundation.

Literature Cited

Amenta, C. A. III, Trahiotis, C., Bernstein, L. R., Nuetzel, J. M. 1987. Some physical and psychological effects produced by selective delays of the envelope of narrow bands of noise. *Hearing Res.* 29:147–61

Angell, J. R., Fite, W. 1901. The monaural localization of sound. *Psychol. Rev.* 8:225–46

Batteau, D. W. 1967. The role of the pinna in human localization, *Proc. R. Soc. London Ser. B* 168:158–80

Batteau, D. W. 1968. Listening with the naked ear. In *The Neuropsychology of Spatially Oriented Behavior*, ed. S. J. Freedman, pp. 109–33. Homewood, IL: Dorsey Press

Belendiuk, K., Butler, R. A. 1975. Monaural location of low-pass noise bands in the horizontal plane. *J. Acoust. Soc. Am.* 58:701–5

Bernstein, L. R., Trahiotis, C. 1985. Lateralization of sinusoidally amplitude-modulated tones: effects of spectral locus and temporal variation. *J. Acoust. Soc. Am.* 78:514–23

Blauert, J. 1969/1970. Sound localization in the median plane. *Acustica* 22:205–13

Blauert, J. 1974. *Raumliches Hören*. Stuttgart: S. Hirzel

Blauert, J. 1982. Binaural localization: multiple images and application in room- and electroacoustics. In *Localization of Sound: Theory and Application*, ed. R. W. Gatehouse. Groton, CT: Amphora

Blauert, J. 1983. *Spatial Hearing*, Cambridge, MA: MIT Press

Bloom, P. J. 1977a. Creating source elevation illusions by spectral manipulation. *J. Audio Eng. Soc.* 25:560–65

Bloom, P. J. 1977b. Determination of monaural sensitivity changes due to the pinna by use of minimum-audible-field measurements in the lateral plane. *J. Acoust. Soc. Am.* 61:820–28

Boudreau, J. C., Tsuchitani, C. 1968. Binaural interaction in the cat superior olive S segment. *J. Neurophysiol.* 31:442–54

Burger, J. F. 1958. Front-back discrimination of the hearing system. *Acustica* 8:301–2

Butler, R. A. 1969. Monaural and binaural localization of noise bursts vertically in the median sagittal plane. *J. Audit. Res.* 9:230–

Butler, R. A. 1986. The bandwidth effect on monaural and binaural localization. *Hearing Res.* 21:67–73

Butler, R. A. 1987. An analysis of the monaural displacement of sound in space. *Percept. Psychophys.* 41:1–7

Butler, R. A., Flannery, R. 1980. The spatial attributes of stimulus frequency and their role in monaural localization of sound in the horizontal plane. *Percept. Psychophys.* 28:449–57

Butler, R. A., Helwig, C. C. 1983. The spatial attributes of stimulus frequency in the median sagittal plane and their role in sound localization. *Am. J. Otolaryngol.* 4:165–73

Butler, R. A., Levy, E. T., Neff, W. D. 1980. Apparent distance of sounds recorded in echoic and anechoic chambers. *J. Exp. Psychol.: Hum. Percept. Perform.* 6:745–50

Butler, R. A., Planert, N. 1976. The influence of stimulus bandwidth on localization of sound in space. *Percept. Psychol;.* 19:103–8

Clifton, R. K. 1987. Breakdown of echo suppression in the precedence effect. *J. Acoust. Soc. Am.* 82:1834–35

Coleman, P. D. 1963. An analysis of cues to auditory depth perception in free space. *Psychol. Bull.* 60:302–15

Fisher, H. G., Freedman, S. J. 1968. The role of the pinna in auditory localization. *J. Audit. Res.* 8:15–26

Gardner, M. B. 1969. Distance estimation of 0° or apparent 0°-oriented speech signals in anechoic space. *J. Acoust. Soc. Am.* 45:47–53

Gardner, M. B. 1973. Some monaural and binaural facets of median plane localization. *J. Acoust. Soc. Am.* 54:1489–95

Gardner, M. B., Gardner, R. S. 1973. Problem of localization in the medial plane: effect of pinnae cavity occlusion. *J. Acoust. Soc. Am.* 53:400–08

Gaskell, H. 1983. The precedence effect. *Hearing Res.* 11:277–303

Goldberg, J. M., Brown, P. B. 1969. Response of binaural neurons of dog superior olivary complex to dichotic tonal stimuli: some physiological mechanisms of sound localization. *J. Neurophysiol.* 32:613–36

Grantham, D. W. 1986. Detection and discrimination of simulated motion of auditory targets in the horizontal plane. *J. Acoust. Soc. Am.* 79:1939–49

Grantham, D. W. 1989. Motion aftereffects with horizontally moving sound sources in the free field. *Percept. Psychophys.* 45:129–36

Grantham, D. W., Wightman, F. L. 1979. Auditory motion aftereffects. *Percept. Psychophys.* 26:403–8

Hafter, E. R., Dye, R. H. 1983. Detection of interaural differences of time in trains of high-frequency clicks as a function of interclick interval and number. *J. Acoust. Soc. Am.* 73:644–51

Hafter, E. R., Dye, R. H., Nuetzel, J. M., Aronow, H. 1977. Difference threshold for interaural intensity. *J. Acoust. Soc. Am.* 61:829–33

Harris, J. D., Sergeant, R. L. 1971. Monaural/binaural minimum audible angles for a moving sound source. *J. Speech and Hearing Res.* 14:618–29

Hartmann, W. M. 1983. Localization of sound in rooms. *J. Acoust. Soc. Am.* 74:1380–91

Hebrank, J., Wright, D. 1974a. Are two ears necessary for localization of sound sources on the median plane? *J. Acoust. Soc. Am.* 56:935–38

Hebrank, J., Wright, D. 1974b. Spectral cues used in the localization of sound sources on the median plane. *J. Acoust. Soc. Am.* 56:1829–34

Henning, G. B. 1980. Some observations on the lateralization of complex waveforms. *J. Acoust. Soc. Am.* 68:446–54

Holt, R. E., Thurlow, W. R. 1969. Subject orientation and judgement of distance of a sound source. *J. Acoust. Soc. Am.* 46:1584–85

Hubel, D. H., Wiesel, T. N. 1962. Receptive fields, binocular interactions and functional architecture in the cat's visual cortex. *J. Physiol.* 160:106–54

Humanski, R. A., Butler, R. A. 1988. The contribution of the near and far ear toward localization of sound in the sagittal plane. *J. Acoust. Soc. Am.* 83:2300–10

Ivarsson, C., De Ribaupierre, Y., De Ribaupierre, F. 1980. Functional ear asymmetry in vertical localization. *Hearing Res.* 3:241–47

Klumpp, R. G., Eady, H. R. 1956. Some measurements of interaural time difference thresholds. *J. Acoust. Soc. Am.* 28:859–60

Knudsen, E. I. 1982. Auditory and visual maps of space in the optic tectum of the owl. *J. Neurosci.* 2:1177–94

Knudsen, E. I. 1984. Synthesis of a neural map of auditory space in the owl. In *Dynamic Aspects of Neocortical Function,* ed. G. M. Edelman, W. E. Gall, W. M. Cowan, pp. 375–96. New York: John Wiley

Kuhn, G. F. 1977. Model for interaural time differences in the azimuthal plane. *J. Acoust. Soc. Am.* 62:157–67

Kuhn, G. F. 1987. Physical acoustics and measurements pertaining to directional hearing. See Yost & Gourevitch 1987, pp. 3–25

Lappin, J. S., Bell, H. H., Harm, O. J., Kottas, B. 1975. On the relation between time and space in the visual discrimination of velocity. *J. Exp. Psychol.: Hum. Percept. Perform.* 1:383–94

Licklider, J. C. R., Webster, J. C., Hedlum, J. M. 1950. On the frequency limits of binaural beats. *J. Acoust. Soc. Am.* 22:468–73

Makous, J. C., Middlebrooks, J. C. 1990. Two-dimensional sound localization by human listeners. *J. Acoust. Soc. Am.* 87:2188–2200

Masterton, R. B., Imig, T. J. 1984. Neural mechanisms for sound localization. *Annu. Rev. Physiol.* 46:275–87

McFadden, D., Moffitt, C. M. 1977. Acoustic

integration for lateralization at high frequencies. *J. Acoust. Soc. Am.* 61:1604–8

McFadden, D., Pasanen, E. G. 1976. Lateralization at high frequencies based on interaural time differences. *J. Acoust. Soc. Am.* 59:634–39

Mehrgardt, S., Mellert, V. 1977. Transformation characteristics of the external human ear. *J. Acoust. Soc. Am.* 61:1567–76

Mershon, D. H., Bowers, J. N. 1979. Absolute and relative cues for the auditory perception of egocentric distance. *Perception* 8:311–22

Mershon, D. H, King, L. E. 1975. Intensity and reverberation as factors in the auditory perception of egocentric distance. *Percept. Psychophys.* 18:409–15

Middlebrooks, J. C. 1990. Two-dimensional localization of narrowband sound sources. *Assoc. Res. Otolaryngol.* 13:109 (Abstr.)

Middlebrooks, J. C., Green, D. M. 1990. Directional dependence of interaural envelope delays. *J. Acoust. Soc. Am.* 87:2149–62

Middlebrooks, J. C., Makous, J. C., Green, D. M. 1989. Directional sensitivity of sound-pressure levels in the human ear canal. *J. Acoust. Soc. Am.* 86:89–108

Mills, A. W. 1958. On the minimum audible angle. *J. Acoust. Soc. Am.* 30:237–46

Mills, A. W. 1960. Lateralization of high-frequency tones. *J. Acoust. Soc. Am.* 32:132–34

Moiseff, A., Konishi, M. 1981. Neuronal and behavioral sensitivity to binaural time differences in the owl. *J. Neurophysiol.* 1:40–48

Musicant, A. D., Butler, R. A. 1984a. The influence of pinnae-based spectral cues on sound localization. *J. Acoust. Soc. Am.* 75:1195–1200

Musicant, A. D., Butler, R. A. 1984b. The psychophysical basis of monaural localization. *Hearing Res.* 14:185–90

Musicant, A. D., Butler, R. A. 1985. Influence of monaural spectral cues on binaural localization. *J. Acoust. Soc. Am.* 77:202–8

Newsome, W. T., Mikami, A., Wurtz, R. H. 1986. Motion selectivity in macaque visual cortex. III. Psychophysics and physiology of apparent motion. *J. Neurophysiol.* 55:1340–51

Nuetzel, J. M., Hafter, E. R. 1981. Lateralization of complex wave-forms: spectral effects. *J. Acoust. Soc. Am.* 69:1112–18

Oldfield, S. R., Parker, S. P. A. 1984a. Acuity of sound localisation: a topography of auditory space. I. Normal hearing conditions. *Perception* 13:581–600

Oldfield, S. R., Parker, S. P. A. 1984b. Acuity of sound localisation: a topography of auditory space. II. Pinna cues absent. *Perception* 13:601–17

Oldfield, S. R., Parker, S. P. A. 1986. Acuity of sound localisation: a topography of auditory space. III. Monaural hearing conditions. *Perception* 15:67–81

Pantle, A. J., Sekuler, R. W. 1968. Velocity-sensitive elements in human vision: initial psychophysical evidence. *Vis. Res.* 8:445–50

Perrott, D. R., Ambarsoom, H., Tucker, J. 1987. Changes in head position as a measure of auditory localization performance: auditory psychomotor coordination under monaural and binaural listening conditions. *J. Acoust. Soc. Am.* 82:1637–45

Perrott, D. R., Marlborough, K. 1989. Minimum audible movement angle: marking the end points of the path traveled by a moving sound source. *J. Acoust. Soc. Am.* 85:1773–75

Perrott, D. R., Musicant, A. D. 1977. Minimum auditory movement angle: binaural localization of moving sound sources. *J. Acoust. Soc. Am.* 62:1463–66

Perrott, D. R., Tucker, J. 1988. Minimum audible movement angle as a function of signal frequency and the velocity of the source. *J. Acoust. Soc. Am.* 83:1522–27

Phillips, D. P. 1985. Progress in neurophysiology of sound localization. *Annu. Rev. Psychol.* 36:245–74

Pollack, I., Rose, M. 1967. Effect of head movement on the localization of sounds in the equatorial plane. *Percept. Psychophys.* 2:591–96

Rayleigh, Lord. 1907. On our perception of sound direction. *Philos. Mag.* 13:214–32

Roffler, S. K., Butler, R. A. 1968. Factors that influence the localization of sound in the vertical plane. *J. Acoust. Soc. Am.* 43:1255–59

Rose, J. E., Brugge, J. F., Anderson, D. J., Hind, J. E. 1967. Phase-locked response to low-frequency tones in single auditory nerve fibers of the squirrel monkey. *J. Neurophysiol.* 30:769–93

Rose, J. E., Gross, N. B., Geisler, C. D., Hind, J. E. 1966. Some neural mechanism in the inferior colliculus of the cat which may be relevant to localization of a sound source. *J. Neurophysiol.* 29:288–314

Saberi, K., Perrott, D. R. 1990. Minimum audible movement angle thresholds as a function of sound source trajectory. *J. Acoust. Soc. Am.* In press

Sandel, T. T., Teas, D. C., Feddersen, W. E., Jeffress, L. A. 1955. Localization of sound from single and paired sources. *J. Acoust. Soc. Am.* 27:842–52

Searle, C. L., Braida, L. D., Cuddy, D. R., Davis, M. F. 1975. Binaural pinna disparity: another auditory localization cue. *J. Acoust. Soc. Am.* 57:448–55

Searle, C. L., Braida, L. D., Davis, M. F., Colburn, H. S. 1976. Model for auditory localization. *J. Acoust. Soc. Am.* 60:1164–75

Sekuler, R. W., Pantle, A. J. 1967. A model for after effects of seen movement. *Vis. Res.* 88:1–11

Shaw, E. A. G. 1974. Transformation of sound pressure level from the free field to the eardrum in the horizontal plane. *J. Acoust. Soc. Am.* 56:1848–61

Simpson, W. E., Stanton, L. D. 1973. Head movement does not facilitate perception of the distance of a source of sound. *Am. J. Psychol.* 86:151–60

Sorkin, R. D., Wightman, F. L., Kistler, D. S., Elvers, G. C. 1989. An exploratory study of the use of movement-correlated cues in an auditory head-up display. *Hum. Factors* 31:161–66

Stevens, S. S., Newman, E. B. 1936. The localization of actual sources of sound. *Am. J. Psychol.* 48:297–306

Strybel, T. Z., Perrott, D. R. 1984. Discrimination of relative distance in the auditory modality: the success and failure of the loudness discrimination hypothesis. *J. Acoust. Soc. Am.* 76:318–20

Thurlow, W. R., Runge, P. S. 1967. Effect of induced head movements on localization of direction of sounds. *J. Acoust. Soc. Am.* 42:480–88

Trahiotis, C., Bernstein, L. R. 1986. Lateralization of bands of noise and sinusoidally amplitude-modulated tones: effects of spectral locus and bandwidth. *J. Acoust. Soc. Am.* 79:1950–57

Wallach, H. 1939. On sound localization. *J. Acoust. Soc. Am.* 10:270–74

Wallach, H. 1940. The role of head move-

ments and vestibular and visual cues in sound localization. *J. Exp. Psychol.* 27:339–68

Watkins, A. J. 1978. Psychoacoustical aspects of synthesized vertical locale cues. *J. Acoust. Soc. Am.* 63:1152–65

Wightman, F. L., Kistler, D. J. 1989a. Headphones simulation of free-field listening. I. Stimulus synthesis. *J. Acoust. Soc. Am.* 85:858–67

Wightman, F. L., Kistler, D. J. 1989b. Headphone simulation of free-field listening. II. Psychophysical validation. *J. Acoust. Soc. Am.* 85:868–78

Wightman, F. L., Kistler, D., Arruda, M. 1989. The hierarchy of sound localization cues revealed by experiments in a simulated free-field. *Assoc. Res. Otolaryngol.* 12:65 (Abstr.)

Wightman, F. L., Kistler, D. J., Perkins, M. E. 1987. A new approach to the study of human sound localization. See Yost & Gourevitch 1987, pp. 26–48

Woodworth, R. S. 1938. *Experimental psychology.* New York: Holt

Yost, W. A., Gourevitch, G., eds. 1987. *Directional Hearing.* New York: Springer-Verlag

Yost, W. A., Wightman, F. L., Green, D. M. 1971. Lateralization of filtered clicks. *J. Acoust. Soc. Am.* 50:1526–31

Zurek, P. M. 1980. The precedence effect and its possible role in the avoidance of interaural ambiguities. *J. Acoust. Soc. Am.* 67:952–64

Zwislocki, J., Feldman, R. S. 1956. Just noticeable differences in dichotic phase. *J. Acoust. Soc. Am.* 28:860–64

Wenzel, E., Wightman, F., Kistler, D., Foster, S. 1988. Acoustic origins of individual differences in sound localization behavior. *J. Acoust. Soc. Am.* 84 (Suppl 1): S79

Annu. Rev. Psychol. 1991. 42:161–90

HUMAN BEHAVIORAL GENETICS

Robert Plomin and Richard Rende

Center for Developmental and Health Genetics, College of Health and Human Development, The Pennsylvania State University, University Park, Pennsylvania 16802

KEY WORDS: heredity, cognitive abilities, personality, psychopathology, environment

CONTENTS

INTRODUCTION

The modern history of human behavioral genetics began over a century ago with Darwin's cousin, Francis Galton. Reading Darwin's *On the Origin of Species,* Galton was inspired to devote the rest of his life to the investigation of the inheritance of human behavior. During each decade of this century, a few family, twin, and adoption studies of behavior were reported. The first

0066-4308/91/0201-0161$02.00

161

Annual Review of Psychology chapter on behavioral genetics was published in 1960 (Fuller 1960), as was the first textbook in the field (Fuller & Thompson 1960). As environmentalism waned in the 1960s, behavioral genetics began to build momentum. However, the existence of the fledgling field was threatened by the furious response to Arthur Jensen's 1969 paper that broached the topic of genetic differences between ethnic groups. The 1970s were a time of turmoil for the field; but during the 1980s, a remarkable turnaround occurred in which antipathy toward human behavioral genetics turned into acceptance. For example, a survey of over 1000 social and behavioral scientists and educators indicated that most had accepted a significant effect of heredity on IQ scores, traditionally one of the most controversial areas in behavioral genetics (Snyderman & Rothman 1988).

Indeed, the rush of the behavioral sciences away from environmentalism may be going too far, to a view that all behavior is biologically determined. The power of behavioral genetics lies in its ability to consider nurture as well as nature—that is, environmental as well as genetic sources of individual differences in behavior. The evidence from behavioral-genetics research indicates that nongenetic factors are at least as important as genetic factors. Moreover, behavioral-genetics research has yielded breakthroughs in understanding how the environment affects psychological development. For this reason, one focal theme of this review is behavioral genetics and the environment.

The "nature" side of nature-nurture research has been just as exciting in recent years. Behavioral genetics is at the dawn of a new era in which techniques from molecular genetics can be applied to behavior with the goal of identifying sets of specific genes that account for genetic variation in behavior. The far-reaching implications of molecular genetics for behavioral genetics constitute a second theme for our review.

We have the luxury of expanding on these two themes because of the thoroughness of the 1988 *ARP* chapter by Loehlin et al, which reviewed six years (1982–1987) of research in the three major domains of human behavioral genetics research—cognitive abilities and disabilities, personality, and psychopathology. The present review begins with brief updates of these domains for research published or in press in 1988 or 1989. The review then considers two themes in greater detail: what behavioral genetics tells us about the environment, and what molecular genetics can tell us about behavior.

COGNITIVE ABILITIES AND DISABILITIES

Model-fitting analyses of the world's IQ literature continue to yield broad heritability estimates of about .50 (Chipuer et al 1990; Loehlin 1989). What's new is that evidence for nonadditive genetic variance is found when assortative mating is taken into account, and that the magnitude of the effects of shared environment differs for different types of relatives—for example, twins are twice as similar as nontwin siblings in terms of the effects of shared environment. A new unsolved puzzle is that estimates of the heritability of IQ using direct methods (i.e. from the correlations of relatives adopted apart) are greater than those obtained via indirect methods [such as the comparison between identical and fraternal twin correlations or between correlations for nonadoptive and adoptive relatives (Plomin & Loehlin 1989)].

Developmental issues continue to receive increasing attention. For example, a meta-analysis focusing on age was conducted on the basis of 103 papers from 1967 through 1985 that describe twin data for IQ and personality (McCartney et al 1990). The analysis finds a tendency for twin correlations to decrease with age and for heritability to increase—that is, the decrease is greater for fraternal twins than for identical twins. A developmental increase in heritability is strongest for IQ in childhood: An analysis of IQ data from the Colorado Adoption Project indicates that genetic influence on IQ increases steadily between infancy and middle childhood (Fulker et al 1988). Cognitive as well as personality and environmental analyses from the longitudinal Colorado Adoption Project (CAP) at 1, 2, 3, and 4 years of age are summarized in a recent book (Plomin et al 1988a).

Especially important are longitudinal analyses of genetic and environmental change and continuity. For example, a longitudinal analysis of CAP IQ data suggests that phenotypic stability of IQ from year to year during early childhood is largely genetic in origin (Fulker 1988; Phillips & Fulker 1989). However, a 10-year longitudinal analysis from the Texas Adoption Project from childhood to young adulthood suggests that genetics is also a potent source of change (Loehlin et al 1989).

A neglected life-span development issue is the effect of cohort. Cohort changes in IQ heritability were investigated in a large Norwegian twin study for twins born from 1930 through 1960 (Sundet et al 1988). No clear changes were observed despite the more egalitarian social and educational policies implemented in Norway after World War II. As in previous studies in other countries, occupation, education, and IQ were found to be heritable, and genetic covariance among these variables is substantial (Tambs et al 1989). Another multivariate analysis found that the phenotypic covariance among specific cognitive abilities is also due substantially to genetic covariance (Tambs et al 1988), a finding similar to recent results from CAP in childhood (Rice et al 1989).

As compared to psychometric analyses of cognitive abilities, a wider range of heritabilities appears to be emerging from research on information-processing variables (Ho et al 1988a; McGue & Bouchard 1989; Vernon 1989). A new twin study of cognitive abilities includes a 7-hr battery of computer-administered, touch-screen tests of information-processing variables, as well as standard psychometric tests of IQ, specific cognitive abilities, and school achievement for 300 pairs of same-sex twins and 100 nontwin siblings evenly distributed by gender and across ages from 7 to 12 and oversampled at the low and high ends of the IQ distribution (Detterman et al 1990; Thompson et al 1990). As in other studies of adults, preliminary analyses from this study also yield a wide range of heritabilities for information-processing variables. In addition, the study indicates that IQ heritability is greater for lower-ability subjects and that genetic correlations between school achievement and cognitive abilities are substantial.

In the latest in a series of reports from France, the mean IQ of adoptees reared by parents of high socioeconomic status (SES) was higher than that of adoptees reared by low-SES parents (Capron & Duyme 1989). Unlike earlier reports in this series, evidence for genetic influence was also found in that children whose biological parents were of high SES scored higher than children born to low-SES parents. Another recent report concludes that SES of adoptive parents but not biological parents is associated with school failure of adopted children (Duyme 1988). As pointed out by Loehlin et al (1988), significant increases in average IQ might occur through the radical environmental intervention of adoption, but individual differences remain large and these are substantially genetic in origin. Moreover, a review of such studies concludes that they provide modest evidence at best for environmental effects (Locurto 1990).

Finally, an important historical issue concerning behavioral-genetics research on IQ is treated by two books reopening the case of Cyril Burt (Joynson 1989; Fletcher 1990). Both books come to a very different conclusion from the widely accepted view in the Burt biography by Hearnshaw (1979) that behavioral-genetic data on IQ reported by Burt after 1955 were fraudulent.

Concerning cognitive disabilities, an important advance has been made in the context of reading disability. A new method incorporates quantitative measures of dimensions in the analysis of qualitative disorders in order to broach the fundamental issue of the relationship between the normal and abnormal: whether disorders are, etiologically, merely the extremes of continuous dimensions (DeFries & Fulker 1988). For reading disability, the answer appears to be that the magnitude of genetic effects is lower for the disorder of reading disability than for the distribution of individual differences in reading ability (DeFries et al 1987; DeFries & Gillis 1990). The potential importance of this new approach leads us to highlight it later in a section on models. Other analyses of cognitive data for reading-disabled twins have been reported (Ho & Decker 1988, 1989; Ho et al 1988b), and reviews of genetic influence on reading disability (Pennington 1990) and on learning disabilities (Pennington & Smith 1988) are available.

For mental retardation, the "fragile" site on the X chromosome continues to be the focus of major research efforts. Fragile X accounts for at least 2% of the male residents of schools for mentally retarded persons as compared to at least 1 in 2000 live male births, making it the most common cause of familial retardation and the second most common chromosomal cause of mental retardation, exceeded only by Down's syndrome (Neri et al 1988). Recent research suggests unexpected complexity in this syndrome. For example, although the fragile X syndrome is transmitted in many pedigrees as an X-linked recessive marker, cases of transmission through phenotypically normal males have been documented, and its transmission is now thought to be more complicated than that of a single-gene recessive trait. Expression of fragile X is also highly variable; for example, one fifth of males with the fragile X marker are phenotypically normal (Barnes 1989). Recent identification of a DNA marker tightly linked to the fragile X locus is likely to clarify the disorder (Suthers et al 1989).

PERSONALITY

A major event in research on the genetics of personality is the publication of a book by Eaves, Eysenck, and Martin (1989), 15 years in the making, which summarizes the authors' research on personality and attitude questionnaires and their advances in model-fitting. A behavioral-genetics book on personality was also published in the Soviet Union by I. V. Ravich-Shcherbo (1988). The book provides a general review of personality research and features the psychophysiological work of the author's group at the Institute of General and Pedagogical Psychology in Moscow, which has been the most active group of twin researchers in the Soviet Union since proscriptions on such research were lifted in the 1970s. Another important program of research in the Soviet Union involves the work at the Institute of General Genetics in Moscow of Bulayeva and her colleagues, who have compared quantitative genetic parameters across eight human populations of widely varying degrees of isolation and ethnicity (Bulayeva et al 1988, 1989).

An interesting model-fitting analysis of personality data from over 30,000 pairs of twins in four studies in four countries was published in *American Psychologist* (Loehlin 1989). Reports have begun to emerge from two ongoing studies of adults that employ the adoption/twin design. The first personality report from the Minnesota Study of Twins Reared Apart included 44 monozygotic (MZ) and 27 dizygotic (DZ) reared-apart twin pairs whose median age was 41, as well as twins reared together whose average age was 22. This report focused on a new measure, the Multidimensional Personality Questionnaire, and found results typical of personality questionnaires: substantial genetic influence and no influence of shared environment (Tellegen et al 1988). Similar results have been reported for the California Psychological

Inventory (Bouchard & McGue 1990). The study also includes a broad biobehavioral assessment; two recent reports provide evidence for genetic influence for habituation of the skin conductance response (Lykken et al 1988) and for EEG (Stassen et al 1988). The Swedish Adoption/Twin Study on Aging (SATSA), the first behavioral-genetic study of personality later in life, was derived from the Swedish Twin Registry (Pedersen et al 1990). SATSA includes personality data from 99 MZ and 229 DZ reared-apart twin pairs and 160 MZ and 212 DZ matched reared-together twin pairs, whose average age is 60 years. Compared to the literature on twins reared together, SATSA twin correlations are about .10 lower in this older sample, and heritability estimates are also about .10 lower (Bergeman et al 1990a; Pedersen et al 1988, 1989a,b; Plomin et al 1988c). A three-year follow-up has been completed, as well as an in-person session that includes cognitive tests and a health examination (Pedersen et al 1990).

A focus of continued attention is nonadditive genetic influence, suggested when the DZ correlation is less than half the MZ correlation. For example, the first report of a new sample of over 20,554 United States twin pairs suggests that nonadditivity is significant for extraversion and neuroticism, and that it is greatest for males (Eaves et al 1990). Data from twins reared apart can help in disentangling nonadditive genetic variance from violations of the equal-environments assumption for twins reared together. Such comparisons in SATSA suggest the existence of an assimilation effect for identical twins reared together (MZT) that inflates their similarity and is misread as nonadditive genetic variance in studies of twins reared together; despite this MZT assimilation effect, some nonadditive genetic variance is implicated for extraversion (Plomin et al 1990a). Nonadditive genetic variance and MZT assimilation effects are likely to be responsible for the general finding that estimates of heritability from studies of twins reared together exceed estimates from adoption studies of first-degree relatives.

Multivariate analyses continue to be applied to personality. For example, a series of multivariate analyses of items of the Eysencks' personality questionnaire suggests that the genetic structure of the items can differ from the phenotypic structure, especially for the psychoticism dimension (Heath et al 1989a,b; Heath & Martin 1990). A multivariate analysis of fears of twins and their parents finds substantial genetic covariance among several fear factors (Phillips et al 1987). A sibling study suggests that familial factors are responsible for the covariance between early sexual behavior and other deviant behaviors (Rowe et al 1989).

Development has become a focus in personality research as it has in research on cognitive abilities. Evidence continues to mount for the proposition that when developmental changes in heritability are found, heritability increases (Plomin & Nesselroade 1990). Few longitudinal data have been reported; however, research to date suggests that genetic involvement in age-to-age change in adult personality is slight, whereas personality change in childhood is governed substantially by genetic factors (Plomin & Nesselroade 1990). A 10-year follow-up of the Texas Adoption Project sample showed that genetically unrelated individuals reared together did not change in similar ways, nor were personality changes of adopted children predicted by characteristics of biological parents, adoptive parents, or life events (Loehlin et al 1987, 1990). A new area of research involves short-time change (state), which can be investigated as change across situations (Boomsma et al 1989a; Matheny 1989; Plomin & Nesselroade 1990).

Reports of several interesting new measures appeared. For example, a twin study of newborn temperament found no evidence of genetic influence (Riese 1990). A family study of shame and guilt showed substantial parent-offspring correlations (about .40) and assortative mating (about .30; Johnson et al 1989). In analyses of twins, genetic influence was detected using parent and teacher ratings of hyperactive behavior (Goodman & Stevenson 1989) and measures of job satisfaction (Avery et al 1989), suspiciousness (Kendler et al 1987a), masculinity and femininity (Mitchell et al 1989b), and religious interests (Waller et al 1990).

Evolution is seldom considered in behavioral-genetic research. John Paul Scott has written a book that summarizes his thinking about behavioral genetics, especially genetics and social behavior, from an evolutionary perspective (Scott 1989). Other attempts to bring an evolutionary perspective to personality continue, primarily in the context of sociobiology (e.g. Rushton 1989).

PSYCHOPATHOLOGY

Psychopathology continues to be an especially active area of behavioral-genetic research. The thoroughness of the 1988 *ARP* review of psychopathology allows us to focus on the issue of heterogeneity of disorders, a topic that represents a substantial portion of recent behavioral-genetic research on psychopathology. We begin, however, with a brief overview of other recent findings. Recent findings using molecular-genetic techniques are discussed in a later section.

Schizophrenia

Quantitative genetic research on schizophrenia continues to emerge at a fast pace. One particularly interesting finding was reported for the offspring of concordant and discordant twin pairs (Gottesman & Bertelsen 1989). In discordant identical twin pairs, the age-corrected risk for schizophrenia was just as great for the offspring of the normal twin as for the offspring of the schizophrenic twin. This suggests a genetic diathesis that requires an environmental stressor to trigger schizophrenia. However, as the authors indicate, because the number of affected offspring in the study was small, interpretation of these results must be cautious.

Interest continues in examining genetic models of schizophrenia. For example, a mixed-model segregation analysis of Swedish pedigrees was consistent with multifactorial transmission and no major gene effect (Vogler et al 1990). Research also continues on eye movement dysfunction as a possible marker of schizophrenia. A study of the offspring of twins discordant for schizophrenia found similar incidences of eye movement dysfunction in the offspring of both members of each pair (Holzman et al 1988). Whether a single-gene model provides the best fit to such data is currently a topic of debate (Matthysse & Holzman 1989; McGue & Gottesman 1989a). The viral theory of schizophrenia also continues to receive attention (Crow 1989).

Longitudinal studies of schizophrenia have also yielded important information during the past two years. In addition to providing continuing evidence of a genetic contribution to schizophrenia, the longitudinal Finnish Adoptive Family Study of Schizophrenia reported a possible genotype-environment interaction in which a genetic predisposition (a schizophrenic biological mother) in combination with a dysfunctional adoptive family environment increases the likelihood of severe disturbance (Tienari et al 1989). It should be noted, however, that the predisposition to schizophrenia in a child could also result in a disturbed family environment. Longitudinal results also continue to emerge from the New York high-risk study of schizophrenia. There is accumulating evidence that attentional and neuromotor processes in middle childhood may be associated with psychiatric problems in young adulthood in the group at risk for schizophrenia (Cornblatt et al 1989; Erlenmeyer-Kimling et al 1989).

Affective Disorders

Studies of major depression are reviewed in the following section because they focus on the issue of heterogeneity. A few family studies of bipolar disorder have been carried out in recent years (Coryell et al 1989; Strober et al 1988; Winokur & Kadrmas 1989; Zahn-Waxler et al 1988); no twin or adoption studies have been reported. Evidence accumulated over the past decade for significant heritability of bipolar disorder (Blehar et al 1988) has focused efforts on finding genes responsible for the disorder, even though much remains to be done in terms of quantitative genetic analyses, especially in relation to possible heterogeneity within the disorder (Edwards & Watt 1989; Gershon & Goldin 1989; Hodgkinson et al 1990; McGuffin 1988).

Developmental Disorders

The genetics of developmental disorders has begun to receive intensive investigation in recent years (Rutter et al 1990). For example, it now seems clear that autism shows genetic influence (Smalley et al 1988); a recent twin study added further support for this conclusion, as well as suggesting perinatal influence (Steffenburg et al 1989).

Heterogeneity

Perhaps the single most important issue in current behavioral-genetic research on psychopathology is heterogeneity—whether our diagnoses split nature at its joints. Heterogeneity has traditionally referred to phenotypic subtyping based on behavioral symptoms. Phenotypic subtyping also includes so-called endophenotypes (such as eye movement disorder) and responses to drugs (such as dexamethasone suppression); these biological markers have been proposed as indexes of subtypes of schizophrenia and depression, respectively. In addition, investigations of heterogeneity have often involved family studies that ask whether a particular subgrouping of cases shows greater familial incidence of a disorder than another subgrouping.

Although phenotypic or clinical heterogeneity is important, the crucial issue for behavioral-genetic research is whether etiological, especially genetic, heterogeneity occurs (McGuffin et al 1987). The issue of genetic heterogeneity in psychopathology can be seen as a dichotomous version of one of the major advances in quantitative genetics—multivariate analysis of the genetic and environmental etiologies of covariance between traits (Plomin et al 1990b). The genetic correlation is the key concept: To what extent are genetic effects on a certain symptom or syndrome correlated with genetic effects on other symptoms or syndromes? Research on this topic tends to be dominated by "splitters," who are interested in low genetic correlations within a syndrome in order to break down heterogeneity. However, there are also "lumpers," especially in the developmental disorders, who look for genetic correlations indicating that genetic influences spill over beyond the diagnosed disorder to other disorders or to a spectrum of less severe symptoms.

The use of genetic markers makes it possible to assess genetic heterogeneity directly. If a major gene were found for a disorder, we could investigate the extent to which this gene is associated with particular symptoms or with other syndromes. Genetic heterogeneity has a second meaning in linkage studies: Linkage with a particular marker is found in one pedigree but not another, which suggests that different genetic or environmental factors affect other pedigrees.

Traditional attempts to resolve heterogeneity continue to receive attention in recent reports. Schizophrenia has the longest history of such work (Goldstein & Tsuang 1988; Tsuang et al 1990); an elegant explication of the general issue of heterogeneity with regard to schizophrenia is available (McGuffin et al 1987). The classical phenotypically derived subtypes of schizophrenia do not appear to breed true (Gershon et al 1988; Kendler et al 1988; Kendler & Tsuang 1988; Squires-Wheeler et al 1988). In other words, familial cross-correlations for these subtypes are high, suggesting that these phenotypic subtypes are not distinct etiologically.

Heterogeneity has also been a major theme of research on affective disorders. Some consensus has been reached concerning the distinction between bipolar and major (unipolar) depression. Although bipolar manic-depression is reasonably well defined, phenotypic heterogeneity of major depression is a problem for behavioral-genetic research (Blehar et al 1988). As mentioned later, heterogeneity has also been addressed in recent research on alcoholism and autism.

The search for heterogeneity is complex because any characteristic of the individual or his environment could be investigated as a marker of heterogeneity. However, the search has primarily focused on a few obvious candidates. For example, for several disorders, family history vs no family history and early vs late onset have been considered. For schizophrenia, interest continues in comparing cases with and without a family history of psychosis, although no dramatic findings have as yet emerged along these lines (Dalen 1990; Lyons et al 1990a,b); problems with the family history distinction have been discussed (Farmer et al 1990). Early vs late onset has recently been examined as a possible subtyping marker for major depression. For example, prepubertal onset appears to show a higher familial loading than later onset (Orvaschel 1990; Weissman et al 1988). However, prepubertal-onset major depression does not seem to be inherited any more cleanly than other hypothesized subtypes—studies of relatives of children with prepubertal-onset depression indicate that these families show high prevalence of all forms of affective disorders as well as alcoholism (Mitchell et al 1989a; Puig-Antich et al 1989). Early onset, along with criminal behavior, also characterizes one postulated type of alcoholism in males (Gilligan et al 1987). Females do not appear to show the early-onset subtype of alcoholism.

Both early/late onset and family history have been used to distinguish types of Alzheimer's disease. Although previous research had suggested that early-onset cases are heritable but late-onset cases are not, recent work has indicated that both early-onset and late-onset cases may have a genetic basis (Breitner et al 1988; reviewed by Kay 1989). For Alzheimer's disease, attention has been focused on families that show a pattern of autosomal dominant inheritance in contrast to the much more common sporadic cases in which no evidence of family history is found. However, recent evidence suggests that familial Alzheimer's disease is heterogeneous (Bird et al 1989).

In addition to early onset and family history, several other candidates for subtyping markers have been explored. For example, children of parents with recurrent depression (i.e. three or more depressive episodes) show increased rates of psychopathology (Orvaschel et al 1988). However, the types of psychopathology observed include both affective disorders and attention deficit disorders. An interesting approach to within-group heterogeneity in offspring at risk for schizophrenia involves admixture analysis (Moldin et al 1990). Such work revealed a subgroup of the at-risk group with an increased liability to schizophrenia as assessed by a psychometric index derived from the Minnesota Multiphasic Personality Inventory.

Gender is an obvious candidate when, as in the case of alcoholism, the incidence of the disorder differs for males and females. Even when the risk is the same for males and females, as in the case of schizophrenia, different processes could be operative, suggesting etiological heterogeneity. For example, recent work suggests that male and female relatives of male probands have a lower risk for schizophrenia than male and female relatives of female probands (Goldstein & Link 1988; Goldstein et al 1989).

Environmental factors can also be used for purposes of subtyping. For example, the Camberwell Collaborative Depression Study has considered depression associated with stressful life events (Bebbington et al 1988; McGuffin et al 1988a,b). Results from this study suggest that a common familial factor predisposes individuals both to depression and to behavior associated with stressful life events; that this factor might be hereditary is a possibility suggested by a recent twin study of life events (discussed below in the section on genetic influence on environmental measures). These findings suggest that stress aggregates with depression but does not lead to a special subtype of depression.

Rather than using criteria such as early/late onset or familial/sporadic to narrow heterogeneous disorders, some research has explored possible links across disorders. There is a substantial body of literature suggesting that schizoid and schizotypal personality disorders aggregate in the relatives of schizophrenics (Kendler 1988). Evidence also exists for a common genetic component that influences both symptoms of anxiety and symptoms of depression (Kendler et al 1987b); interestingly, environmental factors were largely responsible for differentiation of the syndromes. In two other studies of heterogeneity in depression, cross-familial links were not found, suggesting that familial factors involved in the various disorders are distinct. First, although depression is associated with migraine across individuals, depression in probands is not related to migraine in first-degree relatives (Merikangas et al 1988). Second, panic disorder shows little cross-familiality with depression (Coryell et al 1988).

Research on disorders that appear in childhood have especially tended to broaden rather than narrow the range of symptomatology associated with the disorder. For example, the central question to emerge in research on Tourette syndrome is the relation between cardinal features of the disorder (multiple motor and phonic tics) on the one hand, and obsessive-compulsive behavior and attentional and learning difficulties on the other (Cohen et al 1988; Robertson 1989). Indeed, it has been suggested that the Tourette syndrome spectrum extends to conduct disorders, schizoid behaviors, sleep problems, and affective disorder (e.g. Comings & Comings 1988), although other researchers in the field strongly disagree (Pauls et al 1989; Robertson 1989).

Extending the range of symptomatic concomitants of the fragile X syndrome has also been a theme of recent research for this developmental disorder. Although the fragile X marker is clearly related to mental retardation, a host of other symptoms have been identified (Hagerman & Sobesky 1989). For males, additional forms of disturbance include hyperactivity, attentional deficits, and anxiety (Bregman et al 1988); females have been reported to show increased schizotypal and affective symptomatology (Reiss et al 1988). Additionally, links between the fragile X marker and autism have been suggested for males, including deficits in social interaction, stereotyped behavior, atypical speech and language, and abnormal nonverbal communication (Bregman et al 1988; Reiss & Freund 1990).

In a similar vein, it has been suggested that genetic influence on autism is due to genetic influence on social and cognitive abnormalities (Folstein & Rutter 1988). One study has reported a high incidence of Asperger's syndrome in families of high-functioning autistics (DeLong & Dwyer 1988).

There has been considerable excitement in the field of psychiatric genetics over the possibility that genetic heterogeneity will be pinpointed by molecular-genetic studies—indeed, that a new psychiatric nosology will be established (Mullan & Murray 1989). During the past three years, reports of linkage for bipolar depression and for schizophrenia in some pedigrees but not others suggested the possibility of genetic heterogeneity. However, as discussed below in a section on molecular genetics, the reported linkage for bipolar depression has been retracted, and the schizophrenia linkage has not been replicated. A recent issue of *Schizophrenia Bulletin* reviews etiological heterogeneity in schizophrenia (Schulz & Pato 1989). Some evidence for an X-linked form of bipolar depression exists, but it too has not replicated. The apparent heterogeneity of major depression has deterred linkage studies, although possible linkage on chromosome 9 has been reported (Hill et al 1988; Wilson et al 1989).

Genetic heterogeneity has become a focal point in research on Alzheimer's disease. Two studies have excluded the previously reported linkage to chromosome 21 in both early-onset and late-onset cases (Roses et al 1988; Schellenberg et al 1988). Results such as these are leading to a conclusion that the genetic basis of familial Alzheimer's disease may be more heterogeneous than previously thought (Tanzi et al 1989). However, one recent report has supported the hypothesis of linkage to chromosome 21 (Goate et al 1989). The authors discuss the discrepant results among linkage studies and argue that there is little evidence to support genetic heterogeneity at present. Clearly, additional linkage studies are needed to resolve this issue.

The possibility of establishing genetic heterogeneity via linkage studies is alluring and will no doubt attract increasing research effort. However, much remains to be learned as well from quantitative genetic studies, especially those that assess genetic correlations among symptoms and syndromes.

MODELS AND MODEL-FITTING

We have the pleasure of rectifying the only important omission that we found in the 1988 *Annual Review of Psychology* chapter: Not mentioned was a book that provides an excellent introduction to model-fitting and almost offhandedly provides important behavioral-genetic analyses of personality (Loehlin 1987). In addition, several recent behavioral-genetics books include introductions to model-fitting (Eaves et al 1989; Plomin et al 1988a, 1990b). Of special note is an issue of *Behavior Genetics* devoted to LISREL analyses of twins data (Boomsma et al 1989b).

Advances in model-fitting include continued work on longitudinal models (Hewitt et al 1988; Loehlin et al 1989; Phillips & Fulker 1989), combined multivariate and longitudinal models (Boomsma et al 1989b), the use of delta paths for modeling assortative mating (Phillips et al 1988) and selective placement (Phillips 1989), and the use of multivariate analyses to estimate individual genotypic and environmental factor scores (Boomsma et al 1990).

Particularly important is the development of an approach to compare heritability of dimensions and disorders, which addresses the fundamental question of the etiological association between the normal and abnormal (DeFries & Fulker 1985, 1988). The typical approach in genetic research on disorders is to assess a dichotomy (i.e. affected vs normal) and to employ concordances, or to derive liability (tetrachoric) correlations that assume a continuous distribution although the data are discontinuous. The new approach, which could be dubbed DF (DeFries/Fulker) analysis, requires that probands and their twins are administered a quantitative measure of a disorder-relevant dimension. For some disorders such as mental retardation, this is easy to do because the disorder is diagnosed in relation to a continuous measure, IQ. Often there are obvious parallels between disorders and variations within the normal range such as reading disability, delinquency, alcoholism, anxiety disorders, and unipolar depression. For other disorders, especially rare ones, dimensional parallels are less clear. For example, is a dimension of mood swings related to bipolar manic-depressive disorder?

Autism and schizophrenia have no obvious dimensional equivalent, although both cognitive and social deficits may be related to autism (Rutter et al 1990) and dimensions of schizotypal personality may be related to schizophrenia (Hewitt & Claridge 1989).

If a disorder-relevant quantitative measure sensitive to variability both in the normal range and at the extreme can be employed, DF analysis can provide an estimate of a new quantitative genetic parameter, "group" heritability, which is the extent to which the average difference between probands and the unselected population is due to genetic differences. Group heritability can be estimated, for example, as the differential regression to the population mean for the twins of MZ and DZ probands. Group heritability can be compared to the usual individual heritability estimated from the quantitative measure for unselected twins (or using regression procedures within the selected sample as explained by DeFries & Fulker 1988) to ask whether the disorder is merely the extreme of the normal distribution. This is different from asking whether heritability differs for the extreme of the dimension vs the rest of the distribution. This latter question addresses individual differences at the extreme of a dimension, whereas group heritability assesses the etiology of the average difference between probands and the population.

The DF analysis was first applied to reading disability. Probands and twins were assessed using a continuous discriminant function score of reading-related tests (DeFries et al 1987; DeFries & Gillis 1990). Group heritability was found to be only about half the magnitude of individual heritability, suggesting that reading disability is etiologically different from the continuous dimension of reading ability. A multivariate extension of the DF analysis suggested that phonological coding ability (e.g. speed and accuracy in pronouncing nonwords such as "ter" and "tegwop") may be a key element in the genetics of reading disability (Olson et al 1989). DF analysis has been applied to SATSA personality data; results suggest that the extremes of most dimensions such as neuroticism and somatic complaints are etiologically similar to the rest of the distribution, with the possible exception of depression (Plomin 1990a).

NEW AREAS

The field of health psychology has burgeoned as it becomes increasingly clear that behavior is a major factor in promoting health and in preventing and treating disease (Rodin & Salovey 1989; Taylor 1990). Possible genetic contributions to health psychology variables have hardly been considered. For example, there is next to no research on the genetic and environmental provenances of such favorite health psychology variables as stress, mechanisms for coping, life styles, attributions of self-efficacy and sense of control in relation to health and illness, and nonadherence to regimens of medical treatment, exercise, and nutrition. In addition to univariate behavioral genetic analyses of the variance of such variables, multivariate analyses are needed if we are to understand the genetic and environmental origins of covariance between such variables and health/illness. An example of the kind of work that needs to be done is a twin study that found genetic influence on sports participation and on heart rate, but not on the association between them (Boomsma et al 1989c). Another example is a twin study of heart-rate change during behavioral challenge (Turner 1989).

Behavioral-genetic research relevant to health psychology is currently limited largely to personality and to alcohol use. For example, genetic research on Type A measures continues to show results similar to those for other personality questionnaires (Carmelli et al 1990; Pedersen et al 1989b), including other health-related dimensions such as emotionality, activity, and sensation-seeking (Loehlin et al 1988; Plomin et al 1990c). Rife with implications for health psychology is the emerging finding that environmental measures such as life events and social support show genetic influence (discussed below in the section "Genetic influence on environmental measures").

Although the genetics of alcohol use and abuse has been investigated more than other health-related behaviors (Devor & Cloninger 1989), much remains to be learned. This is an area in which acceptance of genetic influence may have outstripped the data (Searles 1988). Two recent Australian alcohol studies with twins are particularly noteworthy in terms of their implications for health psychology. A questionnaire study found that teenage alcohol consumption but not age of onset of drinking is influenced genetically (Heath & Martin 1988) and that genetic effects on alcohol use are greater for unmarried women than for married women (Heath et al 1989c). Another study in which alcohol was administered to twins showed genetic effects on willingness to drive when drunk (Martin & Boomsma 1989) and on self-reported drunkenness (Neale & Martin 1989). A research design valuable in controlling for genetic factors is the cotwin control study. A recent example is a 12-year prospective study of smoking-discordant identical twins in Finland that showed associations, within pairs of discordant identical twins, between smoking and arteriosclerosis (Haapanen et al 1989) and lung cancer (Kaprio & Koskenvuo 1990.) This finding rules out genetic explanations of these associations for these cases.

Mention should be made here of areas in psychology where there are as yet few signs of genetic research. These areas may prove to be fertile ground for future research. The key feature of such areas is a dearth of research on individual differences. This marks some of the oldest domains of psychology (e.g. perception, learning, and language) as well as some of the newest (e.g. neuroscience and social cognition). In addition to such behavioral domains that are relevant throughout the life span, behaviors important in the context of life events and their transitions represent outstanding opportunities for future research. These possibilities include neonatal behavior; children's relationships with siblings and parents; the stresses of beginning school, of peer relationships, and of adjusting to the educational system; the physical and social transitions of adolescence; entrance into the adult world of work, marriage, and childrearing; and adjustment to the changes of later life.

MOLECULAR GENETICS

Imagine being able to identify behavior-relevant DNA variation directly in individuals rather than resorting to indirect estimates of a genetic component of variance derived from twin and adoption studies. Advances in molecular biology are on the way to making this fantasy a reality. Indeed, we predict that in less than ten years—perhaps by the time of the *Annual Review of Psychology* chapter on human behavioral genetics scheduled for the year 2000—molecular-genetic techniques will have revolutionized human behavioral genetics. It was only ten years ago that the now-standard techniques of the "new genetics" of recombinant DNA were first employed to identify genes responsible for disorders. These techniques include use of restriction enzymes to create recombinant DNA; cloning; use of genetic probes [restriction fragment-length polymorphisms (RFLPs) and variable number tandem repeats (VNTRs)]; and Southern blotting, which hybridizes a probe to DNA. These techniques have been described in relation to behavioral genetics (Plomin et al 1990b).

The pace of developments in this field is breathtaking. The Human Genome Project, whose goal is to map and eventually sequence the entire genome of 3 billion nucleotide bases (National Research Council 1988), will lead to the identification of many more genetic markers, and it will foster technological spin-offs that will facilitate the application of molecular-genetic techniques to the investigation of complex characteristics. For example, new modifications of a technique called subtractive hybridization may eventually make it possible to identify in one analysis all the DNA that differs between groups (e.g. schizophrenic individuals vs unaffected individuals) or even between individuals (Travis & Sutcliffe 1988).

The fast pace of advances makes the forecast very bright for the use of molecular-genetic techniques to investigate behavior and behavioral disorders. However, the weather now is stormy. Two of the most exciting announcements during 1987 and 1988 were the report of linkage of bipolar manic-depression to genetic markers on chromosome 11 in an Amish pedigree (Egeland et al 1987) and the report of linkage of schizophrenia to chromosome 5 in two Icelandic pedigrees (Sherrington et al 1988). The most disappointing developments during 1989 were the retraction of the first finding (Kelsoe et al 1989) and repeated failures to replicate the second (e.g. Kennedy et al 1988; St. Clair et al 1989; Detera-Wadleigh et al 1989). Follow-up work on the original Amish pedigree yielded two new diagnoses of manic-depression, and these cases reduced the evidence for linkage to nonsignificance; moreover, a lateral extension of the original pedigree also failed to replicate the linkage. Some evidence suggests that bipolar manic-depression might show linkage to the X chromosome in some families, despite the frequent occurrence of father-son transmission that rules out a major X-linked gene for manic-depression in the population (Baron et al 1987). Moreover, linkage to the X chromosome has been rejected in an analysis of nine pedigrees (Berrettini et al 1989), and one of the markers claimed to be linked to manic-depression has been found to be located quite far away from the color-blindness loci also claimed to be linked. In addition, an early report of linkage for reading disability on chromosome 15 is also in doubt—only 1 in 21 families now shows a lod score that even approaches significance in this project (Smith et al 1990), and a failure to replicate chromosome 15 linkage for reading disability has been reported (Bisgaard et al 1987).

Type I error may be the explanation for the reported linkages. For example, ascertainment biases could produce false positive results when pedigrees are selected when early linkage results begin to look positive. False positives could also result from multiple testing—that is, testing multiple models of transmission, multiple ways of categorizing the disorder, and multiple markers (Edwards & Watt 1989). For such reasons, psychiatric geneticists have recommended that linkage be considered as established only when it is replicated in more than one pedigree and in more than one laboratory (Merikangas et al 1989). Using these criteria, no linkages have as yet been demonstrated for psychiatric disorders, with the possible exception of Alzheimer's disease.

The mania and subsequent depression surrounding these reports of linkage may serve the useful function of eliciting discussion about the uniqueness of behavior. Behavior is surely the most complex phenotype that can be studied by geneticists because it reflects the functioning of the whole organism and because it is dynamic, changing in response to the environment. Although genes that affect behavioral phenotypes are transmitted hereditarily according to Mendel's laws in the same way as genes that affect any other phenotype, behavior is special in three ways. Unlike the characteristics that Mendel studied in the edible pea, such as smooth vs wrinkled seeds, most behaviors and behavioral disorders are not distributed in simple either/or dichotomies. Second, as discussed below, behavioral traits are substantially influenced by nongenetic factors. Third, behavioral dimension and disorders are likely to be influenced by many genes, each causing small effects. These issues and their implications for linkage analysis have recently been discussed (McGue & Gottesman 1989b; Plomin 1990b).

The problem with current linkage strategies is that they can detect a gene only if the gene is largely responsible for the behavioral disorder. (Disorders rather than dimensions need to be considered here because human linkage analysis has been limited largely to qualitative, either-or traits—that is, the presence or absence of a disorder). Evidence of major-gene effects from segregation analysis of pedigrees can be misleading, as indicated amusingly in an analysis (McGuffin & Hickle 1990) that appears to provide evidence for a major gene causing medical school attendance. It is now generally accepted that no major gene will be found in the population for behavioral disorders. This represents a conceptual shift, because the classical use of linkage focuses on disorders in which a single gene is necessary and sufficient to produce the disorder in all individuals in the population. The exemplar is Huntington's disease, the first disorder mapped to a chromosome using the new RFLP markers (Gusella et al 1983). Huntington's disease has long been linked to a single dominant gene that is lethal later in life regardless of a person's other genes or environment. For just as long a time, we have known that behavioral disorders do not show such clear-cut patterns of single-gene inheritance.

Although it is now recognized that no major gene for behavior or behavioral disorders is likely to be found in the population, current linkage research assumes that a major gene can be found in certain families. For this reason, linkage studies focus on large pedigrees with many affected individuals in the hope of finding a major gene responsible for the disorder in a particular pedigree. In this view, multiple-gene influence is seen at the level of the population because of the interaction among different major genes in different families.

An alternative hypothesis is that major genes influence behavior in neither the population nor the family. Rather, for each individual, many genes may make small contributions towards variability and vulnerability. In this view, the genetic quest is to find, not *the* gene for schizophrenia, but the many genes—and perhaps different sets of genes in different individuals—that increase susceptibility to schizophrenia in a probabilistic rather than pre-determined manner.

Seen from this perspective, reliance on current linkage technology that can only detect major-gene effects seems analogous to losing one's wallet in a dark alley but looking for it in the street because the light is better there (cf Gurling et al 1989). That is, applications of molecular-biology techniques to the study of behavior are unlikely to succeed if they must assume that a major gene is largely responsible for genetic variation either in the population or in a family. One might counter that we have not yet tried hard enough to find major-gene linkages. No one will argue against trying harder; however, during the coming decades closely-spaced genetic markers for nearly all human chromosomes will make it possible to exclude linkage. Although only a small portion of the genome has been excluded for psychopathology, such exclusions may eventually provide the best evidence that human behavioral disorders are not caused by major genes. In the more immediate future a backlash is likely to result from articles that have argued, on the basis of linkage results, for revamping psychiatry as a form of genetic counseling (e.g. Pardes et al 1989).

The point is not that behavior is too complex for molecular biology, but rather that we need to bring the light of molecular biology into the dark alley. New strategies are needed to identify genes that affect behavior, even when they account for only a small amount of variance. That is, we need to use molecular-genetic techniques in a quantitative genetic framework. Association studies can be useful in this context because sample sizes can be increased to provide sufficient power to detect associations that account for small amounts of variance among individuals in a population (Plomin 1990b). Given the pace of developments in molecular biology, the needed strategies are likely forthcoming.

ENVIRONMENT

The fundamental strength of behavioral genetics has been its use of methods that assess both genetic and environmental provenances rather than assuming that either nature or nurture is omnipotent. As noted earlier, antipathy towards the notion of genetic influence on behavior has ebbed noticeably during the past decade, and acceptance of genetic influence is coming in on a high tide—in some areas it looks like a tsunami. With the change of tide, it is important for the second message of behavioral genetics to be heard: The same data that point to significant genetic influence provide the best available evidence for the importance of nongenetic factors. Rarely do behavioral-genetic data yield heritability estimates that exceed 50%, which means that behavioral variability is due at least as much to environment as to heredity. In behavioral genetics, the word *environment* includes any nonhereditary influence, such as biological factors (e.g. physical trauma, nutritional factors, and even DNA itself) in addition to the psychosocial environmental factors that are the focus of most psychological research.

Behavioral genetics can do much more than merely point to the "other" component of variance and note its importance. Indeed, behavioral-genetic research has revealed as much about environmental processes as it has about heredity. As examples, we discuss two developments with far-reaching implications for psychology: nonshared environment and genetic influence on environmental measures.

Nonshared Environment

One of the most important discoveries in human behavioral genetics involves nurture rather than nature: Environmental factors important to development are experienced differently by children in the same family. In the past, the reasonable assumption was made that resemblance within families was caused by environmental factors shared by children growing up together in a family. However, behavioral-genetic research indicates that siblings resemble each other for genetic reasons. What runs in families is DNA, not experiences shared in the home. However, environmental factors are very important even though experiences shared by siblings are not. The significant environmental variation lies in experiences *not* shared by siblings. This implication is consistently supported by data from various designs, such as the direct test of shared environment provided by the resemblance of adoptive siblings, pairs of genetically unrelated children adopted early in life into the same family. This category of environmental influence has been variously called nonshared, E_1, within-family, individual, unique, or specific. A main article in *Behavioral and Brain Sciences* discusses the evidence for and the importance of non-shared environment; the article is followed by 32 commentaries and a response to the commentaries (Plomin & Daniels 1987).

The conclusion that environmental factors operate in a nonshared manner creates new research opportunities for studying environmental influences. It suggests that instead of thinking about the environment on a family-by-family basis, we need to think on an individual-by-individual basis. The critical question is, Why are children in the same family so different? The key to solving this puzzle is to study more than one child per family. The message is not that family experiences are unimportant. The argument is that environmental influences in individual development are specific to each child, rather than general to an entire family.

Recent developments in research on nonshared environment have been described in the first book on the topic (Dunn & Plomin 1990). Research can be categorized into analyses of the nonshared component of variance, attempts to identify nonshared experiences within the family, and exploration of associations between nonshared experiences and behavior. Most is known about the first issue, and important new findings have emerged here concerning IQ. For personality and psychopathology, there is continuing consensus that shared rearing environment is of negligible importance and, thus, that environmental influence is nearly exclusively of the nonshared variety. Aggressive behavior and delinquency show some shared environment, but other areas of personality and psychopathology do not (Plomin et al 1990e). Although shared rearing environment is generally unimportant, work with adults suggests that correlated environments in adulthood might increase personality resemblance of twins (Rose & Kaprio 1988; Rose et al 1988).

A recent surprise is that nonshared environment is of prime importance for IQ as well as for personality and psychopathology. IQ has been thought to be an exception to the rule that environmental influence is nonshared. For example, the average correlation for adoptive siblings is generally reported to be about .30, and data on twins are also consistent with an appreciable shared environment for IQ. However, studies of twins greatly overestimate shared environmental influence because the IQs of fraternal twins are nearly twice as similar as those of nontwin siblings (Plomin 1988). Concerning the substantial adoptive sibling correlation for IQ, earlier studies involved children. However, four recent studies of older adoptive siblings yield IQ correlations of zero on average (Plomin 1988). The most compelling evidence comes from a 10-year longitudinal follow-up of the Texas Adoption Project, which has found that shared environment declines to negligible influence from childhood to early adulthood (Loehlin et al 1989). A longitudinal model-fitting analysis yielded a shared environment estimate of .25 when the children were 8 years old on average, and an estimate of −.11 10 years later. A crucial piece of data is that the IQ correlation for 181 pairs of genetically unrelated siblings was .16 at the first test and −.01 10 years later. This finding suggests that although shared environmental influences are important in childhood, their influence wanes to negligible levels during adolescence. In the long run, environmental effects on IQ are nonshared.

The second research direction attempts to identify specific experiences of siblings that differ. Although research on this topic has just begun, it seems clear that siblings growing up in the same family experience quite different family environments owing to their parents' treatment, their interactions with their siblings, experiences beyond the family, and chance (reviewed by Dunn & Plomin 1990). Concerning the third direction for research, the few initial attempts to relate nonshared environmental factors to sibling differences in outcome are promising (e.g. Baker & Daniels 1990; Daniels 1986; Daniels et al 1985; Dunn et al 1990). As such associations are found, it becomes necessary to disentangle possible genetic sources of these associations. Because siblings differ genetically, associations between differences in their experience and behavioral outcomes may be due to their genetic differences rather than to their nonshared experiences. Identical twins provide a stringent test of differential experiences of siblings that cannot be due to genetic differences within sibling pairs (Baker & Daniels 1990). A major collaborative study to address these issues is under way that involves a national sample of adolescent twins, full siblings, half-siblings, and unrelated siblings visited in their homes for two 3-hr home visits with a focus on differential experiences of children growing up in the same family (Reiss et al, in press).

It is ironic that after decades of environmentalism, the limiting factor in this effort is the need for better measures of the environment. Especially scarce are environmental measures that are specific to a child rather than general to a family, measures of experience (the subjective, experienced environment) in contrast to measures of the objective environment, and measures that move beyond the passive model of the child as merely a receptacle for environmental influence to measures that can capture the child's active selection, modification, and creation of environments.

Genetic Influence on Environmental Measures

Measures once assumed to assess the environment have been shown to be influenced by heredity (Plomin & Bergeman 1990). The first studies on this topic were conducted by Rowe (1981, 1983), who showed that adolescent identical twins are more similar in their perceptions of parental affection than are fraternal twins. It is interesting that perceptions of parental control showed little genetic influence in both studies. These findings were replicated in SATSA analyses of adult twins rating their childhood rearing environment retrospectively 50 years later (Plomin et al 1988b), and genetic influence was also found for adults' ratings of the family in which they are now the parent (Plomin et al 1989). Genetic influence has also been suggested in CAP comparisons between nonadoptive and adoptive siblings for videotaped observations of maternal behavior and for a widely used observation/ interview measure of the home environment (Plomin et al 1988a). CAP analyses suggest that fully half of the associations found between environmental measures and developmental outcomes in infancy and early childhood are mediated genetically.

SATSA analyses have demonstrated that two other major categories of environmental measures—perceptions of life events and social support—also show genetic influence. Life events, especially controllable life events (such as conflict with a spouse), show as much genetic influence as do measures of personality (Plomin et al 1990c). Measures of social support, especially perceptions of the adequacy of support, also indicate genetic influence (Bergeman et al 1990b); the association between social support and sense of well-being appears to be mediated genetically as well (Bergeman et al 1990c).

Which environmental measures are most and least influenced genetically? So far, self-reports and ratings of parental control show little genetic influence compared to other dimensions of parental behavior; controllable life events show more genetic influence than uncontrollable events (such as serious illness of a spouse); and perceptions of the adequacy of social support show more genetic influence than the quantity of social relationships.

What are the processes by which heredity affects measures of environment? In research on measures of the family environment, the obvious candidates— for example, parental IQ and personality in the case of genetic influence on the home environment—do not seem to be the answer (Bergeman & Plomin 1988). Continued research on the genetics of environmental measures is likely to enrich our understanding of the interface between nature and nurture.

CONCLUSIONS

The number of researchers in the field of human behavioral genetics is small compared to that of other fields in psychology, but few fields have yielded so many novel findings during the past two years. Looking back beyond these two years, we are struck by the progress that has been made towards understanding the genetic and environmental provenances of behavior since Galton launched the field a century ago. This sense of contributing to the building of a solid edifice, still far from completion, whose construction stretches back over many generations of researchers, makes it rewarding to be in the field of behavioral genetics. The theory of quantitative genetics, progressive in the philosophy-of-science sense, provides behavioral genetics with strong empirical grounding.

The excitement of the field is fueled by several energy sources. One source is the thrill of looking at old issues from this new perspective and seeing things that have not been seen before. The best recent examples are the discoveries about the environment described above—the importance of nonshared environment and of genetic influence on environmental measures. Another stimulant comes from the rapid development of powerful research tools that make it possible to broach ever more interesting questions. Especially important developments during the past decade include model-fitting, multivariate analysis, and longitudinal analysis. The DF analysis described in this review is yet another example. An emerging development that will affect behavioral genetics more than all of these is the application of molecular-genetic techniques to the analysis of complex quantitative genetic phenotypes, of which behavior is the most complex.

Literature Cited

Avery, R. D., Bouchard, T. J. Jr., Segal, N. L., Abraham, L. M. 1989. Job satisfaction: environmental and genetic components. *J. Appl. Psychol.* 74:187–92

Baker, L., Daniels, D. 1990. Nonshared environmental influences and personality differences in adult twins. *J. Pers. Soc. Psychol.* 58:103–10

Barnes, D. M. 1989. "Fragile X" syndrome and its puzzling genetics. *Science* 243:171–72

Baron, M., Risch, N., Hamburger, R., Mandel, B., Kushner, S. 1987. Genetic linkage between X-chromosome markers and bipolar affective illness. *Nature* 326:289–92

Bebbington, P. E., Brugha, T., MacCarthy, B., Potter, J., Sturt, E., et al. 1988. The Camberwell Collaborative Depression Study. I. Depressed probands: adversity and the form of depression. *Br. J. Psychiatry.* 152:754–65

Bergeman, C. S., Chipuer, H. M., Plomin, R., Pedersen, N. L., McClearn, G. E., et al. 1990a. Genetic and environmental influences on openness to experience, agreeableness, and conscientiousness: an adoption/twin study. *J. Pers.* In press

Bergeman, C. S., Plomin, R. 1988. Parental mediators of the genetic relationship between home environment and infant mental development. *Br. J. Dev. Psychol.* 6:11–19

Bergeman, C. S., Plomin, R., Pedersen, N. L., McClearn, G. E., Nesselroade, J. R. 1990b. Genetic and environmental influences on social support: the Swedish Adoption/Twin Study of Aging (SATSA). *J. Gerontol.* 45:101–6

Bergeman, C. S., Plomin, R., Pedersen, N. L., McClearn, G. E., Nesselroade, J. R. 1990c. Genetic and environmental etiologies of the relationship between social support and emotional well-being. *Psychol. Aging*. In press

Berrettini, W. H., Goldin, L. R., Gelernter, J., Gejman, P. V., Gershon, E. S., Detera-Wadleigh, S. 1989. X-chromosome markers and manic-depressive illness: rejection of linkage to Xq28 in nine bipolar pedigrees. Presented at *1st World Congr. Psychiatr. Genet.*, Cambridge, England

Bisgaard, M. L., Eiberg, H., Moller, N., Niebuhr, E., Mohr, J. 1987. Dyslexia and the chromosome 15 heteromorphism: negative lod score in Danish material. *Clin. Genet.* 32:118–19

Bird, T. D., Sumi, S. M., Nemens, E. J., Nochlin, D., Schellenberg, G., Lampe, T. H., et al. 1989. Phenotypic heterogeneity in familial Alzheimer's disease: a study of 24 kindreds. *Ann. Neurol.* 25:12–25

Blehar, M. C., Weissman, M. M., Gershon, E. S., Hirschfeld, R. M. A. 1988. Family and genetic studies of affective disorders. *Arch. Gen. Psychiatry.* 45:289–92

Boomsma, D. I., Martin, N. G., Molenaar, P. C. M. 1989a. Factor and simplex models for repeated measures: application to two psychomotor measures of alcohol sensitivity in twins. *Behav. Genet.* 19:79–96

Boomsma, D. I., Martin, N. G., Neale, M. C. 1989b. Structural modeling in the analysis of twin data. *Behav. Genet.* 19:5–8

Boomsma, D. I., Molenaar, P. C. M., Oriebeke, J. F. 1990. Estimation of individual genetic and environmental factor scores. *Genet. Epidemiol.* 7:83–92

Boomsma, D. I., van den Bree, M. B. M., Orlebeke, J. F., Molenaar, P. C. M. 1989c. Resemblances of parents and twins in sports participation and heart rate. *Behav. Genet.* 19:123–42

Bouchard, T. J. Jr., McGue, M. 1990. Genetic and rearing environmental influences on adult personality: an analysis of adopted twins reared apart. *J. Pers.* 58:263–92

Bregman, J. D., Leckman, J. F., Ort, S. I. 1988. Fragile X syndrome: genetic predisposition to psychopathology. *J. Autism Dev. Disord.* 18:343–54

Breitner, J. C. S., Silverman, J. M., Mohs, R. C., Davis, K. L. 1988. Familial aggregation in Alzheimer's disease: comparison of risk among relatives of early- and late-onset cases, and among male and female relatives in successive generations. *Neurology* 38:207–12

Bulayeva, K. B., Pavlova, T. A., Isaychev, S. A., Kurbanov, S. K., Shamov, R. I., Skovoroda-Luzin, S. S. 1988. Integral evaluation of phenotypic and genotypic variability of morphological and psychophysiological human traits. *Genetics (USSR)*. 24:2208–13

Bulayeva, K. B., Isaychev, S. A., Pavlova, T. A., Kurbanov, S. K., Shamov, R. I., Sulta-

nova, Z. Kh., Skovoroda-Luzin, S. S. 1989. Phenotypic and genetic differentiation of human populations for morphological and psychophysiological traits. *Genetics (USSR)*. 25:140–49

Capron, C., Duyme, M. 1989. Assessment of effects of socio-economic status on IQ in a full cross-fostering study. *Nature* 340:552–54

Carmelli, D., Rosenman, R. H., Swan, G. E. 1990. The Cook and Medley HO scale: a heritability analysis in adult male twins. *Psychosom. Med.* In press

Chipuer, H. M., Rovine, M., Plomin, R. 1990. LISREL modelling: genetic and environmental influences on IQ revisited. *Intelligence* 14:11–29

Cohen, D. J., Brunn, R. D., Leckman, J. F., eds. 1988. *Tourette's Syndrome and Tic Disorders: Clinical Understanding and Treatment*. New York: John Wiley & Sons

Comings, D. E., Comings, B. G. 1988. A controlled study of Tourette syndrome—revisited: a reply to the letter of Pauls et al. (letter). *Am. J. Hum. Genet.* 43:210–17

Cornblatt, B., Winters, L., Erlenmeyer-Kimling, L. 1989. Attentional markers of schizophrenia: evidence from the New York high-risk study. In *Schizophrenia: Scientific Progress*, ed. S. C. Schulz, C. A. Tamminga, pp. 83–92. New York: Oxford Univ. Press

Coryell, W., Endicott, J., Andreasen, N. C., Keller, M. B., Clayton, P. J., Hirschfeld, R. M. A., et al. 1988. Depression and panic attacks: the significance of overlap as reflected in follow-up and family study data. *Am. J. Psychiatry.* 145:293–300

Coryell, W., Endicott, J., Keller, M., Andreasen, N., Grove, W., Hirschfeld, R. M. A., Scheftner, W. 1989. Bipolar affective disorder and high achievement: a familial association. *Am. J. Psychiatry.* 146:983–88

Crow, T. J. 1989. Viruses and schizophrenia: the virogene hypothesis. *Biologist* 36:10–14

Dalen, P. 1990. Is the familial/sporadic subdivision a method of genetics? *Schizophren. Bull.* In press

Daniels, D. 1986. Differential experiences of siblings in the same family as predictors of adolescent sibling personality differences. *J. Pers. Soc. Psychol.* 51:339–46

Daniels, D., Dunn, J., Furstenberg, F. F. Jr., Plomin, R. 1985. Environmental differences within the family and adjustment differences within pairs of adolescent siblings. *Child Dev.* 56:764–74

DeFries, J. C., Fulker, D. W. 1985. Multiple regression analysis of twin data. *Behav. Genet.* 15:467–73

DeFries, J. C., Fulker, D. W. 1988. Multiple regression analysis of twin data: etiology of deviant scores versus individual differences. *Acta Genet. Med. Gemellol.* 37:205–16

DeFries, J. C., Fulker, D. W., LaBuda, M. C. 1987. Evidence for a genetic aetiology in reading disability of twins. *Nature* 329:537–39

DeFries, J. C., Gillis, J. J. 1990. Etiology of reading deficits in learning disabilities: quantitative genetic analysis. In *Advances in the Neuropsychology of Learning Disabilities: Issues, Methods and Practice*, ed. J. E. Obrzut, G. W. Hynd. Orlando, FL: Academic. In Press

Delong, G. R., Dwyer, J. T. 1988. Correlation of family history with specific autistic subgroups: Asperger's syndrome and bipolar affective disease. *J. Autism Dev. Disord.* 18:93–600

Detera-Wadleigh, S. D., Goldin, L. R., Sherrington, R., Encio, I., de Miguel, C., Berrettini, W., et al. 1989. Exclusion of linkage to 5q11-13 in families with schizophrenia and other psychiatric disorders. *Science* 340:391–93

Detterman, D. K., Thompson, L. A., Plomin, R. 1990. Differences in heritability across groups differing in ability. *Behav. Genet.* In press

Devor, E. J., Cloninger, C. R. 1989. Genetics of alcoholism. *Annu. Rev. Genet.* 23:19–36

Dunn, J., Plomin, R. 1990. *Separate Lives: Why Siblings Are So Different.* New York: Basic Books

Dunn, J., Stocker, C., Plomin, R. 1990. Nonshared experiences within the family: correlates of behavioral problems in middle childhood. *Dev. Psychopathol.* In press

Duyme, M. 1988. School success and social class: an adoption study. *Dev. Psychol.* 24:203–9

Eaves, L. J., Heath, A. C., Neale, M. C., Hewitt, J. K., Martin, N. G. 1990. *Psychol. Sci.* In press

Eaves, L. J., Eysenck, H. J., Martin, N. 1989. *Genes, Culture and Personality.* New York: Academic

Edwards, J. H., Watt, D. C. 1989. Caution in locating the gene(s) for affective disorder. *Psychol. Med.* 19:273–75

Egeland, J. A., Gerhard, D. S., Pauls, D. L., Sussex, J. N., Kidd, K. K. 1987. Bipolar affective disorders linked to DNA markers on chromosome 11. *Nature* 325:783–87

Erlenmeyer-Kimling, L., Golden, R., Cornblatt, B. A. 1989. A taxometric analysis of cognitive and neuromotor variables in children at risk for schizophrenia. *J. Abnorm. Psychol.* 98:203–8

Farmer, A., McGuffin, P., Gottesman, I. I. 1990. The problems and pitfalls of the family history positive and negative dichotomy in classifying schizophrenia. *Schizophren. Bull.* In press

Fletcher, R. 1990. *The Cyril Burt Scandal: Case for the Defence.* New York: Macmillan

Folstein, S. E., Rutter, M. L. 1988. Autism: familial aggregation and genetic implications. *J. Autism Dev. Disord.* 18:3-30

Fulker, D. W. 1988. Genetic and cultural transmission in human behavior. In *Proceedings of the Second International Conference on Quantitative Genetics*, ed. B. S. Weir, E. J., Eisen, M. M. Goodman, G. Namkoong, pp. 318–40. Sunderland, MA: Sinauer

Fulker, D. W., DeFries, J. C., Plomin, R. 1988. Genetic influence on general mental ability increases between infancy and middle childhood. *Nature* 336:767–69

Fuller, J. L. 1960. Behavior genetics. *Annu. Rev. Psychol.* 11:41–70

Fuller, J. L., Thompson, W. R. 1960. *Behavior Genetics.* New York: Wiley

Gershon, E. S., DeLisi, L. E., Hamovit, J., Nurnberger, J. I., Maxwell, M. E., Schreiber, J., et al. 1988. A controlled family study of chronic psychoses. *Arch. Gen. Psychiatry.* 45:328–36

Gershon, E. S., Goldin, L. R. 1989. Linkage data on affective disorders in an epidemiologic context. *Genet. Epidemiol.* 6:201–9

Gilligan, S. B., Reich, T., Cloninger, C. R. 1987. Etiologic heterogeneity in alcoholism. *Genet. Epidemiol.* 4:395–414

Goate, A. M., Haynes, A. R., Owen, J. J., Farrall, M., James, L. A., et al. 1989. Predisposing locus for Alzheimer's disease on chromosome 21. *Lancet* 1:352–55

Goldstein, J. M., Link, B. G. 1988. Gender and the expression of schizophrenia. *J. Psychiatr. Res.* 22:141–55

Goldstein, J. M., Tsuang, M. T. 1988. The process of subtyping schizophrenia: strategies in the search for homogeneity. In *Handbook of Schizophrenia, Volume 3: Nosology, Epidemiology and Genetics*, ed. M. T. Tsuang, J. C. Simpson, pp. 63–83. New York: Elsevier Science

Goldstein, J. M., Tsuang, M. T., Faraone, S. V. 1989. Gender and schizophrenia: implications for understanding the heterogeneity of the illness. *Psychiatry. Res.* 28:243–53

Goodman, R., Stevenson, J. 1989. A twin study of hyperactivity. II. The aetiological role of genes, family relationships and perinatal adversity. *J. Child Psychol. Psychiatry.* 30:691–709

Gottesman, I. I., Bertelsen, A. 1989. Confirming unexpressed genotypes for schizophrenia. *Arch. Gen. Psychiatry.* 46:867–72

Gurling, H. M. D., Sherrington, R. P., Brynjolfsson, J., Read, T., Curtis, D., Mankoo, B. J., et al. 1989. Recent and future molecular genetic research into schizophrenia. *Schizophren. Bull.* 15:373–82

Gusella, J. F., Wexler, N. S., Conneally, P. M., Naylor, S. L., Anderson, M. A., Tanzi, R. E., et al. 1983. A polymorphic DNA marker genetically linked to Huntington's disease. *Nature* 306:234–38

Haapanen, A., Koskenvuo, M., Kaprio, J., Kesäniemi, Y. A., Heikkilä, K. 1989. Carotid arteriosclerosis in identical twins discordant for cigarette smoking. *Circulation* 80:10–16

Hagerman, R. J., Sobesky, W. E. 1989. Psychopathology in Fragile-X syndrome. *Am. J. Orthopsychiatr.* 59:142–52

Hearnshaw, L. S. 1979. *Cyril Burt, Psychologist.* Ithaca, NY: Cornell Univ. Press

Heath, A. C., Eaves, L. J., Martin, N. G. 1989a. The genetic structure of personality. III. Multivariate genetic item analysis of the EPQ scales. *Pers. Indiv. Differ.* 10:877–88

Heath, A. C., Jardine, R., Eaves, L. J., Martin, N. G. 1989b. The genetic structure of personality. II. Genetic item analysis of the EPQ. *Pers. Indiv. Differ.* 10:615–24

Heath, A. C., Jardine, R., Martin, N. G. 1989c. Interactive effects of genotype and social environment on alcohol consumption in female twins. *J. Stud. Alcohol.* 50:38–48

Heath, A. C., Martin, N. G. 1988. Teenage alcohol use in the Australian Twin Register: Genetic and social determinants of starting to drink. *Alcohol. Clin. Exp. Res.* 12:735–41

Heath, A. C., Martin, N. G. 1990. Psychoticism as a dimension of personality: a multivariate genetic test of Eysenck Eysencks' psychoticism construct. *J. Pers. Soc. Psychol.* 58:111–21

Hewitt, J. K., Claridge, G. 1989. The factor structure of schizotypy in a normal population. *Pers. Indiv. Differ.* 10:323–29

Hewitt, J. K., Eaves, L. J., Neale, M. C., Meyer, J. M. 1988. Resolving causes of developmental continuity or "tracking." I. Longitudinal twin studies during growth. *Behav. Genet.* 18:133–51

Hill, E. M., Wilson, A. F., Elston, R. C., Winokur, G. 1988. Evidence for possible linkage between genetic markers and affective disorders. *Biol. Psychiatry.* 24:903–17

Ho, H.-Z., Baker, L. A., Decker, S. N. 1988a. Covariation between intelligence and speed of cognitive processing: genetic and environmental influences. *Behav. Genet.* 18:247–61

Ho, H.-Z., Decker, S. N. 1988. Cognitive resemblance in reading disabled twins. *Dev. Med. Child Neurol.* 30:99–107

Ho, H.-Z., Decker, S. N. 1989. A comparative analysis of cognitive profiles: monozygotic and dizygotic reading-disabled twins. *Read. Writ.: Inderdisc. J.* 1:61–72

Ho, H.-Z., Gilger, J. W., Decker, S. N. 1988b. A twin study of Bannatyne's "genetic dyslexic" subtype. *J. Child Psychol. Psychiatry.* 29:63–72

Hodgkinson, S., Mullan, M. J., Gurling, H. 1990. The role of genetic factors in the aetiology of the affective disorders. *Behav. Genet.* 20:235–50

Holzman, P. S., Kringlen, E., Matthysse, S., Flanagan, S. D., Lipton, R. B., Cramer, G., et al. 1988. A single dominant gene can account for eye tracking dysfunctions and schizophrenia in offspring of discordant twins. *Arch. Gen. Psychiatry.* 45:641–47

Jensen, A. R. 1969. How much can we boost IQ and scholastic achievement? *Harvard Educ. Rev.* 39:1–123

Johnson, R. C., Kim, R. J., Danko, G. P. 1989. Guilt, shame and adjustment: a family study. *Pers. Indiv. Differ.* 10:71–74

Joynson, R. B. 1989. *The Burt Affair.* London: Routledge

Kaprio, J., Koskenvuo, M. 1990. Twins, smoking and mortality: a 12-year prospective study of smoking-discordant twin pairs. *Soc. Sci. Med.* In press

Kay, D. W. K. 1989. Genetics, Alzheimer's disease and senile dementia. *Br. J. Psychiatry.* 154:311–20

Kelsoe, J., Ginns, E. I., Egeland, J. A., Gerhard, D. S., Goldstein, A. M., et al. 1989. Re-evaluation of the linkage relationship between chromosome 11p loci and the gene for bipolar affective disorder in the Old Order Amish. *Nature* 342:238–43

Kendler, K. S. 1988. Familial aggregation of schizophrenia and schizophrenia spectrum disorders. *Arch. Gen. Psychiatry.* 45:377–83

Kendler, K. S., Gruenberg, A. M., Tsuang, M. T. 1988. A family study of the subtypes of schizophrenia. *Am. J. Psychiatry.* 145:57–62

Kendler, K. S., Heath, A., Martin, N. G. 1987. A genetic epidemiologic study of self-report suspiciousness. *Compr. Psychiatry.* 28:187–96

Kendler, K. S., Heath, A., Martin, N. G., Eaves, L. J. 1987. Symptoms of anxiety and symptoms of depression: same genes, different environments? *Arch. Gen. Psychiatry.* 44:451–57

Kendler, K., Tsuang, M. T. 1988. Outcome and familial psychopathology in schizophrenia. *Arch. Gen. Psychiatry.* 45:338–46

Kennedy, J. L., Giuffra, L. A., Moises, H. W., Cavalli-Sforza, L. L., Pakstis, A. J., Kidd, J. R., et al. 1988. Evidence against linkage of schizophrenia to markers on chromosome 5 in a northern Swedish pedigree. *Nature* 336:167–70

Locurto, C. 1990. The malleability of IQ as judged from adoption studies. *Intelligence.* In press

Loehlin, J. C. 1987. *Latent Variable Models: An Introduction to Factor, Path, and Structural Analysis.* Hillsdale, NJ: Lawrence Erlbaum Assoc.

Loehlin, J. C. 1989. Partitioning environmental and genetic contributions to behavioral development. *Am. Psychol.* 44:1285–92

Loehlin, J. C., Horn, J. M., Willerman, L. 1989. Modeling IQ change: evidence from the Texas Adoption Project. *Child Dev.* 60:993–1004

Loehlin, J. C., Horn, J. M., Willerman, L. 1990. Heredity, environment, and personality change: evidence from the Texas Adoption Project. *J. Pers.* 58:221–43

Loehlin, J. C., Willerman, L., Horn, J. M. 1987. Personality resemblance in adoptive families: a 10-year follow-up. *J. Pers. Soc. Psychol.* 53:961–69

Loehlin, J. C., Willerman, L., Horn, J. M. 1988. Human behavior genetics. *Annu. Rev. Psychol.* 39:101–33

Lykken, D. T., Iacono, W. G., Haroian, K., McGue, M., Bouchard, T. J. Jr. 1988. Habituation of the skin conductance response to strong stimuli: a twin study. *Psychophysiology* 25:4–15

Lyons, M. J., Faraone, S. V., Kremen, W. S., Tsuang, M. T. 1990a. Familial and sporadic schizophrenia: a simulation study of statistical power. *Schizophren. Bull.* In press

Lyons, M. J., Kremen, W. S., Tsuang, M. T., Faraone, S. V. 1990b. Investigating putative and environmental forms of schizophrenia: methods and findings. *Int. Rev. Psychiatr.* In press

Martin, N. G., Boomsma, D. I. 1989. Willingness to drive when drunk and personality: a twin study. *Behav. Genet.* 19:97–111

Matheny, A. P. Jr. 1989. Children's behavioral inhibition over age and across situations: genetic similarity for a trait during change. *J. Pers.* 57:215–35

Matthysse, S., Holzman, P. 1989. In reply. *Arch. Gen. Psychiatry.* 46:479–80

McCartney, K., Harris, M. J., Bernieri, F. 1990. Growing up and growing apart: a developmental meta-analysis of twin studies. *Psychol. Bull.* 107:226–37

McGue, M., Bouchard, T. J. Jr. 1989. Genetic and environmental determinants of information processing and special mental abilities: a twin analysis. In *Advances in the Psychology of Human Intelligence,* R. J. Sternberg, ed. 5:7–45. Hillsdale, NJ: Lawrence Erlbaum Assoc.

McGue, M., Gottesman, I. I. 1989a. A single dominant gene still cannot account for the transmission of schizophrenia. *Arch. Gen. Psychiatry.* 46:478–79

McGue, M., Gottesman, I. I. 1989b. Genetic linkage in schizophrenia: perspectives from genetic epidemiology. *Schizophren. Bull.* 15:453–64

McGuffin, P. 1988. Major genes for major affective disorder? *Br. J. Psychiatry.* 153:591–96

McGuffin, P., Farmer, A., Gottesman, I. I. 1987. Is there really a split in schizophrenia? The genetic evidence. *Br. J. Psychiatry.* 150:581–92

McGuffin, P., Hickle, P. 1990. Simulation of Mendelism revisited: the recessive gene for attending medical school. *Am. J. Hum. Genet.* 46:994–99

McGuffin, P., Katz, R., Aldrich, J., Bebbington, P. E. 1988a. The Camberwell Collaborative Depression Study. II. Investigation of family members. *Br. J. Psychiatry.* 152:766–74

McGuffin, P., Katz, R., Bebbington, P. 1988b. The Camberwell Collaborative Depression Study. III. Depression and adversity in the relatives of depressed probands. *Br. J. Psychiatry.* 152:775–82

Merikangas, K. R., Risch, N. J., Merikangas, J. R., Weissman, M. M., Kidd, K. K. 1988. Migraine and depression: association and familial transmission. *J. Psychiatry. Res.* 22:119–29

Merikangas, K. R., Spence, M. A., Kupfer, D. J., Kety, S. 1989. *Linkage studies of bipolar disorder Summary of MacArthur Foundation workshop.* Presented at 1st World Congr. Psychiatr. Genet., Cambridge, England

Mitchell, J., McCauley, E., Burke, P., Calderon, R., Ichloredt, K. 1989. Psychopathology in parents of depressed children and adolescents. *J. Am. Acad. Child Adolesc. Psychiatry.* 28:352–57

Mitchell, J. E., Baker, L. A., Jacklin, C. N. 1989. Masculinity and femininity in twin children: genetic and environmental factors. *Child Dev.* 60:1475–85

Moldin, S. O., Rice, J. P., Gottesman, I. I., Erlenmeyer-Kimling, L. 1990. Psychometric deviance in offspring at risk for schizophrenia. II. Resolving heterogeneity through admixture analysis. *Psychiatry. Res.* In press

Mullan, M. J., Murray, R. M. 1989. The impact of molecular genetics on our understanding of the psychoses. *Br. J. Psychiatry.* 154:591–95

National Research Council. 1988. *Mapping and Sequencing the Human Genome.* Washington, DC: Nat. Acad. Press

Neale, M. C., Martin, N. G. 1989. The effects of age, sex, and genotype on self-report drunkenness following a challenge dose of alcohol. *Behav. Genet.* 19:63–78

Neri, G., Opitz, J. M., Mikkelsen, M., Jacobs, P. A., Davies, K., Turner, G., eds. 1988. X-linked mental retardation. 3. *Am. J. Med. Genet.* 30:(1-2):1–17. Special issue

Olson, R., Wise, B., Conners, F., Rack, J., Fulker, D. 1989. Specific deficits in component reading and language skills: genetic and environmental influences. *J. Learn. Disabil.* 22:339–48

Orvaschel, H. 1990. Psychiatric disorder in high risk children. *J. Am. Acad. Child Adolesc. Psychiatry.* In press

Orvaschel, H., Walsh-Allis, G., Yee, W. 1988. Psychopathology in children of parents with recurrent depression. *J. Abnorm. Child Psychol.* 16:17–28

Pardes, H., Kaufmann, C. A., Pincus, H. A., West, A. 1989. Genetics and psychiatry: past discoveries, current dilemmas, and future directions. *Am. J. Psychiatry.* 146:435–43

Pauls, D. L., Cohen, D. J., Kidd, K. K., Leckman, J. F. 1989. Tourette syndrome and neuropsychiatric disorders: Is there a genetic relationship? (letter). *Am. J. Hum. Genet.* 43:206–9

Pedersen, N. L., Gatz, M., Plomin, R., Nesselroade, J. R., McClearn, G. E. 1989a. Individual differences in locus of control during the second half of the lifespan for identical and fraternal twins reared apart and reared together. *J. Gerontol.* 44:100–5

Pedersen, N. L., Lichtenstein, P., Plomin, R., DeFaire, U., McClearn, G. E., Matthews, K. 1989b. Genetic and environmental influences for Type A–like measures and related traits: a study of twins reared apart and twins reared together. *Psychosom. Med.* 51:428–40

Pedersen, N. L., McClearn, G. E., Plomin, R., Nesselroade, J. R., Berg, S., DeFaire, U. 1990. The Swedish Adoption/Twin Study of Aging: an update. *Acta Genet. Med. Gemellol.* In press

Pedersen, N. L., Plomin, R., McClearn, G. E., Friberg, L. 1988. Neuroticism, extraversion, and related traits in adult twins reared apart and reared together. *J. Pers. Soc. Psychol.* 55:950–57

Pennington, B. F. 1990. Annotation: the genetics of dyslexia. *J. Child Psychol. Psychiatry.* 31:193–201

Pennington, B. F., Smith, S. D. 1988. Genetic influences on learning disabilities: an update. *J. Consult. Clin. Psychol.* 56:817–23

Phillips, K. 1989. Delta path methods for modeling the effects of multiple selective associations in adoption designs. *Behav. Genet.* 19:609–20

Phillips, K., Fulker, D. W. 1989. Quantitative genetic analysis of longitudinal trends in adoption designs with application to IQ in the Colorado Adoption Project. *Behav. Genet.* 19:621–58

Phillips, K., Fulker, D. W., Carey, G., Nagoshi, C. T. 1988. Direct marital assortment for cognitive and personality variables. *Behav. Genet.* 18:347–56

Phillips, K., Fulker, D. W., Rose, R. J. 1987. Path analysis of seven fear factors in adult twin and sibling pairs and their parents. *Genet. Epidemiol.* 4:345–55

Plomin, R. 1988. The nature and nurture of cognitive abilities. In *Advances in the Psychology of Human Intelligence,* ed. R. Sternberg, 4:1–33. Hillsdale, NJ: Lawrence Erlbaum Assoc.

Plomin, R. 1990a. Genetic risk and psychosocial disorders: links between the normal and abnormal. In *Biological Risk Factors for Psychosocial Disorders,* ed. M. Rutter, P. Casaer. London: Cambridge Univ. Press, In press

Plomin, R. 1990b. The role of inheritance in behavior. *Science.* 248:183–88

Plomin, R., Bergeman, C. S. 1990. The nature of nurture: genetic influence on "environmental" measures. *Behav. Brain Sci.* In press

Plomin, R., Chipuer, H. M., Loehlin, J. C. 1990a. Behavioral genetics and personality. In *Handbook of Personality Theory and Research,* L, A. Pervin ed. pp. 225–43. New York: Guilford

Plomin, R., Daniels, D. 1987. Why are children in the same family so different from each other? *Behav. Brain Sci.* 10:1–16

Plomin, R., DeFries, J. C., Fulker, D. W. 1988a. *Nature and Nurture in Infancy and Early Childhood.* New York: Cambridge Univ. Press

Plomin, R., DeFries, J. C., McClearn, G. E. 1990b. *Behavioral Genetics: A Primer.* New York: W. H. Freeman. 2nd ed.

Plomin, R., Lichtenstein, P., Pedersen, N. L., McClearn, G. E., Nesselroade, J. R. 1990c. Genetic influence on life events. *Psychol. Aging.* 5:25–30

Plomin, R., Loehlin, J. C. 1989. Direct and indirect IQ heritability estimates: a puzzle. *Behav. Genet.* 19:331–42

Plomin, R., McClearn, G. E., Pedersen, N. L., Nesselroade, J. R., Bergeman, C. S. 1988b. Genetic influence on childhood family environment perceived retrospectively from the last half of the life span. *Dev. Psychol.* 24:738–45

Plomin, R., McClearn, G. E., Pedersen, N. L., Nesselroade, J. R., Bergeman, C. S. 1989. Genetic influence on adults' ratings of their current family environment. *J. Marriage.* 51:791–803

Plomin, R., Nesselroade, J. R. 1990. Behavioral genetics and personality change. *J. Person.* 58:191–220

Plomin, R., Nitz, K., Rowe, D. C. 1990e. Behavioral genetics and aggressive behavior in childhood. In *Handbook of Developmental Psychopathology*, M. Lewis, S. M. Miller pp. 119–33. New York: Plenum

Plomin, R., Pedersen, N. L., McClearn, G. E., Nesselroade, J. R., Bergeman, C. S. 1988c. EAS temperaments during the last half of the life span: twins reared apart and twins reared together. *Psychol. Aging* 3:43–50

Puig-Antich, J., Goetz, D., Davies, M., Kaplan, T., Davies, S., Ostrow, L., et al. 1989. A controlled family history study of prepubertal major depressive disorder. *Arch. Gen. Psychiatry.* 46:406–18

Ravich-Shcherbo, I. V. 1988. *The Role of Environment and Heredity in the Development of Human Personality*. Moscow: Pedagogika

Reiss, A. L., Freund, L. 1990. Fragile X syndrome, DSM-III-R, and autism. *J. Am. Acad. Child Adolesc. Psychiatry.* In press

Reiss, A. L., Hagerman, R. J., Vinogradov, S., Abrams, M., King, R. J. 1988. Psychiatric disability in female carriers of the Fragile X chromosome. *Arch. Gen. Psychiatry.* 45:25–30

Reiss, D., Hetherington, E. M., Plomin, R. 1990. The separate worlds of teenage siblings: an introduction to the study of the nonshared environment and adolescent development. In *Nonshared Environment*, ed. E. M. Hetherington, D. Reiss, R. Plomin. Hillsdale, NJ: Lawrence Erlbaum Assoc. In press

Rice, T., Carey, G., Fulker, D. W., DeFries, J. C. 1989. Multivariate path analysis of specific cognitive abilities in the Colorado Adoption Project: conditional path model of assortative mating. *Behav. Genet.* 19:195–207

Riese, M. L. 1990. Neonatal temperament in monozygotic and dizygotic twin pairs. *Child Dev.* In press

Robertson, M. M. 1989. The Gilles de la Tourette syndrome: the current status. *Br. J. Psychiatr.* 154:147–69

Rodin, J., Salovey, P. 1989. Health psychology. *Annu. Rev. Psychol.* 40:533–79

Rose, R. J., Kaprio, J. 1988. Frequency of social contact and intrapair resemblance of adult monozygotic cotwins. *Behav. Genet.* 18:309–28

Rose, R. J., Koskenvuo, M., Kaprio, J., Sarna, S., Langinainio, H. 1988. Shared genes, shared experiences, and similarity of personality. *J. Pers. Soc. Psychol.* 54:61–171

Roses, A. D., Pericak-Vance, M. A., Haynes,

C. S., Haines, J. L., Gaskell, P. A., et al. 1988. Genetic linkage studies in Alzheimer's disease (AD). *Neurology* 38 (Suppl. 1):173

Rowe, D. C. 1981. Environmental and genetic influences on dimensions of perceived parenting: a twin study. *Dev. Psychol.* 17:203–8

Rowe, D. C. 1983. A biometrical analysis of perceptions of family environment: a study of twin and singleton sibling kinships. *Child Dev.* 54:416–23

Rowe, D. C., Rodgers, J. L., Meseck-Bushey, S., St. John C. 1989. Sexual behavior and nonsexual deviance: a sibling study of their relationship. *Dev. Psychol.* 25:61–69

Rushton, J. P. 1989. Genetic similarity, human altruism, and group selection. *Behav. Brain Sci.* 12:503–59

Rutter, M., Macdonald, H., Le Couteur, A., Harrington, R., Bolton, P., Bailey, A. 1990. Genetic factors in child psychiatric disorders: II. Empirical findings. *J. Child Psychol. Psychiatry.* 31:39–83

Schulz, S. C., Pato, C. N. 1989. Advances in the genetics of schizophrenia: editors' introduction. *Schizophren. Bull.* 15:361–64

Schellenberg, G. D., Bird, T. D., Wijsman, E. M., Moore, D. K., Boehnke, M., et al. 1988. Absence of linkage of chromosome 21q21 markers to familial Alzheimer's disease. *Science* 241:1507–10

Scott, J. P. 1989. *The Evolution of Social Systems*. New York: Gordon & Breach

Searles, J. S. 1988. The role of genetics in the pathogenesis of alcoholism. *J. Abnorm. Psychol.* 97:153–67

Sherrington, R., Brynjolfsson, J., Petursson, H., Potter, M., Dudleston, K., et al. 1988. Localization of a susceptiblity locus for schizophrenia on chromosome 5. *Nature* 336:164–67

Smalley, S. L., Asarnow, R. F., Spence, M. A. 1988. Autism and genetics: a decade of research. *Arch. Gen. Psychiatry.* 45:953–61

Smith, S. D., Pennington, B. F., Kimberling, W. J., Ing, P. S. 1990. Familial dyslexia: use of genetic linkage data to define subtypes. *J. Am. Acad. Child Psychiatry.* 29:204–13

Snyderman, M., Rothman, S. 1988. *The IQ Controversy, the Media and Public Policy*. New Brunswick, NJ: Transaction Books

Squires-Wheeler, E., Skokol, A. E., Friedman, D., Erlenmeyer-Kimling, L. 1988. The specificity of DSM-III schizotypal personality traits. *Psychol. Med.* 18:757–65

Stassen, H. H., Lykken, D. T., Bomben, G. 1988. The within-pair EEG similarity of twins reared apart. *Eur. Arch. Psychiatry Neurol. Sci.* 237:244–52

St. Clair, D., Blackwood, D., Muir, W., Baillie, D., Hubbard, A., et al. 1989. No linkage of chromosome 5q11-q13 markers to schizophrenia in Scottish families. *Nature* 339:305-8

Steffenburg, S., Gillberg, C., Hellgren, L., Andersson, L., Gillberg, I. C., et al. 1989. A twin study of autism in Denmark, Finland, Iceland, Norway, Sweden. *J. Child Psychol. Psychiatry* 30:405-16

Strober, M., Morrell, W., Burroughs, J., Lampert, C., Danforth, H., Freeman, R. 1988. A family study of bipolar I disorder in adolescence. *J. Affect. Disord.* 15:255-68

Sundet, J. M., Tambs, K., Magnus, P., Berg, K. 1988. On the question of secular trends in the heritability of intelligence test scores: a study of Norwegian twins. *Intelligence* 12:47-59

Suthers, G. K., Callen, D. F., Hyland, V. J., Kozman, H. M., Baker, E., et al. 1989. A new DNA marker tightly linked to the fragile X locus FRAXA. *Science* 246:1298-99

Tambs, K., Sundet, J. M., Magnus, P. 1988. Genetic and environmental effects on the covariance structure of the Norwegian army ability tests: a study of twins. *Per. Indiv. Differ.* 9:791-99

Tambs, K., Sundet, J. M., Magnus, P., Berg, K. 1989. Genetic and environmental contributions to the covariance between occupational status, educational attainment, and IQ: a study of twins. *Behav. Genet.* 19:209-22

Tanzi, R. E., St. George-Hyslop, P. H., Gusella, J. F. 1989. Molecular genetic approaches to Alzheimer's disease. *Trends Neurosci.* 12:152-58

Taylor, S. E. 1990. Health psychology. *Am. Psychol.* 45:40-50

Tellegen, A., Lykken, D. T., Bouchard, T. J. Jr., Wilcox, K. J., Segal, N. L., Rich, S. 1988. Personality similarity in twins reared apart and together. *J. Pers. Soc. Psychol.* 54:1031-39

Thompson, L. A., Detterman, D. K., Plomin, R. 1990. Associations between cognitive abilities and scholastic achievement: genetic overlap but environmental differences. *J. Educ. Psychol.* In press

Tienari, P., Lahti, I., Sorri, A., Naarala, M., Moring, J., Wahlberg, K. 1989. The Finnish Adoptive Family Study of Schizophrenia: Possible joint effects of genetic vulnerability and family environment. *Br. J. Psychiatry* 155 (Suppl. 5):29-32

Travis, G. H., Sutcliffe, J. G. 1988. Phenol emulsion-enhanced DNA-drive subtractive cDNA cloning: isolation of low-abundance monkey cortex-specific mRNAs. *Proc. Natl. Acad. Sci. USA* 85:1696-1700

Tsuang, M. T., Lyons, M. L., Faraone, S. V. 1990. Heterogeneity of schizophrenia: conceptual models and analytic strategies. *Br. J. Psychiatry.* 156:17-26

Turner, J. R. 1989. Individual differences in heart rate response during behavioral challenge. *Psychophysiology* 26:497-505

Vernon, P. A. 1989. The heritability of measures of speed of information-processing. *Pers. Indiv. Differ.* 10:573-76

Vogler, G. P., Gottesman, I. I., McGue, M. K., Rao, D. C. 1990. Mixed model segregation analysis of schizophrenia in the Lindelius Swedish pedigrees. *Behav. Genet.* In press

Waller, N. G., Kojetin, B. A., Bouchard, T. J. Jr., Lykken, D. T., Tellegen, A. 1990. Genetic and environmental influences on religious interests, attitudes, and values: a study of twins reared apart and together. *Psychol. Sci.* 1:138-42

Weissman, M. M., Warner, V., Wickramaratne, P., Prusoff, B. A. 1988. Early-onset major depression in parents and their children. *J. Affect. Disord.* 15:269-77

Wilson, A. F., Tanna, V. L., Winokur, G., Elston, R. C., Hill, E. M. 1989. Linkage analysis of depression spectrum disease. *Biol. Psychiatry.* 26:163-75

Winokur, G., Kadrmas, A. 1989. A polyepisodic course in bipolar illness: possible clinical relationships. *Compr. Psychiatry.* 30:121-27

Zahn-Waxler, C., Mayfield, A., Radke-Yarrow, M., McKnew, D. H., Cytryn, L., Davenport, Y. B. 1988. A follow-up investigation of offspring of parents with bipolar disorder. *Am. J. Psychiatry.* 145:506-9

Annu. Rev. Psychol. 1991. 42:191–212
Copyright © 1991 by Annual Reviews Inc. All rights reserved

MARITAL INTERACTIONS

K. Daniel O'Leary and David A. Smith

Department of Psychology, State University of New York, Stony Brook, New York
11794-2500

KEY WORDS: integration with psychopathology research, prevention, treatment, psychodynamic models of marital adjustment, social learning models of marital adjustment

CONTENTS

INTRODUCTION

Marriage has emerged as an important topic in psychology over the last decade for several reasons. One of the most important is a concern about the divorce rate in the United States and its effects on the quality of life. Divorce rates rose sharply from the 1960s to the 1980s, and the anticipated divorce rate is now approximately 50%. While the divorce rate leveled out in the

0066-4308/91/0201-0191$02.00

1980s, the United States now has the highest divorce rate among major industrialized countries (e.g. Australia, Canada, West Germany, France, Italy, and Japan) of the world (US Bureau of the Census 1990).

This trend is not without consequences. The United States has the world's highest per capita number of children living in single parent families (US Census Bureau 1990). Twenty percent of all children in the United States are in families headed by a single parent, and 50% of all Black children are in such families (Zigler 1985). Depression and suicide among adolescents and young adults are at an all-time high in the United States, and one reason postulated for these increases is the change in family structure with its attendant high rates of marital dissolution (Klerman & Weissman 1990). The association between marital discord and various forms of adult psychopathology such as alcoholism and depression is now becoming increasingly clear (Beach et al 1990; Jacobson et al 1989a). Whether a discordant marriage harms children more than a divorce is now a hotly debated issue (Emery 1989; Wallerstein & Kelly 1980).

Another reason for the emerging interest in marriage and marital therapy is that distressed couples demand help and thereby create a market for therapeutic services. More individuals seek help in mental health clinics for marital problems than for any other single problem. Approximately 40% of all clients in mental health clinics indicate that marital problems are part of their difficulty (Yeroff et al 1981). This need for marital therapy prompted states such as California to train and certify marital and family therapists independent of the traditional training fields of psychiatry, psychology, and social work.

As the divorce rate rose, the need for marital therapy (and mediation or dissolution services) increased. When the impact of relationship factors on psychopathology became more well known, the study of marriage and its impact received greater attention. In turn, a research field largely dominated by sociologists became of special interest to various mental health professionals. The study of the individual gave way to the study of dyads, and the family therapy movement became evident across the world. The American Psychological Association started a Family Psychology Division in 1985 and officially recognized the *Journal of Family Psychology* in 1987. A number of behavior therapists working with children and adolescents gradually expanded their efforts to encompass the larger system, namely, the marriage, as a means of enhancing generalization and treatment gains (O'Leary & Wilson 1987).

Between 1950 and 1966, chapters in the *Annual Review of Psychology* made not a single reference to marriage or marital therapy, and until the mid 1980s this series offered only scattered references to marriage, marital therapy, or marital interaction. Marital issues, however, have been given closer attention in recent *Annual Review of Psychology* chapters on close relationships (Clark & Reis 1988; Huston & Levinger 1978) and family therapy (Bednar et al 1988). A search of the several APA psychology journals that cover issues related to marriage and marital discord *(Journal of Consulting and Clinical Psychology, Journal of Personality and Social Psychology,* and *Developmental Psychology)* indicated that papers on the correlates, predictors, and consequences of marital discord, treatment of marital discord, and family violence appeared with regularity only in the last five years. Maternal employment and public policy issues such as day care that are associated with the changing demographics of marriage and the family have also received frequent attention in our journals recently.

Nonetheless, despite increasing interest in marriage and marital interaction, this is the first chapter in the *Annual Review* devoted to this topic. Consequently, we have been highly selective in our choice of material. We focus our review on theories of marital satisfaction and discord and on the treatment of marital discord because these topics have occupied the largest portion of the clinical psychology literature and are the areas with which we are most closely associated. Because both family systems and social psychology approaches to marriage have received attention in recent issues of the *Annual Review of Psychology* (Clark & Reis 1988; Bednar et al 1988; Huston & Levinger 1978), and because these areas have not been well integrated into the mainstream of clinical theory and research, we do not review them here. We evaluate the effectiveness of prevention efforts and treatment approaches from psychodynamic and social learning perspectives and discuss new directions that marriage research may take in the 1990s. We also explore areas of needed interdisciplinary research across clinical psychology and social psychology at the end of our review.

THEORETICAL MODELS OF MARITAL ADJUSTMENT

Psychodynamic Models of Marital Adjustment

As one of the most venerable and influential traditions in the history of psychology, psychodynamic perspectives on marriage are presented alongside behavioral and family-systems theories in many widely cited surveys of the marital literature (e.g. Jacobson & Gurman 1986; Paolino & McCrady 1978). The psychodynamic orientation toward resolving marital conflict is by far the oldest and most widespread approach to treatment (e.g. Baucom & Hoffman 1986; Beach & O'Leary 1985; Gurman & Kniskern 1978). We examine research from areas directly and indirectly associated with the psychodynamic orientation to see if data can be adduced to support its more central tenets.

There are perhaps no tenets more central to psychodynamic formulations of marital adjustment than those associated with spouse selection. A psychodynamic perspective holds that people consciously and unconsciously seek spouses who gratify narcissistic needs (Dicks 1967; Schutz 1958; Stewart et al 1975; Winch 1958). Dynamic repression of these narcissistic needs and their introjection and projection onto potential partners lead people to prefer spouses who complement their needs. For instance, one partner may be dominant and aggressive while the other is submissive and masochistic; alternatively, one partner may be emotionally detached while the other craves affection (Mittleman 1948). In other words, people select mates who best serve to substitute for some unattained ego ideal. "Couples are usually attracted by shared developmental failures" (Skynner 1976:43). Once established, marital partners have an implicit "contract" to continue to gratify these needs throughout the marriage (Sager 1976).

There are two points in a marriage upon which the need-complementarity hypothesis bears. As already stated, need complementarity is thought to exert an influence upon spouse selection. It is also thought to influence satisfaction in the resulting marriage.

Curiously, few studies have been devoted solely to the issue of spouse selection. The most direct evidence for the existence of need complementarity in spouse selection is found in the behavior genetics literature devoted to assortative mating (e.g. Buss 1984a; Mascie-Taylor & Vandenberg 1988; Phillips et al 1988) and in the personality literature concerned with personal-environment interactions (e.g. Buss 1984b; Caspi & Herbener 1990).

In determining the heritability of psychological characteristics, it is important to know the extent to which parents can be assumed to be randomly paired with respect to each characteristic. Therefore, behavior geneticists have studied the similarity between spouses on a number of personality dimensions. They find not complementarity but similarity of needs influencing spousal selection. For instance, Buss (1984a) found low positive correlations between spouses for most of the 16 personality traits he examined. Similarly, Mascie-Taylor & Vandenberg (1988) and Phillips et al (1988) found fairly consistent evidence for similarity of personality between spouses. Numerous other examples are available (e.g. Phillips et al 1988; see Vandenberg 1972 for a review).

In the personality literature two sources of variance, the person and the situation, are now understood to interact in the determination of behavior. Recent research in this tradition takes marriage to be an important environment within which peoples' dispositions are manifest. Investigators therefore examine the degree to which personality variables influence both spouse selection and marital adjustment. The extent to which people create a marital environment consistent with their own behavioral predilections is of interest not only as it reveals important features of peoples' self-concepts but also as it influences adult personality development.

For example, Buss (1984b) examined spousal correspondence on eight dispositional categories from the Wiggins (1979) interpersonal circumplex and on 800 specific behavioral acts (e.g. "went to a disco", "unplugged my phone for the evening"). Buss (1984b) found moderate positive correlations between spouses for four of the eight dispositional categories. At the level of specific acts, he found substantial correlations within each of the eight categories. In a study of the impact of spouse selection for adult personality development, Caspi & Herbener (1990) also found substantial similarity between spouses using the California Q sort (Block 1971).

A number of studies have examined the association between complementarity and marital satisfaction (e.g. Cattell & Nesselroade 1967; Heiss & Gordon 1964; Murstein 1961, Murstein & Beck 1972; Winch 1958). One study conducted by Meyer & Pepper (1977) exemplifies the results of this research. Using modified versions of 12 scales from Jackson's Personality Research Form (Jackson 1967), they found no evidence of an association between need complementarity and marital adjustment as measured by a modified version of the Lock-Wallace Marital Adjustment Scale (Locke & Wallace 1959). Rather, they found similarity of spouses' needs for affiliation, aggression, autonomy, and nurturance to be associated with marital adjustment. This finding held both for differences in intensity on the same needs (Winch's Type I complementarity) and differences in kind of needs (Winch's Type II complementarity—e.g. high dominance paired with high succorance). Other explicit tests of Winch's Type I and Type II complementarity hypotheses have also proved negative (DeYoung & Fleischer 1976). The association between spouse similarity and marital success is, in fact, highly replicable (e.g. Cattell & Nesselroade 1967; Heiss & Gordon 1964; Murstein 1961; Murstein & Beck 1972). In contrast, only a few studies support need complementarity (Winch 1958; Winch et al 1954), and these have been questioned on both theoretical (e.g. Levinger 1964) and methodological (e.g. Tharp 1963) grounds. It could be argued that measures of personality are poor instantiations of "needs" as conceptualized in psychodynamic theory. However, the Meyer & Pepper (1977) study, for one, used the Personality Research Form (Jackson 1967), a device expressly designed to measure the same Murray (1938) needs upon which the Winch (1958) theory is based.

A longitudinal perspective on the need-complementarity hypothesis was provided in a study by Bentler & Newcomb (1978). The personality similarity of a sample of newly married couples who four years later were divorced was compared to that of a group of couples that remained married. Among the couples who remained married, no traits exhibited significant complementarity. Rather, significant degrees of similarity were found in this group, while the divorced couples were for the most part neither similar nor complementary.

The bulk of the evidence now favors positive assortative mating for personality. Rather than differing in their personalities, spouses tend to be similar; and the degree of similarity is positively correlated with their marital satisfaction. Personality can now take its place alongside physical characteristics, cognitive abilities, age, education, religion, ethnic background, attitudes and opinions, and socioeconomic status (Jensen 1978; Vandenberg 1972) as contributors to marital choice. As stated by Buss, "negative assortative mating in human populations has never been reliably demonstrated (1985:47).

A second major tenet of the psychodynamic formulation of marriage concerns the role each spouse's individual psychosexual development plays in marital functioning. In particular, importance is ascribed to the attachment relationships in spouses' respective families of origin and how "lost aspects of their primary object relations" (Dicks 1967) are manifest in current marital relationships. Comfortable differentiation from the family of origin and nonneurotic resolution of the various psychosexual conflicts are thought to result in levels of individual functioning that form the foundation of satisfactory marital relations (e.g. Framo 1976).

Research regarding the impact of childhood attachment on adult romantic relationships has emerged fairly recently (Feeney & Noller 1990; Hazan & Shaver 1987; Hendrick & Hendrick 1989; Levy & Davis 1988; Main et al 1985; Shaver & Hazan 1988; Shaver et al 1988). Hazan & Shaver (1987) launched this area with an informative survey-based examination of adult romantic relationships. Using fairly literal translations to adult relationships of Bowlby's (1969, 1973, 1980) three styles of infant-parent attachment, they found (a) the relative prevalences of these adult styles were similar to those found in childhood, (b) the experience of love for people in the three types of attachment relationships were consistent with expectations based on theory, (c) subjects' working models of self and relationships were positively correlated to attachment styles, and (d) reports of relationships with parents were meaningfully associated with adult romantic relationships.

Levy & Davis (1988), Hendrick & Hendrick (1989), and Feeney & Noller (1990) have also found attachment styles and romantic orientations to be associated. In general, securely attached persons endorse positive relationship characteristics, avoidant attachments are characteristically mistrusting and fearful, and anxious attachments are typically dependent and otherwise needy. Variables associated with childhood relationships with parents (e.g. "affectionate parental relationship", "separation from mother") were also found to be meaningfully associated with adult romantic relationship attachment styles.

A final tenet worth exploring emerges not as an explicit component of any particular psychodynamic theory about marriage, but rather as an implicit mechanism through which intrapersonal factors bear on the interpersonal marital situation. Specifically, individual levels of neuroticism (broadly defined) are thought to influence directly the adjustment of the couple. These therefore constitute a target of, and justification for, individual rather than couples psychotherapy (e.g. Giovacchini 1965).

The examination of neuroticism has an admirable history in marital research, spawning an impressive set of longitudinal studies (Adams 1946; Bentler & Newcomb 1978; Burgess & Wallin 1953; Kelly & Conley 1987; Terman & Oden 1947; Uhr 1957; Vaillant 1978). Taken together, the results of these studies support the psychodynamic contention that neuroticism, impulsivity, emotional instability, irritability, psychopathology, fearfulness, poor social adjustment, and similar constructs are associated with poor marital adjustment. The mechanisms through which these factors influence marital adjustment require further empirical and theoretical attention.

In 1963 Tharp accurately claimed of the need-complementarity theory of spouse selection that "In marriage research, no other hypothesis produced in the last decade has been as influential (p. 107)", but it would now seem prudent to abandon this account and turn attention to models of mate selection consistent with the robust similarity findings cited above. Notions about the effects of childhood attachment on adult romantic relationships, on the other hand, hold great promise for future clarification of the psychology of marriage.

Social-Learning Models of Marital Adjustment

The social learning approach to marriage is less a unified theoretical position than a collection of empirically established concepts brought to bear on the marital dyad. Its roots lie with Thibault & Kelley's (1959) social exchange theory, but it has evolved over the last 25 years to encompass not only the behavioral economics of the original interdependence models but also cognitive, mediational, and affective components (Baucom & Epstein 1990; O'Leary 1987).

In the behavioral domain, Stuart's (1969) reinforcement model of marital satisfaction spawned research into the day-to-day behaviors of distressed and nondistressed married couples. Distressed couples were shown to engage in fewer recreational activities together (Birchler & Webb 1977), to spend less time together (Williams 1979), and to rate the time spent together more negatively (Williams 1979). During their time together, distressed couples exhibit a lower ratio of pleasing to displeasing behaviors, with displeasing behaviors better able to distinguish the two groups (Margolin 1981). Distressed couples have sex one half to one third as often as nondistressed couples (Barnett & Nietzel 1979; Birchler & Webb 1977).

Particular attention has been paid to verbal behavior in the context of marital problem-solving discussions (Baucom & Adams 1987). In such research, couples are asked to discuss an issue about which they disagree, and the resulting interaction is either audio- or video-taped. As rated by trained observers, in these discussions distressed couples make more negative statements (disagreements, criticisms) and fewer positive ones (e.g. Gottman 1979). Distressed couples are also more confrontive, complaining, and defensive with their spouses than they are with other people (Ting-Toomey 1983). Distressed couples *reciprocate* negative behaviors (i.e. each spouse emits negative behaviors contingent on the partner's emission of others) to a greater degree than the nondistressed, especially during problem-solving communication (Gottman 1979; Margolin & Wampold 1981).

In part because spouses seem to disagree over the occurrence of daily behaviors in their relationship (e.g. Jacobson & Moore 1981), cognitive features began to be incorporated into the previously behavioral model of marriage (Arias & Beach 1987). The cognitive correlates of marital satisfaction have, for the most part, been established through the use of paper-and-pencil self-reports of people's predilections to make certain attributions and appraisals about their spouses and marriages. Distressed couples are less likely to interpret objectively positive behaviors from their spouses as positive, underestimating the positiveness by as much as 50% (Gottman et al 1976). They interpret the intent of their spouse's statements more negatively than they were meant to be (Markman 1981; Schacter & O'Leary 1985). More than their nondistressed counterparts distressed spouses interpret the causes of positive partner behaviors as specific and uncontrollable, the causes of negative partner behaviors as global and pervasive (Fincham & O'Leary 1983).

Programs of research by Fincham & Bradbury (e.g. Fincham & Bradbury 1990), Holtzworth-Munroe & Jacobson (Camper et al 1988; Holtzworth-Munroe 1988; Holtzworth-Munroe & Jacobson 1985; Jacobson et al 1985), and Baucom (Baucom 1987; Baucom, et al 1989a,b) have greatly developed the study of attributions in marriage. Care has been taken to establish the theoretical boundary conditions, measuring devices, samples, and developmental stages of the couples studied. Dissatisfied spouses make attributions that cast their partners' behavior in a negative light. Further, initial findings suggest that attributions predict changes in marital satisfaction and that attributions influence marital satisfaction rather than vice versa (Bradbury & Fincham 1990).

A concern for the affective features of marital satisfaction arose among social learning theorists from two primary sources. First, Gottman's (1979; Gottman et al 1977) extension of his Couples Interaction Scoring System to encompass affect as well as content elements of spousal communication led to the discovery that affective features of communication were more indicative of the current quality of the marriage than were content components (Gottman 1979; Gottman et al 1977; Hahlweg et al 1984a; Schaap 1984). Second, the finding that spouses judged love to be a highly valued characteristic of marriage (Broderick 1981), as well as the troublesome clinical failures in which significant behavioral changes were not associated with changes in levels of caring, led O'Leary et al (1983) to develop the Positive Feelings Questionnaire, a measure that correlates highly with marital satisfaction.

In an extension of the observational coding paradigm, attention has recently been directed at specific affects such as anger, sadness, happiness, and contentment (Gottman & Krokoff 1989; Gottman & Levenson 1986; Smith & O'Leary 1987; Smith et al 1990). Interest in specific affects has led to attempts, using longitudinal designs, to forge links with more basic research in emotion and the structure of affect. Out of this approach has emerged the challenging finding that while current marital satisfaction is negatively associated with expressions of negative emotion, later satisfaction is enhanced by previous arousal and "conflict engagement." In other words, the longitudinal predictors of marital satisfaction differ from its cross-sectional correlates.

The psychophysiological work of Levenson & Gottman (1983, 1985) warrants attention in any discussion of emotion in marriage. They found an association between arousal level of husband and wife measured physiologically and cross-sectionally measured marital satisfaction (Levenson & Gottman 1983). Decreases in marital satisfaction of these same couples over the ensuing three years were subsequently found to be highly predictable from simple levels of autonomic arousal established during the original study (see the section below on physiological predictors of marital satisfaction) (Levenson & Gottman 1985). Here again, then, it appears that the predictors of marital satisfaction differ from its cross-sectional correlates. However, it is unclear how the physiological and affect findings can be integrated. That is, conflict engagement measured through observed affects was associated with increased marital satisfaction in both the Gottman & Krokoff (1989) and Smith et al (1990) studies. But Levenson & Gottman (1985) found that physiological arousal was associated with declines in marital satisfaction over time. There is clearly a degree of discontinuity between measures of emotion that may have important implications for the understanding of the etiology of marital dissatisfaction.

Marital therapy is a domain within which this diverse collection of findings is most readily integrated. Consistent with the available research of their time, marital therapies based on behavioral principles could variously be referred to as "Operant-Interpersonal" (Stuart 1969), "Behavioral" (O'Leary & Turkewitz 1978), "Social Learning-Cognitive" (Jacobson & Holtzworth-Munroe 1986), and "Cognitive-Behavioral-Affective" (Margolin 1987). Behavioral methods of treating discordant spouses have proved exceedingly responsive to basic marital research findings.

PREVENTION AND TREATMENT

Prevention

PREMARITAL RELATIONSHIP ENHANCEMENT   When two people are in love, do they want to know about any problems in their marriage? Generally not. The expression, "blinded by love" conveys a sense of this issue. Nonetheless, certain religious groups require discussion of marriage and potential marital problems before marriage. For example, the Catholic church requires some attendance at Pre-Canna classes before a priest will marry a couple. However, the differential effects of these classes on Catholics are unknown because almost all such couples are required to take them.

One of the most well-developed programs to prevent marital problems was generated by Bernard Guerney and his colleagues (cf Guerney et al 1985). The program is designed for a 2.5-hr/week group format spanning approximately 10 weeks. Comparisons between subjects randomly assigned to the premarital program and a wait-list group indicated that the experimental subjects fared better on measures of empathic skill, expressive skill (appropriate self-disclosure, and nonthreatening openness), understanding, and general satisfaction with their relationships.

Not all premarital programs produce change. The program developed by Guerney and colleagues has been compared with a premarital program similar to Marriage Encounter (ME) in which married couples model how they cope with the joys and sorrows of marriage. The ME-type program also involved discussions of weaknesses in a couple's relationship and potential conflicts in the marriage. The ME group showed no gains in communication skills or in constructive problem solving, whereas the relationship enhancement program evidenced changes on both of these measures (Most & Guerney 1983).

Some evidence indicates that premarital education emphasizing communication and problem-solving skills reduces the divorce rate. Based on several longitudinal studies of early marriage, a model was developed within a social learning framework. It covers many of the issues discussed in the Guerney program and is described as being specifically oriented toward reducing critical comments and encouraging constructive engagement. For example, Markman et al (1988) found that a course of five 3-hr group sessions of premarital education in communication and problem-solving was associated with greater marital satisfaction at both 1.5 and 3 years postmarriage compared to the satisfaction of control subjects who did not receive this intervention. Moreover, couples in the prevention program were significantly less likely to dissolve their relationship three years post marriage (5% vs 24%). These results are certainly impressive and deserving of attempts at replication.

As just indicated, not all premarital programs work equally well, and it is possible that some existing programs used widely in the United States may not have any significant effects on couples. Thus, process research on the effective ingredients of premarital programs as well as comparative outcome research in this area is sorely needed. Use of the treatment outcome and dismantling strategies that have been used effectively in evaluating marital therapy would appear to be promising in this area.

Premarital programs can help couples and reduce divorce rates. A major task in this area, however, is to educate the public about the utility of these programs and to reach the groups that need them most. Premarital programs might well be targeted at high-risk groups such as couples in second marriages and teen marriages.

MARRIAGE ENRICHMENT PROGRAMS   Marriage Encounter is a variation of a religion-based program to help married couples. Started in Spain by a priest in the late 1950s, Marriage Encounter is one of the oldest existing marriage enrichment programs. The program is not well researched, and the few evaluations of it cast doubt on its effectiveness. Of course, almost anyone involved with marital treatment can provide examples of couples who associated great gains in their marriage with the Marriage Encounter weekend retreat. However, couples must be willing to devote a weekend together to ME, and this requirement may effectively screen out the most severely discordant couples. ME couples also are not easily randomly assigned to treatment, though one study indicated that ME couples showed enhanced communication and general marital satisfaction compared to a wait-list control group (Costa 1981).

A more carefully researched marital enrichment program is the Minnesota Couples Group Program. Developed in 1968 by Miller et al (1976), the program is based on a theory of marriage as a growth system. At the heart of the procedure are communication interventions. Skills that receive emphasis are flexibility of interactional style, self-awareness, and elicitation of information from the spouse. Five to seven couples meet with a leader for three hours a week for four weeks. The format is educational, and the book *Alive and Aware: Improving Communication in Relationships* serves as the guide for the groups. Like several behavioral marital therapy programs, this program emphasizes minicontracts in which couples specify certain problem areas and agree to spend time working on resolutions to these problems. Wampler (1982) provided a summary of the outcome research on this marriage enrichment program, and indicated mixed results on self-report measures of communication quality. Only in 7 of the 13 studies reviewed was there an increase in marital satisfaction.

A related program is the Marital Relationship Enhancement Program of Guerney (1977), sometimes called "conjugal therapy." Like the previous program, it uses a group format; but it lasts 16–20 instead of 10–12 hr. A leader helps clients work on areas of their marriage that they find problematic.

Sharing of positive feelings toward one another is encouraged, and communication exercises are emphasized under the guidance of the leader. A number of studies have indicated that this program is effective in increasing trust, intimacy, communication, and general marital satisfaction (Guerney et al 1985). Moreover, comparisons with equally credible programs of a behavioral nature (cf Stuart 1969) indicate that this program is perceived as more worthwhile, exciting, fair, important, and comfortable than the behavioral programs that emphasized reciprocal reinforcement. On the other hand, both programs showed equal improvements on communication, marital adjustment, and cooperation; both showed greater changes on these measures than did wait-list controls.

Of special interest is a study in which experienced marital/family therapists received a three-day training workshop in the marital relationship enhancement program and then provided services to clients using this method. They also provided services to couples using their own preferred method of treatment (psychodynamic, client centered, and behavioral). At the end of ten weeks, couples who received the structured relationship enhancement program fared better than did those who received the therapists' own preferred methods on all three variables studied: marital adjustment, the quality of their relationship, an the quality of their communication (Ross 1981). Some might argue that the specific dependent measures chosen in this study were of greatest relevance to the relationship enhancement group, but these results are still impressive. Most therapists who treat discordant couples would agree that the measures chosen are generally very significant to most couples.

Marital Therapy

Behavioral marital therapy is the most frequently evaluated therapy for the treatment of discordant couples. At least two dozen studies and several reviews provide the empirical base for an evaluation of this therapy. Briefly, behavioral therapy has repeatedly resulted in significant increases in marital satisfaction in diverse laboratories across the United States and Europe (cf Jacobson et al 1984; Hahlweg et al 1984b; Beach & O'Leary 1985). These changes are reasonably well maintained at one year follow-up for those couples who complete therapy (Hahlweg & Markman 1988; O'Leary & Beach 1990). The marital therapy outcome literature is clearly a success story.

At first glance these changes appear impressive. Indeed, depending upon the review, approximately 70–80% of the couples treated in this way improve (cf Baucom & Hoffman 1986). However, when the changes are more closely scrutinized, one's enthusiasm can wane: Only 40–55 percent of couples improve enough to be classified as nondistressed (Baucom & Epstein 1990). For example, on the average, couples move from an extremely dissatisfied evaluation of their marriage at pretreatment to a just satisfactory range at posttreatment (O'Leary & Arias 1983). Unfortunately, no marital therapy investigations have documented whether individuals felt helped when their decision was to terminate their marriage.

In the 1990s, research will attempt to determine whether behavioral marital therapy enables a significant percentage of clients to consider their marriages satisfactory over several years. Passion decreases somewhat over the course of marriage, especially in the first few years, but couples who have found their marriage truly satisfying over many years report that love and sexual attraction remain (Swensen 1985). If so, then sexual excitement and love in a relationship must be addressed more straightforwardly by all therapists.

Classic insight-oriented therapies emphasize unconscious factors thought to influence both choice of mate and the conflicts that develop later in marriage. These therapies no doubt represent a potent influence on the field of marital therapy, yet we were able to find only a few published treatment outcome studies upon which to base an evaluation (Beach & O'Leary 1985). Using these studies, we found no evidence that insight-oriented therapies produced change in communication or marital satisfaction. One problem with the studies we reviewed was that the insight-oriented approaches did not include the directive techniques advocated by prominent psychodynamic therapists (e.g. Sager & Skynner). Nonetheless, one study that included insight and directive techniques (Boelens et al 1980), showed that the insight-oriented approach fared better than a wait-list control on a measure of marital satisfaction.

As a part of the cognitive revolution in psychology, behavioral marital therapy expanded to include cognitive strategies. In fact, therapy texts by leading behavioral marital therapists at the beginning of the 1990s already include or even emphasize cognitive factors (cf Baucom & Epstein 1990). Weiss (1984) aptly noted that in order to be as useful as behavioral marital therapists want them to be, the restructuring techniques of behavioral marital therapy will require conceptual refinement. Such conceptual refinement of cognitive behavioral therapy may have to be tailored to particular types of marital problems [e.g. marital discord and depression of one or both spouses (Beach et al 1990), marital discord and alcoholism of a spouse (McCrady et al 1986)].

Insight approaches used by behavior therapists within a social learning perspective present an interesting conceptual challenge to models of behavioral marital therapy. Snyder & Wills (1989) compared insight-oriented therapy and behavioral therapy to a wait-list control. Both approaches produced significant improvements in general marital satisfaction and, to a lesser extent, a reduction in individual psychological distress. There were no significant differences between the two treatments; both treatments resulted in clinically significant changes in over 60% of couples. The emphasis in the insight-oriented therapy was on interpretation of underlying dynamics that contributed to the current marital difficulties. The emphasis in behavioral marital therapy was on increasing positive interchanges and improving communication. Each therapist provided both insight and behavioral therapy, and it is unclear why this research produced significant and equivalent changes in marital satisfaction while the insight-oriented approaches reviewed earlier did not.

Another interesting development is the use of emotion-focused therapy that incorporates techniques from Gestalt and client-centered therapy. Such therapy emphasizes the identification of underlying vulnerabilities, fears, and unexpressed resentments that contribute to the negative interaction cycles of a discordant marriage. Johnson & Greenberg (1985) found that this approach produced changes in marital satisfaction equivalent to the changes observed in a behavioral marital therapy. Moreover, couples in emotion-focused therapy reported greater intimacy than couples in marital therapy.

These differing therapeutic emphases could be judiciously tailored to the needs of individual clients. Some couples need insight into their problems, some need emotion-focused change, and some need behavioral change. Various combinations of these approaches could be imagined for different clients. One comparison (Jacobson et al 1989b) of a flexible treatment approach with a standard treatment regimen found that the former produced no significantly greater improvement at posttreatment; but because at follow-up the flexible treatment was indeed associated with less deterioration, it is still unclear whether flexible interventions enhance treatment effects. Ingredients common to the different treatment strategies may produce the changes in marital satisfaction across the different therapies.

CHALLENGES AND NEW DIRECTIONS

Special Populations

Marital discord occurs within different contexts, and the etiology and treatment of marital discord may vary greatly depending upon this context. For example, marital treatment is a valuable treatment for depressed women (O'Leary & Beach 1990). Marital treatment alone and marital treatment combined with an alcohol-focused intervention alone were associated with reduced drinking and increased general life satisfaction; neither treatment was associated with increases in marital satisfaction (McCrady et al 1986). Marital treatment for physically abused women and their husbands is controversial, but in many instances it may be critical in the prevention of argument and physical abuse (Adams 1988; Neidig & Friedman 1984; O'Leary & Vivian 1990). Marital treatment for couples in which one spouse tests positive for HIV virus is a high-priority research area, as is marital therapy for AIDS victims. Another area for marital therapy evaluation is treatment of elderly couples. As the population of the United States ages and as it becomes more widely known that partners can be sexually active in old age, treatments with the elderly need evaluation. In sum, there are many populations of maritally discordant individuals who may require variations of standard marital therapy or adjuncts to such therapy.

Love and Intimacy

While affect and intimacy are clearly issues addressed by researchers and clinicians, they have not received much attention in the marital outcome research literature. No method of increasing positive affect or love toward a spouse has been replicated in various clinics. Johnson & Greenberg's (1985) research is intriguing because emotion-focused treatment was associated with greater intimacy than behavioral marital therapy. One of the issues most often addressed by marital therapy clients is their waning love for their partner. Without changes in love or caring for a spouse, marital stability may be of little value; demonstration of such change is certainly a challenge to marital therapists (Margolin 1983).

Physiological Predictors of Marital Satisfaction

Physiological predictors of marital satisfaction may seem far fetched to some, but there is evidence that arousal patterns within a marital-assessment session predict later marital satisfaction (Gottman & Levenson 1986). Greater autonomic activity, such as increased heart rate and more sweating, was associated with greater declines in marital satisfaction across a three-year period. The correlations of the measures of autonomic arousal with declines in marital satisfaction were impressive, but the interpretation of results was not simple. For men, increased heart rate predicted declines in marital satisfaction; for women, skin conductance (sweating) did the same (Levenson & Gottman 1985). While the follow-up data at three years was based on only 19 couples from an original sample of 30, these data provide a basis for an interesting analysis and replication. Replication by an independent laboratory, however, seems crucial since this research produced many intriguing but unexpected findings. The cross-sectional and longitudinal data showed different results; the times originally intended for baseline were later used as actual measures since they correlated with marital discord, and measures of arousal that predicted declines in marital satisfaction for men were different from those of women.

Integration of Clinical and Social Research

Clinical research on marriage has been largely independent of social psychology research. Unfortunately, little cross fertilization has occurred, but we can identify areas that would now profit from a mix of research. For example, interpersonal attraction has long been a major interest of social psychologists studying relationships (cf Murstein 1976), yet this research is not even mentioned in clinical books on marital assessment (cf O'Leary 1987) and treatment (Baucom & Epstein 1990). Commitment has been investigated by social psychologists (Kelley 1983), but again this body of research is seldom mentioned by clinical psychologists—even those who assess commitment to remain in a marriage. Impairing the desired integration has been the use of undergraduate subjects by many social psychologists in their experiments on interpersonal attraction and commitment. Use of diverse subject populations would enhance the generalizability of results and make integration more likely. More theoretically driven research by clinical psychologists would be of greater relevance to social psychologists. Attribution research is one area of social psychology that has had great impact on the psychology of marriage. Interestingly, this research was greatly fostered by a social/developmental psychologist, Fincham, who later received training in clinical psychology and marital therapy (cf Fincham & Bradbury 1990). Perhaps cross-fertilization by postdoctoral training across disciplines would encourage this integration in the attribution area.

Integration with Psychopathology Research

The study of treatment failures would profit from an integration with traditional psychopathology research, for marriage and marital therapy involve individuals who bring their own assets and liabilities to the marriage. Indeed, some bring psychopathologies to the marriage. If they suffer from severe depression, for example, marital therapy may or may not be the treatment of choice (Coyne 1986; O'Leary & Beach 1990). Further, if physical aggression or spouse abuse exists, the appropriateness of marital therapy may be dependent upon the level of physical aggression in the relationship. In some instances, marital therapy may exacerbate the problems in the marriage; in others it may be critical to change. The effects of marital therapy on the high relapse rates of schizophrenics who return to families with high levels of expressed emotion should also be explored (Hooley, 1986).

Process of Therapeutic Change

As comparative outcome studies produce results that indicate no overall differences between treatments such as insight and behavioral marital therapy (Snyder & Wills 1989), the need to study therapeutic processes becomes clear. Fortunately, the research base is large enough to allow an unequivocal claim that marital therapy is effective. We now need to know what produces such changes, and we need to study the treatment failures intensively.

Sophisticated Prediction Models of Marital Discord

Interventions need not be based on a firm etiological base to be clinically effective, but having sophisticated models of the etiology of marital discord could enhance treatment effectiveness. A marital treatment that helps 50% of its client couples to rate their marriages "satisfactory" might be made more effective by means of more sophisticated models of what causes marital discord. It has long been known that discord and divorce can be predicted from assessments of communication and family background (Adams 1946). However, we need models of marital discord that differentiate causal factors and isolate paths of influence. As early as the 1940s, marital discord could be predicted using questionnaire approaches that addressed issues like marital status of parents, educational compatibility, and religious compatibility (Adams 1946). Despite these early studies showing that divorce could be predicted from premarital or early marital assessments, the divorce rate in the United States has climbed dramatically. If individuals enter marriage with the belief that it is more likely to fail than to succeed, the institution may assume a meaning very different from its meaning in the past. Sophisticated models of marital discord may enhance our ability to help troubled partners who want to keep their marriages intact.

Acceptance of the Serious Nature of Marital Discord

When women or men take their own lives, suicide notes reveal that relationship factors are the most common reasons (Bancroft et al 1979). One fourth of all homicide victims in 1984 were related to their assailants, and approximately half of intrafamilial homicides were between partners (Browne 1988). Despite these data, insurance companies do not consider the cost of treatment for marital problems reimbursable. Insurance companies are guided by actuarial data and the profit motive, but as business managers learn of the dramatic impact of marital discord they may push insurance companies or their own companies to provide psychological services for their employees. In January 1990, a survey of small business operators in Ohio suggested that marital problems, not alcohol or drug abuse, was the number one inhibitor of productivity in the workplace (APA Practitioner 1990). This survey attracted national media attention, and such recognition of the cost impact of marital discord, divorce, and work/family conflict may help make marital problems a priority issue for businesses and in turn insurance companies (Barling 1990).

Literature Cited

Adams, C. R. 1946. The prediction of adjustment in marriage. *Educ. Psychol. Meas.* 6:185–93

Adams, D. 1988. In *Feminist Perspectives on Wife Abuse,* ed. K. Yllo, M. Bograd, pp. 176–99. Beverly Hills, CA: Sage

American Psychological Association. 1990. *Pract. Focus* 4:7

Arias, I., Beach, S. R. H. 1987. Assessment of social cognition in the context of marriage. In *Assessment of Marital Discord,* ed. K. D. O'Leary, pp. 109–37. Hillsdale, NJ: Lawrence Erlbaum Assoc.

Barling, J. 1990. *Employment, Stress and Family Functioning.* New York: Wiley

Barnett, L. R., Nietzel, M. T. 1979. Relationship of instrumental and affectional behaviors and self-esteem to marital satisfaction in distressed and nondistressed couples. *J. Consult. Clin. Psychol.* 47:946–57

Baucom, D. H. 1987. Attributions in distressed relations: How can we explain them? In *Heterosexual Relations, Marriage and Divorce,* ed. S. Duck, D. Perlman, pp. 177–206. London: Sage

Baucom, D. H., Adams, A. N. 1987. Assessing communication in marital interaction. See O'Leary, 1987, pp. 139–81

Baucom, D. H., Epstein, N. 1990. *Cognitive-Behavioral Marital Therapy.* New York: Brunner/Mazel

Baucom, D. H., Epstein, N., Sayers, S., Goldman Sher, T. 1989a. The role of cognitions in marital relationships: definitional, methodological, and conceptual issues. *J. Consult. Clin. Psychol.* 57:31–38

Baucom, D. H., Hoffman, J. A. 1986. The effectiveness of marital therapy: current status and application to the clinical setting. See Jacobson & Gurman 1986, pp. 597–620

Baucom, D. H., Sayers, S. L., Duhe, A. 1986b. Attributional style and attributional patterns among married couples. *J. Pers. Soc.* 56:596–607

Bancroft, J., Hawton, K., Simkin, S., Kingston, B., Cumming, C., Whitwell, D. 1979. The reasons people give for taking overdoses: a further inquiry. *Br. J. Med. Psychiatr.* 52:353–65

Beach, S. R. H., O'Leary, K. D. 1985. Current status of outcome research in marital therapy. See L'Abate 1985, pp. 1035–72

Beach, S. R. H., Sandeen, E. E., O'Leary, K. D. 1990. *Depression in Marriage: A Model for Etiology and Treatment.* New York: Guilford

Bednar, R. L., Burlingame, G. M., Masters, K. S. 1988. Systems and family treatment. *Annu. Rev. Psychol.* 39:401–34

Bentler, P. M., Newcomb, M. D. 1978. Longitudinal study of marital success and failure. *J. Consult. Clin. Psychol.* 46:1053–70

Birchler, G. R., Webb, L. 1977. A social learning formulation of discriminating interaction behaviors in happy and unhappy marriages. *J. Consult. Clin. Psychol.* 45:494–95

Block, J. 1971. *Lives Through Time.* Berkeley, CA: Bancroft

Boelens, W., Emmelkamp, P., MacGillavry, D., Markvoort, M. 1980. *Behav. Anal. Modif.* 4:85–96

Bowlby, J. 1969. *Attachment and Loss:* Vol. 1. *Attachment.* New York: Basic Books

Bowlby, J. 1973. *Attachment and Loss:* Vol. 2. *Separation: Anxiety and Anger.* New York: Basic Books

Bowlby, J. 1980. *Attachment and Loss:* Vol. 3. *Loss.* New York: Basic Books

Bradbury, T. N., Fincham, F. D. 1990. Attributions in marriage: review and critique. *Psychol. Bull.* 107:3–33

Broderick, J. 1981. A method for derivation of areas for assessment in marital relationships. *Am. J. Fam. Ther.* 9:25–34

Browne, A. 1988. Family homicide. In *Handbook of Family Violence,* ed. V. B. Van Hasselt, R. L. Morrison, A. S. Bellack, M. Hersen, pp. 271–89. New York: Plenum

Burgess, E. W., Wallin, P. 1953. *Engagement and Marriage.* New York: Lippincott

Buss, D. M. 1984a. Marital assortment for personality dispositions: assessment with three different data sources. *Behav. Genet.* 14:111–23

Buss, D. M. 1984b. Toward a psychology of person-environment (PE) correlation: the role of spouse selection. *J. Pers. Soc.* 47:361–77

Buss, D. M. 1985. Human mate selection. *Am. Sci.* 73:47–51

Camper, P. M., Jacobson, N. S., Holtzworth-Munroe, A., Schmaling, K. B. 1988. Causal attributions for interactional behaviors in married couples. *Cogn. Ther. Res.* 12:195–209

Caspi, A., Herbener, E. S. 1990. Continuity and change: assortative marriage and the consistency of personality in adulthood. *J. Pers. Soc. Psychol.* 58:250–58

Cattell, R. B., Nesselroade, J. R. 1967. Likeness and completeness theories examined by the 16 P.F. measures on stably and unstably married couples. *J. Pers. Soc.* 7:351–61

Clark, M. S., Reiss, H. T. 1988. Interpersonal processes in close relationships. *Annu. Rev. Psychol.* 39:106–72

Costa, L. A. 1981. *The effects of a marriage encounter program on marital communication, dyadic adjustment, and the quality of the interpersonal relationship.* PhD thesis. Univ. Colo., Boulder

Coyne, J. C. 1986. Strategic marital therapy for depression. See Jacobson & Gurman 1986, pp. 495–511

DeYoung, G. E., Fleischer, B. 1976. Motivational and personality trait relationships in mate selection. *Behav. Genet.* 6:1–6

Dicks, H. V. 1967. *Marital Tensions.* New York: Basic Books

Emery, R. E. 1989. *Marriage, Divorce, and Children's Adjustment.* Beverly Hills: Sage

Feeney, J. A., Noller, P. 1990. Attachment style as a predictor of adult romantic relationships. *J. Pers. Soc. Psychol.* 58:281–91

Fincham, F. D., Bradbury, T. N. 1990. Cognition in marriage: a program of research on attributions. In *Advances in Personal Relationships,* ed. D. Perlman, W. Jones, Vol. 2, JAI Press. In press

Fincham, F. D., O'Leary, K. D. 1983. Causal inferences for spouse behavior in maritally distressed and nondistressed couples. *J. Soc. Clin. Psychol.* 1:42–57

Framo, J. 1976. Family origin as a therapeutic resource for adults in marital and family therapy: You can and should go home again. *Fam. Process* 15:193–210

Giovacchini, P. 1965. Treatment of marital disharmonies: the classical approach. In *The Psychotherapies of Marital Disharmony,* ed. B. L. Greene. New York: Free Press

Gottman, J. M. 1979. *Marital Interaction: Experimental Investigations.* New York: Academic

Gottman, J. M., Krokoff, L. J. 1989. Marital interaction and satisfaction: a longitudinal view. *J. Consult. Clin. Psychol.* 57:47–52

Gottman, J. M., Levenson, R. W. 1985. A valid procedure for obtaining self-report of affect in marital interaction. *J. Consult. Clin. Psychol.* 53:151–60

Gottman, J. M., Levenson, R. W. 1986. Assessing the role of emotion in marriage. *Behav. Assess.* 8:31–48

Gottman, J. M., Markman, H., Notarius, C. 1977. The topography of marital conflict: a sequential analysis of verbal and nonverbal behavior. *J. Marriage* 39:461–77

Gottman, J. M., Notarius, C., Markman, H., Bank, S., Yoppi, B., et al. 1976. Behavior exchange theory and marital decision making. *J. Pers. Soc. Psychol.* 34:14–23

Guerney, B. Jr. 1977. *Relationship Enhancement: Skill Training Programs for Therapy, Problem Prevention, and Enrichment.* San Francisco: Jossey-Bass

Guerney, B. G., Guerney, L., Cooney, T. 1985. Marital and family problem prevention and enrichment programs. See L'Abate 1985, pp. 1179–1217

Gurman, A. S., Kniskern, D. P. 1978. Research on marital and family therapy: Progress, perspective, and prospect. In *Handbook of Psychotherapy and Behavior Change: An Empirical Analysis,* ed. S. L. Garfield, A. E. Bergin, pp. 817–901. New York: Wiley. 2nd ed.

Hahlweg, K., Markman, H. J. 1988. Effectiveness of behavioral marital therapy: empirical status of behavioral techniques in preventing and alleviating marital distress. *J. Consult. Clin. Psychol.* 56:440–47

Hahlweg, K., Reisner, L., Kohli, G., Vollmer, M., Schindler, L., et al. 1984. Development and validity of a new system to analyze interpersonal communication: Kategoriensystem für partnerschaftliche Interaktion. In *Marital Interaction: Analysis and Modification,* ed. K. Hahlweg, N. S. Jacobson, pp. 182–98. New York: Guilford

Hahlweg, K., Schindler, L., Revenstorf, D., Brengelmann, J. C. 1984. The Munich marital therapy study. In *Marital Interaction: Analysis and Modification.* ed. K. Hahlweg, N. S. Jacobson, pp. 1–26. New York: Guilford

Hazan, C., Shaver, P. 1987. Romantic love conceptualized as an attachment process. *J. Pers. Soc. Psychol.* 52:511–24

Heiss, J., Gordon, M. 1964. Need patterns and the mutual satisfaction of dating and engaged couples. *J. Marriage* 26:337

Hendrick, C., Hendrick, S. 1989. Research on love: Does it measure up? *J. Pers. Soc.* 56:784–94

Holtzworth-Munroe, A. 1988. Causal attributions in marital violence: theoretical and methodological issues. *Clin. Psychol.* 8:331–44

Holtzworth-Munroe, A., Jacobson, N. S. 1985. Causal attributions of married couples: When do they search for causes? What do they conclude when they do? *J. Pers. Soc. Psychol.* 48:1398–1412

Hooley, J. M. 1986. An introduction to EE measurement and research. In *Treatment of Schizophrenia: Family Assessment and*

Intervention, ed. M. J. Goldstein, K. Hahlweg. Berlin: Springer-Verlag

Huston, T. L., Levinger, G. 1987. Interpersonal attraction and relationships. *Annu. Rev. Psychol.* 29:115–56

Jackson, D. N. 1967. *Personality Research Form Manual.* Goshen, NY: Research Psychologists Press

Jacobson, N. S., Follette, W. C., Elwood, R. W. 1984. Outcome research on behavioral marital therapy: a methodological and conceptual appraisal. In *Marital Interaction: Analysis & Modification,* ed. K. Hahlweg, N. S. Jacobson, pp. 113–29. New York: Guilford

Jacobson, N. S., Gurman, A. S., eds. 1986. *Clinical Handbook of Marital Therapy.* New York: Guilford. 657 pp.

Jacobson, N. S., Holtzworth-Munroe, A. 1986. Marital therapy: a social learning-cognitive perspective. See Jacobson & Gurman 1986, pp. 29–70

Jacobson, N. S., Holtzworth-Munroe, A., Schmaling, K. B. 1989. Marital therapy and spouse involvement in the treatment of depression, agoraphobia, and alcoholism. *J. Consult. Clin. Psychol.* 57:5–10

Jacobson, N. S., McDonald, D. W., Follette, W. C., Berley, R. A. 1985. Attributional processes in distressed and nondistressed married couples. *Cogn. Ther. Res.* 9:35–50

Jacobson, N. S., Moore, D. 1981. Spouses as observers of the events in their relationship. *J. Consult. Clin. Psychol.* 49:269–77

Jacobson, N. S., Schmaling, K. B., Holtzworth-Munroe, A., Klatt, J. L., Wood, L. F., Follette, V. 1989. Research structured vs clinically flexible versions of social learning-base treatments. *Behav. Res. Ther.* 27:173–80

Jensen, A. R. 1978. Genetic and behavioral effects of nonrandom mating. In *Human Variation: Biopsychology of Age, Race, and Sex,* ed. R. T. Osborne, C. E. Noble, N. Wey, pp. 51–151. New York: Academic

Johnson, S. M., Greenberg, L. S. 1985. Differential effects of experiential and problem-solving interventions in resolving marital conflict. *J. Consult. Clin. Psychol.* 53:175–84

Kelley, H. H. 1983. Love and commitment. In *Close Relationships,* ed. H. H. Kelley et al. New York: W. H. Freeman

Kelly, E. L., Conley, J. J. 1987. Personality and compatibility: a prospective analysis of marital stability and marital satisfaction. *J. Pers. Soc. Psychol.* 52:27–40

Klerman, G. L., Weissman, M. M. 1990. Increasing rates of depression. *J. Am. Med. Assoc.* 61:2229–35

L'Abate, L., ed. 1985. *Handbook of Family Psychology and Therapy:* Vol. 2. Homewood, IL: Dorsey

Levenson, R. W., Gottman, J. M. 1983. Marital interaction: physiological linkage and affective exchange. *J. Pers. Soc. Psychol.* 45:587–97

Levenson, R. W., Gottman, J. M. 1985. Physiological and affective predictors of change in relationship satisfaction. *J. Pers. Soc. Psychol.* 49:85–94

Levinger, G. 1964. Note on need complementarity in marriage. *Psychol. Bull.* 61:153–57

Levy, M. B., Davis, K. E. 1988. Lovestyles and attachment styles compared: their relations to each other and to various relationship characteristics. *J. Soc. Pers. Psychol.* 5:439–71

Locke, H. J., Wallace, K. M. 1959. Short marital-adjustment and prediction tests: their reliability and validity. *Marriage Fam. Living* 21:251–55

Main, M., Kaplan, N., Cassidy, J. 1985. Security in infancy, childhood, and adulthood: a move to the level of representation. *Monogr. Soc. Res. Child Dev.* 50:66–104

Margolin, G. 1981. Behavioral exchange in happy and unhappy marriages: a family cycle perspective. *Behav. Ther.* 72:329–43

Margolin, G. 1983. Behavioral marital therapy: Is there a place for passion, play, and other non-negotiable dimensions? *Behav. Ther.* 6:65–68

Margolin, G. 1987. Marital therapy: a cognitive-behavioral-affective approach. In *Psychotherapists in Clinical Practice: Cognitive and Behavioral Perspectives,* ed. N. S. Jacobson, pp. 232–85. New York: Guilford. 451 pp.

Margolin, G., Wampold, B. E. 1981. Sequential analysis of conflict and accord in distressed and nondistressed marital partners. *J. Consult. Clin. Psychol.* 49:554–67

Markman, H. J. 1981. Prediction of marital distress: a 5-year follow-up. *J. Consult. Clin. Psychol.* 49:760–62

Markman, H., Floyd, F., Stanley, S., Storassi, R. 1988. Prevention of marital distress: a longitudinal investigation. *J. Consult. Clin. Psychol.* 56:210–17

Mascie-Taylor, C. G. N., Vandenberg, S. G. 1988. Assortative mating for IQ and personality due to propinquity and personal preference. *Behav. Genet.* 18:339–45

McCrady, B. S., Noel, N. E., Abrahams, D. B., Stout, R. L., Nelson, H. F., Hay, W. M. 1986. Comparative effectiveness of three types of spouse involvement in outpatient behavioral alcoholism treatment. *J. Stud. Alcohol* 47:459–67

Meyer, J. P., Pepper, S. 1977. Need compatibility and marital adjustment in young married couples. *J. Pers. Soc.* 35:331–42

Miller, S., Nunnally, E. W., Wackman, D. B. 1976. Minnesota couples communication program (MCCP): premarital and marital groups. In *Treating Relationships*, ed. D. H. L. Ohlson. Lake Mills, Iowa: Graphic Publishing

Mittleman, B. 1948. Concurrent analysis of marital couples. *Psychoanal. Q.* 17:182–97

Most, R., Guerney, B. 1983. An empirical evaluation of the training of lay volunteer leaders for premarital relationship enhancement. *Fam. Relat.* 32:239–51

Murray, H. 1938. *Explorations in Personality.* New York: Oxford Univ. Press

Murstein, B. I. 1961. A complementary need hypothesis in newly wed and middle aged couples. *J. Abnorm. Soc.* 63:194–97

Murstein, B. I. 1976. *Who Will Marry Whom? Theories and Research in Marital Choice.* New York: Springer

Murstein, B. I., Beck, G. D. 1972. Person perception, marriage adjustment, and social desirability. *J. Consult. Clin. Psychol.* 39:396–403

Neidig, P. H., Friedman, D. H. 1984. *Spouse Abuse: A Treatment Program for Couples.* Champaign, IL: Research Press

O'Leary, K. D., ed. 1987. *Assessment of Marital Discord: An Integration for Research and Clinical Practice.* Hillsdale, NJ: Lawrence Erlbaum. 379 pp.

O'Leary, K. D., Arias, I. 1983. The influence of marital therapy on sexual satisfaction. *J. Sex Marriage Ther.* 3:171–81

O'Leary, K. D., Beach, S. R. H. 1990. Marital therapy: a viable treatment for depression and marital discord. *Am. J. Psychiatr.* 147:183–86

O'Leary, K. D., Fincham, F., Turkewitz, H. 1983. Assessment of positive feelings toward spouse. *J. Consult. Clin. Psychol.* 51:949–51

O'Leary, K. D., Turkewitz, H. 1978. Marital therapy from a behavioral perspective. See Paolino & McCrady 1978, pp. 240–97

O'Leary, K. D., Vivian, D. 1990. Physical aggression in marriage. In *Psychology of Marriage*, ed. F. Fincham, T. Bradbury. New York: Guilford

O'Leary, K. D., Wilson, G. T. 1987. *Behavior Therapy: Application and Outcome*, pp. 253–67. Englewood Cliffs, NJ: Prentice Hall. 2nd ed.

Paolino, T. J. Jr., McCrady, B. S. 1978. *Marriage and Marital Therapy: Psychoanalytic, Behavioral and Systems Theory Perspectives.* New York: Brunner/Mazel. 586 pp.

Phillips, K., Fulker, D. W., Carey, G., Nagoshi, C. T. 1988. Direct marital assort-

ment for cognitive and personality variables. *Behav. Genet.* 18:347–56

Ross, E. R. 1981. *Comparative effectiveness of relationship enhancement and therapist-preferred therapy on marital adjustment.* PhD thesis. Penn. State Univ., University Park

Sager, C. J. 1976. *Marriage Contracts and Couple Therapy.* New York: Brunner/Mazel

Schaap, C. 1984. A comparison of the interaction of distressed and nondistressed married couples in a laboratory situation: literature survey, methodological issues, and an empirical investigation. In *Marital Interaction: Analysis and Modification*, ed. K. Hahlweg, N. S. Jacobson, pp. 133–58. New York: Guilford

Schacter, J., O'Leary, K. D. 1985. Affective intent and impact in marital communication. *Am. J. Fam. Ther.* 13:17–23

Schutz, W. C. 1958. *FIRO: A Three-Dimensional Theory of Interpersonal Behavior.* New York: Rinehart

Shaver, P., Hazan, C. 1988. A biased overview of the study of love. *J. Soc. Pers. Psychol.* 5:473–501

Shaver, P., Hazan, C., Bradshaw, D. 1988. Love as attachment: the integration of three behavioral systems. In *The Anatomy of Love*, ed. R. J. Sternberg, M. L. Barnes, pp. 68–99. New Haven, CT: Yale Univ. Press

Skynner, A. C. R. 1976. *Systems of Family and Marital Psychotherapy.* New York: Brunner/Mazel

Smith, D. A., O'Leary, K. D. 1987. *Affective components of problem-solving communication and their relationships with interspousal aggression.* Presented at 3rd Natl. Fam. Violence Conf., Univ. New Hamp., Durham, NH

Smith, D. A., Vivian, D., O'Leary, K. D. 1990. Longitudinal prediction of marital discord from premarital expressions of affect. *J. Consult. Clin. Psychol.* In press

Snyder, D. N., Wills, R. M. 1989. Behavioral versus insight-oriented marital therapy: effects on individual and interspousal functioning. *J. Consult. Clin. Psychol.* 57:39–46

Stewart, R. H., Peters, T. C., Marsh, S., Peters, M. J. 1975. An object-relations approach to psychotherapy with marital couples, families and children. *Fam. Process* 14:161–78

Stuart, R. B. 1969. Operant interpersonal treatment for marital discord. *J. Consult. Clin. Psychol.* 33:675–82

Swensen, C. H. Jr. 1985. Love in the family. See L'Abate 1985, pp. 357–77

Terman, L. M., Oden, M. H. 1947. *The Gifted Child Grows Up: Twenty-Five Year*

Follow-Up of a Superior Group. Stanford, CA: Stanford Univ. Press

Tharp, R. G. 1963. Psychological patterning in marriage. *Psychol. Bull.* 60:97–117

Tharp, R. G. 1964. Reply to Levinger's note. *Psychol. Bull.* 61:158–60

Thibault, J., Kelly, H. 1959. *The Social Psychology of Groups.* New York: Wiley

Ting-Toomey, S. 1983. An analysis of verbal communication patterns in high and low marital adjustment groups. *Hum. Commun.* 9:306–19

Uhr, L. M. 1957. *Personality changes during marriage.* PhD thesis. Univ. Mich., Ann Arbor

US Bureau of the Census. 1990. *Statistical Abstract of the United States.* 1990. Washington, DC: USGPO

Vaillant, G. E. 1978. Natural history of male psychological health. VI. Correlates of successful marriage and fatherhood. *Am. J. Psychiatr.* 135:653–59

Vandenberg, S. G. 1972. Assortative mating, or who marries whom? *Behav. Genet.* 2:127–57

Yeroff, J., Kulka, R. A., Douvan, E. 1981. *Mental Health in America: Patterns of Help Seeking from 1957 to 1976.* New York: Basic Books

Wallerstein, J. S., Kelly, J. B. 1980. *Surviving the Breakup: How Children Actually Cope with Divorce.* New York: Basic Books

Wampler, K. S. 1982. The effectiveness of the Minnesota Couple Communication Training Program: a review of research. *J. Marriage Fam.* 8:345–55

Weiss, R. L. 1984. Cognitive and behavioral measures of marital interaction. In *Marital Interaction: Analysis and Modification,* ed. K. Hahlweg, N. S., Jacobson. pp. 232–52. New York: Guilford

Wiggins, J. S. 1979. A psychological taxonomy of trait descriptive terms: the interpersonal domain. *J. Pers. Soc. Psychol.* 37:395–412

Williams, A. M. 1979. The quantity and quality of marital interaction related to marital satisfaction: a behavioral analysis. *J. Appl. Behav. Anal.* 12:665–78

Winch, R. F. 1958. *Mate-Selection: A Study of Complementary Needs.* New York: Harper

Winch, R. F., Ktsanes, T., Ktsanes, V. 1954. The theory of complementary needs in mate selection: an analytic and descriptive study. *Am. Sociol. Rev.* 19:241–49

Zigler, E. 1985. Foreward. See L'Abate 1985, pp. x–xii

Annu. Rev. Psychol. 1991. 42:213–37

MOTOR SKILL ACQUISITION

K. M. Newell

Department of Kinesiology, University of Illinois at Urbana-Champaign, Urbana, Illinois 61801

KEY WORDS: motor learning, coordination, motor control, information, representation and action

CONTENTS

INTRODUCTION

Motor skills are usually distinguished from perceptual skills, cognitive skills, communicative skills, and other skill categories; but clearly these traditional distinctions have been made as a matter of heuristic convenience. As a consequence, skill categories reflect primarily differences in scholarly emphasis rather than mutually exclusive avenues of scholarly enquiry. The term

213

0066-4308/91/0201-0213$02.00

motor skills usually refers to those skills in which both the movement and the outcome of action are emphasized.

In this chapter I review certain of the major theoretical issues that have guided the study of motor skill acquisition during the previous 20 years or so. Noble (1968) provided the last related review in this series. An encompassing overview of a century of motor skill acquisition research is that of Adams (1987).

Traditionally, the study of motor skill acquisition is viewed as distinct from the study of the related subdomains of motor control and motor development. Motor learning originated as a branch of experimental psychology and was labeled accordingly to distinguish it from what used to be called verbal learning. The term *motor control* originated in physiology and was taken to represent the neurophysiology of the motor system. A behavioral focus within the study of motor control was initiated with the influential edited book of Stelmach (1976), which examined the processes that support the control of movement. Motor control has since become the predominant theoretical interest of researchers with a behavioral interest in motor skills. Furthermore, with physiology increasingly using macrolevel behavioral experimental strategies and psychology increasingly using more microlevel experimental strategies, it is becoming difficult to draw a line between the physiology and psychology of motor control—an issue Woodworth (1899) thought was irrelevant to the study of movement. In contrast, motor development has always been viewed as distinct from motor learning and motor control because it examined children's motor skills and placed special importance on the study of phylogenetic movement patterns.

In this review I adhere to the traditional domain distinctions and focus on adult motor skill learning. This decision is made at some conceptual cost, however, because it is becoming increasingly clear that the three subdomains of study—motor learning, motor control, and motor development—hold considerable common theoretical ground (see Wade & Whiting 1986). The linkage among these heretofore distinct areas of movement research has been stimulated by contemporary theoretical developments regarding perception and action.

The motor skill acquisition domain also falls on the boundaries of instructional theory, especially with respect to the role that a change agent (such as a teacher, instructor, or coach) may play in facilitating the acquisition of skill. This area of study is sometimes called training, particularly in engineering psychology or human factors research. The contemporary study of motor skill acquisition has tended to deemphasize the role of instructional concepts, implicitly focusing instead on self-generated motor performance enhancement within a variety of contextual and task constraints.

The basic actions of posture, locomotion, and manipulation (and their variations) allow the learner to engage in a variety of motor skills defined by a wide range of task constraints (e.g. those found in athletic, musical, industrial, military, self-help, and vocational contexts). Differences in task constraints have promoted the establishment of separate study domains in both theory and practice. Certain activities, such as those found in sport, tend to emphasize the natural whole-body actions of posture and locomotion, whereas other activities, such as those found in military man-machine contexts, tend to emphasize the manipulative activities of the hands, sometimes with the direct minimization (or even elimination) of the role of movement in the task. Models and theories of motor skill acquisition have tended, as a consequence, to be task and hence context specific. One theme of this review is that a general understanding of task constraints is necessary for the development of broad theoretical perspectives on the acquisition of motor skills.

Like many domains of study in psychology, motor skill acquisition has been influenced, albeit somewhat indirectly, by the information processing framework of the 1950s and 1960s and the subsequent development of general cognitive perspectives on action. Accordingly, I review the major contributions of these theoretical perspectives to some key issues in motor skill acquisition. These issues include: the applicability of a general law to motor skill acquisition; the question of what is learned as reflected in the acquisition of representations of action; and the role of information in motor skill learning. A more recent theoretical influence in motor skill learning research has been the ecological theory of perception and action. Once more relevant to the study of motor control, this theory now also applies to issues in motor learning.

Currently, there is no prevailing theoretical view of motor skill acquisition; indeed, there has not been one since Hull's theory fell from favor during the 1950s. This chapter, therefore reflects the theoretical eclecticism of the last 20 years, but it also indicates significant issues that a general theory of motor skill acquisition must address.

A GENERAL LAW OF MOTOR LEARNING

Investigators of motor skill acquisition have continued to eschew all-incompassing theories of learning. However, the principle that skill learning is continuous has remained an important (although often implicit) general proposition. The established continuous functions created from the learning curves for perceptual-motor skills have been reexamined and compared with the learning functions for a range of cognitive skills. As a consequence of this synthesis, A. Newell & Rosenbloom (1981) have proposed that the power law function is a general law of learning. A contrasting perspective holds that the power law is simply a special case of the general nonlinear integro-differential form of learning (Shaw & Alley 1985).

Motor Learning as a Power Law

It has been known since at least the study of Snoddy (1926) that performance time, when considered as the task criterion in perceptual-motor skills, tends to decrease with practice as a function of a power law. This finding has been replicated in a number of motor performance tasks. The most well-known example of the power law function for performance time is Crossman's (1959) between-subject demonstration of the reduction in the operator's cycle-time in making 10,000,000 cigars over a 7-year period.

A. Newell & Rosenbloom (1981) have discerned the power law function for practice effects in skills beyond those usually classified as perceptual-motor. Indeed, they showed that the general power law fits the practice data much better than exponential functions for a range of cognitive tasks in which performance time is the critical dependent variable. They explained the power law description of learning across tasks with a chunking model of information processing in skill learning, based in part upon Miller's (1956) classic account of information capacity limitations.

The generality of the power law for practice over a range of performance tasks leads naturally to the proposal that it is a universal law of learning not limited to a particular behavioral subdomain; but several limitations of the power law interpretation must be addressed. First, the power law function is typically demonstrated in tasks where time is the dependent variable. There is little evidence of a power law for other motor performance variables. Second, a power law cannot accommodate practice effects where the task dependent variable is on an ordinal scale, such as producing a given set of relative motions. In this situation, the qualitative properties of the coordination mode may change from trial to trial, leading to discontinuous changes over practice time in performance measures. Third, even if performance changes on one variable (even the task criterion variable) as a power law, parallel qualitative changes may occur on other dimensions of performance.

These potential limitations of power law interpretations for both motor skill acquisition and learning in general have not been examined directly owing to (a) the narrow range of task constraints currently used to examine motor performance; (b) the fact that multiple dependent variables are rarely measured in motor learning studies; and (c) the fact that long-term practice studies are now rarely conducted, even in the motor skills domain. In spite of these reservations, the power law function for learning has gained a considerable foothold as the most robust and best-known feature of motor learning (Logan 1988; Salmoni 1989). Indeed, Logan (1988) has remarked that any theory of motor skill acquisition that does not accommodate the power law function for learning can be rejected immediately.

The Power Law—A Special Case of Motor Learning?

A different approach is to view the power law for practice effects in perceptual-motor skills as a special case of learning. That is, in spite of the apparent generality of the power law for practice effects across tasks, studies have still only examined tasks in a narrow segment of the potential state space of learning. In this view, learning is discontinuous or nonlinear, and the constraints of the experimental tasks chosen for study have allowed only the linear portions of that state space to be reflected in the emergent motor performance. Thus, narrow task selection may have served to confirm the a priori theory of a continuous state space for learning that has been exemplified, for example, in information processing models of performance. In the same way, narrow theorizing may have confirmed the a priori selection of highly constrained perceptual-motor and cognitive laboratory tasks for examination. Theory construction and task selection in motor learning have been mutually supporting but limiting endeavors (Newell 1989; Newell et al 1989).

The traditional associative theories of learning (Guthrie, Hull, Thorndike), upon which early motor learning theories were predominantly based, causally specified cumulative continuous changes in behavior. The strength of the representation of movement, such as an S-R bond, was seen to change in a continuous fashion. The more recent motor learning theories of Adams (1971) and Schmidt (1975) have implicitly reiterated this position by accepting the gradual build-up, over practice, of the strength of their respective memory constructs for movement control. Thus the prevailing theoretical bias, together with the accompanying limitation of research tools that emphasize linear analysis techniques (Greeno 1974), has helped sustain continuity as the null hypothesis of the laws of learning.

Shaw & Alley (1985) have outlined, from an ecological perspective on perception and action, a discontinuous or nonlinear approach to considering the laws of learning. They treat perception and action as dual entities in the mathematical sense that the values assumed by the function for perception constrain the course of values assumed by the function for action, and vice versa. Learning is the lawful operation that increases the coordination between the perception and action functions. This proposition treats learning as a functional rather than a function because the learning-to-learn source of variance that coordinates the perception and action dual is a function of functions. Shaw & Alley draw on the field of hereditary mechanics to provide a physical analogy to model the dissipative nature of the learning functional and propose that it will prove to be nonlinear. Within this broader nonlinear view of the laws of learning, the continuous changes in motor performance are considered a special case.

The continuity-discontinuity controversy surrounding the laws of learning can only be examined empirically through consideration of a broader set of task constraints than have been manipulated in traditional and contemporary motor learning studies. The tests to date of the laws of learning have been biased toward confirming the continuity hypothesis as a consequence of the few tasks selected (usually single-degree-of-freedom tasks, such as linear positioning) and the limited amount of practice conducted over a single session (often no more than 100 trials). These task and practice limitations typically require the subject to learn only the scaling of movement amplitude, movement time, or force output in an already established coordination mode (Newell 1985). Rarely studied are the qualitative shifts in the movement dynamics that occur early in the exploratory phase of practice, or the qualitative changes that occur late in practice as a function of the flexible and adaptive qualities of the skilled performer.

Examinations of Shaw & Alley's (1985) proposal of nonlinear integro-differential learning functions for motor skill acquisition require an enriched perceptual-motor environment rather than an impoverished one. An enriched perceptual environment, following Gibson (1966, 1979), has several informational invariants available that could be utilized to organize a stable coordination mode. In the same way, an enriched action environment, following Kugler & Turvey (1987), has several coordination modes that may suffice to provide stable solutions to the task constraints. The mapping of the perceptual informational invariants to the movement kinetic invariants reflects the learning or search through the perceptual-motor workspace.

Shaw & Alley's (1985) proposal emphasizes motor skill acquisition as the learning of the laws that map the dynamics of perception and action, rather than the memory intensive rule-based procedures that reflect what have been loosely called the laws of learning. No direct tests of the Shaw & Alley hypothesis have been conducted, although qualitative changes in the movement dynamics as a function of practice have recently been demonstrated in learning to write (Newell & van Emmerick 1989), throw darts (McDonald et al 1989), juggle (Beek 1989), and ride a ski-simulator (van Emmerick et al 1989). The examination of tasks with a richer perceptual-motor environment than provided by the traditional single-degree-of-freedom tasks (such as linear positioning) is likely to open the door to a more ecologically relevant description and explanation of motor skill acquisition.

As a contrast to Logan's (1988) statement about the primacy of the power law, I suggest that a theory that cannot explain the qualitative discontinuous changes in movement dynamics with practice will lack generality. The experimental strategy of examining the discontinuities of practice effects will also afford an understanding of their continuities. Current evidence suggests that the reverse theoretical and empirical strategy, which has dominated the motor skill acquisition field for the last 100 years, has failed to offer general accounts of the laws of learning.

WHAT IS LEARNED WITH PRACTICE

A fundamental assumption of traditonal and most contemporary theories of motor skill acquisition is that learning is a consequence of the acquisition of more appropriate representations of action. That is, the improved performance over time is due to the acquisition of prescriptions for action that specify the movement dynamics in relation to the task demands. In general, theoretical propositions about the representation of action have shifted over the last two decades from a one-to-one to a one-to-many relation between what is represented and the movement sequence that is produced.

One-To-One Recall-Recognition Processes

A major influence on the motor skill acquisition domain was Adam's (1971) closed-loop theory of motor learning, which proposed a two-state representational scheme for the learning of self-paced positioning movements. One memory state was the *memory trace,* whose role was to select and initiate the movement. The strength of the memory trace was seen as a function of stimulus-response contiguity; it grew as a function of practice trials. The second memory state was the *perceptual trace* which was the image of the correctness of the desired movement; it was based upon prior experience of the sensory consequences (both exteroceptive and proprioceptive) of action. Each movement created a set of associated sensory consequences, and the distribution of these sensory consequences from practice trials formed a modal perceptual trace or memory reference for matching the task demands at hand. In single-degree-of-freedom positioning movements the memory trace had a limited role (what Adams called a modest motor program), and the skill in the task in essence resulted from the formation of an appropriate perceptual trace to evaluate the on-going sensory consequences of movement.

Adam's proposal of two independent memory states for movement initiation and movement evaluation was based primarily on two considerations. First was the logical argument that error nulling closed-loop procedures could not occur if a single mechanism both initiated and evaluated the movement. This was because the sensory consequences of the on-going movement would always be compared against a representation of itself. Second, evidence in the verbal learning domain that recall and recognition could be independently manipulated by certain learning variables supported the proposition that these processes were based on independent memory states. The theory thus proposed dual one-to-one memory processes for the recall and recognition of movement.

Adam's theory stimulated a number of empirical studies of the two-state memory proposal for motor learning in positioning tasks (Adams & Goetz

1973; Adams et al 1972). Other investigators branched out from the confines of slow positioning movements and examined the recall and recognition processes that support rapid short-duration movements, because such movements allowed a cleaner operational distinction between movement initiation and evaluation processes (Newell 1974; Schmidt & White 1972). These experiments demonstrated that the development of movement recognition processes over practice trials with knowledge of results (KR) paralleled those that had traditionally been found for movement recall processes.

A direct test of the two-state recall and recognition memory proposal for movement was conducted by Newell & Chew (1974). After sufficient practice with KR to develop the movement recall and recognition processes, withdrawal of visual and auditory feedback of the movement produced an immediate decrement in movement recognition but not in recall. This differential effect of the feedback variables on recall and recognition processes was taken as evidence for a two-state memory system for movement control.

The concept of independent recall and recognition processes for movement control was preserved in Schmidt's (1975) schema theory of motor learning (see below). The direct empirical examination of the dual-state memory concept for motor learning did not, however, receive subsequent empirical attention. The general influence of the Adams's (1971) theory of motor skill learning faded rapidly with the arrival of schema theory, in part because Adams's theoretical contributions were largely encapsulated within the schema theory. Furthermore, theoretical emphasis in motor control switched from closed-loop to open-loop processes (Keele & Summers 1976; Schmidt 1976) where the role of recognition in both motor control and motor learning was downplayed.

The beginnings of the ecological approach to perception and action were introduced via a challenge both to the two-state concept and to representational accounts of action in general. Turvey (1974) proposed that the problems facing perception theorists and action theorists were very similar. Consequently, similar principles were needed for their solution that would probably prove indigenous to neither. Fowler & Turvey (1978) subsequently outlined a new approach to motor skill acquisition that was based on the emerging ecological perspective on movement coordination and control (Turvey 1977; Turvey et al 1978). A key principle of this perspective was that coordination is a relation defined over the organism and the environment, and that control is the exclusive prerogative of neither. This idea provided a major challenge to prescriptive theories that viewed motor skill learning as the accumulation of more appropriate representations of action, even if these representations were of the one-to-many variety, such as proposed by schema theories.

Schema Representation of Action

Schmidt's (1975) theory of motor learning retained the independent recall and recognition mechanisms for movement advocated by Adams (1971) but gave them a generalized (one-to-many) memory construct through the concept of the schema. The schema is seen as a rule that represents the *relations* between variables rather than the absolute instantiations of the variables themselves. The schema is an old concept in psychology and neurology (e.g. Bartlett 1932; Head 1920) but its links to movement were indirect until Schmidt (1975) merged the intuitions of Pew (1974) on schema and motor learning with the two-state closed-loop theory of Adams (1971).

Two primary theoretical problems motivated the proposal for generalized memory states in motor learning (Pew 1974; Schmidt 1975). First was the storage problem; how many representations of motor programs and closed-loop references could the CNS store? Although this concern was used in support of the schema concept, there was no evidence on this issue. Second was the novelty problem; how could a given motor program in a one-to-one memory framework generate new movement configurations? The schema concept finessed these two theoretical problems. Generalizable schema rules reduced the representation demands on the memory stystem and provided the necessary principles to accommodate new aspects of movement dynamics.

In Schmidt's (1975) theory the relative contributions of the recall and recognition schemata to movement output varied with the task constraints, but the recall schema clearly played a stronger role in determining movement output than in Adams's (1971) theory. The strengths of the recall and recognition schemata were postulated to be built up over practice trials and feedback. The recall schema was based upon the past experience of the relations between the actual outcome and the response specifications. The recognition schema was based on the relations between the initial conditions for action, the movement-produced sensory consequences, and the actual outcomes (KR). The generalized rule allowed the production of so-called new movements within the class of movements for which the schema was established. A major limitation to examining the schema concept in terms of the acquisition, transfer, and retention of motor skill was that no principles were established about what represented a class of movements.

Schmidt (1975) proposed that the schemata rules became more representative of the movement class if a range of movement conditions were experienced in practice. This principle gave rise to the hypothesis that retention and transfer would be facilitated by variable practice in acquisition, because under these conditions the schema rule was both more impervious to decay and more generative in execution. The concept of variability was not limited here to the natural variability that a subject produces in movement dynamics over repeated attempts to attain the same criterion but, in addition, included the variability that accrues from structured practice under a range of task conditions.

The evidence for the benefits of variable practice has largely come from single-degree-of-freedom positioning or timing tasks in which variations in the amplitude or movement-time task constraints were made in both training (usually KR acquisition trials) and transfer (often no-KR trials). For example, Newell & Shapiro (1976) showed that variable practice in a timing task facilitated transfer to a criterion movement time that was outside the range of the initial movement-time practice conditions. McCracken & Stelmach (1977) also found transfer benefits in a timing task from variable practice over a range of amplitudes in producing the criterion movement time. Other similarly designed studies have reported either weak trends for the benefits of variable practice in transfer (e.g. Wrisberg & Ragsdale 1979) or no effects at all (e.g. Zelaznik 1977).

The early evidence for the benefits of variable practice on the transfer of motor skill was not strong (Newell 1981). Some schema studies also tended to confound the manipulation of variability of practice with differences in the similarity between acquisition and transfer task criteria. This is a significant problem because similarity of task stimulus-response conditions is the cornerstone of most traditional accounts of motor skill transfer (Holding 1976). Shapiro & Schmidt (1982) have suggested that the evidence for the benefits of variable practice is stronger in young children than in adults. Certainly a number of motor learning studies in children have demonstrated the facilitative effects of variable practice on subsequent transfer performance (e.g. Kelso & Norman 1978; Moxley 1979), but no study has conducted a direct test of the interaction of age and variable practice.

It appears that the structure of the variable practice schedule is very important in determining the resultant benefits in transfer (Lee et al 1985; Lee 1988). Random practice at a range of task criteria affords better transfer than blocked practice over the same range of practice conditions. Lee (1988) has given a transfer-appropriate processing interpretation to these and related transfer findings. He posits that learning is optimal when the processing activities promoted by the practice conditions are similar to the processing activities required by the transfer test. This view shifts transfer away from the similarity of task stimulus-response properties to similarity of information processing activities—an interpretation concordant with recent attentional theories (not reviewed here) of the acquisition of skill (Schneider & Fisk 1983; Schneider & Shiffren 1977; Shiffren & Schneider 1977).

The process of schema formation is poorly understood. Schmidt (1975) and Keele & Summers (1976) assumed that the schema rule was based on the invariant relations of the movement dynamics, which were independent of the specific muscle groups involved. These invariant characteristics of a movement sequence may not, however, require representation. Indeed, the demonstration of movement invariances in a range of tasks may be a reflection of emergent properties of some other level of organization of the motor system.

Motor learning needs to be reconsidered within a broader framework of how the learner solves the motor problem. This has been a general proposition of cognitive approaches to skill acquisition, but the topic has not been examined systematically from this point of view. The change in performance with practice needs to be examined on an individual-subject basis over individual practice trials. The analysis-of-variance approach to examining performance on blocks of trials does not sufficiently inform about the change in behavior. There have been few studies of the between-trial performance in discrete movement tasks.

Another schema view of action was outlined by Rumelhart & Ortony (1977), an extension of their schema theory for comprehension and knowledge representation. By virtue of its attempt to accommodate the transfer between subactions or classes of movement, Rumelhart & Ortony's theory provided the basis of a view of knowledge and action broader than that offered by Schmidt (1975). On the other hand, its strong roots in the comprehension domain led to its isolation from the motor skill acquisition community, and the theory failed to attract empirical or theoretical attention. A similar fate befell other schema-like cognitive theories either directly or indirectly concerned with motor skill acquisition (Anderson 1976, 1982; Arbib 1980; Norman & Rumelhart 1975; Rumelhart & Norman 1982). It remains to be seen in what way the connectionist approach to cognition will influence the study of human motor skill acquisition.

Problems with Prescriptive Accounts of Motor Learning

The theoretical perspectives on motor learning reviewed above are all prescriptive in the sense of having representational schemes at some level of analysis that prescribe the movement sequence in relation to the task constraints. Learning is viewed as the acquisition of prescriptions for action that will more appropriately satisfy the realization of the task goal. The fundamental differences among the preceding accounts of motor skill acquisition lie in the nature of the representations they posit, which are seen as reflections of what is learned with practice.

Prescriptive approaches to motor skill learning have been challenged on a number of different grounds over the last two decades. The primary challenge came from the emerging ecological approach to perception and action (Fowler & Turvey 1978; Kugler et al 1980; Kugler & Turvey 1987; Turvey & Kugler 1984). Central concerns have been the appropriateness of rule-based accounts of action and the logical difficulties of mapping symbols and dynamics in a principled fashion (Carello et al 1984). Advocates of the ecological position seek the solution in the mapping of perception and action with minimal resort to intelligent operations. Where representation is invoked, it is to be fashioned from law-based dynamic accounts of perception and action rather than from a discrete nonholonomic (non-integrable) symbol system logically separate from the dynamics. This central concern with prescriptive theories of motor skill learning gives rise to a number of subsidiary problems.

Schema theories of motor learning cannot account for the acquisition of new coordination modes or movement forms. As Kugler et al (1980) noted, it is logically difficult for rule-based schema theory to account for the instantaneous production of quadruped-like locomotion by centipedes after all but two pairs of their legs are amputated. Expressed another way, where does the centipede's instantaneous representation of a quadrupedal gait originate? In principle, the schema rule can only accommodate the new scaling of an established coordination mode, and even here, the logic for generalizability of the changing movement dynamics is questionable.

Prescriptive theories of motor learning also have trouble handling logically the compensations to perturbations of an ongoing movement sequence. How does a template-reference-of-correctness concept account for the instantaneous, anatomically distant-in-time-and-space, and functionally specific compensations evident, for example, in sudden and novel perturbations to the jaw in ongoing speech production (Kelso et al 1984)? Expressed another way, where does the closed-loop representation of correctness arise that enables compensation during novel and unexpected perturbation?

The challenge of the ecological position to extant prescriptive accounts of motor skill learning has undoubtedly weakened the influence of information-processing and cognitive accounts of motor skill acquisition in the 1980s. On the other hand, Adams's (1971) theory was limited by design to a very narrow set of task constraints, and this narrowness was fundamentally the cause of its demise. The potential generality to motor skill acquisition of the Schmidt (1975) schema theory was considerably broader but it only stimulated empirical activity on the variability of practice issue. Thus, the Adams and Schmidt theories were already a waning influence in the motor skill acquisition domain by the time the challenge to the prescriptive views arrived.

Motor Skill Acquisition as a Search Strategy

Bernstein's (1967) insights into coordination strongly influenced the development of the ecological approach to action. Bernstein (1967:127) viewed "the coordination of movement as the process of mastering redundant degrees of freedom of the moving organ, in other words its conversion to a controllable system." The process of practice was characterized as the search for the optimal motor solutions to the problem at hand. It is important to note that practicing was seen as repeating the solving of the motor problem rather than repeating a particular solution to the problem.

Consistent with the Bernstein proposals, Fowler & Turvey (1978) interpreted skill acquisition as the search for the optimization of the coordination and control function of several variables. Search strategies reflect the way the perceptual-motor workspace is explored to "solve" the motor problem (Newell et al 1989b). The perceptual-motor workspace is the interface between the relatively high-energy movement-kinetic field and the relatively low-energy information-kinematic flow field—an interface that arises from the complementary influences of the perception-action cycle (Kugler & Turvey 1987; Shaw & Alley 1985). Learning is the coordination of the perceptual environment with the action environment in a way consistent with the task constraints.

In this perspective, Gibson's (1966, 1979) insights about the informational properties that organize the perceptual environment are extended to the complementary action environment. The dynamic organization of the perceptual-motor workspace can be examined through defining the layout of the gradient and singular properties of the perceptual-motor fieldlike spaces that support the macrolevel coordination pattern. The search through this workspace can be analyzed via established search and optimization procedures from biology (Gelfand & Tsetlin 1962) and physical systems.

The significance of this orientation for motor skill acquisition is that it promises to provide a principled way to accommodate the adaptive nature of the dynamics of movement control without resort to the computation-intensive procedures advanced by the prescriptive accounts of skill learning reviewed above. The theoretical and experimental challenge becomes one of identifying critical perceptual and kinetic variables that are being exploited to channel the search for the appropriate mapping of information and movement kinetics in the perceptual-motor workspace. The promise is that there are relatively global macrolevel variables of few degrees of freedom that organize the many microlevel degrees of freedom harnessed in support of action.

A central hypothesis of the search strategy approach (Newell et al 1989b) to motor skill acquisition is that the learning, retention, and transfer of skill in different tasks is dependent on the similarity among the corresponding searches through the equilibrium regions of the perceptual-motor workspace, and relatively independent of the specific effector and manipulanda utilized. The role of search strategies in motor skill acquisition, both in tasks where the perceptual-motor workspace can be specified a priori (Krinskii & Shik 1964) and in the more natural tasks where the workspace can only be modeled post hoc, is currently being examined.

INFORMATION AND MOTOR SKILL ACQUISITION

Information facilitates the changes in motor performance that reflect learning. Different types of information are used in motor skill acquisition, and there have been a number of theoretical interpretations of the role of information. This section is organized around three themes: information as a prescription; information as feedback; and information to channel the search through the perceptual-motor workspace.

Information as a Prescription

The prescriptive accounts of motor skill learning hold that information strengthens the development of the respective memory constructs for action. The development of task-relevant prescriptions for action can be strengthened through the presentation of prior-to-movement information that specifies the to-be-produced outcome and movement dynamics. Instructions or demonstrations convey this prescriptive information (Newell 1981; Newell et al 1985a). Recent empirical work has focused on the role of demonstrations in motor skill learning.

The general evidence in support of the facilitating effect of demonstrations in motor skill acquisition is not strong. This is in part because experiments have tended to use tasks already familiar to the learner. In effect, the information conveyed via the demonstration is often redundant to the learner's task-relevant knowledge.

Bandura's (1977, 1986) social learning theory has stimulated a systematic set of empirical studies on the role of demonstrations in motor skill learning. The theory offers a generative schema-like account of motor learning in which the spatial and temporal elements of the movement are symbolically coded through perceptual cues. The coding of the perceptual cues allows the development of the reference against which movement may be successively modified by appropriate feedback, and used for covert rehearsal techniques. Thus, in this view feedback information is only useful in learning when the appropriate movement reference has been developed.

Carroll & Bandura (1982, 1985, 1987) have examined aspects of these theoretical ideas in a series of experiments that required subjects to learn separate arm and hand postures with specific movements between postures as a function of different modeling and visual control conditions. The results have shown that visual feedback is not useful in the early trials of learning the postural sequences, but it facilitates learning subsequently in the practice sequence; delayed visual monitoring of the just-produced movement does not affect the acquisition process; and the stronger the movement representation (as determined by independent procedures) the more accurate are the subsequent recognition and reproduction of the action patterns. The use of a task that requires the production of a novel movement coordination sequence was instrumental in revealing these systematic effects of observational learning. However, early in practice, learners may not always be able to produce the new coordination mode demonstrated by the model (Martens et al 1976).

Movement related demonstrations can be made to the learner via sensory systems other than the visual system. Newell (1976a) and Zelaznik et al (1978) have shown that auditory demonstrations of the sound associated with rapid movements can effectively convey information about the task movement dynamics. Indeed, in these auditory demonstration protocols, subjects reduced their timing error over a series of practice trials in the absence of KR.

Demonstrations can also provide information about procedural aspects of the task demands that are not directly related to the movement dynamics. In a recent study of different types of augmented information in learning a video-game task, Newell et al (1989a) found that the demonstration of game procedural information was more effective in improving game performance over a 10-hr training period than information and specific practice on the isolated components of the movement dynamics. This finding reveals another way task properties mediate the nature of the appropriate information to support motor skill acquisition.

A major challenge for the motor skill acquisition domain is to understand the nature of the information conveyed in a demonstration. Bandura's (1977, 1986) social learning model fails to address this issue and, in effect, holds that all aspects of the movement dynamics are in some way coded in a memory construct. Schmidt's (1975) schema theory proposed that the relative motion invariances are stored in memory, but no perceptual recognition tests of this hypothesis have been conducted. A perceptual orientation to demonstrations that attempts to understand what information for action is conveyed by a model offers a new approach to this problem (Newell 1985; Scully & Newell 1986).

Information as Feedback

Information feedback is available to the learner both during the ongoing movement sequence (concurrent feedback) and on completion of the movement sequence (terminal feedback). In either case, information can be provided about the outcome of the movement (KR) and/or some aspect of the ongoing movement dynamics (sometimes called knowledge of performance). Information feedback can also be naturally available through the inherent properties of the task constraints, or it can be supplemented via augmented information (i.e. information not normally available from engagement in the task). The distinction between natural and augmented information feedback is not absolute and is inevitably task dependent. The working assumption of the feedback literature has been that the natural and augmented types of information feedback operate on the same principles, but no direct tests of this intuition have been conducted.

CONCURRENT INFORMATION FEEDBACK   There is a long tradition of study-ing the influence of concurrent information feedback on motor skill learning

(Annett 1969; Armstrong 1970). Many studies have demonstrated the facilitative effect of concurrent information feedback on motor performance. The contribution of information from the different sensory systems, whether it is inherent in the task or augmented, varies with the particular task constraints. The positive influence of augmented concurrent information feedback on motor performance is often negated once the supplementary information feedback is removed.

The Adams (1971) and Schmidt (1975) theories of motor skill acquisition incorporated concurrent information feedback into closed-loop accounts of motor learning. In both of these theoretical formulations the ongoing sensory consequences to movement were used in a closed-loop error detection and correction framework. The more information available from sensory channels the stronger and more representative was the development of the respective recognition memory state, which led to a better performance during both KR acquisition trials and when KR was withdrawn.

Adams et al (1972) proposed that the development of the perceptual trace for movement recognition allowed the movement to be executed accurately through concurrent information feedback without external informational support in the form of KR. The perceptual trace provided the evaluation of the movement internally—a process that Adams (1971) called subjective reinforcement. Adams et al (1972) provided evidence for this proposition by showing that positioning movements were more accurate, and that the learner was more able to evaluate the correctness of the movement, when all the sensory channels were available.

The question of what information is available from different sensory systems during movement was never addressed in the closed-loop accounts of movement control. This limitation, together with the increased emphasis given to centralist accounts of motor control during the 1970s and 1980s, contributed to the decline in the study of augmented concurrent information feedback. Concurrent information feedback can clearly have a potent impact on performance according to the task constraints and the nature of the information provided.

TERMINAL INFORMATION FEEDBACK   The presentation of information on completion of the movement sequence has traditionally proved to have a very strong influence on motor skill acquisition (Adams 1971; Bilodeau 1966; Newell 1976b). KR of the outcome of the action has continued to be studied during the past 20 years, but there has also been a new emphasis on information about the dynamics of the just-completed movement.

Adams's (1971) closed-loop theory of motor learning gave a strong role to KR as information in strengthening the two-state memory process. Both the recall and recognition states were postulated to be strengthened over KR practice trials. Schmidt's (1975) schema theory proposed similar learning principles in regard to the necessity and contiguity of KR in motor learning. The informational interpretation of KR was examined by studies that provided direct tests of the processing of KR during motor learning.

Rogers (1974) examined the idea that different precision levels of KR should have differential effects on learning according to the minimal amount of time allowed the learner for processing the information during the post-KR interval. The findings from a micrometer positioning task showed that increased precision of KR up to some point facilitated learning, beyond which decrements in performance occurred. The most beneficial level of KR precision could be changed by varying the duration of the time for information processing during the post-KR interval. Thus higher levels of KR precision could be used effectively with more time for information processing. Similar manipulations have also shown that older children can more effectively utilize more precise levels of KR precision (Newell & Kennedy 1978).

Single-degree-of-freedom positioning or timing tasks do not require much time to process the relevant KR provided. For example, Barclay & Newell (1980) showed that children of 10 years of age only used about 1.5 sec in a self-paced post-KR interval of a timing task study. This finding demonstrates that the manipulations of the post-KR interval have generally been too long to induce information processing effects (Boucher 1974; Magill 1973).

The information processing hypothesis has also been tested by imposing secondary task activity during either the KR-delay interval or the post-KR interval. The basic rationale for this manipulation was that a competing secondary task restricts the capacity remaining for processing the KR. Boucher (1974) showed that reading 4- and 5-syllable words during the post-KR interval produced a detrimental effect in learning a positioning task. In contrast, Magill (1973) failed to find interference effects as a consequence of inserting counting backwards by 3s during the post-KR interval of an angular positioning task. Marteniuk (1986) showed that the influence of information processing activity during the KR-delay interval depended on the relative difficulty of the task and the secondary activity. Thus, the findings in support of the information processing idea that the subject actively operates on the KR information are suggestive rather than decisive, and are strongly influenced by task properties.

The general interpretation of KR studies has been challenged by Salmoni et al (1984), who argue that learning effects for KR can only be inferred if the performance difference from practice with KR is sustained during a subsequent no-KR test phase, such as on a retention test. They have picked up on an earlier finding by Lavery (1962), who showed that while absolute frequency rather than relative frequency of KR presentation was the variable that determined performance level when KR was available, the reverse effect was apparent when performance was subsequently examined over a series of no-KR trials. Using a number of experimental protocols, Schmidt and colleagues (Schmidt et al 1989; Wulf & Schmidt 1989) have provided evidence that the presentation of KR on every trial may not be the most effective KR schedule if performance is to be subsequently evaluated under no-KR conditions.

This proposal for the benefits of relative versus absolute KR effect probably only holds once the learner has produced a performance that is in the ballpark of the task goal. In other words, the intermittent schedule is more appropriate to the maintenance of performance than to the acquisition of new performance states. Furthermore, performance under no-KR conditions is only one possible scenario for transfer and retention tests and therefore should not be taken as the single measure of motor learning. The findings of Schmidt and colleagues clearly suggest some modification to the traditional interpretation of the frequency effects of KR. However, they do not require the formation of new laws of KR as proposed by Salmoni et al (1984).

KR is very effective in single-degree-of-freedom tasks or tasks where the scaling of a given coordination pattern is all that is required to satisfy the task constraints. The usefulness of KR to a learner in acquiring whole body actions, or in tasks where the learner needs to establish a stable coordination mode for the task at hand, has been increasingly questioned over the last 20 years (Fowler & Turvey 1978; Gentile 1972; Newell & Walter 1981). In this situation the learner requires knowledge of performance, or information about the dynamics of the just-produced movement, in addition to KR of the outcome of the action.

Fowler & Turvey (1978) suggested that the information required in the feedback must contain as many degrees of constraint as there are degrees of freedom in the action to be coordinated. This proposal attempts to explain why the single degree of constraint provided by KR is sufficient in single-degree-of-freedom positioning or timing tasks. Newell & McGinnis (1985) suggested a framework by which to determine what information is required by a learner in a given task situation. This framework requires an understanding of the sources of constraint upon action, particularly the role of task constraints (Newell 1986). A number of experimental demonstrations of how task constraints determine the nature of information feedback required by the learner have been provided. It has also been shown that in many task conditions, the use of kinematic and kinetic information feedback facilitates motor learning and performance beyond those reached by means of the presentation of KR alone (Newell & Carlton 1987; Newell et al 1985b; Newell et al 1983, 1987).

The experimental study of kinematic and kinetic information feedback has been limited to one and two-degree-of-freedom task constraints. The generalization of this framework to whole body multiple-degree-of-freedom tasks requires an increased understanding of the nature of what is being regulated in the coordination mode. Furthermore, it needs to be understood that both KR and knowledge of the just-produced dynamics are information feedback and only tell the learner what has happened in regard to the movement dynamics and the outcome. These forms of information feedback do not directly inform the learner about what and how the action should be changed on the next trial. This limitation upon information feedback is particularly evident when a change in the qualitative properties of the coordination mode is required. In this situation a different form of informational support for motor learning is required and is discussed in the next section.

Information to Channel the Search

Information in the ecological approach to perception and action is interpreted as the means via which the learner channels the mapping of information and movement dynamics in the perceptual-motor workspace in a way consistent with the task demands (Kugler & Turvey 1987). After Gibson (1966, 1979), it is assumed that the invariant properties of the environment act as information to guide the exploratory activity of the learner. These informational properties are qualitative in nature and attune the learner to the layout of the perceptual-motor workspace. One important aspect of perceptual learning is the continued differentiation by the learner of the properties of the perceptual-motor workspace. The natural learner-generated search of the perceptual-motor workspace can be supplemented with various forms of augmented information, as described previously, to facilitate the search strategy.

The idea of a natural search through the workspace by the learner is consistent with the traditional concept of discovery learning. The evidence suggests, however, that self-discovery does not always enable the learner to locate a task-appropriate mapping of information and dynamics in the perceptual-motor workspace. Furthermore, even on the occasions where self-discovery affords attainment of the task goal, the process of learning or the search behavior can be very inefficient.

Information can be used, therefore, to channel the search through the perceptual-motor workspace to locate a task-relevant solution to the coordination function. This theoretical framework involves a three-component consideration of augmented information and skill learning (Newell 1990). The first component is understanding the nature of the perceptual-motor workspace in terms of the attractor equilibrium and gradient regions. The second component is understanding the natural search strategies used by learners to explore the space. The third component is the application of augmented information to facilitate the search. These three components are interdependent. This orientation provides a new look at the strengths and weaknesses of traditional prescriptive and feedback accounts of augmented information techniques.

Demonstrations provide some information about the nature of the desired equilibrium set of the perceptual-motor workspace, but they do not inform the learner how to navigate through the space to arrive at the task-relevant solution. In static analogy consider the problems of a traveler being given a map marked only with her current location and final destination. Furthermore, demonstrations do not accommodate the individual nature of the layout of the perceptual-motor workspace.

Information feedback, such as knowledge of results, only informs the learner of performance error in relation to the task criterion. This can be very effective when the perceptual-motor workspace supporting that activity is linear—a condition well approximated in the traditional laboratory tasks that produce the power law for learning. However, feedback cannot provide direct information about how one might search the nonlinear portions of the workspace to produce the qualitative changes necessary to realize new coordination modes.

It has been suggested that a new class of augmented information is required to promote systematic qualitative changes in the coordination mode (Newell et al 1985a; Newell, in press). This information category was labeled transition information. In effect, this information acts as another source of constraint on action in anticipation of producing a qualitative change in the coordination mode. This kind of information should prove valuable in the early stages of acquisition where the learner is attempting to find a new stable equilibrium region in the perceptual-motor workspace.

Instructors of physical activities often provide this information through instructions. The beginning golfer, for example, may be told "Keep your elbow in." The instructor does not intend the learner to keep the elbow in to this degree after she has attained the desired coordination configuration. Rather, this informational constraint acts as a control parameter to change the configuration of the coordination mode. Thus the nature of the information required by the learner seems to depend on the stage of learning. This interaction has not been examined.

Perceptual-motor skills in context have rich sources of information available, but the traditional operational strategy in motor skill acquisition experiments has been to strip away from the learner the support of this information and construct impoverished environments in which skill learning is to take place. This experimental strategy has burdened the learner by providing the constraints to learning. The result has been an emphasis on cognitive operations. The emphasis of the ecological approach to information and motor learning is intimately tied to understanding the natural dynamics of the perceptual-motor workspace.

CONCLUDING REMARKS

The information processing and cognitive frameworks have had considerable impact on concepts of motor skill acquisition domain over the last two decades. In many respects, however, this influence has been indirect. The information processing approach has been concerned primarily with performance, not learning. It has emphasized the processes that support performance. Only the attentional accounts of skill learning (not reviewed here) have treated issues of direct relevance to the changes that occur with practice.

The information processing approach has also given little or no emphasis to the question of *what* information is processed in motor skill acquisition. The focus has been on the *how* of information processing, with no direct examination of the informational support required from the learner. The schema view of motor learning promised a new way to examine the role of information in skill learning but failed to stimulate any empirical activity on this important topic. The revival of interest in learning from a cognitive perspective during the 1980s has largely been oriented to so-called cognitive tasks.

The strong influence of task constraints on motor skill learning is a key point to emerge from the foregoing synthesis. It is usually accepted that skill is specific. This conclusion may arise from the fact that even small changes in the experimental task constraints can lead to large changes in the performance of the learner. The ecological approach to perception and action has offered the beginnings of a new way to consider task analysis: in terms of the perceptual-motor workspace.

The traditional approaches to motor skill acquisition have failed to capture many of the dynamic qualities of the stages of motor skill acquisition exhibited by novice and expert performers. Skill is a reflection of a dynamic exploratory activity, not the stereotypic reproduction of a static representation of action. Current views of skill learning, such as those embedded in a power law view, have failed to capture the richness of the essence of skill and the fullness of the constraints that shape it. The effort to understand the ecologically relevant aspects of task constraints, in relation to the dynamic interface of information and movement, opens the door to a more general theory of motor skill acquisition.

ACKNOWLEDGMENTS

The preparation of this paper was supported in part by NIH grant HD 21212. I would like to thank Richard van Emmerik and Vernon McDonald for helpful comments on an earlier version of the paper.

Literature Cited

Adams, J. A. 1971. A closed-loop theory of motor learning. *J. Mot. Behav.* 3:111–50

Adams, J. A. 1987. Historical review and appraisal of research on the learning, retention, and transfer of human motor skills. *Psychol. Bull.* 101:41–74

Adams, J. A., Goetz, E. T. 1973. Feedback and practice as variables in error detection and correction. *J. Mot. Behav.* 5:217–24

Adams, J. A., Goetz, E. T., Marshall, P. H. 1972. Response feedback and motor learning. *J. Exp. Psychol.* 92:391–97

Anderson, J. R. 1976. *Language, Memory and Thought.* Hillsdale, NJ: Erlbaum. 546 pp.

Anderson, J. R. 1982. Acquisition of cognitive skill. *Psychol. Rev.* 89:369–406

Annett, J. 1969. *Feedback and Human Behavior.* Baltimore: Penguin. 196 pp.

Arbib, M. A. 1980. Interacting schemas for motor control. In *Tutorials in Motor Behavior,* ed. G. E. Stelmach, J. Requin, pp. 71–82. Amsterdam: North-Holland. 680 pp.

Armstrong, T. R. 1970. Feedback and perceptual-motor learning: a review of information feedback and manual guidance training techniques. *Tech. Rep. No. 25,* Hum. Perform. Cent., Univ. Michigan. 66 pp.

Bandura, A. 1977. *Social Learning Theory.* Englewood Cliffs, NJ: Prentice Hall. 247 pp.

Bandura, A. 1986. *Social Foundations of Thought and Action: A Social Cognitive Theory.* Englewood Cliffs, NJ: Prentice Hall. 617 pp.

Barclay, C. R., Newell, K. M. 1980. Children's processing of information in motor skill learning. *J. Exp. Child. Psychol.* 30:98–108

Bartlett, F. C. 1932. *Remembering: A Study in Experimental and Social Psychology.* London: Cambridge Univ. Press. 317 pp.

Beek, P. J. 1989. *Juggling Dynamics.* Amsterdam: Free Univ. Press. 222 pp.

Bernstein, N. A. 1967. *The Coordination and Regulation of Movement.* London: Pergamon Press. 196 pp.

Bilodeau, I. McD. 1966. Information feedback. In *Acquisition of Skill,* ed. E. A. Bilodeau, pp. 255–96. New York: Academic. 539 pp.

Boucher, J.-L. P. 1974. Higher processes in motor learning. *J. Mot. Behav.* 6:131–37

Carello, C., Turvey, M. T., Kugler, P. N., Shaw, R. E. 1984. Inadequacies of the computer metaphor. In *Handbook of Cognitive Neuroscience,* ed. M. S. Gazzaniga, pp. 229–48. New York: Plenum. 416 pp.

Carroll, W. R., Bandura, A. 1982. The role of visual monitoring in observational learning of action patterns: making the unobservable observable. *J. Mot. Behav.* 14:153–67

Carroll, W. R., Bandura, A. 1985. Role of timing of visual monitoring and motor rehearsal in observational learning of action patterns. *J. Mot. Behav.* 17:269–81

Carroll, W. R., Bandura, A. 1987. Translating cognition into action: the role of visual guidance in observational learning. *J. Mot. Behav.* 19:385–98

Crossman, E. R. F. W. 1959. A theory of the acquisition of speed-skill. *Ergonomics* 2:153–66

Fowler, C. A., Turvey, M. T. 1978. Skill acquisition: an event approach with special reference to searching for the optimum of a function of several variables. In *Information Processing in Motor Control and Learning,* ed. G. E., Stelmach, pp. 1–40. New York: Academic. 315 pp.

Gelfand, I. M., Tsetlin, M. L. 1962. Some methods of control for complex systems. *Russ. Math. Surv.* 17:95–116

Gentile, A. M. 1972. A working model of skill acquisition with application to teaching. *Quest* 17:3–23

Gibson, J. J. 1966. *The Senses Considered as Perceptual Systems.* London: George Allen & Unwin. 335 pp.

Gibson, J. J. 1979. *The Ecological Approach to Visual Perception.* Boston: Houghton Mifflin. 332 pp.

Greeno, J. G. 1974. Representation of learning as a discrete transition in a finite state space. In *Contemporary Developments in Mathematical Psychology.* Vol. 1: *Learning, Memory, and Thinking,* ed, D. H. Krantz, R. C. Atkinson, R. D. Luce, P. Suppes, pp. 1–43. San Francisco: Freeman. 299 pp.

Head, H. 1920. *Studies in Neurology,* Vols. I & II. New York: Macmillan. 862 pp.

Holding, D. H. 1976. An approximate transfer surface. *J. Mot. Behav.* 8:1–9

Keele, S. W., Summers, J. J. 1976. The structure of motor programs. In *Motor Control: Issues and Trends,* ed. G. E. Stelmach, pp. 109–42. New York: Academic. 232 pp.

Kelso, J. A. S., Norman, P. E. 1978. Motor schema formation in children. *Dev. Psychol.* 3:529–43

Kelso, J. A. S., Tuller, B., Vatikiotis-Bateson, E., Fowler, C. A. 1984. Functionally specific articulatory cooperation following jaw perturbations during speech: evidence for coordinative structures. *J. Exp. Psychol.: Hum. Percept. Perform.* 10:812–32

Krinskii, V. I., Shik, M. L. 1964. A simple motor task. *Biophysics* 9:661–66

Kugler, P. N., Kelso, J. A. S., Turvey, M. T. 1980. On the concept of coordinative structures as dissipative structures. I. Theoretical lines of convergence. In *Tutorials of Motor Behavior*, ed. G. E. Stelmach, J. Requin, pp. 3–48. Amsterdam: North-Holland. 680 pp.

Kugler, P. N., Turvey, M. T. 1987. *Information, Natural Law, and the Self-Assembly of Rhythmic Movement*. Hillsdale: Erlbaum. 481 pp.

Lavery, J. J. 1962. Retention of simple motor skills as a function of type of knowledge of results. *Can. J. Psychol.* 16:300–11

Lee, T. D. 1988. Transfer-appropriate processing: a framework for conceptualizing practice effects in motor learning. In *Complex Movement Behavior: The 'Motor-Action' Controversy*, ed. O. G. Meijer, K. Roth, pp. 201–15. Amsterdam: North-Holland

Lee, T. D., Magill, R. A., Weeks, D. J. 1985. Influence of practice schedule on testing schema theory prediction in adults. *J. Mot. Behav.* 17:283–99

Logan, G. D. 1988. Toward an instance theory of automatization. *Psychol. Rev.* 95:492–527

Magill, R. A. 1973. The post-KR interval: time and activity effects and the relationship of motor short-term memory theory. *J. Mot. Behav.* 5:49–56

Marteniuk, R. G. 1986. Information processing in movement learning: capacity and structural interference effects. *J. Mot. Behav.* 18:55–75

Martens, R., Burwitz, L., Zuckerman, J. 1976. Modelling effects on motor performance. *Res. Q.* 95:277–91

McCracken, H. D., Stelmach, G. E. 1977. A test of the schema theory of discrete motor learning. *J. Mot. Behav.* 9:193–201

McDonald, P. V., van Emmerik, R. E. A., Newell, K. M. 1989. The effects of practice on limb kinematics in a throwing task. *J. Mot. Behav.* 21:245–64

Miller, G. A. 1956. The magic number seven plus or minus two: some limits on our capacity for processing information. *Psychol. Rev.* 63:81–97

Moxley, S. E. 1979. Schema: the variability of practice hypothesis. *J. Mot. Behav.* 11:65–70

Newell, A., Rosenbloom, P. S. 1981. Mechanisms of skill acquisition and the law of practice. In *Cognitive Skills and Their Acquisition*, ed. J. R. Anderson, pp. 1–55. Hillsdale: Erlbaum. 386 pp.

Newell, K. M. 1974. Knowledge of results and motor learning. *J. Mot. Behav.* 6:235–44

Newell, K. M. 1976a. Motor learning without knowledge of results through the development of a response recognition mechanism. *J. Mot. Behav.* 8:209–17

Newell, K. M. 1976b. Knowledge of results and motor learning. In *Exercise and Sport Science Reviews*, ed. J. Keogh, R. S. Hutton, 4:195–228. Santa Barbara: Journal Publishing Affiliates. 394 pp.

Newell, K. M. 1981. Skill learning. In *Human Skills*, ed. D. H. Holding, pp. 203–26. New York: Wiley. 303 pp.

Newell, K. M. 1985. Coordination, control and skill. In *Differing Perspectives in Motor Learning, Memory, and Control*, ed. D. Goodman, R. B. Wilberg, I. M. Franks, pp. 295–317. Amsterdam: Elsevier. 340 pp.

Newell, K. M. 1986. Constraints on the development of coordination. See Wade & Whiting 1986, pp. 341–60

Newell, K. M. 1989. On task and theory specificity. *J. Mot. Behav.* 21:92–96

Newell, K. M. 1990. Augmented information and the acquisition of skill. In *Motor Learning and Training*, ed. R. Daugs, K. Bliscke. Schormdorf: Hofmann. In press

Newell, K. M., Carlton, M. J. 1987. Augmented information and the acquisition of isometric tasks. *J. Motor Behav.* 19:4–12

Newell, K. M., Carlton, M. J., Fisher, A. T., Rutter, B. G. 1989. Whole-part training strategies for learning the response dynamics of microprocessor driven simulators. *Acta Psychol.* 71:197–216

Newell, K. M., Chew, R. A. 1974. Recall and recognition in motor learning. *J. Mot. Behav.* 6:245–53

Newell, K. M., Kennedy, J. A. 1978. Knowledge of results and children's motor learning. *Dev. Psychol.* 14:531–36

Newell, K. M., Kugler, P. N., van Emmerik, R. E. A., McDonald, P. V. 1989. Search strategies and the acquisition of coordination. In *Perspectives on the Coordination of Movement*, ed. S. A. Wallace, pp. 85–122. Amsterdam: Elsevier. 455 pp.

Newell, K. M., McGinnis, P. M. 1985. Kinematic information feedback for skilled performance. *Hum. Learn.* 4:39–56

Newell, K. M., Morris, L. R., Scully, D. M. 1985. Augmented information and the acquisition of skill in physical activity. In *Exercise and Sport Sciences Reviews*, ed. R. L. Terjung, 13:235–61. New York: Macmillan. 596 pp.

Newell, K. M., Quinn, J. T., Carlton, M. J. 1987. Kinematic information feedback and task constraints. *Appl. Cogn. Psychol.* 1:273–83

Newell, K. M., Quinn, J. T., Sparrow, W. A., Walter, C. B. 1983. Kinematic information feedback for learning a rapid arm movement. *Hum. Mov. Sci.* 2:255–70

Newell, K. M., Shapiro, D. C. 1976. Variability of practice and transfer of training: some evidence toward a schema view of motor learning. *J. Mot. Behav.* 8:233–43

Newell, K. M., Sparrow, W. A., Quinn, J. T. 1985. Kinetic information feedback for learning isometric tasks. *J. Hum. Mov. Stud.* 11:113–23

Newell, K. M., van Emmerik, R. E. A. 1989. The acquisition of coordination: preliminary analysis of learning to write. *Hum. Mov. Sci.* 8:17–32

Newell, K. M., van Emmerik, R. E. A., McDonald, P. V. 1989. On simple movements and complex theories (and vice-versa). *Behav. Brain Sci.* 12:229–30

Newell, K. M., Walter, C. B. 1981. Kinematic and kinetic parameters as information feedback in motor skill acquisition. *J. Hum. Mov. Stud.* 7:235–54

Noble, C. E. 1968. The learning of psychomotor skills. *Annu. Rev. Psychol.* 19:203–50

Norman, D. A., Rumelhart, D. E., and the LNR Research Group, eds. 1975. *Explorations in Cognition.* San Francisco: Freeman. 430 pp.

Pew, R. W. 1974. Human perceptual-motor performance. In *Human Information Processing: Tutorials in Performance and Cognition,* ed. B. H. Kantowitz, pp. 1–39. Hillsdale: Erlbaum. 365 pp.

Rogers, C. A. 1974. Feedback precision and postfeedback interval duration. *J. Exp. Psychol.* 102:604–8

Rummelhart, D. E., Norman, D. A. 1982. Simulating a skilled typist: a study of skilled cognitive-motor performance. *Cognit. Sci.* 1:1–36

Rummelhart, D. E., Ortony, A. 1977. The representation of knowledge in memory. In *Schooling and the Acquisition of Knowledge,* ed. R. C. Anderson, R. J. Spiro, W. E. Montegue, pp. 99–135. Hillsdale: Erlbaum. 448 pp.

Salmoni, A. W. 1989. Motor skill learning. In *Human Skills,* ed. D. H. Holding, pp. 197–227. New York: Wiley. 334 pp.

Salmoni, A. W., Schmidt, R. A., Walter, C. B. 1984. Knowledge of results and motor learning: a review and critical reappraisal. *Psychol. Bull.* 95:355–86

Schmidt, R. A. 1975. A schema theory of discrete motor skill learning. *Psychol. Rev.* 82:225–60

Schmidt, R. A. 1976. Control processes in motor skills. In *Exercise and Sport Sciences Reviews,* ed. J. Keogh, R. S. Hutton, 4:229–61. Santa Barbara: Journal Publishing Affiliates. 394 pp.

Schmidt, R. A., Shapiro, D. C., Young, D. E., Swinnen, S. 1989. Summary knowledge of results for skill acquisition: support

for the guidance hypothesis. *J. Exp. Psychol.: Learn. Mem. Cogn.* 15:352–59

Schmidt, R. A., White, J. L. 1972. Evidence for an error detection mechanism in motor skills: a test of Adams' closed-loop theory. *J. Mot. Behav.* 4:143–54

Schneider, W., Fisk, A. D. 1983. Attention theory and mechanisms for skilled performance. In *Memory and Control of Action,* ed. R. A. Magill, pp. 119–44. Amsterdam: North-Holland. 395 pp.

Schneider, W., Shiffren, R. M. 1977. Controlled and automatic human information processing. I. Detection, search, and attention. *Psychol. Rev.* 84:1–66

Scully, D. M., Newell, K. M. 1986. Observational learning and the acquisition of motor skills: toward a visual perception perspective. *J. Hum. Mov. Stud.* 11:169–86

Shapiro, D. C., Schmidt, R. A. 1982. The schema theory: recent evidence and developmental implications. In *The Development of Movement Control and Coordination,* ed. J. A. S. Kelso, J. E. Clark, pp. 113–50. New York: Academic. 370 pp.

Shaw, R. E., Alley, T. R. 1985. How to draw learning curves: their use and justification. In *Issues in the Ecological Study of Learning,* ed. T. D. Johnson, A. T. Pietrewicz, pp. 275–304. Hillsdale: Erlbaum. 451 pp.

Shiffren, R. M., Schneider, W. 1977. Controlled and automatic human information processing. II. Perceptual learning, automatic attending and a general theory. *Psychol. Rev.* 84:127–90

Snoddy, G. S. 1926. Learning and stability. *J. Appl. Psychol.* 10:1–36

Stelmach, G. E., ed. 1976. *Motor Control: Issues and Trends.* New York: Academic. 232 pp.

Turvey, M. T. 1974. A note on the relation between action and perception. In *Psychology of Motor Behavior and Sport,* ed. M. G. Wade, R. Martens, pp. 307–13. Champaign: Human Kinetics. 356 pp.

Turvey, M. T. 1977. Preliminaries to a theory of action with reference to vision. In *Perceiving, Acting and Knowing,* ed. R. Shaw, J. Bransford, pp. 211–66. Hillsdale: Erlbaum. 492 pp.

Turvey, M. T., Kugler, P. N. 1984. An ecological approach to perception and action. In *Human Motor Actions—Bernstein Revisited,* ed. H. T. A. Whiting pp. 373–412. Amsterdam: North-Holland. 633 pp.

Turvey, M. T., Shaw, R. E., Mace, W. 1978. Issues in the theory of action: degrees of freedom, coordinative structures and coalitions. In *Attention and Performance,* ed. J. Requin, 7:557–95. Hillsdale: Erlbaum. 730 pp.

van Emmerik, R. E. A., Brinker, B. P. L. M.,

Vereijken, B., Whiting, H. T. A. 1989. Preferred tempo in the learning of a gross cyclical action. *Q. J. Exp. Psychol.* 41A:251–62

Wade, M. G., Whiting, H. T. A., eds. 1986. *Motor Development in Children: Aspects of Coordination and Control.* Boston: Martinus Nijhoff. 555 pp.

Woodworth, R. S. 1899. The accuracy of voluntary movements. *Psychol. Rev. Monogr. Suppl.* 3:1–114

Wrisberg, C. A., Ragsdale, M. R. 1979. Further tests of Schmidt's schema theory: development of a schema rule for a coincident timing task. *J. Mot. Behav.* 11:159–66

Wulf, G., Schmidt, R. A. 1989. The learning of generalized motor programs: reducing the relative frequency of knowledge of results enhances memory. *J. Exp. Psychol.: Learn. Mem. Cognit.* 15:748–57

Zelaznik, H. N. 1977. Transfer in rapid timing tasks: an examination of the role of variability in practice. In *Psychology of Motor Behavior and Sport,* ed. D. M. Landers, R. W. Christina, pp. 36–43. Champaign: Human Kinetics. 286 pp.

Zelaznik, H. N., Shapiro, D. C., Newell, K. M. 1978. On the structure of motor recognition memory. *J. Mot. Behav.* 10:313–23

Annu. Rev. Psychol. 1991. 42:239–76

PSYCHOLOGICAL PERSPECTIVES ON NUCLEAR DETERRENCE

Philip E. Tetlock, Charles B. McGuire, and Gregory Mitchell

Department of Psychology, University of California, Berkeley, California 94720

KEY WORDS: nuclear war, international conflict, cognitive and motivational biases, bargaining and negotiation, public opinion and nuclear weapons

CONTENTS

INTRODUCTION

The dramatic events of the 1980s underscore the ambiguity that shrouds the concept of deterrence in general and of nuclear deterrence in particular. The

239

0066-4308/91/0201-0239$02.00

45-year Cold War between the United States and Soviet Union appears finally to have ended. Although few predicted what has occurred, almost no one is now at a loss for explanations. Conservative analysts argue that recent events vindicate the policies of containment and deterrence that the United States has pursued, in one form or another, since World War II. Partisans of the Reagan administration argue, more specifically, that the new Soviet thinking is a response to the hard-line policies of the 1980s and to the technological threat posed by the Strategic Defense Initiative. By contrast, liberal analysts argue that the policies of the 1980s (and, for many, earlier policies as well) were a massive exercise in overkill. The Cold War ended as a result of the internal failures of communist societies. If anything, Gorbachevian policies emerged despite, not because of, the Reagan administration.

Perhaps historians will someday succeed in adjudicating this dispute—although the lack of consensus on the abundantly documented origins of World War I should constrain optimism here. What is most remarkable for current purposes is how easily the disputants could have explained the opposite outcome. If the Soviet Union had moved in a neo-Stalinist direction in the mid-1980s (massive internal repression and confrontational policies abroad), conservatives could have argued that the adversary had merely revealed its true nature, and liberals could have argued that "hard-liners beget hard-liners" in the conflict spiral dynamic. In short, we appear to be in an epistemological quagmire—what Hillel Einhorn (1980) termed an "outcome-irrelevant learning situation."

This chapter draws on psychological and historical evidence to address two seductive but in our view ultimately specious arguments concerning nuclear deterrence: 1. Now that the Cold War has ended, nuclear deterrence is of purely historical interest and we should turn our attention to more pressing economic and ecological problems. 2. If nuclear deterrence is indeed an outcome-irrelevant learning situation, no rational response remains other than total agnosticism. What is left to say?

The first argument can be dispatched much more quickly than the second. Whether the Cold War has ended or is in deep remission, the structural and psychological problems at the core of nuclear deterrence remain. The knowledge of how to construct weapons of mass destruction (nuclear and biochemical) is, for all practical purposes, irreversible. There is no known viable defense against such weapons. National governments jealously guard their control over weapons of mass destruction and try to translate such control into political influence in the international system. And the human beings who rise to positions of authority are capable of extraordinary miscalculations (Jervis 1976; George 1980; Janis 1982, 1989) and of extraordinary fanaticism (Staub 1988). In short, the raw ingredients for disaster are still present. The key question is how history will mix these ingredients: Who will make decisions wth respect to what issues and with what international repercussions?

Granted that there are no "quick fixes" to the nuclear dilemma (Carnesale et al 1983), we still confront the much subtler challenge of agnosticism. It is one matter to note that the threat of nuclear war should still be taken seriously, and quite another to propose serious solutions grounded in empirical knowledge of human nature and societal processes. Skeptics merit a hearing for at least one reason: The central dependent variable of our chapter—nuclear war—has never occurred and may never occur (perhaps a first in *Annual Review* history). Atomic weapons have been used in warfare only at Hiroshima and Nagasaki in 1945. The United States—which possessed overwhelming conventional superiority and a global monopoly on nuclear weapons—used the atomic bomb to force the surrender of an isolated Imperial Japan. We do not have a large data-base of previous wars that we can sift through in search of preconditions of the decision to use these extraordinarily destructive weapons.

Although we lack direct precedents, we risk being overwhelmed by the indirect evidence at our disposal (cf Stern et al 1989). There is no shortage of research on the psychological processes underlying interpersonal, intergroup, and international conflict. If one grants that the same processes that shape these less apocalyptic forms of conflict also bear on the likelihood of nuclear war, then we have a sound logical basis for linking the behavioral sciences to the problems of identifying both plausible pathways to nuclear war and plausible preventive measures. To be sure, the linkages must be made cautiously, with sensitivity to the unique features of the predicament confronting us in the late 20th century: the tremendous accuracy, speed, and power of nuclear weapons; the rapidity with which events in nuclear crises might unfold; and the danger of "losing control" over complex technological systems that no single person fully understands. But the alternative to cautious inductive inference from relevant research must also be kept in mind. To place nuclear war in a category of its own—in which all we know about ourselves is peremptorily deemed irrelevant—is not only difficult to justify, but is also ultimately nihilistic. How can one prepare to avoid an event that transcends existing knowledge? This chapter is premised on the assumption that although there will always be residual uncertainty about whether any given generalization would hold up in a particular war scenario, we have learned a good deal about behavioral processes that bear on the likelihood of war in general and of nuclear war in particular.

This chapter is organized into five sections. The first section sketches the core assumptions of the evolving body of doctrine known as deterrence theory. In succeeding sections, we draw on a variety of evidence—laboratory experiments, qualitative and quantitative historical studies, and computer simulations—to assess the adequacy of this framework. The second section focuses on cognitive, motivational, and political processes that influence the likelihood of deterrence success or failure. The third section treats deterrence as but one category of a broad range of tactics that nations use to influence each other. To achieve desired results, deterrence must frequently be balanced by reassurance—a subtle trade-off that takes different forms in different contexts. The fourth section probes the role of public opinion in national security issues. Finally, the fifth section explores sources of skepticism that social scientists have anything useful to contribute to the nuclear debate. We conclude on a cautiously optimistic note.

CORE PROPOSITIONS OF DETERRENCE THEORY

It is useful to distinguish three distinct, although partly overlapping, genera-tions of deterrence theory in the post-WWII period (Jervis 1979). The first owed much to the insightful observations of Bernard Brodie (1946). Although this first wave had little impact on policy, the second wave, which flourished between 1955 and 1965, was tremendously influential. This influence re-flected the key positions that theorists such as Albert Wohlstetter (1958), Herman Kahn (1961), and William Kaufmann (1956) occupied in the RAND corporation and the Pentagon (Kaplan 1983; Kolkowicz 1987). Second-wave research often took mathematical forms and drew on game-theoretic concepts. Underlying the complex formalisms, however, is a set of starkly simple assumptions concerning the nature of the political world and the best means of coping with that world:

1. The world is a dangerous place. One is confronted by a power-maximizing rational opponent who will capitalize on very opportunity to expand its influence at one's expense. Whenever the option to attack becomes suf-ficiently attractive (i.e. has greater expected utility than other available options), the opponent will do so.
2. To deter aggression, one should issue retaliatory threats that lead one's opponent to conclude that the expected utility of aggression is lower than the expected utility of the status quo.
3. To succeed, deterrent threats must be sufficiently potent and credible to overcome an adversary's motivation to attack. Potential aggressors must believe the deterrer possesses both the resolve and the capability to implement the threat. Deterrence will fail if either of these conditions is not met.

Although deterrence theorists accepted these principles in the abstract, they disagreed vigorously over how to operationalize them in policy. Controversy especially centered on the last two propositions: What types of threats deter aggression? How can threats be made more credible? Some theorists argued that nuclear weapons can only deter attacks on one's own territory ("Type I" or basic deterrence); others argued that nuclear threats can also deter attacks on allies ("Type II" or extended deterrence) (Kahn 1984). For the former camp, nuclear threats were of limited utility because, in McNamara's words, "one cannot fashion a credible deterrent out of an incredible action" (quoted in Freedman 1981:298). Why would a sane American leadership value the political independence of its allies over its own physical survival? This line of argument indicated the need for a massive strengthening of conventional deterrence.

The NATO nations were unwilling, however, to match Soviet spending on conventional forces (Thies 1991), and deterrence theorists sought ways to infuse credibility into the seemingly suicidal threat of nuclear retaliation. One strategy was the "rationality of irrationality." Nuclear threats may gain credibility if one can convince the opponent that one is crazy enough to follow through on them (Schelling 1966; Mandel 1987). Used judiciously, "irrational" threats are effective because "a bluff taken seriously is more useful than a serious threat taken as a bluff" (Kissinger, quoted in Gaddis 1982:300). One danger is that if the threatener does not appear crazy enough, the "bluff" will be called. The strategy can also be dangerous by working too well. For example, during the border skirmishes of the late 1960s, Soviet leaders thought Mao so irrational that he might use nuclear weapons. To preclude this possibility, the Soviets seriously considered a preemptive attack against Chinese nuclear facilities (Whiting 1991).

A second strategy—the "threat that leaves something to chance"— emphasizes the uncertainties inherent in military confrontations (Schelling 1966). Even if both sides want to limit a conflict, once hostilities begin the conflict can escalate far beyond the worst-case expectations of the antagonists. Threats that appear incredible become plausible when two sides find themselves on the "slippery slope" of military engagements in which neither side completely controls the escalation process. From this perspective, American forces in Europe did not need to be sufficient to halt a Soviet invasion; they functioned as a tripwire that raised the likelihood of eventual American nuclear involvement to an unacceptable level. The essence of this strategy is that potential aggressors will be induced to behave cautiously by the nonzero probability that conflicts, once initiated, will lead to "mutual assured destruction" (MAD).

Other deterrence theorists denounced the MAD strategy as morally and intellectually bankrupt. They advocated a "war-fighting" or "countervailing" strategy. Even defensive states need to develop conventional and nuclear capabilities that will give them a wide array of options when faced with a specific challenge. The stated goal was to "prevail" in war with any potential aggressor at any step in the "ladder of escalation" (Kahn 1965). The reasoning was straightforward. If the aggressors know they have nothing to gain by initiating a conflict or moving up the ladder of escalation, they will refrain from doing so (see Jervis 1984 for a critique of this strategy).

In brief, MAD theorists emphasize the existence of secure second-strike forces in both superpowers' arsenals and the dangers of escalation. Their goal is to prevent war by stressing the risk of mutual annihilation. War-fighting theorists are more concerned with what happens should deterrence fail. When faced with a challenge, states need the capability to respond in a controlled manner to contain the damage and yet force opponents to back down (Gray & Payne 1980).

Critics of second-wave deterrence theory and its doctrinal offshoots have objected on both psychological and political grounds. As Jervis (1979) noted, deterrence theory takes conflict for granted and fails to specify when threats should be issued. Classic deterrence theory also says little about how one might change an opponent's motives and transform a competitive relationship into a cooperative one (cf Lindskold et al 1986). Critics have also complained about the theory's exclusive focus on threats and its concomitant neglect of the role that rewards and concessions can play in mitigating conflicts (Jervis 1979). Finally, critics have objected to the notion that decisionmakers in highly stressful international crises are as rational and cool-headed as many deterrence theorists (particularly "war fighters") imply (Holsti & George 1975; Jervis 1979; Morgan 1983; Jervis et al 1985; Holsti 1989). Third-wave researchers have responded to these objections by building psychological and political parameters into deterrence theory. In the next section, we turn to third-wave research.

DETERMINANTS OF DETERRENCE SUCCESS AND FAILURE

Any discussion of deterrence success and failure must confront the serious methodological problems that arise in identifying clear-cut instances of success and failure from the historical record. To be sure, dramatic failures of deterrence as policy are easy to identify. Historical data are, however, sufficiently ambiguous to allow researchers to argue endlessly over whether individual cases also represent failures of deterrence theory (see Orme 1987; Lebow 1987). An equally imposing obstacle is presented by cases of deterrence success: No one knows how to identify them (George & Smoke 1974; Achen & Snidal 1989). When crises do not occur, is it due to the credibility of threats ("successes" for deterrence theory) or to the fact that the other state never intended to attack?

Despite these daunting difficulties, researchers themselves have not been deterred: There is a large (admittedly highly speculative) literature on determinants of deterrence success and failure. We begin by discussing micro processes—cognitive and motivational processes of individual policymakers—and then move on to macro ones (organizational, small group, and domestic processes).

Cognitive Processes

Some versions of deterrence theory assume policymakers act "as if" they were rational beings who possess perfect knowledge of the geopolitical situation. This modest assumption has led critics to complain that the theory lacks "diagnostics" (Jervis 1989a)—it tells us nothing about how policymakers assess threats and opportunities, formulate options, appraise consequences, and choose among options. In the past, such neglect may have been understandable, given our poor understanding of these micro-level processes. There is now, however, a voluminous research literature on judgmental shortcomings that can either exacerbate or mitigate conflict (e.g. Kahneman et al 1982; Abelson & Levi 1985)—a research literature that international relations theorists have put to good use. We highlight here those findings that have strong empirical support in both laboratory and foreign policy contexts.

OVERCONFIDENCE   Laboratory research reveals that people are often excessively confident in their factual judgments and predictions (e.g. Einhorn 1980; Koriat et al 1980). In the foreign policy realm, such overconfidence may lead decisionmakers to: 1. dismiss opposing views out of hand, 2. overestimate their ability to detect subtle clues to the other side's intentions, and 3. assimilate incoming evidence to their existing beliefs (Jervis 1983). Overconfident policymakers in defender states are likely to misapply deterrence strategies—either by failing to respond to potential challenges because of their certainty that no attack will occur (e.g. Israel in 1973 and the Soviet Union in 1941) or by issuing gratuitous threats because of their certainty of attack when no attack is actually planned. Overconfident aggressors are prone to exaggerate the likelihood that defenders will yield to challenges (Lebow 1981). In addition, overconfidence can also produce flawed policies when decisionmakers assess military and economic capabilities. For instance, the mistaken belief that one is militarily superior to a rival may generate risky policies that can lead to costly wars that no one wanted (Levy 1983). A mistaken belief that one is inferior to a rival, on the other hand, can exacerbate conflict in either of two ways (Levy 1983, 1989). One possibility is that such beliefs generate unnecessary arms races as the "weaker" side attempts to catch up. The rival perceives this effort as a bid for superiority, matches it, and sets the stage for the action-reaction pattern of conflict spirals (Jervis 1976). Another possibility is that the "weaker" state will be too quick to yield to a rival's demands. At best, such capitulation produces a diplomatic defeat; at worst, it leads aggressors to up the ante and ultimately produces wars that might have been avoided with firmer initial policies (a widely held view of Chamberlain's Munich appeasement policy of 1938). In a study of the intelligence failures prior to major wars, Ernest May (1984:542) concluded that "If just one exhortation were to be pulled from this body of experience, it would be, to borrow Oliver Cromwell's words to the Scottish Kirk: 'I beseech you in the bowels of Christ think it possible you may be mistaken.' "

THE FUNDAMENTAL ATTRIBUTION ERROR   When assessing the causes of others' behavior, people show a preference for internal, dispositional explanations over external, situational ones (Nisbett & Ross 1980). Insofar as situational determinants are especially important in international politics, this fundamental attribution error may play a critical role in fueling conflict among nations.

The problem can be traced to what international relations theorists call the "security dilemma" (Jervis 1976, 1978): To protect themselves in an anarchic environment (there is no world government), states must seek security either through costly defense programs or by persuading others to defend them by entering entangling alliances. Assessing intentions in such an environment is profoundly problematic. There is no easy way to distinguish between states that are defensively responding to the competitive logic of the situation and states that have expansionist objectives. If everyone assumes the worst, the stage is set for arms races that no one wanted (R. Kramer 1988). The fundamental attribution error exacerbates matters by lowering the perceptual threshold for attributing hostile intentions to other states (Downs 1991). This tendency—in conjunction with the security dilemma—can lead to an inordinate number of "Type I errors" (i.e. exaggerating the hostile intentions of defensively motivated powers). The security dilemma compels even peaceful states to arm; the fundamental attribution error then leads observers to draw incorrect dispositional inferences.

The actor-observer divergence in attributions further complicates matters. National leaders tend to attribute their own military spending to situational pressures. These self-attributions contribute to what White (1984) calls the "injured-innocence mechanism." Policymakers know they arm for defensive reasons and assume that others also know this. They conclude, therefore, that others building up their military capabilities must have aggressive designs.

METAPHORICAL AND ANALOGICAL REASONING   People try to understand novel situations by reaching for familiar concepts. Frequently, those concepts take the form of metaphors and analogies that illuminate some aspects of the new situation but distort or obscure others.

Lakoff & Johnson (1980) argue that metaphors pervade all forms of discourse. Nuclear discourse is no exception. Metaphorical preferences are correlated closely with policy preferences. Consider, for example, the "ladder of escalation" and the "slippery slope" (Jervis 1989b). The former metaphor implies that just as we can easily climb up and down a ladder one step at a time, so can we control the escalation and de-escalation of potential nuclear conflicts (Kahn 1965); the latter metaphor implies that once leaders find themselves in a conflict they can easily lose control and slide helplessly into the nuclear abyss (Schelling 1966). Which metaphor is more accurate? Although it is hard to say (research on crisis decision-making suggests the latter), policymakers appear to base policy decisions on metaphorical underpinnings. "Ladder" adherents support a war-fighting doctrine and counterforce capabilities; although they do not relish the prospect, they believe nuclear war can be controlled. "Slippery slopers," on the other hand, endorse MAD—both as a policy and as strategic reality (Jervis 1989b)—and they fear that, once initiated, superpower conflicts would inevitably escalate to all-out war. They argue that nuclear nations need to avoid crises. Managing them once they break out is too risky. (As President Kennedy said after the Cuban missile crisis, "One can't have too many of these.")

People also give meaning to new situations by drawing on historical precedents (May 1973; Jervis 1976; Gilovich 1981; Holland et al 1986; Neustadt & May 1986; Vertzberger 1986). Although reasonable, this cognitive strategy can be seriously abused. One mistake is focusing on only the most obvious precedent—often the most recent crisis or war (Jervis 1976)—rather than a broad range of precedents. For instance, Khong (1991) documents how American policy during the Vietnam conflict was shaped by its perceived similarity to the Korean war: Once again, a communist army from the north had attacked a pro-Western regime in the south. This diagnosis led to a series of prescriptions and predictions: The United States should resist the aggression with American troops and could expect victory, albeit with considerable bloodshed. A significant side-constraint "lesson" drawn from the Korean conflict was that in Vietnam the United States would have to fight hard but should avoid provoking Chinese entry into the war (Khong 1991).

A second mistake is to focus more on similarities than on differences between the present situation and the preferred precedent. Not only in public but also in private, policymakers rarely engage in balanced comparative assessments of historical cases. From a psychological viewpoint, this result is not surprising. Laboratory research demonstrates that people seek out, and display better recall for, information that confirms their hypotheses (Nisbett & Ross 1980; Skov & Sherman 1986). To invoke the Vietnam example again, American policymakers concentrated on the superficial similarities between the Vietnamese and Korean conflicts while George Ball—virtually alone— noted the differences (e.g. the conventional vs guerilla natures of the conflicts, the degree to which the United States could count on international support) (Khong 1991).

A third mistake is allowing preconceptions to predetermine the conclusions one draws from experience. In the United States, for instance, hawks and doves drew sharply divergent lessons from the Vietnam war (Holsti & Rosenau 1979). Prominent lessons for hawks were that the Soviet Union is expansionist and that the United States should avoid graduated escalation and honor alliance commitments. Prominent lessons for doves were that the United States should avoid guerilla wars, that the press is more truthful than the administration, and civilian leaders should be wary of military advice. Interestingly, no lesson appeared on both the hawk and dove lists. Sharply divergent lessons are not confined to democracies, as a content analysis of Soviet analyses of the Vietnam war revealed (Zimmerman & Axelrod 1981). Different constituencies in the Soviet Union drew self-serving and largely incompatible lessons from the American defeat in Asia. "Americanists" in foreign policy institutes believed Vietnam demonstrated the need to promote detente while restraining wars of national liberation; the military press, by contrast, believed the war demonstrated the implacable hostility of Western imperialism, the need to strengthen Soviet armed forces, and the feasibility and desirability of seeking further gains in the Third World. In summary, although policymakers often use analogies poorly, virtually no one would argue that they should ignore history; rather, the challenge is to employ historical analogies in a more nuanced, self-critical, and multidimensional manner (Neustadt & May 1986; Vertzberger 1986).

BELIEF PERSEVERANCE   Foreign policy beliefs often resist change (Jervis 1976; George 1980; Tetlock & McGuire 1986). Cognitive mechanisms such as selective attention and recall, denial, and biased assimilation of incoming information protect these beliefs from disconfirmation. Consider, for instance, the well-known "inherent bad faith model" of an opponent (Holsti 1967; Stuart & Starr 1981/82): A state is believed to be implacably hostile; contrary indications (e.g. concessions) are ignored, dismissed as propaganda ploys, or interpreted as signs of weakness. Former Secretary of State John Foster Dulles, for instance, held an "inherent bad faith model" of the Soviet Union (Holsti 1967), and many Israelis believe the PLO is implacably hostile (Kelman 1983). Policies of reassurance only tempt such a foe. Although such images are occasionally on the mark, they can produce missed opportunities for conflict resolution. Belief perseverance can also prevent policymakers from shifting to more successful strategies. In World War I, for example, military strategists continued to launch massive infantry charges despite enormous losses, leading two analysts to conclude that "men may die easily, but beliefs do not" (Art & Waltz 1983:13).

Some scholars hold belief perseverance to be "the most pervasive and significant" moderator of deterrence success or failure (Jervis 1983:24).

Aggressors can get away with blatant offensive preparations and still surprise their targets—as long as the target believes that an attack is unlikely (Heuer 1981). An example is Israel's failure to respond to warnings prior to the Yom Kippur war. Israeli leaders believed the Arabs would not attack, given Arab military inferiority, and dismissed contrary signals. Similarly, a nation that does not plan to attack—yet is believed to harbor such plans—will find it difficult to convince the opponent of its peaceful intentions (Jervis 1983).

AVOIDANCE OF VALUE TRADE-OFFS   For an array of cognitive, affective, and political reasons, people find value trade-offs unpleasant and frequently define issues in ways that bypass the need for such judgments (Steinbruner 1974; Jervis 1976; George 1980; Tetlock 1986a; Tetlock & McGuire 1986). Operationalizing a policy of deterrence, however, raises trade-offs that one ignores at one's peril. On the one hand, there is a need to resist exploitation and deter aggression. On the other hand, prudent policymakers should avoid exacerbating the worst-case fears of adversaries. The first value calls for deterrence; the second calls for reassurance. National leaders also confront a conflict between their desire to avoid the devastation of an all-out war and their desire to deter challenges and avoid even limited military skirmishes. Jervis (1984:49) refers to this dilemma as the "great trade-off": "States may be able to increase the chance of peace only by increasing the chance that war, if it comes, will be total. To decrease the probability of enormous destruction may increase the probability of aggression and limited wars." Critics of the "war-fighting" doctrine argue that decreasing the horrors of nuclear war may tempt states to attack under the mistaken assumption that the costs of the resulting war would be tolerable. "War fighters" respond by claiming that the threat of all-out war is so incredible that the aggressor will be tempted to risk challenging the status quo. (Both MAD-adherents and "war fighters" downplay the Jervisian trade-off in their respective policies by claiming that their strategy will simultaneously deter low-level challenges and avoid all-out war.)

There are also higher-order geopolitical trade-offs. Kennedy (1987) describes how great powers over the centuries have consistently failed to manage the three-pronged trade-off among defense spending, productive investment, and consumer spending. Although policymakers must allocate enough resources for defense to deter adversaries, too much defense spending will cut deeply into domestic economic growth (i.e. long-term investment needs) and domestic consumption (i.e. providing a reasonable standard of living for one's citizens).

Research suggests policymakers often avoid trade-offs by (*a*) concentration on a single predominant value to the exclusion of other values (Slovic 1975) or (*b*) the practices of bolstering (Janis & Mann 1977) or "belief system overkill" (Jervis 1976)—that is, by viewing their favored policy as superior to other policies on all relevant value dimensions. Either way, policymakers who fail to acknowledge the trade-off structure of their environment can get into serious trouble: in some cases by provoking conflict spirals when they overemphasize deterrence; in other cases by inviting attacks when they over-emphasize reassurance. Policymakers can also err by (over)protecting their short-term security through heavy defense spending while compromising their long-term security by neglecting investment needs and consumer demands (Kennedy 1987).

Policymakers are not completely oblivious, however, to trade-offs. Two grounds for caution merit note. First, policymakers may know more than they let be known. Acknowledging trade-offs can be politically embarrassing. Second, some policymakers display an awareness of trade-offs even in their public pronouncements. A recent study of the rhetoric of Gorbachev and his political allies reveals considerable sensitivity to the multifaceted trade-offs that must be made if the Soviet Union is, in Gorbachev's words, "to enter the next century in a manner befitting a great power" (Tetlock & Boettger 1989).

EFFECTS OF FRAMING   Prospect theory (Kahneman & Tversky 1979) claims that choice is influenced by how a decision problem is "framed". When a problem is described in terms of potential gains, people are risk averse; when it is described in terms of potential losses, people are risk seeking. This prediction has been supported in both experiments (Bazerman 1986; Tversky & Kahneman 1986; R. Kramer 1988) and case studies of actual foreign policy decisions (Lebow & Stein 1987).

Framing effects can create severe impediments in arms control negotiations (Jervis 1989a; Fischhoff 1990). When negotiators view their own concessions as losses and concessions by the opponent as gains, the subjective value of the former will greatly outweigh the subjective value of the latter. Both sides will therefore perceive a "fair" deal to be one where the opponent makes many more concessions—hardly conducive to reaching agreements. To make matters worse, when both sides distrust each other, concessions by the other side are often minimized for the simple (not necessarily invalid) reason that the other side made them. For instance, in 1981 President Reagan unveiled his "zero-option" proposal calling for the Soviet dismantling of hundreds of intermediate-range nuclear missiles (SS-20s) in Eastern Europe and the Soviet Union while the United States would refrain from deploying new missiles in Western Europe. The Kremlin categorically rejected the proposal. In 1986, however, Gorbachev embraced the original zero-option plan and agreed to eliminate all intermediate-range nuclear missiles on both sides. Gorbachev's concessions stunned many observers, who now assumed that the zero-option must favor the Soviets because of their conventional superiority and urged the United States to back out of the agreement.

To summarize, psychologists have identified a variety of judgmental short-comings. Although most research has taken place in controlled laboratory settings, accumulating case-study and content-analysis evidence indicates that policymakers are not immune to these effects. Researchers have emphasized the role these cognitive processes can play in deterrence failures. Each shortcoming can, however, also strengthen deterrence and limit conflict. Much depends on the geopolitical circumstances. Simplistic analogies some-times lead to correct policies, belief perseverance sometimes prevents us from abandoning veridical assessments of other states, and high-risk policies some-times yield big payoffs. Efforts to eliminate these cognitive biases are likely to be resisted by decisionmaking elites, who argue that these cognitive tendencies are often functional (Tetlock 1986b). Indeed, many biases and errors may be essential components of mental health (Taylor & Brown 1988). Individuals who believe in themselves and project optimism may not only be happier than more realistic souls, they may also be more politically successful (their enthusiasm and drive can be contagious).

In short, decision analysts face an uphill battle convincing skeptics that the benefits of their prescriptions outweigh the costs. Whether they explicitly recognize it or not, policymakers confront a meta-decisionmaking task: decid-ing how to decide. They must balance the estimated benefits of complex, self-critical policy analysis [benefits that Janis (1989) estimates to be quite high] against the psychological and political costs [costs that Tetlock (1986b) estimates to be quite high].

Motivational Processes

Work on the role of motivational processes in international conflict empha-sizes the impact of personal and political needs on policymakers' perceptions and actions. Far from being mutually exclusive processes, cognitive and motivational factors are closely intertwined. Cognitive appraisals activate motives that in turn shape decisionmakers' perceptions of the world (Tetlock & Levi 1982; Sorrentino & Higgins 1986).

MOTIVATED MISPERCEPTIONS   Recent critiques maintain that deterrence theory is fatally flawed (Jervis et al 1985). Credible threats are neither necessary nor sufficient to deter challengers (Lebow 1985a). Challengers act more out of fear than out of greed. Rather than seizing opportunities to make gains, challengers are driven to action to avoid losses (e.g. further erosion of popular support, falling further behind a rival in economic or military power). Egyptian policymakers in 1973, for example, faced enormous domestic prob-lems and attacked Israel not because they thought Israel was weak, but because they had to relieve domestic pressures (Stein 1985).

In such deterrence "failures," challenger states are caught in decisional dilemmas. On the one hand, they face a deteriorating political situation; on the other, the risks of military action are considerable. Confronted with two equally unpleasant alternatives, decisionmakers often rely on a coping strategy known as "defensive avoidance" (Janis & Mann 1977). To reduce stress, decisionmakers (a) procrastinate, (b) delegate the decision to someone else, or (c) bolster the option they initially prefer by generating supporting cognitions. In many situations, the first two options are foreclosed and decisionmakers respond by distorting their perceptions so that they can relieve stress and take action.

Lebow argues that challengers often cope with decisional dilemmas by committing themselves impulsively to attack and then bolstering that decision. Argentina's leaders, for example, felt they had to do something in 1982, decided to invade the Falkland Islands, and then convinced themselves Britain would merely protest (Lebow 1985b). Similarly, in 1962 Soviet leaders reacted to a strategic problem—the vast American superiority in intercontinental ballistic missiles (ICBMs)—by placing intermediate-range missiles in Cuba and then convincing themselves that the United States would accept the fait accompli (Lebow & Stein 1987).

In the cases examined, Lebow and Stein claim that deterrence was properly implemented. Commitments were clearly specified and credible threats issued. Yet the policy failed. Lebow & Stein (1987; Stein 1990) argue that deterrence was the wrong strategy and needed to be supplemented by "reassurance." Reassurance policies are designed to allay the fears of potential challengers by emphasizing the benign nature of one's intentions. The prescription follows from the diagnosis: If fear provokes challenges, then this fear must be put to rest.

Critics have objected on three grounds (Blight 1986; Orme 1987; Tetlock 1987; Achen & Snidal 1989). First, they note that the research is based on an unrepresentative sample of deterrence failures drawn from a much larger unspecified universe of cases. Virtually any social science theory would look bad if one concentrated solely on its predictive failures. Moreover, it is unclear whether Lebow & Stein's cases falsify the predictions of deterrence theory. Failures of deterrence policies are not perforce failures of deterrence theory; the theory predicts numerous failures (Achen & Snidal 1989; Quester 1989). Deterrence theory, for example, does not predict that aggressors will challenge the status quo only when the expected utility of aggression is positive. Aggressors may strike out even when the subjective probability of failure is high—for example, Japan's 1941 decision to attack the United States (Russett 1967; Levi & Tetlock 1980) and Egypt's 1973 decision to attack Israel. From a deterrence perspective, there is nothing odd about long-shot strategic gambles of this sort—as long as the expected utility of aggression is greater than that of the status quo (Levy 1983; Bueno de Mesquita 1985).

Second, the claim of "motivated misperceptions" is problematic. How implausible must perceptions be to count as evidence of motivated error? It is easy for defenders of deterrence (such as Orme 1987) to advance rationalist reinterpretations of historical cases that Lebow invokes as strong support for motivated error in foreign policy. Whether the status quo power adequately communicated its resolve to resist is a difficult judgment call that hinges on nuances of historical interpretation. For instance, whether the British clearly warned the French prior to the Fashoda crisis of 1898 depends on the relative importance one attaches to statements made by key actors at different times and to the parliamentary controversy that ensued after the British undersecretary declared that French penetration into the Sudan would qualify as "an unfriendly act." The judgment also hinges on whether one takes leaders' statements at face value (as reflections of how they see the world) or as forms of strategic posturing (as attempts to intimidate, placate, or otherwise influence other political actors). Strategic impression management may often be a plausible alternative interpretation of statements that political leaders make on the irreversibility of the policies they adopt (see Tetlock & Manstead 1985). The judgment call is made even more difficult by the certainty-of-hindsight bias—the cognitive tendency to view events, in retrospect, as more obviously likely to occur than they appeared beforehand (Fischhoff 1975).

Finally, although the distinction between need-driven and opportunity-driven aggression is psychologically sound, it is of limited practical use. Conflict-spiral and deterrence theorists can apparently generate rival need and opportunity explanations whenever the occasion demands. Was the Soviet ICBM buildup of the 1970s a bid for gain (strategic nuclear superiority and a first-strike capability) or an attempt to achieve parity with American forces? One's answers to questions like this have historically been highly correlated with the emphasis one places on "deterrence" versus "reassurance" (Lebow 1983). Not surprisingly, debates over motives have been notoriously difficult to resolve (Tetlock 1983). Eventually, however, the preponderance of evidence can overwhelm even relatively closed belief systems. Many conservatives in the late 1980s, for example, were willing to abandon a rigid totalitarian model of the Soviet Union in response to the policy initiatives of Gorbachev.

PERSONALITY AND POLICY PREFERENCES   "Neorealists" claim that foreign policy is tightly constrained by the logic of power within the international system (Waltz 1979). From this perspective, individual differences among elites are inconsequential—virtually everyone who matters will agree on what constitutes the "rational" response. Although some crises produce such unanimity (e.g. the American response to the attack on Pearl Harbor), in most cases large differences of opinion arise. By combining laboratory and archival studies, researchers have built a convincing case for systematic personality influences on foreign policy (Greenstein 1975; Hermann 1977; Etheredge 1978a; Tetlock 1983).

One key area of research focuses on "interpersonal generalization theory" which claims that foreign policy preferences are extensions of how people act toward others in their everyday lives. In one archival analysis of disagreements among American policymakers between 1898 and 1968, Etheredge (1978b) found that policy preferences were closely linked to personalities. Elites rated high in interpersonal dominance were more likely to resort to force than their less dominant colleagues. Elites classified as extroverts were more likely to advocate conciliatory policies toward the Soviet Union than their more introverted colleagues. In an extension of this study to 1969–1984, Shepard (1988) replicated Etheredge's finding on dominance but obtained only weak support for the extroversion hypothesis. Laboratory work by Sternberg & Soriano (1984) provided additional evidence of a close relationship between personality variables and preferred methods of resolving interpersonal and international conflicts.

Taken together, these studies suggest that the international environment can be likened to a projective test. When presented with an ambiguous stimulus, people's responses reveal something about their motives, intentions, fears, and hopes. Although these results demonstrate the importance of personality, the policy implications are less straightforward. Some argue that qualified professionals should screen public officials for psychological adjustment (Clark 1971). "Undesirables" should be removed from power or even not allowed to run for office. Such screening measures are not unheard of— American military personnel who handle nuclear weapons are routinely examined for their mental and physical health. At the cabinet level, one can point to Secretary of Defense James Forrestal's forced resignation in 1948 after he manifested signs of severe paranoia. He later leapt to his death from the 16th floor of the Bethesda Naval Hospital after complaining that the Truman administration had selected him "as their Number One target for liquidation as a consequence of his efforts to alert Americans to the Communist menace" (Nathan & Oliver 1976:119). Implementation of psychological screening at the highest decisionmaking level, however, awaits answers to two key questions: 1. How can one prevent partisans of the left and right from building politically loaded definitions of mental health into the assessment process? 2. How can we reconcile such psychological screening with constitutional principles?

Small-Group Processes

Decisionmakers do not operate in a social vacuum. Most national security decisions are collective products—the result of intensive interactions among small groups of decisionmakers, each of whom represents a major bureaucratic or political constituency. The norms and operating procedures of these small groups are important determinants of policy outcomes.

Group dynamics interact with individual cognitive and motivational processes to influence final decisions. Janis (1982), for example, has reviewed considerable historical and experimental research suggesting that, under certain conditions (directive leadership, cohesive group, high external threat, etc), group norms will emerge that exacerbate already dangerous trends in individual judgment. Far from checking bias and error in each other, policymakers in these "groupthink" situations behave in ways that encourage overconfidence, self-righteousness, cognitive rigidity, and excessive optimism and that discourage dissent and the expression of unpopular doubts or opinions. The result, according to Janis, is the undertaking of ill-conceived foreign policy projects that lead to disastrous consequences (e.g. the provoking of Communist Chinese intervention in the Korean war, the abortive Bay of Pigs invasion of Cuba).

Small-group processes do not always, however, make matters worse. Under other conditions (external accountability checks, nondirective leadership, multiple advocacy), group norms can facilitate complex, open-minded analyses of policy options (George 1980; Janis 1982) and confer at least some protection against such judgmental biases as overconfidence, the fundamental attribution error, and belief perseverance (Tetlock & Kim 1987). Janis (1982) cites the development of the Marshall Plan and the handling of the Cuban missile crisis as exemplary models of how group processes can improve the quality of decision-making.

Institutional and Domestic Processes

As war has grown in technological complexity (McNeil 1982), so too have the institutions for waging it. Attempts to escape complexity can, however, trigger disaster. Prior to World War I, for example, the military commanders of the major powers sought to simplify their planning tasks by formulating rigid mobilization schedules that automatically went into effect when certain conditions were met (J. Snyder 1984; Levy 1986). Contemporary strategic analysts are concerned that procedures for the command and control of nuclear forces are dangerously similar to the mobilization plans of 1914 (e.g. Bracken 1983; Blair 1987).

In the nuclear age, military planners confront complex trade-offs in formulating operational plans and designing force structures (Steinbruner 1987). On the one hand, dispersion of command and control centers and the responsibility for launching nuclear weapons diminishes the danger of suffering a "decapitating" first strike. On the other hand, such dispersion is expensive, cumbersome, and increases the danger of an accidental launch.

Adopting a "launch-on-warning" policy virtually ensures that one will be able to unleash a devastating retaliatory response, but such a policy also increases the danger of a nuclear war triggered by a false alarm. A large arsenal of accurate land-based missiles increases one's strategic flexibility, but they also give one a first strike capability that could frighten an opponent into launching a preemptive attack if it believes war is inevitable (i.e. a "use 'em or lose 'em" dilemma). These strategic trade-offs imply that a successful security policy— one neither too weak nor too provocative—depends on decisionmakers who are open-minded and adept at dealing with multidimensional trade-offs.

The complexity, moreover, does not end here. Arms control negotiations add new layers of complexity to an already Byzantine task. Negotiators must play what Putnam (1988) calls a two-level game: They must deal with foreign adversaries and allies ("Level I" games) while they simultaneously placate domestic bureaucracies, special interest groups, and the general public ("Level II" games). American arms control negotiators, for example, presumably try to formulate proposals that not only will be acceptable to their Soviet counterparts but also will be supported by such domestic actors as the Departments of Defense and State, Congress, military contractors, and media elites (Soviet negotiators, of course, face similar pressures) (cf Druckman & Hopmann 1989).

Simply put, "the political complexities for the players in this two-level game are staggering" (Putnam 1988:434). Micro-level processes are likely to be key determinants of winners and losers in such a complex and demanding game. Policymakers unable or unwilling to make the multi-pronged trade-offs demanded by two-level games are likely to fail.

Relationship between Arms Races and War

At present there is little agreement among scholars about whether arms races promote peace or provoke war (Richardson 1960; Wallace 1979, 1980; Weede 1980; Intriligator & Brito 1984). Deterrence theorists argue that arms races prevent war by raising the cost of conflict to the point where potential aggressors are persuaded to accept the status quo. Conflict-spiral theorists argue that arms races cause war by convincing each party to the interaction that they are dealing with an implacably hostile opponent and that war is inevitable. The rising tensions created by the arms race ultimately lead one side to launch a preemptive attack—an act motivated by fear that it will soon be attacked and the belief that preemption is preferable to absorbing the first blow.

Each side is partly correct. Under some conditions, arms races deter war; under other conditions, they exacerbate conflict and promote war. Downs (1991) proposes that three psychological processes help to explain this con-tingent historical relationship: the fundamental attribution error, risky decision-making, and the "ideology of the offensive." The fundamental attribution error leads participants in arms races to overemphasize the dispositional causes of others' military spending. When this "error" is widespread, war becomes more likely. Prospect theory suggests that states lagging behind in an arms race, and particularly states pessimistic about redressing the balance in the future, are likely to risk preemptive wars out of desperation. Other theorists, however, argue that states ahead in an arms race may be more risk acceptant and thus may try to capitalize on their temporary advantage (Morrow 1989). Both viewpoints suggest that races between military equals who match one another's arms buildups are more stable than those in which there is a constant, or a shifting, difference in military power. The "ideology of the offensive" refers to a set of beliefs emphasizing the advantages of preemptive attacks. Some historians believe the "ideology of the offensive" was a key cause of World War I and speculate that contemporary leaders holding similar beliefs could trigger an even more horrible conflagration (J. Snyder 1984; van Evera 1985). Nuclear deterrence, however, may well be robust enough to overcome cognitive biases. The cost of conflict is so obviously high that even declining powers confronted by implacable opponents may prefer the status quo (or perhaps abject surrender) to Armageddon.

Crisis Decision-Making

Most theorists agree that nuclear war will not result from a "bolt out of the blue" attack. The most commonly mentioned scenario has nuclear conflict emerging from a serious crisis that escalates out of control (Allison et al 1985). Not surprisingly, this concern with international crises has given birth to a substantial research literature on crisis decision-making. This literature is methodologically eclectic, encompassing laboratory experiments (where independent variables such as information load and time pressure can be systematically manipulated, and key dependent variables such as decisional quality can be precisely measured) and case studies of actual crises (some of which have, and some of which have not, culminated in war) (G. Snyder & Diesing 1977; Suedfeld & Tetlock 1977; Lebow 1981; J. Snyder 1984; van Evera 1985; Blight 1987, 1990).

In some situations, individuals and groups rise to the challenge and respond in a "rational" manner. For instance, during the Entebbe crisis (Maoz 1981) and the Middle East crisis of 1967 (Stein & Tanter 1980) Israeli policymakers—although under considerable stress—performed effectively: they considered a number of options, assessed the consequences of these options in a probabilistic manner, traded off values, and demonstrated an openness to new information. In other situations, however, individuals and groups respond to the pressure of the moment by relying on many of the shortcuts described earlier: They draw on simplistic metaphors and analogies, they make premature commitments and then escalate, they protect beliefs by assimilating new evidence, and they deny trade-offs (Hermann 1979; Herek et al 1987). Contingency models of decision-making (Janis & Mann 1977; Janis 1982, 1989) seek to bring order to these disparate findings by specifying when we should expect more or less thoughtful information-processing. Much depends on how decisionmakers appraise the situation. If they are caught in a decisional dilemma—forced to choose between two equally unpleasant alternatives—and are pessimistic about the prospects of finding a more palatable alternative in the time available, they are more likely to engage in bolstering and the low-quality information-processing that accompanies it. When decisionmakers are more optimistic about finding an acceptable option, however, they engage in more vigilant information-processing.

Although there is much speculation that nuclear crises will severely degrade the quality of decision-making, evidence for such a relationship is limited. Apropos the Cuban missile crisis—the best, if not the only, case—the evidence about how participants responded to the stress is mixed (at least on the American side; see Blight & Welch 1987), and there are sharp debates concerning the quality of the Executive Committee's deliberations during the crisis (cf Herek et al 1987, 1989; Welch 1989).

SUBSUMING DETERRENCE THEORY INTO A GENERAL THEORY OF INTERNATIONAL INFLUENCE

Deterrence theory focuses on threats as instruments of social influence. From this standpoint, the principal problem is how one can best employ threats to influence opponents. Critics believe that this "deterrence problem" (Achen & Snidal 1989) is too constraining and must be placed in the context of a much broader "foreign policy problem" that explores the conditions under which a wide range of influence strategies are effective in eliciting desired responses from other states (George & Smoke 1974, 1989; Jervis et al 1985; Stein 1990). Excellent reviews of the voluminous literature on bargaining and negotiation strategies exist elsewhere (e.g. Pruitt & Rubin 1986; Patchen 1987, 1988). Our goal here is to offer a condensed summary of work that bears most directly on nuclear deterrence.

Pure Threat Strategies

Threats sometimes work—at least for certain purposes at certain times (McClintock et al 1987; Patchen 1988). Laboratory evidence that threats work comes from bargaining games. Threats of defection have led to beneficial joint outcomes when interests did not conflict (e.g. Friedland 1976; Stech et al 1984), and the mere possession of threat capabilities has reduced defection and increased mutual outcomes in games lacking communication between the parties (W. Smith & Anderson 1975). The evidence is, however, mixed. Other studies have found that threats impede cooperation and lower joint outcomes (Deutsch & Krauss 1960; cf Kelley 1965). Threats have also interfered with cooperation when interests were in conflict (Friedland 1976) and when communication between bargainers was possible (Smith & Anderson 1975). Brehm's (1972) reactance theory suggests that threats may backfire by provoking counter-efforts to assert one's freedom to do what was forbidden.

Evidence from studies of international conflict is equally mixed. Although a "bullying" strategy may be essential against some opponents, the strategy is counterproductive when directed at nations with limited goals (Kaplowitz 1984). Several studies of serious interstate disputes have discovered that even though bullying occasionally yields diplomatic victories, it also often leads to unwanted escalation of severe crises (Leng & Wheeler 1979; Leng & Gochman 1982). Case studies of American foreign policy have drawn a similar conclusion. A strategy of coercive diplomacy emphasizing military threats is appropriate only when restrictive preconditions are met: For example, when the coercer is perceived to be more motivated than the other side to achieve its objectives, when adequate domestic support can be generated for the policy, when there are usable military options, and when the opponent fears escalation more than the coercer (George et al 1971).

Positive Inducements

Since Munich gave appeasement a bad name, international relations theorists have largely neglected the potential utility of positive inducements in foreign affairs (Baldwin 1971; Milburn & Christie 1989). The primary advocates of positive inducements have been conflict-spiral theorists who emphasize the debilitating consequences of action-reaction cycles in international conflict (Deutsch 1983). Although these theorists stress conciliatory gestures, few advocate total unilateral disarmament. And for good reason, too: Experimental evidence indicates that in mixed-motive games, such as the Prisoner's Dilemma, unconditional cooperators are ruthlessly exploited (e.g. Stech et al 1984). In their study of international disputes, Leng & Wheeler (1979) found that nations adopting an appeasement strategy manage to avoid war but almost always suffer a diplomatic defeat. Positive inducements, such as financial rewards for compliance, can also be very expensive if the other side complies (particularly if it quickly becomes satiated and ups its demands for compensation), and they can foster unwanted dependency (Leng 1990). Finally, just as deterrence theorists face difficulties in operationalizing threats, so reinforcement theorists encounter problems in operationalizing rewards, which may be perceived as overbearing, presumptuous, manipulative, or insultingly small or large (Milburn & Christie 1989).

The picture is not completely bleak, however. Komorita (1973), for example, found that unilateral conciliatory acts by one party in an experimental bargaining game resulted in increased communication, perceptions of cooperative intent, and mutually beneficial outcomes. In a study of American-Soviet arms control negotiations between 1969 and 1979, Jensen (1984) found that concessions by one side were almost always met by counter-concessions by the opponent, whereas retractions provoked counter-retractions (see also Stoll & McAndrew 1986).

For the most part, conflict-spiral theorists have stressed the importance of combining conciliatory policy initiatives with adequate military strength and nonprovocative threats. We turn now to these "mixed" strategies.

Mixed-Influence Strategies

Spurred by Robert Axelrod's (1984) *The Evolution of Cooperation,* a great deal of attention has been directed to firm-but-fair approaches to resolving conflict. In this review, we focus on Axelrod's (1984) tit-for-tat strategy (TFT) and Osgood's (1962) strategy of "graduated and reciprocated initiatives in tension-reduction" (GRIT) [useful summaries of other approaches can be found in Fogg (1985) and Patchen (1987)].

TIT-FOR-TAT   TFT is a straightforward strategy. Applied to Prisoner's Dilemma (PD) games, one begins by cooperating and thereafter simply repeats an opponent's previous move: If they cooperated, you cooperate; if they defected, you defect. Considerable research demonstrates that TFT is as effective as it is simple. In two round-robin PD computer tournaments in which numerous strategies were pitted against one another, TFT—the simplest entry in the contest—earned the highest average number of points (Axelrod 1984). In a laboratory simulation of an arms race, Pilisuk & Skolnick (1968) found a preprogrammed matching (TFT) strategy elicited the greatest cooperation from subjects. Moving beyond the laboratory, several studies of international crises have found TFT strategies to be more successful than either pure threat (bullying) or appeasement strategies in avoiding both war and diplomatic defeat (e.g. G. Snyder & Diesing 1977; Leng & Wheeler 1979; Leng & Walker 1982; Huth & Russett 1984, 1988; Huth 1988; Leng 1990).

Axelrod (1984) suggests that TFT works because it is "nice" (never defects first), "perceptive" (quickly discerns the other's intent), "clear" (easy to recognize), "provocable" (quickly retaliates), "forgiving" (willing to abandon defection immediately after the other side's first cooperation), and "patient" (willing to persevere). Pruitt & Kimmel (1977) attribute TFT's success to its ability to communicate two key messages: Exploitation is futile, and cooperation is necessary for higher payoffs. Other researchers believe that TFT works because it triggers a deeply rooted "norm of reciprocity" (G. Snyder & Diesing 1977; Leng & Wheeler 1979).

One major drawback of TFT is that the two parties can easily get caught up in a never-ending series of mutual defections. A possible solution is to respond to defection by the other side with a somewhat smaller defection. Such a move sends the implicit message "I'll retaliate, but I don't want this conflict to escalate." In a computer tournament to test this notion, To (1988) utilized an expanded payoff matrix in which players could respond to cooperation or defection with more or less extreme cooperation or defection of their own. In this tournament, a version of TFT that retaliates with defection one degree less severely than another's defection (a "tit-FOR-TAT" strategy) achieved the highest average score. Downs (1991) argues that a tit-FOR-TAT strategy might be the best way to demonstrate resolve while preventing an arms race from spiraling out of control.

A second drawback of TFT is that it applies primarily to Prisoner's Dilemma games in which both sides prefer mutual cooperation to mutual defection. Many international conflicts, however, may best be described as games of "Deadlock" in which at least one party prefers unilateral defection or mutual defection to cooperation (Oye 1985). In such games, TFT will not induce an opponent to cooperate. In arms races, for example, one or both nations might prefer a mutual buildup to an arms control treaty, especially if trust is low or if there is an opportunity to benefit from the race (a charge often levelled at the "military-industrial complexes" of the superpowers).

A third drawback of TFT is that it implies perfect perception and control—the ability to identify cooperation and defection correctly and to respond to an opponent in ways that will not be misconstrued. In the real world, however, detection is problematic, misperception may be common, and policy implementation is tricky (Oye 1985). Actors can attempt to disguise their actions and sneak in a few defections (e.g. by secretly developing chemical weapons or surreptitiously deploying missiles). The problem of detection is clearly illustrated in arms control negotiations. Difficulties in providing for adequate verification can prolong some negotiations and completely undermine others. In PD games, opponents' moves are unambiguous; in international politics, policymakers must interpret actions that are, to varying degrees, ambiguous. Many Americans, for example, disagreed over whether the recent Soviet nuclear testing moratorium was a "cooperative" initiative or a propaganda ploy designed to lock in place a Soviet advantage. The effects of misperception on the ability of TFT to promote mutual cooperation can be devastating (Jervis 1988). Even when misperceptions are rare, Downs et al (1985) demonstrate that arms races often escalate out of control. Finally, in PD games, the players are "unitary actors" capable of easily implementing either cooperation or defection; in international politics, the players are complex societies, and implementing a specific policy is no easy task (Oye 1985; Downs et al 1985). Even when policymakers realize the desirability of responding in a cooperative or hostile manner, domestic coalitions may block the move or the policy may be poorly implemented. During the Cuban missile crisis, for instance, President Kennedy sought to de-escalate the conflict by sending implicit "cooperative" signals to the Soviets (e.g. by halting all provocative military action against Soviet naval vessels). Unfortunately, the President had a poor understanding of the "rules of engagement" concerning submarines, and the Navy—vigorously implementing its "standard operating procedures" for such situations—continued to force Soviet submarines to surface by employing various provocative tactics (e.g. by harrassing them with sonar or, in one case, dropping low-explosive depth charges) (Sagan 1985).

GRADUATED AND RECIPROCATED INITIATIVES IN TENSION-REDUCTION
Like TFT, GRIT is designed simultaneously to resist exploitation and to shift the interaction onto a mutually beneficial, cooperative plane. GRIT, however, does not assume that the "game" has not yet begun, as does TFT. Rather, GRIT assumes that the parties are already trapped in a costly conflict spiral. To unwind the spiral, Osgood proposed that one side should announce its intention to reduce tensions and then back up its rhetoric with unilateral conciliatory gestures (e.g. troop reductions, missile withdrawals). These actions are designed to convince the opponent of the initiator's peaceful intentions, but they do not seriously weaken the initiator. The opponent is invited to respond with conciliatory gestures, but warned that attempts to exploit the situation will force the initiator to return to more belligerent policies. In contrast to TFT, GRIT is "nicer" (it cooperates in the face of defection) and less "provocable" (it continues to cooperate even when the opponent ignores such moves).

Several studies have demonstrated GRIT's ability to generate cooperation. In one laboratory study, Pilisuk & Skolnick (1968) found GRIT to be more successful than a tit-for-tat strategy in evoking cooperation from an opponent. Moreover, prior communication of intent aided the GRIT strategy but undermined the matching strategy, and GRIT with communication about specific moves elicited the most cooperation. The most impressive experimental evidence comes from the research program of Lindskold (1978, 1979a). The paradigm involves a PD game in which subjects face an opponent (actually, a preprogrammed strategy) who is initially very competitive (to produce a climate of hostility) but then practices GRIT. In the third phase, the simulated other returns to a neutral strategy to test the persistence of GRIT's effects. Key findings from Lindskold's work include: (a) GRIT leads to more integrative agreements than do competitive and no-message strategies (Lindskold & Han 1988); (b) GRIT elicits more cooperation when initiated from a position of strength rather than weakness (a finding that could be invoked as support for major defense buildups in some circumstances as a necessary prelude to GRIT) (Lindskold & Bennett 1973); (c) GRIT's general statement of cooperative intent is more effective than both "if you will cooperate, I will" statements (Lindskold & Finch 1981) and no statements at all (Lindskold et al 1986a), and GRIT statements are particularly effective when repeated and rephrased (Lindskold et al 1986b); (d) GRIT elicits more cooperation than TFT and 50%-cooperative strategies (Lindskold & Collins 1978); and (e) GRIT produces more cooperation than a 50%-cooperative strategy regardless of whether the subject responds before, after, or during the simulated other's response (Lindskold 1979b).

Some historical evidence is also consistent with GRIT. Etzioni (1967) argues that a quasi-GRIT strategy adopted by President Kennedy in 1963 promoted a (short-lived) period of cooperation between the United States and the Soviet Union. GRIT has also been credited with producing the Austrian State Treaty of 1955 (Larson 1987). Furthermore, Soviet initiatives of the 1980s (e.g. withdrawal from Afghanistan, nuclear test moratoria, unilateral troop reductions) are compatible with GRIT and have certainly been instrumental in reducing East-West tensions. Indeed, statements by Gorbachev in response to American claims that the unilateral Soviet moratorium on nuclear explosions was "pure propaganda" demonstrate an intuitive awareness of the strength of a GRIT-type strategy:

> If all that we are doing is indeed viewed as mere propaganda, why not respond to it according to the principle of "an eye for an eye, and a tooth for a tooth"? We have stopped nuclear explosions. Then you Americans could take revenge by doing likewise. You could deal us yet another propaganda blow, say, by suspending the development of one of your strategic missiles. And we would respond with the same kind of "propaganda". And so on and so forth. Would anyone be harmed by competition in such "propaganda"? (*Time,* Sepetmber 9, 1985:23)

Some researchers have suggested that a combination of tit-for-tat and GRIT is the best strategy of conflict management in many situations (Komorita 1973; Patchen 1987; Druckman & Hopmann 1989; Downs 1991). Initial use of a TFT strategy would demonstrate one's willingness to endure a painful stalemate. Conciliatory offers can then be extended with a diminished fear that they will be interpreted as a sign of weakness (cf G. Snyder & Diesing 1977; Leng & Walker 1982). Others, however, argue that the early competitiveness can too easily escalate into all-out war or poison the atmosphere so that later conciliatory gestures will be ignored or discounted.

The superpower detente of the late 1960s and early 1970s provides one example of how a mixed-influence strategy can be applied in practice. In an attempt to build a more stable world order, Nixon and Kissinger sought to shift the superpower relationship from "confrontational competition" to "collaborative competition" in which the United States and the Soviet Union would show restraint both in the Third World and in weapons programs

(Breslauer 1983; George 1983). The essence of American policy during detente was its reliance on carrots and sticks. Carrots included the prospect of enhanced trade and credits, reduced military competition, and access to advanced technology. The sticks included a threat to return to the tensions of the Cold War, a renewed arms race that would seriously strain the Soviet economy, and a suspension of trade that would once again deprive the Soviets of access to American goods. For complex reasons, the Nixon-Kissinger policy ultimately failed, competition in the Third World heated up, and arms control sputtered and eventually stalled with the SALT II treaty (Breslauer 1983; Gaddis 1982). Scholars still debate the causes of the collapse of detente. Was the Soviet Union primarily to blame for exploiting detente by intervening in Angola, Ethiopia, and Afghanistan? Was the Nixon-Kissinger policy ill conceived, poorly implemented, or undermined by Congressional opponents (e.g. the Jackson-Vanik amendment)?

Research on social influence points to a number of conclusions. At a minimum, the findings demonstrate that the simplistic remedies often proposed for complex social conflicts are untenable. An exclusive emphasis on threats can provoke otherwise avoidable conflicts (Leng 1990); so can calls for unilateral disarmament, albeit via a different mechanism—by tempting aggressors. Encouraging, though, is the multi-method convergence suggesting that in many situations a firm-but-fair or reciprocating bargaining strategy works best. The strategy "works best" in that vital interests are protected while conflict is prevented from getting out of control. On a more pessimistic note, current findings are incomplete and poorly integrated. Although we certainly know more than we once did about the conditions under which alternative influence strategies are more or less successful, our "contingent generalizations" (George 1979) are still crude.

Future research on international influence would be well advised to follow the example of Alexander George's (1972, 1980) work on coercive diplomacy in crisis management. George did not presume to tell policymakers whether they should use threats of force in specific crises. On the basis of his own inductive-historical research, he did, however, identify several generic problems that policymakers need to solve in order both to protect "vital national interests" and to avoid war. For instance, policymakers considering the use of a coercive strategy should, at a minimum, consider the following questions: 1. What are the risks of presenting an ultimatum that specifies a deadline for compliance? Can the risks be controlled? 2. How should one calibrate the intensity and timing of threats? 3. How should threats be presented? Should threats be coupled with rewards in a carrot-and-stick package that makes compliance the most attractive option? How can rewards and threats be designed to augment rather than negate each other?

These guidelines highlight the complexity of the issues and the variety of "things that can go wrong" in crisis decision-making. Although policymakers following these guidelines may get into serious trouble (e.g. they may provide the "wrong" answer to a key question), it is reasonable to hypothesize that policymakers who heed these guidelines are less likely to make calamitous miscalculations than policymakers who ignore them.

PUBLIC OPINION AND NUCLEAR WEAPONS

Hundreds of surveys have assessed public attitudes on national security issues (see Russett 1989, for a comprehensive overview). A major goal of this work has been to assess the content, structure, and stability of political beliefs. One consistent finding is that only 5–10% of the American public closely follows foreign affairs. Although aware of major controversies, the public is poorly informed about both arms control and nuclear strategy (Graham 1988). In addition, early survey research indicated that public beliefs lacked ideological coherence (Converse 1964) and were unstable (Almond 1950). These latter conclusions have been seriously qualified (e.g. Shapiro & Page 1988) but not overturned (Kinder & Sears 1985; Sniderman & Tetlock 1986).

American attitudes toward national security issues are well summarized by Yankelovich & Smoke (1988) and Schneider (1987). We focus here on how the public copes with the same nuclear dilemmas that confront policymakers. Overall, survey results are not encouraging for advocates of extended nuclear deterrence and limited war strategies. Few Americans, and even fewer Europeans, believe the United States should be the first to use nuclear weapons, and a substantial majority believe any use of nuclear weapons will lead to an all-out war (Yankelovich & Doble 1984). Advocates of MAD, however, can take comfort in results suggesting that Americans are psychologically prepared to accept mutually assured destruction: The vast majority believe that "nuclear weapons . . . cannot be abolished, and because mankind will maintain its knowledge of how to make them, there can be no turning back to a less threatening time" (Yankelovich & Doble 1984). The public believes attempts to regain American nuclear superiority are misguided, that substantial "overkill" exists in nuclear arsenals, and that negotiations to achieve mutual and verifiable reductions in nuclear weapons are wise.

Since the late 1940s, the American public has appeared to balance two central values: peace and strength (Schneider 1987). In the 1950s and 1960s, there was a bipartisan consensus that America needed to be strong to contain an expansionist Soviet Union. The Vietnam war shattered this consensus (Holsti & Rosenau 1979, 1988), and the early 1970s saw the creation of a fragile "pro-peace" coalition. During this period of detente, important agreements were concluded with the Soviet Union, and defense spending was cut. By 1980, detente had collapsed and a new dominant coalition emphasized greater defense spending and a more assertive foreign policy. This coalition disintegrated in the mid-1980s when the public once again came to favor cuts in defense, improvements in American-Soviet relations, and "fair" arms control agreements. These shifts can be captured by examining support of defense spending. In 1973, only 11% of the public thought the United States spent "too little" on defense. This figure increased during the 1970s until it peaked in 1980 at 56% who believed "too little" was being spent on "the military, armaments and defense". By 1985, Americans were satisfied with the Reagan buildup, and only 14% wanted an increase in defense spending (Schneider 1987). Support for defense spending has eroded in the face of Gorbachev's dramatic reforms in the late 1980s. American political debate by early 1990 focused on the size of the prospective "peace dividend" that would result from cuts in defense spending.

From a theoretical perspective, one can view American attitudes toward nuclear weapons in the postwar period as attempts to cope with the cognitive dissonance aroused by the twin cognitions that a despised adversary has the capacity to destroy you and that there is no effective defense. Dissonance reduction has followed many routes: 1. Some coped by simply not thinking about the nuclear predicament, by forcing such thoughts out of awareness. This argument underlies Lifton's (Lifton & Falk 1982) controversial "psychic numbing" hypothesis—controversial because many people do report thinking about nuclear war, and often those who do not do so have other things on their minds, such as paying the rent, finding a job, and raising children (Schuman et al 1986; T. Smith 1988). 2. Another group—disarmament advocates—reduced dissonance not by avoidance but by actively working for a global ban on nuclear weapons (in effect, eliminating one of the dissonant cognitions). 3. A third group, advocates of strategic defense, sought escape via a belief that an effective defense against nuclear missiles can be found with a little ingenuity (and a lot of cash). 4. "Survivalists" have generally accepted that nuclear war is inevitable, but believe that with proper planning (e.g. fallout shelters) survival is possible (Tyler & McGraw 1983; Fiske 1987). 5. Mikhail Gorbachev has provided Americans with another way of reducing dissonance: an opportunity to perceive a sharply reduced threat from an "evil empire" on its way to reform. Americans have reacted to changes in the Soviet Union by downplaying the Soviet threat (economic challenges from rivals such as Japan are now viewed as posing a far greater threat) and sharply reducing their assessments of the likelihood of nuclear war (Yankelovich & Smoke 1988). For many individuals, the desire to reduce dissonance is so great that they will endorse multiple, and seemingly incompatible, routes to avoiding nuclear war. It is not surprising therefore that some people in the mid-1980s were willing to support both a nuclear freeze and the Strategic Defense Initiative (SDI). As long as the proposal promised to reduce the threat, the public was at least receptive (Graham & Kramer 1986).

These survey results must be interpreted with care. Minor changes in question wording can sometimes have big effects (Tourangeau & Rasinski 1988) by highlighting different facets of complex social issues (e.g. support for arms control depends greatly on whether the question focuses on what one must give up or what the other side must give up). Public support for SDI was particularly vulnerable to such effects. When described as a way to defend cities from attack (which "war fighters" wanted), SDI was widely supported; when described as a limited system to protect missile silos and command centers (which some MAD advocates wanted), a majority rejected the plan (Graham & Kramer 1986; Schneider 1987).

Finally, we turn to the controversy over effects of public opinion on national security policy. Some argue that public opinion is irrelevant, others argue that it is potentially important but under the control of media elites, and still others argue that it is enormously influential. The most plausible position, in our view, is that the two interact in complex ways (Russett 1989). For instance, presidents plummeting in the polls might risk foreign adventures to bolster their support as a result of the (short-lived but replicable) "rally-round-the-flag" phenomenon. In this example, foreign policy is influenced by public attitudes, and these attitudes are in turn responsive to policy decisions. It is hard to argue that public opinion has no impact on policy when elected officials devote so much effort to collecting their own polling data (H. Smith 1988). Public reaction to proposed policies obviously counts for something.

SOURCES OF SKEPTICISM

Some observers have concluded that the psychological and social science literature offers little useful guidance to preventing nuclear war. We examine here four frequently invoked arguments in support of such skepticism. None of these arguments is entirely convincing, although each highlights a valid reason for concern.

The Impact of the Nuclear Revolution

In the pre-nuclear world, the "classic logic" of war prevailed: The victor dictated terms to the loser; if the loser did not acquiesce, the victor could punish without fear of retaliation (e.g. Thucydides 1972 [ca. 400 BC]; von Clausewitz 1976 [1830]. The "nuclear revolution" has changed all this (Mandelbaum 1981; Jervis 1984, 1989b). The existence of secure second-strike forces in nuclear arsenals has profound implications for future wars. Rather than submit to the "winner's" demands, the loser can launch a nuclear attack that will utterly destroy the winner.

The nuclear revolution raises perplexing questions about our ability to generalize from nonnuclear to nuclear decisions. Some analysts claim nuclear weapons have such a powerful effect on policymakers' beliefs and behavior that there is really only one empirical case worth studying: the Cuban missile crisis of 1962 (Blight et al 1987). Others argue that even this case is too outdated to offer lessons for today's policymakers. Still others argue that since the world has never experienced a nuclear war, we have learned nothing about how one might occur or can be prevented. From this viewpoint, beliefs about nuclear deterrence are based on nothing but faith [in Levine's (1991) terms, nuclear deterrence is "nuclear theology"]. As noted at the outset, our position is that cautious inference from the available evidence is preferable— on both logical and ethical grounds—to the alternative of nihilism ('it is impossible to learn anything about nuclear war') and its corollary, subjectivism ('one person's opinion is as good as another's when it comes to the question of how to avoid nuclear war').

Reliance on Historical Counterfactuals

Much of what passes for knowledge in debates over nuclear deterrence consists of highly speculative counterfactual arguments of the form: What would have happened if X had or had not occurred (Nye 1987)? Whereas laboratory scientists can turn to well-designed experiments with control groups to address the causal questions that intrigue them, in nuclear policy debates the control groups exist only in our imaginations. On one side of the debate, deterrence advocates claim that nuclear weapons have "kept the peace" and prevented World War III. On the other side, conflict-spiral theorists argue that by focusing on deterrence American policymakers have squandered numerous opportunities—from Malenkov and Khrushchev to Gorbachev—for promoting international cooperation. Although disciplined use of counterfactual argument is an essential component of good historical scholarship (Bundy 1988; Nye 1988), the counterfactuals in nuclear policy debates are often used more for justification than for impartial analysis.

Counterfactual arguments also play a role in case studies. For instance, Lebow & Stein's (1987) thesis rests on the claim that, in cases where "pure deterrence" failed, a judicious mixture of deterrence and reassurance would have worked. Research on the link between arms races and war runs into the problem of testing two key counterfactuals: 1. What would have occurred in the absence of an arms race when one took place and 2. what difference an arms race would have made when one did not take place (Downs 1991). Current methodological escapes from the counterfactual dilemma number three: laboratory simulations (where systematic control over variables allows comparison among real cases rather than imaginary ones); the method of "structured, focused comparisons" (where analysts select cases that vary on key theoretical dimensions and systematically compare them; George 1979); and sensitivity analysis (where analysts construct multivariate statistical models to estimate the degree to which change in one variable would produce change in another). All three, although imperfect in different ways, are preferable to the alternative of ideologically self-serving use of historical counterfactuals.

Hidden Political Agendas and Value-Driven Social Science

Skeptics also question the political impartiality of psychological work on security issues. Political psychologists, it is argued, are more motivated to advance an ideological agenda than they are to understand the causal dynamics of international conflict. Consider, for instance, White's (1984) call for the West to adopt a posture of "minimal deterrence." White (1984:81) argues that "perhaps ten fairly invulnerable submarines, almost certainly able to destroy the two hundred largest cities in the USSR, would be sufficient to keep the other side from starting a nuclear war. If so, we don't necessarily need anything else for that purpose—not ICBMs, not Pershing IIs, not land-based cruise missiles, perhaps not bombers, and not even a number of nuclear-armed submarines comparable to theirs." This provocative proposal, which included a call for costly improvements in conventional forces, is based on several debatable assumptions: the belief that sudden technological advances will not render the submarines vulnerable to attack, the belief that Western retaliation via relatively inaccurate SLBMs (most of which can destroy cities but not hardened military targets) is a "credible" threat that will deter attacks on the United States, the assessment of the Soviet Union of the late 1970s and early 1980s as a defensive, risk-averse power, and the belief that American ICBMs exacerbate Soviet fears of a first strike and could trigger a preemptive nuclear attack.

Our goal here is not to quarrel with White's recommendations (they bear a striking resemblance to Gorbachev's new thinking on security issues). White's argument, however, can't be deduced from any body of psychological research; his argument rests on a complex mixture of moral, political, and strategic assumptions. One is hard pressed to determine at what point White ceases to speak as a psychologist and begins to speak as a political activist.

Foreign Policy as Art

Existing theories yield conditional generalizations of the form: "Under circumstances x, y, and z, this type of strategy is likely to have these effects; under this other set of circumstances, the same strategy is likely to have this other set of effects." Such statements frustrate policymakers because they beg the question of how one determines whether the preconditions for adopting a strategy have been met. It is one thing to claim that a firm-but-fair strategy usually works better than alternative strategies in promoting mutually advantageous solutions to conflicts of interest; it is quite another to claim that such a strategy should be adopted in a particular context. Before applying any particular contingent generalization, it is necessary to take into account the many circumstances unique to the case at hand, each a potential boundary condition for the "law" one seeks to apply.

Nor do the inferential difficulties end here. Even if we had a sure-fire method of determining that a general principle did apply to a specific case, we would still have to operationalize the theoretical advice. What exactly does it mean to say that the United States should pursue a reciprocity strategy in its security dealings with the Soviet Union or its trade policies with Japan? Reciprocity can be operationalized in a seemingly infinite variety of ways. Does it mean tit-for-tat, or some version of GRIT? Whatever the choice, how exactly does one strike the "right balance" between conciliation and resistance to exploitation? Presumably some kind of corrective feedback mechanism should be built into the policy formula. The key problem then becomes one of response calibration. How does one decide whether a given response by the other side is sufficiently conciliatory or refractory to warrant a response in kind?

CONCLUSION

This chapter reveals the variety of ways psychological theory and research bear on issues of deterrence in general and nuclear deterrence in particular. Converging evidence from radically different research methods points to cognitive, motivational, and social processes that could have a decisive impact (under certain conditions) on war and peace in the nuclear age.

Convincing ourselves is one matter; convincing the world, quite another. Psychologists to date have had little impact on the making of national security decisions (Blight 1987). Psychologists have been much more successful staking their claims to influence elsewhere: in education and child-care, personnel selection and management, and mental health policy. Other professional groups [what Haas (1991) calls epistemic communities] have been much more successful than psychologists in staking their claims on security policy. Economists, game theorists, physicists, and computer systems experts have all argued convincingly that they have something important to offer; the claims of psychologists have tended to be ignored because they are regarded as either obvious or politically naive. Our long-term credibility in the political arena hinges on our ability to sustain an epistemic community devoted to the scientific study of security issues. And it is with our long-term credibility we should be most concerned. The fundamental problems of nuclear deterrence—weapons of mass destruction, no viable defense, a competitive nation-state system, and human beings of limited rationality—will be with us well into the next millennium.

ACKNOWLEDGMENTS

Preparation of this chapter was supported in part by grants from the John D. and Catherine T. MacArthur Foundation. We would like to thank Robert Jervis, Alex George, and Jack Levy for comments on an earlier version of the manuscript.

Literature Cited

Abelson, R. P., Levi, A. 1985. Decisionmaking and decision theory. See Lindzey & Aronson 1985, Vol. 1, pp. 231–310

Achen, C. H., Snidal, D. 1989. Rational deterrence theory and comparative case studies. *World Polit.* 41:143–69

Allison, G. T., Carnesale, A., Nye, J. S. 1985. *Hawks, Doves, and Owls.* New York: W. W. Norton

Almond, G. A. 1950. *The American People and Foreign Policy.* New York: Harcourt, Brace

Art, R. J., Waltz, K. N. 1983. Technology, strategy, and the uses of force. In *The Use of Force,* ed. R. J. Art, K. N. Waltz. Lanham, MD: University Press of America

Axelrod, R. M. 1984. *The Evolution of Cooperation.* New York: Basic

Baldwin, D. A. 1971. The power of positive sanctions. *World Polit.* 24:19–38

Bazerman, M. H. 1986. *Judgment in Managerial Decision Making.* New York: John Wiley & Sons

Blair, B. G. 1987. Alerting in crisis and conventional war. See Carter et al 1987, pp. 75–120

Blight, J. G. 1986. The new psychology of war and peace. *Int. Secur.* 11:175–86

Blight, J. G. 1987. Toward a policy-relevant psychology of avoiding nuclear war: lessons for psychologists from the Cuban missile crisis. *Am. Psychol.* 42:12–29

Blight, J. G. 1990. *The Shattered Crystal Ball: Fear and Learning in the Cuban Missile Crisis.* New York: Rowman & Littlefield

Blight, J. G., Nye, J. S., Welch, D. A. 1987. The Cuban missile crisis revisited. *Foreign Aff.* 66:170–88

Blight, J. G., Welch, D. A. 1987. The eleventh hour of the Cuban missile crisis: an introduction to the ExComm transcripts. *Int. Secur.* 12:5–29

Bracken, P. J. 1983. *Command and Control of Nuclear Forces.* New Haven, CT: Yale Univ. Press

Brehm, J. 1972. *Response to Loss of Freedom: A Theory of Psychological Reactance.* Morristown, NJ: General Learning Press

Breslauer, G. W. 1983. Why detente failed: an interpretation. See George 1983, pp. 319–40

Breslauer, G. W., Tetlock, P. E., eds. 1991. *Learning in U.S. and Soviet Foreign Policy.* Boulder, CO; Westview

Brodie, B. 1946. *The Absolute Weapon.* New York: Harcourt, Brace

Bueno de Mesquita, B. 1985. The war trap revisited: a revised expected utility model. *Am. Polit. Sci. Rev.* 79:156–77

Bundy, M. 1988. *Danger and Survival: Choices about the Bomb in the First Fifty Years.* New York: Random House

Carnesale, A., Doty, P., Hoffman, S., Huntington, S., Nye, J. S., Sagan, S. 1983. *Living with Nuclear Weapons.* Toronto: Bantam

Carter, A., Steinbruner, J. D., Zracket, C., eds. 1987. *Managing Nuclear Operations.* Washington: Brookings Inst.

Clark, K. B. 1971. The pathos of power. *Am. Psychol.* 26:1047–57

Converse, P. E. 1964. The nature of belief systems in mass publics. In *Ideology and Discontent,* ed. D. E. Apter. New York: Free Press

Deutsch, M. 1983. The prevention of World War III: a psychological perspective. *Polit. Psychol.* 4:3–31

Deutsch, M., Krauss, R. M. 1960. The effect of threat on interpersonal bargaining. *J. Abnorm. Soc. Psychol.* 61:181–89

Downs, G. W. 1991. Arms races and war. In *Behavior, Society, and Nuclear War,* Vol. 3, ed. P. E. Tetlock, R. Jervis, P. Stern, J. L. Husbands, C. Tilly. Washington: Oxford Univ. Press

Downs, G. W., Rocke, D. M., Siverson, R. A. 1985. Arms races and cooperation. *World Polit.* 38:118–45

Druckman, D., Hopmann, P. T. 1989. Behavioral aspects of international negotiation. See Tetlock et al 1989, pp. 85–173

Einhorn, H. J. 1980. Overconfidence. *New Direct. Methodol. Soc. Behav. Sci.* 4:1–16

Etheredge, L. S. 1978a. *A World of Men.* Cambridge, MA: MIT Press

Etheredge, L. S. 1978b. Personality effects on American foreign policy 1898–1968: a test of interpersonal generalization theory. *Am. Polit. Sci. Rev.* 78:434–51

Etzioni, A. 1967. The Kennedy experiment. *West. Polit. Q.* 20:361–80

Fischhoff, B. 1975. Hindsight Foresight: the

effect of outcome knowledge on judgment under uncertainty. *J. Exp. Psychol. Hum. Percept. Perform.* 1:288–99

Fischhoff, B. 1990. Nuclear decisions: cognitive limits to the thinkable. See Tetlock et al 1990

Fiske, S. T. 1987. People's reactions to nuclear war: implications for psychologists. *Am. Psychol.* 42:207–17

Fogg, R. W. 1985. Dealing with conflict: a repertoire of creative, peaceful approaches. *J. Confl. Resolut.* 29:330–58

Freedman, L. 1981. *The Evolution of Nuclear Strategy.* London: Macmillan

Friedland, N. 1976. Social influence via threats. *J. Exp. Soc. Psychol.* 12:552–63

Gaddis, J. L. 1982. *Strategies of Containment.* Oxford: Oxford Univ. Press

George, A. L. 1972. The case for multiple advocacy in making foreign policy. *Am. Polit. Sci. Rev.* 66:751–85

George, A. L. 1979. Case studies and theory development: the method of structured, focused comparison. In *Diplomacy: New Approaches in History, Theory, and Policy,* ed. P. Lauren. New York: Free Press

George, A. L. 1980. *Presidential Decisionmaking in Foreign Policy: On the Effective Use of Information and Advice.* Boulder, CO: Westview

George, A. L., ed. 1983. *Managing US-Soviet Rivalry: Problems of Crisis Prevention.* Boulder, CO: Westview

George, A. L., Hall, D. K., Simmons, W. 1971. *The Limits of Coercive Diplomacy.* Boston: Little, Brown

George, A. L., Smoke, R. 1974. *Deterrence in American Foreign Policy: Theory and Practice.* New York: Columbia Univ. Press

George, A. L., Smoke, R. 1989. Deterrence and foreign policy. *World Pol.* 41:170–82

Gilovich, T. 1981. Seeing the past in the present: the effect of associations to familiar events on judgments and decisions. *J. Pers. Soc. Psychol.* 40:797–808

Graham, T. W. 1988. The pattern and importance of public knowledge in the nuclear age. *J. Confl. Resolut.* 32:319–34

Graham, T. W., Kramer, B. M. 1986. ABM and Star Wars: attitudes toward nuclear defense, 1945–1985. *Public Opin. Q.* 50:125–34

Gray, C. S., Payne, K. 1980. Victory is possible. *Foreign Polit.* 39:14–27

Greenstein, F. I. 1975. *Personality and Politics.* New York: W. W. Norton & Co.

Haas, E. B. 1991. Collective learning. See Breslauer & Tetlock 1991

Herek, G. A., Janis, I. L., Huth, P. 1987. Decision making during international crises: is quality of process related to outcome? *J. Confl. Resolut.* 31:203–26

Herek, G. A., Janis, I. L., Huth, P. 1989.

Quality of U. S. decision making during the Cuban missile crisis. *J. Confl. Resolut.* 33:446–59

Hermann, M. G. 1977. *The Psychological Examination of Political Leaders.* New York: Free Press

Hermann, M. G. 1979. Indicators of stress in policymakers during foreign policy crises. *Polit. Psychol.* 1:27–46

Heuer, R. J. 1981. Strategic deception and counterdeception: a cognitive process approach. *Int. Stud. Q.* 25:294–327

Holland, J. H., Holyoak, K., Nisbett, R. E., Thagard, P. 1986. *Induction: Processes of Inference, Learning, and Discovery.* Cambridge, MA: MIT Press

Holsti, O. R. 1967. Cognitive dynamics and images of the enemy. In *Enemies in Politics,* ed. R. Fagan, pp. 25–96. Chicago: Rand McNally

Holsti, O. R. 1989. Crisis decision-making. See Tetlock et al 1989, pp. 1–84

Holsti, O. R., George, A. L. 1975. The effects of stress on the performance of foreign policymakers. *Polit. Sci. Ann.* 6:255–317

Holsti, O. R., Rosenau, J. N. 1979. Vietnam, consensus, and the belief systems of American leaders. *World Polit.* 32:1–56

Holsti, O. R., Rosenau, J. N. 1988. The domestic and foreign policy beliefs of American leaders. *J. Confl. Resolut.* 32:248–94

Huth, P. 1988. Extended deterrence and the outbreak of war. *Am. Polit. Sci. Rev.* 82:423–43

Huth, P., Russett, B. M. 1984. What makes deterrence work? *World Polit.* 36:496–526

Huth, P., Russett, B. M. 1988. Deterrence failure and crisis escalation. *Int. Stud. Q.* 32:29–46

Intriligator, M. O., Brito, D. L. 1984. Can arms races lead to the outbreak of war? *J. Confl. Resolut.* 28:63–84

Janis, I. L. 1982. *Groupthink.* New York: Free Press

Janis, I. L. 1989. *Crucial Decisions: Leadership in Policymaking and Crisis Management.* New York: Free Press

Janis, I. L., Mann, L. 1977. *Decision Making: A Psychological Analysis of Conflict, Choice, and Commitment.* New York: Free Press

Jensen, L. 1984. Negotiating strategic arms control. *J. Confl. Resolut.* 28:535–59

Jervis, R. 1976. *Perception and Misperception in International Politics.* Princeton, NJ: Princeton Univ. Press

Jervis, R. 1978. Cooperation under the security dilemma. *World Polit.* 30:167–214

Jervis, R. 1979. Deterrence theory revisited. *World Polit.* 29:289–324

Jervis, R. 1983. Deterrence and perception. *Int. Secur.* 7:3–30

Jervis, R. 1984. *The Illogic of American Nuclear Strategy.* Ithaca, NY: Cornell Univ. Press

Jervis, R. 1988. Realism, game theory, and cooperation. *World Polit.* 40:317–49

Jervis, R. 1989a. Rational deterrence: theory and evidence. *World Polit.* 41:183–207

Jervis, R. 1989b. *The Meaning of the Nuclear Revolution: Statecraft and the Prospect of Armageddon.* Ithaca, NY: Cornell Univ. Press

Jervis, R., Lebow, R. N., Stein, J. G., eds. 1985. *Psychology and Deterrence.* Baltimore, MD: Johns Hopkins Univ. Press

Kahn, H. 1961. *On Thermonuclear War.* Princeton, NJ: Princeton Univ. Press

Kahn, H. 1965. *On Escalation: Metaphors and Scenarios.* New York: Praeger

Kahn, H. 1984. *Thinking the Unthinkable in the 1980s.* New York: Simon & Schuster

Kahneman, D., Tversky, A. 1979. Prospect theory: an analysis of decision under risk. *Econometrica* 47:263–91

Kahneman, D., Slovic, P., Tversky, A., eds. 1982. *Judgment under Uncertainty: Heuristics and Biases.* Cambridge: Cambridge Univ. Press

Kaplan, F. 1983. *The Wizards of Armageddon.* New York: Simon & Schuster

Kaplowitz, N. 1984. Psychopolitical dimensions of international relations: the reciprocal effects of conflict strategies. *Int. Stud. Q.* 28:373–406

Kaufmann, W. W. 1956. *Military Policy and National Security.* Princeton, NJ: Princeton Univ. Press

Kelley, H. H. 1965. Experimental studies of threats in negotiations. *J. Confl. Resolut.* 9:77–105

Kelman, H. C. 1983. Conversations with Arafat: a social-psychological assessment of the prospects for Israeli-Palestinian peace. *Am. Psychol.* 38:203–16

Kennedy, P. M. 1987. *The Rise and Fall of the Great Powers.* New York: Random House

Khong, Y. F. 1991. The lessons of Korea and the Vietnam decision. See Breslauer & Tetlock 1991

Kinder, D. R., Sears, D. O. 1985. Public opinion and political action. See Lindzey & Aronson 1985, Vol. 2, pp. 659–742

Kolkowicz, R. 1987. Intellectuals and the nuclear deterrence system. In *The Logic of Nuclear Terror,* ed. R. Kolkowicz, pp. 15–46. London: Allen & Unwin

Komorita, S. S. 1973. Concession-making and conflict resolution. *J. Confl. Resolut.* 17:745–62

Koriat, A., Lichtenstein, S., Fischhoff, B.

1980. Reasons for confidence. *J. Exp. Psychol.: Hum. Learn. Mem.* 6:107–18

Kramer, R. M. 1988. Windows of vulnerability or cognitive illusions? Cognitive processes and the nuclear arms race. *J. Exp. Soc. Psychol.* 25:79–100

Lakoff, G., Johnson, M. 1980. *Metaphors We Live By.* Chicago: Univ. Chicago Press

Larson, D. W. 1987. Crisis prevention and the Austrian State Treaty. *Int. Org.* 41:27–60

Lebow, R. N. 1981. *Between Peace and War.* Baltimore, MD: Johns Hopkins Univ. Press

Lebow, R. N. 1983. The deterrence deadlock: Is there a way out? *Polit. Psychol.* 4:333–54

Lebow, R. N. 1985a. Conclusions. See Jervis et al 1985, pp. 203–32

Lebow, R. N. 1985b. Miscalculation in the South Atlantic: the origin of the Falkland War. See Jervis et al 1985, pp. 89–124

Lebow, R. N. 1987. Deterrence failure revisited. *Int. Secur.* 12:197–213

Lebow, R. N., Stein, J. G. 1987. Beyond deterrence. *J. Soc. Issues* 43:5–71

Leng, R. J. 1990. Influence techniques. See Tetlock et al 1990

Leng, R. J., Gochman, C. S. 1982. Dangerous disputes: a study of conflict behavior and war. *J. Confl. Resolut.* 26:664–87

Leng, R. J., Walker, S. G. 1982. Comparing two studies of crisis bargaining: confrontation, coercion, and reciprocity. *J. Confl. Resolut.* 26:571–91

Leng, R. J., Wheeler, H. G. 1979. Influence strategies, success, and war. *J. Confl. Resolut.* 23:655–84

Levi, A., Tetlock, P. E. 1980. A cognitive analysis of Japan's 1941 decision to go to war. *J. Confl. Resolut.* 24:195–211

Levine, R. 1991. Learning in U.S. arms control policy. See Breslauer & Tetlock 1991

Levy, J. S. 1983. Misperception and the causes of war: theoretical linkages and analytical problems. *World Polit.* 36:76–99

Levy, J. S. 1986. Organizational routines and the causes of war. *Int. Stud. Q.* 30:193–222

Levy, J. S. 1989. The causes of war: a review of theories and evidence. See Tetlock et al 1989, pp. 209–333

Lifton, R. J., Falk, R. 1982. *Indefensible Weapons: The Political and Psychological Case against Nuclearism.* New York: Basic

Lindskold, S. 1978. Trust development, the GRIT proposal and the effects of conciliatory acts on conflict and cooperation. *Psychol. Bull.* 85:772–88

Linkskold, S. 1979a. Managing conflict through announced conciliatory initiatives backed with retaliatory capability. In *The Social Psychology of Intergroup Relations,* ed. S. Worchel, pp. 274–87. Monterey, CA: Brooks/Cole

Lindskold, S. 1979b. Conciliation with simultaneous or sequential interaction. *J. Confl. Resolut.* 23:704–14

Lindskold, S., Bennett, R. 1973. Attributing trust and conciliatory intent from coercive power capability. *J. Exp. Soc. Psychol.* 16:187–98

Lindskold, S., Betz, B., Walters, P. 1986. Transforming competitive or cooperative climates. *J. Confl. Resolut.* 30:99–114

Lindskold, S., Collins, M. 1978. Inducing cooperation by groups and individuals: applying Osgood's GRIT strategy. *J. Confl. Resolut.* 22:679–90

Lindskold, S., Finch, M. 1981. Styles of announcing conciliation. *J. Confl. Resolut.* 25:145–55

Lindskold, S., Han, G. 1988. GRIT as a foundation for integrative bargaining. *Pers. Soc. Psychol. Bull.* 14:335–45

Lindskold, S., Han, G., Betz, B. 1986a. The essential elements of communication in the GRIT strategy. *Pers. Soc. Psychol. Bull.* 12:179–86

Lindskold, S., Han, G., Betz, B. 1986b. Repeated persuasion in interpersonal conflict. *J. Pers. Soc. Psychol.* 51:1183–88

Lindzey, G., Aronson, E., eds. 1985. *Handbook of Social Psychology.* New York: Random House. 3rd ed.

Mandel, R. 1987. *Irrationality in International Confrontation.* New York: Greenwood Press

Mandelbaum, M. 1981. *The Nuclear Revolution.* Cambridge: Cambridge Univ. Press

Maoz, Z. 1981. The decision to raid Entebbe: decision analysis applied to crisis behavior. *J. Confl. Resolut.* 25:677–708

May, E. R. 1973. *Lessons of the Past: The Use and Misuse of History in American Foreign Policy.* New York: Oxford Univ. Press

May, E. R. 1984. *Knowing One's Enemies: Intelligence Assessments before the Two World Wars.* Princeton, NJ: Princeton Univ. Press

McClintock, C. G., Stech, F., Beggan, J. 1987. The effects of commitments to threats and promises upon bargaining behaviour and outcomes. *Eur. J. Soc. Psychol.* 17:447–64

McNeil, W. H. 1982. *The Pursuit of Power.* Chicago: Univ. Chicago Press

Milburn, T. W., Christie, D. J. 1989. Rewarding in international politics. *Polit. Psychol.* 10:625–45

Morgan, P. M. 1983. *Deterrence: A Conceptual Analysis.* Beverly Hills, CA: Sage

Morrow, J. D. 1989. A twist of truth: a reexamination of the effects of arms races on the occurrence of war. *J. Confl. Resolut.* 33:500–29

Nathan, J. A., Oliver, J. 1976. *United States Foreign Policy and World Order.* Boston: Little, Brown

Neustadt, R. E., May, E. R. 1986. *Thinking in Time: The Uses of History for Decision-Makers.* New York: Free Press

Nisbett, R. E., Ross, L. 1980. *Human Inference: Strategies and Shortcomings of Social Judgment.* Englewood Cliffs, NJ: Prentice-Hall

Nye, J. S. 1987. Nuclear learning and U.S.-Soviet security regimes. *Int. Org.* 41:371–402

Nye, J. S. 1988. Old wars and future wars: causation and prevention. *J. Interdiscip. Hist.* 18:581–90

Orme, J. 1987. Deterrence failures: a second look. *Int. Secur.* 11:96–124

Osgood, C. E. 1962. *An Alternative to War and Surrender.* Champaign-Urbana, IL: Univ. Illinois Press

Oye, K. A. 1985. Explaining cooperation under anarchy: hypotheses and strategies. *World Polit.* 38:1–24

Patchen, M. 1987. Strategies for eliciting cooperation from an adversary: laboratory and internation findings. *J. Confl. Resolut.* 31:164–85

Patchen, M. 1988. *Resolving Disputes between Nations: Coercion or Conciliation?* Durham, NC: Duke Univ. Press

Pilisuk, M., Skolnick, P. 1968. Inducing trust: a test of the Osgood proposal. *J. Pers. Soc. Psychol.* 8:121–33

Pruitt, D. G., Kimmel, P. R. 1977. Twenty years of experimental gaming: critique, synthesis, and suggestions for the future. *Annu. Rev. Psychol.* 28:363–92

Pruitt, D. G., Rubin, J. Z. 1986. *Social Conflict.* Reading, MA: Addison-Wesley

Putnam, R. D. 1988. Diplomacy and domestic politics: the logic of two-level games. *Int. Org.* 42:427–60

Quester, G. H. 1989. Some thoughts on "deterrence failures." See Stern et al 1989, pp. 52–65

Richardson, L. F. 1960. *Arms and Insecurity.* Pittsburg: Boxwood

Russett, B. M. 1967. Pearl Harbor: deterrence theory and decision theory. *J. Peace Res.* 4:89–106

Russett, B. M. 1989. The democratic governance of nuclear weapons. See Tetlock et al 1989, pp. 174–208

Sagan, S. D. 1985. Nuclear alerts and crisis management. *Int. Secur.* 9:99–139

Schelling, T. C. 1966. *Arms and Influence.* New Haven, CT: Yale Univ. Press

Schneider, W. 1987. "Rambo" and reality: having it both ways. In *Eagle Resurgent?,* ed. K. A. Oye. Boston: Little, Brown

Schuman, H., Ludwig, J., Krosnick, J. A. 1986. The perceived threat of nuclear war, salience, and open questions. *Public Opin. Q.* 50:519–36

Shapiro, R. Y., Page, B. I. 1988. Foreign policy and the rational public. *J. Confl. Resolut.* 32:211–47

Shepard, G. 1988. Personality effects on American foreign policy, 1969–1984: a second test of interpersonal generalization theory. *Int. Stud. Q.* 32:91–123

Skov, R. B., Sherman, S. J. 1986. Information gathering processes: diagnosticity, hypothesis-confirmatory strategies, and perceived hypothesis confirmation. *J. Exp. Soc. Psychol.* 22:93–121

Slovic, P. 1975. Choice between equally-valued alternatives. *J. Exp. Psychol.: Hum. Percept. Perform.* 1:280–87

Smith, H. 1988. *The Power Game.* New York: Ballantine

Smith, T. W. 1988. Nuclear anxiety. *Public Opin. Q.* 52:557–75

Smith, W., Anderson, A. 1975. Threats, communication and bargaining. *J. Pers. Soc. Psychol.* 32:76–82

Sniderman, P. M., Tetlock, P. E. 1986. The interrelationships between political ideology and public opinion. In *Handbook of Political Psychology,* Vol. 2, ed. M. G. Herman, pp. 62–96. San Francisco: Jossey-Bass

Snyder, G. H., Diesing, P. 1977. *Conflict among Nations: Bargaining, Decision Making and System Structure in International Crises.* Princeton, NJ: Princeton Univ. Press

Snyder, J. 1984. *The Ideology of the Offensive: Military Decisionmaking and the Disasters of 1914.* Ithaca, NY: Cornell Univ. Press

Sorrentino, R. M., Higgins, E. T., eds. 1986. *Handbook of Motivation and Cognition: Foundations of Social Behavior.* New York: Guilford

Staub, E. 1988. *The Roots of Evil.* New York: Cambridge Univ. Press

Stech, F., McClintock, C. G., Moss, B. 1984. The effectiveness of the carrot and the stick in increasing dyadic outcomes during duopolistic bargaining. *Behav. Sci.* 29:1–12

Stein, J. G. 1985. Calculation, miscalculation, and conventional deterrence. I: The view from Cairo. See Jervis et al 1985, pp. 34–59

Stein, J. G. 1990. Deterrence and reassurance. See Tetlock et al 1990

Stein, J. G., Tanter, R. 1980. *Rational Decision Making: Israel's Security Choices.* Columbus, OH: Ohio State Univ. Press

Steinbruner, J. D. 1974. *The Cybernetic Theory of Decision: New Dimensions of Political Analysis.* Princeton, NJ: Princeton Univ. Press

Steinbruner, J. D. 1987. Choices and trade-offs. See Carter et al 1987, pp. 535–54

Stern, P. C., Axelrod, R. M., Jervis, R., Radner, R., eds. 1989. *Perspectives on Deterrence.* New York: Oxford Univ. Press

Sternberg, R. J., Soriano, L. 1984. Styles of conflict resolution. *J. Pers. Soc. Psychol.* 47:115–26

Stoll, R. J., McAndrew, W. 1986. Negotiating strategic arms control, 1969–1979. *J. Confl. Resolut.* 30:315–26

Stuart, D. T., Starr, H. 1981/82. The "inherent bad faith model" reconsidered: Dulles, Kennedy, and Kissinger. *Polit. Psychol.* 2:1–33

Suedfeld, P., Tetlock, P. E. 1977. Integrative complexity of communications in international crises. *J. Confl. Resolut.* 21:169–84

Taylor, S. E., Brown, J. D. 1988. Illusion and well-being: a social-psychological perspective on mental health. *Psychol. Rev.* 103:193–210

Tetlock, P. E. 1983. Policymakers' images of international conflict. *J. Soc. Issues* 39:67–86

Tetlock, P. E. 1986a. Psychological research on foreign policy: What do we have to contribute? *Am. Psychol.* 41:557–67

Tetlock, P. E. 1986b. A value pluralism model of ideological reasoning. *J. Pers. Soc. Psychol.* 50:819–27

Tetlock, P. E. 1987. Testing deterrence theory: some conceptual and methodological issues. *J. Soc. Issues* 43:85–91

Tetlock, P. E., Boettger, R. 1989. Cognitive and rhetorical styles of traditionalist and reformist Soviet politicians: a content analysis study. *Polit. Psychol.* 10:209–32

Tetlock, P. E., Jervis, R., Stern, P., Husbands, J. L., Tilly, C., eds. 1989. *Behavior, Society, and Nuclear War,* Vol. 1. Washington: Oxford Univ. Press

Tetlock, P. E., Jervis, R., Stern, P., Husbands, J. L., Tilly, C., eds. 1990. *Behavior, Society, and Nuclear War,* Vol. 2. Washington: Oxford Univ. Press

Tetlock, P. E., Kim, J. I. 1987. Accountability and judgment processes in a personality prediction task. *J. Pers. Soc. Psychol.* 52:700–9

Tetlock, P. E., Levi, A. 1982. Attribution bias: on the inconclusiveness of the cognition-motivation debate. *J. Exp. Soc. Psychol.* 18:68–88

Tetlock, P. E., Manstead, A. S. R. 1985. Impression management versus intrapsychic theories in social psychology: a false dichotomy. *Psychol. Rev.* 92:57–85

Tetlock, P. E., McGuire, C. B. 1986. Cognitive perspective on foreign policy. *Polit. Behav. Ann.* 1:147–79

Thies, W. 1991. Learning in American policy toward Europe. See Breslauer & Tetlock 1991

Thucydides. 1972. [ca. 400 BC]. *The Peloponnesian War*. Transl. R. Warner. Baltimore, MD: Penguin

To, T. 1988. More realism in the prisoner's dilemma. *J. Confl. Resolut.* 32:402–8

Tourangeau, R., Rasinski, K. A. 1988. Cognitive processes underlying context effects in attitude measurement. *Psychol. Bull.* 103:299–314

Tversky, A., Kahneman, D. 1986. Rational choice and the framing of decisions. *J. Bus.* 59:S251–78

Tyler, T. R., McGraw, K. M. 1983. The threat of nuclear war: risk interpretation and behavioral response. *J. Soc. Issues* 39:25–40

van Evera, S. 1985. Why cooperation failed in 1914. *World Polit.* 38:80–117

Vertzberger, Y. 1986. Foreign policy decisionmakers as practical-intuitive historians: applied history and its shortcomings. *Int. Stud. Q.* 30:223–47

von Clausewitz, C. 1976. [1830]. *On War*. Transl. P. Paret, M. Howard. Princeton, NJ: Princeton Univ. Press

Wallace, M. D. 1979. Arms races and escalation: some new evidence. *J. Confl. Resolut.* 23:3–16

Wallace, M. D. 1980. Some persisting findings: a reply to Professor Weede. *J. Confl. Resolut.* 24:289–92

Waltz, K. N. 1979. *Theory of International Politics*. Reading, MA: Addison-Wesley

Weede, E. 1980. Arms and escalation: some persisting doubts. *J. Confl. Resolut.* 24:285–88

Welch, D. A. 1989. Crisis decision making reconsidered. *J. Confl. Resolut.* 33:430–45

White, R. K. 1984. *Fearful Warriors: A Psychological Profile of U.S.-Soviet Relations*. New York: Free Press

Whiting, A. 1991. Soviet policy toward China: 1969–1988. See Breslauer & Tetlock 1991

Wohlstetter, A. 1958. The delicate balance of terror. *Foreign Aff.* 37:211–34

Yankelovich, D., Doble, J. 1984. The public mood: nuclear weapons and the U.S.S.R. *Foreign Aff.* 63:33–46

Yankelovich, D., Smoke, R. 1988. America's "New Thinking". *Foreign Aff.* 67:1–17

Zimmerman, W., Axelrod, R. M. 1981. The "lessons" of Vietnam and Soviet foreign policy. *World Polit.* 34:1–24

Annu. Rev. Psychol. 1991. 42:277–303

MUSIC PSYCHOLOGY: TONAL STRUCTURES IN PERCEPTION AND MEMORY

Carol L. Krumhansl

Department of Psychology, Cornell University, Ithaca, New York 14853-7601

KEY WORDS: music perception, psychoacoustics, music cognition, memory for music, musical pitch

CONTENTS

INTRODUCTION

The psychological literature on music has expanded rapidly during the last two decades. The sheer mass of published reports forces a highly restricted selection of topics. Moreover, a coherent historical or theoretical context is

277

0066-4308/91/0201-0277$02.00

difficult to provide for the wealth of accumulated empirical observations. Historically, two main lines of investigation can be identified. One, in the tradition of Helmholtz (1954), emphasizes perception (of musical pitch, in particular); the other, in the tradition of Seashore (1967), emphasizes performance. The present review focuses on research in the first of these traditions, which seeks an explanation, in psychological terms, for such aspects of musical practice as tuning systems, scale structure, harmony, and melody. Research on the perception of timing, meter, and rhythm is not included as it fits more appropriately with studies of music performance.

Most research in the psychology of music occurs within the frameworks of psychoacoustics, Gestalt psychology, individual-differences psychology, and cognitive psychology; but the influences of developmental, cross-cultural, neuroscience, and computational approaches are also evident. The topics reviewed here trace a shift during the last two decades from psychoacoustic to cognitive orientations. More extended and musically realistic materials tend to be employed, and there is a greater emphasis on learning, memory, and attention. Music is compared with other domains of human behavior that require complex internal representations and processes—e.g. vision and language. Psychological studies depend increasingly on music theory, which helps researchers generate testable hypotheses, directs attention to more interesting and subtle musical questions, and provides a context for interpreting empirical results. The review begins with research in the psychoacoustic tradition which investigates the perceptual effects of isolated tones and intervals. Studies concerned with general principles of tonal organization in melody and harmony are reviewed next. The final sections consider perception and memory of extended sequences and the influences of linguistic and music theories on research in music perception and cognition.

CONSONANCE

Following from the treatise of Helmholtz (1954), the subject of consonance (vs dissonance) has a long tradition of scientific investigation. The multiplicity of methods, results, and theories are not reviewed here (see Malmberg 1918 for an early review). Currently, there appears to be general consensus on two points. First, tonal (or sensory) consonance needs to be distinguished from musical consonance. Tonal consonance refers to the degree to which two simultaneous tones (presented in isolation) sound pleasant, smooth, or blended (Plomp & Levelt 1965). Musical consonance, in contrast, refers to the quality of intervals in a musical context. The latter, while presumed to be related to the former, will also be influenced by the immediate context, the musical style, the musical enculturation of the listener, and other factors (Cazden 1945). With regard to musical enculturation, it should be noted that most of the studies reviewed in this chapter were done with subjects familiar with traditional Western music. A few studies with non-Western music and non-Western listeners are mentioned.

The distinction between tonal and musical consonance has been useful for sharpening the issues investigated in studies of tonal consonance but has divorced them somewhat from musical considerations. Systematic accounts of musical consonance are largely lacking, with the exception of Terhardt's (1974, 1984; Terhardt et al, 1982a,b; Parncutt 1988, 1989) theory of virtual pitch. According to this theory, virtual pitches are heard to the extent that the sounded frequencies match learned harmonic templates. Preliminary results suggest this theory holds some promise to account for such phenomena as the effect of inversion on the consonance of chords, the tone perceived as the root of chords, and the construction of harmonic progressions.

The second point of consensus is that tonal dissonance is best accounted for in terms of beating or roughness. Building on Helmholtz's (1954) basic theory, Plomp & Levelt (1965) proposed a model for computing dissonance. The observation on which their model rests is that the tonal dissonance of an interval formed by simple (sine wave) tones depends on their frequency difference. When the difference is less than a critical bandwidth (the range within which tones interact—in the middle register of the piano, approximately equal to a minor third), the interval is judged dissonant; maximum judged dissonance occurs at about a quarter of a critical bandwidth. Beyond a critical bandwidth, the interval is judged to be consonant. The dissonance of intervals formed by complex (harmonically rich) tones such as those produced by musical instruments is calculated from the dissonance of neighboring harmonics (taking amplitude into account) to give the total dissonance. Calculated values for various types of harmonic tones are presented by Kameoka & Kuriyagawa (1969 a,b), Hutchinson & Knopoff (1978, 1979), and Danner (1985, who also used the values to trace dissonance fluctuations in an atonal composition).

The model predicts that tonal dissonance should be low for intervals with fundamental frequencies (corresponding to the pitches heard) that can be expressed as ratios of small integers, such as the unison $(1:1)$, octave $(1:2)$, perfect fifth $(2:3)$, and perfect fourth $(3:4)$. Somewhat higher dissonance values are predicted for the major sixth $(3:5)$, major third $(4:5)$, minor third $(5:6)$, and minor sixth $(5:8)$. For simple frequency ratios, the lower, more intense harmonics of the two tones either coincide or fall outside the range of interference. For less simple ratios, a greater number of harmonics fall inside the range of interference, causing beating or roughness. Thus, the model is consistent with a large number of perceptual studies showing that judged dissonance increases approximately monotonically with the integers needed to express the fundamental frequency ratios (e.g. Vos & van Vianen 1984). This is true even though the criteria for judging consonance vary widely in the literature. Van de Geer et al (1962) attempted to sort out the relations among the various criteria, many of which are highly subjective (such as "euphonious" and "beautiful"). Investigators have argued for more objective criteria, such as discriminability between pure and mistuned intervals, sensitivity to beats, identification of the direction of mistuning (Vos 1982), and judgments of whether an interval is heard as one or two tones (DeWitt & Crowder 1987, an operationalization of Stumpf's 1883 doctrine of tonal fusion, which holds that combinations of tones differ in the degree to which they fuse).

TUNING AND INTONATION

Recent research has focused less on tonal consonance per se than on the implications the concept may have for musical practice and perception. As has long been recognized, tuning systems cannot be constructed such that all intervals are tuned to their theoretical ratios (Helmholtz 1954; Hall 1973, 1974; Burns & Ward 1982; Rasch 1984). For example, in equal-tempered tuning (in which tones are equally spaced in log frequency), minor thirds are flat (by 16 cents) and major thirds are sharp (by 16 cents) compared to their theoretical values in just intonation (there are 100 cents per semitone). Despite this, equal temperament is the standard for tuning fixed-pitch instruments (such as the piano) because it has the practical advantage that the tuning is equally good in any musical key, permitting modulation and transposition. Singers and players of nonfixed-pitch instruments often deviate markedly from the pure ratios in performance (Francès 1958; Rakowski 1990; Shackford 1961, 1962a,b; Sundberg 1982; and other studies summarized in Ward 1970). Intervals [including the octave (Sundberg & Lindqvist 1973; Ohgushi 1983)] tend to be stretched compared to their theoretical values (except for seconds which tend to be compressed). These observations suggest that the simple-ratio theory of consonance has only indirect bearing on musical practice.

A series of recent studies on interval perception, however, shows listeners are quite sensitive to deviations from simple ratios. The threshold for discriminating between pure and mistuned intervals is in the range of 10–30 cents. Vos (1982, 1984; Vos & van Vianen 1984, 1985) examined the effect of various physical parameters such as spectral frequency, tone duration, and fundamental frequency on thresholds for discriminating between pure and tempered (mistuned) intervals. In many cases, the effects could be attributed to the strength of beats produced by the tempered intervals. However, ratings of subjective purity (Vos 1985) deviated from precise predictions of the model (discussed earlier) of Plomp & Levelt (1965) and Kameoka & Kuriyagawa

(1969a,b), suggesting that modifications are needed. Vos & van Vianen (1985), Hall & Hess (1984), and Elliot et al (1987) found tolerance for mistuning decreased when going from less consonant to more consonant intervals, again implicating absence of beating as a cue for pure tuning. The results of the latter two studies also suggested an additional strategy of matching the intervals to abstract standards of interval sizes.

Taking a somewhat different approach, Mathews & Pierce (1980) used tones with stretched harmonics (the distance between harmonics was expanded by a constant multiplicative factor). They found coinciding harmonics produced a sensation of finality or consonance. In a similar vein, Roberts & Mathews (1984) studied how sensitive listeners are to the intonation of chords formed with nonstandard ratios of fundamental frequencies ($3:5:7$ and $5:7:9$). Again, an effect of coinciding harmonics was found in preference judgments, although some listeners favored slightly mistuned versions both of these and of traditional (major and minor) chords. Using novel stimuli (as in these two studies) has the advantage of allowing effects of psychoacoustic properties to be examined while minimizing the influences of experience or learning. Finally, Rasch (1985) and Vos (1988) recently looked at tuning preferences for longer sequences of simultaneous tones. The former found that mistuning of the intervals of the melody was more disturbing than mistuning of simultaneous (harmonic) intervals, supporting the idea that listeners compare melodic intervals to an abstract interval standard. However, Vos showed that the physical purity of simultaneous fifths and thirds accounted for the acceptability of the sequences in his experiment. Taken together, these studies of musical interval tuning support the view that interference between harmonics is the major influence on judgments of tuning, but additional, nonpsychoacoustic factors or strategies also operate.

CATEGORICAL PITCH PERCEPTION

An apparent paradox arises in the disparity between the accuracy of interval tuning judgments in the studies just reviewed and the deviations from simple-ratio intervals in musical performances. How is it that the sometimes markedly out-of-tune intervals that are performed are not perceived as such? A partial answer to this may be found in studies showing that musically trained subjects perceive intervals categorically. Categorical perception, a phenomenon originally described in the speech literature, is operationally defined (Studdert-Kennedy et al 1970) by: 1. sharp boundaries between category labels assigned to stimuli varying in small steps along a physical continuum, and 2. better discrimination between stimuli in different categories than between stimuli in the same category. (Examples of both criteria are given in the next paragraph.) In the ideal, discrimination performance is no better than the ability to differentially identify the stimuli (in contrast to the more typical psychophysical result that discrimination is much better than absolute identification).

Burns & Ward (1978) found this pattern in their study of melodic intervals ranging from 250 to 550 cents in steps of 12.5 cents. Musically trained listeners abruptly shifted the labels they assigned to intervals along this continuum [from minor third (three semitones) to major third (four semitones), and then from major third to perfect fourth (five semitones)]. Between the points on the continuum where the shifts occurred, there was virtually 100% consistency about the interval label assigned. For example, one subject (C4) consistently labeled all intervals from 350 to 412.5 cents "major third"; below this range intervals were labeled "minor third," above it "perfect fourth." (When additional response labels for quartertones were added in another condition, they were not used consistently, which suggests that these results were not simply a consequence of restricting the responses to traditional interval names.) The discrimination task required listeners to judge which of two intervals was wider, and the data were very close to the predictions from the identification scores. That is, intervals were discriminated only to the extent they were labeled differently, producing peaks at the category boundaries. For example, this same subject was close to chance discriminating between intervals in the range labeled "major third," but was above 75% correct at the ends of the range. Burns & Ward (1978) found no such peaks for musically untrained listeners.

This is perhaps the clearest reported case of categorical perception found for musical intervals, but similar results appear in other studies. Siegel & Siegel (1977a,b) found the following results for musicians with relative pitch (the ability to name tones when a reference pitch is present): 1. sharp identification boundaries; 2. discrete steps in magnitude estimates corresponding to interval category boundaries; 3. no effect on magnitude estimates of changing the range of the stimulus set (i.e. no adaptation effect; Helson 1964); and 4. an inability to distinguish "sharp" and "flat" intervals within categories. Subjects with absolute pitch (the ability to name tones in the absence of a reference pitch) showed the first and third effects when presented with single tones in isolation. Zatorre & Halpern (1979) again found sharp identification boundaries, but here discrimination performance exceeded predictions from the identification responses. The latter result suggests listeners could use acoustic information in addition to the category labels to make the discrimination. The fact that this study, unlike the others, used simultaneous (harmonic) intervals probably contributed to the result; successive (melodic) intervals may be coded more categorically because they require retaining the pitch relations over time. This study also found that the category boundaries could be shifted by preceding the test trials with an adaptor (120 presentations of an interval at one end of the stimulus continuum), a result analogous to adaptation found for speech sounds. Finally, Wapnick et al (1982) investigated whether labeling (of interval category and intonation quality) and discrimination would be more accurate when intervals were presented at the end of a tonal melody. Although performance was better for intervals in context than for isolated intervals, musicians still tended to produce the categorical pattern of results.

The categorical perception of musical intervals suggests that at some level of processing, pitch information is coded with respect to discrete pitch categories corresponding to the intervals in the musical scale. If this is the case, categorical perception should be limited to trained musicians, and indeed large differences as a function of musical training are found in all the studies cited (as well as in Crowder's 1985 study of major and minor triads). Nonmusicians exhibit neither sharp categorical boundaries nor peaks in discrimination functions. That pitch is coded in terms of learned musical categories is further supported by Francès's (1988) finding that listeners notice mistunings of tones less when they conform to the melodic and harmonic tendencies of the tones in the context than when they do not. These findings should not be taken to say, however, that intervals cannot be coded precisely by musicians. The tuning judgments summarized in the last section indicate that, under some circumstances, they can be. Tuning experiments typically use harmonically rich tones and simultaneous (harmonic) intervals, and subjects are often given feedback about whether or not their responses are correct. In contrast, studies showing categorical results typically use sinusoidal tones and successive (melodic) intervals, and no feedback is given. These methodological differences may account in large measure for the different estimates of intonation sensitivity, although no systematic study of these factors has been reported.

ABSOLUTE PITCH PERCEPTION

Absolute pitch refers to the ability to name an isolated musical tone (presented without an objective reference tone) or, conversely, to produce a tone identified by name only. Although the practical significance of this ability for musicians is limited, it has received considerable attention owing to its apparent rarity in the population. Ward & Burns (1982) provide a review of most of the literature on this topic, and a few more recent studies are summarized here. Miyazaki (1988) had listeners assign names to electronically generated sine wave tones (eliminating possible timbral cues of musical instruments such as piano; see Lockhead & Byrd 1981). As in other studies, listeners with absolute pitch showed: 1. high accuracy and short latency of naming; 2. a predominance of octave errors when errors occurred; and 3. a categorical pattern of classifying tones (which differed in steps of 20 cents). The responses of listeners without absolute pitch were slower, more variable, and showed neither a tendency toward octave errors nor sharp categorical boundaries; they apparently relied primarily on an impression of overall pitch height. What is unusual in this study is the prevalence of absolute pitch. In the first experiment, 7 of 10 listeners (university music students) showed absolute pitch. Of the 39 music students in the second study, 12 performed at a rate of 86.7% or better in responding within one semitone. Essentially all of these subjects began musical training at the age of 3–5 years, suggesting that early exposure underlies the ability. Curiously, these subjects did not recognize all 12 tones of the chromatic scale equally well, but were better on the white notes of the piano (and especially the tonally important notes of C major). Although the possibility of a response bias cannot be eliminated, the authors suggest this finding may be related to the fact that early piano and ear training lessons tend to begin with the C major key.

In a somewhat similar vein, Terhardt & Ward (1982) and Terhardt & Seewan (1983) showed a fairly widespread ability to judge whether or not a piece was played in the notated key (indicated to listeners by a simplified score). These studies used as stimuli the initial segments (approximately 5 sec) of Bach's preludes from the *Well-Tempered Clavier*, which were played either in the notated key or transposed up or down by an interval ranging from 1 to 6 semitones. Accuracy rates were surprisingly high. For example, Terhardt & Seewan (1983) found 45% of the listeners (only some of whom claimed absolute pitch) were reliably able to distinguish between the notated key and a transposition by one semitone. The results were similar whether piano or electronic timbres were used. These performance rates exceed what would be predicted based on pitch-naming studies for listeners without absolute pitch, although the specific comparison was not made. Their subjects were not tested on isolated tones, so it is unclear whether they had better pitch-identification abilities than expected or whether identifying keys is a different process from identifying isolated pitches. Both abilities show a bimodal distribution in the population, suggesting they may be related.

Finally, Zatorre & Beckett (1989) recently examined a different question—namely, the nature of the mental code used by musicians with absolute pitch. Such subjects were required to name three successive piano tones after a delay of up to 27 sec. During the retention interval, they performed a verbal interference task (counting backwards by threes) or a musical interference task (humming or singing a chromatic scale). Neither task affected the accuracy of reporting the tones (in contrast to many studies showing interference effects on both musical and verbal memory), suggesting that the mental code is neither exclusively verbal nor exclusively acoustic in nature. Rather, multiple codes appear to be employed, including these and possibly also kinesthetic codes (e.g. specifying the finger position for producing the tone on an instrument).

MODELS OF TONAL RELATIONS

In general, pitch is coded primarily in terms of the intervals between simultaneous and successive pitches. For example, a melody is heard as the same melody even though it begins on a different pitch (is transposed) as long as the intervals between tones are unchanged. Moreover, whereas absolute pitch ability is relatively rare, most musicians have quite accurate relative pitch ability. How is interval information perceived and remembered? In physical terms, tones vary along the continuous dimension of frequency measured in Hertz (cycles per second). The corresponding perceptual attribute—pitch—is a logarithmic function of physical frequency over most of the musical range, and the perceived sizes of musical intervals depend on distances along this logarithmic scale. Additional evidence for the logarithmic scale comes from musical practice. The tones used in music consist of a discrete set of values along this continuum. The chromatic scale of Western music, for example, has 12 semitones per octave that are (in equal-tempered tuning) equally spaced in log frequency. The same pattern repeats in every octave; corresponding tones in the different octaves are given the same name (e.g. C, C#, etc) and are said to be octave-equivalent.

Factors other than distance along this single dimension of pitch also influence the degree to which two tones are perceived as related. Various proposals have been made for summarizing these factors, often in the form of geometric models (reviewed by Shepard 1982). These models variously emphasize different factors: pitch height (the unidimensional scale just described); the chroma circle (on which tones separated by semitones are adjacent and octave-related tones are considered equivalent); the circle of fifths (on which tones separated by perfect fifths, or seven semitones, are adjacent and octave-related tones are considered equivalent); and the sub-cycles generated by major thirds (four semitones) and minor thirds (three semitones).

Models jointly emphasizing pitch height and the chroma circle (producing a helix or variants of it) have been proposed frequently (e.g. Bachem 1950; Shepard 1964; Pikler 1966; and sources cited in these papers). Shepard (1964, 1983 with accompanying sound examples) argued that the sense of chroma (pitch class) is psychologically separate from the sense of overall pitch height. His study employed tones produced according to the following method (variants of which have been employed in numerous subsequent experiments). Each tone consisted of ten sinusoidal components at octave intervals. For example, one tone might consist of Cs sounded in ten octaves, while another of C#s sounded in ten octaves. The amplitudes of the components were determined by a sinusoidal function increasing from threshold at the low end of the frequency range to a maximum in the center of the range, and then decreasing to threshold at the high end of the range. Sounding these tones in succession produces the perception of moving from C to C# but not (owing to the amplitude envelope) of changing pitch height. After continuing the process for a total of 12 steps (with components moving along the chromatic scale), a tone physically identical to the first tone is reached (components are filled in at the bottom of the pitch range as components drop out at the top).

Listeners in Shepard's study (1964) judged two tones as ascending if the distance between components is shorter in the direction of increasing frequency (e.g., a tone with C components followed by a tone with E components) and as descending if the distance is shorter in the direction of decreasing frequency (e.g. a tone with C components followed by a tone with A components). Tones with equal distances in the two directions (e.g. a tone with C components followed by a tone with F# components) were perceived as either ascending or descending (with stable individual differences in the direction of motion, according to Deutsch 1986b, 1987; Deutsch et al 1986; Deutsch et al 1987). From this, Shepard argued for a circular dimension of pitch chroma (with octave-related tones equivalent) that is independent of pitch height. Burns (1981), however, showed the same effects with tones whose components were not separated by octaves, weakening the argument that a circular dimension of chroma (identifying octave-related tones) is implicated. Moreover, Nakajima et al (1988) recently demonstrated a second circular dimension (corresponding to a one-third-octave periodicity) when the components form major triads. Going even further in this direction, Allik et al (1989) provided a general model predicting perceived pitch motion with randomly selected components. For present purposes, it is important to note only that ample evidence from other perceptual studies (and musical practice) supports the notion that tones at octave intervals are in some sense equivalent or at least highly related. In addition, support for the helical model (combining pitch height and the chroma circle) has been obtained recently in a scaling study by Ueda & Ohgushi (1987) in which listeners judged the similarity of pairs of tones generated according to Shepard's (1964) general method.

Other models emphasize different factors that may govern the degree to which tones are heard as related. The dimensions of Lakner's (1960) and Shepard's (1982, "melodic map") models are the chroma circle and the circle of fifths. The models put forth by Longuet-Higgins (1962a,b), Hall (1973, 1974), Balzano (1980), and Shepard (1982, "harmonic map"), which can be traced back to Helmholtz and Euler, are generated by major thirds and perfect fifths. Although these models are intuitively appealing because certain musical structures, such as scales and triadic harmonies, seem to "fall out" of them, direct supporting evidence from perceptual studies is lacking.

Moreover, Krumhansl (1979, 1990a) argued that geometric models of pitch relations are, in general, limited in two important ways when the pitches are heard in context. First, the geometric models just described all assume that intervals of equal size are perceived as equal. This may be true for isolated intervals, but it is not true for intervals in tonal contexts. The tones C and G, for example, were judged by listeners to be more similar or related in the context of a C major key (in which they play the structurally important roles referred to as tonic and dominant, respectively: see next section) than were the tones C# and G#, even though both intervals are perfect fifths. The second limitation is that spatial models cannot depict temporal-order effects because spatial distances are necessarily symmetric. For example, in a C major key context, B followed by C received a higher rating of similarity or relatedness than C followed by B (the B, as a leading tone, tends to be followed by C, the tonic). The appeal of geometric models, however, is that they summarize complex pitch relationships in a form that can easily be understood.

TONAL HIERARCHIES

Krumhansl & Shepard (1979) devised the probe-tone technique to investigate one aspect of how a tonal context influences the perception of musical pitch. Music theorists (e.g. Meyer 1956; Lerdahl 1988) describe a hierarchy of tonal functions, with some tones more stable, structurally significant, or final-sounding than others. In rough categorical terms, the tonic, which heads the hierarchy, is followed by the fifth (dominant) and third (mediant) scale degrees, which are followed by the remaining scale degrees, and finally the nonscale (nondiatonic) tones. In Western music, the seven-tone major and minor diatonic scales are the most frequently used; see Krumhansl (1990a) for a description of their construction. The probe-tone technique, as originally applied, operationalized the notion of a tonal hierarchy as follows. An incomplete C major scale (without the final tonic, C) was sounded in either ascending or descending form. This context, intended to establish the key of C major, was followed on successive trials by each of the chromatic scale pitches in the next octave (the probe tones). Listeners rated how well each tone completed the scale. The ratings of listeners with musical training (instrumental or vocal instruction) conformed to the qualitative predictions of music theory, whereas the ratings of listeners without musical training were dominated by another factor, namely the distance between the probe tone and the last tone of the context.

Krumhansl & Kessler (1982), using different key-defining contexts (tonic triads and chord cadences for both major and minor keys), again recovered the predicted tonal hierarchy in ratings of how well the probe tones "fit with" the contexts. The ratings given the probe tones in major and minor key contexts were then used to obtain a spatial representation of the perceived distances between musical keys. The analysis, which took the following steps, was based on the assumption that closely related keys have similar tonal hierarchies. First, rating profiles for the major and minor keys were shifted to different tonics to produce profiles for all 12 major and 12 minor keys; this was justified by the equivalence of the tonal hierarchies under transposition. Second, all pairs of profiles were correlated to obtain an indirect measure of how closely related each key is to each of the others; keys were considered closely related to the extent that their tonal hierarchies were similar as measured by the correlations. Third, the correlations were analyzed using multidimensional scaling, which produces a spatial representation of points such that interpoint distance is, as much as possible, inversely related to the similarity measures (in this case the correlations of key profiles). The multidimensional scaling solution located the points for the 24 major and minor keys on the surface of a torus in four dimensions. In conformance with musical intuitions (and theoretical predictions—e.g. Schoenberg 1969), the perceived distances between keys were related to two factors: the circle of fifths and the relative and parallel major-minor relations. For example, the C major key had as its neighbors G major (one step "up" the circle of fifths), F major (one step "down" the circle of fifths), A minor (the relative minor), and C minor (the parallel minor). Thus, the information contained in the tonal hierarchy is sufficient to generate a concise and musically interpretable representation of key distance.

One motivation for obtaining the probe-tone ratings with contexts that unambiguously define keys (Krumhansl & Kessler 1982) was to provide standard profiles to compare with probe-tone ratings made with contexts that are less clear tonally. This has been done in a number of cases. Krumhansl & Kessler (1982) used the standard profiles to trace (on the map of musical keys just described) how the sense of key develops and changes over time. Trained musicians rated probe tones presented after each successive chord in nine-chord sequences, some of which contained modulations (changes) between keys. The sense of key was found to develop rapidly, even before the tonic triad was sounded. Shifts to keys that are theoretically closely related were assimilated more readily than shifts to distantly related keys. Thompson (1986), in a similar application to Bach chorales, detected an asymmetry in modulation distance: The initial key continued to have a stronger influence after modulations toward the dominant side of the circle of fifths ("up") than toward the subdominant ("down"). Directional asymmetries also appeared in identification of key changes and judged modulation distance (Thompson &

Cuddy 1989). Krumhansl & Schmuckler (1986) used the standard profiles (Krumhansl & Kessler 1982) to investigate whether listeners can perceive two keys simultaneously using a bitonal passage with materials from two distantly related keys. The tonal hierarchies of the two keys were both evident, but various experimental tasks showed listeners were unable to attend selectively to either one of the two keys. In another study, Krumhansl et al (1987) used contexts drawn from 20th-century atonal (serial) compositions. Listeners with less music training tended to produce probe-tone ratings similar to those of keys (weakly) suggested by the contexts. In contrast, listeners with more such training (particularly academic) tended to produce ratings similar to the tonal hierarchy of a distant key, suggesting they tended to reverse the normal tonal interpretations.

Two studies have adapted the probe-tone technique to non-Western music: Castellano et al (1984) to North Indian music, and Kessler et al (1984) to Balinese music. Both studies found the probe-tone ratings reflected style-appropriate tonal hierarchies, even some produced by listeners unfamiliar with the style. This result may depend on the fact that the contexts preceding the probe tones were relatively complex and explicitly emphasized the structurally important tones. These tones tended to be sounded more frequently, with longer durations, and at prominent positions within the phrases. Thus, these factors may enable listeners to identify the focal tones in novel musical styles. This possibility is supported by an extensive series of experiments conducted by Oram (1989), who investigated whether frequency of occurrence was sufficient to induce a tonal hierarchy as measured in the probe-tone task. In the context sequences, one tone occurred eight times, two others four times, and four others once each. In some cases the tones constituted a diatonic set (the tones of the normal major scale), and in other cases they did not (conforming to no major or minor scale), but in all cases the probe-tone ratings were strongly influenced by the frequency with which the tones appeared in the context. Thus, tone distributions provide a means through which a tonal hierarchy might become established in an unfamiliar style.

Most experiments, however, have focused on pitch structures in Western tonal-harmonic music rather than in earlier or later Western styles or non-Western music. The tonal hierarchies of major and minor keys (as described by music theorists and measured by the probe-tone ratings) influence the degree to which two tones are perceived as related (Krumhansl 1979, 1990a), reaction times in judging key membership (Janata & Reisberg 1988), judgments of phrase endings (Palmer & Krumhansl 1987a,b; Boltz 1989a,b, which also showed influences of rhythmic structure), expectations for melodic continuations (Schmuckler 1989), and patterns of memory confusions (Krumhansl 1979). Moreover, these psychological measures correlate strongly with the distributions of tones in stylistically familiar musical compositions

(Krumhansl 1990a,b), reinforcing the idea that the tonal hierarchies are learned through sensitivity to tone distributions within a stylistic tradition.

HARMONY AND KEY

The first part of this section takes up experimental studies that show effects for chords that are analogous to many of those just described for tones. In the latter part of the section we consider how a key becomes established initially. A tonal context establishes a hierarchy of structural significance, with the I (tonic), V (dominant), and IV (subdominant) heading the hierarchy (Krumhansl et al 1982b; Krumhansl 1990a). These harmonic hierarchies generate the same map of key distance as that generated by the tonal hierarchies (described above) and correlate with the frequency with which chords appear in musical compositions (Krumhansl 1990a). The harmonic hierarchies can also be predicted from the positions of the chord components in tonal hierarchies (Krumhansl & Kessler 1982), suggesting strong interdependencies between the two types of elements: tones and chords. The harmonic functions of chords in keys also affect the degree to which chords are heard as related (Krumhansl et al 1982b; Bharucha & Krumhansl 1983; Krumhansl et al 1982a; Roberts & Shaw 1984) and the probability they are confused in recognition memory (Bharucha & Krumhansl 1983; Krumhansl et al 1982a; Krumhansl & Castellano 1983). Perceived chord relations, in turn, determine harmonic expectancies (Bharucha & Stoeckig 1986, 1987; Schmuckler 1989) and mirror the frequency of chord progressions in music (Krumhansl 1990a). Finally, changing the tonal context produces regular effects on both memory confusions and relatedness judgments (Bharucha & Krumhansl 1983; Krumhansl et al 1982a), indicating strong ties between harmony and key. Bharucha (1987; Bharucha & Olney 1989) has recently developed a connectionist model that accounts for many of these results. Tone units are activated by the events in a musical sequence. Activation then spreads to chord and key units, and continues to reverberate bidirectionally until the network settles into a state of equilibrium. Computer simulations produce many of the same patterns of expectations, relatedness judgments, and memory errors as listeners in the experiments just reviewed.

Thus experiments show numerous parallels between tones and chords in how they are perceived in musical contexts (summarized in Krumhansl 1990a). For both, there is a well-defined hierarchy of structural significance, with harmonic hierarchies dependent on tonal hierarchies. Both mirror the distribution of elements in music, suggesting they are established in the music by repetition and other forms of emphasis, and generate the same measure of interkey distance. Perceived relations between tones and between chords are strengthened for elements that are structurally significant within the tonal context. Moreover, a less-stable element is perceived as more related to a stable element following it than is a more stable element to a less stable element following it. [The tendency to hear the second of two neighboring tones as structurally more stable was codified by Bharucha (1984a) as the melodic anchoring principle.] Analogous results are found in recognition-memory measures and in the fact that listeners remember structurally significant elements better overall. Such studies are concerned with how these musical elements (tones and chords) generally function within the style—that is, in an abstract or normative sense, once the tonality or key has been established.

The problem of how a key becomes established initially has received less attention. Cohen (1977) found music students were quite accurate in producing the tonic of the key of short excerpts from the *Well-Tempered Clavier* (for example, they were 75% correct after hearing just the first four musical events). Butler & Brown (1984) report that three-tone sequences yielded correct judgments of possible tonics 83–91% of the time when the three tones included the tritone formed by the fourth and seventh scale degrees, and 96–98% of the time when the tones were any three other diatonic scale degrees. Their emphasis on the tritone stems from the fact that it (together with any third diatonic tone) uniquely specifies a major key, but their data (even corrected for guessing) do not support the idea that this tritone increases accuracy in judging the tonic (Krumhansl 1990b). Listeners, however, do seem to be aware of the multiple tonics possible when this tritone is absent. Cross et al (1985) found that other three-tone combinations provided clearer tonal cues (especially the first, second, and fourth scale degrees). Brown (1988) demonstrated that the order in which tones appear can have a large effect on key judgments; different tonics were chosen when the same tones were reordered, although general principles for predicting the judgment of tonic remain to be articulated. Finally, two other approaches to understanding the key-finding process take the form of computer algorithms. Longuet-Higgins & Steedman's (1971) algorithm eliminates keys on the basis of whether or not the tones in the musical sample are contained in the diatonic major and minor scales. Krumhansl & Schmuckler's algorithm (described in Krumhansl 1990a) matches (by correlation) the distribution of the tones in the musical sample to the tonal hierarchies of major and minor scales. The second algorithm was found to be more efficient (Krumhansl 1990a), but other factors (particularly temporal order and harmonic implications) may also help listeners ascertain the key quickly so that the tonal and harmonic functions of the sounded events can be appreciated.

CODING MODELS OF MUSIC

The experiments just reviewed describe the perceived relations among the elements of traditional Western music (tones, chords, keys) in an abstract or general sense. They are not concerned with how the elements are employed in simultaneous and successive combinations in specific passages of music. [See Bharucha (1984b) for a discussion of the distinction between tonal hierarchies and event hierarchies as an example of the contrast between stylistic norms and characteristics of particular pieces.] Intuitively, the construction of melodic and harmonic sequences seems to be rule governed. Various suggestions have been made about how to formalize these rules. In an important paper, Simon & Sumner (1968) articulated a number of basic premises that have influenced subsequent theory. First, the psychological purpose of such rules is to enable listeners to develop expectations for successive events ("pattern induction"; see also Meyer 1956). Second, the rules operate on small and well-defined sets of elements ("alphabets" such as chromatic scales, diatonic scales, and triads). Third, the rules can be described using a small number of operators (such as "same" and "next") on the specified alphabet. Fourth, the rules can be applied recursively, producing hierarchically organized patterns of subpatterns. And finally, musical patterns are multidimensional: Patterns exist simultaneously on a number of different levels (metric, rhythmic, melodic, harmonic).

Deutsch & Feroe (1981) proposed a model for representing pitch sequences in tonal music; it follows the general form outlined by Simon & Sumner (1968). The model is perhaps best described with respect to a particular example:

The lowest level shows the actual notes of the passage (from Beethoven, Sonata op. 22). The reference pitch for the whole passage (denoted * at the highest level) is D, the fifth scale tone of the key of the passage, which is G minor. The level below this is represented by the formalism $A = \{(*, 3p); V^7\}$, where the operator p ("predecessor") is applied three times to the alphabet V^7 (the dominant seventh, D F# A C D). In this alphabet, the predecessor of D is C; the predecessor of C is A; and the predecessor of A is F#. This gives the tones D, C, A, and F# shown at the second level from the top of the hierarchy. The next level down is represented by $B = \{(*,s)\}$, where the operator s ("same") means simply that each note is repeated. Finally, the lowest level is represented by $C = \{(p,*); Cr\}$, which means that each note is preceded by its neighbor on the chromatic scale (denoted Cr). This example illustrates a number of basic principles of the model: hierarchical organization, a small set of alphabets and operators, and different alphabets and operators at different hierarchical levels.

In an empirical test, Deutsch (1980) showed that tonal sequences with this kind of hierarchical, rule-governed organization were more accurately recalled than unstructured sequences in a musical dictation task. Moreover, inappropriate temporal segmentation of the rule-governed sequences (breaking up the subgroups) significantly hurt recall. However, Boltz et al (1985) found only weak effects of rule-based patterning; sequences generated by recursive application of rules were better remembered only at certain rates of presentation. Moreover, Boltz & Jones (1986) found that rules at higher hierarchical levels did not consistently aid reproduction of tone sequences. Instead, other factors predominated, such as the number and timing of contour changes (changes from ascending to descending lines or vice versa) and the relative position of melodic and temporal accents. Thus, the rules as formulated have inconsistent effects and interact with other factors, suggesting that further tests are needed to clarify the nature of tonal patterning. Attention might also be directed toward the question of how well such rules characterize actual musical compositions, and whether the sets of rules and/or alphabets might be expanded or modified to allow more flexibility. An additional question is how theoretical descriptions of melody, harmony, rhythm, and meter might be combined, or at least coordinated, to reveal their interdependencies.

LINGUISTIC THEORY APPLIED TO MUSIC

Other suggestions for formally representing musical structure come from analogies to language. Certain structural principles of natural language grammars have been applied to music. Lindblom & Sundberg (1970) argued for a new kind of theory of music that accounts for musical behaviors (composition, performance, perception) the way Chomsky's approach (1968) treats language: ". . . the research problem can in our opinion be formulated in the following fashion: Given a certain well-defined class of melodies what are the principles and laws by means of which the metric, harmonic, and tonal facts of these melodies can be derived?" In an initial contribution along these lines, Lindblom & Sundberg applied rules of linguistic prosody to a set of Swedish nursery tunes, noting that the procedures for deriving a stress or prominence contour from a tree diagram are very similar in the two cases. The system of prominence rules provides a framework for analyzing formally metric, harmonic, and tonal materials; it was used to generate novel but stylistically similar melodies. Variations of a lullaby folk melody were produced by a similar grammar (Sundberg & Lindblom 1976). Other contributions drawing on an analogy between music and language include: a grammar for setting words to music in Gregorian chant (Chen 1983), a grammar for generating jazz chord sequences (Steedman 1984), and computational models for assigning rhythmic and tonal descriptions to performed music (Longuet-Higgins & Steedman 1971; Longuet-Higgins & Lee 1982; Longuet-Higgins & Lisle 1989). Narmour (1989) has recently proposed a theory of melody based on a few elementary principles of similarity, proximity, good continuation, and reversals. These principles produce a small number of archetypal realizations and can be applied recursively to generate multiple hierarchical levels in networks of simultaneous structures.

Currently, the most extensive and influential theory applying linguistic concepts to music is that of Lerdahl & Jackendoff (1983). Their model contains four kinds of structural representations: grouping (which partitions the music into hierarchically organized temporal segments), meter (which assigns periodic patterns of stress), the time-span reduction (which assigns a tree structure specifying the relative dominance of each surface event), and the prolongation reduction (which provides a description, in the form of a tree, of patterns of harmonic tension and relaxation). Parts of this extensive theory have been tested in experimental studies. Deliège (1987) found general support for the grouping principles in judgments of segment boundaries in short musical excerpts. According to the theory, grouping is based on both temporal characteristics (such as slurs, rests, and prolonged sounds) and changes of musical parameters (such as register, dynamics, timbre, and articulation). Clarke & Krumhansl (1990) found that these same kinds of principles operate on a global level, defining major sections within extended pieces. Palmer & Krumhansl (1987a,b) investigated the perception of phrase structure by presenting segments ending at different points in the music. The listeners judged how good or complete a phrase the sounded segment formed, and their responses conformed to two components of the theory: the time-span reduction and the metrical hierarchy (which has since been shown to influence judgments of metrical stability and memory confusions between temporal positions, Palmer & Krumhansl 1990). Finally, Bigand (1990) found evidence that listeners abstract the underlying harmonic structure that is represented by the prolongation reduction. This and other formal theories promise to stimulate a great deal of research in the future about the nature of musical pattern perception. Although currently limited in various ways, these theories provide a framework for understanding music in psychological terms, simultaneously elucidating the music itself and the perceptual and cognitive processes through which it is understood and appreciated. Discussion of some of the promises and problems in this approach can be found in commentaries by West et al (1985), Rosner (1988), and Clarke (1989).

MELODY PERCEPTION AND MEMORY

Theories of melody perception and memory assume that listeners group individual tones into longer temporal units. Principles of a Gestalt nature influence the formation of these units, as has been documented by extensive empirical research (see Bregman 1990; Deutsch 1986a, for reviews). Much of this research uses the methodology of stream segregation, which refers to the perceptual organization of a sequence of (usually rapidly presented) tones into separate acoustic events or "streams." Factors or attributes known to influence whether elements divide into multiple streams include: frequency separation (pitch differences), presence or absence of frequency transitions (glides) between tones, the complexity of the contour (pattern of ups and downs), temporal proximity, rate of presentation, onset and offset asynchrony, timbre differences, spatial location, intensity differences, number of repetitions, attentional instructions, and prior knowledge of the component patterns. It is impossible to review this vast literature here, but two general points should be noted. First, Bregman (1990) argues that the empirical effects reflect fundamental principles that organize the complex acoustic environment into coherent events; sounds from a single source will tend to be continuous; similar in pitch, intensity, and timbre; close in spatial location; and so on. Second, Gestalt principles have influenced various theoretical descriptions of music (e.g. Meyer 1956; Lerdahl & Jackendoff 1983; Narmour 1989), although their applicability to complex and musically representative materials has not been studied systematically. [An important exception is Huron's (1989a,b; Huron & Fantini 1989) analysis of polyphonic music, which relates compositional techniques to the research on stream segregation.]

Specifically musical factors, such as scale structure, harmony, and key also influence the way sequences are encoded and remembered. Results of this kind suggest that listeners interpret the sounded tones by using their knowledge of the interval patterns typical of the style to apprehend and retain larger and more musically meaningful patterns. In an influential early paper along these lines, Dowling (1978) demonstrated the importance of diatonic scale structure in recognition memory for transposed sequences. In the experiment, a target sequence was presented first, followed by two comparison sequences; the listeners were required to say which of the two comparison sequences was the same as the target sequence. One of the comparison sequences was an exact transposition (changing the key, but maintaining the size of the intervals and the contour); the other was a transposition up or down the scale of the target melody (maintaining the key and contour, but altering the size of the intervals). Neither musicians nor nonmusicians could reliably identify the matching melody. Changes of contour were, however, much easier to reject for both groups. From this, Dowling concluded that musical scales provide a basic framework on which the melodic contour is hung.

In an extensive series of studies, Cuddy and collaborators (Cuddy & Cohen 1976; Dewar et al 1977; Cuddy et al 1979; Cuddy et al 1981; Cuddy & Lyons 1981) employed a similar measure of recognition accuracy for transposed sequences. These studies expand the set of musical factors known to influence memory to include: triadic structure, repetition of the tonic, leading tone to tonic ending, harmonic cadence (V–I), modulation within the sequence, and key-distance of transposition (tritone vs dominant). Bartlett & Dowling (1980) also found a key-distance effect such that near-key lures (inexact transpositions) were harder to reject than far-key lures. Studies by Dowling & Bartlett (1981) and DeWitt & Crowder (1986) showed that the relative importance of pitch position within the tonal scale (compared to contour information) increased from short-term to long-term memory [although Dowling (1986) was able to alter the effect by instructions]. These results suggest that knowledge of tonal structure becomes even more important for retaining melodic patterns over longer durations. In a similar spirit, Edworthy (1985) concluded that whereas contour is coded more precisely for shorter sequences and for earlier serial positions in longer sequences, interval information dominates at later serial positions in longer sequences. Finally, Watkins (1985) found a memory advantage for more clearly diatonic sequences. This advantage disappeared, however, when the interval sizes were reduced by a constant (logarithmic) factor; for the resulting sequences, which have abnormal intervals, contour alone influenced recognition performance.

Most of the experiments just reviewed use transposition of short sequences specially constructed to isolate the musical factor(s) of interest. A few studies have used more complex transformations and/or stimulus materials drawn from musical compositions. Recognition of mirror forms [inversion (inverting pitch), retrograde (inverting time), and retrograde inversion (inverting both pitch and time) as employed in 12-tone serial music] has been the focus of a number of experiments (e.g. Francès 1988; Dowling 1972; Krumhansl et al 1987); these find some evidence for perceived melodic invariance under these transformations. Pollard-Gott (1983) used excerpts presenting the two themes from Liszt's Sonata in B minor and their variations. With repeated listenings, the excerpts based on one theme came to be distinguished from the excerpts based on the other theme, as measured in both similarity and classification judgments. Rosner & Meyer's (1982) listeners learned to classify musical excerpts according to their underlying melodic "archetypes" (which describe the process through which a melody moves toward its point of closure; Meyer 1973). Welker (1982) and Carterette et al (1986) demonstrated that listeners abstract the prototypical melody from transformed versions of it. As transformations, the former used inversion, syncopation, reduction of interval size, temporal elaboration, and deletion of a measure from the prototype; the latter used octave displacements (changing contour), altered intervals (preserving contour), changed loudness, and changed note duration. Both studies found regular effects of transformation distance. Finally, Serafine et al's (1989) listeners judged that excerpts with the same hierarchic analysis (Schenker 1979) were similar despite radical harmonic differences on the surface. The perception and memory of musical sequences are thus governed by many different factors, some highly complex and subtle. Future research extending this line of investigation might increasingly draw on music-theoretical concepts of melodic structure.

MELODY AND RHYTHM

The relationship between tonal and rhythmic aspects of music, a centrally important topic, has received relatively little attention. Both theoretically and empirically, these two aspects tend to be treated separately. Clearly, both aspects influence music perception and memory, but it is unclear whether they are truely interactive or simply have additive effects. A number of studies show that rhythmic structure influences judgments of pitch information. Jones et al (1981) found that a target (pitch) interval that is rhythmically differentiated from its context is more accurately perceived (as measured by temporal order judgments) than one that is not. Jones et al (1982) manipulated accent structure and obtained effects on pitch recognition. They proposed that listeners dynamically allocate attentional resources over time (with greater attention at some moments than at others), a theoretical notion elaborated by Jones (1987). Dowling et al's (1987) study required detecting a melody interleaved with distractor tones. The findings indicated attention is directed not only to certain moments in time but also to certain ranges in pitch. The study of dynamic attention allocation over time appears to be a promising approach to expanding theories about attention.

A number of studies examine the combined effects of tonal and rhythmic patterns. In a scaling study of rhythmically varied melodies, Monahan & Carterette (1985) identified three rhythmic and two tonal dimensions underlying judgments of melodic similarity; intersubject trade-offs between the weights for the two kinds of dimensions suggest some measure of independence. Palmer & Krumhansl (1987a,b) found pitch and temporal components made independent and additive contributions to judged phrase structure. However, other results suggest interactions between temporal and pitch patterns. When the patterns are out of phase, recall is impaired (Deutsch 1980; Boltz & Jones 1986; Monahan et al 1987), although this effect is not found consistently (Smith & Cuddy 1989). In addition, Jones et al (1987) found poorer recognition of melodies presented in a rhythm different from the original rhythm, suggesting that these aspects are encoded together in memory. These findings are not necessarily contradictory. Judgments of higher-order properties (memory and similarity of melodies, and judgments of phrase structure) would be expected to show joint influences of the tonal and rhythmic components. To say that they are independent (noninteractive) is simply to say that the effects do not require supposing that additional factors emerge when both tonal and rhythmic components are varied. If the two components are varied in a way that is mutually incompatible or inconsistent, then they may well interfere with one another.

The perception, memory, and production of temporal patterns independent of pitch patterns have been studied extensively. This literature, however, is more closely related to that on musical performance, which is beyond the scope of this review. However, research on the temporal dimension of music has developed along lines parallel to that on musical pitch. Studies of isolated temporal intervals have led to studies of more complex and musically realistic temporal patterns. The results are interpreted in terms of such concepts as grouping, hierarchical organization, rhythm, and meter. Formal models have been proposed and tested, and these draw on concepts from music theory. Finally, structural and interpretative aspects are found to influence expressive timing in musical performances in ways that can be modeled precisely.

Acknowledgement

I am grateful to my colleagues, too numerous to name, who generously provided materials and shared their thoughts about recent developments in the psychology of music. W. Dixon Ward and Lola L. Cuddy made valuable comments on an earlier draft.

Literature Cited

Allik, J., Dzhafarov, E. N., Houtsma, A. J. M., Ross, J., Versfeld, N. J. 1989. Pitch motion with random chord sequences. *Percept. Psychophys.* 46:513–27

Bachem, A. 1950. Tone height and tone chroma as two different pitch qualities. *Acta Psychol.* 7:80–88

Balzano, G. J. 1980. Group-theoretic description of 12-fold and microtonal pitch systems. *Comput. Music J.* 4:66–84

Bartlett, J. C., Dowling, W. J. 1980. Recognition of transposed melodies: a key-distance effect in developmental perspective. *J. Exp. Psychol.: Hum. Percept. Perform.* 6:501–15

Bharucha, J. J. 1984a. Anchoring effects in music: the resolution of dissonance. *Cognit. Psychol.* 16:485–518

Bharucha, J. J. 1984b. Event hierarchies, tonal hierarchies, and assimilation: a reply to Deutsch and Dowling. *J. Exp. Psychol.: General* 113:421–25

Bharucha, J. J. 1987. Music cognition and perceptual facilitation: a connectionist framework. *Music Percept.* 5:1–30

Bharucha, J. J., Krumhansl, C. L. 1983. The representation of harmonic structure in music: hierarchies of stability as a function of context. *Cognition* 13:63–102

Bharucha, J. J., Olney, K. L. 1989. Tonal cognition, artificial intelligence and neural nets. *Contemp. Music Rev.* 4:341–56

Bharucha, J. J., Stoeckig, K. 1986. Reaction time and musical expectancy: priming of chords. *J. Exp. Psychol.: Hum. Percept. Perform.* 12:403–10

Bharucha, J. J., Stoeckig, K. 1987. Priming of chords: spreading activation or overlapping frequency spectra? *Percept. Psychophys.* 41:519–24

Boltz, M. 1989a. Perceiving the end: effects of tonal relationships on melodic completions. *J. Exp. Psychol.: Hum. Percept. Perform.* 15:749–61

Boltz, M. 1989b. Rhythm and "good endings": effects of temporal structure on tonality judgments. *Percept. Psychophys.* 46:9–17

Boltz, M., Jones, M. R. 1986. Does rule recursion make melodies easier to reproduce? If not, what does? *Cognit. Psychol.* 18:389–431

Boltz, M., Marshburn, E., Jones, M. R., Johnson, W. W. 1985. Serial-pattern structure and temporal-order recognition. *Percept. Psychophys.* 37:209–17

Bregman, A. S. 1990. *Auditory Scene Analysis.* Cambridge, MA: MIT Press

Brown, H. 1988. The interplay of set content and temporal context in a functional theory of tonality perception. *Music Percept.* 5:219–50

Burns, E. M. 1981. Circularity in relative pitch judgments for inharmonic complex tones: the Shepard demonstration revisited, again. *Percept. Psychophys.* 30:467–72

Burns, E. M., Ward, W. D. 1978. Categorical perception—phenomenon or epiphenomenon: evidence from experiments in the perception of melodic musical intervals. *J. Acoust. Soc. Am.* 63:456–68

Burns, E. M., Ward, W. D. 1982. Intervals, scales, and tuning. In *The Psychology of Music,* ed. D. Deutsch. New York: Academic

Butler, D., Brown, H. 1984. Tonal structure versus function: studies of the recognition of harmonic motion. *Music Percept.* 2:6–24

Carterette, E. C., Kohl, D. V., Pitt, M. A. 1986. Similarities among transformed melodies: the abstraction of invariants. *Music Percept.* 3:393–410

Castellano, M. A., Bharucha, J. J., Krumhansl, C. L. 1984. Tonal hierarchies in the music of North India. *J. Exp. Psychol.: General* 113:394–412

Cazden, N. 1945. Musical consonance and dissonance: a cultural criterion. *J. Aesthet. Art Crit.* 4:3–11

Chen, M. Y. 1983. Toward a grammar of singing: tune-text association in Gregorian chant. *Music Percept.* 1:84–122

Chomsky, N. 1968. *Language and Mind.* New York: Harcourt, Brace, & World

Clarke, E. F. 1989. Mind the gap: formal structures and psychological processes in music. *Contemp. Music Rev.* 3:1–13

Clarke, E. F., Krumhansl, C. L. 1990. Perceiving musical time. *Music Percept.* 7:213–52

Cohen, A. J. 1977. Tonality and perception: musical scales prompted by excerpts from *Das Wohl temperierte Clavier* of J. S. Bach.

Paper presented at the 2nd Works. Phys. Neuropsychol. Found. Music, Ossiach, Austria.

Cross, I., Howell, P., West, R. 1985. Structural relationships in the perception of musical pitch. In *Musical Structure and Cognition,* ed. P. Howell, I. Cross, R. West. London: Academic

Crowder, R. G. 1985. Perception of the major/minor distinction. II. Experimental investigations. *Psychomusicology* 5:3–24

Cuddy, L. L., Cohen, A. J. 1976. Recognition of transposed melodic sequences. *Q. J. Exp. Psychol.* 28:255–70

Cuddy, L. L., Cohen, A. J., Mewhort, D. J. K. 1981. Perception of structure in short melodic sequences. *J. Exp. Psychol.: Hum. Percept. Perform.* 7:869–83

Cuddy, L. L., Cohen, A. J., Miller, J. 1979. Melody recognition: the experimental application of musical rules. *Can. J. Psychol.* 33:148–57

Cuddy, L. L., Lyons, H. I. 1981. Music pattern recognition: a comparison of listening to and studying tonal structures and tonal ambiguities. *Psychomusicology* 1:15–33

Danner, G. 1985. The use of acoustic measures of dissonance to characterize pitch-class sets. *Music Percept.* 3:103–22

Deliège, I. 1987. Grouping conditions in listening to music: an approach to Lerdahl & Jackendoff's grouping preference rules. *Music Percept.* 4:325–60

Deutsch, D. 1980. The processing of structured and unstructured tonal sequences. *Percept. Psychophys.* 28:381–89

Deutsch, D. 1986a. Auditory pattern recognition. In *Handbook of Perception and Human Performance, Vol. II, Cognitive Processes and Performance,* ed. K. R. Boff, L. Kaufman, J. P. Thomas. New York: Wiley

Deutsch, D. 1986b. A musical paradox. *Music Percept.* 3:275–80

Deutsch, D. 1987. The tritone paradox: effects of spectral variables. *Percept. Psychophys.* 41:563–75

Deutsch, D., Feroe, J. 1981. The internal representation of pitch sequences in tonal music. *Psychol. Rev.* 88:503–22

Deutsch, D., Kuyper, W. L., Fisher, Y. 1987. The tritone paradox: its presence and form of distribution in a general population. *Music Percept.* 5:79–92

Deutsch, D., Moore, F. R., Dolson, M. 1986. The perceived height of octave-related complexes. *J. Acoust. Soc. Am.* 80:1346–53

Dewar, K. M., Cuddy, L. L., Mewhort, D. J. K. 1977. Recognition memory for single tones with and without context. *J. Exp. Psychol.: Hum. Learn. Mem.* 3:60–67

DeWitt, L. A., Crowder, R. G. 1986. Recognition of novel melodies after brief delays. *Music Percept.* 3:259–74

DeWitt, L. A., Crowder, R. G. 1987. Tonal fusion of consonant musical intervals. *Percept. Psychophys.* 41:73–84

Dowling, W. J. 1972. Recognition of melodic transformations: inversion, retrograde, and retrograde inversion. *Percept. Psychophys.* 12:417–21

Dowling, W. J. 1978. Scale and contour: two components of a theory of memory for melodies. *Psychol. Rev.* 85:341–54

Dowling, W. J. 1986. Context effects on melody recognition: scale-step versus interval representations. *Music Percept.* 3: 281–96

Dowling, W. J., Bartlett, J. C. 1981. The importance of interval information in long-term memory for melodies. *Psychomusicology* 1:30–49

Dowling, W. J., Lund, K. M., Herrbold, S. 1987. Aiming attention in pitch and time in the perception of interleaved melodies. *Percept. Psychophys.* 41:642–56

Edworthy, J. 1985. Interval and contour in melody processing. *Music Percept.* 2:375–88

Elliot, J., Platt, J. R., Racine, R. J. 1987. Adjustment of successive and simultaneous intervals by musically experienced and inexperienced subjects. *Percept. Psychophys.* 42:594–98

Francès, R. 1988 [1958]. *The Perception of Music.* Transl. W. J. Dowling. Hillsdale, NJ: Erlbaum

Hall, D. E. 1973. The objective measurement of goodness-of-fit for tunings and temperaments. *J. Music Theory* 17:274–90

Hall, D. E. 1974. Quantitative evaluation of musical scale tunings. *Am. J. Phys.* 48:543–52

Hall, D. E., Hess, J. T. 1984. Perception of musical interval tuning. *Music Percept.* 2:166–95

Helmholtz, H. L. F. 1954 [1885]. *On the Sensations of Tone as a Physiological Basis for the Theory of Music*, ed. & transl. A. J. Ellis, New York: Dover

Helson, H. 1964. *Adaptation-Level Theory.* New York: Harper & Row

Huron, D. 1989a. Voice denumerability in polyphonic music of homogeneous timbres. *Music Percept.* 6:361–82

Huron, D. 1989b. *Voice segregation in selected polyphonic keyboard works of Johann Sebastian Bach.* PhD thesis, School of Music, Univ. Nottingham

Huron, D., Fantini, D. A. 1989. The avoidance of inner-voice entries: perceptual evidence and musical practice. *Music Percept.* 7:43–48

Hutchinson, W., Knopoff, L. 1978. The acoustic component of Western consonance. *Interface* 7:1–29

Hutchinson, W., Knopoff, L. 1979. The significance of the acoustic component of consonance in Western triads. *J. Music. Res.* 3:5–22

Janata, P., Reisberg, D. 1988. Response-time measures as a means of exploring tonal hierarchies. *Music Percept.* 6:161–72

Jones, M. R. 1987. Dynamic pattern structure in music: recent theory and research. *Percept. Psychophys.* 41:621–34

Jones, M. R., Boltz, M., Kidd, G. 1982. Controlled attending as a function of melodic and temporal context. *Percept. Psychophys.* 32:211–18

Jones, M. R., Kidd, G., Wetzel, R. 1981. Evidence for rhythmic attention. *J. Exp. Psychol.: Hum. Percept. Perform.* 7:1059–72

Jones, M. R., Summerell, L., Marshburn, E. 1987. Recognizing melodies: a dynamic interpretation. *Q. J. Exp. Psychol.* 39A:89–121

Kameoka, A., Kuriyagawa, M. 1969a. Consonance theory. Part I. Consonance of dyads. *J. Acoust. Soc. Am.* 45:1451–59

Kameoka, A., Kuriyagawa, M. 1969b. Consonance theory. Part II. Consonance of complex tones and its calculation method. *J. Acoust. Soc. Am.* 45:1460–69

Kessler, E. J., Hansen, C., Shepard, R. N. 1984. Tonal schemata in the perception of music in Bali and the West. *Music Percept.* 2:131–65

Krumhansl, C. L. 1979. The psychological representation of musical pitch in a tonal context. *Cognit. Psychol.* 11:346–74

Krumhansl, C. L. 1990. *Cognitive Foundations of Musical Pitch.* New York: Oxford Univ. Press

Krumhansl, C. L. 1990b. Tonal hierarchies and rare intervals in music cognition. *Mus. Percept.* 7:309–24

Krumhansl, C. L., Bharucha, J. J., Castellano, M. A. 1982a. Key distance effects on perceived harmonic structure in music. *Percept. Psychophys.* 32:96–108

Krumhansl, C. L., Bharucha, J. J., Kessler, E. J. 1982b. Perceived harmonic structure of chords in three related musical keys. *J. Exp. Psychol.: Hum. Percept. Perform.* 8:24–36

Krumhansl, C. L., Castellano, M. A. 1983. Dynamic processes in music perception. *Mem. Cognit.* 11:325–34

Krumhansl, C. L., Kessler, E. J. 1982. Tracing the dynamic changes in perceived tonal organization in a spatial representation of musical keys. *Psychol. Rev.* 89: 334–68

Krumhansl, C. L., Sandell, G. J., Sergeant, D. C. 1987. The perception of tone hierarchies and mirror forms in twelve-tone serial music. *Music Percept.* 5:31–78

Krumhansl, C. L., Schmuckler, M. A. 1986.

The *Petroushka* chord. *Music Percept.* 4:153–84

Krumhansl, C. L., Shepard, R. N. 1979. Quantification of the hierarchy of tonal functions within a diatonic context. *J. Exp. Psychol.: Hum. Percept. Perform.* 5:579–94

Lakner, Y. 1960. A new method of representing tonal relations. *J. Music Theory* 4:194–209

Lerdahl, F. 1988. Tonal pitch space. *Music Percept.* 5: 315–50

Lerdahl, F., Jackendoff, R. 1983. *A Generative Theory of Tonal Music.* Cambridge, MA: MIT Press

Lindblom, B., Sundberg, J. 1970. Towards a generative theory of melody. *Swed. J. Music.* 52:71–88

Lockhead, G. R., Byrd, R. 1981. Practically perfect pitch. *J. Acoust. Soc. Am.* 70:387–89

Longuet-Higgins, H. C. 1962a. Letter to a musical friend. *Music Rev.* 23:244–48

Longuet-Higgins, H. C. 1962b. Second letter to a musical friend. *Music Rev.* 23:271–80

Longuet-Higgins, H. C., Lee, C. S. 1982. The perception of musical rhythms. *Perception* 11:115–28

Longuet-Higgins, H. C., Lisle, E. R. 1989. Modelling musical cognition. *Contemp. Music Rev.* 3:15–27

Longuet-Higgins, H. C., Steedman, M. J. 1971. On interpreting Bach. *Mach. Intell.* 6:221–41

Malmberg, C. F. 1918. The perception of consonance and dissonance. *Psychol. Monogr.* 25:(2, Whole No. 108):93–133

Mathews, M. V., Pierce, J. R. 1980. Harmony and nonharmonic partials. *J. Acoust. Soc. Am.* 68:1252–57

Meyer, L. B. 1956. *Emotion and Meaning in Music.* Chicago: Univ. Chicago Press

Meyer, L. B. 1973. *Explaining Music: Essays and Explorations.* Berkeley: Univ. Calif. Press

Miyazaki, K. 1988. Musical pitch identification by absolute pitch possessors. *Percept. Psychophys.* 44:501–12

Monahan, C. B., Carterette, E. C. 1985. Pitch and duration as determinants of musical space. *Music Percept.* 3:1–32

Monahan, C. B., Kendall, R. A., Carterette, E. C. 1987. The effect of melodic and temporal contour on recognition memory for pitch change. *Percept. Psychophys.* 41:576–600

Nakajima, Y., Tsumura, T., Matsuura, S., Minami, H., Teranishi, R. 1988. Dynamic pitch perception for complex tones derived from major triads. *Music Percept.* 6:1–20

Narmour, E. 1989. The "genetic" code of melody: cognitive structures generated by the implication-realization model. *Contemp. Music Rev.* 4:45–63

Ohgushi, K. 1983. The origin of tonality and a possible explanation of the octave enlargement phenomenon. *J. Acoust. Soc. Am.* 73:1694–1700

Oram, N. 1989. *The responsiveness of Western adult listeners to pitch distributional information in diatonic and nondiatonic melodic sequences.* PhD thesis. Dept. Psychol., Queen's Univ., Kingston, Ontario, Canada

Palmer, C., Krumhansl, C. L. 1987a. Independent temporal and pitch structures in perception of musical phrases. *J. Exp. Psychol.: Hum. Percept. Perform.* 13:116–26

Palmer, C., Krumhansl, C. L. 1987b. Pitch and temporal contributions to musical phrase perception: effects of harmony, performance timing, and familiarity. *Percept. Psychophys.* 41:505–18

Palmer, C., Krumhansl, C. L. 1990. Mental representations for musical meter. *J. Exp. Psychol.: Hum. Percept. Perform.* 16:728–41

Parncutt, R. 1988. Revision of Terhardt's psychoacoustical model of the root(s) of a musical chord. *Music Percept.* 6:65–94

Parncutt, R. 1989. *Harmony: A Psychoacoustical Approach.* Berlin: Springer-Verlag

Pikler, A. G. 1966. Logarithmic frequency systems. *J. Acoust. Soc. Am.* 39:1102–10

Plomp, R., Levelt, W. J. M. 1965. Tonal consonance and critical bandwidth. *J. Acoust. Soc. Am.* 38:548–60

Pollard-Gott, L. 1983. Emergence of thematic concepts in repeated listening to music. *Cognit. Psychol.* 15:66–94

Rakowski, A. 1990. Intonation variants of musical intervals in isolation and in musical contexts. *Psychol. Mus.* 18:60–72

Rasch, R. 1984. Theory of Helmholtz-beat frequencies. *Music Percept.* 1:308–22

Rasch, R. 1985. Perception of melodic and harmonic intonation of two-part musical fragments. *Music Percept.* 2:441–58

Roberts, L. A., Mathews, M. V. 1984. Intonation sensitivity for traditional and nontraditional chords. *J. Acoust. Soc. Am.* 75:952–59

Roberts, L. A., Shaw, M. L. 1984. Perceived structure of triads. *Music Percept.* 2:95–124

Rosner, B. S. 1988. Music perception, music theory, and psychology. In *Explorations in Music, the Arts, and Ideas,* ed. E. Narmour, R. A. Solie. Stuyvesant, NY: Pendragon Press

Rosner, B. S., Meyer, L. B. 1982. Melodic processes and the perception of music. In *The Psychology of Music,* ed. D. Deutsch. New York: Academic

Schenker, H. 1979 [1935]. *Free Composition.* Transl. E. Oster. New York: Longman

Schmuckler, M. A. 1989. Expectation in music: investigations of melodic and harmonic processes. *Music Percept.* 7:109–50

Schoenberg, A. 1969 [1954]. *Structural Functions of Harmony.* New York: Norton Rev. ed.

Seashore, C. E. 1967 [1938]. *Psychology of Music.* New York: Dover

Serafine, M. L., Glassman, N., Overbeeke, C. 1989. The cognitive reality of hierarchic structure in music. *Music Percept.* 6:397–430

Shackford, C. 1961. Some aspects of perception. Part I. Sizes of harmonic intervals in performance. *J. Music Theory* 5:162–202

Shackford, C. 1962a. Some aspects of perception. Part II. Interval sizes and tonal dynamics in performance. *J. Music Theory* 6:66–90

Shackford, C. 1962b. Some aspects of perception. Part III. Addenda. *J. Music Theory* 6:295–303

Shepard, R. N. 1964. Circularity in judgments of relative pitch. *J. Acoust. Soc. Am.* 36:2346–53

Shepard, R. N. 1982. Geometrical approximations to the structure of musical pitch. *Psychol. Rev.* 89:305–33

Shepard, R. N. 1983. Demonstrations of circular components of pitch. *J. Audio Eng. Soc.* 31:641–49

Siegel, J. A., Siegel, W. 1977a. Absolute identification of notes and intervals by musicians. *Percept. Psychophys.* 21:143–52

Siegel, J. A., Siegel, W. 1977b. Categorical perception of tonal intervals: musicians can't tell *sharp* from *flat*. *Percept. Psychophys.* 21:399–407

Simon, H. A., Sumner, R. K. 1968. Pattern in music. In *Formal Representation of Human Judgment,* ed. B. Kleinmuntz. New York: Wiley

Smith, K. C., Cuddy, L. L. 1989. Effects of metric and harmonic rhythm on the detection of pitch alterations in melodic sequences. *J. Exp. Psychol.: Hum. Percept. Perform.* 15:457–71

Steedman, M. J. 1984. A generative grammar for jazz chord sequences. *Music Percept.* 2:52–77

Studdert-Kennedy, M., Liberman, A. M., Harris, K. S., Cooper, F. S. 1970. Motor theory of speech perception: a reply to Lane's critical review. *Psychol. Rev.* 77:234–49

Stumpf, C. 1883. *Tonpsychologie.* Leipzig: S. Hirzel

Sundberg, J. 1982. In tune or not? A study of fundamental frequency in musical practise. In *Tiefenstruktur der Musik* (Festschrift für

Fritz Winckel), ed. C. Dahlhaus, M. Krause. Berlin: Technische Universität

Sundberg, J., Lindblom, B. 1976. Generative theories in language and music descriptions. *Cognition* 4:99–122

Sundberg, J., Lindqvist, J. 1973. Musical octaves and pitch. *J. Acoust. Soc. Am.* 54:922–29

Terhardt, E. 1974. Pitch, consonance and harmony. *J. Acoust. Soc. Am.* 55:1061–69

Terhardt, E. 1984. The concept of musical consonance: a link between music and psychoacoustics. *Music Percept.* 1:276–95

Terhardt, E., Seewan, M. 1983. Aural key identification and its relationship to absolute pitch. *Music Percept.* 1:63–83

Terhardt, E., Stoll, G., Seewan, M. 1982a. Pitch of complex signals according to virtual pitch-pitch theory: tests, examples, and predictions. *J. Acoust. Soc. Am.* 71:671–78

Terhardt, E., Stoll, G., Seewan, M. 1982b. Algorithm for extraction of pitch and pitch salience from complex tonal signals. *J. Acoust. Soc. Am.* 71:679–88

Terhardt, E., Ward, W. D. 1982. Recognition of musical key: exploratory study. *J. Acoust. Soc. Am.* 72:26–33

Thompson, W. F. 1986. *Judgements of key change in Bach chorale excerpts: an investigation of the sensitivity to keys, chords, and voicing.* PhD thesis. Dept. Psychol., Queen's Univ., Kingston, Ontario, Canada

Thompson, W. F., Cuddy, L. L. 1989. Sensitivity to key change in choral sequences: a comparison of single voices and four-voice harmony. *Music Percept.* 7:151–68

Ueda, K., Ohgushi, K. 1987. Perceptual components of pitch: spatial representation using a multidimensional scaling technique. *J. Acoust. Soc. Am.* 82:1193–1200

van de Geer, J. P., Levelt, W. J. M., Plomp, R. 1962. The connotation of musical consonance. *Acta Psychol.* 20:308–19

Vos, J. 1982. The perception of pure and mistuned musical fifths and major thirds: thresholds for discrimination, beats, and identification. *Percept. Psychophys.* 32:297–313

Vos, J. 1984. Spectral effects in the perception of pure and tempered intervals: discrimination and beats. *Percept. Psychophys.* 32:173–85

Vos, J. 1985. Purity ratings of tempered fifths and major thirds. *Music Percept.* 3:221–58

Vos, J. 1988. Subjective acceptability of various regular twelve-tone tuning systems in two-part musical fragments. *J. Acoust. Soc. Am.* 83:2383–92

Vos, J., van Vianen, B. G. 1984. Thresholds for discrimination between pure and tempered intervals: the relevance of nearly coinciding harmonics. *J. Acoust. Soc. Am.* 77:176–87

Vos, J., van Vianen, B. G. 1985. The effect of fundamental frequency on the discriminability between pure and tempered fifths and major thirds. *Percept. Psychophys.* 37:507–14

Wapnick, J., Bourassa, G., Sampson, J. 1982. The perception of tonal intervals in isolation and in melodic context. *Psychomusicology* 2:21–37

Ward, W. D. 1970. Musical perception. In *Foundations of Modern Auditory Theory, Vol. 1,* ed. J. V. Tobias. New York: Academic

Ward, W. D., Burns, E. M. 1982. Absolute pitch. In *The Psychology of Music,* ed. D. Deutsch. New York: Academic

Watkins, A. J. 1985. Scale, key, and contour in the discrimination of tuned and mistuned approximations to melody. *Percept. Psychophys.* 37:275–85

Welker, R. L. 1982. Abstraction of themes from melodic variations. *J. Exp. Psychol.: Hum. Percept. Perform.* 8:435–47

West, R., Howell, P., Cross, I. 1985. Modelling perceived musical structure. In *Musical Structure and Cognition,* ed. P. Howell, I. Cross, R. West. London: Academic

Zatorre, R. J., Beckett, C. 1989. Multiple coding strategies in the retention of musical tones by possessors of absolute pitch. *Mem. Cognit.* 17:582–89

Zatorre, R. J., Halpern, A. R. 1979. Identification, discrimination, and selective adaptation of simultaneous musical intervals. *Percept. Psychophys.* 26:384–95

REFERENCE ADDED IN PROOF

Bigand, E. 1990. Abstraction of two forms of underlying structures in a tonal melody. *Psychol. Music* 18:45–59

Annu. Rev. Psychol. 1991. 42:305–31

PERCEPTION

William P. Banks

Departments of Psychology, Pomona College and The Claremont Graduate School, Claremont, California 91711

David Krajicek

Department of Psychology, The Claremont Graduate School, Claremont, California 91711

KEY WORDS: neuropsychology of perception, artificial intelligence, high-level vision, ecology of perception, observer theory, figure-ground organization

CONTENTS

305

0066-4308/91/0201-0305$02.00

INTRODUCTION

Here we present the theoretical developments and empirical findings that dominate current thinking about perception and show promise of determining the progress of our understanding well into the next century. The important influences originate in three areas: Artificial intelligence (AI); neuroscience; and the descendents of the Gestalt tradition, which constitute modern perceptual psychology. Although the Gestalt descendents are diverse, their lineage influences both their similarities and their disagreements. Included in this category are lines of research deriving from the work of Garner and colleagues (e.g. Pomerantz & Pristach 1990), from the cognitive constructivism of Rock (1983), and from contemporary researchers pursuing modern versions of classic Gestalt questions such as unit formation and figure-ground segregation. We also include in the Gestalt category work normally placed under the rubric of ecological perception—work deriving from J. J. Gibson's approach to perception (Gibson 1950, 1966, 1979). AI and neuroscience have not received explicit coverage in previous chapters on perception in the *Annual Review*.

CHARACTERISTICS OF THE THREE AREAS OF COVERAGE

The AI Approach

The AI approach holds that it is necessary to break the study of perception into three levels of analysis: 1. hardware, 2. algorithms for operation, and 3. the theory of the task to be performed. These levels, which can be applied to any machine or mechanism, must be considered in any complete explanation. Marr & Poggio (1977) illustrate the first two with reference to the hand calculator. Knowledge of the hardware alone is both inadequate and overly detailed as a description of the machine's operation. The calculator's arithmetic algorithms provide a more complete understanding of its operation.

A device that illustrates the third level of analysis is a radio receiver. The frequencies the radio receives and the method of encoding information in them (AM, FM, subcarriers, etc) constrain the structure and operation of the radio in important ways. The theory of the task to be performed is heavily dependent in this case on the "stimulus" the radio picks up. We cannot be said to understand the radio without understanding the stimulus, and knowledge of the stimulus can enable important insights into the functioning of the device. For some purposes, it can tell us all we need to know.

"How do we perceive?" can thus be recast as three separate questions that correspond to the three levels of analysis: 1. What are the physiological mechanisms involved in perception? 2. What is the process of perceiving? 3. What are the properties of the physical world that allow us to perceive? The first two questions are familiar to psychologists. It is easy to see how single-unit recording, neural-net models, and neuropsychological analyses attack the question of the biological hardware involved in perception. The second question occupies the greatest number of psychologists working on perception. Virtually all questions about psychological function fall in this category. Research on areas as diverse as psychophysics, reading, picture naming, pattern recognition, and information processing is devoted to models of the functional properties of the process of perceiving.

The third level of analysis is the description of the perceptual task. We cannot understand how perception takes place without knowing what it is we perceive and what physical aspects of an object are utilized in its perception. AI approaches intend to identify physical constraints on the process of perception in order to determine what perceptual accomplishments the stimulus information will allow. A description of the physical constraints on perception yields so much insight into the process that James Gibson and many of his followers have been accused of believing that nothing more is needed to explain perceptual achievements (cf Haber 1983a).

WHAT AI HAS TO OFFER STUDENTS OF PERCEPTION   The division of the explanation of perception into the three aspects above is a major intellectual tool. Consider, for example, the distinction between the hardware and the algorithmic levels. From an AI perspective, psychological theories are generally at the algorithmic level of analysis—that is, the abstract level specifying how a process works. In AI this level is explicitly distinguished from the hardware implementation of the process. An algorithm can be converted into a program in any of a large set of languages and run on a wide variety of computers.

In psychology the distinction between the perceptual algorithm and the biological hardware on which it hypothetically runs has not been so clearly maintained. Thus several theoretical terms are ambiguous: "Feature detectors," "channels," "inhibition and activation at 'nodes'," and "iconic memory," to name just a few, suggest physiology but are in fact aspects of certain algorithms that hypothetically explain processing. Although the practice of fuzzing the boundary between algorithmic models and hardware implementation is a venerable one in psychology, it only increases the difficulty of eventually integrating the two theoretical levels. When theoretical terms masquerade as physiological ones, speculation advances unchecked by reliable biological underpinnings. In such circumstances the purely theoretical components of research may not be properly tested, and the physiological ones fail to be verified by physiological experiment.

By contrast, the AI approach has often been criticized for neglecting the physical organism and thus being unable to account for such things as the effects of brain damage. However, the separation of the functional or algorithmic account from the neurophysiological one is, in the long run, productive, and we are beginning to see insights that derive from this separation (some discussed below): Ullman's (1986) review of the relation between AI and neuroscience discusses some of these advances.

OBSERVER THEORY   Observer theory is an extremely promising development that has emerged from the AI approach (Bennett et al 1987, 1989, in press). Observer theory began with an analysis of current models explaining such specific perceptual capacities as stereo vision, auditory localization, derivation of depth from motion, and color vision. Bennett et al argue that a structure called the "Observer," common to these models, performs each act of perception. The Observer structure is developed with mathematical rigor (Bennett et al 1987) and discussed in intuitive terms, with many examples (Bennett et al, 1990). The book *Observer Mechanics* (Bennett et al 1989) should be consulted for a full treatment of the approach.

   In essence, an Observer performs inferences. An Observer defines a relation between the class of perceptual premises it receives and its characteristic set of perceptual conclusions or interpretations. A premise can be, for example, a low-level sensory analysis such as the output of a line or edge

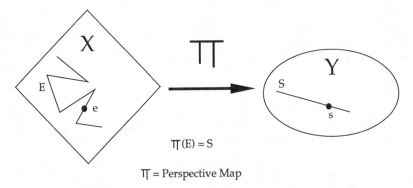

$$\pi(E) = S$$

$$\pi = \text{Perspective Map}$$

X = Possible State of Affairs; Conclusions.   Y = Observations; Premises.

E is an event in X;   S is a set of obervations in Y;
e is a single part of E.   s is a single obervation.

1. Observer has only s or S available (has only members of Y).
2. The observer "knows" that $\pi(E) = s$.
3. The observer's task is, given S, to find the probability of E
   or, given s, was E the cause?

Figure 1 Description of observer theory

detector [what Marr (1976) termed a "primitive assertion"], or it can comprise the higher-level inferences produced by other observers. An inference is a probability estimate applied to members of the characteristic set of interpretations—e.g. the position of a point in 3-space; the hue, saturation, and lightness of a visual region; or the azimuth of a source of sound. In this scheme, Observers perform very specific perceptual tasks, and the inferences they generate can be at the level of early vision or higher. The structure of the Observer captures very well the intrinsically inferential nature of perception. Perception is inferential, not in the sense that our perceptual life is filled with elaborate, clever, unconscious inferences but rather in the sense that perceptual information is formally the minor premise of an inductive syllogism, no matter how precisely it specifies the perceptual object. Perception has the form, "If E, then S; S is given, therefore E is the case." What is available to us is always S; what we "see" is E. (The inductive syllogism is logically invalid. The best one can do is estimate a probability value for E, which is what Observer theory does. For discussion of these points see Cutting 1986a, Ch. 14, 15; Fodor & Pylyshyn 1981; Hoffman & Richards 1984; Pylyshyn 1986, Ch. 6; for a contrary view from theoretical realists who believe perception is direct, see Turvey et al, 1981.)

Bennett et al argue persuasively that Observer theory provides the basis for a unified theory of perception. Observer theory also promises to resolve, or at least to clarify, a number of issues in the field. For example, Bennett et al (in press) discuss how "cognitive penetrability" (the phenomenon involved when a viewer "forces" an ambiguous figure to look one way or another; cf Fodor & Pylyshyn 1981; Pylyshyn 1986) can be described by Observer theory. What is "penetrated" is a supposedly lower level of analysis (where an edge is seen in an array, for example) by a higher level (the description of the scene depicted in the array, for example). Their explanation depends on the way separate Observers can be organized in a system. (Such separate Observers can, of course, exist within single biological individuals.) The input premises for an Observer are not defined exclusively as sensory primitives (e.g. luminance levels); they can also be the output inferences of other Observers. Sets of Observers can be ordered in various ways. A strict linear ordering, in which each Observer takes the output of the Observer below it in the chain and passes its own inferences to the Observer above it, is only the simplest of many possibilities. Networks of many sorts are possible. According to Bennett et al, cognitive penetrability results from a recursion in the network such that a lower Observer can take as input premises the output premises of an Observer at a higher level. The higher-level output could then bias the interpretation that comes from a lower level. The same sort of recursion could explain expectancy effects, some context effects, and many other cognitive influences on perception.

OTHER CONSIDERATIONS REGARDING AI

Does machine perception always tell us something about biological perception? The AI approach to perceptual theory is but one area of AI research. Many AI researchers in perception are simply trying to design machines that accomplish certain perceptual tasks, and they study human perception in the hope of learning something useful in that effort. However, it is unlikely that the constraints of biological evolution and the multiple competencies required of a living organism have produced solutions that apply directly to such single-purpose engineering problems. To attempt to implement the biological strategies of perception in a perceiving machine seems to some as foolish as designing airplanes with flapping wings. By the same token a machine model of perception may tell us surprisingly little about human perception.

Can perception be modeled by a Turing machine? Bennett et al (1987) have recently challenged the assumption that human perception can be modeled completely by AI techniques. They base their challenge upon Observer theory, which they propose as a general formal foundation for perceptual models. Automata theory and the theory of the Turing machine provide a formal structure for understanding all specific computations. The question then arises whether an Observer is a Turing machine. If it is not, and if the thesis is correct that all perceptual acts are performed by Observers, then perception can not be modeled rigorously or completely by AI techniques.

Bennett et al conclude that Turing machines constitute a subclass of Observers, which they term "Turing observers." This categorization leaves a large class of non-Turing Observers, which Turing machines cannot simulate. Bennett et al suggest that most psychologically plausible Observers actually fall in the non-Turning category. They give as one example of these the Observer that recovers the 3-D structure of moving points from dynamic images. They discuss how some, but not all, non-Turing Observers can be approximated by Turing machines. Their conclusions have far-reaching implications for all theoretical approaches to perception, not just those based on computer simulations (for example, Jackendoff 1987; Pylyshyn 1986). Any modeling approach that assumes essentially Turing simulation, whether explicitly or not, will not account for all perceptual capacities and will thus fail as a general theory. The use of computer programs to test perceptual theories is in this view limited to special cases, and unless there are Turing-simulable alternatives to non-Turing human perceptual abilities, perception machines based on computers will not satisfactorily simulate human perception. If no such alternatives exist, then a divergence between engineering approaches to perception and AI-oriented theories of perception is inevitable, and perceiving machines will eventually be as different from animate perceivers as flying machines are from birds.

Neuropsychological Approach to Perception

Neuropsychologists have analyzed patterns of cognitive disassociation resulting from brain injury. Cognitive neuropsychology has thus provided information on perceptual processing that frequently challenges accounts of perception derived from purely behavioral studies. Such information often suggests new theoretical accounts that would seem implausible on the basis of behavior alone.

Many theories and models have assumed a physiological basis for large classes of perceptual phenomena. By so doing they have opened themselves to influence by concepts derived from neurophysiological investigations (Fechner 1860; Helmholtz 1867; Mach 1914). The Gestalt hypothesis of cortical field interaction was influenced (indeed falsified) by the finding of Lashley et al (1951), using a physiological preparation, that interactions among isomorphs of visual patterns on the visual cortex could not possibly account for Gestalt grouping effects or distortions in memory for patterns. The concept of lateral inhibition figured importantly in von Bekéséy's sensory models of the basilar membrane and of sensory functioning in general. Lateral inhibition has been a primitive concept in explanations of visual phenomenon at least since Mach (1914), even though the physiological evidence for lateral inhibition did not come until Hartline & Ratliff (1957) established lateral inhibitory effects in the visual system of the *Limulus*.

Single-unit recording from neurons in the visual system of vertebrates has brought a wealth of information, most of it completely unexpected by perceptual theorists. The retinal simple cells found by Kuffler (1953) seemed to send the visual cortex a blurred image, of limited usefulness. The simple, complex, and hypercomplex receptive fields found by Hubel & Wiesel (1962, 1968) did not fit into any existing schemes of perception. It was not until computational approaches to perception began to analyze the requirements for vision that a principled account of perception could be based on them (cf Marr 1982).

The discovery of "maps" in cortex of various high-level features in visual space [Kaas (1987) presents a general review; see also Zeki (1981)] has had considerable and rapid influence on perceptual theory (cf Treisman 1988; Treisman & Gelade 1980).

Human cognitive neuropsychology differs from the neurophysiological approach in several important ways. First, neuropsychology is almost entirely observational; it generally studies the results of brain damage caused by strokes, war, and accidents. Single-unit recordings and other invasive techniques can be used only sparingly and to promote the welfare of the patient. However, recent developments in neurological imaging, such as positron emission tomography (PET) scans and magnetic resonance imaging (MRI), have added considerable power to the observational repertory of neuropsychology and have even allowed experimental access to some questions.

Second, neuropsychology generally looks at the brain correlates of high-level human cognitive abilities. The traditional neurophysiological approach tends to concentrate on the neural substrate for the registration of simple stimulus features. At present, therefore, neuropsychology provides virtually our only window on the biological hardware underlying complete acts of perception or cognition.

Third, neuropsychology analyzes *dissociation* syndromes. Patterns of cognitive deficit following brain injury are investigated to see which aspects of functioning are lost and which are preserved. The results are often surprising. Deficits can be extremely specific, and specific patterns of functioning can be preserved relatively intact in the face of major deficits in some areas. Here we contrast the disassociation approach with the *association* approaches of strictly clinical neuropsychology. The latter look for patterns of co-occurrence among deficits in order to localize areas of damage. Patterns of association are dubious indicators of correlation in processing mechanisms across tasks. For example, if two entirely separate functions happen to occupy adjacent locations in cortex they will covary in their response to brain damage.

This brings us to a fourth assumption of the cognitive neuropsychological approach: modularity of function. The approach seeks to identify processing units (modules) in the brain and determine their interconnections. Modules are, by assumption, special-purpose information-processing units that receive input and produce a specific output. [Fodor (1983) develops the concept in detail.] A word-recognition module, for example, would transform an input stimulus (perhaps produced by an earlier module) into an output code that corresponds to the word and that can be used by later modules. A module should be independent of other modules, producing its output without influence from them. If a module is lost, a specific function is lost. Only functions that depend on the lost module will be affected.

There are many alternatives to the modular view, of which the most commonly held is that mental functioning depends on a generalized ability distributed over the whole brain. The debate between the modular view and the wholistic view has deep roots in the history of neuropsychology (Hughlings Jackson 1932). Evidence now appears to favor something like a modular view for the cognitive and perceptual abilities that have been investigated (cf Ellis & Young 1988; Gardner 1983; Humphreys & Riddoch 1987a).

The neuropsychological approach further attempts to associate modular functions with specific brain areas and to identify the functional associations among these with actual neural connections. Such a program, if successful, would result in a functional "map" of the brain that could be overlaid on an anatomical map. The functional map would show what deficits would be associated with lesions to various areas or with disconnection of the neural fibers connecting the areas. The latter sort of damage, known as a disconnection syndrome, provides some credibility to this approach.

WHAT NEUROPSYCHOLOGY HAS TO OFFER STUDENTS OF PERCEPTION Neuropsychological investigations provide the opportunity to obtain converging information on perceptual processes. At the behavioral level, many models may fit the available data. Rather than attempting to design more experiments of questionable diagnosticity, one might profitably seek neurophysiological data that constrain the choice among models. Julesz (1989) has remarked on exactly this beneficial interaction between AI models (which tend to be too powerful to be disconfirmed by behavioral data) and neurophysiological data (which can provide independent—and strong—constraints on modeling).

LIMITS OF THE NEUROPSYCHOLOGICAL APPROACH   The idea that a particular location in the brain is the site of neural hardware for a specific ability has always been problematic. To support an association between a single site and a single function on the basis of observed deficits after specific injury, the researcher needs evidence against a number of alternative hypotheses. One such alternative is that the site in question is only a way station between other areas that actually accomplish the processing. Another is that the observed damage has affected several complexly related small sites rather than a single simple large one. Still another alternative hypothesis is that clinical observations involve whole syndromes of damage. A stroke, for example, endangers all brain areas served by the damaged artery, even if they are functionally unrelated. The commonly observed patterns of deficit following stroke may thus result from damage to a number of different processing functions. In such cases the evidence required to isolate processing modules would come from an extremely small proportion of cases in which the deficits normally seen to be correlated are disassociated.

Finally, note the reliance on negative evidence of the conclusion that two apparently different functions rely on the same processing module: Support for this conclusion comes only from continued failure to find cases of disassociation.

Current Gestalt Theory

As E. G. Boring noted, by 1950 Gestalt psychology had ceased to exist as a school. Its influence has continued, however, and many of the questions that occupied it are still under active and fruitful investigation. The issues inherited from the Gestalt movement include perceptual organization, figure-ground segregation, and perceptual combination of attributes.

Gibsonian ecological perception shares the Gestalt hypothesis that perception is determined by the stimulus configuration presented to the viewer; it shares, as well, the Gestalt rejection of any process that mediates construction of perceptions from sensations. Even the Gibsonian (1979) doctrine of affordances was anticipated by the Gestalt movement (Koffka 1935:7; Köhler 1929, Introduction). The seemingly antithetical cognitive constructivism of Rock (cf Rock 1983) and his colleagues also has roots in the Gestalt tradition. It breaks from this tradition largely because it has turned up phenomena that seem to require the assumption of intelligent perceptual processes. To us it appears that Rock's approach derives from the Gestalt question, "Why do things look as they do?" while the Gibsonian approach derives more from the Gestalt program to examine how perception and action are determined by environmental structure.

Overview of the Three Approaches to Investigating Perception

Each of the approaches sketched above is incomplete as a theoretical basis for understanding perception. The ecological approach is valuable in specifying stimulus invariants and emphasizing how stimulus information supports perception—matters essential to an understanding of perceptual competence. Knowledge about the information available in the stimulus may save us the theoretical embarrassment of needlessly hypothesizing elaborate constructive or inferential processes. However, the ecological approach fails to specify the mechanisms needed to "pick up" the information available in the stimulus. Without postulating mechanisms of perception, we cannot properly explain perceptual phenomena involving cognitive penetration [Rock (1983) discusses many such phenomena; see also Gilchrist (1977, 1980)].

The AI approach aims for an integrated account of stimulus information and the processes that operate on it, but it formulates these processes at a general, functional level, without reference to the specific biological hardware they may run on. It will require a whole new theoretical and empirical effort to relate the progress that has been made in AI modeling of perception to what we know about brain mechanisms of perception.

Nor can the neuropsychological approach stand alone. It is better at determining where a process takes place than how that process works, and it needs the other two areas of theory to be complete.

An AI approach using the three levels of analysis discussed above combines the elements of a complete theory of perception. The first level, hardware, corresponds to the neuropsychological approach; the second, computational theory, describes the attempts at functional accounts of perception and is where most of the effort of AI is expended; and the third, operating environment (the stimulus), corresponds to the ecological approach. There are signs of growing dialog among the approaches—e.g. a text/monograph and several volumes of integrative contributions (Bruce & Green 1985; Humphreys & Riddoch 1987a); and research, such as Julesz's (1989) or Kosslyn's (1988; Kosslyn et al 1990), that uses behavioral, neurophysiological, and AI considerations to constrain theory [see also Ullman's (1986) review of the relation between AI and the neurosciences]. The major integrative models of perception developed by Grossberg and his colleagues pay careful attention to all three areas (e.g. Carpenter & Grossberg 1988; Grossberg 1987). We also note research from an ecological perspective that investigates how a computational mechanism might make use of stimulus information (Todd & Reichel in press). Finally, Richards (1988) has developed what he terms "Natural Computation" as an area and has put together an accessible and comprehensive set of readings to cover it. Natural computation, while heavily influenced by AI, integrates the other two approaches productively.

HIGH-LEVEL VISION

How do we see and identify objects? This basic question has proved an extremely difficult one, and traditional theories have fallen far short of an answer.

A "Phonology" for Object Recognition

Biederman (1987, 1988) has proposed a theory of visual object recognition he terms Recognition-by-Components (RBC). The theory approaches the problem of how we recognize the many objects we do [as many as 30,000 by Biederman & Ju's (1988) estimate] in much the way that a phonological theory approaches the problem of recognizing the large set of words available to a language user. In both cases competence in dealing with the extremely large set is based on use of a much smaller set of components, of which members of the larger set are constructed. [Biederman (1988) discusses this theoretical strategy in detail.] Spoken words are decomposed into 20–50 phonemes, depending on the language. In Biederman's theory of visual recognition, objects are decomposed into 24 (Biederman 1989) to 36 Biederman 1987) *geons* (*geo*metrical *ions*). The geons are simple shapes that have several important properties: they are discriminable from each other on the basis of viewpoint-invariant features (cf Lowe 1984), and they are resistant to visual noise.

Biederman (1987) proposes that object recognition begins with extraction of geons. Geons are isolated as parts of objects by a procedure that uses concavities in the surface (see also Hoffman & Richards 1984) in conjunction with features of the image that are likely to represent edges of parts rather than accidental alignments of elements of a single part (Pentland 1986). When the representations of geons are activated, activation of object models can begin.

Biederman (1987) presented a flow chart model of processing in which functional components were interconnected to perform the operations assumed by RBC theory. This model provided the basis for the tests he presented. Subsequently, Biederman and colleagues (Hummel et al 1988) developed a connectionist model of recognition based on RBC theory. This model has four layers, beginning with edge orientation and curvature recognition and ending with identification of geons. The model accomplishes many object-recognition tasks: It can learn to overcome noise, it can recognize geons of any size, location, or rotation, it can recognize multiple instances of the same geon, and it can recognize many different simultaneously present geons. The model comes just short of recognizing complete objects. What it lacks is the ability to specify completely how the geons are connected (a given set of geons can make a number of different objects, depending on how they are connected).

The RBC model has not yet been extensively tested, but it appears to be a major advance in object-recognition theory. Many of its assumptions are based on AI considerations, and it shows great promise of being implemented in an object-recognition computer program. Tests with human subjects also show it to be a plausible psychological model of object perception. Still other evidence may come from neuropsychology. Some forms of visual agnosia (loss of recognition abilities) seem to imply difficulties with exactly the processes assumed in the RBC model. For example, Humphreys & Riddoch's (1987d) extensive case study of "John" concluded that his dysfunction is best described as "integrative agnosia"—loss of the ability to "bind together" the local parts of objects simultaneously to form a coherent whole. The RBC model would characterize this deficit as an inability to combine geons correctly into recognizable objects.

A Cognitive Neuropsychological Model of Object Perception

Kosslyn and his colleagues (Kosslyn et al 1990) have developed a comprehensive model of visual object recognition and identification that combines approaches from neuropsychology and AI. This is a systematic examination of agnosias and their interpretation within a model of visual recognition. The model postulates a number of processing subsystems ("centers") based on neurophysiological and neuroanatomical evidence and organized in a manner consistent with the same evidence. While the model has been developed with the perceptual capacities of the normally functioning adult in mind, it has been tested primarily by checking how well it predicts the effects of brain damage. When the model is damaged in various ways, a wide variety of clinical dysfunctions can be simulated, many of which result from several distinct forms of simulated brain damage. Although their reports on the dysfunctions do not always discriminate among the possible underlying patterns of damage, the authors describe how tests might be made. Such a use of simulation may offer means of distinguishing among a dysfunction's possible etiologies. Clinical observations based upon a few diagnostic tasks may lump together deficits resulting from very different patterns of damage, and an incorrect picture of brain function may emerge. Kosslyn et al's model enables theorists to go beyond the original set of diagnostic tasks and thus to consider differences among members of a given diagnostic group.

Ellis & Young (1988) present a number of vision models based on processing centers and interconnections, among them models of object recognition, optic aphasia, recognition and comprehension of the spoken word, spelling, and perception of written words in reading. Still another descriptive model is presented by Coslett & Saffran (1989). These models are based upon patterns of disassociation and other neuropsychological data, but they have not been integrated into a larger model. On the contrary, it is often difficult to see how they are related. While these models serve well the purpose of organizing the phenomena in their domains, they do not combine within a model of perceptual functioning.

Humphreys & Riddoch (1987bc) consider several alternative models of visual agnosia, one a cascade model of picture naming with three separate levels (cf Humphreys et al 1988) and another, in an information-processing format, intended to explain access to semantic information from visually presented objects; but these, too, fail of more general explanatory power.

Finally, we refer the reader to Shepp & Ballesteros (1989) for recent accounts of various approaches to object perception.

PERCEPTUAL PSYCHOLOGY

Perceptual Features

FEATURE INTEGRATION THEORY   Feature integration theory (FIT) is a theoretical approach to perception and attention developed by Treisman and her colleagues. The central tenet of FIT is that different sensory features of an object (e.g. color, form, orientation) are coded in specialized modules or "maps" (Treisman 1988; Treisman & Gelade 1980; Treisman & Gormican 1988; Treisman & Schmidt 1982). This central assumption is supported by neurophysiological evidence that the mammalian visual system has a large number of spatially separate maps devoted exclusively to encoding specific features of the visual environment (Kaas 1987; Zeki 1981). According to the model, when an object is presented to the visual system, its features are separately registered on different maps; perceptual processing requires that the features be retrieved from those maps and appropriately associated with the object. The reintegration of sensory features from different maps requires a location-based attentional mechanism (Treisman & Gelade 1980; Treisman & Gormican 1988; Treisman & Schmidt 1982). To put the theory somewhat colloquially, attention serves as the "glue" that binds features from different modules together appropriately.

FIT has predicted a number of phenomena that without the theoretical assumptions of the model would seem surprising. One is the phenomenon of illusory conjunctions: When attention is occupied, objects in a single visual array can trade features. Treisman & Schmidt (1982) found that an array containing, say, a red square and a green circle would sometimes be reported by subjects as very clearly containing a red circle and a green square when a concurrent attentionally demanding task was given. The central role of attention in FIT has been supported by Prinzmetal et al's (1986a) finding that advance knowledge of the location of a stimulus array slightly reduces the time it takes a subject to detect single-feature targets within an array of single-feature distractors but gives a much larger reduction in latency for targets composed of conjunctions of features. Furthermore, illusory conjunctions of simple features (as in Treisman & Schmidt 1982) were more likely to occur for stimuli that appeared at unexpected locations than for those at expected locations. According to FIT, advance knowledge of location allows subjects to orient their attentional mechanism to a given location and properly conjoin target features.

FIT accurately predicts the finding that increasing the number of conjunction distractors increases the time it takes to identify a target whose identity is defined as the conjunction of two or more simple features. This set-size effect does not occur with single-feature targets and distractors; in a search for a target defined by a single feature, the search time increases little with the number of nontarget elements in the array. The function is essentially flat, and Treisman refers to detection of the target in this condition as "pop-out." According to the theory, in the conjunctions of features, a serial, self-terminating application of an attentional mechanism is necessary to test for the proper conjunction of the features of each stimulus individually. Thus, when subjects are searching for conjunctions they must attend to individual items, and the search time increases roughly linearly with display size. On the other hand, to find a single-feature target among single-feature distractors, the subject need only monitor the activity of the "module" or feature map devoted to the feature in question. This allows for the detection of the target regardless of distractor set size, and the item "pops out."

Recently, a number of researchers have shown that searches for conjunction targets can occur in parallel (e.g. McLeod et al 1988; Nakayama & Silverman 1986a). For example, Wolfe et al (1989) have shown that searches for triple conjunctions are quicker than those for double conjunctions and can be independent of set size. To account for this difference they propose a two-stage, Guided-Search model (see below) in which simple feature information is first processed in parallel and then used to guide attention in the search for target conjunctions. Searches for triple conjunctions are easier than searches for double conjunctions because input from the processing of three features can guide the attentional mechanism more effectively than that of only two.

Cave & Wolfe (1990) designed their Guided Search model to retain the virtues of FIT while accounting for fast conjunction searches. Guided Search adds a serial stage to an earlier parallel stage of search. Even though the parallel stage does not successfully locate the target, it produces an activation map of the array that the serial stage can use. In a series of simulations, Cave & Wolfe show that the activation map can guide the serial stage to the target with essentially parallel-search. Their model resembles Neisser's (1967) two-stage schema, having a parallel preattentive process followed by a serial attentive process. A model of the same form for a similar task was also proposed by Hoffman (1978, 1979).

How many different feature maps operate, according to FIT (or modified FIT)? Besides orientation, color, and shape, such other features as motion and depth have been considered (e.g. Nakayama & Silverman 1989b; Steinman 1987). Most identifications of basic features have relied on converging evidence from a number of different empirical tests (see Treisman 1988). Neuropsychological studies show promise in providing likely feature candidates, although some predictions suggested by single-cell recordings have not been verified.

Duncan & Humphreys (1989) have shown that FIT has difficulty in explaining variations in search efficiency across different letter-search tasks. First, with stimulus characters of large enough angular subtense, no set-size effect is found, even if the target has no unique feature. Second, with heterogeneous nontargets, large set-size effects are found even when the target does have a unique feature. To account for these letter-search effects, Duncan & Humphreys (1989) propose an alternative model in which FIT's dichotomy between serial and parallel search is abandoned for an account based on search efficiency. In all cases, search efficiency is influenced by the similarity between target and nontargets. Search difficulty increases with increasing similarity between target and nontarget and decreasing similarity among nontargets.

The first step in the Duncan & Humphreys model involves the registration of all stimuli in parallel. At this stage inputs are subject to perceptual grouping (i.e. Gestalt grouping, segmentation) and are weighted according to their correspondence to an internal template. Similar inputs have a tendency to be grouped together, and suppression (or activation) of one input can spread to other inputs it is grouped with. The degree of spread among inputs is proportional to the strength of the perceptual grouping. When the task involves similar nontargets, suppression of any one nontarget will spread to related nontargets. Much like the process of lateral inhibition, this spread of suppression sharpens sensitivity to the target input, increasing search efficiency. Decreasing letter size makes it difficult to distinguish targets from nontargets. This inability to distinguish inputs interferes with the template-matching process and thus with the differential assignment of weights to target (activation) and nontargets (suppression). Furthermore, spreading suppression also hinders the process of target identification since the target presumably receives inhibition from similar, or indistinguishable, nontargets. This model neatly explains a number of other findings both anomalous to and consistent with FIT (Duncan & Humphreys 1989).

EARLY VISUAL MEMORY   Under the heading of early visual memory we include what has been termed visible persistence, presumably of static arrays (cf Coltheart 1980; Haber 1983b), along with preattentive storage of other types of visual information (e.g. Irwin et al 1983). All have the common property that visual information of varius types remains available when the visual stimulus is no longer available.

Many investigators have suggested that iconic memory might serve as a mechanism by which information from successive saccades is integrated (e.g. Banks 1982; Banks & Barber 1977; Breitmeyer 1984). Recently, Irwin et al (1990) have provided evidence that visual information is maintained across fixations and checked against information gleaned from successive fixations. After a saccade an object does not change position in relation to other objects in the visual field. Such an assertion of perceptual stability fits nicely with Gibson's view that stimulus invariants allow perceivers to view the world as continuous and stable (Irwin et al 1990).

Other research on persistence of vision has focused on components such as spatial frequency resolution (DiLollo & Woods 1981), factors that influence duration (DiLollo & Hogben 1985, 1987; DiLollo & Bourassa 1983), preattentive effects (Holding & Orenstein 1983; Orenstein & Holding 1987), and underlying mechanisms of storage (DiLollo & Dixon 1988; Yeomans & Irwin 1985; Loftus & Hanna 1990).

Figural Processes

Gestalt psychology's concern with "figure" and "ground" continues to bear fruit. The account of Gestalt grouping processes is divided into two general questions: What determines grouping or object-formation? and What are the effects of grouping on perceptual processing?

DETERMINANTS OF PERCEPTUAL OBJECTS   Texture is a powerful figure-ground determinant. One model of texture segregation is based on the detection of geometric features of a pattern (Beck 1982; Marr 1976). Julesz (1981, 1984a,b, 1986) has labeled these features textons. Elongated blobs (e.g. rectangles, ellipses, line segments, widths, lengths), endpoints of elongated blobs (terminators), and intersections of blobs (line crossings) have all been identified as textons. Texture segregation is said to occur rapidly by preattentive detection of differences in texton type or texton density.

On a purely descriptive level there is general consensus on the elements (i.e. textons) that mediate texture segregation. However, there is no general agreement on the process by which segregation proceeds (cf Enns 1986). For example, Taylor & Badcock (1988) have shown that density differences may not be detected in the way initially predicted by texton theory. Pashler (1988) has proposed spatially specific detectors of the boundaries between textures, whose outputs can be pooled for higher-level processing.

A second model posits that segregation may be accomplished via differences in the outputs of spatial-frequency channels (Caelli 1985; Beck et al 1987; Graham 1981; Grossberg & Mingolla 1985). Spatial-frequency channels are independent, parallel neural channels made up of receptive fields and distributed throughout the representations of the visual field (Graham 1985, 1989). Klymenko & Weisstein (1986) presented subjects with ambiguous figures like the Peter-Paul goblet with high-frequency sine gratings in one region and low-frequency gratings in the other. The region with the higher spatial frequency was more likely to be seen as figure. Sutter et al (1990) have shown that an explanation based on spatial-frequency channels can account for changes in perceived texture as a function of changes in element contrast spacing. They also propose a more complicated spatial-frequency model, which relies on complex filtering strategies, to give a general account of texture segregation in many different situations. Julesz (1989), however, has shown some exceptions to the spatial-frequency account of texture segregation.

Texture segregates figures from the background rapidly and without the need for inspection, in what can be called a "bottom-up" manner. There is also evidence for "top-down" influences on figural segregation. Often just as rapid, these mechanisms depend on conceptual or categorical information rather than physical features of the array. Peterson and her colleagues (Peterson 1986; Peterson & Hochberg 1983, 1989; Hochberg & Peterson 1987; Peterson & Gibson, in press) have investigated effects of priming of interpretations (cf Carr et al 1982) and of structural prototypicality in determining the perceptual organization of an array. While many models of object recognition assume that figure-ground organization takes place as a necessary step before object recognition, Peterson et al show figural effects on segregation. Thus, figural properties, which many theories assume are consequences of figure-ground segregation, are involved in the generation of perceptual figures. Therefore some interaction between bottom-up and top-down processes seems necessary to create figural segregation. This interaction is modeled in the Peterson et al model. The neural net models of Grossberg (1987), Carpenter & Grossberg (1988), and Grossberg et al (1989), very different in structure, also assume an interactive process, as does McClelland (1990). Mumford et al (1987) concluded that two processes, edge detection and "region growing"—rather different from those considered above, but still at separate processing levels—could operate interactively in figure-ground segregation.

Pomerantz & Pristach (1990) argue that perceptual grouping results from emergent features created by the configuration of elements in an array. Combinations of elements create new features that resist analysis into parts, so that the original elements are difficult to process (Pomerantz 1986). Pomerantz & Pristach argue that emergence of features rather than a perceptual "glue" or active bonding process makes separate attention to elements difficult. The texton theory of segregation is not supported by their research; they note that they are investigating form discrimination, which may have properties different from those of texture discrimination.

EFFECTS OF PERCEPTUAL GROUPING   Many investigators have examined the effects of grouping on other processes. Banks & Prinzmetal (1976) and Prinzmetal & Banks (1977) showed that membership in a group can camouflage an item and make it more difficult to detect than if it is not so grouped, even when its proximity to the grouped items is controlled. Prinzmetal (1981) showed that illusory conjunctions of features (Treisman & Schmidt 1982) are more likely to take place within a group than between items in different groups, again with proximity relations controlled. Treisman (1982) found that subjects searched serially through groups of items for conjunctively defined objects in an array but searched for single features without regard for groups. She suggested that preattentive grouping creates separate feature maps within each separable dimension rather than one global configuration. Prinzmetal & Millis-Wright (1984) showed that grouping, defined by orthographic structure of briefly presented words, determines the illusory spread of color over the letters. (We term the previously undocumented illusion of a color spreading from some letters to others in a word the *Prinzmetal Illusion*.) Prinzmetal et al (1986b) also showed the effect of orthographic structure on perception of words. Prinzmetal & Keysar (1989) explain these and other effects, such as neon color spreading, in a unified theory postulating that perceptual grouping localizes perceptual features encoded in "maps" (Kaas 1987; Zeki 1981) that have poor spatial resolution.

Wong & Weisstein (1982, 1983) found that detectability of a high-spatial-frequency stimulus was better when it was presented against figure than when it was presented against ground in a simple array divided into figure and ground perceptually. They found, conversely, that a stimulus that was low-pass filtered spatially was better seen when placed in the ground than in the figure.

ECOLOGY OF PERCEPTION

Layout and Locomotion

Two research programs of the ecological movement, perception of spatial layout and perception of self-motion, have recently received some overdue attention. Haber (1985) provided a theory, a measurement technique, and some data on the metric structure of how people perceive the spatial layout of real scenes. Cutting and his colleagues have investigated spatial layout in cinema (Cutting 1986b, 1987), pictures (1988), and simulated spatial gradients (Cutting & Millard 1984) and arrays (Bruno & Cutting 1988). Todd & Reichel (1990) have investigated the visual information that specifies the shape of smoothly curving surfaces. They concluded that nonmetric, ordinal relations between areas are critical. They also showed that occlusion contours are a primary source of information about surface structure.

R. Warren & Wertheim (1990) have edited a book on the topic of the perception and control of self-motion that includes contributions on a wide variety of topics from many points of view. Wallach's review (1987) of self-motion in perception of the environment and Cutting's (1986a) treatment of transformations of the visual array during motion are also of interest. W. Warren and his colleagues have made careful analyses of the information in optical flow that gives the perception of the direction of self-motion (Warren & Hannon 1988; Warren et al 1988). They have also measured the optical information used to control step length in running (Warren et al 1986) and body posture in walking through doorways (Warren & Whang 1987; Warren 1988).

Extraction of Shape

How perceivers derive the 3-D shape of an object from surface properties, motion, or 2-D projections is a topic shared by the AI and ecological traditions. The theoretical goal is the same in both cases: to determine how the optical information can specify the shape and what aspect of this information is used by the visual system. Ramachandran (1988) and chapters in Richards (1988) give reviews of current approaches to 3-D shape perception. (See also citations in the previous section.) The research has investigated effects of surface shading (e.g. Todd & Mingolla 1983, 1984; Mingolla & Todd 1986), local curvature (Beusmans et al 1987; Stevens 1987, 1988), motion (Braunstein & Andersen 1984; Doner et al 1984; Ullman 1984; Todd 1985), and projective 2-D shape (Richards & Hoffman 1985; Richards et al 1988). Tarr & Pinker (1989) have investigated the orientation dependency of object recognition. They argue that shapes are represented in memory in multiple orientation-specific views and that seen forms are mentally rotated to match them. However Jolicoeur (1988) found different effects of orientation for left-right judgments and for shape naming. He suggests a single-process model for left-right orientation judgments and a more complex dual-process model for shape recognition. While most research is on visual form perception, several interesting lines of investigation involve the perception and recognition of objects by touch (Klatsky et al 1988; Richards 1988: Ch. 5) and hearing (cf Richards 1988: Ch. 4).

LOGIC OF PERCEPTION

This section takes its name from the work of Rock (1983), who has developed the most inclusive and empirically plausible explanation of perceptual effects that seem to require intelligent activity on the part of the perceiver. Rock's approach treats perception as a process of problem solving. Perceptual or sensory information is termed the "support" for perception, much as evidence or data is taken as support for an argument or a theoretical position. The product of perceptual activity is a description of the object of perception. Thus, in perceiving, the perceiver uses the available information and searches for more in order to construct or test an encoded description of the event.

Demonstrations supporting this account of perception are often striking and clever. In one, for example, subjects were shown two lights alternately illuminated in a dark room. The time between illuminations was set to produce apparent motion. Once subjects reported seeing the (apparent) motion, the room lights were turned on and subjects were shown an opaque panel hanging between the lights. The experimenter then falsely claimed, backed by a faked demonstration, that the alternating illumination of the lights was caused by the panel's swinging to cover one light, then the other. Exposed once again to the experiment's initial conditions, subjects no longer reported seeing motion. Some now said they saw occlusion of the lights from the inner side as the panel (supposedly) slid over them from the center.

This and the numerous other experiments discussed by Rock illustrate a common phenomenon: People's descriptions of what they see are influenced by many factors in addition to the elements present in the stimulus array. According to Rock, people "take account of" these additional factors in describing what they see. The process could hardly be more cognitive; it is as though the perceiver is using a problem-solving strategy that considers many sources of information beyond anything available in the array. [Gogel and colleagues have investigated cognitive influences such as memory of the sizes of objects on perceived distance (see, for example, Gogel & Da Silva 1987; Gogel 1990).]

The "intelligence" of perception has some peculiar aspects. For example, in the apparent-motion effect discussed above, the effect of believing in an opaque occluder makes sense, but why do some subjects persist in seeing apparent motion even after they have been told that stationary lights are actually being turned on and off electronically? How smart is perception, after all? Aware of this issue, Rock does not claim for perception the logical approach of a rational decision-maker. Perception, he maintains, has a "logic" of its own that is often inaccessible to conscious, declarative knowledge. I can be aware of the true state of affairs in an illusory array and yet be fully subject to the illusion. In such a case no amount of thought can change my perception. If perception "takes account of" extra-stimulus knowledge, how can this be?

Bennett et al (1990) consider perception to be the product of Observer-structured modules that are only partially cognitively penetrable. Judgments, extra-stimulus information, and the output of other modules may be among the premises these modules take, but they do not have available (or simply cannot use) all of the information available to consciousness. The peculiar "logic" they display may thus result from the limited facts they can consider or from the rules of inference they use. As Searle (1990) has remarked, these functions may behave "as if" intelligent, but careful experiments may show that intelligence to be spurious.

Rock's notions suggest a set of goals for perceptual theory—namely, to isolate and understand these "intelligent" functions and determine their origins. They may well originate in evolutionary adaptations to the perceptual tasks confronting organisms. Consider an approach that assumes "intelligence" behind the perceptual system's ability to dismiss low-probability stimulus configurations. For example, a "T" intersection of lines is less likely to be the result of a fortuitous coincidence of edges than it is to result from interposition of one object in front of another (cf Richards 1988, for examples of this sort; Biederman, 1987). Rather than assume every such perception to derive from an intelligent estimate of probability, one could look for perceptual mechanisms produced by evolutionary pressures that have this effect. [See Searle (1990) for a discussion of this mode of explanation of perceptual intelligence.]

Information Pick-up vs Logic of Perception

Rock's approach could hardly be more different from that of the ecologists. Rock is concerned with what things look like, while the ecologists are concerned with the actions things afford. Rock studies the perceptual "taking account" of various sorts of information both inside and outside the perceived array; ecologists study the structure of the available information and how much of it is "picked up." Rock's experiments carefully control the available information and often focus on illusions. Ecologists prefer to study natural information; they eschew illusions.

Despite these differences, which sometimes trigger the sort of emotional responses that lead to religious wars, we suggest Observer theory (Bennett et al 1990) as a basis for resolution on some points. The ecologists must recognize that a scientific account will need a mechanistic account, and the Observer structure comes close to the flavor of their approach. The "intelligence" of Rock's mechanisms must also succumb to analysis, and again Observer theory seems appropriate. Such issues as cognitive penetrability (or the lack of it in an otherwise "intelligent" processor) are well captured by Observer theory. Even the controversial Gibsonian theory of affordances has an explanation from Observer theory, as Bennett et al (1990) explain: If what is perceived is the inference generated by an Observer, then an Observer that generates such inferences as "sit-on-able" will create perceptions of affordances, which to the perceiver might as well be in the perceived object.

MODULES, OBSERVERS, AND BRAIN LOCI

Much of our discussion has touched on assumptions that have not yet been fully worked out, much less tested. We have assumed that modules have some sort of explanatory status, but their definition has been rather loose and variable since Fodor (1983) developed the concept. In current neuroscience we find modular explanations at a general level but little agreement on modules across explanations. One approach to clarifying matters might be to assume that the basic modules are, simply, Observers. Such an equation would give us a workable operational definition of a module, it would create a connection between two areas of inquiry, and it might simplify things greatly. Still another step would be to determine whether individual brain loci of information processing can be modeled as Observers. If they can, the connections created among the three areas discussed here might be enormously productive.

Literature Cited

Banks, W. P. 1983. On the decay of the icon. *Behav. Brain Sci.* 6:14

Banks, W. P., Barbar, G. 1977. Color information in iconic memory. *Psychol. Rev.* 84:536–46

Banks, W. P., Prinzmetal, W. 1976. Configurational effects in visual information processing. *Percept. Psychophys.* 19:361–67

Beck, J. 1982. Texture segmentation. In *Organization and Representation in Perception*, ed. J. Beck, pp. 285–318. Hillsdale, NJ: Erlbaum

Beck, J., Sutter, A., Ivry, R. 1987. Spatial frequency channels and perceptual grouping in texture segregation. *Comput. Vis. Graph. Image Process.* 37:299–325

Bennett, B. M., Hoffman, D. D., Prakash, C. 1987. Perception and computation. *Proc. IEEE 1st Int. Conf. Comput. Vis., London*, pp. 356–64

Bennett, B. M., Hoffman, D. D., Prakash, C. 1989. *Observer Mechanics: A Formal Theory of Perception.* New York: Academic

Bennett, B. M., Hoffman, D. D., Prakash, C. 1990. Unity of perception. Also available as Univ. Calif. Irvine Math. Behav. Sci. Memo 90–13

Beusmans, J. M. H., Hoffman, D. D., Bennett, B. M. 1987. Description of solid shape and its inference from occluding contours. *J. Opt. Soc. Am.* 4:1155–67

Biederman, I. 1987. Recognition-by-components: a theory of human image interpretation. *Psychol. Rev.* 94:115–47

Biederman, I. 1988. Aspects and extensions of a theory of human image understanding. In *Computational Human Vision: An Interdisciplinary Perspective*, ed. Z. Pylyshyn, pp. 370–428. Norwood, NJ: Ablex

Biederman, I. 1989. Higher-level vision. In *An Invitation to Cognitive Science*, ed. D. N. Osherson, H. Lasnik, S. Kosslyn, J. Hollerbach, E. Smith, N. Bloch. Cambridge, MA: MIT Press

Biederman, I., Ju, G. 1988. Surface vs. edge-based determinants of visual cognition. *Cognit. Psychol.* 20:38–64

Boring, E. G. 1950. *A History of Experimental Psychology.* New York: Appleton-Century-Crofts. 2nd ed.

Braunstein, M. L., Andersen, G. J. 1984. Shape and depth perception from parallel projections of three-dimensional motion. *J. Exp. Psychol. Hum. Percept. Perform.* 10:749–60

Breitmeyer, B. G. 1984. *Visual Masking: An Integrative Approach.* New York: Oxford Univ. Press

Bruce, V., Green, P. R. 1985. *Visual Perception: Physiology, Psychology and Ecology.* Hillsdale, NJ: Erlbaum

Bruno, N., Cutting, J. E. 1988. Minimodularity and the perception of layout. *J. Exp. Psychol. Gen.* 117:161–70

Caelli, T. 1985. Three processing characteristics of visual texture segmentation. *Spatial Vis.* 1:19–30

Carpenter, G. A., Grossberg, S. 1988. Self-organizing neural network architectures for real-time adaptive pattern recognition. In *Neural and Synergetic Computers*, ed. H. Haken. New York: Springer-Verlag

Carr, T. H., McCauley, C., Sperber, R. D., Parmelee, J. 1982. Words, pictures, and priming: on semantic activation, conscious identification, and the automaticity of information processing. *J. Exp. Psychol.: Hum. Percept. Perform.* 8:757–77

Cave, K. R., Wolfe, J. M. 1990. Modelling the role of parallel processing in visual search. *Cognit. Psychol.* 22:225–71

Coltheart, M. 1980. Iconic memory and visible persistence. *Percept. Psychophys.* 27:183–228

Coslett, H. B., Saffran, E. M. 1989. Preserved object recognition and reading comprehension in optic aphasia. *Brain* 112:1091–1110

Cutting, J. E. 1986a. *Perception with an Eye for Motion.* Cambridge, MA: MIT Press

Cutting, J. E. 1986b. The shape and psychophysics of cinematic space. *Behavior, Research Methods, Instruments, & Computers*, 18, 551–558

Cutting, J. E. 1987. Rigidity in cinema seen from the front row, side aisle. *J. Exp. Psychol.: Hum. Percept. Perform.* 13:323–34

Cutting, J. E. 1988. Affine distortions of pictorial space: some predictions for Goldstein (1987) that La Gournerie (1859) might have made. *J. Exp. Psychol.: Hum. Percept. Perform.* 14:305–11

Cutting, J. E., Millard, R. T. 1984. Three gradients and the perception of flat and curved surfaces. *J. Exp. Psychol. Gen.* 113:198–216

DiLollo, V., Bourassa, C. M. 1983. Temporal integration following intensification of long-lasting visual displays. *Vis. Res.* 23:677–87

DiLollo, V., Dixon, P. 1988. Two forms of persistence in visual information processing. *Percept. Psychophys.* 14:671–81

DiLollo, V., Hogben, J. H. 1985. Suppression of visible persistence. *J. Exp. Psychol.: Hum. Percept. Perform.* 11:304–16

DiLollo, V., Hogben, J. H. 1987. Suppression of visible persistence as a function of spatial separation between inducing stimuli. *Percept. Psychophys.* 41:345–54

DiLollo, V., Woods, E. 1981. Duration of visible persistence in relation to range of spatial frequencies. *J. Exp. Psychol. Hum. Percept. Perform.* 7:754–69

Doner, J., Lappin, J. S., Perfetto, G. 1984. Detection of three-dimensional structure in moving optical patterns. *J. Exp. Psychol.: Hum. Percept. Perform.* 10:1–11

Duncan, J., Humphreys, G. W. 1989. Visual search and stimulus similarity. *Psychol. Rev.* 96:433–58

Ellis, A. W., Young, A. W. 1988. *Human Cognitive Neuropsychology.* Hillsdale, NJ: Erlbaum

Enns, J. T. 1986. Seeing textons in context. *Percept. Psychophys.* 26:195–205

Fechner, G. T. 1860. *Elemente der Psychophysik.* Leipzig: Breecktkopf and Härtel

Fodor, J. A. 1983. *The Modularity of the Mind: An Essay on Faculty Psychology.* Cambridge, MA: MIT Press

Fodor, J. A., Pylyshyn, Z. W. 1981. How direct is visual perception? Some reflections on Gibson's 'Ecological Approach'. *Cognition* 9:139–96

Gardner, H. 1983. *Frames of Mind.* New York: Basic Books

Gibson, J. J. 1950. *Perception and the Visual World.* Boston: Houghton Mifflin

Gibson, J. J. 1966. *The Senses Considered as Perceptual Systems.* Boston: Houghton Mifflin

Gibson, J. J. 1979. *The Ecological Approach to Visual Perception.* Boston: Houghton Mifflin

Gilchrist, A. L. 1977. Perceived lightness depends on perceived spatial arrangement. *Science* 195:185–87

Gilchrist, A. L. 1980. When does perceived lightness depend on perceived spatial arrangement? *Percept. Psychophys.* 28:527–38

Gogel, W. C. 1990. A theory of phenomenal geometry and its applications. *Percept. Psychophys.* 48:105–23

Gogel, W. C., Da Silva, J. A. 1987. A two-process theory of the response to size and distance. *Percept. Psychophys.* 41:220–38

Graham, N. 1981. Psychophysics of spatial frequency channels. In *Perceptual Organization,* ed. M. Kubovy, J. R. Pomerantz, pp. 1–26. Hillsdale, NJ: Erlbaum

Graham, N. 1985. Detection and identification of near-threshold visual patterns. *J. Opt. Soc. Am. A.* 2:1468–82

Graham, N. 1989. *Visual Pattern Analyzers.* New York: Oxford Univ. Press

Grossberg, S. 1987. Cortical dynamics of three-dimensional form, color, and brightness perception. I. Monocular theory. *Percept. Psychophys.* 41:87–116

Grossberg, S., Mingolla, E. 1985. Neural dynamics of perceptual grouping: textures, boundaries, and emergent features. *Percept. Psychophys.* 38:141–71

Grossberg, S., Mingolla, E., Todorović, D. 1989. A neural network architecture for preattentive vision. *IEEE Trans. Biomed. Eng.* 36:65–84

Haber, R. N. 1983a. Visual perception during the last one hundred years. *Acad. Psychol. Bull.* 5:141–54

Haber, R. N. 1983b. The impending demise of the icon: a critique of the concept of iconic storage in visual information processing. *Behav. Brain Sci.* 6:1–11

Haber, R. N. 1985. Toward a theory of the perceived spatial layout of scenes. *Comput. Vis. Graph. Image Process.* 1:1–40

Hartline, H. K., Ratliff, F. 1957. Inhibitory interaction of receptor units in the eye of *Limulus. J. Gen. Physiol.* 40:357–76

Helmholtz, H. von. 1962 [1867]. *Treatise on Physiological Optics, Vol. III.* Transl. from the 3rd German ed.; ed. J. P. C. Southall. New York: Dover Publications

Hochberg, J., Peterson, M. A. 1987. Piecemeal organization and cognitive components in object perception: perceptually coupled responses to moving objects. *J. Exp. Psychol. Gen.* 116:370–80

Hoffman, D. D., Richards, W. A. 1984. Parts of recognition. *Cognition* 18:65–96

Hoffman, J. E. 1978. Search through a sequentially presented visual display. *Percept. Psychophys.* 23:1–11

Hoffman, J. E. 1979. A two-stage model of visual search. *Percept. Psychophys.* 25:319–27

Holding, D. H., Orenstein, H. B. 1983. Sensory storage of fragmentary displays. *Percept. Motor Skills* 57:1283–94

Hubel, D. H., Wiesel, T. N. 1962. Receptive fields, binocular interaction and functional architecture in the cat's visual cortex. *J. Physiol. (London)* 160:106–54

Hubel, D. H., Wiesel, T. N. 1968. Receptive fields and functional architecture of monkey striate cortex. *J. Physiol. (London)* 195:215–43

Hughlings Jackson, J. 1932. *Selected Writings.* London: Hodder and Stoughton

Hummel, J. E., Biederman, I., Gerhardstein, P. C., Hilton, H. J. 1988. From image edges to geons: a connectionist approach. In *Proc. 1988 Connect. Models Summer School,* ed. D. Touretsky, G. Hinton, T. Sejnowski, pp. 462–71. San Mateo: Morgan Kaufman

Humphreys, G. W., Riddoch, M. J., eds. 1987a. *Visual Object Processing: A Cognitive Neuropsychological Approach.* Hillsdale, NJ: Erlbaum

Humphreys, G. W., Riddoch, M. J. 1987b. Cognitive neuropsychology and visual object processing. See Humphreys & Riddoch 1987a, pp. 1–16

Humphreys, G. W., & Riccoch, M. J. 1987c. The fractionation of visual agnosia. See Humphreys & Riddoch 1987a, pp. 281–306

Humphreys, G. W., Riddoch, M. J. 1987d. *To See But Not to See: A Case Study of Visual Agnosia.* Hillsdale, NJ: Erlbaum

Humphreys, G. W., Riddoch, M. J., Quinlan, P. T. 1988. Cascade processes in picture identification. *Cognit. Neuropsychol.* 5:67–104

Irwin, D. E., Yantis, S., Jonides, J. 1983. Evidence against visual integration across saccadic eye movements. *Percept. Psychophys.* 34:49–57

Irwin, D. E., Zacks, J. L., Brown, J. S. 1990. Visual memory and the perception of a stable visual environment. *Percept. Psychophys.* 47:35–46

Jackendoff, R. S. 1987. *Consciousness and the Computational Mind.* Cambridge, MA: MIT Press

Jolicoeur, P. 1988. Mental rotation and the identification of disoriented objects. *Can. J. Psychol.* 42:461–78

Julesz, B. 1981. Textons, the elements of texture perception, and their interactions. *Nature* 290:91–97

Julesz, B. 1984a. Adaptation in a peephole: a texton theory of preattentive vision. In *Sensory Experience, Adaptation, and Perception: Festschrift for Ivo Kohler,* ed. L. Spillman, B. R. Wooten. Hillsdale, NJ: Erlbaum

Julesz, B. 1984b. Toward an axiomatic theory of preattentive vision. In *Dynamic Aspects of Neocortical Function,* ed. G. M. Edelman, W. E. Gall, W. M. Cowan. New York: Wiley

Julesz, B. 1986. Texton gradients: the texton theory revisited. *Biol. Cybern.* 54:245–51

Julesz, B. 1989. Concepts in early vision. In *Synergetics of Cognition,* ed. H. Haken, M. Stadler. New York: Springer-Verlag

Kaas, J. H. 1987. The organization of neocortex in mammals: implications for theories of brain function. *Annu. Rev. Psychol.* 38: 129–51

Klatsky, R. L., Lederman, S., Reed, C. 1988. Haptic integration of object properties: texture, hardness, and planar contour. *J. Exp. Psychol.: Hum. Percept. Perform.* 15:45–57

Klymenko, V., Weisstein, N. 1986. Spatial frequency differences can determine figureground organization. *J. Exp. Psychol.: Hum. Percept. Perform.* 12:324–30

Koffka, K. 1935. *Principles of Gestalt Psychology.* New York: Harcourt, Brace and World

Kosslyn, S. M. 1988. Aspects of a cognitive neuroscience of mental imagery. *Science* 240:1621–26

Kosslyn, S., Flynn, A., Amsterdam, J. B., Wang. G. 1990. Components of high-level vision: a cognitive neuroscience analysis and accounts of neurological syndromes. *Cognition* 34:203–77

Köhler, W. 1929. *Gestalt Psychology.* New York: Liveright

Kuffler, S. W. 1953. Discharge patterns and functional organization of mammalian retina. *J. Neurophysiol.* 16:37–68

Lashley, K. S., Chow, K. L., Semmes, J. 1951. An examination of the electrical field theory of cerebral integration. *Psychol. Rev.* 58:123–36

Loftus, G. R., Hanna, A. M. 1990. The phenomenology of spatial integration: data and models. *Cognit. Psychol.* In press

Lowe, D. G. 1984. *Perceptual organization and visual recognition.* PhD thesis, Dept. Comput. Sci., Stanford Univ.

Mach, E. 1959 [1914]. *The Analysis of Sensations.* New York: Dover

Marr, D. 1976. Early processing of visual information. *Philos. Trans. R. Soc. London Ser. B, Biol. Sci.* 275:483–524

Marr, D. 1982. *Vision.* San Francisco: W. H. Freeman

Marr, D., Poggio, T. 1977. From understanding computation to understanding neural circuitry. *Neurosci. Res. Prog. Bull.* 15:470–88

McClelland, J. L. 1990. Stochastic interactive activation and the effect of context on perception. *Cognit. Psychol.* In press

McLeod, P., Driver, J., Crisp, J. 1988. Visual search for a conjunction of movement and form is parallel. *Nature* 332:154–55

Mingolla, E., Todd, J. T. 1986. Perception of solid shape from shading. *Biol. Cybern.* 53:137–51

Mumford, D., Kosslyn, S. M., Hillger, L. A., Herrnstein, R. J. 1987. Discriminating figure from ground: the role of edge detection and region growing. *Proc. Natl. Acad. Sci. USA* 84:7354–58

Nakayama, K., Silverman, G. H. 1986a. Serial and parallel encoding of visual feature conjunctions. ARVO Suppl. to *Invest. Ophthalmol. Vis. Sci.*

Nakayama, K., Silverman, G. H. 1986b. Serial and parallel processing of visual feature conjunctions. *Nature* 320:264–65

Neisser, U. 1967. *Cognitive Psychology.* New York: Appleton-Century-Crofts

Orenstein, H. B., Holding, D. H. 1987. Attentional factors in iconic memory and visible persistence. *Q. J. Exp. Psychol.* 39A:149–66

Pashler, H. 1988. Cross-dimensional interaction and texture segregation. *Percept. Psychophys.* 43:307–18

Pentland, A. P. 1986. Perceptual organization

and the representation of natural form. *Artif. Intell.* 28:293–331

Peterson, M. A. 1986. Illusory concomitant motion in ambiguous stereograms: evidence for nonstimulus contributions to perceptual organization. *J. Exp. Psychol.: Hum. Percept. Perform.* 12:50–60

Peterson, M. A., Gibson, B. S. 1991. The initial identification of figure-ground relationships: contributions from shape-recognition routines. *Bull. Psychonom. Soc.* In press

Peterson, M. A., Hochberg, J. 1983. Opposed-set measurement procedure: a quantitative analysis of the role of local cues and intention in form perception. *J. Exp. Psychol.: Hum. Percept. Perform.* 9:183–93

Peterson, M. A., Hochberg, J. 1989. Necessary considerations for a theory of form perception: a theoretical and empirical reply to Boselie and Leeuwenberg (1986). *Perception* 18:105–19

Pomerantz, J. R. 1986. Overview of visual form perception. In *Perception of Speech and Visual Form: Theoretical Issues, Models, and Research*, ed. E. C. Schwab, H. C. Nusbaum. New York: Academic

Pomerantz, J. R., Pristach, E. A. 1990. Emergent feature, attention and perceptual glue in visual form perception. *J. Exp. Psychol.: Hum. Percept. Perform.* 15:635–49

Prinzmetal, W. 1981. Principles of feature integration in visual perception. *Percept. Psychophys.* 30:330–40

Prinzmetal, W., Banks, W. P. 1977. Good continuation affects visual detection. *Percept. Psychophys.* 21:389–95

Prinzmetal, W., Keysar, B. 1989. Functional theory of illusory conjunctions and neon colors. *J. Exp. Psychol.: Gen.* 118:165–90

Prinzmetal, W., Millis-Wright, M. 1984. Cognitive and linguistic factors affect visual feature integration. *Cognit. Psychol.* 16:305–40

Prinzmetal, W., Presti, D. E., Posner, M. I. 1986. Does attention affect visual feature integration? *J. Exp. Psychol.: Hum. Percept. Perform.* 12:361–70

Prinzmetal, W., Treiman, R., Rho, S. H. 1986. How to see a reading unit. *J. Mem. Lang.* 25:361–69

Pylyshyn, Z. W. 1986. *Computation and Cognition.* Cambridge, MA: MIT Press

Ramachandran, V. S. 1988. Perceiving shape from shading. *Sci. Am.* 241:76–83

Richards, W., ed. 1988. *Natural Computation.* Cambridge, MA: MIT Press

Richards, W., Hoffman, D. D. 1985. Codon constraints on closed 2D shapes. *Comput. Vis. Graph., Image Process.* 31:265–81

Richards, W., Koenderink, J. J., Hoffman, D. D. 1988. Inferring three-dimensional shapes

from two-dimensional silhouettes. In *Natural Computation*, ed. W. Richards, pp. 125–37. Cambridge, MA: MIT Press

Rock, I. 1983. *The Logic of Perception.* Cambridge, MA: MIT Press

Searle, J. R. 1990. Consciousness, explanatory inversion and cognitive science. *Behav. Brain Sci.* In press

Shepp, B. E., Ballesteros, S., ed. 1989. *Object Perception: Structure and Process.* Hillsdale, NJ: Erlbaum

Steinman, S. B. 1987. Serial and parallel search in pattern vision. *Perception* 16:389–99

Stevens, K. A. 1987. Visual object perception from a computational perspective. See Humphreys & Riddoch 1987a, pp. 17–42

Stevens, K. A. 1988. The line of curvature constraint and the interpretation of 3D shape from parallel surface contours. In *Natural Computation*, ed. W. Richards, pp. 107–14. Cambridge, MA: MIT Press

Sutter, A., Beck, J., Graham, N. 1990. Contrast and spatial variables in texture segregation: testing a simple spatial-frequency channels model. *Percept. Psychophys.* In press

Tarr, M. J., Pinker, S. 1989. Mental rotation and orientation dependable in shape recognition. *Cogn. Psychol.* 21:233–82

Taylor, S., Badcock, D. 1988. Processing feature density in preattentive perception. *Percept. Psychophys.* 44:551–62

Todd, J. T. 1985. Perception of structure from motion: is projective correspondence of moving elements a necessary condition? *J. Exp. Psychol.: Hum. Percept. Perform.* 11:689–710

Todd, J. T., Mingolla, E. 1983. Perception of surface curvature and direction of illumination from patterns of shading. *J. Exp. Psychol.: Hum. Percept. Perform.* 9:583–95

Todd, J. T., Mingolla, E. 1984. Simulation of curved surfaces from patterns of optical texture. *J. Exp. Psychol.: Hum. Percept. Perform.* 10:734–39

Todd, J. T., Reichel, F. D. 1990. Ordinal structure in the visual perception and cognition of smoothly curved surfaces. *Psychol. Rev.* In press

Treisman, A. 1982. Perceptual grouping and attention in visual search for features and for objects. *J. Exp. Psychol. Hum. Percept. Perform.* 8:194–214

Treisman, A. 1988. Features and objects: the Fourteenth Bartlett Memorial Lecture. *Q. J. Exp. Psychol.* 40A:201–37

Treisman, A., Gelade, G. 1980. A feature integration theory of attention. *Cognit. Psychol.* 12:97–136

Treisman, A., Gormican, S. 1988. Emergent features, attention and object perception. *J.*

Exp. Psychol.: Hum. Percept. Perform. 10:12–31

Treisman, A., Schmidt, N. 1982. Illusory conjunctions in the perception of objects. *Cognit. Psychol.* 14:107–41

Turvey, M. T., Shaw, M. E., Reed, E. S., Mace, W. M. 1981. Ecological laws of perceiving and acting: in reply to Fodor and Pylyshyn (1981). *Cognition* 9:237–304

Ullman, S. 1984. Visual routines. *Cognition* 18:97–159

Ullman, S. 1986. Artificial intelligence and the brain: computational studies of the visual system. *Annu. Rev. Neurosci.* 9:1–26

Wallach, H. 1987. Perceiving a stable environment when one moves. *Annu. Rev. Psychol.* 38:1–27

Warren, R., Wertheim, A. H. 1990. *Perception and Control of Self-Motion.* Hillsdale, NJ: Erlbaum

Warren, W. H. 1988. Action modes and laws of control for the visual guidance of action. In *Complex Movement Behaviour: The Motor-Action Theory Controversy,* ed. O. G. Meijer, K. Roth. North-Holland: Elsevier

Warren, W. H., Hannon, D. J. 1988. Direction of self-motion is perceived from optical flow. *Nature* 336:162–63

Warren, W. H., Whang, S. 1987. Visual guidance of walking through apertures: body-scaled information for affordances. *J. Exp. Psychol.: Hum. Percept. Peform.* 13:371–83

Warren, W. H., Morris, M. W., Kalish, M. 1988. Perception of translational heading from optical flow. *J. Exp. Psychol.: Hum. Percept. Perform.* 14:646–60

Warren, W. H., Young, D. S., Lee, D. N. 1986. Visual control of step length during running over irregular terrain. *J. Exp. Psychol.: Hum. Percept. Perform.* 12: 259–66

Wolfe, J., Cave, K. R., Franzel, S. L. 1989. A modified feature integration model for visual search. *J. Exp. Psychol.: Hum. Percept. Perform.* 15:419–33

Wong, E., Weisstein, N. 1982. A new perceptual context-superiority effect: Line segments are more visible against a figure than against a ground. *Science* 218:587–89

Wong, E., Weisstein, N. 1983. Sharp targets are detected better against a figure and blurred targets are detected better against a background. *J. Exp. Psychol.: Hum. Percept. Perform.* 9:194–202

Yeomans, J. M., Irwin, D. E. 1985. Stimulus duration and partial report performance. *Percept. Psychophys.* 37:163–69

Zeki, S. M. 1981. The mapping of visual functions in the cerebral cortex. In *Brain Mechanisms of Sensation,* ed. Y. Katsuki, R. Norgren, M. Sato. New York: Wiley

Annu. Rev. Psychol. 1991. 42:333–76

MEMORY AND AGING: FOUR HYPOTHESES IN SEARCH OF DATA

Leah L. Light

Pitzer College, Claremont, California 91711

KEY WORDS: memory self-efficacy, semantic deficits in old age, processing resources, indirect tests of memory

CONTENTS

Older adults complain more about memory than younger adults. Moreover, in laboratory tests of memory, adults over 60 perform less well than adults in

333

their 20s on free recall, cued recall, and recognition memory for lists of words or sentences (e.g. Burke & Light 1981; Craik 1977; Guttentag 1985; Howe 1988; Hultsch & Dixon 1990; Poon 1985). Although such results might be attributed to the artificiality of standard laboratory tests of memory, older adults also score lower on memory tasks designed to have greater ecological validity (West 1986). For example, older adults have poorer memory for prose passages (Cohen 1988; Hartley 1989; Zelinski & Gilewski 1988b), for information from simulated medicine labels (Morrell et al 1989), for the buildings on the major thoroughfares of towns in which they have resided for long periods (Rabbitt 1989), for the appearance of common objects such as coins and telephones (Foos 1989b), for the activities they have performed (Kausler & Lichty 1988), and for names and faces of people (Bahrick 1984; Cohen & Faulkner 1986; Maylor, 1990b).

This chapter examines several perspectives on the nature of memory impairment in old age. The approaches taken range from the optimistic view that poorer memory in old age arises from inefficient use of encoding and retrieval strategies, a problem subject to remedial intervention, to less optimistic views that declining memory ability is the consequence of irreversible age-related changes in basic mechanisms underlying cognition. The classes of hypotheses to be considered are that age-related impairments in memory are the consequence of 1. failures of metamemory, 2. defective semantic encoding, 3. failures of deliberate recollection, and 4. diminished processing resources.

FAILURES OF METAMEMORY

The term "metamemory" was originally used to refer to cognitions about memory—in particular, knowledge of the memory demands imposed by different tasks or situations as well as strategies that might be used to improve memory in these situations (Flavell & Wellman 1977). More recently, the domain of metamemory has been expanded to include memory monitoring (self-knowledge about current memory use, contents, and states) and memory self-efficacy (beliefs about one's own memory abilities). When applied to the study of age-related impairments in memory, the metamemory perspective gives rise to several hypotheses—i.e. that older adults remember less well because they have erroneous beliefs about the nature of memory and the strategies appropriate for use in different memory tasks, because they are less likely to use task-appropriate strategies spontaneously, or because they monitor their encoding and retrieval processes less effectively.

Deficient Knowledge about Memory

It is conceivable that older adults have difficulty remembering new information simply because they have incorrect beliefs about the nature of task demands and, as a result, fail to engage in appropriate encoding or retrieval strategies. This possibility can be disposed of quickly. The evidence suggests that younger and older adults share a set of beliefs about the properties of memory tasks (e.g. Hultsch et al 1987; Loewen et al, in press; Perlmutter 1978; Williams et al 1983). For instance, Loewen et al (1991) found no reliable age differences in response to questions about the relative memorability of information varying in degree of interest, familiarity, relatedness, concreteness, personal significance or involvement, or bizarreness. One study suggests that older adults may experience some difficulty in acquiring knowledge about the efficacy of new strategies. Brigham & Pressley (1988) found that younger, but not older adults, came to prefer the more effective keyword technique to the less effective sentence-generation technique for learning meanings of words that are used infrequently after exposure to both study methods. Inasmuch as the experiment involved a within-subjects design, it is possible that older adults did not learn to assess the differential effectiveness of the two study methods because they could not remember which items were associated with which mnemonic.

Deficient Strategy Use

Three reasons have been proposed for expecting older adults to use less-effective encoding and retrieval strategies: disuse, diminished attentional capacity, and reduced sense of mastery (self-efficacy) in memory tasks.

DISUSE   According to the disuse view, memory-enhancing strategies are required less as people move further away from the educational system; because capacity demands are reduced, memory strategies play a smaller role in the lives of older adults. According to this view, findings from laboratory studies that older adults remember less than younger adults are merely artifacts of comparing younger students with older nonstudents.

Several lines of evidence indicate the inadequacy of this view. First, there have been several questionnaire studies of the effects of aging on reported use of strategies in everyday life (e.g. Cavanaugh 1986–1987; Cavanaugh et al 1983; Cavanaugh & Poon 1989; Dixon & Hultsch 1983b; Dobbs & Rule 1987; Gilewski et al 1990; Hultsch et al 1987; Loewen et al 1991; Perlmutter 1978); these suggest only small (if any) differences between age groups in reported frequency of strategy use, with the exception that older adults may rely more on external memory aids, while younger adults use more internally based mnemonics. Moreover, the role of strategies in everyday life has probably been overestimated, inasmuch as even young adults rarely report using deliberate mnemonic strategies (Intons-Peterson & Fournier 1986).

Second, if age-related differences in remembering new information derive from age-related differences in current educational status, they should disappear when young students are compared to old students or when younger nonstudents are compared to older nonstudents. But they do not (e.g. Hartley, 1986; Parks 1986; Salthouse et al 1988a).

Third, according to the disuse perspective, experts who continue to be active in their domains of expertise should experience continued memory demands in these domains and would therefore be expected to show preserved memory in these domains; but such preservation does not seem to occur for the domains of bridge (Charness 1987), chess (Charness 1981), or spatial abilities (Salthouse et al 1990). Although Arbuckle et al (1990) found no age-related differences in memory for information about music when they tested people knowledgeable about this subject matter, there were none in memory for information about dogs either. It was thus impossible to tell if the lack of age-related differences for music is due to continuing domain-specific engagement or to overall memory equivalence in the two samples.

Fourth, extended strategy training should, on this view, eliminate age-related differences, but it does not (Kliegl et al 1989). Thus, there is no support for the disuse hypothesis.

DIMINISHED ATTENTIONAL CAPACITY   A popular hypothesis is that older adults are less likely than younger ones to engage in appropriate self-initiated encoding or retrieval strategies because the aging process is associated with reduced attentional capacity, a capacity taxed by use of strategies. It has been claimed that older adults will elect to use such strategies less frequently than younger adults, or to use different, less taxing, strategies (e.g. Craik 1977; Craik & Rabinowitz 1984; Guttentag 1985; Hasher & Zacks 1979; Perlmutter & Mitchell 1982; see Bäckman 1989 for a similar position). A corollary to this production-deficiency hypothesis is that the performance of older adults may be "repaired" by guiding encoding through the use of orienting tasks and by using less effort-demanding recognition tests (rather than recall) to assess memory (e.g. Craik 1977, 1983, 1986).

Several factors militate against acceptance of this view. The hypothesis that reduced use of mnemonic strategies is a consequence of reduced attentional capacity in old age has not, to our knowledge, been tested empirically. There is no evidence that differences in strategy use are associated with differences in attentional capacity in any age group. Moreover, Cohen (1988) pointed out that use of different strategies by younger and older adults should give rise to qualitative rather than merely quantitative differences in performance, but qualitative differences are rarely obtained. In general, experimental manipulations of encoding or retrieval conditions that benefit the young benefit the old to about the same extent (e.g. Arbuckle et al 1990; Bäckman & Mäntylä 1988; Brigham & Pressley 1988; Mueller et al 1986; Puglisi & Park 1987; Rabinowitz & Craik 1986; Rankin & Firnhaber 1986; Rebok & Balcerak 1989; see Burke & Light 1981 for a review).

A few examples will illustrate this point. Young adults demonstrate better recall and recognition after generating words to cues (e.g. HOT-C___: give an antonym) than after reading them; this is called "the generation effect" (e.g. Jacoby & Dallas 1981). An important aspect of Craik's (1977, 1986) theoretical position is that older adults engage in less deep or less elaborative semantic encoding than younger adults and thus that ensuring semantic encoding through orienting tasks should reduce age differences, especially when performance is assessed by recognition. Because generation of targets during encoding presumably forces semantic processing, age-related differences should be reduced for "generate" relative to "read" conditions. However, younger and older adults benefit equally from generation, even when tested by recognition (Johnson et al 1989; McDaniel et al 1989; McFarland et al 1985; Mitchell et al 1986; Rabinowitz 1989b).

As a second example, consider the picture superiority effect. Pictures are remembered better than words, presumably because their names are also encoded, producing either a richer representation or representations in two different codes (Paivio 1971). Rissenberg & Glanzer (1986) found that younger, but not older adults recalled pictures better than words when they were not asked to name the pictures, though both age groups demonstrated the picture superiority effect when pictures were named and words were read. Rissenberg & Glanzer attribute this pattern of findings to lack of spontaneous naming of pictures in the old. Interestingly enough, Bäckman's (1989) compensation hypothesis also predicts that the possibility of dual encoding for pictures should result in smaller age-related differences for picture memory than for word memory. Neither of these patterns is the norm, however, because most studies report comparable picture superiority effects for young and old (e.g. Park et al 1983; Pezdek 1983; Puglisi et al 1988). In a related vein, the compensation hypothesis also predicts that age-related differences should be small or nonexistent for memory of televised events because of the bisensory information afforded by this medium. Cavanaugh (1983) obtained this result for high-verbal-ability but not for low-verbal-ability adults. Moreover, Stine et al (1990) found no indication that reading or watching televised news segments while also listening to them eradicated age-related differences.

A cornerstone of the production-deficiency hypothesis is that older adults encode more superficially than younger ones—i.e. that they are less apt to engage in deep semantic processing (see Burke & Light 1981 for a review). Several findings call this view into question. There is no difference across age in the degree to which semantic (category) cues improve performance relative to free recall or structural cues (the first two letters of a word) for target words studied without encoding cues (Rankin & Hinrichs 1983). Because retrieval cues are believed to be effective only when they map onto information encoded during input (Tulving 1983), the presumption is that semantic encoding is equivalent across age. A similar interpretation can be given to the finding of constancy across age in the effects of semantic and acoustic cues on recall, following semantic or acoustic encoding (West & Cohen 1985). Finally, Shaw & Craik (1989) presented younger and older adults with words paired with letter, rhyme, or category/description cues at both study and test. Younger adults scored higher than older adults with letter and rhyme cues, but there was no age-related difference for the semantic cues. These results argue against strategy differences between younger and older adults. If older adults attend more to superficial aspects of information while younger adults attend more to meaning, we would expect superficial cues (e.g. letters or rhymes) to be more beneficial to the old, semantic cues to the young; but this does not occur. Moreover, as discussed below, older adults remember less about nonsemantic contextual information than do younger ones, whereas a superficial-encoding hypothesis might predict that they should be better at this than younger adults are.

MEMORY SELF-EFFICACY   It has recently been suggested that older adults believe their memory abilities to be poor and that this lack of self-efficacy with respect to memory has untoward consequences for performance (e.g. Bandura 1989; Berry 1989; Berry et al 1989; Cavanaugh & Green 1990; Dixon & Hultsch 1983b). The gist of the argument is that older adults lack a sense of mastery for memory abilities, either because they have observed changes in their own memory or because their culture teaches that memory declines are both inevitable and irremediable. As a result, older adults may not try as hard as younger ones to remember. They then remember less, experience reduced feelings of self-efficacy, and so on. There is evidence for some but not all aspects of this argument.

Considerable energy has gone into the development of psychometrically sound instruments to measure stable conceptualizations of memory self-efficacy. These include both general measures of attitudes towards and knowledge about memory, such as the Metamemory in Adulthood or MIA scale (Dixon & Hultsch 1983a,b; Hultsch et al 1987; Hultsch et al 1988) and the Memory Functioning Questionnaire or MFQ (Gilewski et al 1990), as well as instruments tied more closely to predicting performance in particular situations (e.g. Berry et al 1989). Although the wording of questionnaires is critical, there is evidence from these instruments for reduced sense of mastery on memory tasks in old age (for reviews see Dixon 1989, Gilewski & Zelinski 1986, and Zelinski & Gilewski 1988a).

Further, there is some evidence for the predictive validity of memory self-efficacy measures (for reviews see Berry et al 1989; Hultsch et al 1988; Gilewski & Zelinski 1986, 1988; Zelinski & Gilewski 1988a; Zelinski et al 1990), although the amount of variability in performance accounted for is disappointingly low. However, there is no strong evidence that self-efficacy beliefs bear a causal relation to memory performance; indeed, there is some evidence that the reverse may be true—i.e. that self-efficacy beliefs are influenced by performance (Hertzog et al 1990; Lachman & Leff 1989). As Bandura (1989) has noted, it is crucial to demonstrate that self-efficacy measures are related not only to performance but to behaviors conducive to good performance, such as degree of effort or persistence in memory tasks. To date, there have been no published studies reporting such relationships. It is interesting in this vein to note that MIA and MFQ assessments of knowledge about tasks and reported use of strategies do not load on the same factors as memory self-efficacy items, suggesting that reported use of strategies and beliefs about memory demands are unrelated to self-efficacy beliefs. Further, reported strategy use is not a potent predictor of memory in older adults (Cavanaugh & Poon 1989; Dixon & Hultsch 1983a), though it accounts for some variability in the performance of the young.

Memory Monitoring

The studies reviewed above do not offer much support for the view that age-related differences in memory arise from the use of inefficient encoding strategies by the old. The possibility remains that older adults might be less able to monitor memory—that is, they might be less aware of their memory states as indexed by feelings of knowing, congruence between predicted and actual memory performance, or assessment of test readiness. There is, however, no consistent evidence that this is the case. Older adults are at least as adept as younger adults in assessing feelings of knowing, such as are involved in predicting recognition of currently unrecallable information (e.g. Lachman et al 1979; Butterfield et al 1988). Younger and older adults do not differ in ability to predict which items they will be able to remember when memorability is assessed on an item-by-item basis as items are studied (Rabinowitz et al 1982; but see Shaw & Craik 1989 and Lovelace & Marsh 1985 for quite small age-related differences favoring the young) or to postdict the correctness of responses after they have been made (Devolder et al 1990; Lovelace & Marsh 1985; Perlmutter 1978; but see Brigham & Pressley 1988 for conflicting evidence). Young and old are equally good at predicting memory span (Devolder et al 1990; Murphy et al 1981), though conflicting results are found for lists of words, prose passages, or face-name pairings when memory level is predicted prior to list study (Bruce et al 1982; Brigham & Pressley 1988; Devolder et al 1990; Hertzog et al 1990; Perlmutter 1978; Rebok & Balcerak 1989). Finally, Zabrucky et al (1987) found no evidence for age-related differences in monitoring comprehension of prose.

The preponderance of the evidence thus supports the proposition that age-related differences are small or nil in most aspects of memory monitoring.

There is, nonetheless, some evidence that older adults may have difficulty in assessing their test-readiness. A number of studies have found that older adults do not adjust their study times in accordance with the difficulty of the material to be learned (e.g. Cohen 1981; Murphy et al 1981; Murphy et al 1987; Zacks & Hasher 1988); that is, they do not give themselves enough study time to bring their performance up to the level of younger adults. This presupposes that given unlimited time, younger and older adults would have equivalent performance. However, older adults do not benefit disproportionately from incresed study time or from self-paced conditions (e.g. Craik & Rabinowitz 1985; Rabinowitz 1989a). Thus, inadequate study time cannot explain age-related memory decrements. Further, the relation between study time and memory is far from simple; longer study does not always insure better memory even in young adults (Mazzoni et al 1990). Hence, study-time data are not easy to interpret.

Summary

There is little support for hypotheses that failures in metamemory are responsible for age differences in memory. Younger and older adults hold similar beliefs about the demands of different situations requiring memory. There is scant evidence for dramatic age-related differences either in the use of mnemonic techniques in everyday life or in benefits that accrue from providing guidance at study or retrieval. Younger and older adults are equally skilled in memory monitoring, with the possible exception that older adults may not be as good at gauging their test-readiness. Evaluation of the view that age-related decrements in memory stem from lowered self-efficacy is premature, given that the appropriate causal links have yet to be established between memory beliefs and performance in the old. As a final observation here, we reiterate one of the most striking features of the literature on memory and aging: the overall absence of cross-over interactions, in which older adults perform less well than younger ones in some conditions but better than they in others. This lack of interactions strongly suggests that age differences in memory are quantitative rather than qualitative—i.e. they are the product of a deficit in one or more fundamental processes, not the result of differences in strategy use.

SEMANTIC DEFICIT HYPOTHESIS

One reading of the view that memory impairment in old age is due to impoverished semantic encoding is that it is language comprehension, not self-initiated strategy use, that is impaired in old age. Because comprehension is necessary for retention, problems in language comprehension would lead to memory decrements. For instance, Craik & Byrd (1982) postulated that aging is associated with "an attenuation or shrinkage in the richness, extensiveness, and depth of processing operations at both encoding and retrieval," that "older subjects' encodings will contain less associative and inferential information," and "that an encoded event is less modified by the specific context in which it occurs for the older person and that this difference leads to a less distinctive (and thus less memorable) encoding of the event" (p. 208).

These claims have been tested within the framework of network theories of memory (e.g. Anderson 1983). According to Anderson, all factual knowledge, both semantic and episodic, is organized in networks consisting of nodes, which stand for concepts or propositions, with these nodes being connected by associative pathways. When a concept is encountered, its node is activated, and activation also spreads along associative pathways to related nodes, making them more available for additional cognitive processing. Spreading activation is viewed as the mechanism underlying retrieval of both semantic and episodic information. An important distinction in spreading-activation models is between automatic and attentional or effortful processes (Neely 1977; Posner & Snyder 1975). Automatic processes are believed to arise from a rapid spread of activation and are not subject to the influence of expectations, whereas attentional processes have a slow rise time and are driven by expectations.

Activation processes, both automatic and attentional, play an important part in natural-language understanding. They have been implicated in perception of words in spoken or written form (McClelland & Rumelhart 1981), in determining the syntactic structure of sentences (Tanenhaus et al 1987), and in deriving the meanings of single sentences and entire discourses (Kintsch 1988). Activation of pragmatic or general world knowledge embodied in schemata is necessary for making inferences, for establishing the topic of a discourse, and for determining the antecedents of pronouns. Hence, differences across age in the way knowledge is represented in memory or in the way activation proceeds could result in comprehension differences. Because it is the result of comprehension processes that is ultimately stored in memory (Anderson 1983; Craik 1983), age-related differences in comprehension would lead to age-related differences in retention. The remainder of this section is devoted to analysis of the specific claims 1. that older adults' encodings are less rich, extensive, and deep; 2. that encoding deficits underlie memory problems; 3. that older adults' encodings have less associative or inferential content; and 4. that older adults' encodings are more general, in that they rely less on specific contextual information.

Richness, Extensiveness, and Depth of Encoding

The terms "rich," "extensive," and "deep" can be understood in terms of network models of memory. Anderson (1983) has proposed that deep or elaborative processing involves increasing the number of associative pathways between ideas, and that elaboration may involve activation of prior schemata or general world knowledge. Such encodings might be considered to be "richer." The notion of extensiveness may similarly be construed in terms of the number of pathways activated during encoding. Age-related differences in encoding could arise either because the content or organization of knowledge is different in young and old adults, so that the pattern of connections in the network differs across age, or because of differences in the nature of activation processes. If younger and older adults do not share the same system of meanings for words or the same general fund of pragmatic information, comprehension differences would not be surprising. Similarly, age-related differences in amount of activation, extent of activation, or rate of spread of activation could determine the likelihood that particular nodes receive activation from associated nodes. The available evidence, however, is consistent with the conclusion that neither the organization of concepts nor the characteristics of semantic activation varies with age.

REPRESENTATION OF KNOWLEDGE   There is clear evidence for stability in patterns of word associations across the adult years (Bowles et al 1983; Burke & Peters 1986; Howard, 1979a,b; Lovelace & Cooley 1982; Nebes & Brady 1988; Scialfa & Margolis 1986; Stine et al 1986). Category judgment latencies are equally affected by exemplar typicality in younger and older adults, suggesting stable organization of the representation of categories across the adult years (Byrd 1984; Hertzog et al 1986; Howard 1979a, 1980, 1983a; Mueller et al 1980; Nebes et al 1986; Petros et al 1983). Also, there appear to be no age-related differences in the representation of culturally defined scripted activities (Hess 1985; Light & Anderson 1983), though scripts based on individual experiences may vary across age (Ross & Berg 1991; Hess 1991). Thus, there is constancy throughout adulthood in the representation of knowledge as assessed by the tasks enumerated above.

SPREADING ACTIVATION   Studies of semantic priming in lexical decision, word naming, and judgments of semantic relatedness offer no evidence for age-related differences in extent or breadth of activation when type of associate is varied (Howard et al 1981) or when strength of association between prime and target is varied (Balota & Duchek 1988; Nebes et al 1986). In these tasks, the extent of priming is evaluated by comparing latencies when the target is preceded by a related prime to latencies when the target is preceded by an unrelated prime or a neutral prime. In lexical decision (the task most frequently used to assess age-related differences in priming), the results reveal remarkable similarity across age in the extent of priming and no evidence for reduced benefits or costs when latencies following related and unrelated primes are compared to latencies following neutral primes (Bowles & Poon 1985; Burke et al 1987; Burke & Yee 1984; Chiarello et al 1985; Howard 1983b; Howard et al 1981; Howard et al 1986b; Madden 1986, 1988, 1989). Benefits are believed to reflect a mix of automatic and attentional processes whereas costs are believed to be the result of attentional processes only; thus, these results point to the lack of age-related differences in either automatic or attentional components of activation.

One conflicting outcome was reported by Howard et al (1986b), who found that older adults showed facilitation from related primes only at long prime-to-target intervals. Because facilitation at short prime-to-target intervals is believed to arise solely from automatic processes, this result suggests an age-related slowing of automatic processes. However, other studies of lexical decision (Burke et al 1987; Madden 1989) and word naming (Balota & Duchek 1988) have not observed interactions of age and prime-to-target interval.

Overall, then, there is little evidence for age-related differences in the organization of knowledge. In addition, the amount, breadth, and rate at which activation spreads from concept to concept within a semantic network appear to be similar across ages. This last conclusion is potentially damaging not only to hypotheses that age-related decrements in memory are due to problems in language comprehension but also to more general theories that memory deficits in old age arise from cognitive slowing (e.g. MacKay & Burke 1990; Salthouse 1985a). However, MacKay & Burke (1990) note that older adults have more practice with semantically associated words, increasing the strength of their connections relative to younger adults, and that because of the many interconnections between nodes in a semantic network, there may be a summation of priming that masks age deficits in this domain. They also point out that the paradigms used to examine semantic priming may differentially benefit older adults because they do not put limitations on response time. Because older adults have longer absolute response times than younger adults, there is more time for priming to spread from prime to target. Hence, they recommend the use of deadline procedures (which eliminate this problem by requiring responses to be made within particular periods) to study the effects of age on semantic priming.

Before leaving this topic, we should also note that, although the currently available evidence supports the conclusion that *semantic* priming is preserved in old age, older adults do experience increased word-finding problems that suggest deficits in activation of orthographic or phonological information from concepts. Thus, older adults have reduced output on verbal fluency tasks (e.g. McCrae et al 1987; Obler & Albert 1985), are less accurate in naming to definition and in confrontation naming of pictures (Albert et al 1988; Borod et al 1980; Bowles & Poon 1985; Van Gorp et al 1986), and have more tip-of-the-tongue experiences (Burke et al 1988; Cohen & Faulkner 1986; Maylor 1990b). However, it is unlikely that age-related changes in the activation of orthographic and phonological representations of concepts influence semantic encoding in old age.

Encoding and Memory

Anderson (1983) has explicitly claimed that spreading activation is the mechanism of retrieval in both priming studies and in memory for new information. The view that older adults' memory problems are due to age-related differences in spreading activation would then predict that studies examining memory for words involved in priming tasks should show reduced priming in the old whenever the old perform less well in recall or recognition. However, none of the studies that have examined both priming and subsequent retention have shown the predicted pattern. Younger adults score higher on recall and recognition than older adults despite age invariance in magnitude of semantic priming in lexical decision (Burke et al 1987; Burke & Yee 1984; Howard 1983b; Howard et al 1981; Howard et al 1986b; Madden 1986) and category-judgment tasks (Mitchell & Perlmutter 1986). Mitchell (1989) found that recall and recognition of pictures used in a naming task were poorer in older adults, although no age-related differences in repetition priming of naming latencies were observed. Further, when correlations between the magnitude of priming and the accuracy of subsequent recall were examined in several of these studies, they were not found to be reliable. Hence, reduced comprehension, as measured by semantic priming, does not seem to be the cause of age-related differences in memory.

Encoding Inferences

Current models of discourse comprehension assume that inferences based on activation of general world knowledge are necessary for understanding (e.g. Kintsch 1988) and that certain kinds of inferences are made on-line during discourse comprehension (e.g. O'Brien et al 1988). The issue here is whether aging affects the likelihood that such inferences will be made and, later, stored. When comprehension is examined during or immediately after a sentence is read, there is no evidence that younger and older adults differ in how readily they draw inferences about the instruments with which verbs are used (Burke & Yee 1984), about the properties of nouns relevant in particular sentence contexts (Burke & Harrold 1988), about the antecedents of pronouns (Light & Albertson 1988; Light & Capps 1986), or about the antecedents of noun-phrase anaphors (Light & Albertson 1988; Zelinski 1988; but see Hasher & Zacks 1988 for evidence that older adults may be slower here). Even with longer passages or with delays between study and test, age-related differences are not invariably obtained (Belmore 1981; Hess & Arnould 1986;

Light & Anderson 1983; Rebok et al 1988; Reder et al 1986; Zabrucky et al 1987; Zelinski & Miura 1988).

Studies that find age differences in the likelihood of drawing inferences typically do not use on-line procedures. For instance, some studies have used implicational cues for recall (Till 1985; Till & Walsh 1980), but these studies confound processes operating at storage with those operating at retrieval and do not permit inferences about encoding. Age-related differences are also found when some information must be held in memory until other facts needed to draw an inference are presented (Cohen 1979, 1981; Foos 1989a; Hasher & Zacks 1988; Light & Albertson 1988; Light & Anderson 1985; Light & Capps 1986; Light et al 1982; Zacks & Hasher 1988; Zacks et al 1987). Thus, forgetting of relevant information, inability to activate previously presented information when subsequent relevant information is given, and/or inability to combine unrelated facts when these are not presented in an optimal order may all contribute to problems in forming inferences. The results of these studies, taken as a package, strongly suggest that difficulties in drawing inferences on-line do not contribute to impoverished semantic encoding and poorer memory, but rather that, at least under some conditions, memory problems produce comprehension problems.

General Encoding

Rabinowitz et al (1982) hypothesized that, owing to reduced attentional resources, older adults might not form distinctive, contextually specific encodings of new information, but rather would encode events "in the same old way" from one occasion to the next. In terms of network models, the suggestion is that when older adults encounter a concept, the pattern of activation does not depend on the specifics of the situation but only on the strengths of preexisting associations. Evidence for this hypothesis comes from encoding-specificity experiments modeled after those of Thomson & Tulving (1970), who presented subjects with both weakly and strongly associated pairs to study and then tested them with either strong or weak associates as retrieval cues. Targets from both strongly and weakly associated pairs were better remembered when study and test cues were the same. Further, targets from the weak-weak condition were better remembered than those from weak-strong condition, suggesting that strength of prior association is less crucial than compatibility of study and test cues in terms of activation at retrieval. Rabinowitz et al (1982) found this pattern of results for their younger subjects, but their older subjects' recall did not differ in the weak-weak and weak-strong conditions. They interpreted their findings to mean that the encodings of older adults are not as distinctive as those of younger adults and that core meanings of words are activated whenever they occur regardless of the context in which they occur. Simon (reported in Craik & Simon 1980) presented younger and older adults with sentences containing words from taxonomic categories. She found that for older subjects the category names (which had not been presented) were better retrieval cues than other sentence words for these category members, while sentence words were better cues for the younger adults (see Perlmutter 1979 and Rabinowitz et al 1982 for similar findings). This, too, is taken as evidence that older adults encode more generally than younger ones.

There are, however, several problems with this conclusion. First, some studies purporting to find age-correlated differences in encoding specificity in fact did not obtain reliable interactions of context with age when appropriate indexes of memory were used (Hess 1984; Hess & Higgins 1983). Second, younger and older adults have been shown to have similar patterns of results, at least in some conditions, in variants of the Thomson & Tulving study (Park et al 1987; Puglisi et al 1988). Third, younger and older adults sometimes show similar effects of context in studies of episodic priming; recognition is faster when a word is preceded by another word studied in close proximity to it originally (Hasher & Zacks 1988; Howard et al 1986a; Rabinowitz 1986). Fourth, studies of word recognition and naming (e.g. Cohen & Faulkner 1983; Nebes et al 1986; see Light 1988 for a review) as well as studies of immediate memory for sentences (Wingfield et al 1985) find that older adults rely at least as much as younger ones on prior semantic and syntactic context. Fifth, the studies reviewed above which demonstrate that younger and older adults are equally likely to make certain kinds of inferences during sentence comprehension offer no support for concluding that there are age-related differences in use of context to particularize word meaning. On the contrary, the evidence strongly suggests constancy across age here.

Summary

Our literature review offers no support for the claim that deficits in semantic processing underlie memory problems in old age. The organization of knowledge is stable across the adult years. Moreover, none of the specific claims about the relation between language comprehension and memory, addressed above, are supported by the data. Older adults do not seem to differ from younger ones in rate, breadth, or amount of spreading activation, in likelihood of making inferences, or in use of context to particularize word meanings. They do, however, differ in memory. Such results are embarrassing for network models, which predict that age-related differences in memory should be accompanied by age-related differences in comprehension because the retrieval mechanisms involved in encoding and subsequent recall or recognition are the same. They also contradict models predicting such age-related differences because of reduced processing resources (see below).

IMPAIRMENT OF DELIBERATE RECOLLECTION

During the last several years, cognitive psychologists have given increasing attention to measures of memory that do not require intentional or conscious recollection of a prior experience but that simply permit the effects of that prior experience to be manifested in the performance of some task. Such indexes of memory are called *indirect* measures to contrast them with more traditional *direct* measures of memory, such as recall and recognition. For instance, on an indirect test of memory, subjects may be asked to complete the fragment of a word, given some of its letters, as in _E_D_L_M (Tulving et al 1982); to complete the stem of a word such as ATT__ (Graf & Mandler 1984); to read spatially transformed or visually degraded words (Jacoby & Dallas 1981; Moscovitch et al 1986); or to decide whether a string of letters is a word in a lexical decision task (Scarborough et al 1977). In these tasks, memory is inferred from a facilitation in performance when words encountered earlier in the experiment are involved. This facilitation in processing previously experienced stimuli in comparison to processing new stimuli is known as *repetition priming*.

There is considerable evidence that anterograde amnesics who have no conscious recollection of the circumstances of prior encounters show normal or near normal repetition priming of single words (for reviews see Cohen 1984; Squire 1987). Anterograde amnesics show little memory for new associations when tested with direct measures of memory, but there is evidence (somewhat controversial) that in mild amnesics indirect measures reveal evidence for learning of new associations (Graf & Schacter 1985; Moscovitch et al 1986; Schacter & Graf 1986; Shimamura & Squire 1989). Because of the possibility that the same brain structures (e.g. the hippocampus) are affected in amnesia and normal aging (Moscovitch 1982), there has been considerable interest in determining the extent to which the nature of the memory impairment is the same in these two populations. Thus, the question is whether older adults, like amnesics, show impaired memory when tested by recall or recognition (which require deliberate recollection) but show normal memory when tested by indirect measures. For single-item priming, the evidence suggests that this may be the case, though the evidence is less clear with respect to priming of new associations.

For single items, similar levels of priming across age have been found for word fragment completion (Light et al 1986), word stem completion (Howard 1988b; Light & Singh 1987; but see Chiarello & Hoyer 1988, Davis et al 1990, and Hultsch et al 1991 for a different conclusion), perceptual identification of degraded words (Light & Singh 1987), picture naming (Mitchell 1989; Mitchell et al 1990), lexical decision (Moscovitch 1982), category judgments (Rabbitt 1982, 1984), spelling of homophones in accordance with a previously biased meaning (Howard 1988b; but see Davis et al 1990, and Rose et al 1986 for a different result), and free association to a category name (Light & Albertson 1989). In most of these studies, the same individuals were tested on both direct and indirect meaures of memory. Although age-related differences were almost invariably observed on direct measures of memory, such differences on indirect measures of memory were more often than not small and unreliable.

One troublesome finding in these studies is that while age-related differences in priming are small and usually unreliable, they often do favor younger adults. Indeed there are reliable findings of better performance by the young (e.g. Chiarello & Hoyer 1988; Davis et al 1990; Howard 1988a; Hultsch et al 1991; Rose et al 1986; see Mitchell 1989 and Mitchell et al 1990 for a summary). Such findings may indicate real differences in the processes underlying priming that are too small to be detected with conventional sample sizes. Alternatively, the small advantage in priming observed in the young may result from an intrusion of deliberate recollection into priming tasks. Younger adults perform better than older adults on deliberate memory tasks. They may consequently be more likely to realize that they are producing previously seen list members during priming tasks, and having noticed this, they may be more likely to continue doing so deliberately. Evidence indicates that such problems may occur in priming tasks that require production of the target word, such as word association (Light & Albertson 1989) and homophone spelling (Howard 1988b).

Evidence from direct measures of memory indicates that older adults have difficulty forming new associations (Light & Burke 1988). If the difficulty lies in formation of new associations rather than in deliberate recollection, older adults should have reduced associative priming as well as reduced recall and recognition when memory for new associations is examined. However, age-related differences in priming of new associations are sometimes observed (Howard 1988b; Howard et al 1986a; Moscovitch et al 1986) and sometimes not (Hasher & Zacks 1988; Howard 1988a,b; Howard et al 1986a; Moscovitch et al 1986; Rabinowitz 1986). Because conditions of presentation and type of indirect memory test vary across studies, it is difficult to isolate the reasons for the discrepant findings. Howard (1988b) suggests that single presentations, long study-to-test delays, less elaboration-inducing study conditions, and test order (forward vs backward associations) may all affect performance. It may also be the case that different conditions must be met for priming of new associations to be obtained in different paradigms; for instance, Moscovitch et al found preserved priming for new associations in both younger and older adults in a degraded-stimulus reading task despite the fact that the study conditions were not designed to foster elaborative encoding. Even when priming of new associations is preserved, however, older adults show substantial impairment on recall and recognition tests that require conscious recollection.

What are we to make of these results? From an empirical standpoint, they suggest that older adults show impairment only when deliberate recollection is necessary. This impairment may not be restricted to situations involving new learning inasmuch as older adults also have increased word-finding difficulties, as evidenced in verbal fluency tasks, confrontation naming, and tip-of-the-tongue experiences (see Light 1987, 1990 and Light & Burke 1988 for reviews). From a theoretical standpoint, finding spared performance on indirect measures of memory coupled with impaired performance on recall and recognition poses an interpretive puzzle. Several different accounts have been offered. Here we evaluate three of these: spared activation and impaired contextual processing, impaired self-initiated constructive activity, and multiple memory systems.

Spared Activation and Impaired Processing of Contextual Information

Many contemporary accounts of memory distinguish between (*a*) mechanisms dependent on activation or perceptual familiarity of items and (*b*) mechanisms dependent on memory for new associations, either associations between events experienced simultaneously or between events and the environmental or cognitive contexts in which they occur (e.g. Gillund & Shiffrin 1984; Jacoby & Dallas 1981; Jacoby et al 1989; Mandler 1980). The importance of contextual information in determining the accuracy of memory is also recognized by single-process theories, which emphasize the similarity between current experiences and memorial representations of prior events (e.g. Eich 1985; Hintzman 1988). Further, ability to remember such contextual details as perceptual information, spatiotemporal information, thoughts and feelings, and cognitive operations performed as an event is experienced is believed to underlie reality monitoring, the discrimination between fact and fantasy (Johnson & Raye 1981; Johnson et al 1988).

One explanation of repetition priming effects is that they require only activation of preexisting memory representations, whereas recall and recognition require more elaborative processing of contextual information (e.g. Graf & Mandler 1984). According to this view, the pattern of findings in old age implies that activation processes are spared, whereas contextual information processing is impaired (Light et al 1986; Light & Singh 1987; see also Balota et al 1989 and Rabinowitz 1984 for related views). Evidence that semantic activation processes are intact has already been reviewed, and the issue of whether this is true for all activation is taken up below. Here, we address the question of impaired contextual information processing in old age.

When asked about nonsemantic attributes of events, older adults recall less information than younger adults. Thus, older adults are less adept at monitoring the sources of information they have received. They are not as good at recalling whether information was presented auditorily or visually (Kausler & Puckett 1981a; Lehman & Mellinger 1984, 1986; McIntyre & Craik 1987), in upper or lower case letters (Kausler & Puckett 1980, 1981a), in a male voice or a female voice (Kausler & Puckett 1981b), or in a particular color (Park & Puglisi 1985). Similarly, older adults have more trouble than younger adults in remembering whether they saw a word or generated it from a clue (Mitchell et al 1986; Rabinowitz 1989b), in remembering whether they learned a fact in an experimental setting or knew it before (Janowsky et al 1989; McIntyre & Craik 1987), in judging an act as one that was carried out rather than only planned or imagined (Cohen & Faulkner 1989; Guttentag & Hunt 1988, but see Kausler et al 1985b for a different finding), in monitoring whether an act has already been performed (Koriat et al 1988), in deciding whether a word was thought or said (Hashtroudi et al 1989), and in remembering which of two orienting tasks they used during encoding (Brigham & Pressley 1988; Mueller et al 1986). Older adults are more susceptible to the effects of misleading information presented after they witness a series of events, suggesting that they are confused about the source of the information (Cohen & Faulkner 1989). In addition, older adults are more likely than younger ones to call a previously seen face "famous" when it is encountered later, indicating faulty source attribution (Dywan & Jacoby 1990). Finally, as discussed below, younger adults remember more temporal and spatial information than older ones.

Although the evidence reviewed here supports the idea that older adults have impaired memory for context, there are reasons for being cautious in accepting the conclusion that faulty contextual information processing is the cause of impaired deliberate recollection in the old. Studies in which younger and older adults were queried about contextual details have often failed to assess memory for the target information, leaving open the possibility that older adults remember less contextual information because they remember less target information. Examining context memory only for items correctly identified as previously studied—i.e. conditionalizing on correct target memory, a strategy used by some researchers, does not solve the problem where there are age differences in target memory, because guessing rates for contextual information may vary across ages (Batchelder & Riefer 1989). Further, Denney et al (1991) have found that memory for context is no more impaired than memory for target information, suggesting that a general age deficit in memory encompasses both target and context memory. Also, despite evidence that semantic priming is intact in old age, there is reason to believe that activation may be impaired in old age. Finally, it has been suggested (e.g. Craik et al 1990) that source-monitoring deficits are associated with frontal lobe dysfunction. If age-related impairments in remembering new information arise from inefficient hippocampal function, memory for context and content may involve different mechanisms. Indeed, Kliegl & Lindenberger (1988) found that equating younger and older adults on memory for target information did not eliminate age differences in memory for context; if contextual information is critically involved in memory for targets, we might have expected that age differences in memory for context would disappear under these conditions, but they did not.

Deficient Self-Initiated Constructive Operations

Some investigators have proposed that indirect measures of memory are data driven rather than conceptually driven (e.g. Jacoby & Dallas 1981; Roediger & Blaxton 1987). They argue that indirect tests of memory depend on the physical similarity between the materials studied and the test items to a greater extent than do direct tests of memory. In this vein, Craik (1983) has suggested that sizable age-related differences in memory should be expected on tasks that require self-initiated constructive operations and afford little environmental support for retrieval (e.g. free recall), whereas age-related differences should be minimal on tasks that provide substantial environmental support (e.g. perceptual identification). Indeed, there is evidence that among direct measures of memory, those that afford more retrieval support show smaller age-related differences (Craik & McDowd 1987).

The retrieval support hypothesis focuses on the physical similarity between study materials and retrieval cues provided at test; it leads to the prediction that if amount of retrieval support is held constant across classes of memory tasks, age-related differences should be similar on direct and indirect measures. However, when amount of environmental support is held constant by using the same cues for both direct and indirect tasks, reliable age-related differences are found on the former but not the latter (Howard 1988b; Light & Albertson 1989; Light & Singh 1987). For instance, using three-letter word stems as cues, Light & Singh (1987) found reliable age-related differences for cued recall but not for word completion, suggesting that the crucial variable is not amount of environmental support for retrieval but intention to remember. Nonetheless, one could argue that these findings do not constitute a definitive test of the retrieval support hypothesis. It is possible that varying amount of retrieval support within cued recall or word-fragment completion (e.g. by varying the number of letters in the fragment) would reveal that older adults are differentially benefited by increased retrieval support. Such studies have yet to be performed.

An added source of difficulties for the retrieval support hypothesis comes from research on prospective memory tasks that involve remembering to do something in the future. The retrieval support hypothesis predicts that older adults should be especially impaired on such tasks because of the lack of environmental support for retrieval. However, there is no consistent evidence for age-related differences favoring the young on prospective memory tasks (e.g. Dobbs & Rule 1987; Einstein & McDaniel 1990; Maylor 1990a; Moscovitch 1982; Sinnott 1986).

Multiple Memory Systems Approach

In 1972 Tulving proposed that there are two memory systems, semantic memory and episodic memory. According to this distinction, semantic memory is the store of knowledge needed for language use while episodic memory stores information about temporally dated episodes or events, and the temporal-spatial relations among events. Although the form in which particular experiences enter episodic memory can be heavily influenced by information in semantic memory, via encoding processes, these two systems can operate fairly independently. In a recent modification of his position, Tulving (1985) outlined a monohierarchical arrangement of three systems, with procedural memory containing semantic memory as its single specialized subsystem, and semantic memory, in turn, containing episodic memory as its single specialized subsystem. Mitchell (1989) has proposed that only episodic memory is impaired in old age whereas both semantic memory and procedural memory remain intact. Repetition priming effects, in this view, reflect processes occurring in procedural memory, and constancy across age in repetition priming is consistent with intact procedural memory. There are several difficulties with this position. For one thing, it is not clear either that semantic memory is totally preserved or that episodic memory is totally impaired in old age (Light & Burke 1988; Salthouse 1988a). For instance, word-finding difficulties increase in old age. Similarly, findings of constancy across age in repetition priming can be taken as support for the view that encoding of new information (which involves episodic memory processes) is not a problem for the old but that retrieval is. Moreover, it is not always clear how to classify processes. As an example, consider strategies. Strategies may be treated as aspects of general world knowledge and therefore as part of semantic memory, or they may be treated as procedures for acquisition or retrieval of new information. If they are classified as procedures, then any age-related impairment in use of strategies must count as evidence against sparing of procedural memory.

There are additional difficulties in accepting this view, some empirical and some theoretical. Squire (1987) has identified several different categories of procedural learning, including cognitive skill learning, perceptual learning, motor skill learning, and classical conditioning in addition to repetition priming. It is thus important to ask whether these other varieties of procedural learning are spared in old age. A review of the literature suggests that this may not be the case. Older adults are not as adept in learning the Tower of Hanoi problem as younger ones (Charness 1987). Older adults are slightly impaired relative to younger adults in learning to read geometrically transformed scripts (Moscovitch et al 1986). Learning and retention of motor skills decline with age (e.g. Salthouse & Somberg 1982; Welford 1985; Wright & Payne 1985). There is also evidence that older adults do not develop the classically conditioned eyeblink response as readily as younger adults (e.g. Solomon et al 1989; Woodruff-Pak & Thompson 1988). Thus, if one accepts Squire's taxonomy, it is an oversimplification to say that older adults have preserved procedural memory. Even if one disagrees with this particular classificatory scheme, it is nonetheless clear that there are a great many indirect measures of memory (Richardson-Klavehn & Bjork 1988). It is highly unlikely that all of these measures will prove amenable to the same theoretical analysis or that all of them will be found to be dependent on the same cognitive or brain structures (Squire 1987; Tulving & Schacter 1990). Hence, it would be surprising if all such measures were to prove equally insensitive to aging.

Summary

There is sufficient evidence for us to conclude that older adults have a specific problem in retrieving new information when deliberate recollection is required, but that indirect measures of memory reveal smaller (or possibly nonexistent) age-related differences. However, there are still a number of unknowns here. Although most studies report stability across age when indirect measures of memory for single items are used, the extent to which this is also true for new associations is unclear. Moreover, the mechanisms underlying this pattern of spared and impaired performance cannot yet be identified. For instance, it is uncertain whether the same mechanisms underlie problems in recollection of recent events and in retrieval of old knowledge (e.g. word-finding problems as demonstrated by reduced verbal fluency and increased frequency of tip-of-the-tongue experiences), whether memory for contextual information plays a crucial role in differentiating between performance on priming tasks and on direct measures of memory, or whether it is necessary to postulate different memory systems, one spared and one intact, to account for the findings.

REDUCED PROCESSING RESOURCES

In this section, we discuss the possibility that age-related changes in memory across the adult years arise from changes in fundamental processing mechanisms such as reduced attentional capacity, reduced working-memory capacity, or cognitive slowing. In short, we assess the adequacy of the processing resource hypothesis as it applies to memory in old age. Navon (1984) defined the concept of processing resources as "any internal input essential for processing (e.g. locations in storage, communication channels) that is available in quantities that are limited at any point in time" (p. 217). Salthouse (1988c,d) includes in this category speed of processing, as well as attention and working-memory capacity. Although it has never been clear whether speed of mental operations should be classed as a processing resource per se or whether the speed with which mental processes can be carried out is itself dependent on the amount of processing resources allocated to the task at hand, we follow the convention in cognitive aging research of treating cognitive slowing under the rubric of processing resource explanations.

The relationships among attentional, working-memory capacity, and speed conceptualizations of processing resources are complex and it is often difficult to distinguish among them. For instance, Baddeley (1986) described working memory as "a system for the temporary holding and manipulation of information during the performance of a range of cognitive tasks such as comprehension, learning, and reasoning" (p. 34). In Baddeley's (1986) model, working memory consists of a central executive that "has attentional capacities and is capable of selecting and operating control processes" (p. 71), together with a set of slave systems that have specialized storage functions. The approach taken by many workers in cognitive aging reflects this idea that lower capacity in the central executive constrains performance in the elderly by placing limits on storage and/or manipulation of information. The contributions of attentional and working-memory concepts are hard to separate here inasmuch as working-memory involves attention. Similarly, an unresolved issue is whether the principal limitation in working memory in old age is storage capacity (e.g. Foos 1989a; Parkinson et al 1985; Zacks & Hasher 1988), efficiency of performing or managing sequences of operations (e.g. Campbell & Charness 1991; Charness & Campbell 1988; Gick et al 1988; Morris et al 1988; Stine & Wingfield 1987), ability to perform mental operations while simultaneously preserving the products of intermediate operations (Salthouse & Mitchell 1989), or mental slowing (e.g. Campbell & Charness 1991; see Salthouse 1990, for discussion of these issues). Despite the difficulties in distinguishing among different classes of processing resource hypotheses, we treat them separately because each has given rise to different experimental paradigms in the study of memory and aging.

Reduced Attentional Capacity

Three themes have predominated in research on the role of reduced attentional resources in memory in old age. One theme, addressed above, focuses on the possible effects of reduced attentional capacity on strategy use in old age. A second theme centers on the question of whether older adults incur greater costs when asked to learn or retrieve information under divided attention conditions. The third theme deals with a specific claim by Hasher & Zacks (1979) that only those aspects of memory that are effortful are impaired in old age while those aspects of memory that are automatic (i.e. demand little or no attentional capacity) are spared. In particular, Hasher & Zacks suggested that memory for temporal, spatial, and event-frequency information should be stable across the adult years. It is to the second and third themes that we now turn.

DIVIDED ATTENTION COSTS   The assumptions underlying both attentional and working-memory explanations of cognitive impairment in old age are 1. that tasks vary in the extent to which they require processing resources, 2. that resource capacity is a stable trait-like property of individuals, and 3. that, on average, older people have fewer processing resources than younger people. To the extent that this set of assumptions is valid, predictions with respect to aging are straightforward. When two tasks must be carried out simultaneously, provided that they are difficult enough, the performance of older adults will suffer more than that of younger adults. The evidence on these points is less clear-cut than the predictions.

Early studies of age-related differences in divided attention focused principally on a single paradigm, dichotic listening, and yielded inconsistent outcomes (Somberg & Salthouse 1982). Subsequent studies have employed a variety of paradigms, but the outcomes have continued to be mixed with respect to the question of whether older adults suffer greater decrements than younger adults when asked to remember under dual-task rather than single-task conditions. With respect to short-term or working memory, the findings also lack uniformity. Wickens et al (1987) observed no greater divided-attention costs in the old with a memory search task. Others, however, have (e.g. Baron & Mattila 1989; Madden et al 1989). Even when single-task performance on letters and digits was equated across age, older adults had greater divided-attention costs when these two-span tasks were combined (Salthouse et al 1984). The latter result conflicts with a finding by Baddeley et al (1986) that there was no age-related difference in vulnerability to distraction when a span task was combined with a tracking task. Further, in a series of experiments, Craik and his colleagues have found no age-related differences in the disruptive effects of divided attention in a working-memory task, even under conditions in which age differences would be expected, such as greater memory load or task complexity (Gick et al 1988; Morris et al 1990; Morris et al 1988). Tun (1989) examined the effects of divided attention on tone response time while reading prose. There did not seem to be any greater slowing for the old than for the young under divided-attention conditions, but the number of observations was very small. Taken together, these results make it clear that we do not yet understand the conditions under which greater divided-attention costs will be found for older adults in working-memory tasks.

Given that the deleterious effects of age on memory have been attributed to reduced attentional capacity in the old, it is surprising how few studies have actually examined the effects of divided attention on long-term memory. Park and her colleagues have reported a series of studies which suggest that dividing attention during encoding may be especially deleterious for the old. In two studies, the effects of divided attention during encoding reduced memory more for the old than the young, but the interaction was apparently not reliable (Park et al 1986; Park et al 1987), while in two others the interactions between attentional status and age were reliable (Puglisi et al 1988; Park et al 1989). Park et al (1989) did not find an interaction between age and attentional demands at recall on amount recalled, suggesting that the attentional demands of retrieval do not vary with age. This result conflicts with findings by Macht & Buschke (1983), who found greater slowing of responses in a secondary task during recall in the old, as well as with findings by Craik & McDowd (1987) of greater absolute (but not relative) costs for the old associated with cued recall than with recognition.

Two points should be made about these results. First, it is not obvious why encoding should be more susceptible to increased divided-attention costs in the old. Proponents of production deficiency or semantic deficit hypotheses would argue that these results indicate increased attentional needs for semantic processing in old age, but studies comparing divided-attention costs during on-line semantic processing in younger and older adults afford no consistent support for this view (e.g. Duchek 1984; Kellas et al 1988; Lorsbach & Simpson 1988; Nestor et al 1989; Madden 1987). With the exception of Duchek's (1984), however, none of these studies involved retention paradigms. Thus, this is an issue needing further examination. Second, the lack of coherent findings with respect to divided-attention costs during retrieval is potentially damaging to the view that memory deficits in old age are due to inadequate environmental support for retrieval. According to this view, reduced attentional capacity is responsible for problems in self-initiated retrieval operations, and older adults would be expected to show greater divided-attention costs during retrieval.

MEMORY FOR TEMPORAL, SPATIAL, AND FREQUENCY INFORMATION
Considerable evidence, most of it negative, has now accrued on the issue of whether memory for temporal, spatial, and event-frequency information is age invariant. With regard to temporal information, younger adults are better than older adults in reconstructing the order of a list of words or activities (Kausler et al 1985a; Kausler et al 1988; Naveh-Benjamin 1990), in choosing the most recent of two items (McCormack 1982), and in deciding in which of

two or more lists an item was presented (Kliegl & Lindenberger 1988; McCormack 1984). Even studies that do not show reliably superior performance by younger adults demonstrate a trend in this direction (McCormack 1981; Perlmutter et al 1981), so there are no discrepant results here. Further, Allen (1990) has obtained evidence for impairment in memory for order information immediately after encoding.

Similarly, the evidence argues convincingly against age invariance in memory for spatial information. Younger adults show better memory for the locations of structures on a schematic map (Bruce & Herman 1986; Light & Zelinski 1983; Zelinski & Light 1988); for the positions of letters, words, pictures, or objects in a matrix (Cherry & Park 1989; Naveh-Benjamin 1987, 1988; Pezdek 1983; Puglisi et al 1985; Salthouse et al 1988a); for the positions of chess pieces on a chess board (Charness 1981); for left-right positions of pictures presented singly or in pairs (Park et al 1982); and for the locations of pictures or words on a page (Park et al 1983; but see Ellis et al 1987, and McCormack 1982 for contradictory outcomes). There has been some controversy over whether age-related differences in spatial memory can be eliminated by use of naturalistic contexts (Sharps & Gollin 1987; Waddell & Rogoff 1981), but age-related differences favoring young adults have been observed in studies involving large-scale real-life environments (Evans et al 1984; Kirasic 1988), suggesting that such differences are not an artifact of the use of laboratory tasks.

The situation with respect to memory for event frequency is more complex. While some studies have reported age-related differences favoring the young (e.g. Freund & Witte 1986; Hasher & Zacks 1979; Kausler et al 1982; Kausler et al 1984; Salthouse et al 1988a), others have found no effects of age (e.g. Attig & Hasher 1980; Ellis et al 1988; Kausler et al 1985b). Lack of age-related differences in some experiments may be due to ceiling effects, as memory for frequency appears to be quite accurate under the conditions tested in developmental research.

One could argue that memory for event frequency is automatic because it is so clearly better than chance under a wide variety of encoding conditions (Sanders et al 1987). However, as Naveh-Benjamin (1988) points out, this is not a satisfactory criterion for assigning automaticity, inasmuch as processes believed to involve effort or attention, such as recall or recognition, also produce above-chance performance. Further, there are surely a number of different processes involved in encoding and retrieving information about event frequency. For instance, Jonides & Naveh-Benjamin (1987) have suggested that two mechanisms are responsible for remembering frequency of occurrence, a direct coding mechanism that is attentional and an indirect mechanism that estimates event frequency from some properties of the memory trace itself. The indirect mechanism is thought not to be attention dependent. We might thus suppose that age-related differences in event frequency, which are sometimes obtained, are due solely to the direct coding mechanism. This is not likely, however, since there is reason to believe that the memory traces of older adults, on which the indirect mechanism relies, are also less adequate than those of younger adults. Further, there may be age-related differences in retrieving event frequency even if there are no such differences in encoding frequency information (but see Kausler 1990 for counterarguments). Thus, even if one found consistent age-related differences in memory for event frequency, attributing these to age-related impairments in specific underlying mechanisms would by no means be straightforward.

There are other fundamental problems here as well. Hasher & Zacks (1979, 1984) suggested that in addition to developmental invariance, a number of other criteria must be jointly satisfied before a process can be classified as automatic. These include lack of sensitivity to intentionality of encoding or to variations in encoding strategies, lack of disruption by concurrent processing demands, lack of sensitivity to conditions of training or feedback, immunity to variations of organismic states, and absence of a large range of ability across individuals. Recent research has shown that these criteria cannot be satisfied for encoding of spatial, temporal, or event-frequency information (e.g. Greene 1984; Jonides & Naveh-Benjamin 1987; Naveh-Benjamin 1988, 1989, 1990; Sanders et al 1987). Hence, in addition to failing the developmental criterion, processes involved in memory for these aspects of events do not pass other tests of automaticity. In short, this is not a promising domain for framing questions about the role of attentional processes in age-related differences in memory.

Reduced Working-Memory Capacity

Three approaches to the investigation of the effects of reduced working-memory capacity on cognitive aging may be identified. One approach to the investigation of age-related changes in working-memory capacity involves what Salthouse (1990) has labeled within-context assessment. The hallmark of tasks used for within-context assessment is that capacity limitations are inferred from performance on tasks not designed specifically for this purpose. For instance, Light et al (1982) argued that working-memory limitations accounted for the failure of older adults to integrate information across several premises even when these premises could be recognized accurately. Light & Capps (1986) found that older adults were equally good at identifying the antecedents of pronouns when memory load was low (i.e. there was no material intervening between a sentence containing a pronoun and a sentence containing its antecedent), but they did observe an age-related difference when two sentences intervened. Light & Albertson (1988) also found that backgrounding information by shifting the topic had a more deleterious effect on ability to detect anomalies in short prose passages in older adults than in younger adults; they attributed this difference to reduced ability to retain prior relevant information. Kemper (1986) found that older adults experienced more difficulty in imitating left-branching sentences than young adults; such sentences are more complex syntactically than right-branching sentences, and comprehending them is believed to place greater burdens on working memory.

In a series of studies using within-context assessments of working-memory capacity, Salthouse and his colleagues have carefully manipulated complexity by varying the number of identical mental operations that must be carried out within a task. Examples of such tasks include varying the number of relevant premises that must be integrated in verbal reasoning (Salthouse et al 1989b), varying the number of folds in a piece of paper that must be kept track of before a hole is punched and the appearance of the unfolded paper is tested (Salthouse et al 1989b), and varying the number of frames that must be integrated in a spatial visualization task (Salthouse 1987; Salthouse & Mitchell 1989; Salthouse et al 1989a). In each case, older adults were more adversely affected by increasing complexity, permitting the inference that aging is associated with reduced working-memory capacity. Moreover, Salthouse et al (1989b) found reliable correlations between slopes of the complexity functions for verbal reasoning and paper folding tasks, suggesting that the same underlying processes are tapped by these two tasks.

Despite this impressive set of results, not all within-context assessments of working memory have produced age-related performance decrements. For instance, Light & Anderson (1985) found no interaction between age and number of sentences intervening between a pronoun and its antecedent. Increasing propositional density of sentences of constant length (a manipulation that also increases syntactic complexity) does not differentially impair gist recall in the old (Stine et al 1986). Varying the size of a concurrent memory load affects sentence verification latencies in younger and older adults to the same extent (Morris et al 1990; Morris et al 1988). In addition, within-context measures of working-memory capacity are as yet untried as predictors of performance on other cognitive tasks sensitive to age.

The second approach to the role of working-memory capacity in producing age-related decrements in memory involves development of individual-difference measures. The goals of this research are twofold: to establish that reliable age-related differences on such measures may be obtained, and to use the measures as predictors of performance in other domains, such as memory for text, reasoning, or spatial integration. Age-related differences have been obtained on a variety of indexes of working-memory capacity including backward digit span (e.g. Charness 1987; Salthouse 1988b; but see Light & Anderson 1985), sentence span (e.g. Gick et al 1988; Light &

Anderson 1985; Wingfield et al 1988; but see Hartley, 1986, 1988), and several types of computation spans (e.g. Braune & Wickens 1985; Dobbs & Rule 1989; Salthouse 1988b, 1990; Salthouse & Mitchell 1989), among others (see Salthouse 1988b for a review).

Efforts to use indexes of working-memory capacity as predictors of age-related differences in memory have met with only moderate success. Although some studies have found that partialing out a measure of working-memory capacity leads to attenuation of age-related differences in performance (Pratt et al 1989; Salthouse 1988c,d; Salthouse et al 1988b; Stine & Wingfield 1987; Stine et al 1990), others have not (Hartley 1986; Light & Anderson 1985). The proportion of age-related variation in performance attributable to working-memory capacity is small enough (probably less than 50%) to discredit strong versions of the hypothesis that working-memory differences are the sole mediators of performance decrements in old age (Salthouse 1988c, 1990; Salthouse et al 1988b). This problem is not unique to memory; similar failures to obtain support for strong versions of the working-memory hypothesis have been obtained for problem solving (Charness 1987), integrative verbal reasoning (Salthouse et al 1989b), spatial paper folding (Salthouse et al 1989b), and a host of other tasks (Salthouse et al 1988b).

A third approach to the study of working-memory declines in old age comes from a recent suggestion by Hasher & Zacks (1988) that older adults do not have reduced working-memory capacity, but rather that as a consequence of the diminished efficiency of inhibitory processes, the contents of working memory may differ in young and old. Older adults may be more likely to entertain thoughts that are off the goal path, such as personally relevant thoughts, contextually inappropriate interpretations of words or phrases subject to multiple interpretation, and daydreams. If true, this would help to explain why older adults remember less target information than do younger ones and are less successful in integrating successive parts of a discourse. The evidence is, however, not wholly consistent either on the claim that older adults have reduced inhibition or on the claim that older adults have different, less relevant mental contents.

With respect to the claim that older adults have reduced inhibitory functioning, the evidence from selective-attention paradigms, the principal testing ground for this idea, indicates that older adults have difficulty in rejecting distracting information in some but not all situations (see McDowd & Birren 1990 for a review). For instance, older adults are more susceptible to the Stroop effect (Cohn et al 1984; Comalli et al 1962) and show less diminution with practice of Stroop-like inhibition in a mental arithmetic task (Rogers & Fisk 1991). On the other hand, Plude & Doussard-Roosevelt (1989) found no special disadvantage of increasing number of distractors for older adults in a visual search task when the target was defined by a single feature, though the old suffered more than the young when the target was defined by a conjunction of features. Hence, it is not yet clear how general a problem older adults have with respect to inhibitory processes.

More specific claims with respect to the contents of working memory also lack universal support. Contrary to expectation, daydreaming and task-unrelated thoughts appear to decrease in old age (Giambra 1989). Intrusions in recall, which may be taken as indications of irrelevant working-memory contents, are sometimes found to be more prevalent in old age (e.g. Stine & Wingfield 1987) and sometimes they are not (e.g. Light & Albertson 1988; Light & Anderson 1983; Perlmutter 1978; Zelinski & Miura 1988). Further, the inhibition hypothesis predicts phenomena that do not occur. For instance, the associations of older adults should be more idiosyncratic, but they are not (e.g. Burke & Peters 1986; Howard 1980; Light & Anderson 1983). Also, older adults should show less particularization of word meanings in context because of interference from competing meanings, but as we saw earlier, this is not the case. Finally, as we saw above, older adults remember less, not more, contextual information than younger adults, though this information is often irrelevant to the primary goal of remembering target information.

In support of the reduced inhibition thesis, there is evidence that older adults are more likely simultaneously to entertain two competing inferences in memory (Hamm & Hasher 1990) and to be less slowed when it is necessary to produce a previously inhibited response (Hasher et al 1989; McDowd & Oseas 1990). Also, older adults report better memory for thoughts and feelings surrounding an event than do younger adults, and they recall more thoughts and feelings and less perceptual and spatial information than younger adults (Hashtroudi et al 1990). Nevertheless, the link between increased presence of task-unrelated thoughts and impaired memory in old age has yet to be established; there is no compelling evidence that older adults recalled less perceptual and spatial information *because* they recalled more thoughts and feelings. Also, people whose speech consists of sequences of loosely associated topics with much extraneous information do not seem to remember less (Gold et al 1988).

Cognitive Slowing

There is abundant evidence that aging is accompanied by slower responding in almost every task in which response speed has been assessed, including rate of rehearsal during a memory task (Salthouse 1980), rate of scanning in memory search tasks (e.g. Cerella 1985; Cerella et al 1980; Fisk et al 1988), and rate of responding in primary and secondary memory tasks (Waugh et al 1978). This general slowing has given rise to what is known as "the complexity hypothesis"—i.e. that latencies of older adults are longer than latencies of younger adults by a constant proportion. This slowing has been hypothesized as due to greater noise in the nervous system (e.g. Salthouse & Lichty 1985;

Cremer & Zeef 1987), broken or attenuated neural connections (Cerella 1990), weakened linkage strength between connections (MacKay & Burke 1990), or an increase in the proportion of information lost at each step of processing (Myerson et al 1990; see Salthouse 1985a,b for a review).

Some theorists have suggested that deficits in transmission of activation in a network can account for important aspects of age-related memory impairment without invoking attentional concepts. For instance, Salthouse (1988b) has noted that slower transmission of activation can result in a smaller number of connected nodes being activated, leading to less elaborated memory traces. Similarly, MacKay & Burke (1990) have described mechanisms whereby transmission deficits can prevent the formation of new associations or cause activation failures in existing connections (resulting in retrieval failures such as the tip-of-the-tongue experience). Myerson et al (1990) have noted that slowing of transmission cannot be compensated by increased durations of study time, so that age-related differences should not be eliminated by providing unlimited presentation time (see above). Baddeley et al (1975) found that memory span is related to rate of pronunciation in young adults. Pronunciation times increase with age, suggesting that reductions in span in older adults are due to increases in pronunciation time (Balota & Duchek 1988), though this has yet to be demonstrated in a single study in which both span and pronunciation time measures are obtained for young and old adults.

Despite these conceptual successes, however, empirical efforts to demonstrate that memory decrements in old age stem either solely or in large measure from cognitive slowing have not met with much success. Salthouse (1985a) used digit symbol substitution performance as an index of cognitive speed and examined the pattern of intercorrelations among age, speed, and performance on several memory measures, including a number of span tasks, a supraspan task (eight trials on seven pairs of letters of digits), free recall of word lists, paired associate learning, and spatial recall. In most cases, partialing out speed reduced the correlation between age and performance, at least somewhat. However, the correlations did not all drop to zero, as would be expected if slowing were the sole basis of age-related memory impairment. A particular source of embarrassment to the slowing theory is the finding in this study that as amount to be remembered increased, the match between predictions from general slowing and experimental findings worsened. Salthouse argues that failures of prediction could be due to excessive dependency on strategies in some taks or to the inadequacy of the digit symbol task as a measure of processing rate. With respect to the latter possibility, he argues that the digit symbol task may be an appropriate measure of active but not passive processing and that spatial memory may involve passive processing. These explanations are clearly post hoc.

Salthouse (1988d) obtained some success in using the digit symbol measure of speed as a predictor of age-related differences in verbal and spatial memory. However, these results were not replicated by Salthouse et al (1988b), who found little evidence that speed accounts for much of the age-related variability in paired-associate learning, memory for activities, spatial memory, temporal memory, or memory for event frequency. In a study of aging and individual differences in memory for written discourse, Hartley (1988) found both a general slowness factor and a specific-process slowing factor. The former, but not the latter, appeared to be important in predicting discourse memory either for the whole sample of young, middle-aged, and older adults or for predicting performance of just the older adults. On the other hand, Kliegl & Lindenberger (1988) found that the rate of presentation that produced 50% recall of a list of words was a strong predictor of list memory at other fixed presentation rates. Overall, then, there is little consistent empirical support for the hypothesis that slowing accounts for memory differences in old age.

Summary

In this section, evidence pertaining to the hypotheses that age differences in retention of new information are the result of changes in attentional capacity, working-memory capacity or content, or cognitive slowing has been reviewed. The picture with respect to attentional capacity is at best mixed, with some studies finding greater divided attention costs for old than for young adults on processes thought to be critical for encoding or retrieval, and other studies finding equivalent costs across age. [A similar inconsistency is found in domains other than memory (McDowd & Birren 1990).] Attempts to evaluate the attentional capacity hypothesis have also been hampered by the lack of clarity as to the nature of the concepts of attention or effort, making it difficult to develop individual-difference measures of this alleged processing resource (Salthouse 1988d). The precise manner in which attention might affect the operation of mechanisms responsible for storage and retrieval of information has not been specified, making resolution of conflicting findings difficult, if not impossible.

With respect to working-memory capacity, the outlook appears to be somewhat brighter. Measures of working-memory capacity that reliably discriminate between younger and older adults have been developed. Models exist that specify the role of working memory for some areas of cognition, such as prose memory (Kintsch & van Dijk 1978; Spilich 1983) and mental computation (Charness & Campbell 1988). Further, working-memory capacity appears to account for some, though unfortunately not nearly all or even most of the age-related difference in retention.

Nevertheless, discrepant findings have been reported and there are some conceptual problems as well. For instance, measures of working memory do not correlate strongly with each other (Light & Anderson 1985; Salthouse 1988d), suggesting that they do not tap the same resource. One possibility is that there is no single entity called working memory but rather a number of different working memories that are domain-specific (e.g. Baddeley et al 1985; Turner & Engle 1989). If this were so, it would account for the low correlations between indexes of working memory. In addition, the relatively small attenuation in correlations between age and performance when indexes of working memory are partialed out could be due to mismatch between the domains tapped by the individual difference measure and the retention task. The search for a general indicator of working memory would also be futile. Moreover, a defining characteristic of working memory is that capacity must be allocated between concurrent processing and storage demands. Hence, older adults should be increasingly disadvantaged when such demands are increased, but this is not always the case (see Salthouse 1990 for a review).

A number of problems beset the hypothesis that general slowing is responsible for age-related differences in memory. There is little consistent empirical support for this view. At a conceptual level, it encounters some of the same difficulties we have already seen. The approach taken by Salthouse (e.g. 1985a, 1988d; Salthouse et al 1988b) presupposes that slowing is general and that it therefore makes sense to use a single behavioral indicator of slowing such as performance on the digit symbol task. However, it is by no means clear that a single slowing parameter suffices to describe the relation between old and young latencies (e.g. Cerella 1985, 1990; Hertzog et al 1986; Baron & Mattila 1989; Rogers & Fisk 1990). Salthouse himself (1985a) suggested that active and passive slowing rates might be different. Certainly, if slowing is domain specific, use of a single indicator of slowing in correlational studies is unlikely to produce consistent outcomes with respect to the extent to which partialing out speed reduces age-performance correlations.

In addition, the complexity hypothesis has its own difficulties at the present time. The exact form of the relationship between latencies of younger and older adults is in dispute (e.g. Cerella, 1985, 1990; Hale et al 1987; Myerson et al 1990). Studies employing both reaction time and electrophysiological indexes of slowing (i.e. the P300) find that the functions relating young and old reaction times and young and old P300 measures have different forms (e.g. Bashore et al 1989). Cerella (1985, 1990) has claimed that there is more slowing of cognitive operations than of sensorimotor processes, but this claim has been challenged (Strayer et al 1987).

Cerella (1990) has hailed the general-slowing hypothesis as producing great theoretical coherence because it replaces "the myriad task-specific explanations of age effects that have proliferated in the literature" (p. 217) with a single mechanism; thus, according to Cerella, "cognitive aging reemerges as a subfield of neurophysiology rather than cognitive psychology" (p. 217). This strong testimonial for the slowing hypothesis surely needs tempering in the face of the points enumerated above. Further, without more specific models of how neural slowing affects performance, it will not be possible to have principled methods for deciding which tasks should show similar slowing rates (see Rogers & Fisk 1990, for an example). Finally, it is not obvious how to extend the insights of the slowing hypothesis to response measures other than latencies. The order of difficulty of memory units or propositions in prose stays the same across the adult years (Rubin 1985; Stine & Wingfield 1988). Thus, Stine & Wingfield (1988) find linear relationships between the probabilities that a proposition is recalled by young and older adults. The similarity between these functions and between latency functions is notable. However, the slope of the function relating young and old recall varied considerably with propositional density, suggesting that the amount recalled by the old is not a constant proportion of the amount recalled by the young in different situations. Again, without a clear model explaining why this should be the case, the regularity of the relationships between young and old accuracies or between young and old latencies seems to be an interesting empirical fact rather than an explanation of age-related impairment in cognition.

The appeal of processing resource approaches is that they are general enough to encompass not only memory but all aspects of cognition. The danger of these approaches is that without specification of the precise mechanisms involved and adequate assessment of both the resource demands of particular tasks and the resources available to individuals at a given moment, there is a serious risk of circularity. That is, finding age-related differences on some task can lead to the conclusion that the task was demanding of processing resources whereas failure to find such differences can lead to the inference that the task is automatic (Light & Burke 1988; Salthouse 1988c). An example of this problem is the distinction between direct and indirect measures of memory. As discussed above, age-related differences appear to be much larger on direct measures of memory, and repetition priming (at least of single items) is relatively spared in amnesia as well. Some researchers have claimed (e.g. Light et al 1986; Squire 1987) that direct and indirect measures differ in their capacity requirements, with indirect measures relying on more automatic processes. However, the empirical basis for such claims is slim, and there is evidence that amnesics and older adults can show learning on tasks that require attentional capacity (Howard & Howard 1989; Nissen & Bullemer 1987). Hence the distinction between direct and indirect measures probably does not lie in degree of automaticity.

CONCLUSION

Four classes of explanation for age-related decrements in memory have been examined. These hypotheses, taken individually or collectively, do not provide an adequate account for the observed patterns of spared and impaired function found in old age. The absence of cross-over interactions involving age argues against strategy hypotheses, as does the finding that younger and older adults generally benefit to about the same extent from manipulations designed to guide encoding or retrieval. The evidence also runs counter to the view that problems in language comprehension are responsible for memory decrements in old age. There is reason to believe that age-related decrements in memory for new information are not generalized, but rather may be confined to situations in which deliberate recollection is required, with sparing of memory tapped by indirect measures. However, there is as yet no adequate explanation for this pattern of results. Nor is it known whether the same mechanisms can account for problems in retrieving old and new information. Finally, all variants of the processing resource hypothesis considered here are unsatisfactory both because of conflicting experimental outcomes and because of lack of clarity about the concepts involved.

ACKNOWLEDGMENT

Preparation of this chapter was supported by National Institute on Aging Grant AG02452. The author thanks Deborah Burke for helpful comments.

Literature Cited

Albert, M. S., Heller, H. S., Milberg, W. 1988. Changes in naming ability with age. *Psychol. Aging* 3:173–78

Allen, P. A. 1990. Influence of processing variability on adult age differences in memory distribution of order information. *Cognit. Dev.* In press

Anderson, J. A. 1983. A spreading activation theory of memory. *J. Verb. Learn. Verb. Behav.* 22:261–95

Arbuckle, T. Y., Vanderleck, V. F., Harsany, M., Lapidus, S. 1990. Adult age differences in memory in relation to availability and accessibility of knowledge-based schemas. *J. Exp. Psychol.: Learn. Mem. Cogn.* 16:305–15

Attig, M., Hasher, L. 1980. The processing of frequency occurrence information by adults. *J. Gerontol.* 35:66–69

Bäckman, L. 1989. Varieties of memory compensation by older adults. In *Everyday Cognition in Adulthood and Late Life,* ed. L. W. Poon, D. C. Rubin, B. A. Wilson, pp. 509–44. New York: Cambridge Univ. Press

Bäckman, L., Mäntylä, T. 1988. Effectiveness of self-generated cues in younger and older adults: the role of retention interval. *Int. J. Aging Hum. Dev.* 26:241–48

Baddeley, A. 1986. *Working Memory.* Oxford: Clarendon Press

Baddeley, A., Logie, R., Bressi, S., Della Sala, S., Spinnler, H. 1986. Dementia and

working memory. *Q. J. Exp. Psychol.* 38A:603–18

Baddeley, A., Logie, R., Nimmo-Smith, I., Brereton, N. 1985. Components of fluent reading. *J. Mem. Lang.* 24:119–31

Baddeley, A. D., Thomson, N., Buchanan, M. 1975. Word length and the structure of short-term memory. *J. Verb. Learn. Verb. Behav.* 14:575–89

Bahrick, H. P. 1984. Memory for people. In *Everyday Memory, Actions and Absent-Mindedness,* ed. J. E. Harris & P. E. Morris, pp. 19–34. New York: Academic

Balota, D. A., Duchek, J. M. 1988. Age-related differences in lexical access, spreading activation, and simple pronunciation. *Psychol. Aging* 3:84–93

Balota, D. A., Duchek, J. M., Paullin, R. 1989. Age-related differences in the impact of spacing, lag, and retention interval. *Psychol. Aging* 4:3–9

Bandura, A. 1989. Regulation of cognitive processes through perceived self-efficacy. *Dev. Psychol.* 25:729–35

Baron, A., Mattila, W. R. 1989. Response slowing of older adults: effects of time-limit contingencies on single- and dual-task performances. *Psychol. Aging* 4:66–72

Bashore, T. R., Osman, A., Heffley, E. F. III. 1989. Mental slowing in elderly persons: a cognitive psychophysiological analysis. *Psychol. Aging* 4:235–44

Batchelder, W. H., Riefer, D. M. 1989. *Multinomial processing models of source monitoring. Tech. Rep. MBS 89-07. Irvine: Univ. Calif., Irvine Res. Unit in Math. Behav. Sci.

Belmore, S. M. 1981. Age-related changes in processing explicit and implicit language. *J. Gerontol.* 36:316–22

Berry, J. M. 1989. Cognitive efficacy across the life span: introduction to the special series. *Dev. Psychol.* 25:683–86

Berry, J. M., West, R. L., Dennehey, R. L. 1989. Reliability and validity of the memory self-efficacy questionnaire. *Dev. Psychol.* 25:701–13

Borod, J. C., Goodglass, H., Kaplan, E. 1980. Normative data on the Boston Diagnostic Aphasia Examination, Parietal Lobe Battery, and the Boston Naming Test. *J. Clin. Neuropsychol.* 2:209–15

Bowles, N. L., Poon, L. W. 1985. Aging and retrieval of words in semantic memory. *J. Gerontol.* 40:71–77

Bowles, N. L., Williams, D., Poon, L. W. 1983. On the use of word association norms in aging research. *Exp. Aging Res.* 9:175–277

Braune, R., Wickens, C. D. 1985. The functional age profile: an objective decision criterion for the assessment of pilot performance capacities and capabilities. *Human Factors* 27:681–93

Brigham, M. C., Pressley, M. 1988. Cognitive monitoring and strategy choice in younger and older adults. *Psychol. Aging* 3:249–57

Bruce, P. R., Coyne, A. C., Botwinick, J. 1982. Adult age differences in metamemory. *J. Gerontol.* 37:354–57

Bruce, P. R., Herman, J. F. 1986. Adult age differences in spatial memory: effects of distinctiveness and repeated experience. *J. Gerontol.* 41:774–77

Burke, D. M., Harrold, R. M. 1988. Automatic and effortful semantic processes in old age: experimental and naturalistic approaches. In *Language, Memory and Aging*, ed. L. L. Light, D. M. Burke, pp. 100–16. New York: Cambridge Univ. Press

Burke, D. M., Light, L. L. 1981. Memory and aging: the role of retrieval processes. *Psychol. Bull.* 90:513–46

Burke, D. M., Peters, L. 1986. Word associations in old age: evidence for consistency in semantic encoding during adulthood. *Psychol. Aging* 1:283–92

Burke, D. M., White, H., Diaz, D. L. 1987. Semantic priming in young and older adults: evidence for age-constancy in automatic and attentional processes. *J. Exp. Psychol.: Hum. Percept. Perform.* 13:79–88

Burke, D., Worthley, J., Martin, J. 1988. I'll never forget what's-her-name: aging and the tip of the tongue experience. In *Practical*

Aspects of Memory: Current Research and Issues, ed. M. M. Gruneberg, P. Morris, & R. N. Sykes, 2:113–18. New York: Wiley

Burke, D. M., Yee, P. L. 1984. Semantic priming during sentence processing by young and older adults. *Dev. Psychol.* 20:903–10

Butterfield, E. C., Nelson, T. O., Peck, V. 1988. Developmental aspects of the feeling of knowing. *Dev. Psychol.* 24:654–63

Byrd, M. 1984. Age differences in the retrieval of information from semantic memory. *Exp. Aging Res.* 10:29–33

Campbell, J. I. D., Charness, N. 1991. Age-related declines in working-memory skills: evidence from a complex calculation task. *Dev. Psychol.* In press

Cavanaugh, J. C. 1983. Comprehension and retention of television programs by 20- and 60-year olds. *J. Gerontol.* 38:190–96

Cavanaugh, J. C. 1986–1987. Age differences in adults' self-reports of memory ability: It depends on how and what you ask. *Int. J. Aging Hum. Dev.* 24:271–77

Cavanaugh, J. C., Grady, J. G., Perlmutter, M. A. 1983. Forgetting and use of memory aids in 20 to 70 year olds' everyday life. *Int. J. Aging Hum. Dev.* 17:113–22

Cavanaugh, J. C., Green, E. E. 1990. I believe, therefore I can: self-efficacy beliefs in memory aging. In *Aging and Cognition: Mental Processes, Self-Awareness, and Interventions*, ed. E. A. Lovelace, pp. 189–230. Amsterdam: Elsevier. In press

Cavanaugh, J. C., Poon, L. W. 1989. Metamemorial predictors of memory performance in young and older adults. *Psychol. Aging* 4:365–68

Cerella, J. 1985. Information processing rates in the elderly. *Psychol. Bull.* 98:67–83

Cerella, J. 1990. Aging and information-processing rate. In *Handbook of the Psychology of Aging*, ed. J. E. Birren & K. W. Schaie, pp. 201–21. New York: Academic. 3rd ed.

Cerella, J., Poon, L. W., Williams, D. M. 1980. Aging and the complexity hypothesis. In *Aging in the 1980s: Psychological Issues*, ed. L. W. Poon, pp. 332–40. Washington, DC: Am. Psychol. Assoc.

Charness, N. 1981. Aging and skilled problem solving. *J. Exp. Psychol.: Gen.* 110:21–38

Charness, N. 1987. Component processes in bridge bidding and novel problem-solving tasks. *Can. J. Psychol.* 41:223–43

Charness, N., Campbell, J. I. D. 1988. Acquiring skill at mental calculation in adulthood: a task decomposition. *J. Exp. Psychol.: Gen.* 117:115–29

Cherry, K. E., Park, D. C. 1989. Age-related differences in three-dimensional spatial memory. *J. Gerontol.: Psychol. Sci.* 44: P16–22

Chiarello, C., Church, K. L., Hoyer, W. J. 1985. Automatic and controlled semantic priming: accuracy, response bias, and aging. *J. Gerontol.* 40:593–600

Chiarello, C., Hoyer, W. J. 1988. Adult age differences in implicit and explicit memory: time course and encoding effects. *Psychol. Aging* 3:358–66

Cohen, G. 1979. Language comprehension in old age. *Cognit. Psychol.* 11:412–29

Cohen, G. 1981. Inferential reasoning in old age. *Cognition* 9:59–72

Cohen, G. 1988. Age differences in memory for text: production deficiency or processing limitations? See Burke & Harrold 1988, pp. 171–90

Cohen, G., Faulkner, D. 1983. Word recognition: age differences in contextual facilitation effects. *Br. J. Psychol.* 74:239–51

Cohen, G., Faulkner, D. 1986. Memory for proper names: age differences in retrieval. *Br. J. Dev. Psychol.* 4:187–97

Cohen, G., Faulkner, D. 1989. Age differences in source forgetting: effects on reality monitoring and eyewitness testimony. *Psychol. Aging* 4:10–17

Cohen, N. J. 1984. Preserved learning capacity in amnesia: evidence for multiple memory systems. In *Neuropsychology of Memory,* ed. L. R. Squire & N. Butters, pp. 83–103. New York: Guilford Press

Cohn, N. B., Dustman, R. E., Bradford, D. C. 1984. Age-related decrements in Stroop color test performance. *J. Clin. Psychol.* 40:1244–50

Comalli, P. E. Jr., Wapner, S., Werner, H. 1962. Interference effects of Stroop color-word test in childhood, adulthood, and aging. *J. Genet. Psychol.* 100:47–53

Craik, F. I. M. 1977. Age differences in human memory. In *Handbook of the Psychology of Aging,* ed. J. E. Birren, K. W. Schaie, pp. 384–420. New York: Van Nostrand Reinhold

Craik, F. I. M. 1983. On the transfer of information from temporary to permanent storage. *Philos. Trans. R. Soc. London Ser. B* 302:341–59

Craik, F. I. M. 1986. A functional account of age differences in memory. In *Human Memory and Cognitive Capabilities,* ed. F. Klix, H. Hagendorf, pp. 409–22. Amsterdam: Elsevier

Craik, F. I. M., Byrd, M. 1982. Aging and cognitive deficits: the role of attentional resources. In *Aging and Cognitive Processes,* ed. F. I. M. Craik & S. Trehub, pp. 191–211. New York: Plenum

Craik, F. I. M., McDowd, J. 1987. Age differences in recall and recognition. *J. Exp. Psychol.: Learn., Mem., Cogn.* 13:474–79

Craik, F. I. M., Morris, L. W., Morris, R. G., Loewen, E. R. 1990. Relations between source amnesia and frontal lobe functioning in older adults. *Psychol. Aging* 5:148–51

Craik, F. I. M., Rabinowitz, J. C. 1984. Age differences in the acquisition and use of verbal information: a tutorial review. In *Attention and Performance. X. Control Of Language Processes,* ed. H. Bouma, D. G. Bouwhuis, pp. 471–99. Hillsdale, NJ: Erlbaum

Craik, F. I. M., Rabinowitz, J. C. 1985. The effects of presentation rate and encoding task on age-related memory deficits. *J. Gerontol.* 40:309–15

Craik, F. I. M., Simon, E. 1980. Age differences in memory: the roles of attention and depth of processing. In *New Directions in Memory and Aging,* ed. L. W. Poon, J. L. Fozard, L. S. Cermak, D. Arenberg, L. W. Thompson, pp. 95–112. Hillsdale, NJ: Lawrence Erlbaum Assoc.

Cremer, R., Zeef, E. J. 1987. What kind of noise increases with age? *J. Gerontol.* 42:515–18

Davis, H. P. et al. 1990. Lexical priming deficits as a function of age. *Behav. Neurosci.* 104:288–97

Denney, N. W., Miller, B. V., Dew, J. R., Levav, A. L. 1991. An adult developmental study of contextual memory. *J. Gerontol.: Psychol. Sci.* In press

Devolder, P. A., Brigham, M. C., Pressley, M. 1990. Memory performance awareness in young and older adults. *Psychol. Aging* 5:291–303

Dixon, R. A. 1989. Questionnaire research on metamemory and aging: issues of structure and function. See Bäckman 1989, pp. 394–415

Dixon, R. A., Hultsch, D. F. 1983a. Metamemory and memory for text relationships in adulthood: a cross-validation study. *J. Gerontol.* 38:689–94

Dixon, R. A., Hultsch, D. F. 1983b. Structure and development of metamemory in adulthood. *J. Gerontol.* 38:682–88

Dobbs, A. R., Rule, B. G. 1987. Prospective memory and self-reports of memory abilities in older adults. *Can. J. Psychol.* 41:209–22

Dobbs, A. R., Rule, B. G. 1989. Adult age differences in working memory. *Psychol. Aging* 4:500–3

Duchek, J. M. 1984. Encoding and retrieval differences between young and old: the impact of attentional capacity usage. *Dev. Psychol.* 20:1173–80

Dywan, J., Jacoby, L. L. 1990. Effects of aging and source monitoring: differences in susceptibility to false fame. *Psychol. Aging* 5:379–87

Eich, J. M. 1985. Levels of processing, encoding specificity, elaboration, and CHARM. *Psychol. Rev.* 92:1–38

Einstein, G. O., McDaniel, M. A. 1990. Normal aging and prospective memory. *J. Exp. Psychol.: Learn. Mem., Cogn.* 16:717–26

Ellis, N. R., Katz, E., Williams, J. E. 1987. Developmental aspects of memory for spatial locations. *J. Exp. Child Psychol.* 44:401–12

Ellis, N. R., Palmer, R. L., Reeves, C. L. 1988. Developmental and intellectual differences in frequency processing. *Dev. Psychol.* 24:38–45

Evans, G. W., Brennan, P. L., Skorpanich, M. A., Held, D. 1984. Cognitive mapping and elderly adults: verbal and location memory for urban landmarks. *J. Gerontol.* 39:452–57

Fisk, A. D., McGee, N. D., Giambra, L. M. 1988. The influence of age on consistent and varied semantic-category search performance. *Psychol. Aging* 3:323–33

Flavell, J. H., Wellman, H. M. 1977. Metamemory. In *Perspectives on the Development of Memory and Cognition*, ed. R. V. Kail Jr., J. W. Hagen, pp. 3–33. Hillsdale, NJ: Erlbaum

Foos, P. W. 1989a. Adult age differences in working memory. *Psychol. Aging* 4:269–75

Foos, P. W. 1989b. Age differences in memory for two common objects. *J. Gerontol.: Psychol. Sci.* 44:P178–80

Freund, J. L., Witte, K. L. 1986. Recognition and frequency judgments in young and elderly adults. *Am. J. Psychol.* 99:81–102

Giambra, L. M. 1989. Task-unrelated-thought frequency as a function of age: a laboratory study. *Psychol. Aging* 4:136–43

Gick, M. L., Craik, F. I. M., Morris, R. G. 1988. Task complexity and age differences in working memory. *Mem. Cogn.* 16:353–61

Gilewski, M. J., Zelinski, E. M. 1986. Questionnaire assessment of memory complaints. In *Handbook for Clinical Memory Assessment of Older Adults*, ed. L. W. Poon, pp. 93–107. Washington, DC: Am. Psychol. Assoc.

Gilewski, M. J., Zelinski, E. M., Schaie, K. W. 1990. The Memory Functioning Questionnaire for assessment of memory complaints in adulthood and old age. *Psychol. Aging*. In press

Gillund, G., Shiffrin, R. M. 1984. A retrieval model for both recognition and recall. *Psychol. Rev.* 91:1–67

Gold, D., Andres, D., Arbuckle, T., Schwartzman, A. 1988. Measurement and correlates of verbosity in elderly people. *J. Gerontol.: Psychol. Sci.* 43:P27–33

Graf, P., Mandler, G. 1984. Activation makes words more accessible, but not necessarily more retrievable. *J. Verb. Learn. Verb. Behav.* 23:553–68

Graf, P., Schacter, D. L. 1985. Implicit and explicit memory for new associations in normal and amnesic subjects. *J. Exp. Psychol.: Learn., Mem., Cogn.* 11:501–18

Greene, R. L. 1984. Incidental learning of event frequency. *Mem. Cogn.* 12:90–95

Guttentag, R. E. 1985. Memory and aging: implications for theories of memory development during childhood. *Dev. Rev.* 5:56–82

Guttentag, R. E., Hunt, R. R. 1988. Adult age differences in memory for imagined and performed actions. *J. Gerontol.: Psychol. Sci.* 43:P107–8

Hale, S., Myerson, J., Wagstaff, D. 1987. General slowing of nonverbal information processing: evidence for a power law. *J. Gerontol.* 42:131–36

Hamm, V. P., Hasher, L. 1990. *Age and the Formation of Inferences*. Manuscript submitted for publication

Hartley, J. T. 1986. Reader and text variables as determinants of discourse memory in adulthood. *Psychol. Aging* 1:150–58

Hartley, J. T. 1988. Aging and individual differences in memory for written discourse. See Burke & Harrold 1988, pp. 36–57

Hartley, J. T. 1989. Memory for prose: perspectives on the reader. See Bäckman 1989, pp. 135–56

Hasher, L., Rypma, B., Stoltzfus, E., Zacks, R. T. 1989. *Age deficits in inhibitory mechanisms: data and theory*. Paper presented at the Meet. Psychonom. Soc., Atlanta

Hasher, L., Zacks, R. T. 1979. Automatic and effortful processes in memory. *J. Exp. Psychol.: Gen.* 108:356–88

Hasher, L., Zacks, R. T. 1984. Automatic processing of fundamental information: the case of frequency of occurrence. *Am. Psychol.* 39:1372–88

Hasher, L., Zacks, R. T. 1988. Working memory, comprehension, and aging: a review and a new view. In *The Psychology of Learning and Motivation*, ed. G. H. Bower, 22:193–225. New York: Academic

Hashtroudi, S., Johnson, M. K., Chrosniak, L. D. 1989. Aging and source monitoring. *Pschol. Aging* 4:106–12

Hashtroudi, S., Johnson, M. K., Chrosniak, L. D. 1990. Aging and qualitative characteristics of memories for perceived and imagined complex events. *Psychol. Aging* 5:119–26

Hertzog, C., Dixon, R., Hultsch, D. F. 1990. Relationships between metamemory, memory predictions, and memory task performance in adults. *Psychol. Aging* 5:215–27

Hertzog, C., Raskind, C. L., Canon, C. J. 1986. Age-related slowing in semantic information processing speed: an individual differences analysis. *J. Gerontol.* 41:500–2

Hess, T. M. 1984. Efforts of semantically related and unrelated contexts on recognition memory of different-aged adults. *J. Gerontol.* 39:441–51

Hess, T. M. 1985. Aging and context influences on recognition memory for typical and atypical script actions. *Dev. Psychol.* 21:1139–51

Hess, T. M. 1991. Adult age differences in script content and structure. In *Everyday Memory and Aging: Current Research and Methodology*, ed. R. L. West, J. D. Sinnott. New York: Springer-Verlag. In press

Hess, T. M., Arnould, D. 1986. Adult age differences in memory for explicit and implicit sentence information. *J. Gerontol.* 2:191–94

Hess, T. M., Higgins, J. N. 1983. Context utilization in young and old adults. *J. Gerontol.* 38:65–71

Hintzman, D. L. 1988. Judgments of frequency and recognition memory in a multiple-trace memory model. *Psychol. Rev.* 95:528–51

Howard, D. V. 1979a. *Category norms for adults between the ages of 20 and 80*. Tech. Rep. NIA-79-1. Washington, DC: Georgetown Univ.

Howard, D. V. 1979b. *Restricted word association norms for adults between the ages of 20 and 80*. Tech. Rep. NIA-79-2. Washington, DC: Georgetown Univ.

Howard, D. V. 1980. Category norms: a comparison of the Battig and Montague (1969) norms with the responses of adults between the ages of 20 and 80. *J. Gerontol.* 35:225–31

Howard, D. V. 1983a. A multidimensional scaling analysis of aging and the semantic structure of animal names. *Exp. Aging Res.* 9:27–30

Howard, D. V. 1983b. The effects of aging and degree of association on the semantic priming of lexical decisions. *Exp. Aging Res.* 9:145–51

Howard, D. V. 1988a. Aging and memory activation: the priming of semantic and episodic memories. See Burke & Harrold, pp. 77–99

Howard, D. V. 1988b. Implicit and explicit assessment of cognitive aging. In *Cognitive Development in Adulthood: Progress in Cognitive Development Research*, ed. M. L. Howe, C. J. Brainerd, pp. 3–37. New York: Springer-Verlag

Howard, D. V., Heisey, J. G., Shaw, R. J. 1986a. Aging and the priming of newly learned associations. *Dev. Psychol.* 22:78–85

Howard, D. V., Howard, J. H. Jr. 1989. Age differences in learning serial patterns: direct versus indirect measures. *Psychol. Aging* 4:357–64

Howard, D. V., McAndrews, M. P., Lasaga, M. I. 1981. Semantic priming of lexical decisions in young and old adults. *J. Gerontol.* 36:707–14

Howard, D. V., Shaw, R. J., Heisey, J. G. 1986b. Aging and the time course of semantic activation. *J. Gerontol.* 41:195–203

Howe, M. L. 1988. Measuring memory development in adulthood: a model-based approach to disentangling storage-retrieval contributions. See Howard 1988b, pp. 39–64

Hultsch, D. F., Hertzog, C., Dixon, R. A. 1987. Age differences in metamemory: resolving the inconsistencies. *Can. J. Psychol.* 41:193–208

Hultsch, D. F., Hertzog, C., Dixon, R. A., Davidson, H. 1988. Memory self-knowledge and self-efficacy in the aged. See Howard 1988b, pp. 65–92

Hultsch, D. F., Masson, M. E. J., Small, B. J. 1991. Adult age differences in direct and indirect tests of memory. *J. Gerontol.: Psychol. Sci.* In press

Intons-Peterson, M. J., Fournier, J. 1986. External and internal memory aids: When and how often do we use them? *J. Exp. Psychol.: Gen.* 115:267–80

Jacoby, L. L., Dallas, M. 1981. On the relationship between autobiographical memory and perceptual learning. *J. Exp. Psychol.: Gen.* 110:306–40

Jacoby, L. L., Woloshyn, V., Kelley, C. 1989. Becoming famous without being recognized: unconscious influences of memory produced by dividing attention. *J. Exp. Psychol.: Gen.* 118:115–25

Janowsky, J. S., Shimamura, A. P., Squire, L. R. 1989. Source memory impairment in patients with frontal lobe lesions. *Neuropsychologia* 27:1043–56

Johnson, M. K., Foley, M. A., Suengas, A. G., Raye, C. L. 1988. Phenomenal characteristics of memories for perceived and imagined autobiographical events. *J. Exp. Psychol.: Gen.* 117:371–76

Johnson, M. K., Raye, C. L. 1981. Reality monitoring. *Psychol. Rev.* 88:67–85

Johnson, M. M. S., Schmitt, F. A., Pietrukowicz, M. 1989. The memory advantages of the generation effect: age and process differences. *J. Gerontol.: Psychol. Sci.* 44:P91–94

Jonides, J., Naveh-Benjamin, M. 1987. Estimating frequency of occurrence. *J. Exp. Psychol.: Learn., Mem., Cogn.*, 13:230–40

Kausler, D. H. 1990. Automaticity of encoding and episodic memory processes. See Cavanaugh & Green 1990, pp. 29–67

Kausler, D. H., Hakami, M. K., Wright, R. 1982. Adult age differences in frequency judgments of categorical representations. *J. Gerontol.* 37:365–71

Kausler, D. H., Lichty, W. 1988. Memory for

activities: rehearsal-independence and aging. See Howard 1988a, pp. 93–131.

Kausler, D. H., Lichty, W., Davis, T. M. 1985. Temporal memory for performed activities: intentionality and adult age differences. *Dev. Psychol.* 21:1132–38

Kausler, D. H., Lichty, W., Freund, J. S. 1985. Adult age differences in recognition memory and frequency judgments for planned versus performed activities. *Dev. Psychol.* 21:647–54

Kausler, D. H., Lichty, W., Hakami, M. K. 1984. Frequency judgments for distractor items in a short-term memory task: instructional variations and adult age differences. *J. Verb. Learn. Verb. Behav.* 23:660–68

Kausler, D. H., Puckett, J. M. 1980. Adult age differences in recognition memory for a nonsemantic attribute. *Exp. Aging Res.* 6:349–55.

Kausler, D. H., Puckett, J. M. 1981a. Adult age differences in memory for modality attributes. *Exp. Aging Res.* 7:117–25

Kausler, D. H., Puckett, J. M. 1981b. Adult age differences in memory for sex of voice. *J. Gerontol.* 36:44–50

Kausler, D. H., Salthouse, T. A., Saults, J. S. 1988. Temporal memory over the adult lifespan. *Am. J. Psychol.* 101:207–15

Kellas, G., Simpson, G., Ferraro, F. R. 1988. Aging and performance: a mental workload analysis. In *Psychology and Productivity,* ed. P. Whitney & R. B. Ochsman, pp. 35–49. New York: Plenum

Kemper, S. 1986. Imitation of complex syntactic constructions by elderly adults. *Appl. Psycholinguist.* 7:277–88

Kintsch, W. 1988. The role of knowledge in discourse comprehension: a construction-integration model. *Psychol. Rev.* 95:163–82

Kintsch, W., van Dijk, T. A. 1978. Toward a model of context comprehension and production. *Psychol. Rev.* 85:363–94

Kirasic, K. C. 1988. Aging and spatial cognition: current status and new directions for experimental researchers and cognitive neuropsychologists. In *Cognitive Approaches to Neuropsychology,* ed. J. M. Williams, C. J. Long, pp. 83–100. New York: Plenum

Kliegl, R., Lindenberger, U. 1988. *A mathematical model of proactive interferences in cues recall: localizing adult age differences in memory functions.* Paper presented at the Cognit. Aging Conf., Atlanta

Kliegl, R., Smith, J., Baltes, P. B. 1989. Testing-the-limits and the study of adult age differences in cognitive plasticity of a mnemonic skill. *Dev. Psychol.* 25:247–56

Koriat, A., Ben-Zur, H., Sheffer, D. 1988. Telling the same story twice: output monitoring and age. *J. Mem. Lang.* 27:23–39

Lachman, J. L., Lachman, R., Thronesbery, C. 1979. Metamemory through the adult life span. *Dev. Psychol.* 15:543–51

Lachman, M. E., Leff, R. 1989. Perceived control and intellectual functioning in the elderly: a 5-year longitudinal study. *Dev. Psychol.* 25:722–28

Lehman, E. B., Mellinger, J. C. 1984. Effects of aging on memory for presentation modality. *Dev. Psychol.* 20:1210–17

Lehman, E. B., Mellinger, J. C. 1986. Forgetting rates in modality memory for young, mid-life, and older women. *Psychol. Aging* 1:178–79

Light, L. L. 1988. Language and aging: competence versus performance. In *Emergent Theories of Aging,* ed. J. E. Birren, V. L. Bengtson, pp. 177–213. New York: Springer

Light, L. L., Albertson, S. 1988. Comprehension of pragmatic implications in young and older adults. See Burke & Harrold 1988, pp. 133–53

Light, L. L., Albertson, S. A. 1989. Direct and indirect tests of memory for category exemplars in young and older adults. *Psychol. Aging* 4:487–92

Light, L. L., Anderson, P. A. 1983. Memory for scripts in young and older adults. *Mem. Cogn.* 11:435–44

Light, L. L., Anderson, P. A. 1985. Working-memory capacity, age, and memory for discourse. *J. Gerontol.* 40:737–47

Light, L. L., Burke, D. M. 1988. Patterns of language and memory in old age. See Burke & Harrold 1988. pp. 244–71

Light, L. L., Capps, J. L. 1986. Comprehension of pronouns in young and older adults. *Dev. Psychol.* 22:580–85

Light, L. L., Singh, A. 1987. Implicit and explicit memory in young and older adults. *J. Exp. Psychol.: Learn., Mem., Cogn.* 13:531–41

Light, L. L., Singh, A., Capps, J. L. 1986. Dissociation of memory and awareness in young and older adults. *J. Clin. Exp. Neuropsychol.* 8:62–74

Light, L. L., Zelinski, E. M. 1983. Memory for spatial information in young and old adults. *Dev. Psychol.* 15:543–51

Light, L. L., Zelinski, E. M., Moore, M. 1982. Adult age differences in reasoning from new information. *J. Exp. Psychol.: Learn., Mem., Cogn.* 8:435–47

Loewen, E. R., Shaw, R. J., Craik, F. I. M. 1991. Age differences in components of metamemory. *Exp. Aging Res.* In press.

Lorsbach, T. C., Simpson, G. B. 1988. Dual-task performance as a function of adult age and task complexity. *Psychol. Aging* 3:210–12

Lovelace, E. A., Cooley, S. 1982. Free associations of older adults to single words and conceptually related word triads. *J. Gerontol.* 37:432–37

Lovelace, E. A., Marsh, G. R. 1985. Prediction and evaluation of memory performance by young and older adults. *J. Gerontol.* 40:192–97

Macht, M. L., Buschke, H. 1983. Age difference in cognitive effort in recall. *J. Gerontol.* 38:695–700

MacKay, D. G., Burke, D. M. 1990. Cognition and aging: a theory of new learning and the use of old connections. In *Aging and Cognition: Knowledge Organization and Utilization*, ed. T. M. Hess, pp. 213–64. Amsterdam: North Holland

Madden, D. J. 1986. Adult age differences in visual word recognition: semantic encoding and episodic retention. *Exp. Aging Res.* 12:71–77

Madden, D. J. 1987. Aging, attention, and the use of meaning during visual search. *Cognit. Dev.* 2:201–16

Madden, D. J. 1988. Adult age differences in the effects of sentence context and stimulus degradation during visual word recognition. *Psychol. Aging* 3:167–72

Madden, D. J. 1989. Visual word identification and age-related slowing. *Cognit. Dev.* 4:1–29

Madden, D. J., Blumenthal, J. A., Allen, P. A., Emery, C. F. 1989. Improving aerobic capacity in healthy older adults does not necessarily lead to improved cognitive performance. *Psychol. Aging* 4:307–20

Mandler, G. 1980. Recognizing: the judgment of previous occurrence. *Psychol. Rev.* 87:252–71

Maylor, E. A. 1990a. Age and prospective memory. *Q. J. Exp. Psychol.* 42A. In press

Maylor, E. A. 1990b. Recognizing and naming faces: aging, memory retrieval and the tip of the tongue state. *J. Gerontol.: Psychol. Sci.* In press

Mazzoni, G., Cornoldi, C., Marchitelli, G. 1990. Do memorability ratings affect study-time allocation? *Mem. Cogn.* 18:196–204

McClelland, J. L., Rumelhart, D. E. 1981. An interactive activation model of context effects in letter perception. Part 1. An account of basic findings. *Psychol. Rev.* 88:375–407

McCormack, P. D. 1981. Temporal coding by young and elderly adults: a test of the Hasher-Zacks model. *Dev. Psychol.* 17:509–15

McCormack, P. D. 1982a. Coding of spatial information by young and elderly adults. *J. Gerontol.* 37:80–86

McCormack, P. D. 1982b. Temporal coding and study-phase retrieval in young and elderly adults. *Bull. Psychonom. Soc.* 20:242–44

McCormack, P. D. 1984. Temporal coding by young and elderly in a list-discrimination setting. *Bull. Psychonom. Soc.* 22:401–2

McCrae, R. R., Arenberg, D., Costa, P. T. 1987. Declines in divergent thinking with age: cross-sectional, longitudinal, and cross-sequential analyses. *Psychol. Aging* 2:130–37

McDaniel, M. A., Ryan, E. B., Cunningham, C. J. 1989. Encoding difficulty and memory enhancement for young and old readers. *Psychol. Aging* 3:333–38

McDowd, J. M., Birren, J. E. 1990. Aging and attentional processes. See Cerella 1990. pp. 222–33

McDowd, J. M., Oseas, D. M. 1990. *Aging, inhibitory processes, and negative priming.* Paper presented at the Cognit. Aging Conf., Atlanta

McFarland, C. E. Jr., Warren, L. R., Crockard, J. 1985. Memory for self-generated stimuli in young and old adults. *J. Gerontol.* 40:205–7

McIntyre, J. S., Craik, F. I. M. 1987. Age differences in memory for item and source information. *Can. J. Psychol.* 41:175–92

Mitchell, D. B. 1989. How many memory systems? Evidence from aging. *J. Exp. Psychol.: Learn., Mem., Cogn.* 15:31–49

Mitchell, D. B., Brown, A. S., Murphy, D. R. 1990. Dissociations between procedural and episodic memory: effects of time and aging. *Psychol. Aging* 5:264–76

Mitchell, D. B., Hunt, R. R., Schmitt, F. A. 1986. The generation effect and reality monitoring: evidence from dementia and normal aging. *J. Gerontol.* 41:79–84

Mitchell, D. B., Perlmutter, M. 1986. Semantic activation and episodic memory: age similarities and differences. *Dev. Psychol.* 22:86–94

Morrell, R. W., Park, D. C., Poon, L. W. 1989. Quality of instructions on prescription drug labels: effects on memory and comprehension in young and old adults. *Gerontologist* 29:345–54

Morris, R. G., Craik, F. I. M., Gick, M. L. 1990. Age differences in working memory tasks: the role of secondary memory and the central executive. *Q. J. Exp. Psychol.* 41A:67–86

Morris, R. G., Gick, M. L., Craik, F. I. M. 1988. Processing resources and age differences in working memory. *Mem. Cogn.* 16:362–66

Moscovitch, M. 1982. A neuropsychological approach to perception and memory in normal and pathological aging. See Craik & Byrd 1982, pp. 55–78

Moscovitch, M., Winocur, G., McLachlin, D. 1986. Memory as assessed by recognition and reading time in normal and memory-impaired people with Alzheimer's disease and other neurological disorders. *J. Exp. Psychol.: Gen.* 115:331–46

Mueller, J. H., Kausler, D. H., Faherty, A., Oliveri, M. 1980. Reaction time as a function of age, anxiety, and typicality. *Bull. Psychonom. Soc.* 16:473–76

Mueller, J. H., Wonderlich, S., Dugan, K. 1986. Self-referent processing of age-specific material. *Psychol. Aging* 1:293–99

Murphy, M. D., Sanders, R. E., Gabriesheski, A. S., Schmitt, F. A. 1981. Metamemory in the aged. *J. Gerontol.* 36:185–93

Murphy, M. D., Schmitt, F. A., Caruso, M. J., Sanders, R. E. 1987. Metamemory in older adults: the role of monitoring in serial recall. *Psychol. Aging* 2:331–39

Myerson, J., Hale, S., Wagstaff, D., Poon, L. W., Smith, G. A. 1990. The information loss model: a mathematical theory of age-related cognitive slowing. *Psychol. Rev.* 97:

Naveh-Benjamin, M. 1987. Coding of spatial location information: an automatic process? *J. Exp. Psychol.: Learn., Mem., Cogn.* 13:595–605

Naveh-Benjamin, M. 1988. Recognition memory of spatial location information: another failure of automaticity. *Mem. Cogn.* 16:437–45

Naveh-Benjamin, M. 1990. Coding of temporal order information: an automatic process? *J. Exp. Psychol.: Learn., Mem., Cogn.* 16:117–26

Navon, D. 1984. Resources—a theoretical soup stone? *Psychol. Rev.* 91:216–34

Nebes, R. D., Boller, F., Holland, A. 1986. Use of semantic context by patients with Alzheimer's disease. *Psychol. Aging* 1:261–69

Nebes, R. D., Brady, C. B. 1988. Integrity of semantic fields in Alzheimer's disease. *Cortex* 24:291–99

Neely, J. H. 1977. Semantic priming and retrieval from lexical memory: roles of inhibitionless spreading activation and limited-capacity attention. *J. Exp. Psychol.: Gen.* 106:226–54

Nestor, P. G., Parasuraman, R., Haxby, J. V. 1989. Attentional costs of mental operations in young and old adults. *Dev. Neuropsychol.* 5:141–58

Nissen, M. J., Bullemer, P. 1987. Attentional requirements of learning: evidence from performance measures. *Cognit. Psychol.* 19:1–32

Obler, L. K., Albert, M. L. 1985. Language skills across adulthood. In *Handbook of the Psychology of Aging*, ed. J. E. Birren, K. W. Schaie, pp. 463–73. New York: Van Nostrand Reinhold. 2nd ed.

O'Brien, E. J., Schank, D. M., Myers, J. L.,

Rayner, K. 1988. Elaborative inferences during reading: Do they occur on-line? *J. Exp. Psychol.: Learn., Mem., Cogn.* 14:410–20

Paivio, A. 1971. *Imagery and Verbal Processes*. New York: Holt, Rinehart and Winston

Park, D. C., Puglisi, J. T. 1985. Older adults' memory for the color of pictures and words. *J. Gerontol.* 40:198–204

Park, D. C., Puglisi, J. T., Lutz, R. 1982. Spatial memory in older adults: effects of intentionality. *J. Gerontol.* 37:330–35

Park, D. C., Puglisi, J. T., Smith, A. D. 1986. Memory for pictures: Does an age-related decline exist? *Psychol. Aging* 1:11–17

Park, D. C., Puglisi, J. T., Smith, A. D., Dudley, W. N. 1987. Cue utilization and encoding specificity in picture recognition by older adults. *J. Gerontol.* 42:423–25

Park, D. C., Puglisi, J. T., Sovacool, M. 1983. Memory for pictures, words, and spatial location in older adults: evidence for pictorial superiority. *J. Gerontol.* 38:582–88

Park, D. C., Smith, A. D., Dudley, W. N., La Fronza, V. N. 1989. Effects of age and a divided attention task presented during encoding and retrieval on memory. *J. Exp. Psychol.: Learn., Mem., Cogn.* 15:1185–91

Parks, C. W. Jr., Mitchell, D. B., Perlmutter, M. 1986. Cognitive and social functioning across adulthood: age or student status differences? *Psychol. Aging* 1:248–54

Parkinson, S. R., Inman, V. W., Dannenbaum, S. E. 1985. Adult age differences in short-term forgetting. *Acta Psychol.* 60:83–101

Perlmutter, M. 1978. What is memory aging the aging of? *Dev. Psychol.* 14:330–45

Perlmutter, M. 1979. Age differences in adults' free recall, cued recall, and recognition. *J. Gerontol.* 34:533–39

Perlmutter, M., Metzger, R., Nezworski, T., Miller, K. 1981. Spatial and temporal memory in 20 and 60 year olds. *J. Gerontol.* 36:59–65

Perlmutter, M., Mitchell, D. B. 1982. The appearance and disappearance of age differences in adult memory. See Craik & Byrd 1982, pp. 127–44

Petros, T. V., Zehr, H. D., Chabot, R. J. 1983. Adult age differences in accessing and retrieving information from long-term memory. *J. Gerontol.* 38:589–92

Pezdek, K. 1983. Memory for items and their spatial locations by young and elderly adults. *Dev. Psychol.* 19:895–900

Plude, D. J., Doussard-Roosevelt, J. A. 1989. Aging, selective attention, and feature integration. *Psychol. Aging* 4:98–105

Poon, L. W. 1985. Differences in human memory with aging: nature, causes, and clinical implications. See Obler & Albert 1985, pp. 427–62

Pratt, M. W., Boyes, C., Robins, S., Manchester, J. 1989. Telling tales: aging, working memory, and the narrative cohesion of story retellings. Dev. Psychol. 25:628–35

Posner, M. I., Snyder, C. R. R. 1975. Attention and cognitive control. In Information Processing and Cognition, ed. A. Solso, pp. 55–85. Hillsdale, NJ: Erlbaum

Puglisi, J. T., Park, D. C. 1987. Perceptual elaboration and memory in older adults. J. Gerontol. 42:160–62

Puglisi, J. T., Park, D. C., Smith, A. D., Dudley, W. N. 1988. Age differences in encoding specificity. J. Gerontol.: Psychol. Sci. 43:P145–50

Puglisi, J. T., Park, D. C., Smith, A. D., Hill, G. W. 1985. Memory for two types of spatial location: effects of instructions, age, and format. Am. J. Psychol. 98:101–18

Rabbitt, P. 1989. Inner-city decay? Age changes in structure and process in recall of familiar topographical information. See Bäckman 1989, pp. 284–99

Rabbitt, P. M. A. 1982. How do old people know what to do next? See Craik & Byrd 1982, pp. 79–98

Rabbitt, P. M. A. 1984. How old people prepare themselves for events which they expect. See Craik & Rabinowitz 1984, pp. 515–527

Rabinowitz, J. C. 1984. Aging and recognition failure. J. Gerontol. 39:65–71

Rabinowitz, J. C. 1986. Priming in episodic memory. J. Gerontol. 41:204–13

Rabinowitz, J. C. 1989a. Age deficits in recall under optimal study conditions. Psychol. Aging 4:378–80

Rabinowitz, J. C. 1989b. Judgments of origin and generation effects: comparisons between young and elderly adults. Psychol. Aging 4:259–68

Rabinowitz, J. C., Ackerman, B. P., Craik, F. I. M., Hinchley, J. L. 1982. Aging and metamemory: the roles of relatedness and imagery. J. Gerontol. 37:688–95

Rabinowitz, J. C., Craik, F. I. M. 1986. Prior retrieval effects in young and older adults. J. Gerontol. 41:368–75

Rabinowitz, J. C., Craik, F. I. M., Ackerman, B. P. 1982. A processing resource account of age differences in recall. Can. J. Psychol. 36:325–44

Rankin, J. L., Firnhaber, S. 1986. Adult age differences in memory: effects of distinctive and common encodings. Exp. Aging Res. 12:141–46

Rankin, J. L., Hinrichs, J. V. 1983. Age, presentation rate, and the effectiveness of

structural and semantic cues. J. Gerontol. 38:593–96

Rebok, G. W., Balcerak, L. J. 1989. Memory self-efficacy and performance differences in young and old adults: the effect of mnemonic training. Dev. Psychol. 25:714–21

Rebok, G. W., Montaglione, C. J., Bendlin, G. 1988. Effects of age and training on memory for pragmatic implications in advertising. J. Gerontol: Psychol. Sci. 43:P75–78

Reder, L. M., Wible, C., Martin, J. 1986. Differential memory changes with age: exact retrieval versus plausible inference. J. Exp. Psychol.: Learn. Mem., Cogn. 12:72–81

Richardson-Klavehn, A., Bjork, R. A. 1988. Measures of memory. Annu. Rev. Psychol. 39:475–543

Rissenberg, M., Glanzer, M. 1986. Picture superiority in free recall: the effects of normal aging and primary degenerative dementia. J. Gerontol. 41:64–71

Roediger, H. L. III, Blaxton, T. A. 1987. Effects of varying modality, surface features, and retention interval on priming in word-fragment completion. Mem. Cogn. 15:379–88

Rogers, W. A., Fisk, A. D. 1990. A reconsideration of age-related reaction time slowing from a learning perspective: age-related slowing is not just complexity-based. Learn. Indiv. Diff. 2:161–79

Rogers, W. A., Fisk, A. D. 1991. Age-related differences in the maintenance and modification of automatic processes: arithmetic Stroop interference. Hum. Factors. In press

Rose, T. L., Yesavage, J. A., Hill, R. D., Bower, G. H. 1986. Priming effects and recognition memory in young and elderly adults. Exp. Aging Res. 12:31–37

Ross, B. L., Berg, C. A. 1991. Examining idiosyncracies in script reports across the life span: distortions or derivations of experience. See Hess 1991, In press

Rubin, D. C. 1985. Memorability as a measure of processing: a unit analysis of prose and list learning. J. Exp. Psychol.: Gen. 114:213–38

Salthouse, T. A. 1985a. A Theory of Cognitive Aging. Amsterdam: North-Holland

Salthouse, T. A. 1985b. Speed of behavior and its implications for cognition. See Obler & Albert 1985, pp. 400–26

Salthouse, T. A. 1987. Adult age differences in integrative spatial ability. Psychol. Aging 2:254–60

Salthouse, T. A. 1988a. Effects of aging on verbal abilities: examination of the psychometric literature. See Burke & Harrold 1988, pp. 17–35

Salthouse, T. A. 1988b. Initiating the formalization of theories of cognitive aging. *Psychol. Aging* 3:3–16

Salthouse, T. A. 1988c. Resource-reduction interpretations of cognitive aging. *Dev. Rev.* 8:238–72

Salthouse, T. A. 1988d. The role of processing resources in cognitive aging. See Howard 1988b, pp. 185–239

Salthouse, T. A. 1990. Working memory as a processing resource in cognitive aging. *Dev. Rev.* 10:101–24

Salthouse, T. A., Babcock, R. L., Skovronek, E., Mitchell, D. R. D., Palmon, R. 1990. Age and experience effects in spatial visualization. *Dev. Psychol.* 26:128–36

Salthouse, T. A., Kausler, D., Saults, J. S. 1988a. Investigation of student status, background variables, and feasibility of standard tasks in cognitive aging research. *Psychol. Aging* 3:29–37

Salthouse, T. A., Kausler, D. H., Saults, J. S. 1988b. Utilization of path-analytic procedures to investigate the role of processing resources in cognitive aging. *Psychol. Aging* 3:158–66

Salthouse, T. A., Lichty, W. 1985. Tests of the neural noise hypothesis of age-related cognitive change. *J. Gerontol.* 40:443–50

Salthouse, T. A., Mitchell, D. R. D. 1989. Structural and operational capacities in integrative spatial ability. *Psychol. Aging* 4:18–25

Salthouse, T. A., Mitchell, D. R. D., Palmon, R. 1989a. Memory and age differences in spatial manipulation ability. *Psychol. Aging* 4:480–86

Salthouse, T. A., Mitchell, D. R. D., Skovronek, E., Babcock, R. L. 1989b. Effects of adult age and working memory on reasoning and spatial abilities. *J. Exp. Psychol.: Learn., Mem., Cogn.* 15:507–16

Salthouse, T. A., Rogan, J. D., Prill, K. A. 1984. Division of attention: age differences on a visually presented memory task. *Mem. Cogn.* 12:613–20

Salthouse, T. A., Somberg, B. L. 1982. Skilled performance: effects of adult age and experience on elementary processes. *J. Exp. Psychol.: Gen.* 111:176–207

Sanders, R. E., Gonzalez, E. G., Murphy, M. D., Liddle, C. L., Vitina, J. R. 1987. Frequency of occurrence and the criteria for automatic processing. *J. Exp. Psychol.: Learn., Mem., Cogn.* 13:241–50

Scarborough, D. L., Cortese, C., Scarborough, H. S. 1977. Frequency and repetition effects in lexical memory. *J. Exp. Psychol.: Hum. Percept. Perform.* 3:1–17

Sharps, M. J., Gollin, E. S. 1987. Memory for object locations in young and elderly adults. *J. Gerontol.* 42:336–41

Schacter, D. L., Graf, P. 1986. Preserved learning in amnesic patients: perspectives from research on direct priming. *J. Clin. Exp. Neuropsychol.* 6:727–43

Scialfa, C. T., Margolis, R. B. 1986. Age differences in the commonality of free associations. *Exp. Aging Res.* 12:95–98

Shaw, R. T., Craik, F. I. M. 1989. Age differences in predictions and performance on a cued recall task. *Psychol. Aging* 4:131–35

Shimamura, A. P., Squire, L. R. 1989. Impaired priming of new associations in amnesia. *J. Exp. Psychol.: Learn., Mem., Cogn.* 15:721–28

Sinnott, J. D. 1986. Prospective/intentional and incidental everyday memory: effects of age and passage of time. *Psychol. Aging* 1:110–16

Solomon, P. R., Pomerleau, D., Morse, D. L., Bennett, L., James, J. 1989. Acquisition of the classically conditioned eyeblink response in humans over the life span. *Psychol. Aging* 4:34–41

Somberg, B. L., Salthouse, T. A. 1982. Divided-attention abilities in young and old adults. *J. Exp. Psychol.: Hum. Percep. Perform.* 8:651–63

Spilich, G. J. 1983. Life-span components of text processing: structural and procedural differences. *J. Verb. Learn. Verb. Behav.* 22:231–44

Squire, L. R. 1987. *Memory and Brain*. New York: Oxford Univ. Press

Stine, E. L., Wingfield, A. 1987. Process and strategy in memory for speech among younger and older adults. *Psychol. Aging* 2:272–79

Stine, E. A. L., Wingfield, A. 1988. Memorability functions as an indicator of qualitative age differences in text recall. *Psychol. Aging* 3:179–83

Stine, E. A. L., Wingfield, A., Myers, S. D. 1990. Age differences in processing information from television news: the effects of bisensory augmentation. *J. Gerontol.: Psychol. Sci.,* 45:P1–8

Stine, E. L., Wingfield, A., Poon, L. W. 1986. How much and how fast: rapid processing of spoken language in later adulthood. *Psychol. Aging* 1:303–11

Strayer, D. L., Wickens, C. D., Braune, R. 1987. Adult age differences in the speed and capacity of information processing. 2. An electrophysiological approach. *Psychol. Aging* 2:99–110

Tanenhaus, M. K., Dell, G. S., Carlson, G. 1987. Context effects and lexical processing: a connectionist approach to modularity. In *Modularity in Knowledge Representation and Natural-Language Understanding*, ed. J. L. Garfield, pp. 83–110. Cambridge, MA: MIT Press

Thomson, D. M., Tulving, E. 1970. Associative encoding and retrieval: weak and strong cues. *J. Exp. Psych.* 86:255–62

Till, R. E. 1985. Verbatim and inferential memory in young and elderly adults. *J. Gerontol.* 40:316–23

Till, R. E., Walsh, D. A. 1980. Encoding and retrieval factors in adult memory for implicational sentences. *J. Verb. Learn. Verb. Behav.* 19:1–16

Tulving, E. 1972. Episodic and semantic memory. In *Organization of Memory*, ed. E. Tulving, W. Donaldson, pp. 382–403. New York: Academic

Tulving, E. 1983. *Elements of Episodic Memory.* Oxford: Clarendon Press

Tulving, E. 1985. How many memory systems are there? *Am. Psychol.* 40:385–98

Tulving, E., Schacter, D. L. 1990. Priming and human memory systems. *Science* 247:301–6

Tulving, E., Schacter, D. L., Stark, H. A. 1982. Priming effects in word-fragment completion are independent of recognition memory. *J. Exp. Psychol.: Learn., Mem., Cogn.* 8:336–42

Tun, P. A. 1989. Age differences in processing expository and narrative text. *J. Gerontol.: Psychol. Sci.* 44:P9–15

Turner, M. L., Engle, R. W. 1989. Is working memory capacity task dependent? *J. Mem. Lang.* 28:127–54

Van Dijk, T. A., Kintsch, W. 1983. *Strategies of Discourse Comprehension.* New York: Academic

Van Gorp, W., Satz, P., Kiersch, M. E., Henry, R. 1986. Normative data on the Boston Naming Test for a group of normal older adults. *J. Clin. Exp. Neuropsychol.* 8:702–5

Waddell, K. J., Rogoff, B. 1981. Effect of contextual organization on spatial memory of middle-aged and older women. *Dev. Psychol.* 17:878–85

Waugh, N. C., Fozard, J. L., Thomas, J. C. 1978. Retrieval time from different memory stores. *J. Gerontol.* 33:718–24

Welford, A. T. 1985. Practice effects in relation to age: a review and a theory. *Dev. Neuropsychol.* 1:173–90

West, R. L. 1986. Everyday memory and aging. *Dev. Neuropsychol.* 2:323–44

West, R. L., Cohen, S. L. 1985. The systematic use of semantic and acoustic processing by younger and older adults. *Exp. Aging Res.* 11:81–86

Wickens, C. D., Braune, R., Stokes, A. 1987. Age differences in the speed and capacity of information processing. 1. A dual-task approach. *Psychol. Aging* 2:70–78

Williams, S. A., Denney, N. W., Schadler,

M. 1983. Elderly adults' perception of their own cognitive development during the adult years. *Int. J. Aging Hum. Dev.* 16:147–58

Wingfield, A., Lahar, C. J., Stine, E. A. L. 1989. Age and decision strategies in running memory for speech: effects of prosody and linguistic structure. *J. Gerontol.: Psychol. Sci.* 44:P106–13

Wingfield, A., Poon, L. W., Lombardi, L., Lowe, D. 1985. Speed of processing in normal aging: effects of speech rate, linguistic structure, and processing time. *J. Gerontol.* 40:579–85

Wingfield, A., Stine, E. A. L., Lahar, C. J., Aberdeen, J. S. 1988. Does the capacity of working memory change with age? *Exp. Aging Res.* 14:103–7

Woodruff-Pak, D. S., Thompson, R. F. 1988. Classical conditioning of the eyeblink response in the delay paradigm in adults aged 18–83 years. *Psychol. Aging* 3:219–29

Wright, B. M., Payne, R. B. 1985. Effects of aging on sex differences in psychomotor reminiscence and tracking proficiency. *J. Gerontol.* 40:179–84

Zabrucky, K., Moore, D., Schultz, N. R. Jr. 1987. Evaluation of comprehension in young and old adults. *Dev. Psychol.* 23:39–43

Zacks, R. T., Hasher, L. 1988. Capacity theory and the processing of inferences. See Burke & Harrold 1988, pp. 154–70

Zacks, R. T., Hasher, L., Doren, B., Hamm, V., Attig, M. S. 1987. Encoding and memory of explicit and implicit information. *J. Gerontol.* 42:418–22

Zelinski, E. M. 1988. Integrating information from discourse: Do older adults show deficits? See Burke & Harrold 1988, pp. 117–32

Zelinski, E. M., Gilewski, M. J. 1988a. Assessment of memory complaints by rating scales and questionnaires. *Psychopharmacol. Bull.* 24:523–29

Zelinski, E. M., Gilewski, M. J. 1988b. Memory for prose and aging: a meta-analysis. See Howard 1988b, pp. 134–58

Zelinski, E. M., Gilewski, M. J., Anthony-Bergstone, C. R. 1990. The Memory Functioning Questionnaire: Concurrent validity with memory performance and self-reported memory failures. *Psychol. Aging.* 5:388–99

Zelinski, E. M., Light, L. L. 1988. Young and older adults' use of context in spatial memory. *Psychol. Aging* 13:99–101

Zelinski, E. M., Miura, S. A. 1988. Anaphor comprehension in young and older adults. *Psychol. Aging* 3:292–99

Annu. Rev. Psychol. 1991. 42:377–99

SOCIAL MOTIVATION

Russell G. Geen

Department of Psychology, University of Missouri, Columbia, Missouri 65211

KEY WORDS: anxiety, evaluation apprehension, social facilitation, social loafing

CONTENTS

INTRODUCTION

"Failure," Ruskin (1907/1963) observed, "is less frequently attributable to either insufficiency of means or impatience of labor, than to a confused understanding of the thing actually to be done" (p. 1). This maxim may be taken as a word of advice to anyone writing a review on social motivation at the end of the 1980s. At present, definition of the subject to be reviewed is not a simple matter. During the decade just ended, three reviews bearing the title "Social Motivation" appeared in the *Annual Review of Psychology,* and each differed considerably from the others in scope and emphasis. In addition, motivation was not a popular construct among theorists of social behavior during the 1980s. It was, in fact, seldom identified, even as its effects were described. Instead, motivational processes often had to be inferred from

0066-4308/91/0201-0377$02.00

specific behaviors—such as self-presentation, maintenance of self-esteem, and attributional strategies—that are more customarily explained in terms not of motivation, but of cognition.

In delineating the subject of this review an admittedly arbitrary approach was adopted for the sake of clarity. First, the conditions of social motivation were defined as those in which the person is in direct contact with another person or a group of other persons, such as an audience, a group of coactors, or a partner in interaction. Second, the effect of the social presence was defined as nondirective; the social entity does not provide specific cues to the individual about how to act in the situation. For example, direct social influence, persuasion, or attempts at attitude modification fall outside the present definition of a social motivational phenomenon. Third, this socially engendered effect on the individual is considered an intrapsychic state capable of initiating and/or intensifying behavior.

Given these definitions, there exists a circumscribed literature on what appears to be an implicit need of individuals to avoid criticism or negative evaluation by others when the others are in a position to exercise judgment. This literature describes the study of two of social psychology's oldest problems—social facilitation and the loss of individual motivation in groups, often called the Ringelmann effect. It can be argued that this evaluation apprehension is derived from a more basic motive of individuals to present themselves to others in such a way that a favorable impression is created and approval is obtained. Failure to elicit a desired impression results in both a state of negative affect and self-defensive behaviors. It can be argued further that the self-presentation motive is a facet of a still more basic need for inclusion and for role fulfillment within society. Viewed in this way the specific topics of this review—social facilitation, social loafing, and social anxiety—represent more than just three subjects that commanded interest in the late 1980s; they constitute in addition three aspects of a larger and broader discussion of the fundamental bases of social motivation.

SOCIAL FACILITATION

The study of the social facilitation of individual behavior has undergone considerable change since Zajonc revived interest in it in 1965. This interest reached its peak during the mid-1970s. In the 12 years between Zajonc's paper and the review by Geen & Gange (1977), most of the theories of social facilitation still extant were formulated. To understand the changes that have come about in thinking on social facilitation since 1977 it is necessary to note that theoretical explanations have generally involved two sequential steps. The first we may call the impact of the presence of others on the person, which creates an intrapsychic state that mediates subsequent behavior. The second is some intervening process animated by that state, which leads to the facilitation effect. In terms of the drive-arousal hypothesis that dominated early research, the first step was expressed in the proposition that the presence of others increases arousal. The second step, agreed upon by all investigators working within the drive-theoretical tradition, consisted of the multiplication of drive with habit strength to increase response potential. As Geen & Gange observed in 1977, this rationale accounted for most of the findings at that time. More recent approaches to social facilitation continue to describe both the initial impact of social presence and processes produced by that impact. The conceptual language, however, now goes beyond that of drive theory.

The Arousal Hypothesis

MERE PRESENCE AND EVALUATION APPREHENSION   Discussions of the nature of the impact of social settings on individuals once revolved almost exclusively around the question of whether others could arouse the individual by their "mere presence" or whether they had to be regarded by the person as potential evaluators of performance. This matter is still being investigated. Guerin (1986) reviewed all studies purporting to investigate social facilitation and isolated 287 that did not involve imitation, group discussion, or social reinforcement. A further refinement left 85 studies that contrasted the behavior of subjects working alone with that of subjects in the presence of a "passive, nondirective other." Finally, the application of several additional criteria designed to rule out the possibility of evaluation of the subject, either implicit or explicit, left only 13 studies that provided adequate tests of the "mere-presence" hypothesis. Guerin conducted three reviews. Analysis of the 13 studies of the mere-presence effect revealed that such an effect is found only when the presence of the other person creates uncertainty in the subject. In some studies the behavior of the other person is unpredictable; in others the person's behavior is predictable but the person cannot be monitored. This conclusion supports both the monitoring theory of social facilitation proposed by Guerin & Innes (1982) and Zajonc's (1980) suggestion that the mere presence of others elevates drive level by creating uncertainty.

Guerin's subsequent reviews covered studies in which either another person observed the subject or the experimenter was present with the subject. In both cases the social-facilitation effect was found in a predominance of studies, and it was especially robust when the experimenter was perceived to be an evaluator of the subject's performance. These conclusions therefore support the theory that the social-facilitation effect is associated with increased apprehension in anticipation of negative outcomes (Geen & Gange 1977). Guerin concludes that at least two social-facilitation phenomena have been shown. One is linked to threat, personal space, and defense; the other is associated with seeking and maintaining social approval.

PRIOR EXPECTANCIES OF SUCCESS AND FAILURE   The hypothesis that social facilitation is a product of evaluation apprehension has been supported by studies showing that prior experiences of success and failure affect performance during observation by an audience. Early studies (e.g. Geen 1979) showed that observation was associated with poor performance on complex tasks only when the subject had first experienced failure. In an experiment by Sanna & Shotland (1990), subjects who were first given a success experience and then observed subsequently performed better on a complex task than did subjects who had first succeeded and then performed alone. In addition, subjects who had first failed and were then observed performed more poorly than control subjects who performed alone without a prior success or failure experience. The social-facilitation effect was therefore found to be related to expectancies of negative evaluation but not to expectancies of positive evaluation (cf Geen & Gange, 1977).

EFFECTS OF GROUP SIZE   In a series of studies, Seta and his associates have investigated the effects on performance of varying the size and composition of audiences. The results of these investigations support the hypothesis that social-facilitation effects are mediated by evaluation apprehension. This line of research poses the question of what happens when additional persons are added to an observing and potentially evaluative audience. Seta and his associates have proposed that the overall effects of such additions on subsequent evaluation apprehension involve both averaging and summative processes. In a task situation the overall level of apprehension is a function of both the subject's initial level of concern over performance and the amount of concern introduced by the presence of spectators. The addition of an observer will increase evaluation apprehension if the amount of subjective concern associated with that person exceeds the weighted average of concern associated initially with the task and that associated with previously existing observers. If concern over an additional observer is less than that weighted average, evaluation apprehension should be reduced by the addition. In both cases an averaging process predicts the outcome. In a study designed to test the averaging hypothesis, Seta et al (1989b) found that an audience comprised of four persons of high status led to greater anxiety than one comprised of two high-status persons, whereas an audience of two high- and two low-status persons produced less anxiety than one comprised of just two high-status observers. This outcome is consistent with the assumption that evaluation-apprehension effects due to the status of the observers average as the number of observers is increased. Seta et al (1989a) found that errors on a difficult paired-associates learning task were reduced when a low-status observer was added to one of high status, a finding consistent with the evaluation-apprehension approach to social facilitation.

Seta et al (1989a) have also shown that effects of increasing group size may be summative when more than a few persons are added. In the first of two experiments they showed that ratings of anxiety were reduced when two persons of low status joined two of high status in an audience, whereas anxiety was not significantly reduced when two low-status people joined two of intermediate status. These outcomes are consistent with the averaging hypothesis. In the second experiment it was found that adding two low-status members to two of high status again reduced anxiety but that adding 32 low-status members increased anxiety above that experienced in the presence of two high-status persons.

PHYSIOLOGICAL AROUSAL   The several versions of the drive theory of social facilitation all assume that the presence of others is associated with increased levels of arousal. However, Geen & Bushman (1989) reviewed studies designed to test this assumption and concluded that the evidence for it is weak. The measure most often cited in support of the arousal hypothesis is palmar sweat, but studies using this measure may be open to criticism on methodological grounds. Moreover, studies in which arousal is inferred from tonic electrodermal measures provide little support for the hypothesis that the presence of others is arousing. What support can be marshaled for the hypothesis is limited to studies of phasic skin-conductance responses. Finally, the evidence from cardiovascular studies does not reveal a consistent relationship between the presence of others and increases in heart rate.

DISTRACTION   For several years the work of Baron and his colleagues has shown that socially engendered arousal may be to some extent a function of distraction while the subject attempts to perform a task. The most recent evidence for this hypothesis has been reviewed by both Baron (1986) and Geen (1989). It must be concluded that distraction, uncertainty, and evaluation apprehension are all possible consequences of social settings and that all may be antecedents of arousal. It is possible, of course, that being distracted during the performance of a task, especially one in which the person is highly involved, may cause increased anxiety if the person believes that the distraction could bring about failure. In a similar way, uncertainty about the behavior of others can be a source of anxiety if the others are thought to be possible sources of disapproval or threat of rejection. Social monitoring may represent a search for cues of approval or disapproval from observers.

SELF-PRESENTATION   The argument that social-facilitation effects can reflect subjects' needs to present a desired self-image to other people has been put forth by several theorists (e.g. Baumeister 1982; Bond 1982). Geen (1989) has reviewed several studies that implicate self-presentation motives as important mediators of the social-facilitation effect. In these studies, the most important consequence of the audience or coaction situation is not the energization of responses but how the social setting influences the behaviors aimed at either making a good impression or avoiding a bad one. Such findings may be adduced as evidence against the arousal hypothesis of social facilitation, but they are not necessarily antithetical to that position. Evaluation apprehension, which plays a major role in social facilitation, may be a product of the self-presentation process. Baumeister (1982) asserts that the desire to make a good impression is a fundamental motive and that fear of negative evaluation arises when the person has some concern over being able to present the self adequately. Thus, the argument that social facilitation involves self-presentation motives is not necessarily an alternative to the arousal hypothesis.

CONCLUSION   From the foregoing, we may conclude that arousal is still to be considered an important intervening variable in social facilitation but that arousal should now be thought of more as an aversive affective state than as physiological activation. Moreover, such arousal is at least to some degree a consequence of apprehension over being evaluated by others. This latter state, in turn, arises from a more fundamental need to present the self to others in such a way that a desired impression will be made. (The basis for this self-presentational need is discussed below.) It should be emphasized that distraction, uncertainty, and evaluation apprehension may all occur in social settings. Furthermore, all may be precursors of socially engendered arousal and all may be associated with anxiety. Which process predominates may be determined by specific conditions.

Attentional Effects in Social Facilitation

DISTRACTION AND COGNITIVE OVERLOAD   In a major review, Baron (1986) has made a significant departure from the position that he and his colleagues took in the past. Whereas Baron formerly considered distraction-engendered conflict to be a source of drive, he now (1986) defines it as a condition for cognitive overload. This shift in theoretical emphasis is due in part to the lack of evidence linking social presence to physiological arousal and in part to the desirability of relating distraction-conflict theory to other topics in distraction research, such as persuasion. The attentional conflict produced by distraction places demands on the person that may exceed the person's finite attentional capacity. It is assumed that as demands for attention increase, less capacity remains for other activities such as problem solving.

One immediate consequence of an overtaxed attentional system is a selective narrowing of attention to a small number of central stimuli. This reduction of the range of cue utilization, described by several writers (e.g. Geen

1980), represents the creation of a system of attentional priorities caused by a breakdown in parallel processing. The person must attend to a few stimuli at a time because the ability to process several alternative inputs has been momentarily disrupted. Reduction in the range of stimuli to which the person attends has effects on performance similar to those hitherto attributed to increased drive. Simple tasks require attention to a small number of central cues, whereas complex tasks demand attention to a wide range of cues. If we assume that stimulus overload motivates elimination of cues over a given range regardless of whether the task is simple or complex, it should terminate attention to irrelevant distractors when the task is easy but cause interference with important task-related stimuli when the problem is more complex. The consequence for behavior is improvement of performance on the simple task (through elimination of distractors) but impairment of performance on the complex task (because of diminished attention to central cues).

AROUSAL AND COGNITIVE OVERLOAD   Geen (1989), while agreeing with Baron on the importance of attentional factors in social facilitation, does not in the process reject the arousal hypothesis. Geen (1989) noted that one version of the attentional approach to social facilitation includes the premise that attentional overload is arousing and that selective attention is a means of reducing this aversive state (e.g. Hockey 1979). The outcome of any of the conditions linked to arousal—evaluation apprehension and uncertainty, as well as distraction—may be cognitive overload and the corresponding restriction of attention.

Two recent studies suggest that audience presence can influence attentional processes related to utilization or organization of information. In one, Seta et al (1988) gave subjects a list of words to be sorted into categories. Subjects worked either alone or before a one-way mirror behind which an audience of five people supposedly sat. Relative to subjects who worked alone, those who had been informed that they were being observed showed less shared-feature clustering in free recall, even though the amount recalled in both conditions was the same. The presence of the audience apparently diminished available processing resources and thereby reduced the likelihood of organizational processing.

The results of a study by Cacioppo et al (1990) indicate that mere observation produces increased arousal only in response to some change in the environment. Skin conductance and heart rate were monitored in female subjects as they sat passively. Half were led to believe that they could be observed by the experimenter and half that they could not be observed. Following the baseline measurement period a series of ten orienting tones was presented. Being observed had no effect on the subjects' heart rates or skin conductance levels during the baseline period. Observed subjects did, however, show skin conductance responses of greater magnitude to the first tone of the series than did nonobserved subjects. This effect of observation on the conductance response habituated quickly across trials. The Cacioppo et al (1990) experiment suggests that mere observation may facilitate an electrodermal response to environmental change. Exactly how this happens cannot be determined from the data of this single exploratory study. Being observed may influence attention to stimuli in the ways suggested above. If observed subjects experience a narrowed range of attention, they may be less distracted by peripheral stimuli than unobserved subjects, and consequently more likely to attend to the initial orienting tone.

SOCIAL LOAFING

An apparent loss of motivation in groups, first noted by Ringelmann in 1913 (see Kravitz & Martin 1986), has been labelled *social loafing* in a series of experiments by Latané and his associates. In general, these studies have shown that individual output in a wide variety of tasks decreases as the number of persons in the group is increased. Early tests of the loafing phenomenon involved simple physical acts such as shouting and clapping individually or in groups (Latané et al 1979). Subsequent studies have shown considerable generality of the effect, with loafing occurring in such outcomes as ratings of the quality of written material (Petty et al 1980), maze performance (Jackson & Williams 1985), creativity (Harkins & Jackson 1985), vigilance (Harkins 1987), thought listing (Brickner et al 1986), swimming (Williams et al 1989), and cognitive judgments (Weldon & Gargano 1988). The data on social loafing are consistent with one of the major premises of social impact theory (Latané & Nida 1980; Jackson 1987): When a person is a member of a group subjected to social forces, the impact of those forces on each person in the group is diminished in inverse proportion to the strength (e.g. status, power), immediacy, and number of persons in the group. The exact form of the functional relationship is an inverse power function having an exponent with a value of less than one.

Causes of Social Loafing

OUTPUT EQUITY   From a number of studies addressed to the question of why social loafing occurs, three explanations have emerged. One is that subjects adjust their outputs to what they perceive to be the output of others in the group and try to achieve a level of equity. This explanation is based on the assumption that subjects in groups expect their partners to loaf and hence loaf themselves rather than put out an unequitable amount of effort. The results of an experiment by Jackson & Harkins (1985) show this effect. Subjects manifested social loafing by shouting more when alone than when in pairs only when they had no information concerning their partners' intended level of effort. When informed that the partner intended to expend either a high or a low amount of effort on the task, subjects likewise expended high or low levels of effort, respectively. The findings of Jackson & Harkins (1985) may represent a case of social comparison, in that the partner's behavior may provide information about the level of effort that is normal in an otherwise ambiguous situation. Alternatively, they may show the operation of what Kerr (1983) has called the "sucker effect": A subject may believe working vigorously while the other does not looks foolish.

EVALUATION APPREHENSION   Another explanation of social loafing is that the desire to loaf is a response to tasks that are tiring, uninteresting, or otherwise not likely to engage the subject's involvement, and that loafing will occur unless social constraints against it are implemented. Kerr & Bruun (1981) have labeled this the "hide-in-the-crowd" explanation, indicating that the presence of group members provides a cover of anonymity for the unmotivated individual. This cover is facilitated by the usual practice in loafing experiments of pooling the subjects' outputs. It would follow that any treatment designed to remove anonymity and make the individual's performance observable would reduce social loafing. Such a treatment was used by Williams et al (1981), who found that when subjects were told that individual responses could be identified they shouted as much in groups as they did when alone.

Making the subject's responses identifiable introduces the possibility that subjects become apprehensive about being evaluated by the experimenter, and that this is why they do not loaf under nonanonymous conditions. This should be especially true when subjects also believe that their responses are being compared to the responses of their coactors, so that they are effectively in competition with the others. Harkins & Jackson (1985) tested this idea by manipulating identifiability and evaluation potential separately; the former was done through use of either pooled or individual data, and the latter by having subjects and coactors work on either the same or different tasks. The task was a commonly used "creativity" task: to generate as many uses as possible for common objects. All subjects worked in groups of four persons. The results indicated that subjects who worked on the same task as did the others and whose output was individually identifiable generated more uses for the objects than did subjects in all other conditions. The condition designed to create evaluation apprehension thus facilitated the emission of responses in the context of a small group.

As noted above, the tasks used in social loafing studies may be intrinsically uninteresting—i.e. subjects are not motivated to expend much effort on them. If experiments involve tasks that engage the interest or concern of the subject, a necessary condition for social loafing should be absent and the effect should not be found. Brickner et al (1986) found evidence supporting this conclusion. Subjects, all of whom were college students, were instructed to list their thoughts about the implementation of general comprehensive examinations as a requirement for graduation. A high level of involvement was created in some subjects by telling them such exams were planned for their school in the coming semester; other subjects were told either that the exams would be started later or that they were under consideration at another school. In addition, the thoughts listed by each subject were either separately identifiable or pooled with those of other subjects. Brickner and her colleagues (1986) found that when the topic was introduced with the less involving instructions, subjects generated fewer thoughts when responses were pooled than when they were identifiable, thus replicating the social loafing effect. However, when the topic was made more involving, no differences in thought listing were found as a function of identifiability. Social loafing was therefore eliminated through use of an involving task but was observed when the situation provided neither a source of intrinsic motivation nor an external constraint against loafing.

That evaluation apprehension serves as a powerful motivator of behavior is not surprising, as the research on social facilitation has shown. Harkins (1987) has argued that the coaction model in social-facilitation studies and the social-loafing model actually represent two sets of comparisons within a single two-dimensional model defined by the variables Evaluation Apprehension and Coaction. Social loafing is described by Harkins as an evaluation-apprehension effect within a coaction setting. Four conditions can occur: subject alone, evaluated (A/E); coactors present, evaluated (C/E); subject alone, not evaluated (A/NE); and coactors present, not evaluated (C/NE). Noting that most coaction experiments in the tradition of social-facilitation research involve a covert element of evaluation potential (cf Geen et al 1988), Harkins describes such experiments as comparisons between the A/E and the C/E conditions. For reasons noted above, he defines social loafing experiments as comparisons between the C/E and the C/NE conditions. The true A/NE condition is relatively rare in studies of social motivation.

If one assumes that motivation to perform varies from low to moderate to high as a function of evaluation and coaction, then a study implementing this design would yield two main effects and no interaction. In two experiments in which subjects worked either alone or in the presence of a coactor and in which subjects' responses were either identifiable or pooled, Harkins (1987) found main effects for coaction and identifiability, and no interaction. This finding is therefore consistent with Harkins's hypothesis that social loafing is a case of the evaluation apprehension effect (cf Harkins & Szymanski 1987).

Evaluation apprehension has been linked, at least theoretically, to the concept of drive in the literature on social facilitation (Geen 1989). If absence of evaluation apprehension is what characterizes the social loafing effect, this effect should be accompanied by relatively low drive. Jackson & Williams (1985) found that identifiability of responses inhibited performance on a difficult task but tended to facilitate performance on a difficult task among subjects who worked in pairs. Subjects whose responses could be identified in this coaction setting also performed worse than subjects who worked alone when difficult mazes were given, but performed better than lone subjects on easy mazes. The latter finding replicates the social-facilitation effect associated with drive. The authors concluded that social loafing is associated with decreased drive. Results essentially comparable to those of Jackson & Williams, in that they also suggest arousal reduction under conditions of social loafing, have been reported by Griffith et al (1989).

A study by Bartis et al (1988) found results consistent with the drive-theoretical conclusions of Jackson & Williams. In addition to counting the total number of uses for objects generated on the creativity task described above, these investigators also obtained ratings from judges of the creativity of the uses produced. Under conditions where each individual's product could be identified, subjects generated more responses than under conditions when responses were pooled, but these responses were rated as less creative. Increased drive, by energizing dominant responses at the expense of subordinate (but possibly more creative) ones, would be expected to have this effect.

MATCHING TO STANDARD   The third and most recent explanation of social loafing is that such behavior occurs when some standard of performance is absent. Studies conducted since Harkins's 1987 paper indicate that apprehension over evaluation by others may be only one of a larger class of explanations of social loafing subsumed by the concept of matching-to-standard. The findings of these studies show that even in the absence of cues for evaluation by the experimenter, social loafing may be eliminated by the invocation of salient standards of comparison to the subjects' output. In the first of two experiments, Szymanski & Harkins (1987) gave subjects, who were run individually, the task of listing uses for objects, with instructions that the outputs would be either identifiable or pooled with those of other participants. Within each condition, half the subjects were informed of the "average number of uses generated by students in [previous] research," whereas the other half were told that the standard could not be revealed. Even when responses were pooled, subjects who had been given a standard for performance showed no evidence of loafing, reporting as many object uses as did subjects whose responses could be identified. The findings of the second experiment replicated those of the first and showed in addition that subjects who did not learn of the standard generated as few uses as those to whom no standard had even been mentioned. The latter condition is typical of those used in previous loafing experiments. In general, therefore, the explicit statement of a performance standard was sufficient to eliminate social loafing.

Giving subjects a standard based on the previous performance of others actually introduces two possible incentives. One is to appraise exactly how well they (i.e. the subjects) are performing, and the other is to perform better than others who have done the task. Goethals & Darley (1987) have named these incentives, respectively, self-knowledge and self-validation. Subjects in the Szymanski & Harkins (1987) study may have been motivated by either or both of these incentives. In a subsequent experiment, Harkins & Szymanski (1988) manipulated an objective standard of performance rather than a social one, so that subjects could obtain self-knowledge but not self-validation. A visual signal-detection task was used, with subjects' responses either monitored or not monitored by the experimenter. Half the subjects were given feedback concerning their detection accuracy and half were not; half the subjects were informed how many signals would be presented, and half were not. The latter manipulation thus instituted an objective standard for half the subjects.

Harkins & Szymanski (1988) found, as expected, that when the experimenter could monitor subjects' performance, the error rate was uniformly low, regardless of whether or not feedback and a standard were provided. The unique finding of the study was that subjects who were not monitored but were given the performance standard committed as few errors as those who were monitored. This was true, moreover, whether or not they received feedback about how well or poorly they were performing. Merely having the opportunity to match an objective standard was sufficiently motivating for subjects to eliminate errors, even if they had no way of knowing how closely their performance matched that standard. This finding does not demonstrate that subjects were motivated by a desire for self-knowledge, because without feedback self-knowledge was impossible. Instead it appears to show that subjects are motivated by the *salience* of certain standards in the situation, and that reminders of such standards may be adequate to arouse recognition of salient goals. Raising the possibility of comparing one's work to a self-standard also introduces the possibility of self-evaluation, which has been shown to elicit evaluation anxiety (Leary et al 1986a). It is possible, therefore, that introducing a standard of comparison, either personal or social, reduces social loafing by increasing evaluation apprehension.

In a major extension of the theory of social comparisons, Goethals & Darley (1987) have also proposed that such comparisons may also be made at the level of the group rather than the individual. Following Tajfel & Turner's (1986) premise that a positive social identity may be attained through membership in a successful group, these theorists have proposed that persons are motivated to seek information about group performance. Harkins & Szymanski (1989) have applied this reasoning to the social-loafing model by hypothesizing that loafing may be eliminated not only through establishment of personal and social standards, but also through making salient the standard for the group. Subjects working in groups of three at either a signal-detection task or generation of uses for objects were told either that they would or would not be given information about how well their group had performed. For both tasks, the provision of a group standard of comparison eliminated social loafing in much the same way as provision of individual standards had done in earlier studies cited above.

Related Concepts

Social loafing is similar in some ways to two other phenomena found in the literature on group motivation losses. These are the *free rider* and *sucker* effects (e.g. Kerr 1983). Free-riding occurs when each member of a group perceives that there is a high probability that some other member will solve the problem at hand and that the benefits from the other's performance will accrue to all members. Given this perception, each person concludes that his or her output is dispensable, and exerts little effort as a result. As the size of the group increases, the probability likewise increases that someone else in the group will solve the problem. Thus dispensability of individual effort increases with group size. The sucker effect describes motivation loss among group members who imagine that others in the group are free-riding. Rather than exert effort while others do not, the person achieves a sort of equity by reducing his or her output.

Conclusions

Social loafing is usually discussed as a phenomenon of motivation loss in groups. However, recent evidence, especially that from the programmatic studies of Harkins and his colleagues, suggests another interpretation. Social loafing may be due not so much to a group-engendered loss of motivation as to the facilitation of performance decrements motivated by other conditions. For various reasons individuals may not be motivated to exert effort on a group task. Believing their efforts to be unnecessary, they may be content to let others do the work. They may wish to avoid putting out more than their fair share of effort. The task may be uninteresting. When subjects believe they are safely anonymous in the group, they will, given such low motivation to perform, become loafers.

If the group task is one that increases subjects' involvement, the motivational basis for loafing is removed and such behavior does not occur. Even when the hypothesized conditions for low motivation are present, removing the cover provided by the group context introduces evaluation apprehension, which reduces loafing. Finally, the introduction of salient standards to which output can be compared brings about increased motivation and a consequent reduction in loafing. These standards may be personal or linked to the output of the group. The idea that introduction of group and personal standards increases motivation is consistent with several recent theoretical formulations pertaining to the self. For example, Breckler & Greenwald (1986) have argued that individuals select their behaviors in order to secure a favorable self-image, to receive a positive evaluation from other people, and to live up to the goals and standards of important reference groups. It could be argued that subjects who foreswear social loafing despite low intrinsic motivation do so because of salient private, public, or collective standards. Below, I propose that evaluations of the self that are based on personal standards of competence and those based on social standards are related, in that both pertain to the person's sense of social inclusion.

SOCIAL ANXIETY

Theory and research on both social facilitation and social loafing suggest that evaluation apprehension is an important motive for human behavior in social settings. Each phenomenon may therefore be thought of as a manifestation, in some ways, of a more general influence of social anxiety. This subject has received considerable attention in its own right. The study of social anxiety has received much of its impetus from the theoretical work of Schlenker & Leary (1982), who defined the effect within the context of self-presentation and impression formation. Schlenker & Leary define social anxiety as the state created when a person is motivated to make a certain impression on an audience, either real or imagined, but doubts that this impression can be made. In the language of traditional expectancy-value theory, social anxiety is a product of desire for a highly valued outcome (a good impression) and a low expectancy of attainment of that outcome. Persons may also show a characteristic disposition to experience social anxiety in social settings; this disposition is referred to as social anxiousness.

Impression Management and Self-Presentation

IMPRESSION MOTIVATION   Leary & Kowalski (1990) have described in detail the motivation that underlies the impression-management process. Their analysis divides impression management into two sequential processes, *impression motivation* and *impression construction,* the first of which is relevant to the subject of this review. The concept of impression motivation follows from the assumption that people have such interpersonal behavioral goals as maintenance of self-esteem and development of personal identity.

Impression motivation is a function of three variables related to the seeking of social rewards: the relevance of impression management to the attainment of these goals, the values attached to the goals, and the degree of discrepancy between the impression currently being made by the person on others and the desired impression. Each of these variables—goal-relevance of behavior, goal value, and perceived discrepancy—is the product of both situational and dispositional factors.

Impression management is thus attempted when the person has certain social goals and thinks certain behaviors are instrumental to attaining those goals. The person thus behaves as a direct function of the strength of these two variables. When the person does not believe that impression management will be successful (i.e. expectancy is low), social anxiety results.

OUTCOME AND EFFICACY EXPECTANCIES   The expectancy component in social anxiety and social anxiousness can in turn be broken down into two different expectancies, in line with Bandura's recently developed theory of self-efficacy (e.g. Bandura 1988). Leary & Atherton (1986) have distinguished between a self-presentation efficacy expectancy (how probable a person believes it is that he or she can enact a behavior chosen to make an impression) and a self-presentation outcome expectancy, (how probable a person believes it to be that proper execution of the chosen behavior will make the desired impression). Both types of expectancy are correlated with situational social anxiety and with social anxiousness. In a study by Maddux et al (1988), subjects were given a set of scenarios describing potentially anxiety-arousing situations; both outcome and efficacy expectancies were assessed. Both expectancies were negatively correlated with social anxiousness and with subjects' estimates of how anxious they would feel in the situations described.

Why should a distinction be made between outcome and efficacy expectancies if both are correlated in the same way to social anxiety? As yet we have no evidence pertaining to this matter, although Leary & Atherton (1986) have theorized that varying combinations of the two may have different effects on outcomes other than social anxiety. For example, the combination of low efficacy expectancy and high outcome expectancy might cause the person to attribute difficulties in self-presentation to personal inadequacies and thereby elicit feelings of helplessness and self-criticism. The combination of high efficacy expectancy and low outcome expectancy, on the other hand, might lead to the angry conclusion that ineffective impression management is due not to personal inability but to rejection by the other person(s). Research is needed on the question of how social anxiety combines with other possible effects of low expectancies to create complex response patterns in impression management.

Effects of Social Anxiety

INHIBITION OF BEHAVIOR   Social anxiety essentially inhibits behavior. It may, for example, bring about disengagement—avoidance of social situations, withholding of communication (Daly & Stafford 1984), or breaking of eye contact (Leary 1983)—or replacement of meaningful communication with innocuous sociability (Leary 1983). Leary et al (1987) provide evidence that social anxiety is associated with a passive and self-defensive style of verbal behavior in two-person interaction. Leary & Atherton (1986) have suggested two ways in which low self-presentation efficacy expectancies may link social anxiety and behavioral inhibition. One possibility is that low efficacy expectancies may independently elicit anxiety and cause the withholding of relevant behaviors. Another is that anxiety, which is a response to behavior that is inadequate to social demands, serves as a cue indicating low self-efficacy. This latter expectancy of low self-efficacy would then inhibit social behavior. Leary & Atherton have therefore stated two possible reasons for the correlation between self-efficacy expectancies and social anxiety. In the first case, low self-efficacy expectancies are a cause of anxiety, as well as of behavioral inhibition. In the second, anxiety is a cause of low self-efficacy expectancies. Which of the two explanations is correct cannot be determined from the data now available.

If social anxiety is a threat cue for defensive inhibition and avoidance, it should be an especially powerful one when the person attributes it to internal and personal factors rather than to external and situational ones. In a study designed to test this possibility, Leary et al (1986b) asked subjects to imagine themselves as actors in a set of relaxed or nervous scenarios. Subjects who attributed nervousness to such internal factors as personality and ability showed the highest positive correlations among rated nervousness, social avoidance, and social inhibition (the latter measures were obtained from personality scales). Subjects who attributed relaxation to internal causes showed the highest negative correlation between rated relaxation and avoidance inhibition.

Leary (1986) has also shown that when subjects misattribute the arousing effects of social anxiety to an external stimulus, they show less arousal than when they do not misattribute such effects. In this study some subjects were led to believe, as they conversed with another person, that any arousal they felt was due to noise in the laboratory, whereas others were told that noise would have no such arousing effect. Subjects in the latter condition showed higher pulse rates during the interaction than those in the former, and this effect was most pronounced among subjects who were high in social anxiousness.

IDENTITY ORIENTATION   That dispositional social anxiousness moderates the effects of situation on social anxiety is documented in several of the studies cited in this review. Another such moderating variable is *identity orientation*. As has already been noted, the self may be defined in terms of standards that are either personal or social (Breckler & Greenwald 1986). Social and personal orientations are independent dimensions of identity (Cheek & Briggs 1982). Theoretically, a person may base his or her identity on both personal and social standards. However, most research on identity has concentrated on persons in whom one or the other orientation predominates. Barnes et al (1988) classified subjects as either high or low in both personal and social identity by means of Cheek's Aspects of Identity Questionnaire (Cheek 1989). When they then informed some subjects that their performance on a forthcoming test would be made known to the experimenter's assistant, those high in social identity exhibited more anxiety than did those low in social identity. No such effect of social identity was found among subjects who were not told that their performance would be reported to another.

Motivational Basis for Self-Presentation

Social anxiety is rooted in the process of self-presentation. It represents an undesirable byproduct of failed impression management. Why is self-presentation so important that its failure causes such an aversive outcome? To answer this question we must first note that impression management involves two motives (Baumeister & Tice 1986; Leary & Kowalski 1990). One is the familiar one of manipulating an audience for some immediate social or material gain. The other is the construction of a desired self-concept. The person establishes a self by obtaining the acceptance and approval of that self by others (e.g. Schlenker 1986). Social anxiety is linked to the second of these motives. Failure to create a desired impression on others weakens one's sense of identity.

FEAR OF DEATH   Greenberg et al (1986) have suggested that human culture, by providing a drama within which each person may play a part, provides a buffer against the dread of facing one's own vulnerability and mortality. The person is motivated toward successful fulfillment of a desired role within the cultural drama. Meeting cultural standards brings social approval and maintains self-esteem. Failure to meet the demands of one's socially appointed role brings the threat of exclusion and loss of the social buffer against the terror of death. Evaluation apprehension therefore takes on an existential dimension.

FEAR OF EXCLUSION   A related theory has been outlined by Baumeister & Tice (1990) and elaborated by Leary (1990). Both of these viewpoints stress a potentially adaptive side of social anxiety. According to these theorists, social anxiety may serve as a warning signal tending to prevent behavior that would endanger survival by making the person appear unattractive or useless to the collective. Anxiety interrupts such behavior, focuses attention on the improper behavior, and motivates the person to seek alternative courses of action.

NEGOTIATION OF REALITY   Among alternative courses of action are the wide array of cognitive strategies shown in several recent research programs on maintenance of self-esteem. Most of these have been reviewed extensively in other contexts and they are mentioned here only to acknowledge their relevance to the position being taken. They include the self-serving attributional bias (McFarland & Ross 1982), excuse-making (Basgall & Snyder 1988), symbolic self-completion (Wicklund & Gollwitzer 1982), denial (Janoff-Bulman & Timko 1987), and self-handicapping (Baumgardner & Arkin 1987; Shepperd & Arkin 1989). Each strategy can be thought of as a process whereby the individual attempts to escape blame or criticism for actual or expected failures by attributing the failure to nonpersonal causes. Another reaction to personal failure may be identification with a stigmatized social group, with the expectation that social disapproval following failures may then be explained away as social prejudice (Crocker & Major 1989). All of these mechanisms are motivated by a need to avoid negative information about the self; all involve adaptive illusions. Snyder & Higgins (1988) have subsumed all such illusions in the concept of *negotiation of reality*—the integration of active coping processes into one's theory of the self for protective and defensive reasons.

ESCAPE FROM SELF AND DECONSTRUCTION   Baumeister (1990) has noted that when alteration of behavior in response to anxiety is not possible, the anxiety state itself can become the immediate problem from which the person seeks escape by any available means. One means may be escape from self-awareness through cessation of meaningful thought. This process, called *cognitive deconstruction* by Baumeister, involves such alterations in thought as a narrow focus on the immediate situation, a preoccupation with procedural details at the expense of broader perspectives, passivity, and closed-mindedness.

CONCLUDING COMMENTS

The three phenomena discussed in this review—social facilitation, social loafing, and self-presentation—reveal an underlying social motive linked to evaluation apprehension and fear of disapproval. This motive manifests itself in a number of behaviors and behavioral strategies that, at first glance, appear unrelated. Moreover, it arises from a more fundamental need to belong to, and be approved of by, important social groups. It motivates the person's self-presentation and elicits aversive affective arousal when inclusion and approval are threatened.

The motive described here has been adduced as the basis for other social phenomena. In earlier literature on motivation and personality, it formed the basis for fear of failure in the study of achievement motivation (Atkinson 1974) and, more recently, it underlies the theory of test anxiety (e.g. Sarason 1980). The related concepts of evaluation apprehension and need for social approval are also implicated in certain formulations that posit the existence of social demands on the self. Dweck & Leggett (1988), for example, have proposed that an orientation of helplessness, approval-seeking, and social anxiety constitutes one of the two observed patterns of adaptive behavior. Higgins (1987, 1988) has noted three possible versions of self—the *actual* self, the *ideal* self, and the self as it *ought* to be. The latter is the self version defined by the expectancies and demands of others or oneself. It is "your representation of the attributes that someone (yourself or another) believes you should or ought to possess (i.e., a representation of someone's sense of your duty, obligations, or responsibilities)" (Higgins 1987:321). The ideal self is the representation of attributes to which one aspires. When the person perceives that the "actual self" is in conflict with the "ought self," the result is fear, restlessness, and anxiety. The motive of evaluation apprehension also has some features in common with what Deci & Ryan (1985) have called the *control orientation,* in which either other people or the introjected values of others dominate the individual.

The motive to seek approval from others (and to fear social rejection) has traditionally been contrasted with the motive to achieve (e.g. Atkinson, 1974) or to meet some internalized standard. Dweck & Leggett (1988) have identified the latter as the basis for *mastery-oriented* behavior, the counterpart of the helpless orientation (cf Elliott & Dweck 1988). Higgins (1987, 1988) regards it as the basis for the "ideal" as opposed to the "ought" self. For Deci & Ryan, this motive arises from an *autonomy orientation,* in which "people use available information to make choices and to regulate themselves in pursuit of self-selected goals" (Deci & Ryan 1985:154). To go back even further, differentiating between social approval and mastery motivation is part of an older and more basic distinction between deficit motivation (as reflected in homeostatic theories) and growth or competence motivation, ideas that are consistent with the assumptions of humanistic psychology (e.g. White 1959).

As was noted elsewhere in this review, however, some recent theoretical formulations tend to weaken this classic dichotomy. Self-enhancement, growth motivation, and the need for competence may also be animated by a need for social inclusion. People may develop a sense of personal competence through successful enactment of socially useful and approved behaviors that increase the probability of acceptance and inclusion. Thus the two apparently contrasting motives may both arise from a single underlying one: the need to be included and socially relevant.

The two motives described here may also be related to two modes of self-presentation. One, usually called self-enhancement, involves behaviors that build up the self-image and establish the person as ambitious and competent. The other, referred to as self-protective behavior, involves actions that simply allow the person to avoid looking incompetent or ridiculous. The basis for individual differences in these self-presentational styles is not well understood. One antecedent may be a trait of generalized self-esteem. Persons whose behavior exhibits high levels of this trait tend to develop a self-enhancing style whereas those low in self-esteem tend to develop a self-protective one. The development of this trait may depend upon the person's history of rewards and punishments for past self-presentations and the extent of the person's repertoire of self-presentational skills (Baumeister et al 1990). It is also possible that persons inherit a tendency toward restraint and social inhibition that could mediate the development of a self-protective style. Recent studies by Kagan and his associates show evidence of such a hereditary disposition (e.g. Kagan et al 1988).

In the introduction, I noted that during the 1980s motivation and cognition were sometimes invoked as alternative explanations of behavior. The once formidable wall separating the two constructs may now have been breached. Signs of a rapprochement between cognition and motivation are abundant, as the material in this review has shown. Some of the lines along which this joining of concepts will occur have been set forth in a timely and authoritative volume edited by Sorrentino & Higgins (1986). The continuation of this development makes social motivation a topic with great promise and potential for psychologists of the 1990s.

ACKNOWLEDGMENT

I thank Vernon Forbes for his valuable assistance in the literature search.

Literature Cited

Atkinson, J. W. 1974. The mainsprings of achievement-oriented activity. In *Motivation and Achievement,* ed. J. W. Atkinson & J. O. Raynor, pp. 13–41. Washington, DC: Winston

Bandura, A. 1988. Self-efficacy conception of anxiety. *Anx. Res.* 1:77–98

Barnes, B. D., Mason, E., Leary, M. R., Laurent, J., Griebel, C., Bergman, A.

1988. Reactions to social vs. self-evaluation: moderating effects of personal and social identity orientations. *J. Res. Pers.* 22:513–24

Baron, R. S. 1986. Distraction-conflict theory: progress and problems. *Adv. Exp. Soc. Psychol.* 19:1–40

Bartis, S., Szymanski, K., Harkins, S. G. 1988. Evaluation and performance: a two-edged knife. *Pers. Soc. Psychol. Bull.* 14:242–51

Basgall, J. A., Snyder, C. R. 1988. Excuses in waiting: external locus of control and reactions to success-failure feedback. *J. Pers. Soc. Psychol.* 54:656–62

Baumeister, R. F. 1982. A self-presentational view of social phenomena. *Psychol. Bull.* 91:3–26

Baumeister, R. F. 1986. *Public Self and Private Self.* New York: Springer-Verlag

Baumeister, R. F. 1990. Anxiety and deconstruction: on escaping the self. In *Self-Inference Processes: The Ontario Symposium,* Vol. 6. ed. J. M. Olson, M. P. Zanna, Hillsdale, NJ: Erlbaum

Baumeister, R. F., Tice, D. M. 1986. Four selves, two motives, and a substitute self-regulation model. See Baumeister 1986, pp. 63–74

Baumeister, R. F., Tice, D. M. 1990. Anxiety and social exclusion. *J. Soc. Clin. Psychol.* 9:165–95

Baumeister, R. F., Tice, D. M., Hutton, D. G. 1990. Self presentation motivations and personality differences in self-esteem. *J. Pers.* 57:547–79

Baumgardner, A., Arkin, R. M. 1987. Coping with the prospect of social disapproval: strategies and sequelae. In *Coping with Negative Life Events: Clinical and Social Psychological Perspectives,* ed. C. R. Snyder, C. E. Ford, pp. 323–46. New York: Plenum

Bond, C. F. 1982. Social facilitation: a self-presentational view. *J. Pers. Soc. Psychol.* 42:1042–50

Breckler, S. J., Greenwald, A. G. 1986. Motivational facets of the self. In *Handbook of Motivation and Cognition,* ed. R. M. Sorrentino & E. T. Higgins, pp. 145–64. New York: Guilford

Brickner, M. A., Harkins, S. G., Ostrom, T. M. 1986. Effects of personal involvement: thought-provoking implications for social loafing. *J. Pers. Soc. Psychol.* 51:763–69

Cacioppo, J. T., Rourke, P. A., Marshall-Goodell, B. S., Tassinary, L. G., Baron, R. S. 1990. Rudimentary psychological effects of mere observation. *Psychophysiology* 27:177–86

Cheek, J. M. 1989. Identity orientations and self-interpretation. In *Personality Psychology: Recent Trends and Emerging Directions,* ed. D. M. Buss, N. Cantor, pp. 275–85. New York: Springer-Verlag

Cheek, J. M., Briggs, S. R. 1982. Self-consciousness and aspects of identity. *J. Res. Pers.* 16:401–8

Crocker, J., Major, B. 1989. Social stigma and self-esteem: the self-protective properties of stigma. *Psychol. Rev.* 96:608–30

Daly, J. A., Stafford, L. 1984. Correlates and consequences of social-communicative anxiety. In *Avoiding Communication,* ed. J. A. Daly & J. C. McCroskey, pp. 125–43. Beverly Hills, CA: Sage

Deci, E. L., Ryan, R. M. 1985. *Intrinsic Motivation and Self-Determination in Human Behavior.* New York: Plenum

Dweck, C. S., Leggett, E. L. 1988. A social-cognitive approach to motivation and personality. *Psychol. Rev.* 95:256–73

Elliott, E. S., Dweck, C. S. 1988. Goals: an approach to motivation and achievement. *J. Pers. Soc. Psychol.* 54:5–12

Geen, R. G. 1979. Effects of being observed on learning following success failure experiences. *Motiv. Emotion* 3:355–71

Geen, R. G. 1980. Test anxiety and cue utilization. In *Test Anxiety: Theory, Research, and Applications,* ed. I. G. Sarason, pp. 43–61. Hillsdale, NJ: Erlbaum

Geen, R. G. 1989. Alternative conceptions of social facilitation. In *The Psychology of Group Influence,* ed. P. Paulus, pp. 15–51. Hillsdale, NJ: Erlbaum. 2nd ed.

Geen, R. G., Bushman, B. J. 1989. The arousing effects of social presence. In *Handbook of Social Psychophysiology,* ed. H. Wagner & A. Manstead pp. 261–81. London: Wiley

Geen, R. G., Gange, J. J. 1977. Drive theory of social facilitation: twelve years of theory and research. *Psychol. Bull.* 84:1267–88

Geen, R. G., Thomas, S. L., Gammill, P. 1988. Effects of evaluation and coaction on state anxiety and anagram performance. *Pers. Indiv. Diff.* 6:293–98

Goethals, G. R., Darley, J. M. 1987. Social comparison theory: self-evaluation and group life. In *Theories of Group Behavior,* ed. B. Mullen, G. R. Goethals, pp. 21–47. New York: Springer-Verlag

Greenberg, J., Pyszczynski, T., Solomon, S. 1986. The causes and consequences of a need for self-esteem: a terror management theory. See Baumeister 1986, pp. 189–212

Griffith, T. L., Fichman, M., Moreland, R. L. 1989. Social loafing and social facilitation: an empirical test of the cognitive-motivational model of performance. *Basic Appl. Soc. Psychol.* 10:253–71

Guerin, B. 1986. Mere presence effects in humans: a review. *J. Exp. Soc. Psychol.* 22:38–77

Guerin, B., Innes, J. M. 1982. Social facilitation and social monitoring: a new look at Zajonc's mere presence hypothesis. *Br. J. Soc. Psychol.* 21:7–18

Harkins, S. G. 1987. Social loafing and social facilitation. *J. Exp. Soc. Psychol.* 23:1–18

Harkins, S. G., Jackson, J. M. 1985. The role of evaluation in eliminating social loafing. *Pers. Soc. Psychol. Bull.* 11:456–65

Harkins, S. G., Szymanski, K. 1987. Social

loafing and social facilitation: new wine in old bottles. In *Rev. Pers. Soc. Psychol.* 9:167–88

Harkins, S. G., Szymanski, K. 1988. Social loafing and self-evaluation with an objective standard. *J. Exp. Soc. Psychol.* 24:354–65

Harkins, S. G., Szymanski, K. 1989. Social loafing and group evaluation. *J. Pers. Soc. Psychol.* 56:934–41

Higgins, E. T. 1987. Self-discrepancy: a theory of relating self and affect. *Psychol. Rev.* 94:319–40

Higgins, E. T. 1988. Self-discrepancy theory: What patterns of self-beliefs cause people to suffer? *Adv. Exp. Soc. Psychol.* 22:93–196

Hockey, R. 1979. Stress and cognitive components of skilled performance. In *Human Stress and Cognition: An Information-Processing Approach,* ed. V. Hamilton, D. M. Warburton. New York: Wiley

Jackson, J. M. 1987. Social impact theory: a social forces model of influence. See Goethals & Darley, pp. 111–24

Jackson, J. M., Harkins, S. G. 1985. Equity in effort: an explanation of the social loafing effect. *J. Pers. Soc. Psychol.* 49:1199–1206

Jackson, J. M., Williams, K. D. 1985. Social loafing on difficult tasks: Working collectively can improve performance. *J. Pers. Soc. Psychol.* 49:937–42

Janoff-Bulman, R., Timko, C. 1987. Coping with traumatic events: the role of denial in light of people's assumptive worlds. See Baumgardner & Arkin 1987, pp. 135–59

Kagan, J., Reznick, J. S., Snidman, N. 1988. Biological bases of childhood shyness. *Science* 240:167–71

Kerr, N. L. 1983. Motivation losses in small groups: a social dilemma analysis. *J. Pers. Soc. Psychol.* 45:819–28

Kerr, N. L., Bruun, S. E. 1981. Ringelmann revisited: alternative explanations for the social loafing effect. *Pers. Soc. Psychol. Bull.* 7:224–31

Kravitz, D., Martin, B. 1986. Ringelmann rediscovered: the original article. *J. Pers. Soc. Psychol.* 50:936–41

Latané, B., Nida, S. 1980. Social impact theory and group influence: a social engineering perspective. See Geen 1980, pp. 3–34

Latané, B., Williams, K., Harkins, S. 1979. Many hands make light the work: the cases and consequences of social loafing. *J. Pers. Soc. Psychol.* 37:822–32

Leary, M. R. 1983. *Understanding Social Anxiety: Social, Personality, and Clinical Perspectives.* Beverly Hills, CA: Sage

Leary, M. R. 1986. The impact of interactional impediments on social anxiety and self-presentation. *J. Exp. Soc. Psychol.* 22:122–35

Leary, M. R. 1990. Responses to social exclusion: social anxiety, jealousy, loneliness, depression, and low self-esteem. *J. Soc. Clin. Psychol.* 9:221–29

Leary, M. R., Atherton, S. C. 1986. Self-efficacy, social anxiety, and inhibition in interpersonal encounters. *J. Soc. Clin. Psychol.* 4:256–67

Leary, M. R., Kowalski, R. M. 1990. Impression management: a literature review and two-component model. *Psychol. Bull.* 107:34–47

Leary, M. R., Barnes, B. D., Griebel, C. 1986. Cognitive, affective, and attributional effects of potential threats to self-esteem. *J. Soc. Clin. Psychol.* 4:461–74

Leary, M. R., Knight, P. D., Johnson, K. A. 1987. Social anxiety and dyadic conversation: a verbal response analysis. *J. Soc. Clin. Psychol.* 5:34–50

Leary, M. R., Atherton, S. C., Hill, S., Hur, C. 1986. Attributional mediators of social inhibition and avoidance. *J. Pers.* 54:704–16

Maddux, J. E., Norton, L. W., Leary, M. R. 1988. Cognitive components of social anxiety: an investigation of the integration of self-presentation theory and self-efficacy theory. *J. Soc. Clin. Psychol.* 6:180–90

McFarland, C., Ross, M. 1982. Impact of causal attributions on affective reactions to success and failure. *J. Pers. Soc. Psychol.* 43:937–46

Petty, R. E., Harkins, S. G., Williams, K. D. 1980. The effects of group diffusion of cognitive effort on attitudes: an information-processing view. *J. Pers. Soc. Psychol.* 38:81–92

Ruskin, J. 1907/1963. *The Seven Lamps of Architecture.* London: Everyman's Library

Sanna, L. J., Shotland, R. L. 1990. Valence of anticipated evaluation and social facilitation. *J. Exp. Soc. Psychol.* 26:82–92

Sarason, I. G., ed. 1980. *Test Anxiety: Theory, Research, and Applications.* Hillsdale, NJ: Erlbaum

Schlenker, B. 1986. Self-identification: toward an integration of the private and public self. See Baumeister 1986, pp. 21–62

Schlenker, B. R., Leary, M. R. 1982. Social anxiety and self-presentations: a conceptualization and model. *Psychol. Bull.* 92:641–69

Seta, C. E., Seta, J. J., Donaldson, S., Wang, M. A. 1988. The effects of evaluation on organizational processing. *Pers. Soc. Psychol. Bull.* 14:604–9

Seta, J. J., Crisson, J. E., Seta, C. E., Wang, M. A. 1989a. Task performance and perceptions of anxiety: averaging and summation in an evaluative setting. *J. Pers. Soc. Psychol.* 56:387–96

Seta, J. J., Wang, M. A., Crisson, J. E., Seta,

C. E. 1989b. Audience composition and felt anxiety: impact averaging and summation. *Basic Appl. Soc. Psychol.* 10:57–72

Shepperd, J. A., Arkin, R. M. 1989. Determinants of self-handicapping: task importance and the effects of preexisting handicaps on self-generated handicaps. *Pers. Soc. Psychol. Bull.* 15:101–12

Snyder, C. R., Higgins, R. L. 1988. Excuses: their effective role in the negotiation of reality. *Psychol. Bull.* 104:23–35

Sorrentino, R. M., Higgins, E. T., eds. 1986. *Handbook of Motivation and Cognition.* New York: Guilford

Szymanski, K., Harkins, S. G. 1987. Social loafing and self-evaluation with a social standard. *J. Pers. Soc. Psychol.* 53:891–97

Tajfel, H., Turner, J. 1986. The social identity theory of intergroup behavior. In *Psychology of Intergroup Relations,* ed. S. Worchel, W. Austin, pp. 33–48. Chicago: Nelson-Hall

Weldon, E., Gargano, G. M. 1988. Cognitive loafing: the effects of accountability and shared responsibility on cognitive effort. *Pers. Soc. Psychol. Bull.* 14:159–71

White, R. W. 1959. Motivation reconsidered: the concept of competence. *Psychol. Rev.* 66:297–333

Wicklund, R. A., Gollwitzer, P. M. 1982. *Symbolic Self-Completion.* Hillsdale, NJ: Erlbaum

Williams, K. D., Harkins, S. G., Latané, B. 1981. Identifiability as a deterrent to social loafing: two cheering experiments. *J. Pers. Soc. Psychol.* 40:303–11

Williams, K. D., Nida, S. A., Baca, L. D., Latané, B. 1989. Social loafing and swimming: effects of identifiability on individual and relay performance of intercollegiate swimmers. *Basic Appl. Soc. Psychol.* 10:73–81

Zajonc, R. B. 1965. Social facilitation. *Science* 149:269–74

Zajonc, R. B. 1980. Compresence. See Latané & Nida 1980, pp. 35–60

Annu. Rev. Psychol. 1991. 42:401–25

SOCIAL FACTORS AND PSYCHOPATHOLOGY: Stress, Social Support, and Coping Processes

James C. Coyne

University of Michigan Medical School, Department of Family Practice, Ann Arbor, Michigan 48109-0708

Geraldine Downey

University of Denver, Department of Psychology, Denver, Colorado 80208

KEY WORDS: depression, domestic violence, interpersonal

CONTENTS

"Stress, Social Support, and Coping Processes" was the subtitle of the last *Annual Review* chapter on social factors in psychopathology (Kessler et al 1985). Whereas earlier reviews (King 1978; Strauss 1989; Dohrenwend &

0066-4308/91/0201-0401$02.00

Dohrenwend 1981; Eron & Peterson 1982) had been concerned primarily with group differences in psychopathology, the attention Kessler et al (1985) gave to race, gender, and socioeconomic factors comprised part of a larger discussion of how support and coping influence adaptation to stress. Continuing trends in the field warrant that we, too, emphasize stress, support, and coping processes.

Over the past decade there has been an avalanche of studies that have adopted the "stress process" hypothesis, which explains psychopathology in terms of exposure to stress and ameliorative factors (mainly social support and coping). This model is currently the dominant research approach to the relationship between social factors and psychopathology. One citation analysis concluded that the study of stress, anxiety, depression, and support, has become the single most active research front in social science (Garfield 1987). While methodological and theoretical advances evident in some recent studies have addressed several of the problems and ambiguities that Kessler et al identified as hampering our understanding of the stress process, they have also revealed additional problems. We have learned much about the shortcomings of ostensibly superior methodologies and about the limitations of attempts to relate social factors and psychopathology in a simple, unambiguous way.

Other developments suggest the need for changes in current approaches and emphases in studying social factors in psychopathology. First, just as psychiatrists have begun again to use formal diagnosis, epidemiologists have turned from representing psychopathology as a continuum of distress to viewing it in terms of categorical diagnoses. Self-report symptom checklists have given way to semi-structured interviews with formal diagnostic criteria. Although this is a recent change, accumulating findings already call into question many of our assumptions about the nature of psychopathology and how it should be studied. Second, researchers have become increasingly aware of the intergenerational transmission of family disruption, troubled relationships, and childhood adversity (Elder et al 1986; Quinton & Rutter 1988) and of the scope of intimate violence and its consequences for mental health (Koss 1990). The growing recognition of high rates of childhood physical and sexual victimization in the pasts of adult psychiatric patients (Bryer et al 1987) challenges what has been the rather exclusive focus of stress research on temporally proximal stressors in understanding the etiology of disorder. Evidence that spouse abuse is prevalent has also accumulated, and attention has been drawn to its possible etiological significance in psychopathology (Walker 1987). Finally, research on assortative mating (Merikangas 1982), marital problems associated with psychopathology (Weissman 1987), concurrent psychological distress in adults who live with depressed persons (Coyne et al 1987), and psychological disturbance in their offspring (Downey

& Coyne 1990) has complicated the effort to understand psychopathology in terms of individuals confronting stressful events, mobilizing support, and engaging in problem- and emotion-focused coping. Such studies suggest the need to examine how interdependent individuals adapt to stress within the context of troubled relationships.

Research on social factors and psychopathology is at a critical juncture. There are ample reasons to doubt the adequacy not only of current concepts and methods but also of the questions being addressed. It is difficult to do research that substantially advances our knowledge of basic issues. We are faced with a choice. Should we continue to do studies that arrive at foregone conclusions simply by exploiting the nonindependence of measures? (Such studies inevitably find that stress is generally bad, that perceiving relationships as supportive is good, and that coping—though this is difficult to demonstrate—must be good.) Or should we undertake the much more difficult task of identifying the complex and dynamic links among persons' experiencing recurrent periods of disruption and dysfunction in their lives, how they lead their lives, and the nature of their social contexts?

THE RELATIONSHIP BETWEEN DISTRESS AND PSYCHOPATHOLOGY: A CHANGING VIEW

Focus on Diagnosis

Following decades of theoretical and empirical disrepute, formal diagnosis in psychiatry was enthusiastically reborn in the 1970s (Klerman 1989; Robins & Helzer 1986). In the preceding period, mental disorder and normal functioning had been conceived as aspects of a single continuum—a view compatible with etiological theories that emphasized social rather than constitutional factors. In reaction to this view and to more broadly based criticisms of the field of psychiatry, psychiatric researchers undertook to develop reliable and valid diagnostic criteria based on clearly defined symptoms involving minimal etiological inferences (Klerman 1989). Among methodological innovations was the development of semi-structured interviews to obtain standardized information about the person's history, social functioning, and symptom status—e.g. the Schedule for Affective Disorders and Schizophrenia (SADS; Endicott & Spitzer 1978), the NIMH Diagnostic Interview Schedule (DIS; Robins et al 1981), and the Structured Clinical Interview for DSM-III (SCID). Operational criteria and algorithms for assigning persons to diagnostic categories were also specified (Feighner et al 1972; Spitzer et al 1978), and this approach was adopted in the DSM-III (American Psychiatric Association 1980).

More than previous chapters on the topic of social factors in psychopathology we can draw on studies that use direct interview assessment of the signs and symptoms of psychopathology and well-specified diagnostic criteria with improved reliability. We integrate studies of psychiatric patients with community studies employing interview-based diagnosis. We pay particular attention to results emerging from the NIMH Epidemiologic Catchment Area Study (ECA; Regier et al 1984), which utilized the DIS with over 18,000 persons in 5 communities.

We have much more to say about depressive disorders than about other forms of psychopathology. This could be justified by the prevalence of depression and the social costs associated with it, but there are more basic conceptual and methodological reasons for the literature's greater attention to depression. Until publication of the DSM-IIIR (American Psychiatric Association 1987), hierarchical rules caused the diagnosis of an anxiety disorder to be preempted by the diagnosis of another disorder (e.g. depression or schizophrenia). When such rules are relaxed it becomes apparent that generalized anxiety and phobias are as common as major depression. Furthermore, over their lifetimes, most persons who become depressed have another diagnosable disorder, the most common being an anxiety disorder (Robins & Regier 1991). Another reason for the lack of attention to anxiety disorders is that the widely used SADS does not produce such a diagnosis. With the advent of DSM-IIIR, the SCIDS, and the DIS, the relationships among social factors and anxiety disorders will undoubtedly receive more attention. Already, the ECA study has found that panic disorder is associated with as much social impairment, marital dysfunction, and suicidal tendency as major depression, and these relationships are not explained by the frequent association of panic disorder with depression (Markowitz et al 1989).

The attention to diagnosable disorder—in particular to the study of depression—can be seen as the third stage of research on social factors in psychopathology. Early studies focused on the social correlates of general malaise (Gurin et al 1960; Langner 1962). The next stage centered on self-reported symptoms of depression (Radloff 1975; Kaplan et al 1987). Measures of general malaise and of depressive symptoms are highly correlated, and so they were usually related to psychosocial factors in similar ways. The belief that depression could be construed as being on a continuum with distress led to the additional assumption that the social correlates of general malaise and depressive symptoms were related to clinical depression in similar ways. This conveniently sanctioned the use of self-report symptom inventories in place of more expensive structured interviews, and it permitted the generalization to clinical depression from questionnaire surveys of normal populations.

However, as findings based on self-report surveys and structured interviews have been compared, problems with this assumption have emerged. Most people from community samples with high scores on self-report depression scales do not meet the diagnostic criteria for clinical depression. Many of the depressive symptoms identified in this way indicate only mild and transient distress (Coyne & Gotlib 1983). One can even score in the "depressed" range on such a questionnaire without having a single symptom that would contribute to a diagnosis of major depression (Schulberg et al 1985). Finally, current self-report depression scales may do as good a job of identifying anxiety disorders as they do of identifying clinical depression (Hough et al 1985).

Particularly relevant to understanding the relation between social factors and psychopathology are recurrent findings that self-reported symptoms and interview-based diagnosis of depression have different social correlates. Poverty is associated both with a heightened risk of a DSM-III diagnosis (Holzer et al 1986) and with more depressive symptoms, but it does not increase the risk of major depression (Weissman 1987). Some other chronic stressors (e.g. having a handicapped child) are associated with substantial increases in depressive symptoms, but not with greater risk of major depression (Breslau & Davis 1986). Whereas both minor and major life events are related to increases in depressive symptoms, it appears that only serious life events requiring long-term adjustment predict subsequent clinical depression (Brown & Harris 1978). Thus, if one is interested in predicting depressive symptoms, stronger correlations are obtained with a broad sampling of major and minor events, and current life-event inventories seem to have adopted a philosophy of "more is better." Yet only about a dozen items on a typical inventory are consistently related to clinical depression (Dohrenwend et al 1986), and broader samplings of events produce an underestimate of the strong association found with the dirty dozen. Brugha et al (1985) found that 12 of 67 categories of life events accounted for 77% of the events with etiological significance and that these events alone entailed greater relative risk for depression than the full list.

Difficulties in generalizing about depression on the basis of self-reported symptoms have only begun to be documented, but it is obvious this practice entails considerable confusion. The social correlates of distress and depressive symptoms remain a viable topic of research. Level of depressive symptoms predicts symptoms nine years later (Kaplan et al 1987) and risk for depressive disorder in the more immediate future (Lewinsohn et al 1988). Even in the absence of a diagnosable disorder, depressive symptoms are associated with more functional impairment than diabetes or hypertension (Wells et al 1989). However, studies of depressive symptoms are not justified if depressive disorders are the phenomena of interest. While most clinically depressed persons have scores in the depressed range on self-report questionnaires (although see Hopkins et al 1989), comparatively few persons with high scores would be diagnosed with depression. Thus such a diagnosis will have fewer correlates with more common social factors than does a high score on a depression questionnaire (Robins et al 1977). This implies that many findings from self-report questionnaires will not generalize to those based on categorical diagnoses of depression.

In sum, the study of how social factors affect depressive disorder is distinct from the study of the social correlates of distress. As we come to terms with this, a needed shift from self-reported symptoms to interview-based diagnosis will make it considerably more costly to study psychopathology. As if this were not problem enough, accumulating studies of social factors and the nature and course of psychopathology suggest a host of other complications.

An Emerging View of Depression and Other Psychopathology

We now probably know more about the natural history of depressive disorders than we do about that of other disorders, although long-term longitudinal studies are documenting the variable, episodic course of schizophrenia (Harding et al 1987). It was once assumed that depression occurs in a single episode that usually resolves without enduring impairment. We now believe depression is best conceptualized as a recurrent, episodic condition with a heterogeneous course, associated with varying degrees of social impairment, recovery, and susceptibility to relapse. Most people who experience major depression will have at least one subsequent episode; fewer than half recover without relapse in a two-year period; and one fifth do not recover in the two-year period (Keller 1985). One quarter will suffer six or more episodes in their lifetimes, and after the onset of major depression, 20% of each sufferer's lifetime will be spent in a depressive episode (Angst 1986). As many as 40% of depressed persons have a "double depression," with major depression superimposed on a preexisting dysthymia that may persist after recovery from the acute episode of major depression and increase the risk for recurrence (Keller & Shapiro 1982).

Most studies of the stress-depression relation attempt to address the implications of stress for the onset of psychopathology, whether it is measured as an increase in symptoms or a diagnosis. With a few notable exceptions, study designs reflect the implicit assumption that the stress-psychopathology relation works similarly for everyone and at all stages of the disorder (Hammen et al 1986). It has been noted that studies of the relation between life events and increase of symptoms should take into account symptom status prior to the event (Depue & Monroe 1986; Hammen et al 1986), but there has been too little attention to the history of prior episodes.

A prospective community study of depressive disorder illustrated complications that can arise when this problem is ignored (Lewinsohn et al 1988). Persons who were maritally distressed but not clinically depressed at an initial interview exhibited a heightened risk of depression eight months later, suggesting that marital distress is a risk factor for depression. However, the strongest predictor of depression during the study period was a history of depression: Over 90% of the persons who became depressed in the eight-month period had been depressed previously. When this factor was controlled, the increased risk associated with marital problems disappeared. Thus many prospective studies that purport to examine the antecedents of depression may actually be identifying precipitants of its recurrence and/or residual effects of past occurrences. Given the recurrent, episodic nature of depression, efforts to disentangle the effects of prior episodes from enduring social factors may prove difficult.

Implications for the Study of Social Factors and Psychology

The view that depression and other psychopathologies are recurrent and episodic requires an even more complex conceptualization than the diathesis-stress models currently in the ascendant. The recognition that most people confronted with severe stress do not develop psychopathology has prompted the suggestion that becoming depressed depends on a preexisting vulnerability to depression. Proposed causes of vulnerability include biological dysregulation (Goplerud & Depue 1985), negative self-concept (Hammen 1988), and coping strategies such as rumination (Nolen-Hoeksema 1987).

Such diathesis-stress models are a considerable advance over the less sophisticated view that everyone is equally susceptible to stress. However, this approach to linking person and context in the course of psychopathology has important limitations. Most crucial are the nondynamic nature of the model (it views psychopathology as a status rather than a process that unfolds over time) and its neglect of changes in vulnerability over time. The vulnerabilities identified have generally been viewed as fixed attributes of the person that interact with contextual stressors to influence the onset of psychopathology. Such a view ignores how vulnerabilities to psychopathology originate, what circumstances maintain or modify them, and what personal and social resources are available to confront stress.

The emerging view of depression and other psychopathologies is that they have a variable, episodic course that is influenced by a changing environment. Thus, in understanding the implications of social factors for a disorder, we must be concerned not only with the onset of a disorder, but also with stage in the life course of the disorder (e.g. whether it is a first or later episode) and the cumulative effects of experiences with disorder and dysfunction. We must also be aware of the interplay between the disorder and the normative developmental tasks of adulthood. Persons who experience psychopathology may spend considerable portions of their adult life in recurrent episodes of disturbance with interludes of wellness or residual distress. During this time, they may also face such tasks as completing their education, pursuing vocational goals, marrying, becoming parents, and perhaps getting divorced and married again.

Difficulties with adult social roles both contribute to and are in turn increased by depression. The interplay between depression and role functioning is well illustrated by the study of depressed mothers (Downey & Coyne 1990), whose conflicts with their children further exacerbate their distress and vice versa.

Childhood experience has also been linked with adult role functioning in ways that affect risk for psychopathology (Elder et al 1986; Quinton & Rutter 1988). Whereas there is growing evidence that early loss of a parent per se does not greatly affect subsequent risk for psychopathology (Brier et al 1988), prolonged family disruption in childhood may do so both directly and by being linked to adversity in adulthood. For example, in two independent samples Brown and his colleagues (Harris et al 1987) documented a link between lack of care in childhood (following loss of a mother) and affective disturbance in adult women, an influence mediated by premarital pregnancy and marital dysfunction. Specifically, they reported that such inadequate care increases the risk of early premarital pregnancy, which in turn increases the risk of marriage to an undependable partner. Marriage to such a partner, in addition to being low in intimacy, increases the risk both of serious life events (such as trouble with the law, discoveries of infidelities, and threats of eviction) and of poverty. Such findings indicate the value of a life-course developmental perspective alert to how individuals' strengths and vulnerabilities, their manifestations of psychopathology, and their social environments constrain and influence each other in different ways over time. Although the application of such a perspective to psychopathology is just beginning (Cummings & Cicchetti 1990; Strauss et al 1985; Walker 1990), its contribution to a broader understanding of how persons and contexts are linked in the course of development has been well established (Bronfenbrenner 1988; Elder et al 1986; Bolger et al 1988).

THE STRESS PROCESS

Stress

Studies documenting the association between scores on inventories of life events, on the one hand, and either self-report depression scores or diagnoses, on the other, have supported the development of the stress model of psychopathology, but the weakness of the relationships typically found has been a major source of frustration (Dohrenwend & Dohrenwend 1981). Various efforts at improving the inventories (e.g. increasing the range of events sampled and including respondents' ratings of events' stressfulness) have failed to increase their predictive power appreciably and have introduced new problems of interpretation (Kessler et al 1985). The limitations of checklist inventories as a means of assessing the stress-psychopathology association may be fundamental.

Items on life-event checklists are ambiguous and "thin descriptions" (Geerwitz 1973) of complex situations. Not only the interpretation of an event, but also its character and the circumstances surrounding it must differ between persons. Citing the case of a respondent whose husband had just died, but who had not seen him in two years, Shrout et al (1989) note the shortcomings of checklist assessments of even normatively severe events. A promising alternative to self-report checklists are semi-structured interviews. These can either (a) allow raters to take into consideration situational and personal factors that influence the threat posed by events (Brown & Harris 1978) or (b) use descriptive information about what actually happened before, during, and after each event to identify potent life events (Dohrenwend et al 1986). The key difference between the two interview-based approaches is that the former utilizes contextual factors (i.e. having preexisting debts and dependent children) to make judgments about the severity of the threat posed by an event, whereas the latter focuses exclusively on features of the event itself (being laid off owing to a plant closing rather than being fired) to arrive at consensual judgments.

Interview approaches to life events have generally attempted to ascertain whether or not the events in question occurred independently of the respondent's prior symptoms and behavior. As a result they have demonstrated strong relationships between the occurrence of independent events and risk for depression (Brown & Harris 1978; Shrout et al 1989), the onset of acute schizophrenia (Day et al 1987), and schizophrenic relapse (Ventura et al 1989). Finlay-Jones & Brown (1981) demonstrated some specificity in the relationship between classes of events and combinations of depression and anxiety. For instance, loss events much more frequently preceded the onset of pure depression and mixed anxiety/depression than they did the onset of pure anxiety; danger events preceded anxiety but not pure depression. Mixed anxiety/depression was preceded by events that involved both threat and loss. Dohrenwend et al (1986) found that disruptive loss events that were independent of the individual's behavior increased the risk for both onset and recurrence of major depression, whereas a variety of life events (including those related to health problems, role performance, and loss in the social network) predicted depression only in individuals with a history of recurrent psychopathology.

Research focusing on events shown to be independent of the individual's psychopathology or behavior is important, but an exclusive focus on such events can be misleading and may prevent other issues from being addressed. For example, early research found that an increase in arguments with their husbands was the single most frequent life change reported by depressed women for the months prior to the onset of depression (Paykel et al 1969). Today, however, life-events researchers rarely include marital turmoil or other interpersonal disputes in their assessments, the independence of events and pathology being too difficult to establish. Yet establishing the role of interpersonal conflict in the onset and recurrence of depression is crucial. Difficulties in interpersonal relationships, the most common form of stress (Bolger et al 1989), may be the most important precipitants of depression.

There are other reasons for giving more consideration to stress that cannot be presumed to be independent of the psychological state and behavior of the individuals confronting it. McGuffin et al (1988) found that first degree relatives of depressed persons had personally experienced more life events immediately prior to the inquiry than had relatives of controls (even excluding events related to the depressed proband). This raises the possibility that the tendency to experience adversity may be familial. The mechanism of transmission remains unclear. Akiskal (1989) has found that losses of parent(s) early in life are associated not with overt mood disorders but with immaturity, hostile dependency, manipulativeness, impulsiveness, and low threshold for alcohol and drug abuse in adulthood. Without directly affecting the lifetime risk for depression, these characteristics may precipitate life events that then trigger depression earlier in life and result in more frequent episodes of depression. Similarly, the 40% of depressed patients who have personality disorders experience more life stress, an earlier onset of depression, and poorer recovery than those without such disorders (Black et al 1988; Phofl et al 1984). If we take seriously the need for an interactive developmental conception of psychopathology, we must study potentially nonindependent life events, which may both express and influence vulnerability to depression.

How are past episodes of depression and susceptibility to life events related? A number of studies have found that elevated rates of negative events are more likely to precede early episodes of depression than later episodes (Dolan et al 1985; Ezquiga et al 1987; Perris 1984). Thus persons who have repeated episodes of depression may differ in kind from those who have single or few episodes. These findings have also been interpreted in terms of a biological sensitizing effect (Post et al 1986), such that the threshold of stress necessary to precipitate depressive episodes lowers with their repetition. However, it should be noted that whether depression is associated with neuroendocrine markers or vegetative symptoms does not strongly reduce its correlation to life events (Dolan et al 1985). Furthermore, repeated episodes of depression may have analogous sensitizing effects on the sufferer's social environment, causing support and tolerance for dysfunctional behavior progressively to decrease (Coyne et al 1990).

Research into the effects of chronic stress on psychopathology continues to lag behind the study of life events. The contribution of chronic stress to risk for depression is presumed to be smaller than that of acute severe events (Brown & Harris 1978), but methodological expediency is probably the major factor for ignoring chronic stress (Kessler et al 1985). It is difficult to show that chronic stress exists independent of an earlier disorder and, given a chronic source of stress, to determine why an individual becomes depressed at a certain point.

Pearlin (1989) has challenged the notion that life events indicate "a discrete change rather than a marker or surrogate indicator of an ongoing life course in a particular social context" (p. 244). A focus on life events may distract us from the problematic and relatively intractable continuities in persons' lives. As noted above, certain childhood adversities may be linked to adverse environments in adulthood in ways beyond the control of the individual, such that both "independent" stressful events and chronic stressors are more likely to befall persons raised in adverse environments (Quinton & Rutter 1988; Harris et al 1987). We should be careful not to minimize such continuities in people's life situations. We must also be careful not to infer personal short-comings, poor coping, or incompetency from what are actually effects of enduring features.

One can readily see in much of the earlier research on stress and psychopathology an effort to approximate the experimental control lost in the shift from laboratory studies to field research. Investigators construed life events as experiments provided by nature. Researchers attempted to identify situations in which people's experiences of life events were analogous to random protocol assignments in an experimental manipulation. But truly random events may not be the most common or the most theoretically interesting precipitants of psychopathology, nor is it clear that many stressful events of interest are actually independent from individuals' life courses. Efforts to grapple with the basic interdependence of individual and context have led to a new set of theoretical questions and methodological challenges, which may ultimately result in abandonment of the laboratory experiment and the tidy ANOVA-based experimental design as metaphors for understanding the relationship between social factors and psychopathology.

Social Support

Early studies of the social networks of psychiatric patients found those of psychotics to be smaller and kin-based and those of neurotics to be looser and sparser than those of controls (Kessler et al 1985; see Mueller 1980 for a review). More recently, the bulk of research has focused on the perceived supportiveness of relationships, asking how well social support buffers the effects of stress and what contribution it makes directly to mental health (see

Cohen & Wills 1985; Lin et al 1986). Most of this research is based on depression questionnaire scores rather than depressive disorder, and persistent ambiguities are evident with respect to what measures of perceived support capture. Curiously, although the perception of support is assumed to reflect what is conveyed in supportive transactions. Reports of having sought (Coyne et al 1981; Lieberman & Mullin 1978) or received (Barrera 1981) support are related negatively to adaptational outcomes.

Compared with controls, persons with DSM III diagnoses of depression report less contact with friends, fewer friends nearby who can help, less satisfaction with friends and relatives, less confiding in their spouses, and less satisfactory marital relationships (Leaf et al 1984). These findings parallel those for depressed patients (Billings & Moos 1984). The quality of close relationships, notably that with the spouse, correlates more positively with DSM III diagnosis than does the quality of more distant relationships (Leaf et al 1984). The same holds for new cases of depression (Brown & Harris 1978). A number of studies have now replicated Brown & Harris's (1978) findings that depression in the face of life events or chronic difficulties is more likely when an intimate relationship with a spouse is lacking. It appears that the lack of an intimate relationship is also a risk factor for depression in the absence of life events—i.e. intimacy has direct as well as buffering effects (See Oatley & Bolton 1985 for a review).

Such findings of an association between measures of support and adaptational outcomes do not justify the conclusion that the supportiveness of relationships protects against depression (House et al 1988). Social support may not be a fundamentally unipolar construct. That is, while reports of "low support" may sometimes reflect the absence of a supportive relationship, they may more often signify the presence of a negative, conflictive relationship (Coyne & Bolger 1990). Perceived-support scales anchored by "high" and "low" support do not permit distinguishing these alternative meanings of low support.

Negative features of social relationships appear to correlate more strongly than positive features with measures of both perceived support and psychological symptoms (Fiore et al 1983; Pagel et al 1987; Rook 1984). "It is primarily the problematic features that cause, maintain, or fail to reduce psychological symptoms" (Pagel et al 1987:794). The ECA study has yielded provocative data on this issue (Weissman 1987). The risk of clinical depression for people who are married and can talk to their spouses is modestly lower than that of people who are single, separated, or divorced. This reduction may be viewed as a benefit of emotional support or intimacy, a positive effect of a good marriage, and thus a finding consistent with the conventional interpretation of the benefits of social support. Yet this positive effect is dwarfed by the negative one of being married and unable to talk to one's spouse. The adjusted odds-ratio for depression associated with being married and unable to talk to one's spouse was over 25 for both men and women. This effect size is extraordinary for epidemiological studies. As a concurrent association, it does not address questions of causality, but it offers evidence for the view that we may need to turn the concept of social support on its head. The apparent benefits of having support may in large part represent freedom from the deleterious effects of relationships that are conflictful, insecure, or otherwise not sustaining.

Such a change in interpretive perspective has profound conceptual and theoretical implications. The question of how social support buffers stress is supplemented by that of how involvement in dysfunctional relationships impairs coping with stress. Instead of focusing on social transactions presumed to convey support, we emphasize the conflict, inhibited communication, and lack of stability in close relationships that reduce the sense of support. In addition, if the observed association between social support and depression has its greatest effects in intimate relationships, and if the negative features of such relationships are more important than the positive, then literatures on marital distress and depression (Coyne et al 1990) and on expressed emotion (Hooley et al 1986) become especially relevant to our field.

A growing literature documents the complex relation between marital problems and depression, but a sense that such findings concern only marital quality has limited the attention accorded them in discussions of social support. Roy (1978) found that women reporting a lack of intimacy with their husbands were but a subset of those reporting a "bad marriage"; having a bad marriage, not the lack of a confiding relationship per se, leaves women at risk for depression. A number of studies suggest that spouses corroborate depressed persons' negative reports about the quality of their marriages (Coleman & Miller 1975; Kahn et al 1985; Merikangas et al 1985). Simply being married predicts slower recovery (George et al 1989) and diminished response to antidepressant treatment (Keller et al 1984). This effect of marital status may reflect the poorer outcomes for the considerable proportion of depressed persons who have marital problems, both in the short (Rounsaville et al 1979) and longer term (Rounsaville et al 1980). Other studies relate attitudes of the spouse to potential for relapse. Leff & Vaughn (1985) found that most spouses of depressed persons were critical of them; level of hostile criticism from the spouse, a key component of expressed emotion, strongly predicted patient relapse. Hooley et al (1986) replicated this finding (see Coyne et al 1990 for a more extensive review of the marriage and depression literature).

If the effects of social support on depression derive largely from problematic relationships, how should we distinguish between low support and stress? Lennon (1989) proposed that "the distinction between stressors and support blurs when we conceptualize the unit of study as actors embedded in social relations . . . [because] support and stressors often reside in the same set of interactions and cannot be understood apart from this relational context" (p. 262). And just as we need to understand how stress is embedded in life course and context, we need to understand how dysfunction in close relationships comes about and is perpetuated. Persons who spend a considerable portion of their adult lives in episodes of psychological disturbance may have difficulty maintaining a satisfactory relationship, but there are also questions of selective and assortative mating (Merikangas 1982). Brown et al (1986) found that depressed women with marital difficulties tended to be married to husbands whom raters found to be "grossly undependable." Several studies suggest that women's relationships with their spouses may be important mediators of the association between childhood adversity and depression in adulthood, and that the background of the spouse is a crucial determinant of the quality of this relationship. Indeed, it has been suggested that women whose background makes them particularly vulnerable to depression tend to marry men unable to provide a positive intimate relationship, and that early adverse experiences may in large part exert their effects through the selection of the spouse (Parker & Hadzi-Pavlovic 1984; Birtchnell 1980; Quinton, Rutter, & Liddle 1984).

The concept of social support was originally seen as a balance to the more negative view that social relationships were sources of stress. It was further intended to call attention to resources that might buffer or attenuate the effects of life events and other stressors. It now appears that a heterogeneous set of conditions influences perceptions of support but that the negative features of relationships may predominate. Theoretical formulations and techniques of assessing support have not yet come to terms with this balance.

Coping

Over the past decade, a consensus has developed on the basic dimensions of coping and how to assess them. Coping has been conceptualized in terms of approach-vs-avoidance (Suls & Fletcher 1985) and in terms of appraisal, problem focus, and emotion focus (Billings & Moos 1984). Appropriate self-report checklists have been developed. Lazarus & Folkman's (1984) distinction between problem-focused and emotion-focused coping has been by far the most influential conceptualization, and various versions of their Ways of Coping Checklist (WOCC) have been utilized in literally hundreds of studies (Stone et al, in press). In such research, respondents nominate a stressful recent incident and pick checklist items that reflect the thoughts and behaviors they have used to cope with it. Such assessments of coping in specific stressful episodes may be aggregated across situations or combinations of persons and situations (e.g. depressed persons coping with work problems or situations involving loss). Lazarus & Folkman's work on stress and coping has also been influential in establishing the notion that dispositional measures of coping do not adequately characterize the range of coping strategies used in dealing with complex situations. Cohen (1987) argues, for example, that because such measures may inadvertently tap personality (rather than coping strategies that predict adaptational outcomes), situational assessments of the kind provided by the WOCC are needed.

Despite the recent outpouring of studies, research on coping and psychopathology still lags considerably behind studies of other aspects of the stress process. The bulk of research relates current distress (rather than depressive disorder) to retrospective reports of coping with stressful episodes. A few studies have used repeated assessments to insure that the distress is not transient (Coyne et al 1981; Folkman & Lazarus 1986). These find that persons with chronic depressive symptoms do more wishful thinking, escape-avoidance, confrontation, and support-seeking. Such studies depict how distressed persons cope, not how coping reduces or exacerbates the effects of stress or how poor coping precedes the development of distress. It is also important to note that depressive symptoms and depressive disorders are different measures and may correlate differently with coping (Rhode et al 1990).

Studies of depressed patients have generally employed coping measures other than the WOCC. Depressed patients reported doing less problem-solving and more emotional discharge than controls on a brief measure of how they coped with a recent life event (Billings & Moos 1984); they reported socializing less and engaging in fewer distracting activities, and they rated themselves as more passive (Parker & Brown 1982). Differences between depressed persons and controls may be substantially reduced (Billings & Moos 1985) or disappear (Parker et al 1986) when the patients recover. In the only prospective study of coping and clinical depression to date, ineffective escapism was related to increases in depressive symptoms and new diagnosis of depression, but cognitive self-control and solace seeking were not (Rhode et al 1990).

The availability of theoretically derived and easily administered instruments for assessing coping represents an important advance in the field. Overall, however, the results from coping studies have not yet been particularly informative. They offer little wisdom about how to avoid becoming depressed, and little advice to improve the coping of persons vulnerable to depression or other forms of psychopathology. Generally speaking, research utilizing either measures of distress or diagnoses finds that particular coping patterns are positively related to symptoms or to the probability of being depressed; few or no strategies are found to be negatively related (Miller et al 1985; Coyne et al 1981; Parker & Brown 1982; Pearlin et al 1981; Aldwin & Revenson 1987). This positive correlation may reflect nothing more than the fact that the respondents were already distressed when they began coping with a specific incident; it may indicate that coping efforts become more intense but unfocused when things are not going well. One could conclude from the current literature that coping does little to buffer or attenuate stress; or, believing such a conclusion premature, one could find the research to date inadequate to determine whether the way one copes can reduce the potential for distress or depressive disorder.

Like checklist inventories of life events, coping checklists may open up an area of research without providing much in the way of definitive findings. A single, relatively brief checklist may be insufficient to capture the patterns of coping relevant to our purposes. It may be infeasible to assess the course and content of a stress episode by means of the respondent's choices among dichotomous items devoid of temporal sequence or narrative. We may also err in believing that checklists assess the competencies of the respondent. How one copes is constrained by how other persons involved in a stressful exchange cope (Kahn et al 1985). Differences in how people report they cope may reflect differences in their circumstances, and these may not readily be eliminated by matching or statistical controls. Thus, studies designed to identify the competencies that buffer individuals from the effects of stress almost inevitably confound competency both with level of upset at the time of the episode and with situational factors such as the quality of relationships with other persons involved in the incident.

Advances in the study of coping will likely have to follow the path set by innovations in the study of stress: namely, a reliance on semi-structured interviews and the judgments of trained raters to establish the details of how a stressful encounter unfolds and how well, given its circumstances, it is handled. Statements about effective and ineffective coping will undoubtedly have to be phrased in more specific terms. In our reviews of stress and social support we highlighted the importance of interpersonal discord. It is likely that studies of coping will need to give more attention to how people manage their close relationships. The basic dimensions of problem- and emotion-focused coping will need to be supplemented by considerations of *relationship-focused* coping: how people in distress deal with those with whom they have enduring relationships—others who offer advice, can have influence on the situation, and to some degree share their fate, despite disagreements and even hostility (Coyne & Smith 1991).

Violence, Sexual Abuse, and Other Victimization

These topics are seldom broached in discussions of stress and coping processes or in more general discussions of the role of social factors in psychopathology, but evidence is mounting that they are significant. Past or current victimization appears to be "a strong risk factor for the development of . . . lifetime mental health problems" (Kilpatrick et al 1987:65). Although reliable information on the prevalence of physical and sexual abuse is sparse, available data suggest high rates of violence against women. For example, Koss (1988) noted that 38–67% of women experience sexual abuse or assault before age 18 and almost one third of married women report violence in their current marriage. Systematic information on victimization history is not typically obtained from psychiatric patients. However, when such information is actively sought, a considerable proportion of both inpatient and outpatient women report physical and sexual abuse in childhood and in the recent past (Herman 1986; Carmen et al 1984; Jacobson & Richardson 1987).

Studies of the relation between victimization and specific disorders are limited. Nonetheless, physical and sexual victimization by strangers as well as by parents and spouses have been linked with a variety of disorders. Female victims of sexual abuse and assault may be the single largest group experiencing post-traumatic stress disorder (Koss 1990; Foa et al 1987). A childhood history of repeated victimization contributes in important ways to personality disorders (Bryer et al 1987), in particular to dissociative disorders. Ellis et al (1981) reported that 20% of adult survivors of rape and incest were seriously depressed and another 25% were moderately depressed. Childhood physical abuse has also been linked with adult depression and substance abuse (Holmes & Robins 1988).

According to Gelles & Straus (1988), women in violent marriages are compromised in nearly every area of their physical and mental health. Violence that is severe and recurrent leaves victims feeling depressed, demoralized, and powerless. Further investigation of the association between victimization and psychopathology is needed.

Cycles of abuse may be perpetuated across generations, although the extent of cross-generational continuity has not yet been established (Widom 1989a,b). Conversely, persons who have not been abused themselves are unlikely to become abusive adults (Kaufman & Zigler 1987; Quinton & Rutter 1988). Yet the continuities between childhood experience and victimization in adulthood are not clear-cut. Walker (1987) reports that most women in violent marriages were not abused as children. On the other hand the experience of childhood victimization appears to increase the risk of troubled relationships in adulthood (Koss 1990).

Intergenerational continuity of abuse is not inevitable. Several studies have identified a triad of factors that distinguish mothers who broke out of the cycle of abuse from those who abused their own children. The former were more likely to have received support from a nonabusive adult as a child, to have a supportive mate, and to have a reliable income (Egeland et al 1988; Quinton et al 1984; Hunter & Kilstrom, 1979). Egeland et al found that mothers who reenacted their maltreatment with their own children had themselves been more severely maltreated; they were more anxious, dependent, immature, and depressed than the nonabusive mothers. Such personality characteristics, which may be consequences of severe childhood abuse, may reduce the likelihood of positive adult relationships. Thus, salutary spousal relationships may be most difficult to achieve for those who most need them.

Obtaining valid information on victimization and its role in psychopathology is difficult. Many victims of domestic violence probably do not report the abuse in response to life-events checklist items about criminal victimization. Whether they endorse more specific items about rape, incest, or physical abuse is also questionable. Presumably many victims of spousal violence report a lack of social support from the spouse, but it is inappropriate to construe such marital problems as lack of perceived support. Coping inventories must generally miss how the threat of violence conditions coping efforts. Abused women expend considerable effort to prevent angering their spouses (Gelles & Straus 1988; Walker 1987). Such efforts often compromise potentially supportive relationships with other network members. Thus the experience of marital violence and the threat of its recurrence affect stress and coping processes in crucial ways difficult to identify without knowing that such a threat exists. Similarly, the experience of victimization in childhood may condition adult stress and coping processes.

Past applications of survey methodology to the study of victimization have been severely criticized on methodological grounds. In particular, it has been suggested that surveys may underestimate the prevalence of victimization and overestimate the role of victims in eliciting it (Yllö 1988). Many of the concerns we have raised here about survey and checklist methodologies are particularly applicable to the study of victimization. We hope future *Annual Review* chapters on social factors in psychopathology will be able to draw on a larger body of methodologically sound studies of victimization. Until this is possible, the absence of reference to victimization in discussions of social factors in psychopathology stands as a criticism of the field, not an indication that the factor is insignificant.

COMMENTARY

The momentum that has made studies of stress processes and depression and anxiety the most active research front in the social sciences is likely to continue. Yet a variety of factors will limit the further contribution of most of this literature to our understanding of the relationship between social factors and psychopathology. It is time for a parting of ways between researchers who are primarily interested in self-reported distress and depressive symptoms and those who are interested in psychopathology. The issue involves more than a difference between the adaptational outcomes to be examined. The emerging view of psychopathology outlined here dictates a fundamentally different and more complex set of research questions than is required in the study of social factors in distress. Diagnosable psychopathology is likely to have fewer social correlates than does distress. A past history of disturbance is likely to be a marker for increased susceptibility to other risks, including social factors; but such a history is also likely to be a major determinant of the adversities confronting the individual, the resources that are available, and how the stress process unfolds. In turn, there may be largely uncharted, long-term, reciprocal influences between social factors and vulnerability. In ways we are only beginning to grasp, tendencies to experience psychopathology, the major life contexts in which individuals find themselves, and how they meet developmental tasks are complexly intertwined over time.

Here we focus mainly on depression, but as the results of the ECA study become available and the newer diagnostic tools find wider application, our knowledge of the relationship of social factors to other diagnoses, particularly anxiety disorders, should also greatly increase. It remains to be seen to what extent current social factors, prior experience, and constitutional vulnerabilities determine which forms of psychopathology are manifested. Because individuals tend to be diagnosed with disorder more than once over the life course, this question is likely to prove difficult. We should also be alert to the possibility that similar social correlates may reflect very different processes. Thus, persons with a lifetime diagnosis of schizophrenia are more likely to be divorced than persons with major depressive disorder (Robins & Regier 1991), but the reasons for the two sets of divorces may be quite different.

The life-course perspective that we recommend here for the study of social factors and psychopathology requires a change in approach away from many of the simple questions of cause and effect that have dominated the field. Far too often, researchers use statistical analyses as if to approximate a controlled experiment with random assignment. For instance, it is misleading to interpret a regression analysis as indicating that "when marital support is controlled, the use of confrontative coping becomes a predictor of becoming depressed in the next six months." Such a conclusion neglects a host of complex relationships among history of depression, risk for recurrence, choice of mate, inter-episode adjustment, likelihood and specific nature of marital problems, and types of stressful episodes likely to require coping. As Meehl (1970) argued earlier and Lieberson (1985) has cogently demonstrated more recently, many efforts of social scientists to disentangle causal influences are hopelessly confused (see also Kessler 1987), and the study of social factors and psychopathology is rich with examples of this. Rather than strive for a control we cannot achieve, we can learn much about key influences by simply examining the nature of the nonrandom combinations of variables we would normally control (Lieberson 1985). Thus, rather than control current symptoms as a nuisance variable, we should examine how symptoms affect susceptibility to life events (see Hammen et al 1986).

Here we challenge the very identity of key variables in the stress process. Seemingly independent life events may be markers for other current adversities, or they may be the direct and indirect results of past experiences, including childhood adversity and victimization, previous episodes of psychopathology, and mate selection. Perceived support may often best be viewed as the absence of particular kinds of adversity in interpersonal relationships, and these adversities might just as well be seen as strains or chronic stressors. Assessments of coping may be unable to distinguish coping skills from distress and situational factors, including the key people in an individual's life. Matters do not always get this confusing, but we must not assume that stress is what a life-event inventory assesses, that social support is what a social support scale assesses, and that a coping checklist assesses coping and not stressor support. We should not attribute more precision to our concepts than is afforded by the life courses and social contexts of the individuals we study.

Finally, we doubt that various checklists adequately capture the patterns in the particulars of people's lives. The limitations of such instruments may be fundamental, and their objectivity illusory, particularly when it comes to substantive interpretation of their correlates. The use of semi-structured interviews and trained raters may be indispensable for addressing many theoretical questions about the relationships between social factors and psychopathology. When criteria are well specified and raters well trained, the validity of such data will undoubtedly exceed that of investigators' blind inferences about what circumstances led a respondent to endorse an item on a checklist.

Literature Cited

Akiskal, H. S. 1989. New insights into the nature and heterogeneity of mood disorders. *J. Clin. Psychol.* 50(5):6–12

Aldwin, C. M., Revenson, T. A. 1987. Does coping help? A reexamination of the relation between coping and mental health. *J. Pers. Soc. Psychol.* 53:337–48

Angst, J. 1986. The course of affective disorders. *Psychopathology* 19(2):47–52

American Psychiatric Association. 1980. *Diagnostic and Statistical Manual of Mental Disorders.* Washington, DC: Am. Psychiatr. Assoc. 3rd ed.

American Psychiatric Association. 1987. *Diagnostic and Statistical Manual of Mental Disorders.* Washington, DC: Am. Psychiatr. Assoc. 3rd rev. ed.

Barrera, M. Jr. 1981. In *Social Networks and Social Support,* ed. B. H. Gottlieb, pp. 69–96. Beverly Hills, CA: Sage Press

Billings, A. G., Moos, R. H. 1984. Coping, stress, and social resources among adults with unipolar depression. *J. Pers. Soc. Psychol.* 46:877–91

Billings, A. G., Moos, R. H. 1985. Life stressors and social resources affect posttreatment outcomes among depressed patients. *J. Abnorm. Psychol.* 94:140–53

Birtchnell, J. 1980. Women whose mothers died in childhood: an outcome study. *Psychol. Med.* 10:699–713

Black, D. W., Bell, S., Hulbert, J., Nasrallah, A. 1988. The importance of Axis II disorders in patients with major depression: a controlled study. *J. Affect. Disord.* 14:115–22

Bolger, N., Caspi, A., Downey, G., Moorehouse, M., eds. 1988. *Persons in Context: Developmental Processes.* NY: Cambridge Univ. Press

Bolger, N., DeLongis, A., Kessler, R. C., Shilling, E. A. 1989. Effects of daily stress on negative mood. *J. Pers. Soc. Psychol.* 57:808–18

Breslau, N., Davis, G. C. 1986. Chronic stress and major depression. *Arch. Gen. Psychol.* 43:309–14

Brier, A., Kelsoe, J. C., Kirwin, P. D., Beller, S. A., Wolkowitz, O. M., Pickar, D. 1988. Early parental loss and development of adult psychopathology. *Arch. Gen. Psychol.* 45:87–93

Bronfenbrenner, U. 1988. Interacting systems in human development. Research paradigms: past and future. In *Persons in Context: Developmental Processes,* ed. N. Bolger, A. Caspi, G. Downey, M. Moorehouse. New York: Cambridge Univ. Press

Brown, G. W., Harris, T. D. 1978. *Social Origins of Depression: A Study of Psychiatric Disorder in Women.* New York: Free Press

Brown, G. W., Bifulco, A., Harris, T., Bridge, L. 1986. Life stress, chronic subclinical symptoms and vulnerability to clinical depression. *J. Affect. Disord.* 11:1–19

Brugha, T., Bebbington, P., Tennant, C., Hurry, J. 1985. The list of threatening experiences: a subset of 12 life event categories with considerable long-term contextual threat. *Psychol. Med.* 15:189–91

Bryer, J. B., Nelson, B. A., Miller, J. B., Krol, P. A. 1987. Childhood sexual and physical abuse as factors in adult psychiatric illness. *Am. J. Psychol.* 144:1426–30

Carmen, E., Rieker, P., Mills, T. 1984. Victims of violence and psychiatric illness. *Am. J. Psychol.* 141:378–83

Cohen, F. 1987. Measurement of coping. In *Stress and Health: Issues in Research Methodology,* ed. S. V. Kasl, C. L. Cooper, pp. 283–305. John Wiley: New York

Cohen, S., Wills, T. A. 1985. Stress, social support, and the buffering hypothesis. *Psychol. Bull.* 98:310–57

Coleman, R. E., Miller, R. E. 1975. The relationship between depression and marital maladjustment in a clinic population: a multitrait-multimethod study. *J. Consult. Clin. Psychol.* 43:647–51

Coyne, J. C., Aldwin, C., Lazarus, R. S. 1981. Depression and coping in stressful episodes. *J. Abnorm. Psychol.* 90:439–47

Coyne, J. C., Bolger, N. 1990. Doing without social support as an explanatory concept. *J. Soc. Clin. Psychol.* 9:148–58

Coyne, J. C., Burchill, S. A. L., Stiles, W. B.

1990. An interactional perspective on depression. In *Handbook of Social and Clinical Psychology: The Health Perspective,* ed. C. R. Snyder & D. O. Forsyth. NY: Pergamon

Coyne, J. C., Gotlib, I. H. 1983. The role of cognition in depression: a critical appraisal. *Psychol. Bull.* 94:472–505

Coyne, J. C., Smith, D. A. F. 1991. Couples coping with myocardial infarction: wives' distress and the couple's relationship-focused coping. *J Per & Soc Psychol.* In press

Coyne, J. C., Kessler, R. C., Tal, M., Turnbull, J., Wortman, C., Greden, J. 1987. Living with a depressed person: burden and psychological distress. *J. Consult. Clin. Psychol.* 55:347–52

Cummings, E. M., Cicchetti, D. 1990. Toward a transactional model of relations between attachment and depression. In *Attachment in the Preschool Years: Theory, Research, and Intervention,* ed. M. T. Greenberg, D. Cicchetti, E. M. Cummings. Chicago: Univ. Chicago Press

Day, R., Nielsen, J. A., Korten, A., Ernberg, G., Dube, K. C., Gebhart, J., et al 1987. Stressful life events preceding the acute onset of schizophrenia: a cross-national study from the World Health Organization. *Cult. Med. Psychiatry* 11:123–205

Depue, R. A., Monroe, S. M. 1986. Conceptualization and measurement of human disorder in life stress research: the problem of chronic disturbance. *Psychol. Bull.* 99(1):36–51

Dohrenwend, B. S., Dohrenwend, B. P. 1981. Life stress and illness: formulation of the issues. In *Stressful Life Events and Their Contexts,* B. S. Dohrenwend, B. P. Dohrenwend. New York: Prodist

Dohrenwend, B. S., Dohrenwend, B. P. 1981. Social and cultural influences on psychopathology. *Annu. Rev. Psychol.* 25:417–52

Dohrenwend, B. P., Shrout, P. E., Link, B. G., Skodol, A. E., Martin, J. L. 1986. Overview and initial results from a risk factor study of depression and schizophrenia. In *Mental Disorders in the Community: Progress and Challenge,* ed. J. E. Barrett, pp. 184–215. New York: Guilford Press

Dolan, R. J., Calloway, S. P., Fonagy, P., De Souza, F. V. A., Wakeling, A. 1985. Life events, depression, and hypothalamic-pituitary-adrenal axis function. *Br. J. Psychol.* 147:429–33

Downey, G., Coyne, J. C. 1990. Children of depressed parents: an integrative review. *Psychol. Bull.* 108:50–76

Egeland, B., Jacobvitz, D., Sroufe, L. A. 1988. Breaking the cycle of abuse. *Child Dev.* 59:1080–88

Elder, G. H. Jr., Caspi, A., Downey, G.

1986. Problem behavior and family relations: life course and intergenerational themes. In *Human Development and the Life Course: Multidisciplinary Perspectives,* ed. A. Sorensen, F. Weinert, L. Sherrod. Hillsdale, NJ: Erlbaum

Ellis, E. M., Atkeson, B. M., Calhoun, K. S. 1981. An assessment of long term reaction to rape. *J. Abnorm. Psychol.* 90:263–66

Endicott, J., Spitzer, R. L. 1978. A diagnostic interview: the schedule for affective disorders and schizophrenia. *Arch. Gen. Psychol.* 35:837–44

Eron, L. S., Peterson, R. A. 1982. Abnormal behavior: social approaches. *Annu. Rev. Psychol.* 33:231–36

Ezquiaga, E., Gutierrez, J. L. A., Lopez, A. G. 1987. Psychosocial factors and episode number in depression. *J. Affect. Disord.* 12:135–38

Feighner, J. P., Robins, E., Guze, S., et al. 1972. Diagnostic criteria for use in psychiatric research. *Arch. Gen. Psychol.* 26:57–63

Finlay-Jones, R. A., Brown, G. W. 1981. Types of stressful life event and the onset of anxiety and depressive disorders. *Psychol. Med.* 11:803–15

Fiore, J., Becker, J., Coppell, D. A. B. 1983. Social network interactions: a buffer or a stress? *Am. J. Commun. Psychol.* 11:423–40

Foa, E. B., Olasov, B., Stekette, G. S. 1987. *Treatment of rape victims.* Paper presented at the Conf. State of the Art in Sexual Assault, Charleston, South Carolina

Folkman, S., Lazarus, R. S. 1986. Stress processes and depressive symptomatology. *J. Abnorm. Psychol.* 95(2):107–13

Garfield, E. 1987. The 1983 articles most cited in the SSCI 1983–1985. *Curr. Contents* 43(17):3–9

Geerwitz, C. 1973. *The Interpretation of Culture.* New York: Basic Books

Gelles, R. J., Straus, M. A. 1988. *Intimate Violence.* New York: Touchstone

George, L. K., Blazer, D. G., Hughes, D. C., Fowler, N. 1989. Social outcome and the outcome of major depression. *Br. J. Psychol.* 154:478–85

Goplerud, E., Depue, R. A. 1985. Behavioral response to naturally occurring stress in cyclothymia and dysthmia. *J. Abnorm. Psychol.* 94:128–39

Gurin, G., Veroff, J., Feld, S. 1960. *Americans View Their Mental Health.* New York: Basic Books

Hammen, C. 1988. Self cognitions, stressful events, and the prediction of depression in children of depressed mothers. *J. Abnorm. Child. Psychol.* 16:347–60

Hammen, C., Mayol, A., DeMayo, R., Marks, T. 1986. Initial symptom levels and the life-event-depression relationship. *J. Abnorm. Psychol.* 95(2):114–22

Harding, C. M., Brooks, G. W., Ashikaga, T., Strauss, J. S., Breier, A. 1987. The Vermont longitudinal study of persons with severe mental illness. I: Methodology, study sample, and overall status 32 years later. *Am. J. Psychol.* 144:718–26

Harris, T., Brown, G. E., Bifulco, A. 1987. Loss of parent in childhood in adult psychiatric disorder: the role of social class and premarital pregnancy. *Psychol. Med.* 17:163–83

Herman, J. L. 1986. History of violence in an outpatient population. *Am. J. Orthopsychiatry* 56:137–41

Holmes, S. J., Robins, L. N. 1988. The role of parental disciplinary practices in the development of depression and alcoholism. *Psychiatry* 51:24–36

Holzer, C., Shea, B., Swanson, J., Leaf, P., Myers, J., George L., et al. 1986. The increased risk for specific psychiatric disorders among persons of low socioeconomic status. *Am. J. Soc. Psychol.* 6:259–71

Hooley, J. M., Orley, J., Teasdale, J. D. 1986. Levels of expressed emotion and relapse in depressed patients. *Br. J. Psychol.* 148:642–47

Hopkins, J., Campbell, S. B., Marcus, M. 1989. Postpartum depression and postpartum adaptation: overlapping constructs? *J. Affect. Disord.* 17:251–54

Hough, R. L., Landsuerk, J. A., Stone, J. D., Jacobson, G. F. 1985. *Comparison of Psychiatric Screening Questionnaires for Primary Care Patients.* Final Rep. NIMH Contract No. 278-81-0036

House, J. S., Landis, K. R., Umberson, D. 1988. Social relationships and health. *Science* 241:540–45

Hunter, R., Kilstrom, N. 1979. Breaking the cycle in abusive families. *Am. J. Psychol.* 136:1320–22

Jacobson, A., Richardson, B. 1987. Assault experiences of 100 psychiatric inpatients: evidence of the need for routine inquiry. *Am. J. Psychol.* 144:900–13

Kahn, J., Coyne, J. C., Margolin, G. 1985. Depression and marital conflict: the social construction of despair. *J. Soc. Pers. Relat.* 2:447–62

Kaplan, G., Roberts, R., Camacho-Dickey, T., Coyne, J. C. 1987. Psychosocial predictors of depression: a nine-year follow-up study. *Am. J. Epidemiol.* 125:206–20

Kaufman, J., Zigler, E. 1987. Do abused children become abusive parents? *Am. J. Orthopsychiatry* 57:186–92

Keller, M. B. 1985. Chronic and recurrent affective disorders: incidence, course, and influencing factors. *Adv. Biochem. Psychopharmacol.* 40:111–20

Keller, M. B., Shapiro, R. W. 1982. "Double depression": superimposition of acute depressive episodes on chronic depressive disorders. *Am. J. Psychol.* 139:438–42

Keller, M. B., Klerman, G. L., Lavori, P. W., Coryell, W., Endicott, J., Taylor, J. 1984. Long-term outcome of episodes of major depression: clinical and public health significance. *J. Am. Med. Assoc.* 252:788–92

Kessler, R. C. 1987. The interplay of research design strategies and data analysis procedures in evaluating the effects of stress on health. In *Stress and Health: Issues in Research Methodology*, ed. S. V. Kasl, C. L. Cooper. New York: John Wiley

Kessler, R. C., Price, R. H., Wortman, C. B. 1985. Social factors in psychopathology: stress, social support, and coping processes. *Annu. Rev. Psychol.* 36:531–72

Kilpatrick, D. G., Saunders, B. E., Beronen, L. J., Best, C. L., Von, J. M. 1987. Criminal victimization: lifetime prevalence, reporting to police, and psychological impact. *Crime Delinq.* 33:479–89

King, L. M. 1978. Social and cultural influences on psychopathology. *Annu. Rev. Psychol.* 29:405–33

Klerman, G. L. 1989. Psychiatric diagnostic categories: issues of validity and measurement. *J. Health Soc. Behav.* 30:26–32

Koss, M. P. 1990. The women's mental health research agenda. Violence against women. *Am. Psychol.* 45:374–80

Koss, M. P. 1988. *The Women's Mental Health Research Agenda.* Rockville, MD: Natl. Inst. Ment. Health, Off. Women's Progr.

Langner, T. S. 1962. A twenty-two item screening score of psychiatric symptoms indicating impairment. *J. Health Hum. Behav.* 3:269–76

Lazarus, R. S., Folkman, S. 1984. *Stress, Appraisal, and Coping.* New York: Springer

Leaf, P. J., Weissman, M. M., Myers, J. K., Tischler, G. L., Holzer, C. E. 1984. Social factors related to psychiatric disorder: the Yale Epidemiologic Catchment Area Study. *Soc. Psychol.* 19:53–61

Leff, J. P., Vaughan, C. 1985. *Expressed Emotion in Families.* New York: Guilford Press

Lennon, M. C. 1989. The structural contexts of stress. *J. Health Soc. Behav.* 30:241–56

Lewinsohn, P. M., Hoberman, H. M., Rosenbaum, M. 1988. A prospective study of risk factors for unipolar depression. *J. Abnorm. Psychol.* 97:251–64

Lieberman, M. S., Mullin, T. J. 1978. Does help help? The adaptive consequences of obtaining help from professionals and social networks. *Am. J. Commun. Psychol.* 6:499–517

Lieberson, S. 1985. *Making It Count: The Improvement of Social Theory and Research.* Berkeley: Univ. Calif. Press

Lin, N., Dean, A., Ensel, W. 1986. *Social Support, Life Events and Depression.* Orlando, FL: Academic

Markowitz, J. S., Weissman, M. M., Ouellette, R., Lish, J. D., Klerman, G. L. 1989. Quality of life in panic disorder. *Arch. Gen. Psychol.* 46:984–92

McGuffin, P., Bebbington, P. 1988. The Camberwell collaborative depression study. III. Depression and adversity in the relatives of depressed patients. *Br. J. Psychol.* 152:775–82

Meehl, P. E. 1970. Nuisance variables and the ex post facto design. In *Minnesota Studies in the Philosophy of Science.* Vol. 4. *Analyses of Theories and Methods of Physics and Psychology*, ed. M. Radner, S. Winokur. Minneapolis: Univ. Minnesota Press

Merikangas, K. R. 1982. Assortative mating for psychiatric disorders and psychological traits. *Arch. Gen. Psychol.* 39:1173–80

Merikangas, K. R., Prusoff, B. A., Kupfer, D. J., Frank, E. 1985. Marital adjustment in major depression. *J. Affect. Disord.* 9:5–11

Miller, P., Surtees, P. G., Kreitman, N. B., Ingham, J. B., et al. 1985. Maladaptive coping in reactions to stress: a study of illness inception. *J. Nerv. Mental Disord.* 173:707–16

Mueller, D. P. 1980. Social networks: a promising direction for research on the relationship of the social environment to psychiatric disorder. *Soc. Sci. Med.* 14A:147–61

Nolen-Hoeksema, S. 1987. Sex differences in unipolar depression: evidence and theory. *Psychol. Bull.* 10(2):259–82

Oatley, K., Bolton, W. 1985. A social-cognitive theory of depression in reaction to life events. *Psychol. Rev.* 3:372–88

Pagel, M. D., Erdly, W. W., Becker, J. 1987. Social networks: We get by with (and in spite of) a little help from our friends. *J. Pers. Soc. Psychol.* 53:793–804

Parker, G., Brown, L. 1982. Coping behaviors that mediate between life events and depression. *Arch. Gen. Psychol.* 39:1386–91

Parker, G., Brown, L., Blignault, I. 1986. Coping behaviors as predictors of the course of clinical depression. *Arch. Gen. Psychol.* 43:561–65

Parker, G., Hadzi-Pavlovic, D. 1984. Modification of levels of depression in mother-bereaved women by prenatal and marital relationships. *Psychol. Med.* 14:125–35

Paykel, E. S., Myers, J. K., Dienelt, M. N., Klerman, G. L., Lindenthal, J. A., Pepper, M. P. 1969. Life events and depression: a controlled study. *Arch. Gen. Psychol.* 21:753–57

Pearlin, L. I. 1989. The sociolological study of stress. *J. Health Soc. Behav.* 30:241–56

Pearlin, L. I., Lieberman, M. S., Menaghan, E. G., Mullan, J. T. 1981. The stress process. *J. Health Soc. Behav.* 22:337–56

Perris, H. 1984. Life events and depression. *J. Affect. Disord.* 7:11–24

Phofl, B., Stangl, D., Zimmerman, M. 1984. The implications of DSM III-R personality disorders for patients with major depression. *J. Affect. Disord.* 7:309–18

Post, R. M., Rubinow, D. R., Bellenger, J. C. 1986. Condemning and sensitization in the longitudinal course of affective illness. *Br. J. Psychol.* 149:191–201

Quinton, D., Rutter, M., Liddle, C. 1984. Institutional rearing, parenting difficulties and marital support. *Psychol. Med.* 14:107–24

Quinton, D., Rutter, M. 1988. *Parenting Breakdown.* Aldershot, England: Avebury

Radloff, L. 1975. Sex differences and depression: the effects of occupational and marital status. *Sex Roles* 1:249–65

Regier, D. A., Myers, J. K., Kramer, M., et al. 1984. The NIMH Epidemiologic Catchment Area Program: historical context, major objectives, and study population characteristics. *Arch. Gen. Psychol.* 41:934–41

Rhode, P., Lewinsohn, P. M., Tilson, M., Seeley, J. 1990. The dimensionality of coping and its relation to depression. *J. Pers. Soc. Psychol.* 58:499–511

Robins, L. N., Regier, D., eds. 1991. *Psychiatric Disorder in America.* NY: Free Press. In press

Robins, L. N., Helzer, J. E. 1986. Diagnosis and clinical assessment: the current state of psychiatric diagnosis. *Annu. Rev. Psychol.* 37:409–32

Robins, L. N., Davis, D., Wish, E. 1977. Detecting predictors of rare events: demographics, family and personal deviance as predictors of stages in the progression to narcotic addiction. In *Origins and Course of Psychopathology,* ed. J. Strauss, H. M., Babigian, M. Roff. New York: Plenum

Robins, L. N., Helzer, J. E., Croughan, J. L., Williams, J. B., et al. 1981. *The NIMH Diagnostic Interview Schedule.* Version III. Washington, DC: Publ. Health Serv. (HSS) ADM-1-423 (5/81, 8/81)

Rook, K. 1984. The negative side of social interaction: impact on psychological well-being. *J. Pers. Soc. Psychol.* 46:109–18

Rounsaville, B. J., Prusoff, B. A., Weissman, M. M. 1980. The course of marital disputes in depressed women: a 48-month follow-up study. *Compr. Psychol.* 21:111–18

Rounsaville, B. J., Weissman, M. M., Prusoff, B. A., Herceg-Baron, R. L. 1979. Marital disputes and treatment outcome in depressed women. *Compr. Psychol.* 20:483–90

Roy, A. 1978. Risk factors and depression in Canadian women. *J. Affect. Disord.* 3:69–70

Rutter, M. 1966. *Children of Sick Parents.* Oxford: Oxford Univ. Press

Schulberg, H. C., Saul, M., McClelland, M., et al. 1985. Assessing depression in primary medical and psychiatric practices. *Arch. Gen. Psychol.* 42:1164–70

Shrout, P. E., Link, B. G., Dohrenwend, B. P., Skodol, A. E., Stueve, A., Mirotznik, J. 1989. Characterizing life events as risk factors for depression: the role of fateful loss events. *J. Abnorm. Psychol.* 98(4):460–67

Spitzer, R. L., Endicott, J., Robins, E. 1978. Research diagnostic criteria: rationale and reliability. *Arch. Gen. Psychol.* 35:773–82

Stone, A. A., Kennedy-Moore, E., Newman, M. G., Greenberg, M., Neale, J. M. 1990. Conceptual and methodological issues and current coping assessments. In *Personal Coping Theory, Research, and Application,* ed. B. N. Carpenter. NY: Guilford. In press

Strauss, J. S. 1989. Subjective experience of schizophrenia: toward a new dynamic psychiatry—II. *Schizophr. Bull.* 15:179–87

Strauss, J. S., Hisham, H., Lieberman, P., Harding, C. M. 1985. The course of psychiatric disorder. III: Longitudinal principles. *Am. J. Psychol.* 142:289–96

Suls, J., Fletcher, B. 1985. The relative efficacy of avoidant and nonavoidant coping strategies: a meta-analysis. *Health Psychol.* 4(3):249–88

van der Kolk, B. A. 1987. The psychological consequences of overwhelming life experiences. In *Psychological Trauma,* ed. B. A. van der Kolk. Washington, DC: Am. Psychiatric Press

Ventura, J., Nuechterlein, K. H., Lukoff, D., Hardesty, J. P. 1989. A prospective study of stressful life events and schizophrenic relapse. *J. Abnorm. Psychol.* 4:407–11

Walker, E. F. 1990. *Schizophrenia: A Life-Span Developmental Perspective.* NY: Academic. In press

Walker, L. E. 1987. Psychology and violence against women. *Am. Psychol.* 44:695–702

Walker, L. E. 1979. *The Battered Woman.* New York: Harper & Row Publishers

Weissman, M. M. 1987. Advances in psychiatric epidemiology: rates and risks for depression. *Am. J. Publ. Health* 77:445–51

Wells, K. B., Stewart, A., Burnam, M. A., et al. 1989. The functioning and well-being of depressed patients: results from the medical outcome study. *J. Am. Med. Assoc.* 262:914–19

Widom, C. S. 1989a. Does violence beget violence? A critical examination of the literature. *Psychol. Bull.* 106:3–28

Widom, C. S. 1989b. The cycle of violence. *Science* 244:160–66

Yllö, K. 1988. Political and methodological debates in wife abuse research. In *Feminist Perspectives on Wife Abuse,* ed. K. Yllö, M. Bograd. Newbury Park, CA: Sage Publications

Annu. Rev. Psychol. 1991. 42:427–58

ORGANIZATIONAL BEHAVIOR: WHERE WE'VE BEEN, WHERE WE'RE GOING

Charles A. O'Reilly III

School of Business Administration, University of California, Berkeley, California 94720

KEY WORDS: Micro-OB, Macro-OB, Organizational Psychology

CONTENTS

In 1979, Terry Mitchell, author of the first *Annual Review of Psychology* chapter on organizational behavior (OB), noted that OB "has become a distinct discipline with a focus on individual and group behavior in the organizational context" (1979:244). In the 11 years since this first chapter, there have been five additional reviews of OB (Cummings 1982; Staw 1984;

0066-4308/91/0201-0427$02.00

Schneider 1985; House & Singh 1987; Ilgen & Klein 1989). Ilgen & Klein (1989) call attention to the cognitive revolution that has characterized much theory and research in OB. House & Singh (1987) offered an in-depth treatment of leadership and reminded us to consider the ramifications of organizational evolution as we study processes within organizational settings. Schneider (1985) noted the importance of distinguishing between the individual and group levels of analysis in our research. Staw (1984) focused on the more applied aspects of OB as seen in the typical outcome variables used by OB researchers. Cummings (1982) called attention to macro-OB topics and highlighted methodological advances. Each of these chapters provides a rich cross-section of the field during the past 11 years.

Other important books, updates, and summaries have also appeared. For example, a recent issue of the *American Psychologist* was devoted to the changing face and place of work. In the introductory article, Offermann & Gowing (1990) discuss the future challenges facing both scholars and practitioners interested in organizations. They note the dramatic changes in the demography of the US workforce, the increased competition and challenges of maintaining productivity in a global environment, and the enormous impacts on organizations these will bring. How does research in the field of organizational behavior fit with these changes?

As we enter the 1990s, it seems useful to reflect broadly on what has changed in OB research since 1979 and to consider where the field is headed. This chapter is organized around three general questions. First, "Where has the field of organizational behavior been?" The six *Annual Review* chapters and other research summaries and journal contents offer a clear record of the trends and progress of the last decade.

Second, "Where is the field of OB today?" An answer can be found in the major organizational behavior journals published during the period 1987–1990 [i.e. *Academy of Management Journal* (AMJ), *Academy of Management Review* (AMR), *Administrative Science Quarterly* (ASQ), *Journal of Applied Psychology* (JAP), and *Organizational Behavior and Human Decision Processes* (OBHDP)]. These journals form the core for North American OB researchers. Other psychology and sociology journals (e.g. *Journal of Personality and Social Psychology, American Journal of Sociology*) and more international journals (e.g. *Journal of Occupational Psychology, Human Relations*) also publish relevant research. A content analysis of the types of articles published in these core journals as well as a review of the research published in a broad set of relevant journals will define the current state of OB research.

Finally, "Where is the field of OB going?" Based on emerging trends in research and exogenous changes in organizations and their environments, suggestions are made about areas of research that appear to offer promise for the construction of new theories and better insight into organizational phenomena.

WHERE HAS THE FIELD OF ORGANIZATIONAL BEHAVIOR BEEN?

What Is OB?

Each of the previous *Annual Review* chapters on the field has offered a definition of organizational behavior. Some authors have defined it in terms of its disciplines. Schneider (1985), for instance, defines OB as "the confluence of individual, group, and organizational studies flowing from industrial-organizational (I/O) psychology and organization and management theory (OMT) with headwaters in psychology (social, psychometrics), sociology (organizational, work, and occupational), and management (scientific, human relations)" (p. 574). Barry Staw (1984) focuses on the fundamental bifurcation in the field between the micro side (with its roots in psychology) and the macro side (drawing from sociology, political science, and economics). OB functions almost as two separate disciplines, with the macro researchers typically identifying with the American Sociological Association and the micro researchers with the American Psychological Association. This schizophrenic orientation is heightened by the tension between basic and applied research: Macro researchers are characteristically interested in broad theories and descriptive, empirical research not aimed at application, while micro researchers tend toward narrower theories and research topics involving application.

Fortunately, micro and macro research interests intersect at several points. The first is in the professional association, the Academy of Management, and its major journals, *The Academy of Management Journal* and the *Academy of Management Review.* These publications, along with others such as *Administrative Science Quarterly* and *Human Relations,* publish a blend of micro- and macro-OB studies. Second, as shown below, the tendency is growing for micro and macro studies to draw from each other's theory and research (Pfeffer 1982), and attention to issues of cross-level theory and research is increasing (e.g. Capelli 1990). Given the scope of the field and the interests of readers of the *Annual Review,* the present chapter reviews primarily material in micro-OB. Reviews of macro topics are available in the *Annual Review of Sociology.*

Themes in OB Research

Over the past decade, the micro-OB themes most frequently researched and reviewed have been: job attitudes; motivation; leadership; job design; individual differences; and outcomes such as absenteeism, turnover, and performance. While progress has been made, many of the discipline's theoretical streams have reached the point of diminishing returns. Many early theories of motivation, leadership, and job design have now been well researched. Recent studies tend to clarify fine theoretical points or establish boundary conditions rather than set off in new directions. For example, in the late 1970s, competing theories of job design created a lively intellectual dispute, and various theories of leadership competed actively for attention; but much of this theoretical foment has receded over the last ten years. Several books and chapters have provided authoritative summaries of research areas (e.g. Griffin 1987; Locke & Latham 1990; Vroom & Jago 1988), but few new theories or topics have emerged to focus attention. Many researchers now exhibit a more methodological orientation, with numerous meta-analytic studies summarizing areas of study (e.g. McEvoy & Cascio 1989; Wanous et al 1989).

While the micro side of OB seems to be in a dormant period, attention and interest have shifted substantially to the macro side. In 1979, 70% of the studies published in the *Academy of Management Journal* were on micro topics. By 1989 this figure had fallen to 38%. *Annual Review* authors in 1982, 1984, 1985, and 1987 called for more attention to cross-level research, studies that incorporate both individual and group or organizational-level variables. Mitchell (1979) and Ilgen & Klein (1989) both noted that micro-OB may have focused too narrowly, concentrating on rigorous empirical studies at the expense of more encompassing theory. Indeed micro-OB has attended to a comparatively narrow range of topics during the past decade.

WHERE IS THE FIELD OF MICRO-OB TODAY?

For the years 1987, 1988, and early 1990, all articles published in *JAP, AMJ, AMR, ASQ, OBHDP,* and the annual *Research in Organizational Behavior* volumes edited by Cummings & Staw and Staw & Cummings (1987–1989), were classified into content categories (e.g. test validation, job design, leadership, strategy, groups, etc). The proportion of studies published on particular topics was then used as an indicator of research interest.

Several themes defining the field of OB are notable. First, while both *JAP* and *OBHDP* remain almost exclusively micro or psychological in their orientation, the three major cross-disciplinary journals (*AMJ, AMR,* and *ASQ*) are now predominantly macro. For example, fewer than 40% of the articles published in *AMJ* are micro, while fewer than 20% of *AMR* and *ASQ* papers could be considered fundamentally psychological. This represents a significant shift in the field toward such macro topics as strategy and organizational design—approximately 40% of articles in *AMJ* during 1987–1990 were on strategy, organizational design, or control. A decade ago a comparable proportion of studies would have been on work attitudes and motivation.

On the micro side, the tally shows much of the research focused on methodological or validation issues. During the period reviewed here, almost 30% of articles published in *JAP* were methodological (e.g. validity generalization). If, for purposes of this review, one ignores more traditional industrial/organizational studies (e.g. performance appraisal, jury selection, training, human factors) and focuses primarily on traditional micro-OB topics, most research during 1987–1990 has centered on five areas: motivation (61 studies); work attitudes such as job satisfaction and commitment (38 studies); job analysis and task design (34 studies); studies of turnover and absenteeism (32); and leadership (21 studies). Not surprisingly, these have also been the topics most often reviewed by *Annual Review of Psychology* authors.

In 1979, Terry Mitchell organized his chapter around job attitudes, motivation, and leadership, taking a more pessimistic view of research on personality and individual differences. The following sections briefly review the five topic areas in micro-OB that received the most research attention during 1987–1990. Let's see what, if anything, has changed in the intervening decade.

Motivation

Over the past several years, motivation has been the most frequently researched topic in micro-OB, with over 60 studies published. In their recent review, Katzell & Thompson (1990) define work motivation as "a broad construct pertaining to the conditions and processes that account for the arousal, direction, magnitude, and maintenance of effort in a person's job" (p. 144). Under this general definition, a variety of new approaches have been suggested. Hyland (1988), for example, proposes a control-theory framework in an effort to integrate early motivational theories, including those by Atkinson, Deci, and Locke. In this view, behavior is explained in terms of variation in either the amount of energy invested in specific goals, the goals themselves, or the organization of the goals. Klein (1989) also proposes a control-theory model to integrate earlier work. Both of these approaches are ambitious but at present lack empirical support. Guastello (1987) also offers a new perspective, suggesting that motivation may best be explained using nonlinear catastrophe models. He offers some evidence for these nonlinear effects in explaining academic performance. Other novel approaches to motivation include the use of scripts as determinants of behavior (Lord & Kernan 1987) and a focus on the role of language in motivation theory (Sullivan 1988). Kanfer & Ackerman (1989) offer both a theoretical perspective and relevant empirical evidence demonstrating how motivation and cognitive ability can be integrated within an information-processing framework. They show, for instance, how interventions designed to engage motivational processes may impede task learning if presented before the subject understands the task. Their results suggest that researchers must pay greater attention to interactions between cognitive abilities and motivational interventions.

While these represent less frequently used motivational theories, the bulk of the empirical research in organizational behavior continues to focus on two dominant theories: goal setting and equity. A resurgence of interest in intrinsic motivation has occurred primarily in social psychology.

GOAL SETTING   This approach continues to attract the bulk of research attention, with over 20 studies published in the past few years. Locke & Latham (1990) have published the definitive book on the subject, *A Theory of Goal Setting and Task Performance,* in which they summarize and integrate research done over 25 years and encompassing over 500 experiments and 40,000 subjects. Their comprehensive review treats the efforts of such researchers as Earley (e.g. Earley et al 1989), Hollenbeck (e.g. Hollenbeck et al 1989), and Erez (e.g. Erez & Earley 1987). In their Chapter 2, Locke & Latham summarize the core findings of this stream of research: goal difficulty is linearly related to performance; and the establishment of specific, difficult goals is associated with levels of performance higher than those associated with instructions to do your best or with an absence of assigned goals. Further, goal commitment is crucial to the effectiveness of goal setting (e.g. Locke et al 1988). Overall, this work is broad, deep, and, as Locke & Latham (1990) stress, useful to practitioners.

Two noteworthy studies illustrate this general approach. Pritchard et al (1988) report the results of an extraordinary field study using five intact work groups studied over two years. The study involved multiple, sequential examinations (using the researchers' own productivity measurement system) of how feedback, goal setting, and incentives affected group productivity. Group-level feedback increased productivity an average of 50% over baseline, group goal setting increased productivity another 25%, and incentives increased productivity still further. This study, complex and careful, provides convincing evidence for the utility of goal setting, feedback, and incentives in attempts to increase group productivity.

In a second notable study, Latham, Erez, and Locke (Latham et al 1988) jointly designed an experiment to resolve their conflicting findings. Previous research by Erez and her colleagues had shown that participation in goal setting was crucial to obtaining goal commitment. Latham and his colleagues had found that assigned goals were generally as effective as those set participatively. In collaboration with Locke, a set of definitive experiments was jointly designed and conducted. Results showed that previous differences had resulted from Erez's "tell" instructions under the assigned-goals condition versus Latham's "tell and sell." Together, the experiments conducted by Latham et al (1988) showed that the motivational effects of assigned goals are as powerful as those of participatively set goals in generating goal commitment and subsequent performance.

EQUITY THEORY   Equity theory has continued to attract substantial attention, with 13 studies during 1987–1989. Much of the current interest is focused on issues of procedural and distributive justice (e.g. Greenberg 1987a). A core problem with equity theory has been that in emphasizing the results of reward-allocation, researchers have typically ignored reactions to how the decision leading to the results was made. Evidence, however, suggests that people may react differently to the same inequity depending on their beliefs about how the inequity was created. Greenberg (1987b), for instance, offers an interesting taxonomy based on how various equity theories focus attention on the processes used to make decisions.

Evidence for the general validity of equity theory and data on the effects of both procedural and distributive justice continue to accumulate. For example, Greenberg (1988), in a clever field experiment involving the office relocation of insurance company employees, finds that workers reassigned to higher-status offices raised their performance while those reassigned to lower-status offices lowered their performance levels, both predictions consistent with equity theory. Folger & Konovsky (1989), in a study of employee reactions to pay raises, found that distributive justice considerations better accounted for variance in satisfaction, while procedural justice accounted for greater variance in several other work attitudes. In a laboratory study, Greenberg (1987c) found that subjects were most concerned with procedural justice when they were underrewarded.

Several new theoretical variants of equity theory have also been developed. Lind & Tyler (1988) proposed a group-value approach to procedural justice. Tyler's results (1989) suggest that judgments about the fairness of the process may affect both preferences for the procedure and assessments of procedural justice. Folger (1986) has proposed a referent-cognitions-theory (RCT) approach to procedural justice that emphasizes the role decision-making procedures play in shaping perceptions of unfair treatment. Cropanzano & Folger (1989) found that subjects who expressed a preference for how their performance was to be judged and then were told that their preference had not been heeded were more likely to complain of unfair treatment than subjects who were not given a choice. Other research has also demonstrated that feelings about equity may be affected by individual preferences and interpersonal factors (Dalton et al 1987; Griffith et al 1989; Huseman et al 1987; Rasinski 1987). These refinements and extensions in theory continue to make equity an active topic in micro-OB.

INTRINSIC MOTIVATION   In 1979, Mitchell noted that one of the new directions in research on motivation was based on Deci's (1975) finding that when people are engaged in intrinsically interesting tasks, added external rewards (e.g. monetary payments) may decrease task interest. Similarly, people who can be induced to engage in a task without extrinsic rewards may subsequently evaluate the task on its intrinsic properties, even when such tasks seem uninteresting. Extending this early theory, Deci & Ryan (1985) have argued that contextual factors do not determine behavior in any straightforward sense; instead, individuals provide psychological meaning, referred to as "functional significance," to those contextual factors. Of central importance is whether people construe contexts as supporting their autonomy (e.g. encouraging them to make their own choices) or controlling their behavior. Deci & Ryan (1987) have recently extended their theory and conclude, based on a wide range of evidence, that "when the context is autonomy supportive, people initiate regulatory processes that are qualitatively different from those that are initiated when the functional significance of the events or context is controlling" (p. 1033). In their view, what distinguishes intrinsic and extrinsic motivation is whether an activity is engaged in for its inherent satisfaction or done to obtain a separable goal.

Deci et al (1989) offer empirical evidence that supervisors' support for self-determination increased subordinate trust and satisfaction. Other studies have obtained similar results (e.g. Cellar & Wade 1988). In general, how contextual cues affect motivation depends on the nature and salience of an individual's performance goals. When an individual is engaging in a task for intrinsic rather than instrumental reasons, extrinsic rewards and feedback typically reduce interest, whereas the opposite is not the case (e.g. Harackiewicz et al 1987; Sansone et al 1989). Cellar & Barrett (1987) suggest that these results may stem from different scripts or labels applied to the activity (e.g. play vs work). Hirst (1988) demonstrated that task interdependence and goal setting can affect intrinsic motivation. Using 64 managers engaged in two laboratory tasks, he showed that for each independent activity, setting specific, difficult goals increased intrinsic motivation while the same goal-setting process reduced intrinsic motivation when the tasks were reciprocally interdependent. He interpreted these findings as showing that task interdependence provides more opportunities for subjects to experience feelings of competence.

While findings such as these generally support Deci & Ryan's (1987) theory, questions still exist about the circumstances under which extrinsic reinforcers impair intrinsic motivation. Scott et al (1988), for instance, have shown that adding a monetary incentive increased task performance without diminishing intrinsic interest. In an analysis of a 114-month data series from a unionized iron foundry, Wagner et al (1988) found that a nonmanagerial incentive system had positive long-term effects on productivity. These results suggest the importance of understanding the individual's motives for engaging in a task, and of recognizing that people have both instrumental and intrinsic interests. Research has not yet clarified these distinctions sufficiently. Nevertheless, given the prevalence of extrinsic reinforcers in organizations and the frequent need for initiative and innovation among workers, interest in intrinsic motivation appears to be important for future organizations.

Overall, motivation continues to generate a great deal of research, both in what Katzell & Thompson (1990) refer to as exogenous theories (those concerned with independent variables that can be changed by external agents, such as goals or reinforcements) and in endogenous theories (those focused on internal processes that mediate the effects of work conditions on performance, such as equity and attributions). Most recent research has centered on the three major theories discussed. Other work has examined individual differences, such as needs (Raven 1988), self-esteem (Sandelands et al 1988), and Type A patterns (Spence et al 1989). The importance of the topic of motivation for practitioners is likely to increase in the next decade as the number of new workers entering the work force declines. Offermann & Gowing (1990) report that in the 1970s there were about 3 million new workers per year. By 1995 there will be 1.3 million fewer workers, in absolute terms, in the 18–24-year-old cohort. The number of people aged 48–53 will increase by 67% between 1986 and 2000. These are massive changes. At lower organizational levels, there may be significant labor shortages; and in the middle of the hierarchy, promotion rates may slow considerably. Issues of motivation for younger, older, and ethnically diverse workers will likely become more salient.

Work Attitudes

Work-related attitudes (e.g. job satisfaction, commitment, and self-reported stress) comprise the second most frequently published topic in micro-OB. Work attitudes are typically defined as positive or negative evaluations about aspects of one's work environment. While much of this research is conventional, concerned with the development and validation of attitude measures (e.g. Ironson et al 1989) or investigating antecedents and consequences of job attitudes (e.g. Frone & McFarlin 1989; Meyer et al 1989), new and exciting research has begun to explore the basic nature of affect in the workplace (e.g. Levin & Stokes 1989), the relationship between moods and work outcomes (Meyer & Shack 1989; Sinclair 1988), and the expression of emotion at work (Rafaeli & Sutton 1989). This research shows great promise for clarifying and extending our understanding of work-related attitudes.

JOB SATISFACTION   In spite of substantial evidence that it is not consistently linked to performance (e.g. Staw 1984), job satisfaction remains the single most frequently studied job attitude, accounting by some estimates for over 4000 published studies (O'Connor et al 1978). Researchers continue to develop and refine measures of job satisfaction. Roznowski (1989), for instance, suggests improvements to Smith et al's (1969) Job Descriptive Index (JDI), the most frequently used measure of job satisfaction. Ironson et al (1989) describe the construction of a global satisfaction measure, the Job in General scale. Using over 9000 respondents, they argue that global and facet satisfaction scales may not be equivalent. Other researchers continue to develop alternative satisfaction scales (Kerber & Campbell 1987; Scarpello & Vandenberg 1987), including instruments intended to determine whether job satisfaction measures are comparable (e.g. Brief & Roberson 1989; Sawyer 1988) or susceptible to method bias (Spector 1987).

Researchers continue to explore the antecedents and consequences of job satisfaction. For example, questions still exist about the nature of the association between age and job satisfaction. In a meta-analysis, Brush et al (1987) report positive associations between age and satisfaction, while Kacmar & Ferris (1989) find support for both a linear and a U-shaped relationship. Pond & Geyer (1987) find that employee age is associated with the relation between perceived job alternatives and satisfaction. Tsui & O'Reilly (1989) argue that demographic effects may be nonlinear, with increasing distance (in tenure, age, race, and education) between superiors and subordinates having progressively larger effects. They show, for example, that increasing variation in demographic attributes between superiors and subordinates have negative effects on job attitudes beyond what is captured by simple demographic variables.

Several studies have focused on how satisfaction at work is related to satisfaction away from the job. Shaffer (1987) suggested that the inconclusiveness of such studies may be explained by the varying background experiences of the workers in the samples. Contrary to previous reviews, Tait et al (1989) found considerable overlap between work and nonwork satisfaction, with stronger associations for men than for women, in studies published prior to 1974. In a related vein, Parasuraman et al (1989) reported lower levels of job satisfaction among husbands of employed women than among husbands of housewives.

An interesting dispute in the literature concerns the degree to which job satisfaction may be dispositional. The controversy was provoked largely by the studies of Staw and his colleagues (Staw et al 1986; Staw & Ross 1985), who provided evidence suggesting that affective responses to work may be stable over time and across jobs. This position has been vigorously attacked by situationists in a resurrection of the person-situation debate (e.g. Davis-

Blake & Pfeffer 1989). Gerhart (1987), for example, criticizes the original Staw research and uses longitudinal data to assess the impact of changes in job complexity on job satisfaction. He argues that over a three-year interval job complexity significantly affects subsequent job satisfaction. However, Gerhart also finds previous job satisfaction to predict current satisfaction and acknowledges the importance of both. In a provocative study of 34 pairs of identical twins, Arvey et al (1989) reported that roughly 30% of variance in general job satisfaction was due to genetic factors. (The investigators attempted to control for job characteristics.) Other studies, notably those showing the stability of negative affect as a disposition (e.g. Levin & Stokes 1989), raise interesting issues about the causes and consequences of job satisfaction. These significant new approaches may extend the study of job satisfaction in useful ways.

COMMITMENT   In 1979, Mitchell noted that research in organizational commitment was relatively new. By 1985, a substantial amount of research had accumulated, with the Organizational Commitment Questionnaire (OCQ) representing the dominant approach (Mowday et al 1982). By this point, however, Schneider (1985) noted that some confusion had developed in defining the construct. Although progress is being made, some of this confusion still exists.

First, what is commitment and how does it differ from similar constructs such as job involvement and satisfaction? Mowday et al (1982) define commitment in terms of an individual's identification with and involvement in a focal organization. Their measure, the OCQ, includes assessments of motivation, intent to remain, and identification. Several researchers have examined the factor structure of the OCQ and reported multiple factors rather than a unidimensional structure (e.g. Tetrick & Farkas 1988). Others have suggested that there may be two types of commitment; one attitudinal (reflecting identification) and the other behavioral (indicating an intent to stay) (Meyer & Allen 1984). McGee & Ford (1987) report that there may be even more dimensions. Using the Meyer & Allen (1984) measures, they found a single dimension for affective commitment and two dimensions for continuance commitment (one based on having few employment alternatives, the second on the personal sacrifice associated with leaving the organization). Affective commitment was correlated negatively with few employment alternatives and positively with personal sacrifice. O'Reilly & Chatman (1986) argue that part of the confusion surrounding the construct stems from a failure to differentiate between the antecedents to commitment and the consequences of being committed. They suggest distinguishing commitment (psychological attachment resulting from identification and internalization) from compliance. Caldwell et al (1990) report two factor-analytically derived dimensions, one defined by identification [similar to that of Mowday et al (1982)] and one based on compliance or instrumental attachment [similar to the continuance commitment of Meyer & Allen (1984)]. Other studies have broadened the notion of commitment to include commitment to careers (Blau 1988) and to the union (e.g. Klandermans 1989; Magenau et al 1988; Tetrick et al 1989). Other research has shown that commitment is empirically distinct from related constructs such as job satisfaction and job involvement (Brooke et al 1988; Farkas & Tetrick 1989; Glisson & Durick 1988; Meyer et al 1989).

Numerous other investigations have explored both the antecedents and the consequences of commitment. Several studies have shown that organizational attributes such as structure, human-resource practices, reward systems, and leadership may affect individual commitment (DeCotiis & Summers 1987; Glisson & Durick 1988; Luthans et al 1987; Mottaz 1988). In an interesting qualitative study of a college basketball team, Adler & Adler (1988) identified five elements essential to the development of intense loyalty: domination by a strong leader, identification with the group and its leader, commitment through investment and public expression, integration into cohesive groups, and clarity of goals and expectations. These socialization experiences appear similar to the processes that lead to behavioral commitment (Staw & Ross 1989) and are often found in high-involvement organizations (Galanter 1989; Lawler 1988; O'Reilly 1989).

Continuing interest in organizational commitment stems in part from the generally positive consequences that result when organizations have committed members. Research findings continue to show that higher levels of commitment are related to lower turnover intentions (Shore & Martin 1989), lower actual turnover (Farkas & Tetrick 1989; O'Reilly & Chatman 1986), and higher job performance (Meyer et al 1989). Randall (1987), however, doubted that the consequences of high employee commitment are uniformly positive and suggested that negative personal and organizational consequences may stem from family tensions and lack of organizational flexibility. In a partial test of the latter suggestion Romzek (1989) investigated the relationship between job commitment and satisfaction (both in and out of work). She reported that the consequences of employee commitment for the individual are positive, supporting the notion that psychological attachment to an organization may yield personal benefits and contradicting the idea that individuals must pay a high price for high levels of organizational commitment.

STRESS   During 1987–1990, 19 studies focused on the determinants of job stress. Several suggest that the lack of clarity in previous research on the topic stems from the multidisciplinary nature of the field and the overreliance on self-report measures (Handy 1988; Steffy & Jones 1988). Brief et al (1988) offer provocative evidence that a person's disposition toward negative affectivity may inflate reports of stress. Convincing evidence exists for the relationship between certain aspects of job design and increased stress, although the evidence for moderator effects remains mixed (Dooley et al 1987; Frone & McFarlin 1989; Martocchio & O'Leary 1989; Sutton & Rafaeli 1987). Spector et al (1988) find both convergent and discriminant validity for the associations between stress and job autonomy, workload, number of hours worked, and number of people worked for. Martin & Wall (1989) report increased stress from jobs with increased attentional demand and cost responsibility. In a new book, Karasek & Theorell (1990) conclude that stress is a function of what they call "decision latitude"—whether the incumbent has a chance to use skills, exercise initiative, and otherwise control the working conditions. Tetrick & LaRocco (1987) also report that understanding and control can moderate reports of stress, as can support from others (Barling et al 1987; Russell et al 1987) and stress management interventions (Bruning & Frew 1987; Jones et al 1988). A comprehensive review and critique of stress management interventions (Ivancevich et al 1990) concludes that much of our present knowledge about these techniques is based on methodologically weak research, although more rigorous studies are appearing at a slowly increasing rate.

AFFECT AND MOOD   Research in the area of positive/negative affect and mood promises to reorient our thinking about work attitudes. In 1982, Zevon & Tellegen (1982) suggested that positive and negative affect might be separate dimensions, not opposite ends of the same continuum as assumed in most research on job attitudes. In a short time frame, the two feelings may appear inversely related, since we typically have a dominant affective response to a stimulus; but Diener & Emmons (1985) have cleverly demonstrated how, over time, positive and negative affect are independent constructs. Watson & Tellegen (1985) confirmed the two-factor structure of mood. They showed that high positive affect reflects the degree to which a person feels enthusiastic, active, and alert. Low positive affect is characterized by sadness and lethargy. High negative affect is a general dimension of subjective distress and unpleasurable engagement including feelings of anger, disgust, and guilt. Low negative affect is characterized by feelings of calmness and serenity. Watson & Tellegen (1985) offer a circumplex of moods defined by the positive and negative axes that has been replicated several times (e.g. Russell et al 1989a). Most recently, Meyer & Shack (1989) have shown how the two mood dimensions may relate to basic personality structures.

Drawing upon this work, a number of researchers have developed measurements of positive and negative affect. Watson et al (1988) developed a brief, easy to administer 10-item mood scale, the Positive and Negative Affect Schedule (PANAS). Russell et al (1989b) constructed the Affect Grid, a single-item scale, designed as a quick means of assessing affect along the dimensions of pleasure-displeasure and arousal-sleepiness. Burke et al (1989) offer four unipolar factors assessing each of the four affective states.

Recognizing that positive and negative affect are separate dimensions and that these affective states may be dispositional has fundamental implications for the study of work attitudes. For instance, even transitory positive moods have been shown to increase helping behavior (Carlson et al 1988), increase the likelihood of accepting feedback (Esses 1989), result in more positive impressions of others (Forgas & Bower 1987), and facilitate creative problem solving (Isen et al 1987). Positive mood states have also been found to affect subjects' utility estimates (e.g. Isen et al 1988). Negative affect has been shown to increase perceived stress, health care needs (Salovey & Birnbaum 1989), and the accuracy of perceptions (e.g. Sinclair 1988). Shelley Taylor (1989) has summarized much of this research in a recent book.

The recognition that affect cannot be adequately assessed as a single dimension and that affect may have a dispositional component raises important questions about traditional work attitudes, such as satisfaction (Levin & Stokes 1989), job stress (Burke et al 1989), and even outcomes such as absenteeism (George 1989) and group behavior (George 1990). Indeed, as Sutton & Rafaeli (1988) have shown, the question of how emotion is displayed at work has been underresearched (e.g. Rafaeli 1989; Rafaeli & Sutton 1987, 1989). The general approach to work-related attitudes appears to be undergoing a provocative reappraisal.

Job Design

In his 1984 review, Barry Staw identified research on job design as the most active forum for work on job attitudes. During the 1970s, most of this research was based on Hackman & Oldham's Job Characteristics Theory (1980). This formulation posited that five job characteristics (skill variety, task identity, task significance, autonomy, and feedback) contribute to internal work motivation and job attitudes. This approach is based on a need-fulfillment notion that certain job characteristics are associated with increased motivation. In the late 1970s, Salancik & Pfeffer (1977, 1978) criticized this approach and proposed an alternative Social Information Processing (SIP) view, which claimed that task perceptions and affective responses were functions of social cues. These alternative perspectives sparked substantial debate and research (e.g. Roberts & Glick 1981). In reviewing this literature, Ilgen & Klein (1989) conclude that "The primary conclusion to be drawn from this work is that social cues do affect perceptions of job characteristics and affective responses to jobs" (Griffin 1987; Griffin et al 1987).

Although evidence for an integrated perspective seems convincing, research continues on both sides of the debate (Hogan & Martell 1987; Kilduff & Regan 1988). Several recent studies, for example, have proposed revisions of the original Job Diagnostic Survey (JDS) (Idaszak et al 1988; Idaszak & Drasgow 1987; Kulik et al 1988). Zaccaro & Stone (1988), in a study of chemical plant employees, confirmed the relationship between JDS-based measures and job satisfaction but also found effects for job characteristics not assessed with the JDS, leading them to conclude that use of the JDS alone may needlessly restrict researchers' ability to explain outcomes such as job satisfaction and intent to leave. They argue that two non-JDS measures, job-related danger and intellectual demand, are also important. Other researchers have also suggested the need for better measures of task complexity (Campbell 1988; Gerhart 1988). From an SIP viewpoint, Kulik (1989) has shown that judgments of a job's motivating potential may depend on the categorizations made by respondents; that is, individuals may use protypical categories to assess a job's motivating potential rather than systematically evaluating job characteristics. Sandelands & Calder (1987) found that subjects may organize perceptions of tasks in ways not adequately captured through a priori measurement schemes. James & James (1989) explored the larger question of how individuals impute meaning to their work environments. Using a hierarchical cognitive model they find a single, general factor underlying several different measures and conclude that people may evaluate work based on a simple notion of how its facets are personally beneficial.

Staw & Boettger (1990) address a new topic, task revision. They argue that an overlooked aspect of job design is the ability and willingness of job incumbents to correct faulty procedures. Results of several laboratory experiments show that goal setting inhibited task revision while accountability pressures facilitated it. Overall, however, the excitement in job design research shown in the late 1970s has diminished, with most current efforts falling into the realm of extensions or refinements of existing theories.

An interesting perspective on the current state of job design research is offered by Campion (1988), who notes that in micro-OB most research has focused on the motivational properties of jobs. However, other active streams of research on job design in disciplines such as industrial engineering, ergonomics, and human information processing, have had different outcome measures in mind. For example, using a sample of 92 jobs and over 1000 respondents, he shows that different job attributes are systematically related to different job outcomes and largely independent of each other and of individual moderator effects. Perceptual and motor skill assessments, for example, were strongly related to reliability of performance but not to job attitudes. Campion concludes that, independent of the types of jobs, nature of the instruments used, or level of analysis, a comprehensive theory of job design needs to be interdisciplinary. He offers a useful taxonomy. This suggestion seems particularly appropriate since most of the industrial psychological research on job analysis has proceeded virtually independently of interest in job design (e.g. Harvey & Lozada-Larsen 1988; Mullins & Kimbrough 1988).

Turnover and Absenteeism

During the past three years over 30 studies of absenteeism and turnover have been published. In general, these investigations try either (a) to predict absenteeism or turnover by using an arbitrary set of predictors or by selecting variables from one or another model of the withdrawal process (e.g. Frayne & Latham 1987; Griffeth & Hom 1988; Inwald 1988) or (b) to improve prediction through the identification of moderator variables (e.g. Carsten & Spector 1987; Kanfer et al 1988; Parkes 1987).

For instance, direct associations between turnover and job satisfaction have typically not been large—usually less than r = .40 (Carsten & Spector 1987). This has led researchers to search for potential moderators of this relationship. Several studies have shown that people are less likely to leave their jobs when the external labor market makes leaving one's job costly or when alternative employment opportunities are fewer (Capelli & Chauvin 1990; Rusbult et al 1988; Withey & Cooper 1989). Carsten & Spector (1987) showed that satisfaction-turnover relationships were stronger when alternative job opportunities were plentiful. Others have argued that the use of self-report measures of job alternatives is flawed (Steel & Griffeth 1989). In a meta-analysis of studies of turnover and employee performance, McEvoy & Cascio (1987) found that turnover is generally lower among good performers. In a field study of new employees, Kanfer et al (1988) found that poor performers were more likely to leave in the first year than were good performers; poor performers were absent more frequently during this period. Analogous studies have found moderators of absenteeism to include variables such as body weight (Parkes 1987), organizational policies (Farrell & Stamm 1988; Majchrzak 1987) and gender (Hackett 1989). In an interesting field study of underground coal miners, Goodman & Garber (1988) showed that absenteeism was related to increased chances of accidents when such absenteeism lessened familiarity with job procedures. In another interesting approach, Mathieu & Kohler (1990) showed that group-level absence significantly predicted subsequent individual absence beyond that predicted by previous individual absence. This evidence suggests that group-level factors may influence individual absence behavior.

While these studies add useful increments to our knowledge about absenteeism and turnover, perhaps the most interesting developments in this area have been methodological. Two techniques with origins in biomedical statistics—survival analysis and event history models—are particularly well suited to longitudinal analysis of data with such binary dependent variables as absenteeism and turnover. While these models have been widely used in sociology (Tuma & Hannan 1984), they have only recently been introduced into the micro-OB literature (e.g. Fichman 1988, 1989; Peters & Sheridan 1988). Morita et al (1989) provide an excellent introduction to survival analysis of turnover, while Harrison & Hulin (1989) provide an equally lucid application of event history models to absenteeism.

Both of these approaches allow time to be included as a variable in the research design. Harrison & Hulin (1989), for example, note that the typical study of absenteeism uses measures created by aggregating either the frequency or duration of absences over an arbitrary period. Such measures are rarely normally distributed, and the arbitrary selection of a time frame for aggregation can create difficulties in assessing causality. By their estimate, 25 of 27 studies of absenteeism published during 1982–1986 failed to take these biases into account and used inappropriate analyses.

The advantage of survival analysis is that one can simultaneously examine the relationships of occurrence and timing of turnover. These statistical models are based on the probability that an event of interest (e.g. turnover or absence) will occur for a given individual in a specified time interval. These estimated probabilities can be related to linked variables of theoretical interest. Problems of right- or left-censored data can also be accommodated. O'Reilly et al (1989) used event history models to examine the impacts of work group demography and social integration on turnover. They found that heterogeneity in group composition based on date of entry led to decreased social integration. This, in turn, led to subsequent turnover. These data analytic approaches are both more appropriate and more powerful elucidators of behavioral processes that unfold over time than the static analyses often seen in the literature. They should permit future research to examine the causes of absenteeism and turnover more carefully.

Leadership

Leadership has continued to attract considerable research attention over the past three years, with more than 20 studies published. Indeed, Bass (1981) estimates that over 5000 studies of leadership have been published. Several excellent reviews of this topic are available, so extensive coverage need not be provided here. House & Singh (1987) provide a comprehensive review of much of the recent literature, and a number of other excellent chapters and books have been published recently (Fiedler & Garcia 1987; Vroom & Jago 1988; Yukl 1989).

Hollander & Offerman (1990) have summarized the development and current state of leadership research. They call attention to an important distinction often overlooked in discussions of this area: that between supervision and executive leadership. This is more than a troublesome methodological oversight. Leadership research originated in studies of what should properly be labeled supervision, and many current theories also focus on the interaction between the supervisor and his or her subordinates (e.g. Crouch & Yetton 1987; Keller 1989; Vecchio 1987, 1990). More recently, interest has emerged in the broader construct of executive leadership and how this affects the entire organization (e.g. Conger & Kanungo 1987; Gardner 1990). Here the concern is primarily with the leader's ability to affect large numbers of followers, not simply immediate subordinates. These two very different topics are likely to require different theoretical underpinnings.

With respect to supervision, research based on theories of superior-subordinate continues, albeit at a slow pace. Recent studies treat path-goal notions (Keller 1989), superior-subordinate interaction (Crouch & Yetton 1988; Sutton & Woodman 1989; Turban & Jones 1988), situational leadership (Hammer & Turk 1987; Vecchio 1987), operant approaches (Komaki et al 1989), and tests of the Vroom-Yetton model (Crouch & Yetton 1987; Curtis 1989). In general, these provide refinements to well-developed theories.

A more active and innovative stream of research focuses on executive leadership. Here a debate continues over whether leadership exists as a useful construct. On the one side are claims that leadership may be more subjective than objective. Meindl & Ehrlich (1987) suggest that the leadership concept has a romantic and heroic quality unrelated to observable practices. Cronshaw & Lord's (1987) laboratory study suggests that organizational participants may rely on simple cognitive heuristics such as categorization in forming leadership impressions. On the other side of the debate are those who argue that executive leadership is an observable and influential phenomenon. Thomas (1988), for example, in a reanalysis and replication of an early study critical of the executive leadership concept, found that new Chief Executive Officers had a substantial impact on firm performance beyond that accounted for by year, company, or industry. He reported that over 60% of the variance in profit and sales of UK retail stores was associated with changes in the top executive. Day & Lord (1988) suggested that executive leadership can explain as much as 45% of an organization's performance. In a study of nuclear power plants, Osborn & Jackson (1988) showed that some styles of executive leadership can increase safety risks.

Several approaches to characterizing executive leadership have been taken. Bass (1985) differentiated between transactional leadership centered on social exchange principles and transformational leadership based on charisma, shared visions, and strong leader-follower identification. Some evidence is available that supports this distinction. Hater & Bass (1988) found top-performing managers to be significantly higher than ordinary managers on dimensions of charisma and individualized consideration (treating subordinates as individuals, teaching, etc). Subordinates rated these leaders more effective than those practicing transactional leadership. In a 1989 working paper, R. J. House, W. D. Spangler, and J. Woycke used the notions of charisma and transformational leadership to explain significant variance in experts' ratings of Presidential performance. Others have suggested that charismatic leadership may be an important and underresearched ingredient in organizational success (Conger & Kanungo 1988; Kuhnert & Lewis 1987).

I agree with House & Singh's (1987) assessment that the field of leadership has advanced significantly over the past several years. Many of the theories reviewed by Mitchell in 1979 have come to fruition. With substantial empirical evidence accumulating, the central issues of many of these theories seem well explicated. Recent efforts to understand the impact of executive leadership and the motives underlying its various styles raise interesting new possibilities (e.g. Biggart & Hamilton 1987; Meindl 1989).

Summary

Micro-OB is in a fallow period. Useful micro-OB work is being done, but more excitement and attention are currently being generated by macro-OB. The areas of micro-OB that Mitchell considered dominant—job attitudes, motivation, leadership, and individual differences—remain the most frequently researched areas today, though today they may generate less intellectual excitement.

The motivation domain is dominated by well-researched theories. Goal-setting, the most often investigated area, has demonstrable validity and practical utility. Studies in this vein aim mainly to clarify portions of the theoretical framework. Equity (most frequently in the form of procedural and distributive justice) is similarly well researched. While clever work continues (Greenberg 1988), most studies are directed toward refinements within the existing framework (e.g. Miller & Grush 1988). The same applies to studies of intrinsic motivation.

Studies of job design and work attitudes (e.g. satisfaction, commitment, and stress) are largely variations on familiar themes. While much of this work provides useful refinements of measures and tests designed to clarify previous ambiguities, few advances into new theoretical domains are apparent—with the notable exception of research on affect and emotion. Here, new theories and interesting empirical work have begun and may result in some important rethinking of these topics.

Studies of absenteeism and turnover attempt to identify moderators that can increase the predictive power of existing models. The excitement in this area is primarily methodological, with a set of more appropriate and powerful survival analysis techniques being brought to bear. These approaches may help clarify early research and enhance new theories.

Finally, research on leadership continues to add refinements to existing theories, with some interest emerging in charisma and executive leadership. This interest may benefit us by requiring more ambitious studies in which the outcomes will necessarily be organizational variables rather than the attitudes and behaviors of subordinates.

WHERE IS THE FIELD OF MICRO-OB GOING?

Two themes seem to characterize recent trends in micro-OB research. First, increased attention is being paid to the influence of context upon individuals and groups in organizations (Capelli 1990). This interest is manifest in the study of organizational demography (Zenger & Lawrence 1989), the reemergence of the person-situation debate (Mitchell & James 1989), studies of organizational culture (Rousseau 1990), and a concern about the impact of physical space on organizational members (Oldham 1988). Second, the growing influence of macro-OB theories is creating an awareness of the potential contribution of sociological approaches to OB. For example, interest in internal labor markets (Capelli 1990), growth and decline processes (Sutton 1990), and executive team dynamics (Mascarenhas 1989) is increasing.

The Importance of Context

Organizations are fundamentally relational entities. As Pfeffer (1983) has pointed out, the distributional properties of groups and organizations can have important effects beyond those of the group's simple demographic characteristics; that is, the composition of units may explain group interaction patterns better than simple demographics can (e.g. O'Reilly et al 1989). This observation is hardly a new one, and previous *Annual Review* authors have regularly called for more attention to cross-level theory and research. Indeed, many of our theories are explicitly situational, often invoking variables at a higher level of analysis as moderators of cause and effect relationships. For example, the use of social information processing notions in job design explicitly acknowledges the influence of social norms on respondents' interpretations of job characteristics (Griffin 1987); and organizational policies may affect judgments about equity (e.g. Folger & Konovsky 1989). However, two aspects of the research in the past few years appear different and noteworthy: the number of studies explicitly considering cross-level effects, and the increasing number of studies assessing compositional effects.

Several studies have used social-network methods to address relational aspects of organizations. Nelson (1989) investigated the relationship between social networks and conflict in 20 organizational units. He found that low-conflict organizations were characterized by a larger number of strong intergroup ties. Krackhardt & Porter (1985, 1986) also used a sociometric approach to examine the impact of employee turnover on the attitudes of those who remained with the company. Their approach blended both micro and macro theories of turnover and demonstrated how neither of these perspectives alone could adequately explain the attitudes of employees who did not leave. Use of social-network methodologies can enable researchers to operationalize such constructs as informal organizational structures in ways that permit cross-level analysis and theory construction (Krackhardt 1989).

The relational or compositional effects of groups can readily be seen in studies of organizational demography. Several previous studies have shown that, beyond simple demographic effects, increased heterogeneity in work groups can lead to increased turnover (e.g. O'Reilly et al 1989). Zenger & Lawrence (1989) have also shown that the dispersion of age and tenure within groups does affect critical communication patterns. Other studies show that these variations influence innovation (Bantel & Jackson 1989) and salary (Berkowitz et al 1987; Pfeffer & Davis-Blake 1987). Markham (1988), for instance, found no pay-for-performance relation at the individual level of analysis and suggests the need to consider group-level effects. Other studies of group performance reiterate the necessity of considering both exogenous determinants (such as labor market factors) and group effects (such as norms and structure) (e.g. Argote 1989; Argote et al 1989; David et al 1989).

The influence of context on individuals is also revealed by social psychological studies of social loafing—the phenomenon of people generating less effort when working together than when working alone (e.g. Earley 1989). Studies have shown that when subjects performing in groups cannot be evaluated, either by themselves or others, they expend less effort on physical and cognitive tasks than when they can be evaluated (Price 1987; Weldon & Mustari 1988). Reducing this tendency requires the promulgation of standards that allow the group and/or others to evaluate individual contributions to performance (Harkins & Syzmanski 1989).

Students of OB have begun to understand how group demography and dynamics affect both the members and the functioning of groups with respect to communication, social interaction, and group development (Gersick 1988, 1989; O'Reilly et al 1989; Zenger & Lawrence 1989). The very composition of the group may have important effects on individual outcomes, beyond what is normally captured in measures of individual attributes (Tsui & O'Reilly 1989). As Sundstrom et al (1990:130) note in their review of research on work team effectiveness, "For researchers, an obvious next step is to study the *demographics of work groups* or the prevalence of various applications of work teams and their organizational contexts" (italics in the original). Large-scale changes in workforce demography are now occurring, and it will be useful to understand how they will affect individuals and groups within organizations.

Both the *Academy of Management Review* (e.g. Mitchell & James 1989) and the *Journal of Vocational Behavior* (e.g. Caplan 1987) have recently devoted special issues to a reemergence, in a temperate form, of the person-situation debate. In two important studies, Wright & Mischel (1987, 1988) have argued that dispositional constructs such as traits summarize specific condition-behavior contingencies; that is, dispositional statements are viewed as clusters of if-then propositions that implicitly reflect both the situation and the person. They note (1988:455) that "the study of dispositional constructs requires an analysis of the specific situations in which people believe dispositionally relevant behavior will occur."

In the current version of the debate both sides acknowledge that the person and the situation interactively affect attitudes and behavior (Davis-Blake & Pfeffer 1989; Kenrick & Funder 1988; Schneider 1987). Needed now are careful specification of the theory and measurement of the effects; and in this regard, progress is being made. Caldwell & O'Reilly (1990) have shown how Q-sort techniques can be used to describe both situations and people and to assess the fit of one to the other. They report significant correlations between person-job fit and performance.

Concern about contextual effects can also be seen in the burgeoning literature on organizational culture. Although scholars differ over how culture should be defined or measured (Rousseau 1990), most agree that it helps to determine how well an individual fits into an organization (Rynes & Gerhart 1990). Using a Q-sort approach to assess individual and organizational values, J. A. Chatman (unpublished working paper) and O'Reilly et al (1990) found highly significant associations between person-organization fit and outcomes such as performance, job attitudes, and turnover. Similar approaches to the measurement of person-situation congruence have been reported by Enz (1988) and Meglino et al (1989). Much of the current fascination with organizational culture stems from an awareness of the importance of person-context effects at the individual, group, and organizational levels (e.g. Rousseau 1990; Saffold 1988; Wiener 1988).

The Impact of Macro-OB Theory

As the proportion of macro-OB studies in the literature has increased, so has the opportunity for the blending of psychology and sociology. For instance, a number of studies of internal labor markets and career dynamics have begun to draw upon theories from sociology, economics, and psychology. Bills (1987), in a detailed case study of three organizations, shows how internal labor markets are constructed, based partially on managerial beliefs. Other studies have shown that internal labor markets and careers are often quite different from what pure disciplinary theories would suggest, reflecting forces such as political pressures and individual tastes (Di Prete 1987; West et al

1987). Forbes (1987), for example, blends both psychological and sociological reasoning to explain patterns of early intraorganizational mobility.

Other researchers have combined macro and micro theories to explain the growth and decline of organizations. Boeker (1989) and Romanelli (1989) have explored how early strategic choices can affect the probability of survival of new organizations. Boeker (1989) shows that one determinant of strategy is the founder's background and previous experience. Bird (1988) discusses how entrepreneurs' states of mind set the form and direction of their organizations. Similarly, Cameron et al (1987), Hambrick & D'Aveni (1988), and others (e.g. McKinley 1987; Weitzel & Jonsson 1989) have explored how the process of organizational decline can affect micro-OB processes such as leadership, conflict, and decision-making. Sutton (1990) provides a comprehensive review of this literature and offers a social psychological perspective for integrating many of these findings. These studies note the influence of growth and decline processes on psychological dynamics within the organization. For example, Mascarenas (1989) found that strategic group dynamics were significantly affected by whether the unit was in a period of economic growth or decline. Others have noted the critical function served by top management teams and the importance of investigating the dynamics of their interaction (Hambrick 1987; Tushman et al 1986). Similar effects of external economic conditions have been seen on individual-level phenomena such as turnover and satisfaction relationships (Capelli 1990; Capelli & Chauvin 1990). Together, these more macro studies are increasing micro researchers' awareness of the importance of economic and sociological theories. They offer interesting opportunities for cross-disciplinary research that can broaden the focus of micro-OB.

CONCLUSIONS

First, there is room for optimism: Many of the theories that characterized the field over the past decade have been carefully investigated and, in some instances, shown to be valid and useful. Second, the field of micro-OB is in a period of consolidation, with much of the work concentrating on mature streams of research; the macro side of the field appears to be generating more intellectual excitement at the present. Third, several new and promising trends are emerging from the basic disciplines. As Ilgen & Klein (1989) note, development in the disciplines often takes several years to emerge in micro-OB. New themes from personality, social psychology, and sociology are beginning to be reflected in micro-OB research. Needed is a broadening of micro-OB theory and research to address the micro side of macro topics, such as the social psychology of top management teams, the goal-setting aspects of organizational reward systems, or the grounding of economic models in a more complex and realistic understanding of motivation. As massive demographic changes occur over the next decade, some of the recent research on context and cross-disciplinary influences is likely to become more important. Just as research over the past 20 years has reflected the abundance of new workers, the next decade's problems will reflect the organizational consequences of the aging of the baby boom generation and the shortage of new entrants into the work force. Micro-OB research cannot help but reflect these changes.

ACKNOWLEDGMENTS

I am grateful for the help of John Anderson, Glenn Carroll, and Barry Staw in structuring the review. I thank Dave Caldwell and Frances Van Loo for suggestions in revising it. Vicki Milledge provided immense help with the bibliography. The Institute of Industrial Relations and IBER provided research support.

Literature Cited

Adler, P. A., Adler, P. 1988. Intense loyalty in organizations: a case study of college athletics. *Admin. Sci. Q.* 33:401–17

Argote, L. 1989. Agreement about norms and work-unit effectiveness: evidence from the field. *Basic Appl. Soc. Psychol.* 10:131–40

Argote, L., Turner, M. E., Fichman, M. 1989. To centralize or not to centralize: the effects of uncertainty and threat on group structure and performance. *Org. Behav. Hum. Decis. Processes* 43:58–74

Arvey, R. D., Bouchard, T. J. Jr., Segal, N. L., Abraham, L. M. 1989. Job satisfaction: environmental and genetic components. *J. Appl. Psychol.* 74:187–92

Bantel, K. A., Jackson, S. E. 1989. Top management and innovations in banking: does the composition of the top team make a difference? *Strat. Manage. J.* 10:107–24

Barling, J., Bluen, S. D., Fain, R. 1987. Psychological functioning following an acute disaster. *J. Appl. Psychol.* 72:683–90

Bass, B. M. 1981. *Stogdill's Handbook of Leadership.* New York: Free Press. Rev. & exp. ed.

Bass, B. M. 1985. *Leadership and Performance Beyond Expectations.* New York: Free Press

Berkowitz, L., Fraser, D., Treasure, F. P. 1987. Pay equity, job gratifications, and comparisons in pay satisfaction. *J. Appl. Psychol.* 72:544–51

Biggart, N. W., Hamilton, G. G. 1987. An institutional theory of leadership. *J. Appl. Behav. Sci.* 23:429–41

Bills, D. B. 1987. Costs, commitment, and rewards: factors influencing the design and implementation of internal labor markets. *Admin. Sci. Q.* 32:202–21

Bird, B. 1988. Implementing entrepreneurial ideas: the case for intention. *Acad. Manage. Rev.* 13:442–53

Blau, G. J. 1988. Further exploring the meaning and measurement of career commitment. *J. Vocat. Behav.* 32:284–97

Boeker, W. 1989. Strategic change: the effects of founding and history. *Acad. Manage. J.* 32:489–515

Brief, A. P., Burke, M. J., George, J. M., Robinson, B. S., Webster, J. 1988. Should negative affectivity remain an unmeasured variable in the study of job stress? *J. Appl. Psychol.* 73:193–98

Brief, A. P., Roberson, L. 1989. Job attitude organization: an exploratory study. *J. Appl. Soc. Psychol.* 19:701–16

Brooke, P. P. Jr., Russell, D. W., Price, J. L. 1988. Discriminant validation of measures of job satisfaction, job involvement, and organizational commitment. *J. Appl. Psychol.* 73:139–45

Bruning, N. S., Frew, D. R. 1987. Effects of exercise, relaxation, and management skills training on physiological stress indicators: a field experiment. *J. Appl. Psychol.* 72:515–21

Brush, D. H., Moch, M. K., Pooyan, A. 1987. Individual demographic differences and job satisfaction. *J. Occupat. Behav.* 8:139–55

Burke, M. J., Brief, A. P., George, J. M., Roberson, L., Webster, J. 1989. Measuring affect at work: confirmatory analyses of competing mood structures with conceptual linkage to cortical regulatory systems. *J. Pers. Soc. Psychol.* 57:1091–1102

Caldwell, D. F., Chatman, J. A., O'Reilly, C. A. III. 1990. Building organizational commitment: a multi-firm study. *J. Occupat. Psychol.* 63:245–61

Caldwell, D. F., O'Reilly, C. A. III. 1990. *Measuring person-job fit using a profile comparison process.* Presented at Annu. Meet. Acad. Manage., 50th, San Francisco

Cameron, K. S., Kim, M. U., Whetten, D. A. 1987. Organizational effects of decline and turbulence. *Admin. Sci. Q.* 32:222–40

Campbell, D. J. 1988. Task complexity: a review and analysis. *Acad. Manage. Rev.* 13:40–52

Campion, M. A. 1988. Interdisciplinary approaches to job design: a constructive replication with extensions. *J. Appl. Psychol.* 73:467–81

Capelli, P. 1990. The missing role of context in OB: developing a mezoscopic link to organizational theory and the external environment. *Res. Org. Behav.* 12

Capelli, P., Chauvin, K. 1990. An interplant test of the efficiency wage hypothesis. *Q. J. Econ.* In press

Caplan, R. D. 1987. Person-environment fit theory and organizations: commensurate dimensions, time perspectives, and mechanisms. *J. Vocat. Behav.* 31:248–67

Carlson, M., Charlin, V., Miller, N. 1988. Positive mood and helping behavior: a test of six hypotheses. *J. Pers. Soc. Psychol.* 55:211–29

Carsten, J. M., Spector, P. E. 1987. Unemployment, job satisfaction, and employee turnover: a meta-analytic test of the Muchinsky model. *J. Appl. Psychol.* 72: 374–81

Cellar, D. F., Barrett, G. V. 1987. Script processing and intrinsic motivation: the cognitive sets underlying cognitive labels. *Organ. Behav. Hum. Decis. Processes* 40:115–35

Cellar, D. F., Wade, K. 1988. Effect of behavioral modeling on intrinsic motivation and script-related recognition. *J. Appl. Psychol.* 73:181–92

Chatman, J. A. 1989. Improving interactional organizational research: a model of person-organization fit. *Acad. Manage. Rev.* 14: 333–49

Conger, J. A., Kanungo, R. N. 1987. Toward a behavioral theory of charismatic leadership in organizational settings. *Acad. Manage. Rev.* 12:637–47

Conger, J. A., Kanungo, R. N. 1988. The empowerment process: integrating theory and practice. *Acad. Manage. Rev.* 13:471–82

Cronshaw, S. F., Lord, R. G. 1987. Effects of categorization, attribution, and encoding processes on leadership perceptions. *J. Appl. Psychol.* 72:97–106

Cropanzano, R., Folger, R. 1989. Referent cognitions and task decision autonomy: be-

yond equity theory. *J. Appl. Psychol.* 74: 293–99

Crouch, A., Yetton, P. 1987. Manager behavior, leadership style, and subordinate performance: an empirical extension of the Vroom-Yetton conflict rule. *Organ. Behav. Hum. Decis. Processes* 39:384–96

Crouch, A., Yetton, P. 1988. Manager-subordinate dyads: relationships among task and social contact, manager friendliness and subordinate performance in management groups. *Organ. Behav. Hum. Decis. Processes* 41:65–82

Cummings, L. L. 1982. Organizational behavior. *Annu. Rev. Psychol.* 33:541–80

Cummings, L. L., Staw, B. M. 1987. *Research in Organizational Behavior.* Greenwich, CT: JAI Press. 9th ed.

Cummings, L. L., Staw, B. M. 1989. *Research in Organizational Behavior.* Greenwich, CT: JAI Press. 11th ed.

Curtis, R. L. 1989. Leadership decision making in a service organization: a field test of the Vroom-Yetton model. *Hum. Relat.* 42:671–89

Dalton, D. R., Todor, W. D., Owen, C. L. 1987. Sex effects in workplace justice outcomes: a field assessment. *J. Appl. Psychol.* 72:156–59

David, F. R., Pearce, J. A. II, Randolph, W. A. 1989. Linking technology and structure to enhance group performance. *J. Appl. Psychol.* 74:233–41

Davis-Blake, A., Pfeffer, J. 1989. Just a mirage: the search for dispositional effects in organizational research. *Acad. Manage. Rev.* 14:385–400

Day, D. V., Lord, R. G. 1988. Executive leadership and organizational performance: suggestions for a new theory and methodology. *J. Manage.* 14:453–64

Deci, E. L. 1975. *Intrinsic Motivation.* New York: Plenum

Deci, E. L., Connell, J. P., Ryan, R. M. 1989. Self-determination in a work organization. *J. Appl. Psychol.* 74:580–90

Deci, E. L., Ryan, R. M. 1985. *Intrinsic Motivation and Self-Determination in Human Behavior.* New York: Plenum Press

Deci, E. L., Ryan, R. M. 1987. The support of autonomy and the control of behavior. *J. Pers. Soc. Psychol.* 53:1024–37

DeCotiis, T. A., Summers, T. P. 1987. A path analysis of a model of the antecedents and consequences of organizational commitment. *Hum. Relat.* 40:445–70

Diener, E., Emmons, R. A. 1985. The independence of positive and negative affect. *J. Pers. Soc. Psychol.* 47:1105–17

DiPrete, T. A. 1987. Horizontal and vertical mobility in organizations. *Admin. Sci. Q.* 32:422–44

Dooley, D., Rook, K., Catalano, R. 1987. Job

and non-job stressors and their moderators. *J. Occupat. Psychol.* 60:115–32

Earley, P. C., Connolly, T., Ekegren, G. 1989. Goals, strategy development, and task performance: some limits on the efficacy of goal setting. *J. Appl. Psychol.* 74:24–33

Earley, P. C. 1989. Social loafing and collectivism: a comparison of the United States and the People's Republic of China. *Admin. Sci. Q.* 34:565–81

Enz, C. 1988. The role of value congruity in intra-organizational power. *Admin. Sci. Q.* 33:284–304

Erez, M., Earley, P. C. 1987. Comparative analysis of goal-setting strategies across cultures. *J. Appl. Psychol.* 72:658–65

Esses, V. M. 1989. Mood as moderator of acceptance of interpersonal feedback. *J. Pers. Soc. Psychol.* 57:769–81

Farkas, A. J., Tetrick, L. E. 1989. A three-wave longitudinal analysis of the causal ordering of satisfaction and commitment on turnover decisions. *J. Appl. Psychol.* 74:855–68

Farrell, D., Stamm, C. L. 1988. Meta-analysis of the correlates of employee absence. *Hum. Relat.* 41:211–27

Fichman, M. 1988. Motivational consequences of absence and attendance: proportional hazard estimation of a dynamic motivation model. *J. Appl. Psychol.* 73:119–34

Fichman, M. 1989. Attendance makes the heart grow fonder: a hazard rate approach to modeling attendance. *J. Appl. Psychol.* 74:325–35

Fiedler, F. E., Garcia, J. E. 1987. *New Approaches to Effective Leadership: Cognitive Resources and Organizational Performance.* New York: Wiley

Folger, R. 1986. A referent cognitions theory of relative deprivation. In *Social Comparison and Relative Deprivation: The Ontario Symposium,* ed. J. M. Olson, C. P. Herman, M. P. Zanna, 4:33–55. Hillsdale, NJ: Erlbaum

Folger, R., Konovsky, M. A. 1989. Effects of procedural and distributive justice on reactions to pay raise decisions. *Acad. Manage. J.* 32:115–30

Forbes, J. B. 1987. Early intraorganizational mobility: patterns and influences. *Acad. Manage. J.* 30:110–25

Forgas, J. P., Bower, G. H. 1987. Mood effects on person-perception judgments. *J. Pers. Soc. Psychol.* 53:53–60

Frayne, C. A., Latham, G. P. 1987. Application of social learning theory to employee self-management of attendance. *J. Appl. Psychol.* 72:387–92

Frone, M. R., McFarlin, D. B. 1989. Chronic occupational stressors, self-focused atten-tion, and well-being: testing a cybernetic model of stress. *J. Appl. Psychol.* 74:876–83

Galanter, M. 1989. *Cults.* New York: Oxford Univ. Press

Gardner, J. W. 1990. *On Leadership.* New York: Free Press

George, J. M. 1989. Mood and absence. *J. Appl. Psychol.* 74:317–24

George, J. M. 1990. Personality, affect, and behavior in groups. *J. Appl. Psychol.* 75:107–16

Gerhart, B. 1987. How important are dispositional factors as determinants of job satisfaction? Implications for job design and other personnel programs. *J. Appl. Psychol.* 72:366–73

Gerhart, B. 1988. Sources of variance in incumbent perceptions of job complexity. *J. Appl. Psychol.* 73:154–62

Gersick, C. J. G. 1988. Time and transition in work teams: toward a new model of group development. *Acad. Manage. J.* 31:9–41

Gersick, C. J. G. 1989. Marking time: predictable transitions in task groups. *Acad. Manage. J.* 32:274–309

Glisson, C., Durick, M. 1988. Predictors of job satisfaction and organizational commitment in human service organizations. *Admin. Q.* 33:61–81

Goodman, P. S., Garber, S. 1988. Absenteeism and accidents in a dangerous environment: empirical analysis of underground coal mines. *J. Appl. Psychol.* 73:81–86

Greenberg, J. 1987a. Reactions to procedural injustice in payment distributions: do the means justify the ends? *J. Appl. Psychol.* 72:55–61

Greenberg, J. 1987b. A taxonomy of organizational justice theories. *Acad. Manage. Rev.* 12:9–22

Greenberg, J. 1987c. Reactions to procedural injustice in payment distributions: do the means justify the ends? *J. Appl. Psychol.* 72:55–61

Greenberg, J. 1988. Equity and workplace status: a field experiment. *J. Appl. Psychol.* 73:606–13

Griffeth, R. W., Hom, P. W. 1988. A comparison of different conceptualizations of perceived alternatives in turnover research. *J. Organ. Behav.* 9:103–11

Griffeth, R. W., Vecchio, R. P., Logan, J. W. Jr. 1989. Equity theory and interpersonal attraction. *J. Appl. Psychol.* 74:394–401

Griffin, R. W. 1987. Toward an integrated theory of task design. *Res. Org. Behav.* 9:79–120

Griffin, R. W., Bateman, T. S., Wayne, S. J., Head, T. C. 1987. Objective and social factors as determinants of task perceptions and responses: an integrated perspective and empirical investigation. *Acad. Manage. J.* 30:501–23

Guastello, S. J. 1987. A butterfly catastrophe model of motivation in organizations: academic performance. *J. Appl. Psychol.* 72: 165–82

Hackett, R. D. 1989. Work attitudes and employee absenteeism: a synthesis of the literature. *J. Occupat. Psychol.* 62:235–48

Hackman, J. R., Oldham, G. R. 1980. *Work Redesign.* Reading, MA: Addison-Wesley

Hambrick, D. C. 1987. The top management team: key to strategic success. *Calif. Manage. Rev.* 30:1–20

Hambrick, D. C., D'Aveni, R. A. 1988. Large corporate failures as downward spirals. *Admin. Sci. Q.* 33:1–23

Hammer, T. H., Turk, J. M. 1987. Organizational determinants of leader behavior and authority. *J. Appl. Psychol.* 72:674–82

Handy, J. A. 1988. Theoretical and methodological problems within occupational stress and burnout research. *Hum. Relat.* 41:351–69

Harackiewicz, J. M., Abrahams, S., Wageman, R. 1987. Performance evaluation and intrinsic motivation: the effects of evaluative focus, rewards, and achievement orientation. *J. Pers. Soc. Psychol.* 53: 1015–23

Harkins, S. G., Szymanski, K. 1989. Social loafing and group evaluation. *J. Pers. Soc. Psychol.* 56:934–41

Harrison, D. A., Hulin, C. L. 1989. Investigations of absenteeism: using event history models to study the absence-taking process. *J. Appl. Psychol.* 74:300–16

Harvey, R. J., Lozada-Larsen, S. R. 1988. Influence of amount of job descriptive information on job analysis rating accuracy. *J. Appl. Psychol.* 73:457–61

Hater, J. J., Bass, B. M. 1988. Superiors' evaluations and subordinates' perceptions of transformational and transactional leadership. *J. Appl. Psychol.* 73:695–702

Hirst, M. K. 1988. Intrinsic motivation as influenced by task interdependence and goal setting. *J. Appl. Psychol.* 73:96–101

Hogan, E. A., Martell, D. A. 1987. A confirmatory structural equations analysis of the job characteristics model. *Organ. Behav. Hum. Decis. Processes* 39:242–63

Hollander, E. P., Offerman, L. R. 1990. Power and leadership in organizations: relationships in transition. *Am. Psychol.* 45:179–89

Hollenbeck, J. R., Williams, C. R., Klein, H. J. 1989. An empirical examination of the antecedents of commitment to difficult goals. *J. Appl. Psychol.* 74:18–23

House, R. J., Singh, J. V. 1987. Organizational behavior: some new directions for I/O psychology. *Annu. Rev. Psychol.* 38:669–718

Huseman, R. C., Hatfield, J. D., Miles, E. W. 1987. A new perspective on equity theory: the equity sensitivity construct. *Acad. Manage. Rev.* 12:222–34

Hyland, M. E. 1988. Motivational control theory: an integrative framework. *J. Pers. Soc. Psychol.* 55:642–51

Idaszak, J. R., Bottom, W. P., Drasgow, F. 1988. A test of the measurement equivalence of the revised job diagnostic survey: past problems and current solutions. *J. Appl. Psychol.* 73:647–56

Idaszak, J. R., Drasgow, F. 1987. A revision of the Job Diagnostic Survey: elimination of a measurement artifact. *J. Appl. Psychol.* 72:674–82

Ilgen, D. R., Klein, H. J. 1989. Organizational behavior. *Annu. Rev. Psychol.* 40:327–51

Inwald, R. E. 1988. Five-year follow-up study of departmental terminations as predicted by 16 preemployment psychological indicators. *J. Appl. Psychol.* 73:703–10

Ironson, G. H., Smith, P. C., Brannick, M. T., Gibson, W. M., Paul, K. B. 1989. Construction of a job in general scale: a comparison of global, composite, and specific measures. *J. Appl. Psychol.* 74:193–200

Isen, A. M., Daubman, K. A., Nowicki, G. P. 1987. Positive affect facilitates creative problem solving. *J. Pers. Soc. Psychol.* 52:1122–31

Isen, A. M., Nygren, T. E., Ashby, F. G. 1988. Influence of positive affect on the subjective utility of gains and losses: it is just not worth the risk. *J. Pers. Soc. Psychol.* 55:710–17

Ivancevich, J. M., Matteson, M. T., Freedman, S. M., Phillips, J. S. 1990. Work stress management interventions. *Am. Psychol.* 45:252–61

James, L. A., James, L. R. 1989. Integrating work environment perceptions: explorations into the measurement of meaning. *J. Appl. Psychol.* 74:739–51

Jones, J. W., Barge, B. N., Steffy, B. D., Fay, L. M., Kunz, L. K., et al. 1988. Stress and medical malpractice: organizational risk assessment and intervention. *J. Appl. Psychol.* 73:727–35

Kacmar, K. M., Ferris, G. R. 1989. Theoretical and methodological considerations in the age-job satisfaction relationship. *J. Appl. Psychol.* 74:201–7

Kanfer, R., Ackerman, P. L. 1989. Motivation and cognitive abilities: an integrative/aptitude-treatment interaction approach to skill acquisition. *J. Appl. Psychol.* 74:657–90

Kanfer, R., Crosby, J. V., Brandt, D. M. 1988. Investigating behavioral antecedents of turnover at three job tenure levels. *J. Appl. Psychol.* 73:331–35

Karasek, R., Theorell, T. 1990. *Healthy Work: Stress, Productivity, and the Reconstruction of Working Life.* New York: Basic Books

Katzell, R. A., Thompson, D. E. 1990. Work motivation: theory and practice. *Am. Psychol.* 45:144–53

Keller, R. T. 1989. A test of the path-goal theory of leadership with need for clarity as a moderator in research and development organizations. *J. Appl. Psychol.* 74:208–12

Kenrick, D., Funder, D. 1988. Profiting from controversy: lessons from the person-situation debate. *Am. Psychol.* 43:23–35

Kerber, K. W., Campbell, J. P. 1987. Component structure of a measure of job facet satisfaction: stability across job levels. *Educ. Psychol. Meas.* 47:815–23

Kilduff, M., Regan, D. T. 1988. What people say and what they do: the differential effects of informational cues and task design. *Organ. Behav. Hum. Decis. Processes* 41:83–97

Klandermans, B. 1989. Union commitment: replications and tests in the Dutch context. *J. Appl. Psychol.* 74:869–75

Klein, H. J. 1989. An integrated control theory model of work motivation. *Acad. Manage. Rev.* 14:150–72

Komaki, J. L., Desselles, M. L., Bowman, E. D. 1989. Definitely not a breeze: extending an operant model of effective supervision to teams. *J. Appl. Psychol.* 74:522–29

Krackhardt, D. 1989. *Graph theoretical dimensions of informal organizations.* Presented at Annu. Meet. Acad. Manage., 49th, Washington, DC

Krackhardt, D., Porter, L. W. 1985. When friends leave: a structural analysis of the relationship between turnover and stayer's attitudes. *Admin. Sci. Q.* 30:242–61

Krackhardt, D., Porter, L. W. 1986. The snowball effect: turnover embedded in communication networks. *J. Appl. Psychol.* 71:50–55

Kuhnert, K. W., Lewis, P. 1987. Transactional and transformational leadership: a constructive/developmental analysis. *Acad. Manage. J.* 12:648–57

Kulik, C. T. 1989. The effects of job categorization on judgments of the motivating potential of jobs. *Admin. Sci. Q.* 34:68–90

Kulik, C. T., Oldham, G. R., Langner, P. H. 1988. Measurement of job characteristics: comparison of the original and the revised job diagnostic survey. *J. Appl. Psychol.* 73:462–66

Latham, G. P., Erez, M., Locke, E. A. 1988. Resolving scientific disputes by the joint design of crucial experiments by the antagonists: application to the Erez-Latham dispute regarding participation in goal setting. *J. Appl. Psychol.* 73:753–72

Lawler, E. E. 1988. Choosing an involvement strategy. *Acad. Manage. Exec.* 11:197–204

Levin, I., Stokes, J. P. 1989. Dispositional approach to job satisfaction: role of negative affectivity. *J. Appl. Psychol.* 74:752–58

Lind, E. A., Tyler, T. R. 1988. *The Social Psychology of Procedural Justice.* New York: Plenum

Locke, E. A., Latham, G. P. 1990. *A Theory of Goal Setting and Task Performance.* Englewood Cliffs, NJ: Prentice Hall

Locke, E. A., Latham, G. P., Erez, M. 1988. The determinants of goal commitment. *Acad. Manage. Rev.* 13:23–39

Lord, R. G., Kernan, M. C. 1987. Scripts as determinants of purposeful behavior in organizations. *Acad. Manage. Rev.* 12:265–77

Luthans, F., Baack, D., Taylor, L. 1987. Organizational commitment: analysis of antecedents. *Hum. Relat.* 40:219–35

Magenau, J. M., Martin, J. E., Peterson, M. M. 1988. Dual and unilateral commitment among stewards and rank-and-file union members. *Acad. Manage. J.* 31:359–76

Majchrzak, A. 1987. Effects of management policies on unauthorized absence behavior. *J. Appl. Behav. Sci.* 23:501–23

Markham, S. E. 1988. Pay-for-performance dilemma revisted: empirical example of the importance of group effects. *J. Appl. Psychol.* 73:172–80

Martin, R., Wall, T. D. 1989. Attentional demand and cost responsibility as stressors in shop floor jobs. *Acad. Manage. J.* 32:69–86

Martocchio, J. J., O'Leary, A. M. 1989. Sex differences in occupational stress: a meta-analytic review. *J. Appl. Psychol.* 74:495–501

Mascarenhas, B. 1989. Strategic group dynamics. *Acad. Manage. J.* 32:333–52

Mathieu, J. E., Kohler, S. S. 1990. A cross-level examination of group absence influences on individual absence. *J. Appl. Psychol.* 75:217–20

McEvoy, G. M., Cascio, W. F. 1987. Do good or poor performers leave? A meta-analysis of the relationship between performance and turnover. *Acad. Manage. J.* 30:744–62

McEvoy, G. M., Cascio, W. F. 1989. Cumulative evidence of the relationship between employee age and job performance. *J. Appl. Psychol.* 74:11–17

McGee, G. W., Ford, R. C. 1987. Two (or more?) dimensions of organizational commitment: reexamination of the affective and continuance commitment scales. *J. Appl. Psychol.* 72:638–42

McKinley, W. 1987. Complexity and administrative intensity: the case of declining organizations. *Admin. Sci. Q.* 32:87–105

Meglino, B. M., Ravlin, E. C., Adkins, C. L. 1989. A work values approach to corporate culture: a field test of the value congruence process and its relationship to individual outcomes. *J. Appl. Psychol.* 74:424–32

Meindl, J. R. 1989. Managing to be fair: an exploration of values, motives, and leadership. *Admin. Sci. Q.* 34:252–76

Meindl, J. R., Ehrlich, S. B. 1987. The romance of leadership and the evaluation of organizational performance. *Acad. Manage. J.* 30:91–109

Meyer, G. J., Shack, J. R. 1989. Structural convergence of mood and personality: evidence for old and new directions. *J. Pers. Soc. Psychol.* 57:691–706

Meyer, J. P., Allen, N. J. 1984. Testing the "side-bet theory" of organizational commitment: some methodological considerations. *J. Appl. Psychol.* 69:372–78

Meyer, J. P., Paunonen, S. V., Gellatly, I. R., Goffin, R. D., Jackson, D. N. 1989. Organizational commitment and job performance: it's the nature of the commitment that counts. *J. Appl. Psychol.* 74:152–56

Miller, L. E., Grush, J. E. 1988. Improving predictions in expectancy theory research: effects of personality, expectancies, and norms. *Acad. Manage. J.* 31:107–22

Mitchell, T. R. 1979. Organizational behavior. *Annu. Rev. Psychol.* 30:234–82

Mitchell, T. R., James, L. R. 1989. Introduction and background. *Acad. Manage. Rev.* 14:331–32

Morita, J. G., Lee, T. W., Mowday, R. T. 1989. Introducing survival analysis to organizational researchers: a selected application to turnover research. *J. Appl. Psychol.* 74:280–92

Mottaz, C. J. 1988. Determinants of organizational commitment. *Hum. Relat.* 41:467–82

Mowday, R. T., Porter, L. W., Steers, R. M. 1982. *Employee Commitment, Turnover and Absenteeism.* New York: Academic

Mullins, W. C., Kimbrough, W. W. 1988. Group composition as a determinant of job analysis outcomes. *J. Appl. Psychol.* 73:657–64

Nelson, R. E. 1989. The strength of strong ties: social networks and intergroup conflict in organizations. *Acad. Manage. J.* 32:377–401

O'Connor, L. J., Peters, L. H., Gordon, S. M. 1978. The measurement of job satisfaction: current practices and future considerations. *J. Manage.* 4:17–26

O'Reilly, C. A. 1989. Corporations, culture, and commitment: motivation and social control in organizations. *Calif. Manage. Rev.* 31:9–25

O'Reilly, C. A., Caldwell, D. F., Barnett, W. P. 1989. Work group demography, social integration, and turnover. *Admin. Sci. Q.* 34:21–37

O'Reilly, C. A. III, Chatman, J. A. 1986. Organizational commitment and psychological attachment: the effects of compliance, identification, and internalization on prosocial behavior. *J. Appl. Psychol.* 71:492–99

O'Reilly, C. A. III, Chatman, J. A., Caldwell, D. F. 1990. *People and organizational culture: a Q-sort approach to assessing person-organization fit.* Presented at Annu. Meet. Acad. Manage., 50th, San Francisco

Offerman, L. R., Gowing, M. K. 1990. Organizations of the future: changes and challenges. *Am. Psychol.* 45:95–108

Oldham, G. R. 1988. Effects of changes in workspace partitions and spatial density on employee reactions: a quasi-experiment. *J. Appl. Psychol.* 73:253–58

Osborn, R. N., Jackson, D. H. 1988. Leaders, riverboat gamblers, or purposeful unintended consequences in the management of complex, dangerous technologies. *Acad. Manage. J.* 31:924–47

Parasuraman, S., Greenhaus, J. H., Rabinowitz, S., Bedeian, A. G., Mossholder, K. W. 1989. Work and family variables as mediators of the relationship between wives' employment and husbands' well-being. *Acad. Manage. J.* 32:185–201

Parkes, K. R. 1987. Relative weight, smoking, and mental health as predictors of sickness and absence from work. *J. Appl. Psychol.* 72:275–86

Peters, L. H., Sheridan, J. E. 1988. Turnover research methodology: a critique of traditional designs and a suggested survival model alternative. *Res. Pers. Hum. Res. Manage.* 6:231–62

Pfeffer, J. 1982. *Organizations and Organization Theory.* Marshfield, MA: Pitman

Pfeffer, J. 1983. Organizational demography. *Res. Org. Behav.* 5:299–357

Pfeffer, J., Davis-Blake, A. 1987. The effect of the proportion of women on salaries: the case of college administrators. *Admin. Sci. Q.* 32:1–24

Pond, S. B. III, Geyer, P. D. 1987. Employee age as a moderator of the relation between perceived work alternatives and job satisfaction. *J. Appl. Psychol.* 72:552–57

Price, K. H. 1987. Decision responsibility, task responsibility, identifiability, and social loafing. *Org. Behav. Hum. Decis. Processes* 40:330–45

Pritchard, R. D., Jones, S. D., Roth, P. L.,

Stuebing, K. K., Ekeberg, S. E. 1988. Effects of group feedback, goal setting, and incentives on organizational productivity. *J. Appl. Psychol.* 73:337–58

Rafaeli, A. 1989. When clerks meet customers: a test of variables related to emotional expressions on the job. *J. Appl. Psychol.* 74:385–93

Rafaeli, A., Sutton, R. I. 1987. Expression of emotion as a part of the work role. *Acad. Manage. Rev.* 12:23–37

Rafaeli, A., Sutton, R. I. 1989. The expression of emotion in organizational life. *Res. Org. Behav.* 11:1–42

Randall, D. M. 1987. Commitment and the organization: the organization man revisited. *Acad. Manage. Rev.* 12:460–71

Rasinski, K. A. 1987. What's fair is fair—or is it? Value differences underlying public views about social justice. *J. Pers. Soc. Psychol.* 53:201–11

Raven, J. 1988. Toward measures of high-level competencies: a re-examination of McClelland's distinction between needs and values. *Hum. Relat.* 41:281–94

Roberts, K. H., Glick, W. 1981. The job characteristics approach to task design: a critical review. *J. Appl. Psychol.* 66:193–217

Romanelli, E. 1989. Environments and strategies of organization start-up: effects on early survival. *Admin. Sci. Q.* 34:369–87

Romzek, B. S. 1989. Personal consequences of employee commitment. *Acad. Manage. J.* 32:649–61

Rousseau, D. 1990. Quantitative assessment of organizational culture: the case for multiple measures. In *Frontiers in Industrial and Organizational Psychology,* ed. B. Schneider. In press

Roznowski, M. 1989. Examination of the measurement properties of the job descriptive index with experimental items. *J. Appl. Psychol.* 74:805–14

Rusbult, C. E., Farrell, D., Rogers, G., Mainous, A. G. III. 1988. Impact of exchange variables on exit, voice, loyalty, and neglect: an integrative model of responses to declining job satisfaction. *Acad. Manage. J.* 31:599–627

Russell, D. W., Altmaier, E., Van Velsen, D. 1987. Job-related stress, social support, and burnout among class room teachers. *J. Appl. Psychol.* 72:269–74

Russell, J. A., Lewicka, M., Niit, T. 1989a. A cross-cultural study of a circumplex model of affect. *J. Pers. Soc. Psychol.* 57:848–56

Russell, J. A., Weiss, A., Mendelsohn, G. A. 1989b. Affect grid: a single-item scale of pleasure and arousal. *J. Pers. Soc. Psychol.* 57:493–502

Rynes, S., Gerhart, B. 1990. Interviewer assessments of applicant "fit": an exploratory investigation. *Person. Psychol.* In press

Saffold, G. S. III. 1988. Culture traits, strength, and organizational performance: moving beyond "strong" culture. *Acad. Manage. Rev.* 13:546–58

Salancik, G. R., Pfeffer, J. 1977. An examination of need-satisfaction models of job attitudes. *Admin. Sci. Q.* 22:427–56

Salancik, G. R., Pfeffer, J. 1978. A social information processing approach to job attitudes and task design. *Admin. Sci. Q.* 23:224–53

Salovey, P., Birnbaum, D. 1989. Influence of mood on health-relevant cognitions. *J. Pers. Soc. Psychol.* 57:539–51

Sandelands, L. E., Brochner, J., Glynn, M. A. 1988. If at first you don't succeed, try, try, again: effects of persistence-performance contingencies, ego involvement, and self-esteem on task persistence. *J. Appl. Psychol.* 73:208–16

Sandelands, L. E., Calder, B. J. 1987. Perceptual organization in task performance. *Org. Behav. Hum. Decis. Processes* 40:287–306

Sansone, C., Sachau, D. A., Weir, C. 1989. Effects of instruction on intrinsic interest: the importance of context. *J. Pers. Soc. Psychol.* 57:819–29

Sawyer, J. E. 1988. Measuring attitudes across job levels: when are scale scores truly comparable? *Org. Behav. Hum. Decis. Processes* 42:324–42

Scarpello, V., Vandenberg, R. 1987. The Satisfaction with My Supervisor Scale: it's utility for research and practical applications. *J. Manage.* 13:447–66

Schneider, B. 1985. Organizational behavior. *Annu. Rev. Psychol.* 36:573–611

Schneider, B. 1987. E = f(P,B): the road to a radical approach to person-environment fit. *J. Vocat. Behav.* 31:353–61

Scott, W. E. Jr., Farh, J., Podsakoff, P. M. 1988. The effects of "intrinsic" and "extrinsic" reinforcement contingencies on task behavior. *Org. Behav. Hum. Decis. Processes* 41:405–25

Shaffer, G. S. 1987. Patterns of work and nonwork satisfaction. *J. Appl. Psychol.* 72:115–24

Shore, L. M., Martin, H. J. 1989. Job satisfaction and organizational commitment in relation to work performance and turnover intentions. *Hum. Relat.* 42:625–38

Sinclair, R. C. 1988. Mood, categorization breadth, and performance appraisal: the effects of order of information acquisition and affective state on halo, accuracy, information retrieval, and evaluations. *Org.*

Behav. Hum. Decis. Processes 42:22–46

Smith, P. C., Kendall, L. M., Hulin, C. L. 1969. *The Measurement of Satisfaction in Work and Retirement*. Chicago: Rand-McNally

Spector, P. E. 1987. Method variance as an artifact in self-reported affect and perceptions at work: myth or significant problem? *J. Appl. Psychol.* 72:438–43

Spector, P. E., Dwyer, D. J., Jex, S. M. 1988. Relation of job stressors to affective, health and performance outcomes: a comparison of multiple data sources. *J. Appl. Psychol.* 73:11–19

Spence, J. T., Pred, R. S., Helmreich, R. L. 1989. Achievement strivings, scholastic aptitude, and academic performance: a follow-up to "Impatience versus achievement strivings in the type A pattern". *J. Appl. Psychol.* 74:176–78

Staw, B. M. 1984. Organizational behavior: a review and reformation of the field's outcome variables. *Annu. Rev. Psychol.* 35:627–66

Staw, B. M., Bell, N. E., Clausen, J. A. 1986. The dispositional approach to job attitudes: a lifetime longitudinal test. *Admin. Sci. Q.* 31:56–77

Staw, B. M., Boettger, R. 1990. Task revision as a form of work performance. *Acad. Manage. J.* 33:534–59

Staw, B. M., Cummings, L. L. 1988. *Research in Organizational Behavior*. Greenwich, CT: JAI Press. 10th ed.

Staw, B. M., Ross, J. 1985. Stability in the midst of change: a dispositional approach to job attitudes. *J. Appl. Psychol.* 70:469–80

Staw, B. M., Ross, J. 1989. Understanding behavior in escalation situations. *Science* 246:216–20

Steel, R. P., Griffeth, R. W. 1989. The elusive relationship between perceived employment opportunity and turnover behavior: a methodological or conceptual artifact? *J. Appl. Psychol.* 74:846–54

Steffy, B. D., Jones, J. W. 1988. Workplace stress and indicators of coronary-disease risk. *Acad. Manage. J.* 31:686–98

Sullivan, J. J. 1988. Three roles of language in motivation theory. *Acad. Manage. Rev.* 13:104–15

Sundstrom, E., De Meuse, K. P., Futrell, D. 1990. Work teams: applications and effectiveness. *Am. Psychol.* 45:120–33

Sutton, C. D., Woodman, R. W. 1989. Pygmalion goes to work: the effects of supervisor expectations in a retail setting. *J. Appl. Psychol.* 74:943–50

Sutton, R. 1990. Organizational decline processes: a social psychological perspective. *Res. Org. Behav.* 12

Sutton, R. I., Rafaeli, A. 1987. Characteristics of work stations as potential occupational stressors. *Acad. Manage. J.* 30:260–76

Sutton, R. I., Rafaeli, A. 1988. Untangling the relationship between displayed emotions and organizational sales: the case of convenience stores. *Acad. Manage. J.* 31:461–87

Tait, M., Padgett, M. Y., Baldwin, T. T. 1989. Job and life satisfaction: a reevaluation of the strength of the relationship and gender effects as a function of the date of the study. *J. Appl. Psychol.* 74:502–7

Taylor, S. E. 1989. *Positive Illusions*. New York: Basic Books

Tetrick, L. E., Farkas, A. J. 1988. A longitudinal examination of the dimensionality and stability of the organizational commitment questionnaire (OCQ). *Educ. Psychol. Measure.* 48:723–35

Tetrick, L. E., LaRocco, J. M. 1987. Understanding, prediction, and control as moderators of the relationships between perceived stress, satisfaction, and psychological well-being. *J. Appl. Psychol.* 72:538–43

Tetrick, L. E., Thacker, J. W., Fields, M. W. 1989. Evidence for the stability of the four dimensions of the commitment to the union scale. *J. Appl. Psychol.* 74:819–22

Thomas, A. B. 1988. Does leadership make a difference to organizational performance? *Admin. Sci. Q.* 33:388–400

Tsui, A. S., O'Reilly, C. A. III. 1989. Beyond simple demographic effects: the importance of relational demography in superior-subordinate dyads. *Acad. Manage. J.* 32:402–23

Tuma, N. B., Hannan, M. T. 1984. *Social Dynamics: Models and Methods*. New York: Academic

Turban, D. B., Jones, A. P. 1988. Supervisor-subordinate similarity: types, effects, and mechanisms. *J. Appl. Psychol.* 73:228–34

Tushman, M., Newman, W. H., Romanelli, E. 1986. Convergence and upheaval: managing the unsteady pace of organizational evolution. *Calif. Manage. Rev.* 29:1–16

Tyler, T. R. 1989. The psychology of procedural justice: a test of the group-value model. *J. Pers. Soc. Psychol.* 57:830–38

Vecchio, R. P. 1987. Situational leadership theory: an examination of a prescriptive theory. *J. Appl. Psychol.* 72:444–51

Vecchio, R. P. 1990. Theoretical and empirical examination of cognitive resource theory. *J. Appl. Psychol.* 75:141–47

Vroom, V. H., Jago, A. G. 1988. *The New Leadership: Managing Participation in Organizations*. Englewood Cliffs, NJ: Prentice Hall

Wagner, J. A. III, Rubin, P. A., Callahan, T.

J. 1988. Incentive payment and nonmanagerial productivity: an interrupted time series analysis of magnitude and trend. *Org. Behav. Hum. Decis. Processes* 42:47–74

Wanous, J. P., Sullivan, S. E., Malinak, J. 1989. The role of judgment calls in meta-analysis. *J. Appl. Psychol.* 74:259–64

Watson, D., Clark, L. A., Tellegen, A. 1988. Development and validation of brief measures of positive and negative affect: the PANAS scales. *J. Pers. Soc. Psychol.* 54:1063–70

Watson, D., Tellegen, A. 1985. Toward a consensual structure of mood. *Psychol. Bull.* 98:219–35

Weiner, Y. 1988. Forms of value systems: a focus on organizational effectiveness and cultural change and maintenance. *Acad. Manage. Rev.* 13:534–45

Weitzel, W., Jonsson, E. 1989. Decline in organizations: a literature integration and extension. *Admin. Sci. Q.* 34:91–109

Weldon, E., Mustari, E. L. 1988. Felt dispensability in groups of coactors: the effects of shared responsibility and explicit anonymity on cognitive effort. *Org. Behav. Hum. Decis. Processes* 41:330–51

West, M. A., Nicholson, N., Rees, A. 1987. Transitions into newly created jobs. *J. Occupat. Psychol.* 60:97–113

Wiener, Y. 1988. Forms of value systems: a focus on organizational effectiveness and cultural change and maintenance. *Acad. Manage. Rev.* 13:534–45

Withey, M. J., Cooper, W. H. 1989. Predicting exit, voice, loyalty, and neglect. *Admin. Sci. Q.* 34:521–39

Wright, J. C., Mischel, W. 1987. A conditional approach to dispositional constructs: the local predictability of social behavior. *J. Pers. Soc. Psychol.* 53:1159–77

Wright, J. C., Mischel, W. 1988. Conditional hedges and the intuitive psychology of traits. *J. Pers. Soc. Psychol.* 55:454–69

Yukl, G. A. 1989. *Leadership in Organizations.* Englewood Cliffs, NJ: Prentice Hall

Zaccaro, S. J., Stone, E. F. 1988. Incremental validity of an empirically based measure of job characteristics. *J. Appl. Psychol.* 73:245–52

Zenger, T. R., Lawrence, B. S. 1989a. Organizational demography: the differential effects of age and tenure distributions on technical communication. *Acad. Manage. J.* 32:353–76

Zevon, M. A., Tellegen, A. 1982. The structure of mood change: an ideographic/nomothetic analysis. *J. Pers. Soc. Psychol.* 42:111–22

Annu. Rev. Psychol. 1991. 42:459–91

EVOLUTIONARY PERSONALITY PSYCHOLOGY

David M. Buss

Department of Psychology, University of Michigan, Ann Arbor, Michigan
48109-1346

KEY WORDS: Personality, evolution, strategy, psychological mechanism

CONTENTS

A new discipline is emerging called "evolutionary psychology." Its central aim is to identify psychological mechanisms and behavioral strategies as

459

evolved solutions to the adaptive problems our species has faced over millions of years. Because personality psychology is dedicated to studying human nature in all of its individually different manifestations, this field is uniquely positioned to contribute to, and become informed by, evolutionary psychology.

This review differs from previous ones in articulating an evolutionary metatheory to organize the diverse strands of current personality research and to clarify many of its core concerns. These include: clarifying the debate about personality consistency, clarifying the causal status of dispositions, understanding interactionism, identifying important features of context, identifying the structure of goal-directed strategies, explaining the origins of individual differences, and placing the five-factor model of personality in adaptive context. In clarifying these issues, several crucial misunderstandings must be corrected—the "sociobiological fallacy," the "fundamental situational error," and the "fallacy of genetic determinism."

WHY DOES PERSONALITY PSYCHOLOGY NEED EVOLUTIONARY THEORY?

A recent review of the personality literature argued that "psychology in general, and personality theory and assessment in particular, have paid a high price for refusing to follow physics' model" (Rorer & Widiger 1983). My view is precisely the opposite. Physics provides a very poor model for psychology because the principles that govern purely physical phenomena are fundamentally different from those that govern organic life. If I walk around on bare feet for a few weeks, my soles and heels develop thick calluses. Callus-producing mechanisms are complex environment-contingent adaptations that become activated in response to friction; they function to protect the anatomical and physiological structures beneath the skin. If I ride around in my car for a few weeks, however, my tires do not grow thicker. My feet, as much subject to the laws of physics as my tires, are in addition shaped by organic natural selection. They exhibit adaptations that exist because of the fitness benefits they conferred in the past.

Only three theories have been proposed to account for the origins of these complex organic mechanisms known as adaptations. The first is evolution by natural selection (Darwin 1859; Hamilton 1964). The second is "creationism." The third is "seeding theory," the idea that extraterrestrial organisms visited the earth many years ago and planted the seeds of life. Creationism and seeding theory, largely incapable of being verified or disproved by observation or experiment, are not scientific theories. Evolution by natural selection, in contrast, is a powerful and well-articulated theory that has successfully organized and explained thousands of diverse facts in a principled way (Alexander 1979).

Evolutionary theory promises to circumvent the plethora of seemingly arbitrary personality theories by anchoring a theory of human nature in processes known to govern all life. There is no reason to believe that humans are exempt from the organizing forces of evolution by natural selection. Personality theories inconsistent with evolutionary theory stand little chance of being correct.

PERSONALITY COMPRISES PSYCHOLOGICAL MECHANISMS AND BEHAVIORAL STRATEGIES

The Fundamental Situational Error

It does not seem to be generally recognized in personality and social psychology that *all* observable behavior is the product of mechanisms residing within the organism, combined with environmental and organismic inputs that activate those mechanisms (Cosmides & Tooby 1987). No behavior can be produced in the absence of mechanisms. There is no such thing as a purely environmental or situational cause of behavior. If a person responds to the presence of a group by conforming (e.g. Asch 1955) or by social loafing (Latane 1981) but a cockroach, a rat, or a chimpanzee does not conform or loaf in response to identical environmental inputs, then there must be something about the *psychological mechanisms* of humans that differs from those of the cockroach, rat, or chimp.

Such mechanisms are a necessary and central part of any sensible causal explanation of observed behavior. The fundamental situational error is to assume that, because situational variance can "account for" behavioral variance (e.g. changes in situation can be correlated with changes in obedience, conformity, social loafing), a coherent explanatory account need not invoke stable psychological mechanisms (e.g. dispositions, decision-rules, structures, processes) residing within the organism. Without internal mechanisms there can be no behavior. The fundamental situational error is as often committed in sociobiology and behavioral ecology as in personality and social psychology (see Symons 1990).

At some fundamental level of description, evolution by natural selection is the process that creates physiological, anatomical, and psychological mechanisms. Therefore the crucial question is not *whether* evolution is relevant to the understanding of human behavior but how it is relevant.

Problem-Specificity of Psychological Mechanisms

How has biological evolution affected psychological mechanisms? A continuum of possible answers can be evaluated. At one end is the possibility that natural selection has produced in humans a few domain-general mechanisms—e.g. a capacity to learn by operant conditioning or to reason inductively. If this were the case, then psychologists could legitimately focus on how these domain-general mechanisms develop more or less arbitrary psychological structures during ontogeny (i.e., study learning histories and schedules of reinforcement). Evolutionary theory would not further illuminate psychology and could be largely ignored. The assumption of domain-general psychological mechanisms, promulgated in this century by Watson (1924) and Skinner, remains implicit in much current psychological theory (see Rozin & Schull 1988 and Symons 1987 for useful discussions).

At the other end of the continuum is the possibility that natural selection has created many domain-specific psychological mechanisms that solve particular adaptive problems (Cosmides & Tooby 1987; Symons 1987). Evolutionary theory can become a scientifically useful metatheory for personality psychology to the degree that human psychological mechanisms (a) operate according to different principles across different adaptive domains, (b) number in the dozens, hundreds, or thousands, and (c) are complex solutions to specific adaptive problems.

Human psychological mechanisms undoubtedly vary in domain-generality. Some apparently solve a specific problem (e.g. an 8–24-month-old's fear of strangers solves a safety problem), whereas others may solve several problems (e.g. mechanisms of status striving partially solve the problems of attracting mates and of securing resources for offspring). Recent work in evolutionary psychology, however, suggests that the effects of natural selection cannot have produced solely or even primarily a few domain-general mechanisms (Barkow et al 1990; Cosmides & Tooby 1987; Symons 1987, 1990; Tooby & Cosmides 1990a).

There are two bases for this conclusion, one empirical and one conceptual. First, many experiments in the past 25 years have documented systematic violations of proposed domain-general "laws" of learning (Herrnstein 1977; Rozin & Schull 1989). Consider the fact that the objects of human fears and phobias are not a random assortment: More people fear heights, snakes, darkness, spiders, and strangers than fear guns, cars, or electrical outlets (Seligman 1972). Humans are apparently predisposed to learn more easily and rapidly to avoid some things (e.g. those that were environmentally hazardous earlier in human evolution) than others (e.g. those that are environmentally novel). Recent evolutionary psychological findings in aggression, attraction (Langois & Roggman 1990), social exchange (Cosmides 1989), self-deception (Lockard & Paulhus 1988), decision theory (Cooper 1987), psychophysics of perception (Shepard 1984), language (Pinker & Bloom 1990), and many others all point to a single powerful conclusion: Human psychology involves many complex and domain-specific mechanisms, each suited to serve a particular function.

A second rationale for conceptualizing psychological mechanisms as numerous, specific, and complex derives from the nature and number of the adaptive problems that humans and their ancestors have faced. Consider, as an analogy, animal adaptations favoring physical survival. Most terrestrial mammals have evolved solutions to the survival problems of extreme heat (sweat glands or other evaporation mechanisms), cold (shivering), diseases and parasites (immune system), predators (specific evasive capacities), wounds (blood clotting), and what food objects to consume (taste preferences for sugar, salt, and fat). In the realm of reproduction, many primate species have had to solve the social problems of intrasexual competition, mate attraction, mate selection, mate retention, hierarchy negotiation, coalition-building, dyadic reciprocal alliance formation, and parental investment, to name just a few. Now, sweat glands do nothing to solve the problem of what foods to put into one's mouth or how to combat parasites. Solutions to the problem of attracting mates contribute little toward solving the problem of detecting nonreciprocators in social exchange. Different problems typically select for different adaptive solutions; natural selection results in a multiplicity of specific adaptations over time. Evolutionary psychologists expect psychological mechanisms to be many and domain-specific.

The Sociobiological Fallacy

Evolutionary psychology is best regarded as a theory about the origins, rather than the content, of human nature (Symons 1990; Tooby & Cosmides 1989). Some sociobiological writings err by assuming that natural selection has produced in humans a general motivation to maximize one's inclusive fitness—i.e. a domain-general psychological mechanism such as an "inclusive fitness maximizer."[1] One problem with this view is that fitness cannot be tracked within an individual's lifetime; only correlates of fitness (such as mating success or food acquisition) can be tracked. A second problem is that what constitutes fitness differs radically across species, sexes, ages, and adaptive domains. Hence, even in principle, there can be no domain-general way to maximize fitness or reproductive success. Humans thus cannot have psychological mechanisms the goal of which is to maximize reproductive success (either consciously or unconsciously). Instead, we have mechanisms that exist in their present form because in our evolutionary past they successfully solved specific adaptive problems. The fact that successful solutions evolve through a process of differential reproductive success does not mean that the solution mechanisms are domain-general fitness maximizers.

Behavioral Strategies, Tactics, and Acts

Personality psychologists seek to characterize relatively enduring or stable human *psychological mechanisms,* including the qualitative and quantitative

[1]Inclusive fitness may be defined as "the sum of an individual's Darwinian fitness (personal reproductive success) and his or her influence upon the Darwinian fitness of relatives, weighted according to their coefficients of relatedness to the focal individual" (Daly & Wilson 1983:393).

ways such mechanisms differ across individuals (e.g. Tellegen 1990). Psychological mechanisms evolve because they have behavioral consequences. Status-striving mechanisms, for example, could not evolve unless they reliably produced classes of acts that actually led to the increase or maintenance of positions within social hierarchies. Thus, behavioral strategies, tactics, and classes of acts are an essential part of a correct description of evolved psychological mechanisms. In this view, a general theory of personality must correlate evolved psychological mechanisms, their accompanying behavioral strategies, and the specific adaptive problems they were designed to solve.

EVOLUTIONARY FOUNDATIONS OF PERSONALITY

Adaptive Problems and Their Solutions

Adaptive problems are of two major kinds—those of individual survival and those of reproduction. All living organisms have ancestors who successfully solved survival and reproductive problems. Some solutions are anatomical, some are physiological, and some entail psychological mechanisms whereby information is processed according to decision rules that produce output that solves a particular adaptive problem.[2] Some adaptive solutions occurred long ago in the mammalian and primate lineages that led to humans. Each species, however, possesses adaptations that are unique as well as those shared with some other species.

SURVIVAL PROBLEMS   Darwin (1859) identified many of an organism's major survival problems, subsumed by what he called the "hostile forces of nature." These include food shortages, harsh climate, disease, parasites, predators, and other natural hazards. Evolved psychological contributions to the solutions to some of these (e.g. fear of strangers) are of concern to personality psychologists. However, because differential *reproductive* success is the key process in evolution by natural selection, reproductive problems, many of which are inherently social, are more central to evolutionary personality psychology, as illustrated below.

---

[2]I provisionally define an evolved "psychological mechanism" as a set of processes inside an organism that 1. exist in the form they do because they (or other mechanisms that reliably produce them) solved specific problems of individual survival or reproduction; 2. take only certain classes of input, where input (a) can be either external or internal, (b) can be actively extracted from the environment or passively received from the environment, and (c) specifies to the organism the particular adaptational problem it is facing; and 3. transform that information into output through a procedure (e.g. decision rule) where output (a) regulates physiological activity, provides information to other psychological mechanisms, or produces action, and (b) solves a particular adaptational problem. Species have evolved psychologies to the degree that they possess mechanisms of this sort.

REPRODUCTIVE PROBLEMS   Major classes of problems that humans (like many species before them) have had to solve for successful reproduction were: 1. *successful intrasexual competition:* besting members of one's own sex to gain access to desirable members of the opposite sex; 2. *mate selection:* choosing from the pool of potential mates those with the greatest reproductive value; 3. *successful conception:* engaging in the necessary social and sexual behaviors to fertilize a mate, or to become fertilized by a mate; 4. *mate retention:* preventing the encroachment of intrasexual competitors as well as preventing one's mate from defecting or deserting (this problem arises only when pursuing a long-term mating strategy, and does not apply to mating strategies tailored to brief, opportunistic copulation); 5. *reciprocal dyadic alliance formation:* initiating dyadic relationships characterized by cooperation and reciprocity; 6. *coalition-building and maintenance:* participating in cooperative groups whose interests are more closely aligned with group members than with competing groups (Manson & Wrangham 1990; Tooby & Cosmides, 1988); 7. *parental care and socialization:* engaging in actions to ensure the survival and reproductive success of one's offspring; and 8. *extra-parental kin investment:* incurring costs to self that benefit nondescendant genetic relatives.[3]

Each of these problems subsumes a host of subproblems. Successful intrasexual competition among humans, for example, probably entails: (*a*) acquisition of resources required by a potential mate (e.g. Townsend 1989), (*b*) successful negotiation of social hierarchies (Kyl-Heku 1990), (*c*) formation of successful reciprocal alliances and coalitions (Cosmides 1989), (*d*) appeasement, or at least not nonalienation, of relatives and friends of the potential mate (Buss 1988a,b), (*e*) successful courtship of the potential mate (Buss 1988a,b), and (*f*) derogation of intrasexual competitors to the potential mate (Buss & Dedden 1990). A personality psychologist who understands in detail the survival and reproduction problems confronting early humans (and their ancestor species) is in a position to identify the relatively enduring psychological solutions.

THE LIMITATIONS OF EVOLUTIONARY THEORY: CONSTRAINTS ON THE DETECTION AND PREDICTION OF ADAPTATIONS   While general evolutionary theory broadly outlines what is *unlikely* to have evolved (e.g. adaptations that favor other species or conspecific competitors), it can rarely specify what *must* have evolved. Nothing in general evolutionary theory could have predicted, for example, such adaptations as a turtle's shell, a giraffe's neck, human hairlessness, bipedal locomotion, or a universal language grammar.

---

[3]Of course solutions to some of these problems (e.g. coalition-building and reciprocal alliance formation) contribute to individual survival as well as to reproduction.

Evolution-based models of particular adaptive domains, in contrast, can sharply constrain the range of possible adaptations and thus have predictive and heuristic value. For example, we can predict that in species (such as ours) that engage in protracted social exchange, mechanisms for detecting cheaters must evolve (Cosmides 1989). Likewise, species (such as ours) that form social hierarchies must have mechanisms for monitoring status, position, and reputation (Buss 1986; Stone 1989). There is no substitute for specific evolutionary models of particular content domains such as social exchange (Cosmides 1989), coalition formation (Tooby & Cosmides 1988), and hierarchy negotiation (Stone, 1989). It is at the level of evolution-based models of particular adaptive domains, rather than at the level of general evolutionary theory, that specific hypotheses can be confirmed or falsified.

Several other cautions should be noted. First, some biological phenomena arise through processes other than natural selection. Examples include those due to genetic drift, pleiotropy, or chance (see Dawkins 1982). Second, some mutations may be neutral with respect to natural selection, and thus endure without being adaptive. Third, the scientific standards of evidence for invoking the concept of adaptation are often difficult to meet (Williams 1966).

Finally, cleaving psychological and behavioral phenomena into functionally significant units remains a central and extraordinarily difficult theoretical task for the evolution-minded psychologist. Evolutionary psychology attempts to ground its description of basic psychological mechanisms in adaptive function and by so doing escapes arbitrariness.

Human Nature

All "grand" theories of personality have hypotheses about the contents of human nature as their core, be they motives for sex and aggression (Freud), self-actualization (Maslow), effectance (White), striving for superiority (Adler), or striving for status, power, popularity, or intimacy (Hogan, McAdams, McClelland, Wiggins). Even the most radical behaviorist has an implicit theory of human nature—i.e. that it consists of a few domain-general psychological mechanisms such as those of operant conditioning (Symons 1987). If humans have a nature different from that of the gorilla, dog, rat, or cockroach, what are its contents and how can we discover them?

In a recent special issue of the *Journal of Personality,* Tooby & Cosmides (1990b) argue that human nature comprises the species-typical solutions that humans have evolved in response to the selective pressures we faced in our ancestral conditions. They argue that the constraints of sexual recombination and the necessarily polygenic nature of complex adaptations virtually dictate a human nature that is unitary, although susceptible to quantitative variation. This renders unlikely the idea of distinct "personality types" based on entirely different sets of genes. Despite the clear-cut genetic distinction between them, even males and females are expected to share a universal functional structure in most respects, differing only in those domains where they have faced recurrently different adaptive problems.

Several recent articles attempt to identify the particulars of this unitary human nature. Wiggins (1990), for example, argues that two motivational modes, agency (strivings for power and mastery that differentiate the individual) and communion (striving for intimacy, union, and solidarity with others), provide conceptual coordinates for understanding interpersonal behavior. He reviews the literature on agency and communion from a variety of theoretical perspectives, including an evolutionary one. Sex differences in agency and communion (e.g. men's greater levels of physical aggressiveness; women's greater levels of empathy) may stem from the distinct reproductive problems that men and women have faced in ancestral environments—problems of gaining access to mates through intrasexual competition and problems of elevated parental investment in children.

Hogan (1990) argues that the basic human motivators are status and popularity. According to Hogan the most important social problems early humans had to solve to survive and reproduce involved establishing cooperative relations with other members of the group and negotiating hierarchies. Achieving status and popularity likely conferred a host of reproductively relevant resources, including better protection, more food, and more desirable mates.

Like Wiggins and Hogan, Baumeister (1990) notes the importance of group living. He proposes that anxiety is a species-typical adaptation that prevents social exclusion. Those who were indifferent to being excluded by others may have experienced lower reproductive success than those whose psychological mechanisms caused them to maintain inclusion in the group by avoiding acts that might elicit criticism.

The importance of group living is also evident in the work of Cosmides (1989). She concludes, from an evolutionary analysis, that in complex reciprocal social exchange, individuals would be favored who possessed psychological mechanisms that would alert them to "cheaters"—i.e. those who take without giving. Her evidence that humans now exhibit such a mechanism for detecting cheaters shows how psychologists can experimentally document domain-specific adaptations that comprise important parts of human nature.

Daly & Wilson (1990) use evolution-based reasoning to argue that Freud's universal Oedipal complex is inconsistent with evolutionary biology. Using Trivers's (1974) theory of parent-offspring conflict, they argue that Freud failed to distinguish two sorts of conflict—an early nonsexual father-son conflict over how a mother's reproductive efforts should be expended, and a later sexual rivalry not over the mother (who is probably of low fertility at that point) but over possible mates. Daly & Wilson review previous data and present new data refuting the central Freudian claim of a same-sex contingency in parent-offspring antagonism during the Oedipal phase. They thus use an evolutionary analysis and empirical data to provide a more accurate portrait of human nature.

These recent evolutionary trends in personality theory, however, represent exceptions to the historical norm. Personality theories have typically been formulated in innocence of the processes that shaped personality. Consider, for instance, Epstein's (1990) claim that "the person in everyday life is motivated to live his or her life in an emotionally satisfying way. . . . Personal theories of reality have four basic functions: to assimilate the data of reality . . . [, to] maintain a favorable pleasure-pain balance, to maintain relatedness to others; and to maintain a favorable level of self-esteem" (p. 166). Epstein may well have hit upon some key insights, but the theory does not explain why human nature should be so constructed.

An evolutionary perspective can provide constraints upon otherwise unanchored assertions about motivation. For example, evolutionary thinking points to particular others with whom people will strive to "maintain relatedness"—those who make good reciprocal allies (Cosmides 1989), those elevated in social hierarchies (Stone 1989), mates of high reproductive value (Buss 1989a), those who are genetically related (Hamilton 1964), and those who will make good members of one's coalition (Tooby & Cosmides 1988). These five types of relationships—dyadic alliances, hierarchical relationships, mateships, kinships, and coalitions—subsume most important human relationships. People do not simply "maintain relatedness," they nurture and train their children in particular ways (Low 1989), help their coalitions to out-compete other coalitions, cooperate with their reproductively valuable mates, protect and defend their kin, and exchange reproductively relevant resources with allies.

Progress in identifying the fundamental psychological mechanisms and behavioral strategies that comprise human nature should accelerate once the study of these mechanisms is based on careful analysis of the fitness problems that humans likely had to solve in ancestral conditions. Those who failed to solve these problems were not our ancestors; whatever mechanisms led directly to their failure we did not inherit. Current humans and their functional mechanisms are all products of evolutionary success.

Goal-Directed Tactics and Strategies as Units of Analysis

Evolved psychological mechanisms do not reside passively within the skulls of humans. They propel us to act toward particular goals, the attainment of which historically led to reproductive success. The actions generated by psychological mechanisms are not mere "physicalistic acts" (Fiske 1988), but rather are charged with emotion and are specific to context. Indeed, goal-directed behavioral strategies compose part of the essential description of evolved psychological mechanisms.

An emerging trend within the field of personality psychology has been the proposal and exploration of tactics and strategies as units of analysis (Buss & Cantor 1989; Pervin 1989). These have been given different labels by different investigators: personal projects and acts that accomplish them (Little 1989), life tasks and the strategies used to accomplish them (Cantor 1990; Langston & Cantor 1989; Zirkel & Cantor 1990), personal strivings and their act instantiations (Emmons 1990), current concerns (Klinger 1975), and reproductively relevant goals and the tactics used to accomplish them (Buss 1988a,b). These investigators share the idea that humans deploy cognitive, motivational, emotional, and behavioral strategies to accomplish particular goals (e.g. Carver & Scheier 1990; Pervin 1989).

Many researchers study aspects of these units on which individuals differ. People differ, for example, in their use of defensive pessimism as a cognitive strategy (Cantor 1990), in the degree to which they feel that their various projects conflict (Little 1989), and on the efforts they apportion to intimacy and achievement (Emmons 1990). The fascinating diversity of human strategies and strivings, however, should not divert investigators from the likelihood that at some fundamental level of description many goals will be shared by all humans.

Humans speak a diversity of languages, but the "language organ" has evolved in all humans and shows strong evidence of adaptive design (Pinker & Bloom 1990). Humans eat diverse foods, but all humans share taste preferences for substances rich in fat, sugar, salt, and protein (Rozin 1976). Science usually proceeds by discovering the deep structure that accounts for the complex and variegated surface structure. Geologists, for example, were bewildered by complex and apparently unique phenomena such as volcanoes, earthquakes, continental drift, and mountain formations until plate tectonic theory showed them all to be caused by interactions among the underlying plates on which continents and oceans rest. Personality psychology may now be positioned to make an analogous scientific advance, but it cannot do so without understanding the fundamental mechanisms that underlie manifest diversity.

The goal-based research programs pursued by different investigators often identify similar fundamental goals. Consider these examples: "To make attractive women [men] notice me more" (personal striving), "to have sex" (personal project), "to get a boyfriend [girlfriend]" (life task), "to attract mates" (evolutionary life task), and "to maintain my marital relationship" (current concern). From an evolutionary perspective, all these forms of effort constitute mating effort and are thematically related to reproduction. Successful mating is a task that must be accomplished for sexual reproduction.

Individuals whose psychological properties led them to succeed at this task are our ancestors. The fact that the theme of successful mating emerges repeatedly from goal-based personality research suggests that these methods provide powerful tools for exploring functionally significant life tasks.

Two other behaviors that have major evolutionary significance are the negotiation of hierarchies and the formation of reciprocal alliances (Buss 1986). Surveys repeatedly show people listing such personal goals as getting a promotion, graduating from university, being more productive at work, dominating people in certain situations, and making friends (Emmons 1990). Because position within social hierarchies historically bestowed on the successful a host of reproductively relevant resources (e.g. more food and better mating opportunities), rising in hierarchies or status-striving likely constitutes a major species-typical goal of humans (Betzig 1986; Buss 1986; Hogan, 1983; Sadalla et al 1987; Symons 1990). Because establishing cooperative social exchanges represents an effective form of reproductive competition, reciprocal alliance formation should also comprise a major motive of humans (Axelrod 1984; Cosmides 1989; Trivers 1971).

It is not by chance that so much attention has been paid to human motives such as achievement (McClelland 1989), power (Winter 1987), and intimacy (McAdams 1988). Not by chance do power and love emerge consistently and cross-culturally as the two most important axes of interpersonal behavior (Carson 1990; Kiesler 1990; White 1980; Wiggins 1990). These goals are framed in somewhat different ways for different individuals, and the strategies used to attain them vary; but such individual variability should not lead us to ignore shared features of our evolved human nature. Human effort (strivings, projects, tasks, concerns, and their attendant strategies and acts) is commonly directed by goals that historically have been linked with inclusive fitness. Goals and their attendant strategies across the life span are likely to be a central focus of personality research in the 1990s (see Caspi & Bem 1990; Eder 1989; Helson & Picano 1990; Ozer & Gjerde 1989).

Goal-directed strategic effort arises from psychological mechanisms that owe their existence and form to evolution by natural selection. Although most goal-based research has focused on consciously articulated tasks, nothing in an evolutionary perspective requires that humans be aware of either the psychological mechanisms or the ultimate functions of goal pursuit. The crucial issue is whether these strivings and their underlying psychological mechanisms show evidence of function and meet rigorous standards of evidence for adaptation. For example, such mechanisms should show evidence of efficiency, economy, precision, and complexity of design that is uniquely tailored to solving a particular problem. Furthermore, a plausible account of a history of selection that could have created them and evidence of species-typicality of functional design add greater credence to a hypothesized adaptation. The discovery of a species-typical goal-structure underlying observed behavioral strategies will constitute a major and lasting scientific advance in personality psychology.

Personality as the Adaptive Landscape: The Five-Factor Model in Evolutionary Perspective

A previous *Annual Review* chapter (Digman 1990) thoroughly reviewed the empirical work on the five-factor model of personality (see also Botwin & Buss 1989; John 1990; Peabody & Goldberg 1989; Watson 1989). The five factors, variously labeled, are: surgency (extraversion), agreeableness, conscientiousness (will to achieve), emotional stability, and intellect (openness). This work is primarily descriptive and shows the robustness of the five-factor model across time, contexts, cultures, and data sources. One need not believe that there are *only* five important personality dimensions (e.g. DeRaad & Hoskens 1990; Tellegen 1985) to reach the conclusion that these five should be included in any major personality taxonomy. Descriptive work documents the robustness of these factors, but does not elucidate why they are so frequently found.

From an evolutionary perspective, there are three ways to explain the prominence of the five factors: 1. These factors may represent fundamental differences in the strategies humans use to accomplish species-typical goals; 2. they may, on the other hand, signify mere "noise" in the system— variations that were neutral with respect to natural selection, and hence evolutionarily unimportant; or 3. the five factors may summarize the most important dimensions of the social landscape to which humans have had to adapt (Buss 1989c). I consider the third option first.

The core of the "personality as the adaptive landscape" view is that perceiving, attending to, and acting upon differences in others is crucial for solving problems of survival and reproduction. One piece of evidence favoring this view is the finding that trait terms are inherently evaluative. Peabody (1985) found that fewer than 3% of trait terms were evaluatively neutral; more than 97% have definite evaluative (as well as descriptive) aspects (see also Hofstee 1990). Hogan (1990) argues that trait terms reflect observer evaluations of others as potential contributors to, or exploiters of, the group's resources. Borkenau (1990) proposes that traits are evaluative goal-based social categories and provides evidence for this view. For example, individuals must evaluate the conscientiousness (Factor III) of others in order to decide whom to trust with tasks. Borkenau argues that a selective advantage would accrue to persons with the ability to perceive and act upon these major individual differences in others. In a similar vein, Graziano & Eisenberg (1990) place agreeableness (Factor II) in evolutionary perspective, arguing that coordinated group action is best accomplished when individuals are willing to cooperate and conform to group norms, and suspend their individual concerns for the good of the group (see Wiggins 1990 for a similar account). This implies that it is crucial for people to evaluate individual differences in agreeableness for deciding on group inclusion.

As a species humans live in groups (e.g. Tooby & DeVore 1987). Groups historically afford protection from predators, protection from marauding males, the possibility of cooperative hunting of large game, and a pool of potential mates. But groups also impose costs. With group living comes an intensification of competition, risk of communicable diseases, depletion of resources, and aggression from other group members. Other humans are our primary "hostile force of nature." Other humans define many of the problems to which we must adapt, and are capable of facilitating or interfering with our reproductive strategies (cf Byrne & Whiten 1988).

I have hypothesized (1989c) that personality traits such as surgency, agreeableness, and conscientiousness are the most important psychological dimensions of our social adaptive landscape. They provide information for answering adaptively important life questions: Who is high or low in the social hierarchy? Who is likely to rise in the future? Who will make a good member of my coalition? Who possesses the resources that I need? Who will share their resources with me? With whom should I share my resources? Who can I go to for advice? Whom can I depend on when in need? With whom should I mate? Who will be a good cooperator and reciprocator? Who might do me harm? Whom can I trust? Who will betray my trust? I hypothesize that people have evolved psychological mechanisms sensitive to individual differences in others that are relevant to answering these critical questions.

Human groups are 1. often intensely hierarchical, with important reproductive resources closely linked with position in the hierarchy (e.g. Hogan 1983; Lopreato 1984), and 2. characterized by elevated forms of *cooperation* and *reciprocal alliance formation* compared with all other mammalian species (Axelrod 1984; Tooby & Cosmides 1989; Trivers 1971). The importance of hierarchy suggests that *location* of others in the hierarchy and differences in the *proclivities* of others to ascend in the hierarchy are extremely important features of the human adaptive landscape. The prevalence of reciprocal alliance formation suggests that a second critical feature of the human adaptive landscape is the differential proclivity of others to "cooperate" or to "aggress."

I have argued (1989c) that the persistent emergence of surgency (Factor I) and agreeableness (Factor II) as the two major axes in interpersonal taxonomies and as the first two factors in personality-descriptive taxonomies (McCrae & Costa 1989; Trapnell & Wiggins in press) results from the advantage humans gain from discerning others' hierarchical positions and proclivities to form reciprocal alliances. During the course of human evolution, individuals who were able to discern accurately and act upon these dimensions of their social context likely attained a reproductive advantage over those who failed to discern them. Studies of competition and mating support specific predictions from an evolutionary analysis of these features of the human adaptive landscape (Buss 1989c).

In sum, the five factors of personality, in this account, represent important dimensions of the social terrain that humans were selected to attend to and act upon. Whenever individuals differ in ways relevant to the problems of survival and reproduction that humans must solve, a selective advantage would accrue to those whose capacity to discern the differences enabled them to increase their inclusive fitness.

We turn now to the question of why there would be such important differences among individuals to begin with.

Explaining the Origins of Individual Differences—Dispositions as Evolved Problem-Solving Strategies

Evolutionary accounts of the origins of individual differences fall into three basic categories: 1. Individuals may differ in their adaptive *strategies*; 2. individual differences could be incidental by-products of strategy differences; or 3. individual differences could be the product of noise in the system (e.g. mutations that were selectively neutral, and hence not eliminated by natural selection). Although the "incidental by-product" and "noise" accounts are viable alternatives, the "strategic differences" account is the most intriguing theoretical possibility, and so I examine it in detail.

There are four major evolutionary routes to the emergence of consistent individual differences in dispositional strategies (discussed further below): 1. *heritable alternative strategies:* genetically based strategy differences due to frequency-dependent selection or selection within alternative niches (cf Tooby & Cosmides 1990a; Hamilton 1987); 2. *heritable calibration of psychological mechanisms:* where the adaptive optimum has changed or fluctuated over time or place, producing heritable variation in the calibration or threshold of a species-typical mechanism; 3. *situationally contingent alternative strategies:* situational activation of different strategies, all of which comprise a species-typical repertoire inherent in each individual; and 4. *developmental calibration of psychological mechanisms:* where individually different experiences during development calibrate or set a threshold on a species-typical mechanism in a continuous fashion, producing a distribution of individual differences.

To illustrate these alternatives, consider the findings on individual differences in mating strategies in frogs (Howard 1981). Dominant males emit loud croaks that attract female frogs. Smaller male frogs sometimes sit silently nearby and intercept females as they approach the resonant croaks—a "satellite" strategy. If genetic differences limit each frog to one of the two behaviors then we have here an example of heritable alternative mating strategies. In contrast, if all male frogs can use either strategy and the observed behavior varies directly with the circumstances (e.g. whether or not larger frogs dominate the pond), then this example shows environmentally contingent alternative strategies. A third possibility might occur when the optimum threshold for shifting from a dominant strategy to a satellite strategy has fluctuated over time or across niches occupied by these frogs. In this case, there could be heritable differences in the threshold for shifting from one strategy to another *or* environmental calibration of the threshold for shifting from one strategy to another.

HERITABLE ALTERNATIVE STRATEGIES   Tooby & Cosmides (1990a) outline the observations that would support heritable determination of dispositional strategies: 1. For each putative strategy a range of personality variables should covary in an organized, coordinated fashion; 2. the variables must covary in ways that fulfill criteria for adaptation, and 3. the alternative dispositions should show evidence of frequency-dependent selection (i.e. that the adaptive payoff of any one type decreases when the relative frequency of that type increases in the population). Of course behavioral genetic methods must show that the individual differences are heritable.

These standards of evidence are extraordinarily difficult to meet. The male-female difference does meet these rigorous standards (cf Buss 1990; Savin-Williams & Weisfeld 1989). Men and women differ on a suite of personality and physiological variables that covary in an adaptive fashion and show evidence of frequency-dependent selection (Symons 1979). Although no other proposed personality types or differences have yet been shown to meet these standards, there are several promising candidates.

Snyder et al (1986) and Gangestad & Simpson (1990) have identified a suite of personality characteristics that covary with female "sociosexual orientation" (the latter captures an individual's tendency to form long-lasting mateships rather than seek brief sexual encounters); and there is evidence that this suite is heritable (see also Rowe et al 1989). These researchers argue that women using the short-term strategy increase their chances of being inseminated by men with greater attractiveness, whereas women using the long-term strategy elicit more substantial male parental investment. Gangestad & Simpson (1990) report empirical evidence of bimodality in sociosexual orientation, thus supporting one prediction from their theory. This theory (which requires further empirical testing—e.g. to determine whether the characteristics in question are maintained through frequency-dependent selection) illustrates the possibility of heritable alternative strategies within sex. In addition, because sociosexual orientation is clearly linked with surgency (Factor I) and conscientiousness (Factor III), this research provides compelling links among traditionally conceived personality variables, the concept of dispositions as strategies, and evolutionary theory.

HERITABLE CALIBRATION OF THRESHOLDS ON PSYCHOLOGICAL MECHA-NISMS   Most personality dispositions seem to be continuously distributed in the population, an observation that raises doubt that they represent heritable alternative adaptations. However, the moderate heritability associated with these continuous distributions (e.g. Bouchard & McGue 1990; Eysenck 1990; Goldsmith 1989; Loehlin et al 1990) is compatible with the hypothesis that the adaptive optima for some strategies have fluctuated over time or place.

Zuckerman (1990), for example, argues that heritable individual differences in sensation-seeking may represent variation in tendencies or thresholds for approaching or avoiding resources (including mates), with different thresholds carrying costs as well as benefits. In ancestral environments, those with a greater tendency to seek sensation may have obtained reproductive resources through vigorous approach behaviors but may have incurred substantial risk in the process. Those with a lesser tendency to seek sensation may have avoided these risks but also failed to accrue the reproductive benefits probabilistically associated with approach. Because sensation-seeking is normally rather than bimodally distributed, different thresholds for sensation seeking are evidently not distinct alternative strategies. But they may represent differences in threshold setting that signify past environments or niches that imposed different adaptive optima. Niches where food resources were scarce, for example, may have favored a lower threshold for risk-taking and sensation-seeking, whereas niches where resources were reliably present may have favored a higher threshold for risk-taking.

Personality dimensions tend to be continuously rather than bimodally distributed. Variation in surgency, conscientiousness, emotional stability, and openness-intellect (but not agreeableness) is moderately heritable (Plomin & Nesselroade 1990). These findings are consistent with, but do not prove, the hypothesis that these major personality dimensions represent heritable calibration of basic psychological mechanisms. They rule out the hypothesis that such individual differences represent disjunctive alternative strategies. This explanation of individual differences remains speculative because we lack precise knowledge of the relevant environmental fluctuations.

DEVELOPMENTAL OR SITUATIONAL CALIBRATION OF PSYCHOLOGICAL MECHANISMS   Evidence of low heritability of personality factors is compatible with the hypothesis of environmentally contingent strategies of either the disjunctive or the continuous variety (cf Crawford & Anderson 1989). Since these strategies are possessed by all members of a species, genetic variation cannot account for them. Instead, individuals differ as a function of variable external conditions.

Two programs of research in personality psychology have explored environment-contingent species-typical strategies. Draper & Belsky (1990) propose that people whose fathers were present during early childhood exhibit delayed puberty, delayed onset of sexual activity, stability in adult pair-bonding, and a set of personality characteristics that includes low self-monitoring and high cooperativeness (high agreeableness in five-factor models). People whose fathers were absent during early childhood develop an alternative personality constellation and reproductive strategy involving early onset of puberty and sexual activity, unstable pair-bonding in adulthood, low parental investment, high self-monitoring, and high aggressiveness.

The Draper-Belsky theory is consonant with a recent report that the agreeable-aggressive dimension on five-factor models differs from the other four in showing low heritability (Plomin & Rende 1991). Individual differences in agreeableness appear to stem from environmental, not genetic differences. The fact that developmental studies show aggressiveness to be fairly stable over time (Olweus, 1979) suggests that developmental calibration probably occurs early in life. Thus if any important personality difference results from developmental calibration of genetically invariant psychological mechanisms, the agreeableness factor is the most promising candidate.

These are not, of course, the only possibile explanations for the origins of individual differences. The "incidental by-product" and "noise" accounts cannot be ruled out (Tooby & Cosmides 1990a). Similarly, some personality differences may be the incidental by-product of assortative mating or other processes known to increase genetic variance. There is evidence, for example, that at least some individual differences in IQ are due to the incidental effects of assortative mating for intelligence over the past four or five generations—a process in part attributable to cultural institutions such as places of higher education. In cases like these, it would be mistaken to view individual differences as evolved strategic differences.

All these accounts are recent and require more systematic research before firm conclusions can be reached. Personality psychologists in the 1990s will likely focus on testing these alternative explanations of the origins and nature of individual differences. The concept of dispositions as strategies (whether due to basic genetic differences, to heritable calibration of psychological mechanisms, to situational elicitation of strategies possessed by all, or to developmental threshold calibration of psychological mechanisms) should stimulate personality study in the next decade.

Interim Summary

Evolutionary personality theory involves the following essential components:

1. *Identification of the adaptive problems confronted by ancestral human populations* (with an emphasis on social problems). This task includes characterizing the probable *human adaptive landscape* of that period—that is,

the challenges and benefits produced by conspecific competitors and cooper-ators. These fellow humans likely differed in major ways, as in their hierar-chical proclivities (surgency), their willingness to cooperate (agreeableness), their capacity for reliable work and enduring commitment (conscientious-ness), their ability to handle stress (emotional stability), and their propensity for innovation or astuteness in solving problems (openness, intellect).

2. *Correlation of currently observable personality factors with the pro-posed problems of ancestral populations,* to support the hypothesis that the former evolved because they were solutions to the latter. Such adaptations include relatively enduring psychological mechanisms and the behavioral strategies they produce.

3. *Identification of the major individual differences in the ways humans adopt and deploy dispositional strategies.*

CLARIFYING CORE CONTROVERSIES IN PERSONALITY PSYCHOLOGY

Evolutionary thinking can guide personality theory and research in several ways: 1. It can suggest important domains of inquiry (e.g. hierarchies, coalitions, alliances, kinships, mateships); 2. it "prevents certain kinds of errors . . . and raises suspicions of certain explanations or observations" (Lloyd 1979:18); 3. it "provides a sound criterion for recognizing significant observations on natural phenomena" (p. 18); 4. it lends precision to otherwise unanchored and vague assertions about human nature (e.g. predicts the specific others with whom people will strive to "maintain relatedness"); 5. it explicates observed personality phenomena within a broader theoretical framework (e.g. views five-factor models in the context of the problems of adaptation humans must have solved); and 6. in delimited domains it can sometimes correctly predict previously unobserved phenomena (e.g. Cos-mides 1989).

Evolutionary psychology also provides a useful framework for reevaluating several core controversies in the field. It can, for example, help to clarify the debate about personality consistency, clarify the causal status of personality dispositions, explain interactionism, identify the most important features of context and environment, and clarify the roles of emotion, motivation, and culture in personality functioning.

An Evolutionary Resolution of the Personality Consistency Debate: Enduring Psychological Mechanisms and Discriminative Manifest Behavior

The issue of personality consistency has generated much debate over the past two decades (see Ozer 1986). It is now clear that many of the alternative hypotheses about traits (e.g. that findings of consistency reflect mere "semantic similarity" of trait judgments, or that traits are constructs residing solely "in the eyes of the beholder") can be ruled out (Kenrick & Funder 1988; Mervielde & Pot 1989). Modest agreement can be found across different observers for some traits (Funder 1989). Factors such as friendliness appear to generalize across target persons varying in sex and familiarity (Moskowitz 1988). Nonetheless, high cross-situational consistency in manifest acts is rarely found, and behavior shows marked sensitivity to even slight variations in situations (e.g. Wright & Mischel 1987).

Evolutionary psychology offers one conceptual clarification relevant to issues of personality consistency debate by distinguishing (a) evolved psychological mechanisms from (b) manifested psychology and behavior (Tooby & Cosmides 1990a). According to an evolutionary psychological perspective, basic psychological mechanisms that have evolved because they solved problems of survival and reproduction will be relatively stable over time. Exceptions would be those that change as a function of life history—e.g. intensification of mating effort at the onset of puberty and a shift from mating effort to parental effort after the birth of a child. Personality, in the sense of a collection of psychological mechanisms, will typically be reasonably consistent over time.

Manifest psychology and behavior, however, result from the interaction between evolved psychological mechanisms and the environmental factors that activate them differentially across individuals. Behavior will thus be highly context dependent and discriminative for at least three reasons. First, each person confronts different problems over time and over situations (e.g. problems of social exchange, hierarchy negotiation, coalition formation), which activate different psychological mechanisms and produce different behavior. The mechanisms activated when threatened by an angry man with a clenched fist differ from those activated when engaged in a mutually beneficial cooperative exchange. Although the manifest behavior will differ along the agreeable-aggressive dimension, the psychological mechanisms remain stable and reliably activated when confronted with those classes of contextual inputs.

Second, each psychological mechanism can generate a host of diverse acts, depending on context, each of which performs the mechanism's function. The status-striving mechanisms hypothesized to underlie surgency, for example, produce acts as diverse as working long hours, socializing selectively, suggesting a new idea to the group, and deceptively exaggerating one's current status (Kyl-Heku 1990). Different acts can express a mechanism that evolved because it once solved a single kind of problem. Third, an act may represent the merged outputs of several psychological mechanisms. According to this view, consistency in personality must be sought at the level of basic psychological mechanisms and the events that reliably activate them, not [as has typically been the case in personality psychology (e.g. Mischel & Peake 1982)] at the level of manifest behavior.

The apparent opposition frequently drawn between "personality consistency" and "behavioral discriminativeness and specificity" disappears according to this analysis. Evolutionary accounts predict that manifest behavior will be highly discriminative and sensitive to context, while the underlying psychological mechanisms remain stable over time and reliably activated when exposed to the same contextual inputs. Variable contextual inputs into stable psychological mechanisms produce discriminative manifest behavior.

Within this formulation, there are four primary contexts in which personality is expected to differ in consistent ways between individuals:

1. When there exist alternative genetic determinants of personality strategies or thresholds (e.g. those that specify male and female personality differences, the restricted and unrestricted types of sociosexuality posited by Gangestad and Simpson, and the heritable differences in sensation-seeking postulated by Zuckerman).

2. When early environments shunt different individuals into different developmental strategies or set different thresholds on psychological mechanisms (e.g. the personality effects of the early absence or presence of the father, posited by Belsky & Draper).

3. When different individuals currently occupy different niches that reliably evoke different behavioral frequencies (e.g. inhabiting a local environment populated with cheaters may elicit consistent noncooperation whereas an environment populated with cooperators would elicit cooperation).

4. When individual differences in ability or morphology produce differences in the effectiveness with which alternative strategies can be adopted or carried out (e.g. mesomorphs may adopt a more aggressive, physically intimidating strategy because they can enact it with greater effectiveness than can ectomorphs).

Prior accounts of personality consistency (or apparent inconsistency) have sometimes emphasized consistency at the "intrapsychic" level (e.g. Allport 1937; Block 1968; Wachtel 1973). These accounts, however, provide no explanation for why there would be stable psychological mechanisms in the first place. Evolutionary personality psychology is an attempt to lend precision to otherwise vague assertions about "intrapsychic consistency" by providing specific accounts of (*a*) psychological mechanisms as evolved solutions to adaptational problems and (*b*) the conditions that reliably activate these mechanisms (e.g. Buss 1989; Cosmides 1989).

An Evolutionary Perspective on Interactionism

Formulating an adequate concept of interactionism has been a major goal of personality psychology at least since Murray (1938). Although interactions in the ANOVA (analysis of variance) sense generally fail to capture the essence of interactionism in any dynamic sense (Golding 1975), no subsequent interactionist framework has gained broad endorsement, in spite of the fact that most personality psychologists claim to be interactionists.

Recent developments have centered on the role of persons in selecting, evoking, cognitively restructuring, and manipulating features of their environments (e.g. Buss 1987; Caspi & Bem 1990; Caspi & Herbener 1990; Coyne et al 1990; Emmons et al 1986; Hettema 1989; Kenrick et al 1990a; Plomin et al 1977; Scarr & McCartney 1983; Swann et al 1989; Van Heck 1990). These active and reactive person-generated processes create links between features of persons and features of their environments.

Aggressive children, for example, apparently expect others to be hostile, thereby eliciting hostility from others and creating an environment populated with more belligerent acts than the one created by children who are less aggressive (Dodge & Coie 1987). People selectively attend to and elicit behaviors from others that confirm their prior self-concepts (cf Markus & Cross 1990; Swann et al 1989). Adults select as mates those with similar personality dispositions, attitudes, and interests, thus creating an enduring environment that they may inhabit for years or decades (Caspi & Herbener 1990). Ill-tempered boys tend to discontinue their educations earlier, achieve lower occupational status, and suffer divorce more frequently than better-tempered ones (e.g. Caspi & Bem 1990). Selection, evocation, and manipulation describe interactional processes that link features of persons with features of their environments, creating person-environment correspondences.

Specific evolutionary models of goals and life tasks provide theoretical frameworks to predict particular forms of person-environment interaction. There is replicable evidence, for example, that reproductively valuable[4] women can and do select as mates surgent men capable of providing abundant social and material resources for them and their children, thus creating a material and experiential world different from that obtainable by women of lower mate value (Borgerhoff Mulder 1988; Buss 1989a). Similarly, reproductively damaging acts and attributes evoke social revulsion in others (e.g. incompetence, deviance, unattractiveness, adultery, mate poaching, aggression) (Baumeister & Tice 1990). Finally, manipulation is predictably directed toward the same proximate goals (e.g. status attainment, competition for mates, and alliance formation) that led to reproductive success among our ancestors (Buss 1988a,b).

---

[4]Reproductive value is defined actuarially in units of expected future reproduction—the extent to which persons of a given age and sex will contribute, on average, to the ancestry of future generations.

These evolution-based examples of person-environment interactions are merely illustrative, and provide no magical formula for predicting interactions in other content domains. Because many psychological mechanisms are expected to be domain-specific, there is no substitute for developing specific conceptual models of person-environment interactions within each particular adaptive domain. The processes of selection, evocation, and manipulation, however, represent interactive processes that occur in many domains of personality functioning. Conjoined with evolution-based models, they provide a powerful interactionist framework.

Context, Situation, and Environment

Personality psychologists know that human behavior is highly sensitive to context, but we have not yet determined which features or dimensions of context are important or the ways they are important (but see Van Heck 1990). From an evolutionary psychological perspective, the organism is the final arbiter of important contextual dimensions. Indeed, the psychological mechanisms produced by natural selection are sensitive only to certain forms of environmental input: "The environment, per se, is powerless to act on the psyche of an animal, except in ways specified by the developmental programs and psychological mechanisms that already happen to exist in that animal at a given time. . . . The actual relationship between environment and behavior is created . . . by the nature and design of the information processing mechanisms that happen to exist in the animal" (Tooby & Cosmides 1990a:4).

"Organism" and "situation" do not independently affect personality or behavior. It makes no sense to create a "taxonomy of situations" independent of the psychological mechanisms within humans. Psychological mechanisms evolved because they receive, process, and respond only to certain forms of environmental input. In this view, the dimensions of contextual input important for persons depend on the proximate goals toward which humans direct action and the specific psychological mechanisms activated by each proximate goal. When hunger mechanisms are activated and the proximate goal is food consumption, the relevant contextual dimensions involve substances that differ in their nutritive value, locations that vary in the likelihood of containing such substances, and the costs and benefits of actions that could be used to acquire those substances. Because our personality strategies are facilitated and obstructed primarily by other humans, our most important contextual input is social (see the section above on personality as the adaptive landscape). Evolved psychological mechanisms ensure that these key contextual dimensions will be value-laden. Just as fruits of varying ripeness differ in nutritive value, potential mates differ in mate value, potential cooperators differ in coalition value, and potential friends differ in dyadic alliance value.

Natural selection has created in humans psychological mechanisms that are highly sensitive to context, not rigid "instincts" that operate regardless of context. Progress in understanding which dimensions of context are important will rest on jettisoning the view that context can be understood independently of the proximate goals and psychological mechanisms of the person. Understanding the importance of context depends on progress in understanding our evolved psychological mechanisms. The environment experienced by an organism is itself the product of evolution.

Emotions, Desires, Preferences: Evolved Psychological Mechanisms That Signal Adaptively Significant Features of the Environment

The study of emotions, broadly conceived to include affect, mood, desire, arousal, attraction, repulsion, and preference, provides one path for identifying adaptively relevant environmental input. These organismic processes have received increasing attention within personality psychology in the past decade (e.g. Clark & Watson 1988; Kagan 1989; Larsen & Kasimatis 1990; Lazarus 1990; Revelle 1990; Tellegen 1985; Watson 1989). Several lines of work have explored the adaptive functions of the emotions, preferences, and desires.

Ellsworth & Smith (1988), for example, documented patterns of appraisal that support the hypothesis that emotions solve adaptational problems. Sadness, for example, produces an expression of distress that elicits aid from others. In a related series of studies, I (1989b) proposed that the exhibition of anger alerts others to the angry person's sense that his/her strategy has been interfered with, and signals a demand that the interference be removed (see also Frijda 1988). Because men and women enact somewhat different sexual strategies, the events that lead to strategic interference in this domain should differ between the sexes. I found that women were far angrier than men about sexual aggressiveness in the opposite sex, whereas men were angrier than women about sexual withholding by the opposite sex. This observation supports Trivers's hypothesis of a link between parental investment and choosiness and the hypothesis that anger functions to alert people to strategic interference. In another line of work, Nesse (1990) developed a taxonomy of the specific functions of different forms of fear and panic. Social anxiety, for example, apparently alerts the organism to threats to status and group membership (see also Baumeister & Tice 1990). Panic, to take another example, is provoked by imminent attack.

People anticipate with pleasure or revulsion the prospect of eating certain foods in ways that reveal our evolved adaptations to food consumption problems (e.g. positive affect to sweet food; negative affect to bitter, sour, or putrid food). Analogously, our affective reactions to potential coalition members, rivals, or mates reveal our evolved adaptations to social problems.

The universal desire of women for men who show cues to resource acquisition (e.g. ambition, industriousness, status) and the universal desire that men express for women who show cues to reproductive value (e.g., youth, physical attractiveness) are affective reactions that reveal our evolved solutions to two types of mating problem (Buss 1989a).

The emotion of jealousy has received increasing research attention. The evidence is strong that jealousy is a major cause of intersexual violence worldwide, particularly violence perpetrated by men against their mates (Daly & Wilson 1988). Among men, jealousy is elicited by suspicions or evidence of sexual infidelity, likely functioning as an evolved mechanism to guard against paternity uncertainty (Daly et al 1982). Consistent sex differences in the focus of jealousy have been documented, with men focusing on the sexual aspects and women focusing more on the loss of time, attention, and resources from the primary relationship (Teismann & Mosher 1978; White & Mullen 1989). Finally, there is evidence that women sometimes intentionally elicit male jealousy (e.g. by showing interest in, or attention to, another man) as a tactic for retaining their mates (Buss 1988b).

Emotions, mood states, preferences, and desires are clearly products of natural selection. The structure of affect and social preferences shows remarkable cross-cultural generality (e.g. Buss et al 1990; Russell et al 1989). Emotions signal adaptationally significant features of context and environment. The field should experience a surge of interest in linking these states to traditional dimensions of personality and understanding their functions in the evolved psychology of humans (e.g. Tellegen 1985; Tooby & Cosmides 1990b).

Culture and Personality

Most personality research tends to be parochial in that it is formulated and carried out within one culture. With the recent establishment of the *European Journal of Personality* there has been an increasing output of cross-cultural personality research (e.g. Angleitner et al 1990; Hettema 1989; Hofstee 1990; Strelau et al 1989; Van Heck 1990). There are both conceptual and empirical benefits to be derived from cross-fertilization among personality psychologists from around the world.

Some of the most important and enduring questions in the field require cross-cultural study. The question posed by Goldberg (1981) a decade ago and more recently by John (1990), "Is the five-factor model of personality universal?", has yet to be answered. However, using Filipino samples Church & Katigbak (1989) provide non-Western support for the five-factor model. A recent study of 37 societies from around the world found that kindness (Factor 2), dependability (Factor 3), emotional stability and maturity (Factor 4), and intelligence (roughly Factor 5) were among the most highly valued of 31 possible characteristics in potential mates (Buss et al 1990). These findings point to the intriguing possibility that the five-factor model may indeed describe universal adaptation-relevant dimensions of human action and value.

Although evolutionary hypotheses often concern species-typical, sex-typical, or age-graded mechanisms, culture provides important input to those mechanisms. The premium placed on physical courage and aggressiveness among the Yanomamo of South America (Chagnon 1988), for example, is apparently linked with levels of violence higher than those in Iceland, Denmark, or Canada (Daly & Wilson 1988). Indeed, there is evidence that among the Yanomamo killing rivals currently leads to elevated status and reproductive success (Chagnon 1989).

Socialization practices are widely believed to influence the personality characteristics of children, but little is known about them cross-culturally. In perhaps the most extensive cross-cultural study yet conducted, Low (1989) examined the socialization training of personality (e.g. surgency, agreeableness, and conscientiousness) in 93 societies. Low found striking support for three evolution-based predictions about childhood training: 1. Boys, across cultures, are trained to show greater fortitude, aggression, and self-reliance than girls; 2. girls, across cultures, are trained to be more responsible, obedient, and restrained than boys (especially sexually restrained); and 3. the more polygynous the society, the more intensely boys were trained to be competitive strivers. These findings highlight the heuristic value of evolutionary thinking in identifying important variation, as well as uniformity, across cultures.

Culture, however, cannot be understood independently of our evolved psychological mechanisms (Tooby & Cosmides 1989). Individuals are not passive receptacles of cultural influence, they are active self-interested strategists whose psychological mechanisms dispose them to act selectively on adaptationally relevant dimensions of environmental input—perhaps most importantly on input from one's social group and culture. Our evolved psychology is necessary for, not separate from, cultural processes. In spite of the tremendous practical difficulties, cross-cultural research will be indispensable for answering many of the most important questions in evolutionary personality psychology.

CONCLUSION

Evolutionary metatheory provides a systematic framework for the central conceptual issues in personality psychology. Personality theory, in this view, must include a nonarbitrary characterization of human nature, including specification of 1. the major goals toward which humans direct action (problems that historically had to be solved to enable reproductive success), 2. the psychological mechanisms that have evolved because they solved these problems, and 3. the species-typical and individually different behavioral strategies, activated by psychological mechanisms, that people deploy to reach goals or solve adaptive problems.

Goal-directed tactics and strategies, therefore, are promising units for personality psychology. Although there exists substantial variability in how individuals frame their goals and devote their problem-solving effort, evolutionary considerations suggest a non-arbitrary species-typical structure to both the goals and the means of their attainment. Discovery of the underlying species-typical goal structure and the corresponding evolved strategic solutions will constitute a major and lasting scientific contribution of personality psychologists informed by evolutionary theory.

Coherent individual differences of the sort embodied by the five-factor model of personality will be analyzed at two related levels. The first focuses on individual strategists and conceptualizes dispositions as evolved problem-solving mechanisms, either heritably based or differentially activated by environmental contingencies. The second focuses on the environment composed of other people, who are the main facilitators and obstructors of our social strategies. The five personality factors, in this view, represent important features of the human "adaptive landscape." Those who had the capacity to perceive and act upon these major individual differences in others had a selective advantage when it came to negotiating hierarchies, selecting and attracting mates, and forming effective coalitions with other humans.

The debates about personality consistency, the importance of environmental context, and interactionism are clarified within an evolutionary metatheory. The consistency debate is clarified by distinguishing between evolved psychological mechanisms and manifest behavior. Consistency will be found at the level of psychological mechanisms and the environmental inputs that predictably activate them; specificity of behavior will be found in the adaptational problems that humans confront across different situations and in the context-dependent strategic solutions that they deploy to solve them. Personality is expected to be highly consistent at the level of psychological mechanisms but highly discriminative at the level of overt behavior.

Although the field has increasingly recognized the importance of context and the discriminativeness of behavior, commensurate gains have not been made in identifying which dimensions of context or situation are important. From the perspective of evolutionary psychology, evolved mechanisms within the organism determine which environmental inputs will be attended to, processed, and acted upon. Therefore, the importance of a given situational dimension depends on the adaptational problems that humans have confronted over evolutionary history and on the psychological and behavioral strategies that have evolved as solutions to those problems. Contexts, environments, and situations cannot affect behavior except through these mechanisms. Therefore, the relevant environmental dimensions are themselves a product of human evolution; they cannot be properly understood without understanding the evolved mechanisms of the organism. Studies of emotion, affect, desire, and preference provide important routes for revealing the environmental problems to which we are the evolved solutions.

Evolutionary personality psychology, however, is neither simple nor easy. It requires a non-trivial mastery of evolutionary biology. Many attempts to use evolutionary theory have been conceptually sloppy. Some have committed the "sociobiological fallacy" by assuming that humans have as a psychological goal the maximization of inclusive fitness. Others have erred in seeking in evolution a justification of particular political views. Still others err in adopting the view that evolutionary theory implies genetic determinism in the sense of intractability and lack of environmental influence. These misunderstandings must be eliminated before the field can progress.

Evolutionary metatheory, properly conceived, provides for personality psychology the grand framework it seeks, and which has been missing almost entirely from its core formulations. Such theory links the field with what is known about the processes that govern all forms of life. It provides a powerful heuristic for identifying the central human goals and the psychological and behavioral strategic means deployed to obtain those goals. Evolutionary personality psychology gives us the tools for understanding the core of our human nature and the most important ways in which we differ from one another.

ACKNOWLEDGMENTS

The chapter profited greatly from the support and commentary of many friends and colleagues. Among them are members of the *Evolutionary Psychology Group* at the Center for Advanced Study in Palo Alto: Leda Cosmides, Martin Daly, John Tooby, and Margo Wilson; members of the *Cultural Evolution Faculty Seminar* at Michigan: Allan Gibbard, Larry Hirschfield, Ron Kessler, Hazel Markus, Richard Nisbett, and Claude Steele; members of the *Evolution and Human Behavior Program* at Michigan, especially Randolph Nesse and Valerie Stone; members of my *Evolutionary Psychology* graduate seminar, especially Todd DeKay, Bruce Ellis, David Schmitt, and Tim Ketelaar; and friends and colleagues Bob Emmons, Robert Hogan, Doug Kenrick, Randy Larsen, Jeff McCrae, Dan Ozer, Chris Peterson, Aaron Pincus, Larry Pervin, Robert Plomin, Cindy Rehfues, Auke Tellegen, and Jerry Wiggins. Support for this chapter was also provided by the Center for Advanced Study in the Behavioral Sciences (including NSF Grant BNS98-00864 and the Gordon P. Getty Trust), and NIMH Grant MH-44206-01 to the author.

Literature Cited

Alexander, R. D. 1979. *Darwinism and Human Affairs*. Seattle: Univ. Washington Press

Allport, G. W. 1937. *Personality: A Psychological Interpretation*. New York: Holt

Angleitner, A., Buss, D. M., Demtroder, A. 1990. A cross-cultural comparison using the act frequency approach (AFA) in West Germany and the United States. *Eur. J. Pers.* In press

Asch, S. 1955. Opinions and social pressures. *Sci. Am.* 193:31–35

Axelrod, R., ed. 1984. *The Evolution of Cooperation*. NY: Basic Books

Barkow, J., Cosmides, L., Tooby, J. 1990. *The Adapted Mind*. NY: Oxford Univ. Press. In press

Baumeister, R. F., Tice, D. M. 1990. Anxiety and social exclusion. *J. Soc. Clin. Psychol.* 9:165–95

Betzig, L. L., ed. 1986. *Despotism and Differential Reproduction: A Darwinian View of History*. Hawthorne, NY: Aldine

Block, J. 1968. Some reasons for the apparent inconsistency of personality. *Psychol. Bull.* 70:210–12

Borgerhoff Mulder, M. 1988. Kipsigis bridewealth payments. In *Human Reproductive Behavior: A Darwinian Perspective*, ed. L. Betzig, M. Borgerhoff Mulder, P. Turke, pp. 65–82. Cambridge: Cambridge Univ. Press

Borkenau, P. 1990. Traits as ideal-based and goal-derived social categories. *J. Pers. Soc. Psychol.* 58:381–96

Botwin, M., Buss, D. M. 1989. The structure of act report data: Is the five-factor model of personality recaptured? *J. Pers. Soc. Psychol.* 56:988–1001

Bouchard, T. J. Jr., McGue, M. 1990. Genetic and rearing environmental influences on adult personality: an analysis of adopted twins reared apart. *J. Pers.* 58:263–92

Buss, D. M. 1989a. Sex differences in human mate preferences: evolutionary hypotheses tested in 37 cultures. *Behav. Brain Sci.* 12:1–49

Buss, D. M. 1989b. Conflict between the sexes: strategic interference and the evocation of anger and upset. *J. Pers. Social Psychol.* 56:735–47

Buss, D. M. 1989c. *A strategic theory of trait usage: personality and the adaptive landscape*. Presented at Invited Workshop on Personality Language, Univ. Groningen, Groningen, Netherlands

Buss, D. M. 1988a. The evolution of human intrasexual competition: tactics of mate attraction. *J. Pers. Soc. Psychol.* 54:616–28

Buss, D. M. 1988b. From vigilance to violence: tactics of mate retention in American

undergraduates. *Ethol. Sociobiol.* 9:291–317

Buss, D. M. 1987. Selection, evocation, and manipulation. *J. Pers. Soc. Psychol.* 53:1214–21

Buss, D. M. 1986. Can social science be anchored in evolutionary biology? *Rev. Eur. Sci. Soc.* 24:41–50

Buss, D. M., Cantor, N., eds. 1989. *Personality Psychology: Recent Trends and Emerging Directions*. NY: Springer-Verlag

Buss, D. M., Dedden, L. 1990. Derogation of competitors. *J. Soc. Pers. Relat.* 7:395–422

Buss, D. M., et al. 1990. International preferences in selecting mates: a study of 37 societies. *J. Cross Cult. Psychol.* 21:5–47

Byrne, R., Whiten, A., eds. 1988. *Machiavellian Intelligence*. Oxford: Clarendon Press

Cantor, N. 1990. From thought to behavior: "having" and "doing" in the study of personality and cognition. *Am. Psychol.* 45:735–50

Carson, R. C. 1990. The social-interactional viewpoint. In *The Clinical Psychology Handbook*, ed. M. Hersen, A. E. Kazdin, A. S. Bellack. New York: Pergamon. 2nd ed. In press

Carver, C. S., Scheier, M. F. 1990. Principles of self-regulation: action and emotion. In *Handbook of Motivation and Cognition: Foundations of Social Behavior*, ed. E. T. Higgins, R. M. Sorrentino, 2:3–52. NY: Guilford

Caspi, A., Bem, D. J. 1990. Personality continuity and change across the life course. In *Handbook of Personality Theory and Research*, ed. L. A. Pervin. New York: Guilford Press

Caspi, A., Herbener, E. S. 1990. Continuity and change: assortative marriage and the consistency of personality in adulthood. *J. Pers. Soc. Psychol.* 58:250–58

Chagnon, N. 1988. Life histories, blood revenge, and warfare in a tribal population. *Science* 239:985–92

Church, A. T., Katigbak, M. S. 1989. Internal, external, and self-report structure of personality in a non-Western culture: an investigation of cross-language and cross-cultural generalizability. *J. Pers. Soc. Psychol.* 57:857–72

Clark, L. A., Watson, D. 1988. Mood and the mundane: relations between daily life events and self-reported mood. *J. Pers. Soc. Psychol.* 54:296–308

Cooper, S. 1987. Decision theory as a branch of evolutionary theory: a biological derivation of the savage axioms. *Psychol. Rev.* 94:395–411

Cosmides, L. 1989. The logic of social exchange: has natural selection shaped how humans reason? *Cognition* 31:187–276

Cosmides, L., Tooby, J. 1987. From evolution to behavior: evolutionary psychology as the missing link. In *The Latest on the Best: Essays on Evolution and Optimality*, ed. J. Dupre. Cambridge: MIT Press

Coyne, J. C., Burchill, S. A. L., Stiles, W. B. 1990. An interactional perspective on depression. In *Handbook of Social and Clinical Psychology: The Health Perspective*, ed. C. R. Snyder, D. O. Forsyth. NY: Pergamon

Crawford, C. B., Anderson, J. L. 1989. Sociobiology: an environmentalist discipline? *Am. Psychol.* 44:1449–59

Daly, M., Wilson, M. 1990. Is parent-offspring conflict sex-linked? Freudian and Darwinian models. *J. Pers.* 58:163–90

Daly, M., Wilson, M. 1988. *Homicide*. NY: Aldine deGruyter

Daly, M., Wilson, M. 1983. *Sex, Evolution, and Behavior*. Boston: Willard Grant Press

Daly, M., Wilson, M., Weghorst, S. J. 1982. Male sexual jealousy. *Ethol. Sociobiol.* 3:11–27

Dawkins, R. 1982. *The Extended Phenotype*. Oxford: Oxford Univ. Press

Darwin, C. 1859. *On the Origin of the Species by Means of Natural Selection, or, Preservation of Favoured Races in the Struggle for Life*. London: Murray

DeRaad, B., Hoskens, M. 1990. Personality descriptive nouns. *Eur. J. Pers., Spec. Issue* 4:131–46

Digman, J. 1990. Personality structure: the emergence of the five-factor model. *Annu. Rev. Psychol.* 41:417–40

Dodge, K. A., Coie, J. D. 1987. Social-information-processing factors in reactive and proactive aggression in children's peer groups. *J. Pers. Soc. Psychol.* 53:1146–58

Draper, P., Belsky, J. 1990. Personality development in evolutionary perspective. *J. Pers.* 58:141–62

Eder, R. A. 1989. The emergent personologist: the structure and content of 3 1/2-, 5 1/2-, and 7 1/2-year-olds' concept of themselves and other persons. *Child Dev.* 60:1218–28

Ellsworth, P. C., Smith, C. A. 1988. From appraisal to emotion: differences among unpleasant feelings. *Motiv. Emot.* 12:271–302

Emmons, R. A. 1990. Motives and life goals. In *Handbook of Personality Psychology*, ed. S. Briggs, R. Hogan, W. Jones. Orlando, FL: Academic. In press

Emmons, R. A., Diener, E., Larsen, R. J. 1986. Choice and avoidance of everyday situations and affect congruence: two models of reciprocal interactionism. *J. Pers. Soc. Psychol.* 51:815–26

Epstein, S. 1990. Cognitive experiential self-theory. In *Handbook of Personality Theory and Research*, ed. L. Pervin. NY: Guilford

Eysenck, H. J. 1990. Genetic and environmental contributions to individual differences in personality: the three major dimensions of personality. *J. Pers.* 58:245–62

Fiske, D. W. 1988. From inferred personalities toward personality in action. *J. Pers.* 56:815–33

Frijda, N. H. 1988. The laws of emotion. *Am. Psychol.* 43:349–58

Funder, D. C. 1989. Accuracy in personality judgment and the dancing bear. In *Personality Psychology: Recent Trends and Emerging Directions*, ed. D. M. Buss, N. Cantor, pp. 210–23. NY: Springer-Verlag

Gangestad, S. W., Simpson, J. A. 1990. Toward an evolutionary history of female sociosexual variation. *J. Pers.* In press

Goldberg, L. R. 1981. Language and individual differences: the search for universals in personality lexicons. In *Review of Personality and Social Psychology*, ed. L. Wheeler, pp. 141–65. Beverly Hills, CA: Sage

Golding, S. L. 1975. Flies in the ointment: methodological problems in the analysis of the percentage of variance due to persons and situations. *Psychol. Bull.* 82:278–88

Goldsmith, H. H. 1989. Behavior-genetic approaches to temperament. In *Temperament in Childhood*, ed. G. A. Kohnstamm, J. F. Bates, M. K. Rothbart. NY: Wiley

Graziano, W. G., Eisenberg, N. H. 1990. Agreeableness: a dimension of personality. In *Handbook of Personality Psychology*, ed. S. Briggs, R. Hogan, W. Jones. NY: Academic. In press

Hamilton, W. D. 1987. Discriminating nepotism: expectable, common, overlooked. In *Kin Recognition in Animals*, ed. D. J. C. Fletcher, C. D. Michener. NY: Wiley & Sons

Hamilton, W. D. 1964. The evolution of social behavior. *J. Theor. Biol.* 7:1–52

Helson, R., Picano, J. 1990. Is the traditional role bad for women? *J. Pers. Soc. Psychol.* 59:311–20

Herrnstein, R. J. 1977. The evolution of behaviorism. *Am. Psychol.* 32:593–603

Hettema, P. J., ed. 1989. *Personality and Environment: Assessment of Human Adaptation*. NY: Wiley. 279 pp.

Hofstee, W. K. B. 1990. The use of everyday personality language for scientific purposes. *Eur. J. Pers.* 4:77–88

Hogan, R. 1983. Theory of personality. Nebraska Symposium on Motivation, 1982: Personality—Current Theory and Research, ed. M. M. Page. Lincoln: Univ. Nebraska Press

Howard, R. D. 1981. Male age-size distribution and mating success in bullfrogs. In *Natural Selection and Social Behavior,* ed. R. D. Alexander, D. W. Tinckle. New York: Chiron

Ickes, W., Snyder, M., Garcia, S. 1990. Personality influences on the choice of situations. In *Handbook of Personality Psychology,* ed. S. Briggs, R. Hogan, W. Jones. NY: Academic. In press

John, O. P. 1990. The big-five factor taxonomy: dimensions of personality in the natural language and in questionnaires. In *Handbook of Personality Theory and Research,* ed. L. A. Pervin. NY: Guilford

Kagan, J. 1989. Temperamental contributions to social behavior. *Am. Psychol.* 44:668–74

Kenrick, D. T., McCreath, H. E., Govern, J., King, R., Bordin, J. 1990a. Person-environment intersections: everyday settings and common trait dimensions. *J. Pers. Soc. Psychol.* In press

Kenrick, D. T., Sadalla, E. K., Groth, G., Trost, M. R. 1990b. Evolution, traits, and the stages of human courtship: qualifying the parental investment model. *J. Pers.* 58:97–116

Kenrick, D. T., Funder, D. C. 1988. Profiting from controversy: lessons from the person-situation debate. *Am. Psychol.* 43:23–34

Kiesler, D. J. 1990. Interpersonal methods of assessment and diagnosis. In *Handbook of Social and Clinical Psychology: The Health Perspective,* ed. C. R. Snyder, D. R. Forsyth. Elmsford, NY: Pergamon. In press

Klinger, E. 1975. Consequences of commitment to and disengagement from incentives. *Psychol. Rev.* 82:223–31

Kyl-Heku, L. 1990. *Effects of context and sex on hierarchy negotiation.* PhD thesis. Univ. Michigan

Langois, J. H., Roggman, L. A. 1990. Attractive faces are only average. *Psychol. Sci.* 1:115–21

Langston, C. L., Cantor, N. 1989. Social anxiety and social constraint: when making friends is hard. *J. Pers. Soc. Psychol.* 56:649–61

Larsen, R. J., Kasimatis, M. 1990. Individual differences in entrainment of mood to the weekly calendar. *J. Pers. Soc. Psychol.* 58:164–71

Latane, B. 1981. The psychology of social impact. *Am. Psychol.* 36:343–56

Lazarus, R. S. 1990. Theory-based stress measurement. *Psychol. Inquiry.* 1:3–13

Little, B. R. 1989. Personal projects analysis: trivial pursuits, magnificent obsessions, and the search of coherence. In *Personality Psychology: Recent Trends and Emerging Directions,* ed. D. M. Buss, N. Cantor, pp. 15–31. NY: Springer-Verlag

Lockard, J. S., Paulhus, D. L. 1988. *Self-Deception: An Adaptive Mechanism?* Englewood Cliffs, NJ: Prentice Hall

Loehlin, J. C., Horn, J. M., Willerman, L. 1990. Heredity, environment, and personality change: evidence from the Texas Adoption Project. *J. Pers.* 58:221–44

Loehlin, J. C. 1989. Partitioning environmental and genetic contributions to behavioral development. *Am. Psychol.* 44:1285–92

Lopreato, J., ed. 1984. *Human Nature and Biocultural Evolution.* Boston: Allen & Unwin

Low, B. S. 1989. Cross-cultural patterns in the training of children: an evolutionary perspective. *J. Comp. Psychol.* 103:311–19

Manson, J., Wrangham, R. 1990. The evolution of hominoid intergroup aggression. *Curr. Anthropol.* In press

Markus, H., Cross, S. 1990. The interpersonal self. In *Handbook of Personality Theory and Research,* ed. L. A. Pervin. NY: Guilford

McAdams, D. P. 1988. Biography, narrative, and lives: an introduction. *J. Pers.* 56:1–18

McClelland, D. C. 1989. Motivational factors in health and disease. *Am. Psychol.* 44:675–83

McCrae, R. R., Costa, P. T. Jr. 1989. The structure of interpersonal traits: Wiggins circumplex and the five-factor model. *J. Pers. Soc. Psychol.* 56:586–95

Mervielde, I., Pot, E. 1989. Perceiver and target effects in personality ratings. *Eur. J. Pers.* 3:1–13

Mischel, W., Peake, P. 1982. Beyond déjà vu in the search for cross-situational consistency. *Psychol. Rev.* 89:730–55

Moskowitz, D. S. 1988. Cross-situational generality in the laboratory: dominance and friendliness. *J. Pers. Soc. Psychol.* 54:829–39

Murray, H. A. 1938. *Explorations in Personality.* NY: Oxford

Nesse, R. M. 1990. Evolutionary explanations of emotions. *Human Nature* 1:261–89

Norman, W. T. 1963. Toward an adequate taxonomy of personality attributes: replicated factor structure in peer nomination personality ratings. *J. Abnorm. Soc. Psychol.* 66:574–83

Olweus, D. 1979. Stability of aggressive reaction patterns in males: a review. *Psychol. Bull.* 86:852–79

Ozer, D. J. 1986. *Consistency in Personality: A Methodological Framework.* Berlin: Springer-Verlag

Ozer, D. J., Gjerde, P. 1989. Patterns of personality consistency and change from childhood through adolescence. *J. Pers.* 57:483–507

Paulhus, D. L., Reid, D. B. 1990. Attribution

and denial in socially desirable responding. *J. Pers. Social Psychol.* In press

Peabody, D., Goldberg, L. R. 1989. Some determinants of factor structures from personality-trait descriptors. *J. Pers. Soc. Psychol.* 57:552–67

Peabody, D., ed. 1985. *National Characteristics.* NY: Cambridge Univ. Press

Pervin, L. A. 1990. A brief history of modern personality theory. In *Handbook of Personality Theory and Research,* ed. L. A. Pervin, pp. 3–18. NY: Guildford

Pervin, L. A., ed. 1989. *Goal Concepts in Personality and Social Psychology.* Hillsdale, NJ: Erlbaum

Peterson, C., Seligman, M. E. P., Vaillant, G. E. 1988. Pessimistic explanatory style is a risk factor for physical illness: a thirty-five-year longitudinal study. *J. Pers. Soc. Psychol.* 55:23–27

Pinker, S., Bloom, P. 1990. Natural language and natural selection. *Behav. Brain Sci.* In press

Plomin, R., Nesselroade, J. R. 1990. Behavioral genetics and personality change. *J. Pers.* 58:191–220

Plomin, R., Rende, R. 1991. Human behavioral genetics. *Annu. Rev. Psychol.* 42:161–90

Plomin, R., DeFries, J. C., Loehlin, J. C. 1977. Genotype-environment interaction and correlation in the analysis of human behavior. *Psychol. Bull.* 88:245–58

Read, S. J., Miller, L. C. 1989. Interpersonalism: toward a goal-based theory of persons in relationships. In *Goal Concepts in Personality and Social Psychology,* ed. L. A. Pervin, pp. 413–72. Hillsdale, NJ: Erlbaum

Revelle, W. 1990. Personality, motivation, and cognitive performance. In *Learning and Individual Differences: Abilities, Motivation, and Methodology,* ed. P. Ackerman, R. Kanfer, R. Cudeck. Hillsdale, NJ: Erlbaum. In press

Rorer, L. G., Widiger, T. A. 1983. Personality structure and assessment. *Annu. Rev. Psychol.* 34:431–63

Rowe, D. C., Rodgers, J. L., Meseck-Bushey, S., St. John, C. 1989. Sexual behavior and nonsexual deviance: a sibling study of their relationship. *Dev. Psychol.* 25:61–69

Rozin, P., Schull, J. 1988. The adaptive-evolutionary point of view in experimental psychology. In *Steven's Handbook of Experimental Psychology,* ed. R. C. Atkinson, R. J. Herrnstein, G. Lindzey, R. D. Luce. NY: Wiley. 2nd ed

Rozin, P. 1976. Psychological and cultural determinants of food choice. In *Appetite and Food Intake,* ed. T. Silverstone, pp. 286–312. Berlin: Dahlem Konferenzen

Runyan, W. M. 1988. Progress in psychobiography. *J. Pers.* 56:295–326

Russell, J. A., Lewicka, M., Niit, T. 1989. A cross-cultural study of a circumplex model of affect. *J. Pers. Soc. Psychol.* 57:848–56

Sadalla, E. K., Kenrick, D. T., Vershure, B. 1987. Dominance and heterosexual attraction. *J. Pers. Soc. Psychol.* 52:730–38

Savin-Williams, R. C., Weisfeld, G. E. 1989. An ethological perspective on adolescence. In *Biology of Adolescent Behavior and Development,* ed. G. R. Adams, R. Montemayor, T. P. Gullotta, pp. 249–73. Beverly Hills, CA: Sage

Scarr, S., McCartney, K. 1983. How people make their own environments: a theory of genotype environment effects. *Child Dev.* 54:424–35

Seligman, M. E. P., Hager, J. L., eds. 1972. *Biological Boundaries of Learning.* NY: Appleton-Century-Crofts

Shepard, R. N. 1984. Ecological constraints on internal representation: resonant kinematics of perceiving, imagining, thinking, and dreaming. *Psychol. Rev.* 91:417–47

Snyder, M., Simpson, J. A., Gangestad, S. 1986. Personality and sexual relations. *J. Pers. Soc. Psychol.* 51:181–90

Stone, V. E. 1989. *Perception of status: an evolutionary analysis of nonverbal status cues.* PhD thesis. Stanford Univ., Stanford, Calif., 116 pp.

Strelau, J., Angleitner, A., Ruch, W. 1989. Strelau temperament inventory (STI): general review and studies based on German samples. In *Advances in Personality Assessment,* ed. C. D. Spielberger, J. N. Butcher, 8:187–241. Hillsdale, NJ: Erlbaum

Swann, W. B. Jr., Pelham, B. W., Krull, D. S. 1989. Agreeable fancy or disagreeable truth? Reconciling self-enhancement and self-verification. *J. Pers. Soc. Psychol.* 57:782–91

Symons, D. 1990. On the use and misuse of Darwinism in the study of human behavior. In *The Adapted Mind: Evolutionary Psychology and the Generation of Culture,* ed. J. Barkow, L. Cosmides, J. Tooby. NY: Oxford Univ. Press. In press

Symons, D. 1987. If we're all Darwinians, what's the fuss about? In *Sociobiology and Psychology: Ideas, Issues, and Applications,* ed. C. Crawford, M. Smith, D. Krebs, pp. 121–46. Hillsdale, NJ: Erlbaum

Symons, D. 1979. *The Evolution of Human Sexuality.* NY: Oxford Univ. Press

Teismann, M. W., Mosher, D. L. 1978. Jealous conflict in dating couples. *Psychol. Rep.* 42:1211–16

Tellegen, A. 1990. Personality traits: issues of definition, evidence and assessment. In *Thinking Clearly About Psychology: Essays* in Honor of Paul Everett Meehl, ed. D. Cicchetti, W. Grove. Minneapolis: Univ. Minnesota Press. In press

Tellegen, A. 1985. Structures of mood and personality and their relevance to assessing anxiety, with an emphasis on self-report. In Anxiety and the Anxiety Disorders. ed. A. H. Tuma, J. D. Maser. Hillsdale, NJ: Erlbaum

Tooby, J., Cosmides, L. 1990a. On the universality of human nature and the uniqueness of the individual: the role of genetics and adaptation. J. Pers. 58:17–68

Tooby, J., Cosmides, L. 1990b. The past explains the present: emotional adaptations and the structure of ancestral environments. Ethol. Sociobiol. 11:375–424

Tooby, J., Cosmides, L. 1989. Evolutionary psychology and the generation of culture, Part I: Theoretical considerations. Ethol. Sociobiol. 10:29–49

Tooby, J., Cosmides, L. 1988. The evolution of war and its cognitive foundations. Inst. Evol. Stud. Tech. Rep. No. 88-1.

Tooby, J., DeVore, I. 1987. The reconstruction of hominid behavioral evolution through strategic modeling. In The Evolution of Human Behavior: Primate Models, ed. W. G. Kinzey. Albany, NY: SUNY Press

Townsend, J. M. 1989. Mate selection criteria: a pilot study. Ethol. Sociobiol. 10:214–54

Trapnell, P. D., Wiggins, J. S. 1990. Extension of the Interpersonal Adjective Scales to include the Big Five dimensions of personality (IASR-B5). J. Pers. Soc. Psychol. In press

Trivers, R. L. 1974. Parent-offspring conflict. Am. Zool. 14:249–64

Trivers, R. L. 1971. The evolution of reciprocal altruism. Q. Rev. Biol. 46:35–57

Van Heck, G. L. 1990. Temperament and the person-situation debate. In Explorations in

Temperament, ed. J. Strelau, A. Angleitner. NY: Plenum. In press

Wachtel, P. L. 1973. Psychodynamics, behavior therapy, and the implacable experimenter: an inquiry into the consistency of personality. J. Abnorm. Psychol. 82:324–34

Watson, D. 1989. Strangers' ratings of the five robust personality factors: evidence of a surprising convergence with self-report. J. Pers. Soc. Psychol. 57:120–28

Watson, J. B., ed. 1924. Behaviorism. NY: Norton

White, G. L., Mullen, P. E. 1989. Jealousy: Theory, Research, and Clinical Strategies. NY: Guilford

White, G. M. 1980. Conceptual universals in interpersonal language. Am. Anthropol. 82:759–81

Wiggins, J. S. 1990. Agency and communion as conceptual coordinates for the understanding and measurement of interpersonal behavior. In Thinking Clearly in Psychology: Essays in Honor of Paul E. Meehl, ed. D. Cicchetti, W. Grove. Minneapolis: Univ. Minnesota Press. In press

Williams, G. C. 1966. Adaptation and Natural Selection. Princeton: Princeton Univ. Press

Winter, D. G. 1987. Leader appeal, leader performance, and the motive profiles of leaders and followers: a study of American presidents and elections. J. Pers. Soc. Psychol. 52:196–202

Wright, J. C., Mischel, W. 1987. A conditional approach to dispositional constructs: the local predictability of social behavior. J. Pers. Soc. Psychol. 53:301–22

Zirkel, S., Cantor, N. 1990. Personal construal of life tasks: those who struggle for independence. J. Pers. Soc. Psychol. 58:172–85

Zuckerman, M. 1990. The psychophysiology of sensation seeking. J. Pers. 58:313–45

REFERENCE ADDED IN PROOF

Lloyd, J. E. 1979. Mating behavior and natural selection. Fla. Entomol. 62:17–34

Annu. Rev. Psychol. 1991. 42:493–525

THE CLASSROOM AS A SOCIAL CONTEXT FOR LEARNING

Carol Simon Weinstein

Rutgers Graduate School of Education, New Brunswick, New Jersey 08903

KEY WORDS: classroom ecology, classroom activity segments, sociolinguistic research in classrooms, the classroom as a communicative setting, classroom social interaction

CONTENTS

INTRODUCTION

In order to succeed in school, students must not only achieve academically, they must also learn the norms governing socially appropriate behavior. This is no simple feat. In many ways, the classroom is a curious social setting (Getzels & Thelen 1960; Jackson 1968). Assigned to classes that may contain strangers, perhaps even adversaries, students are expected to interact harmoniously. Crowded together, they are required to ignore the presence of others. Urged to cooperate, they usually work in competition. Pressed to take

493

0066-4308/91/0201-0493$02.00

responsibility for their own learning, they must follow the dictates of a dominant individual—the teacher.

Crowded, competitive, coercive—this portrait highlights social dimensions of the classroom that our familiarity with schools may mask. Yet even this characterization ignores subtleties that students must recognize. Kounin & Sherman (1979) remind us that "the classroom is not a homogenized glob" (p. 150), that it is composed of numerous sub-settings that vary in the kinds of social behaviors they elicit from both teachers and pupils. Ecological psychologists (Gump 1967, 1982; Ross 1984; Stodolsky 1988) have labeled these sub-settings "activity segments." Segments are characterized by an *action structure,* which specifies "who shall do what, to whom, when" (Gump 1982:98), and a *physical milieu,* the "container" for the activity segment. Segments place constraints on the kinds of social interactions that can occur and have implications for other social phenomena, such as the development of friendships and status hierarchies among students. The purpose of this chapter is to examine patterns of social interaction associated with activity segments observed in elementary and secondary classrooms.

Activity Segments and Sociolinguistic Research on Contexts

It appears that a small number of segments is sufficient to describe much of the activity that occurs in classrooms, at least those in the United States. Berliner (1983), for example, identified 11 activity segments in the elementary classrooms he observed (reading circle, seatwork, two-way presentation, one-way presentation, mediated presentation, silent reading, construction, games, play, transition, and housekeeping). Similarly, Gump (1967) found that seven activity segments accounted for more than half of the different activities he observed in third-grade classrooms. Recitations and seatwork were clearly dominant, a finding that has been replicated by others (Burns 1984; Rosenshine 1980; Stodolsky 1988).

Gump's (1982) analysis of activity segments indicates that segments differ along two important dimensions: 1. the extent to which external events (e.g. teacher behavior) stimulate students' attention and participation, and 2. the degree to which participants are interdependent. In addition, a number of researchers have documented differences in student engagement or involvement across settings (see Burns 1984; Kounin et al, 1966; Stodolsky 1988). Until recently, however, we knew little else about the action structures that characterize the various activity segments of the classroom. Within the last two decades, research on classroom contexts has provided a much finer-grained analysis of the program of action in key activity segments (Doyle 1981). Much of this research has been conducted within the paradigms of sociolinguistics (Cazden 1986), microethnography (Erickson & Shultz 1981), and constitutive ethnography (Mehan 1979). In all these approaches, the classroom is viewed as a "communicative setting" in which teachers and pupils collaborate in "instructional conversations" (Green & Wallat 1981). Like the work of ecological psychologists, this perspective also recognizes that the classroom is not an undifferentiated environment, and that each context exerts particular communicative and social demands on participants (Green & Wallat 1981). Indeed, Green & Harker's (1982) definition of a context—a recurrent activity with distinct boundaries and physical character-istics—sounds very much like the ecological psychologists' definition of an activity segment.

A key construct in this research is social or communicative competence: the ability to behave in socially appropriate ways in different contexts (Hymes 1974; Mehan 1980; Shultz & Florio 1979). Competent participation in these contexts requires knowing what context one is in, when contexts are chang-ing, and what behavior is appropriate in each of those contexts (Mehan 1980; Erickson & Shultz 1981). Since the rules governing social interaction are often implicit (Weade & Green 1985), they need to be extracted from observation and interpretation of patterns of action. Often, appropriate be-havior must be inferred from the teacher's oblique statements: "I see someone whose hands are not folded" (Shuy 1988) or "I don't see any hands" (Gum-perz 1981). Pupils must also become sensitive to the contextualization cues (Gumperz 1976) provided by nonverbal behavior—shifts in voice tone and pitch, posture and interpersonal distance, tempo and rhythm of speech and body motion, gaze direction, and facial expression (Erickson & Shultz 1981; Shultz & Florio 1979). Changes in physical milieu may also serve as cues. Fivush (1984), for example, reports that even on the second day of school, kindergartners were able to report the component activities of the school day in the correct temporal sequence; spatial transitions appeared to play a particu-larly important role in signalling a change in activity.

Purpose and Assumptions

The primary focus of this review is the social interaction that occurs as teachers and students work together to accomplish academic tasks.[1] The intent is to describe how appropriate social behavior varies with activity segment and to suggest that students' ability to participate effectively in-fluences opportunity for academic success. Underlying this purpose are four assumptions that have guided the organization of this chapter and the selection of studies.

First, although individual learning is the goal of schooling, formal educa-tion is essentially a social process (Doyle 1986; Florio-Ruane 1989).

[1]The length of the chapter precludes consideration of other topics relevant to the classroom as a social setting—e.g. research on social climate; the socialization and sorting functions of school.

Moreover, as Cazden (1988) observes, this process is heavily dependent on communication: "Spoken language is the medium by which much teaching takes place, and in which students demonstrate to teachers much of what they have learned" (p. 2). This chapter thus emphasizes the ways teachers and students talk with one another and elucidates the communicative demands placed on participants in various classroom contexts.

Second, the social interaction that occurs within each segment is neither entirely prescribed nor totally unconstrained. Erickson (1982) points out that school lessons are located on a continuum between formal ritual and informal spontaneity. Although behavior is guided by the rules and norms of the segment, teachers and students can innovate and adapt to changing circumstances. Thus, an attempt has been made to include research that portrays the typical action structure of each segment, as well as studies that illustrate how teachers and pupils depart from that structure.

A third assumption is that individual and cultural differences influence the development of children's communicative competence in the classroom. Although all children must learn the norms of appropriate classroom talk, this task is particularly difficult when there is discontinuity between the culture of the school and the culture of the home (Cazden 1988; Florio-Ruane 1989; Wilkinson 1982). Furthermore, individual characteristics, such as reticence, dominance, ability level, and gender, may facilitate or impede participation in the action structure of classroom segments. Representative studies depicting these individual and cultural differences are included here.

Finally, it is assumed that experiences in the activity segments of the classroom influence other social phenomena (Gump 1980)—e.g. choice of friends, students' self-perceptions, position in the classroom status hierarchy, and attitudes toward peers from different racial and ethnic groups. Treatment of these issues has been uneven across activity segments, but relevent research is discussed wherever possible.

The Organization and Scope of the Review

This chapter reviews research on five activity segments: recitation, teacher-directed small groups, sharing time, seatwork, and student-directed small groups. Recent empirical data help to clarify the action structure of each of these segments. Thus, the overall framework of the review is derived from the work of ecological psychologists, while the discussions draw from studies conducted within other paradigms—process-product research on effective teaching (Shulman 1986), sociolinguistics, and microethnography.[2] Since most research has been conducted in elementary classrooms, the chapter is oriented toward that level of schooling.

[2]For three extremely helpful, recent reviews on related topics, see Cazden (1986), Gump (1987), and Doyle (1986).

The order in which segments are discussed parallels the extent to which the teacher dominates the interaction, determining who shall speak, to whom, when, and how. As teacher control decreases, opportunities for student interaction increase. For example, in *recitation,* the teacher is firmly in control of the conversation. Student participation is generally limited to short, rapid responses to teacher questions, and there is little interchange among students. *Teacher-directed small groups* exhibit the same patterns of interaction, although the smaller size of the group means that students have both greater opportunity and greater obligation to respond. In *sharing time,* students can speak at length on self-chosen topics; nonetheless, the teacher still selects speakers, monitors the pace of the activity, and evaluates contributions. During *seatwork* segments, students are engaged in individual tasks, while the teacher is often involved in another activity or with a small group. Although interaction among students may be allowed, the teacher still maintains a management role to ensure that conversations remain focused on academic tasks and that students do not become disruptive. Finally, in *student-directed small groups,* the teacher may be even less controlling, and interaction among students is not only encouraged, but required.

A final section of this chapter examines the patterns of behavior surrounding the use of the microcomputer. Microcomputers constitute the most dramatic physical change in classrooms since the construction of open-space schools in the 1960s and 1970s (C. Weinstein 1979). As such, they are bound to have consequences for patterns of social interaction. Indeed, in contrast to initial fears that microcomputers in schools would lead to individual isolation, a number of studies have indicated that computers can bring about increased collaboration among children (Borgh & Dickson 1986; Dickinson 1986; Hawkins et al 1982; Wright & Samaras 1986). The reasons for this increase and the problems it may engender are also discussed here.

THE SOCIAL STRUCTURE OF ACTIVITY SEGMENTS

Recitation

Recitation is the prime example of "classroom talk" (Cazden 1988)—short, quickly paced question-and-answer exchanges between the teacher and the students (Dillon 1983). Sometimes characterized as "quiz shows" (Roby 1988) or "the classroom game" (Bellack et al 1974), recitations have numerous purposes: to check on understanding of previously taught lessons or homework assignments, to drill students on algorithmic material, or to present new material in a way that allows some student involvement ("lecturing in the interrogatory mood"; Roby 1988).

Although the recitation has been repeatedly criticized as a method of instruction, it has shown remarkable persistence (Cuban 1984; Hoetker & Ahlbrand 1969), and several studies have documented the substantial amount of time that students spend in this activity segment. Stodolsky (1988), for example, found that recitation constituted approximately 30% of student "occupancy time" (segment duration multiplied by the number of the students in the segment) in both mathematics and social studies classes.

Despite its unpopularity among educational theorists and reformers, recitation appears to serve several useful functions in the classroom. It ensures curriculum coverage (Wood & Wood 1988); it permits teachers to interact individually with students, even in the context of a whole group lesson; and it encourages relatively high attention levels and alertness among students (Stodolsky et al 1981), particularly when the questions are intellectually demanding (Stodolsky 1988). Cohen (1988) has suggested that the compulsory, unselective nature of the public schools encourages teacher-centered instructional practices like recitations, since they allow teachers to manage classrooms in ways that leave little room for dispute or discussion.

Mehan's (1978, 1979) "constitutive ethnography" of nine lessons in a primary classroom provides a precise analysis of the interaction that occurs during recitations. Mehan identified a basic, three-part interactional unit: teacher initiation, student reply, teacher evaluation (IRE). Within each interactional unit, the teacher not only directs, informs, or elicits information, but also identifies the population of students who are to reply. Orderly interaction is achieved through a turn-allocation process, in which respondents are selected in one of three ways: individual nomination ("What do you think, Susan?"); invitation to bid ("If you know the answer, raise your hand."); and invitation to reply, which allows students to state the answer directly, often in choral response.

McHoul (1978) has also described the turn-taking procedures characteristic of recitations. According to McHoul, recitations fall along a continuum from formal situations, in which turn taking is pre-allocated (e.g. debates and marriage ceremonies), to informal, casual situations (e.g. normal, everyday conversation) in which turns at talk are decided upon "locally," or on a here-and-now basis. In classroom talk, the rules of natural conversation are modified so as to narrow the open-endedness of the situation. Although not as formal as debates, recitations constitute "a heavily pre-allocated system in which the locally managed component is largely the domain of teachers, student participation rights being limited to the choice between continuing or selecting the teacher as next speaker" (p. 211).

Variations in turn-allocation procedures can create substantially different social situations for children. For example, Green et al (1988) examined story-reading/discussion lessons taught by two different teachers to primary-grade students.[3] Although the book, setting, task, and length of each lesson

---

[3]Although Green et al refer to the lessons as discussions, their descriptions and analyses indicate that the lessons can be characterized as recitations.

were the same, the ways the teacher guided the lesson produced different social (and academic) events for the two groups of children. While Teacher G frequently asked questions that were open to any student (i.e. she invited students to bid for the floor), Teacher S tended to nominate individuals. Green et al conclude that a different social structure was established in each lesson: Teacher G's lesson was a group-oriented lesson, while Teacher S's lesson tended to focus on individual teacher-student interaction within a group setting.

Recitations may provide teachers with desired control over participation, pacing, and content, but they constitute a complex social event that the teacher must successfully manage. Within the whole group context, teachers must interact with multiple participants who have differing ability levels and who make simultaneous and competing demands for attention (Doyle 1986; Mehan 1979); they must provide feedback to individuals, yet maintain the flow and momentum of the lesson; they must cope with unpredicted responses from students (Doyle 1986); they must manage the allocation of turns smoothly so there is little overlap (McHoul 1978) and participation is distributed widely and fairly.

Recitations also place special social demands on the students. They must understand when to respond by raising their hands and when to respond chorally (Weade & Evertson 1988). They must understand when the teacher has rejected a response and wants additional volunteers to continue the interaction. This may require sensitivity to cues as subtle as differences in intonation when the teacher repeats the child's answer—for example, falling intonation with a correct response, and rising intonation with an incorrect response (Gumperz 1981). If students wish to initiate interaction, they must learn to identify "seams" in the discourse (i.e. between IRE sequences). If they then wish to "hold the floor," they must make a relevant contribution; and if they are to change the course of the lesson, they must "introduce news" (Mehan 1979).

Occasionally, ambiguity in the teacher's initiation or evaluation makes the task even more difficult for students, resulting in confused replies or violations of the established turn-taking procedure (Gumperz 1981; Mehan 1979). For example, the teacher may unwittingly signal students to both bid for the floor ("Who knows?") and to reply without first obtaining permission to speak ("What is this?"). Farrar (1988) analyzed recitation exchanges in which the teacher asked a yes-no question ("Did you read anywhere that . . . ") but then rejected students' responses ("No," "Uh-uh"). Apparently, the teacher was not really expecting yes or no but was asking for a restatement of information that had appeared in the reading. Students responded to his explicit question, while he was searching for the answer to his implicit question.

Learning the norms that govern recitations is a task that must be achieved by all students if they are to participate effectively in this activity segment.

The task poses special challenges, however, for students who come from cultures in which patterns of interaction are extremely disparate from those of the school (Cazden 1988). A vivid example of this cultural discontinuity is provided by Philips (1972), who explored the reluctance of children on the Warm Springs Indian Reservation to participate in recitations. In this Native American community, children associated almost entirely with kinfolk and were extremely peer-oriented and independent. Learning to carry out tasks usually involved a minimal amount of verbal instruction, and demonstration of competency occurred only after private, self-initiated testing. Participation in social events was accessible to all who attended, with each individual free to determine whether and when to participate. These norms contrast sharply with the "participant structure" (Philips 1972) of recitations, in which participation is controlled by the teacher, there is little interaction among peers, and verbal performance is evaluated publically, even if the individual has not yet achieved competency.

Because of the public evaluation inherent in recitation, ability to participate appropriately may influence students' status in the classroom and their development of friendships. Only a few studies have examined the impact of recitation on students' informal interaction, but these document its powerful effects. Bossert (1979), for example, explored the relationship between classroom social organization and friendship patterns in two third- and two fourth-grade classrooms. In two rooms, teachers primarily used recitation, fostering comparative evaluations of student performance and encouraging the development of an academically based status hierarchy. In these rooms, children segregated themselves into academically homogeneous friendship groups that remained stable throughout the school year. In the other two classrooms, teachers tended to use a "multi-task" organization, in which several different activities occurred simultaneously, or a "class task" organization, in which all children engaged in the same type of activity (e.g. worksheets, independent reading). With these task structures, success on tasks was less visible, and achievement level was less influential in determining friendship choice. Students chose friends and workmates based on similar interests, and groups changed as interests shifted.

More recently, Morine-Dershimer (1983) has pointed out that teachers can create "communicative status" in the classroom through their definition of the task and their questioning strategy. Students with high communicative status are those who participate most and those who are viewed by their peers as "pupils you can learn from." It is interesting that these are not always students who have high status in terms of the more standard variables, such as reading achievement. In one classroom that Morine-Dershimer studied, for example, the teacher seemed to define the task as simply to respond. Here, participation was distributed almost randomly, and the students you could "learn from" were those who both participated frequently and had high status with the teacher. In another class, the task was to produce good, divergent answers. Participation in this class was dominated by those with high academic standing; however, students paid most attention to the comments of those with low academic status. Morine-Dershimer explains this apparent contradiction by contrasting high-achievers' concern about getting the correct answer with low-achievers' willingness to take a risk, "thereby producing ideas that are more divergent (and more interesting)" (p. 656).

Teacher-Directed Small Groups

Teacher-directed small groups are a common segment in early elementary classrooms (Collins 1986; Goodlad 1984), particularly during reading instruction. The typical action structure of these groups is similar to that of recitation (Barr 1989)—the teacher initiates interaction, directs activities, and controls who will participate (Collins 1986). Despite the similarity, however, two unique features of the segment have important social implications. First, the size of the group permits the teacher to introduce modifications of the action structure more easily than in whole-group recitation segments. Second, the ability-based homogeneity of small groups creates the potential for differential treatment of high and low achievers and reinforces the development of an academic status hierarchy in the classroom. Each of these topics is considered briefly below.

Two well-documented modifications of the typical small-group action structure are "reciprocal teaching" (Palincsar & Brown 1985) and the Kamehameha Early Education Program (Au 1980). Both of these represent *instructional* efforts to improve the reading comprehension of at-risk students, but both involve the establishment of new norms for appropriate *social participation*. In reciprocal teaching, students in the small group begin by silently reading the first paragraph of the text material. The teacher then models four comprehension activities—question-asking, summarizing, predicting, and clarifying—and assigns a student to assume the role of group leader for the next paragraph. This student repeats the comprehension routine and selects the next leader. Although the teacher maintains responsibility for monitoring performance, providing feedback, and prompting when necessary, students in reciprocal teaching are far more responsible than students in typical small-group lessons for initiating interaction, asking questions, and evaluating other students' responses.

Another variation in small-group structure is provided by the Kamehameha Early Education Program (KEEP). One aspect of this program has focused on the discontinuity between patterns of verbal interaction common to mainstream culture (i.e. wait to be called on and speak one at a time) and the conversational norms of Hawaiian children. Au (1980) highlighted this cultural discontinuity by analyzing a small-group reading lesson taught by a Hawaiian teacher. She demonstrated that more than half the turns were not single turns; instead they involved joint production and overlapping, characteristics of a major speech event in Hawaiian culture known as the "talk story." Similarly, Au & Mason (1981) compared reading lessons taught by two teachers who varied in amount of prior contact with Hawaiian children. The two teachers managed interaction very differently. The low-contact teacher assigned speaking rights to an individual child, while the high-contact teacher allowed children to produce a joint narration. Moreover, the lessons of the high-contact teacher were characterized by much higher levels of engagement and topically relevant responses. As a result of this research, the KEEP reading program includes small-group lessons in which children are allowed to cooperate in framing answers to questions (Au et al 1985).

In reciprocal teaching and in KEEP, the small-group action structure has been deliberately varied in order to accommodate the special academic or cultural needs of students. Other variations in small-group structure—far more subtle and probably unintended—have also been documented by researchers concerned about the differential treatment of high and low achievers. Although the research is limited, findings suggest that students in high and low groups experience very different social contexts for learning to read (Collins 1986).

First, different norms for behavior are established in the two kinds of groups. In a study of a first-grade classroom, for example, Eder (1982) found that the teacher was quick to reprimand students in the high-achievement groups when they interrupted other students' reading turns to make a topically relevant comment. Students in lower-achievement groups were reprimanded far less often. Not surprisingly, reading turn interruptions decreased over the year in the high group, while they increased for the low group, suggesting that the group environment created by the teacher's behavior is partially responsible for disruptions (Eder & Felmlee 1984). Eder (1981) comments: "Those students who were likely to have more difficulty learning were inadvertently assigned to groups whose social contexts were much less conducive for learning" (p. 159).

Second, low- and high-achievement groups differ with respect to the use of allocated instructional time. Within the group, time appears to be used more efficiently in high groups. For example, McDermott (1977) found that turn-taking in a first-grade high group proceeded efficiently in round-robin fashion, with little time lost between readers. In the low-achievement group, the teacher allowed the students to bid for a turn; consequently, so much time was devoted to deciding who would read next that students spent only one third as much time reading as students in the top group. McDermott suggests that the use of this turn-taking process was not accidental: Having children bid for a turn allowed the teacher to avoid calling on children who could not read. Other research (Grant & Rothenberg 1986) indicates that teachers also seem to be more protective of high-group reading time and to insulate the group from interruptions by other children.

Third, the quality of interaction between students and teacher appears to differ in low- and high-achievement groups. Grant & Rothenberg (1986), for example, found that teachers and students in high groups were more often observed to engage in personal interchanges ("chats"); the high groups were characterized by a warmer emotional climate and pleasant social relationships.

Finally, several studies have demonstrated differences in the kinds of reading activities that occur in low- and high-achievement groups (Allington 1983; Collins 1986). In high groups, the emphasis is on text comprehension. In low groups, instructional time is spent in decoding, with extensive sound-word identification drill. Teachers' responses to students' errors follow a similar pattern: Miscues made by high-group readers prompt a comprehension-focused correction, while identical miscues made by low-group readers prompt a decoding-focused correction (Allington 1980; Collins 1986). These findings suggest that students in the two groups may form substantially different conceptions of what reading is. While high-group readers are likely to see reading as an activity in which one derives meaning from print, low-group readers may equate reading with "sounding-out."

Since reading ability is often viewed as a "proxy for intelligence" (R. Weinstein 1984:244), membership in a reading group may rank students in a status hierarchy that is particularly damaging to the self-perceptions of low-achieving students (Rosenbaum 1984; Rosenholtz & Simpson 1984a,b). Students do use information about group membership to make inferences about reading ability (Filby & Barnett 1982), although a first-grade study by Eder (1983) indicated that within-group comparisons were more salient than across-group comparisons. Nonetheless, even these first-graders became increasingly aware of differences between groups over the course of the year.

Recent research suggests that the negative impact of within-class grouping may depend on the extent to which teachers emphasize differences between high- and low-achieving students (Blumenfeld et al 1982). Mitman & Lash (1988), for example, found that in classes where there were clear cues about the teacher's expectations (e.g. seating by ability level, public comparative evaluations of performance), the gap between the self-perceptions of higher and lower achievers was substantially greater than in lower-cue classes. This "explicitness of expectations" parallels constructs proposed by other researchers. Gamoran (1984), for example, refers to "egalitarian" versus "elitist" use of ability grouping. Rosenholtz & Simpson (1984a,b; Simpson & Rosenholtz 1986) discuss "unidimensional" classrooms, in which clear-cut, stable ability groups allow students to make easy comparisons. Marshall, Weinstein, and their colleagues have investigated "high-differential treatment" versus "low-differential treatment" classrooms (Brattesani et al 1984; Marshall & Weinstein 1984, 1986; Weinstein et al 1987). They conclude that the use of homogeneous ability grouping "may be detrimental only if rigidly enforced and within a context that includes other detrimental features, such as emphasis on overt comparison of ability and statements of negative expectations" (Marshall & Weinstein 1986: 452).

Within-class ability groups may have an impact not only on students' self-perceptions, but also on friendship patterns (Hallinan & Tuma 1978; Rothenberg 1979). Hallinan & Sorensen (1985) found that belonging to the same group affects friendship in three ways: It facilitates interactions, emphasizes students' similarity, and fosters the development of new similarities. These effects are well-illustrated in Rizzo's (1989) recent study of friendship formation in one elementary classroom. Not surprisingly, group assignment proved to be a significant factor. Students in the same group were able to interact not only during meeting time, but also during seatwork, when they worked together on the same assignments.

Emihovich (1981) examined these phenomena in two desegregated kindergartens in a magnet school. In Class A, the teacher established two formal ability groups (the "Tens" and the "Diez"), with most of the black children in the lower group. The clear stratification led to an academically based status hierarchy, in which blacks sank lower and lower. Over the course of the year, there was little evidence of cross-racial play. In Class B, the teacher grouped according to independence, academic ability, and social factors; groups changed frequently and were given no particular labels. Here, play groups were integrated, and the social status of minority children was determined by personal characteristics rather than group membership.

These findings illustrate the particular significance that ability grouping has for social interaction in multi-racial, multi-ethnic classrooms. This issue has been investigated by Hallinan and her colleagues in a series of studies that underscore the naïveté of thinking that mere assignment to the same classroom will promote interracial friendship. Hallinan & Teixeira (1987a), for example, found that whites tended to interact with students in the same ability groups, while blacks were attracted to students with higher status. In another study (Hallinan & Teixeira 1987b), the investigators found that whites were more likely to form cross-race friendships in classrooms where relative academic achievement was deemphasized and where blacks and whites were assigned to the same ability groups. These "status-leveling" factors helped to overcome engrained white resistance to making black friends and seem to be effective in promoting cross-race friendships.

Sharing Time

Sharing time is a unique segment of the classroom in that it is generally the only opportunity for children to speak at length on topics they choose themselves (Cazden 1985, 1988). Despite the apparent openness of the situation, however, the teacher's expectations and evaluative criteria still prevail (Michaels & Foster 1985). Even during sharing time, students must infer the often implicit rules that govern appropriate talk. They must learn what constitutes an acceptable topic and how to present information in a way that others unfamiliar with their personal lives can understand.

Although research on sharing time is limited, Michaels and Cazden have conducted an extensive study of four primary classrooms in the Boston area (see, for example, Cazden 1986, 1988; Michaels 1981, 1984, 1986). Their data illuminate the action structure of sharing-time activities.

Participation in sharing time tends to proceed according to a well-established ritual. In one first-grade classroom, for example, the teacher convened the event according to a standard formula: "Okay, who has something important [interesting, special] to share today?" Children also tend to respond formulaically. Typically, narratives begin with information about time ("Yesterday," "At Thanksgiving") and place ("I was at my grandma's house," "at the beach"). The key agent is then described, and the action begins (Cazden 1988).

Teachers' responses generally fall along a continuum that describes the extent to which the teacher approves of the child's narrative. Teachers may simply express their sense of appreciation ("Wow, that was an exciting story"), or they may make a simple comment or ask a question. At times, they may engage in extended collaborations with children that result in more complete stories than the children would have constructed on their own. Michaels (1986) refers to this activity as building a "scaffolding" for the achievement of a narrative (p. 100). More negative responses include expressions of perplexity, shifts of the topic to one that the teacher values or understands better, or obvious rejections ("That's not a good topic for sharing time").

Sharing time poses special problems for children whose narratives do not conform to teachers' expectations. Michaels (1986) has documented dramatic differences in the sharing-time styles used by black and white children. White children's narratives tend to be "tightly organized, centering on a single topic or a series of closely related topics, with thematic development accomplished through lexical cohesion, and a linear ordering of events, leading quickly to a punch line resolution" (Michaels 1986:102). In contrast, black children tend to use a "topic associating" style in which they relate a series of implicitly linked episodes. These episodic narratives tend to be longer and to have shifting scenes and numerous characters; the links between the scenes are often implicit. This type of discourse is difficult to follow if the teacher expects the discourse to focus on a single topic, to indicate explicitly a shift in topic or setting, and to be grounded both temporally and spatially. The resultant mismatch between the child's sharing-time style and the teacher's implicit model of what constitutes "good sharing talk" may lead to frustration on both sides, particularly as the teacher tries to respond to the child's contribution.

Cazden and Michaels have documented marked differences in teachers' responses to the stories told by black and white children. White teachers often displayed a lack of comprehension and appreciation for the stories told by black children. Hypothesizing that the problem was due to a cultural mismatch, Cazden (1988) presented versions of topic-centered and episodic narratives to black and white adults. Rhythm and intonation were maintained, but black dialect features and social class indicators were removed. White adults found the episodic stories hard to follow and were likely to infer that the narrator was a low achiever. Blacks liked both styles and had little difficulty comprehending the topic-associating stories.

Sharing time can be problematic not only in cases of cultural mismatches, but also when children are extremely reticent about speaking. Evans (1987) examined the interactions between a teacher and both reticent and nonreticent children during sharing time. Reticent children spoke less and engaged in less complex speech. They more often spoke about objects they had brought from home and used shorter utterances. The teacher more frequently directed questions to reticent children, but while peers responded to these as invitations to speak more, reticent children did not. They often answered yes or no or failed to respond at all. Evans attributes this pattern of "labored turn taking" to both anxiety and subtle language delays.

Sharing times that differ from the traditional teacher-directed segment have been studied less frequently. Michaels & Foster (1985) observed a student-run sharing time in which a child was selected each day to be the leader. In this setting, there were norms for appropriate behavior but no teacher-imposed rules governing topic, style, or amount of time that each person could talk. Michaels & Foster discovered two distinct styles of sharing: the lecture/demonstration, in which children presented information about an object or an event; and the performed narrative, a personal account emphasizing interaction between two or more people. The narrative tended to be dramatic, often accompanied by gestures, sound effects, repetitions, and asides. Children showed no preference for either style; in both, a successful sharer was one who attended to and capitalized on audience involvement.

Lazarus & Homer (1980) were able to examine another variation of sharing time when a kindergarten teacher decided that children's inattentiveness required a change in format. The teacher had originally conducted a traditional sharing time in which she directed the speech event from a chair, while the sharer stood next to her facing the other children. In the new format, the teacher sat with the children in a circle; sharing turns were allocated automatically by going around the circle, and children were encouraged to comment and to question one another. After the format change children participated more and the teacher contributed less. More of the total discourse was devoted to elaborations and extensions of the item being discussed. Thus, both the quality and the quantity of children's sharing-time talk increased.

Seatwork

The amount of time that students spend doing independent seatwork assignments has been a cause of concern among educators. The Beginning Teacher Evaluation Study (Fisher et al 1978) found that seatwork constitutes as much as 70% of instructional time, although the percentages vary significantly across content areas (Stodolsky 1988). As Anderson (1985) points out, the extensive use of seatwork is understandable, since it provides an opportunity for the teacher to interact with individuals or to direct a small group while the rest of the class is working independently.

The action structure of seatwork is substantially different from that of other segments. Here, analysis of "who does what to whom" reveals that students are focused on completing individual tasks, often without direction from the teacher or interaction with peers. In seatwork segments, Jackson's (1968) description of classroom life rings particularly true:

> . . . students must try to behave as if they were in solitude, when in point of fact they are not. They must keep their eyes on their paper when human faces beckon. Indeed, in the early grades it is not uncommon to find students facing each other around a table while at the same time being required not to communicate with each other. These young people, if they are to become successful students, must learn how to be alone in a crowd (p. 16).

Since external signals, such as teacher questions, are not present to evoke participant response, seatwork requires that students use self-pacing to sustain activity (Gump 1982). Not surprisingly, seatwork is generally characterized by lower engagement rates than externally paced segments (Fisher et al 1978; Gump 1967; Kounin 1970), although recent data collected by Stodolsky (1988) did not conform to this pattern. The discrepancy may be a function of the grade levels studied, the subject matter, and the cognitive complexity of the assignments.

Engagement in seatwork segments often follows a predictable cycle (deVoss 1979). Students begin to work; their attention wanes; the noise level and other activities increase; the teacher intervenes; the children then return to the assignment. This cycle repeats, until a final "spurt" occurs during which there is a mad rush to complete the work before seatwork time is over. During periods of non-engagement, children sharpen pencils, converse, comb their hair, doodle, or simply watch one another. This behavior is usually acceptable as long as it is quiet, since it does not prevent the teacher from being able to work with an individual or a small group.

Since seatwork is generally an individual enterprise, the ability to remain free of distractions is essential for success (Berliner 1983). Yet seatwork also poses unique social and communicative demands for students; specifically, they must learn the socially appropriate ways to obtain assistance both from the teacher and from peers.

Obtaining the teacher's help can be particularly problematic if he or she is involved in another segment, such as a small reading group, or with another student. If the teacher allows unlimited access, pacing in the teacher-directed activity can slow down, and pupil involvement can drop dramatically. Merritt (1982a,b) studied the way students not currently working with the teacher solicit attention and help. She called these solicitations "service-like events," not unlike the kinds of moves made by customers trying to get a clerk's attention in a store (Cazden 1988). Merritt found that solicitations were most likely to be positively received if students made a nonverbal approach to the teacher. This allowed teachers to maintain control of the interaction and to initiate the contact when they could "slot out" of the main activity. The likelihood of receiving help was also dependent on the anticipated nature of the soliciting child's request (especially how long it was likely to take) and the phase of the teacher's activity. Slot-outs were more likely to occur when there was verbal "down time" in the main activity. Merritt also found that teachers split their communication modalities (e.g. between verbal and nonverbal; or by distinctions in tone or rhythm of their verbal modality) in order to attend to both activities. These splits provide a good example of what Kounin (1970) referred to as "overlapping"—the ability to deal with simultaneous situations without becoming immersed in one and ignoring the other.

In addition to learning the socially acceptable ways to obtain the teacher's help, students must understand (and perhaps work around) the norms surrounding peer assistance. Sometimes, giving or receiving help is tantamount to cheating (Rizzo 1989). In such situations, the students' need to follow the teacher's directions (and to stay out of trouble) may clash with their need to obtain help or to assist friends who are having difficulty (Bloome & Theodorou 1988). To resolve this conflict, students must create an "underground" for covert peer interaction (Hatch 1986; Sieber 1979).

Even in situations where peer assistance is permitted or encouraged, not all students are able to take advantage of their peers' expertise. Cohen (1984) hypothesized that classroom social status affects frequency of student interaction, which in turn affects amount of learning. She observed children in nine bilingual classrooms (grades 2–4) working in shifting groups at learning centers. Children were told they had the right to ask for help and also had the duty to assist anyone who asked for help. She found that status was positively related to amount of peer interaction; moreover, the more children talked and worked together, the more they learned from the curriculum. She concludes: "Those children with high social status have more access to peer interaction that, in turn, assists their learning. In other words, the rich get richer. This is the dilemma of using peer interaction . . ." (p. 184).

Cohen's findings are echoed by Cooper et al (1982), who observed that certain children are at the "crossroads of learning exchanges" (p. 76). These students not only receive the most unsolicited help, but they are also the most sought out as consultants. Others are neglected individuals—"omega children" (Garnica 1981)—who rarely initiate interaction and whom other children seldom engage in conversation. Garnica provides a poignant example of the omega child's plight by contrasting two conversations among small groups of kindergarten children who are coloring a picture. In both situations, the target child needs a marker that another child is using. The successful "bidder" requests the marker directly ("I need green. When you're done can I have it?"), and his request is ultimately successful. In contrast, the omega child repeatedly attempts to obtain the marker (e.g. "How'r ya doing with that pink?" "Could I use some pink?"), but her bids are either rejected or ignored. When the pink marker is eventually "auctioned" off to another child, the omega child offers no protest and quietly selects another color.

Garnica's findings are consistent with a description of the "effective speaker" provided by Wilkinson and her colleagues (Wilkinson & Calculator 1982a,b; Wilkinson & Spinelli 1983). Their data indicate that students are more likely to get appropriate responses if their requests are direct and on-task, perceived as sincere, made to a designated listener, and revised if initially unsuccessful. While most children make on-task, sincere requests to a designated listener, there appear to be substantial individual differences with respect to the directness of a request and the degree to which students revise their requests and try again.

Data also suggest that help-seeking may be ineffective if it is interpreted by peers as lazy or excessive (i.e. asking for the answer rather than assistance with the process; asking for help when you haven't worked hard to solve the problem yourself). Nelson-Le Gall & Glor-Scheib (1986) found a significant negative correlation between peer ratings of social attractiveness and excessive help-seeking in mathematics classes (although not in reading).

Student-Directed Small Groups

The lack of opportunity for students to work together in peer-directed small groups is well documented (Gerleman 1987; Goodlad 1984; Lockheed &

Harris 1984). Graybeal & Stodolsky (1985), for example, found that peer work groups had a 4.6% occupancy time (segment duration multiplied by the number of students in the segment) in fifth-grade mathematics classes and 12% occupancy time in fifth-grade social studies classes. Moreover, these small percentages actually reflect a wide variety of interactive situations, from students being permitted to help one another during seatwork assignments to true cooperative learning groups in which children work together toward a common goal (Graybeal & Stodolsky 1985; Stodolsky 1984).

This lack of student interaction is not surprising, given teachers' responsibility for keeping order and moving through the curriculum. In the crowded, complex world of the classroom, both are more easily achieved in situations that allow teachers to control content, pacing, and patterns of participation. Small-group work dictates that teachers give up their role as "direct supervisor" of student behavior and performance and assume the unfamiliar—and perhaps uncomfortable—roles of "supportive supervisor" (Cohen 1986), facilitator, consultant, and "human relations trainer" (Kagan 1985).

Small-group situations also place unfamiliar social demands on students. In order to participate appropriately, they must replace traditional classroom norms (e.g. listening to the teacher, ignoring other students) with the norms required by group work. They must learn to listen to one another, to allocate turns for speaking, and to manage time and task (Cohen 1986). They must also initiate, explain, and even evaluate the contributions of their peers.

Learning to adopt the roles normally assigned to the teacher may not be easy. Students who are used to passivity may be unwilling to assume a more active role (Lazarowitz et al 1985). Some may have difficulty providing coherent, complete explanations for their peers (Webb & Kenderski 1984), while others may lack the skills needed to obtain responses to their questions (Wilkinson & Calculator 1982a,b; Wilkinson & Spinelli 1983). In groups that perceive the task to be too difficult or too easy, students may focus on getting through the assignment as quickly as possible (Webb 1980). The development of a status hierarchy within the group may result in undesirable domination by some, and nonparticipation and withdrawal by others (Cohen 1986; Dembo & McAuliffe 1987). Students whose cultural backgrounds have fostered a competitive orientation may find cooperative situations particularly difficult (Philips 1972; Kagan et al 1985).

Recent research has indicated that patterns of interaction in small groups are influenced by group composition, particularly with respect to ability level and gender. Webb and her colleagues (Webb 1982a,b; Webb & Cullian 1983; Webb & Kenderski 1984) have compared interaction among junior-high and high-school students working on mathematics tasks in homogeneous versus heterogeneous ability groups. In homogeneous groups, they found that students were less likely to receive a response to their questions (Webb 1982b; Webb & Cullian 1983). Since research has consistently demonstrated that providing explanations is positively related to achievement (Peterson et al 1984; Swing & Peterson 1982; Webb 1985) while not receiving an explanation is negatively related to achievement (Webb 1985), these data suggest that mixed-ability groups are preferable. Further research, however, has shown that heterogeneous groups composed of high-, medium-, and low-achieving students are detrimental for medium-ability students, who tend to be left out of the interaction (Peterson et al 1981; Webb & Kenderski 1984). Medium-ability students appear to receive more explanations and to achieve best in uniform ability groups or in heterogeneous groups with only two ability levels (Webb 1982a). Indeed, Webb (1985) contends that two-level groups (high-medium or medium-low) are most beneficial for all students.

One study by Webb (1984) indicated that interaction in small mathematics groups is also affected by the ratio of females to males. In groups where females outnumbered males, the females tended to direct most of their comments and questions to the males and to achieve less than males. In majority-male groups, females tended to be ignored and again showed somewhat lower achievement than males. In groups with equal numbers of males and females, patterns of interaction and achievement were similar for males and females.

These gender findings can be interpreted as evidence of the higher social status of males (particularly in a mathematics context). Research by Lockheed and her colleagues (Lockheed et al 1983; Lockheed & Harris 1984) suggests that gender functions as a "diffuse status characteristic" when there is no substantive basis for determining an individual's competence and leadership ability. Small-group experiences may actually reinforce rather than counteract gender stereotypes, with girls perceived as less competent and less leaderlike. Data suggest, however, that perceptions can be altered by specific training designed to improve peer perceptions of girls' competence.

Several structured programs of cooperative learning have been developed to avoid the problems characteristic of small groups and to encourage norms of effort and mutual support. Designed for use at any grade level and in most school subjects, all of the cooperative learning strategies are characterized by heterogeneous groups working together to achieve a common goal (Slavin 1983, 1985). These strategies can be viewed as systematic variations of the action structure of peer-directed small groups.

Student Team Learning methods were developed and studied at Johns Hopkins University (Slavin 1990). In Student Teams–Achievement Divisions (STAD), the teacher presents a lesson, and students then work within their teams on academic tasks. Their objective is to ensure that all team members master the material. Finally, students take individual quizzes, and team scores are derived from members' individual improvement over their own past performance. Teams that meet designated criteria receive certificates or other rewards. In Teams-Games-Tournaments (TGT), the quizzes are replaced by tournaments in which students compete with same-ability members of other teams.

In Jigsaw, one of the earliest cooperative learning methods (Aronson et al 1978), heterogeneous teams work on academic material that has been divided into sections. Each team member reads only one section. The teams then disband, and students meet in "expert groups" with others who have been assigned the same section. Working together, they learn the material and then return to their home teams to teach it to their teammates. Since everyone is responsible for learning all the material, successful task completion requires students to cooperate. Jigsaw also includes team-building activities and training to improve communication and tutoring skills. In Jigsaw II (Slavin 1985), a modification developed by the Johns Hopkins researchers, all students in a team read the entire assignment. They are then assigned a particular topic on which to become an expert. Like STAD, Jigsaw II uses individual quizzes and team scores based on individual improvement.

Learning Together methods (Johnson & Johnson 1987) emphasize the social skills needed for successful group work. Students are taught to trust one another, to communicate accurately and unambiguously, to accept and support one another, and to resolve conflicts constructively. Generally, students hand in a single product and receive praise for working together well and for their performance on the group task.

Group Investigation (Sharan & Sharan 1976, 1989–1990), a fourth cooperative learning method, places students in small groups to investigate topics from a unit being studied by the entire class. Each group further divides their topic into individual subtopics and then carries out the research. Students work together to find resource materials, to collect and analyze information, and to plan and present a report, demonstration, play, learning center, or exhibition for the class. Evaluation focuses on both learning and affective experiences; assessment procedures may include comments from peers, students' self-evaluations, and questions submitted by groups for a common test, as well as evaluation by the teacher.

The differences in these cooperative learning methods reflect alternative ways of solving the problems inherent in peer-directed small groups. For example, in order to minimize the possibility that one student will do most of the group's work, individual accountability is central to many of the methods (e.g. individual quizzes in STAD; tournaments in TGT; individual assignments in Jigsaw, Jigsaw II, and Group Investigation). The methods also provide incentives to cooperate by offering team rewards and recognition (e.g. STAD, TGT, and Jigsaw II) or designing tasks so that they require interdependence (e.g. Jigsaw and Group Investigation). Some explicitly teach the social skills needed for group work (e.g. Jigsaw and Learning Together). Finally, to ensure that all students can contribute to the group's efforts, methods base team scores on students' improvement over past performance or assign students their own topics to master.

Despite their similarities, the cooperative learning methods differ substantially with respect to the social relationships established among students, both within groups and between groups. For example, in STAD and TGT, students engage in peer tutoring on well-defined tasks provided by the teacher. Since teams contain both high- and low-status students, it is likely that a status hierarchy will emerge within the group (Kagan 1985; Sharan 1980) whereby low achievers and minorities will tend to be cast in the role of tutee. This seems less likely to occur in Jigsaw, since each team member is responsible for a unique section of the material, and high-status individuals must listen to low-status peers in order to learn about the whole topic. Similarly, in Group Investigation, each team member researches a different subtopic, and the task structure is intended to foster inquiry, problem-solving, and exchange of ideas, rather than dyadic tutoring; nonetheless, a status hierarchy may still emerge during group discussion and planning (Kagan 1985).

Between-group relationships also vary considerably across methods. In STAD, there is no actual interaction among members of different teams; furthermore, since all groups can meet the established criteria for reward or recognition, competition between teams is tempered. In contrast, the tournaments of TGT foster strong intergroup competition. Indeed, Kagan et al (1985) have suggested that TGT be reconceptualized as a mixed cooperative-competitive classroom structure. In Jigsaw and Jigsaw II, between-team cooperation is facilitated through the use of expert groups. Jigsaw reinforces this cooperation by providing individual grades only; Jigsaw II uses the same reward structure as STAD and TGT. In Group Investigation, a steering committee of representatives from each group coordinates activities and resources and encourages between-team cooperation; since teams are not vying for rewards, there is little basis for competition.

Research examining the effects of cooperative learning methods has generally demonstrated their positive impact on social relationships among students of different races and ethnic backgrounds. Slavin (1990) recently reviewed 19 studies that met rigorous criteria for duration (at least four weeks) and methodological soundness. The studies spanned grades 2 through 12 and involved black, Anglo, and Mexican-American students in the United States (e.g. Kagan et al 1985), Middle Eastern and European Jews in Israel (Sharan et al 1984), and recent European and West Indian immigrants and Anglo-Canadians in Toronto (Ziegler 1981). Sixteen of the 19 studies demonstrated positive effects on some dimension of friendship. A notable example is the Elementary School Study, a part of the Riverside Cooperative Learning Project (Kagan et al 1985). This study involved 35 student teachers and approximately 900 elementary school students (grades 2–4 and grades 5–6) in one of three classroom structure conditions—STAD, TGT, and "traditional." Results indicated that cooperative methods were superior for producing positive race relations, prosocial development, and classroom climate for all students. Indeed, the most dramatic finding of the study was the impact on race relations. While segregation among students increased with grade level in the traditional classrooms, "same-ethnicity dropped out as a significant predictor of friendship in the cooperative classrooms at both grade levels" (p. 307).

Given the forces operating against the formation of cross-racial, cross-ethnic bonds, the impact of cooperative learning is impressive. Indeed, even shorter-term studies have found positive effects. For example, Warring et al (1985) found that cooperative conditions promoted cross-race (and cross-sex) interactions even when implemented for approximately one hour a day for two weeks. Moreover, the results do not appear to be restricted to studies that rely only on sociometric instruments or peer-rating scales. Johnson & Johnson (1981a), for example, examined the impact of cooperative methods on fourth-grade students' behavior during free-time periods. Students in the cooperative condition engaged in significantly more cross-ethnic interaction during this unstructured time.

Cooperative learning strategies have also been shown to improve relationships between academically handicapped and normal-progress students (Johnson et al 1983; Slavin 1990). Research has generally used sociometric measures of friendship ("Who are your friends in this class?"), although a few have used sociometric rejection measures ("Who would you not want to have in your group?"). Madden & Slavin (1983) used both types of assessment to examine the impact of STAD in third-, fourth-, and sixth-grade classrooms containing mainstreamed academically handicapped students. Results indicated that the rejection of mainstreamed students by normal-progress students was significantly decreased by the cooperative treatment; however, positive choices of mainstreamed students as friends or preferred workmates were not affected by the intervention.

Behavioral observations have been used by researchers investigating the effects of Learning Together methods on the acceptance of academically and emotionally handicapped students. Although the results have been mixed, there is some evidence that cooperative learning can affect students' behavior during unstructured times when students can choose their workmates. Johnson & Johnson (1981b), for example, found that students assigned to a cooperative condition engaged in more cross-handicap interaction during post-instruction free time than students assigned to the individualistic condition. In a long-term study by Lew et al (1986), four socially isolated, special-needs children were assigned to heterogeneous groups to study vocabulary words. Over a period of more than five months, the groups worked under varying conditions of interdependence. The results indicated that during free-choice study periods, the frequency of voluntary association between the socially isolated students and their classmates increased. Although simply working in cooperative groups had a positive effect on voluntary association, the effect was even greater with the addition of reward for group mastery of the material and for exhibiting specific collaborative behaviors.

MICROCOMPUTERS AND SOCIAL INTERACTION

When computers enter the social context of the classroom, they raise innumerable questions for teachers (Sheingold et al 1984): What are computers and software good for? What can students learn from computer experiences? How should computers fit into the physical organization of the room? How does computer technology relate to traditional curricula and modes of learning? Teachers' answers to these questions determine the role of the computers in the classroom and the impact they have on social interaction.

Amarel (1983) has noted that the interactive space between students and the computer can be viewed as a subsetting of the classroom, much like recitations, teacher-directed small groups, and seatwork. Yet, it is difficult to specify the norms for appropriate behavior in this setting or to describe the communicative demands placed on students, since computers can be used in strikingly different ways. Microcomputers can provide opportunities for students to complete drill and practice exercises; to engage in problem-solving and exploration through games and simulations; and to experience the writing process—to compose, edit, revise, and publish. Such uses constitute distinct "micro-settings," each with its own demands and limits on behavior (Amarel 1983).

In addition, different teachers may implement very different rules governing social interaction at the computer. Some may restrict computer use to one student at a time, while others may encourage pairs or small groups of students to work together. Olson (1988) provides a vivid example of such differences. At Spruce Grove, computers were integrated into the regular curriculum of the fifth–sixth-grade class that Olson observed. Here, the teacher allowed children to have frequent, regular access to computers and encouraged them to cooperate. In Maple Hills, computers were viewed more as a formal exercise than as an aid to curriculum delivery. The computers were centralized in a small laboratory that could accommodate six or seven children at a time. Concerned with maintaining order, the teacher in this school did not allow children to collaborate.

Despite the marked differences in current computer practices, research indicates that the computer can be a powerful catalyst for social interaction (Borgh & Dickson 1986; Dickinson 1986; Hawkins et al 1982; Wright & Samaras 1986). Clements & Nastasi (1988) compared interaction among first- and third-grade children participating in computer-assisted instruction (CAI) or Logo (Papert 1980)—two distinctly different computer environments. Whereas CAI provides "electronic worksheets" designed to teach specific skills, Logo allows students to construct computer programs that create graphics by moving a triangular shape around the screen. Randomly assigned to one of the two environments, pairs of children spent an equivalent amount of time working cooperatively (60–70%) and exhibited the same amount of conflict. However, the Logo group demonstrated a higher percentage of conflict resolution. Clements & Nastasi speculate that Logo enhances conflict resolution since children cannot continue playing unless they arrive at consensus; in contrast, CAI allows children to continue, even though they disagree, simply by taking turns.

A recent study by Genishi (1988) underscores the notion that computer use is often "a social event" (p. 197). Genishi observed the behavior of 20 kindergarten children participating in a Logo lesson in a computer laboratory. She found that "the appearance of any image on the screen, whether expected or not, was an occasion for comment or inquiry. . . . The public nature of the screen made cooperation (and competition) natural" (p. 197).

This "public nature" of computers is one explanation for the increased collaboration observed in numerous classrooms (Hawkins et al 1984). A second explanation involves the limited number of computers in classrooms. Since computers are a scarce resource, teachers often assign children to work in pairs or in small groups (Daiute 1985). Third, teachers may lack familiarity with computers and may therefore be more willing to share responsibility for instruction with child experts or "computer jocks" (Amarel 1983). Finally, the novelty of the computer creates a situation in which no one is quite sure what children are supposed to be doing; thus, the normal constraints on collaboration do not apply (Hawkins et al 1984).

At times, the increased collaboration stimulated by computers may be problematic. As Sheingold et al (1984) observe, children "do not necessarily possess good collaborative skills for jointly solving problems . . ., nor are they necessarily skilled at making use of human resources other than teachers in their work" (p. 59). To avoid the problems inherent in true collaboration, students may opt to designate distinct roles for different children—as in the case of two children who decided, "I'm the thinkist, you're the typist" (Sheingold et al 1984:59). Young children, in particular, may engage in activities akin to associative play, in which they monitor each other's behavior while waiting for their own turn (Emihovich 1989).

A case study reported by Daiute (1985) provides insight into the difficulties experienced by two young boys using the computer for joint composition. Although computers facilitate the process of editing and revising, each child was extremely reluctant to change the other's writing. Moreover, because of the boys' different personalities and work styles, their collaborative efforts resulted in stories that were less coherent than stories they wrote individually.

Heap (1989) describes the contrasting situation of a class in which first-graders had established very clear social norms about the rights and responsibilities of students involved in collaborative writing on the computer. Children who were writing at the computer could choose a helper to be a "technical advisor." Each child had a carefully designated role to play with respect to composition and inputting text. The writer was primarily responsible for composing, while the advisor had the "license" to input because of his or her greater expertise.

Students' seating arrangements were a physical manifestation of the social rules governing their collaboration on the computer. Students vied to sit in the "driver's seat," the chair directly in front of the computer. Heap observes:

> Whoever got to the computer center first would slide into the driver's seat. At the arrival of the designated writer, the helper usually moved over to the right side seat. . . . When the writer got up, the helper sometimes slid left into the driver's seat. On the writer's return, the helper usually moved back to the right side seat. In disputes over who had the right to sit where, the children formulated to each other what the rules for seating were (p. 284).

These disputes about seating indicate students' concern about controlling the writing process. As Heap reminds us, the problem of control is "endemic" to collaboration (p. 285).

CONCLUDING COMMENTS

In the 1980 volume of the *Annual Review of Psychology,* Gump called for a "science of settings" in order to understand the school as a social situation (p. 59). Although we are far from that goal, research conducted within the last 15 years has added considerably to our knowledge of "who does what to whom" in key settings of the classroom. What lessons can we learn from this research? Are there any themes that cut across activity segment boundaries?

First, the studies reviewed in this chapter illustrate how students' ability to participate in socially appropriate ways influences their opportunity to achieve academic success. If students call out during recitations, instead of bidding for an opportunity to respond, the teacher may reject even correct contributions. Sharing-time narratives that do not conform to the teacher's model of "good talk" are likely to meet with disapproval. Students who need the teacher's help during seatwork may be ignored unless they make a nonverbal approach to the teacher during "down time." Requests for peer assistance may also fail if students do not frame their requests directly or if they are perceived as not having tried hard enough. Pupils who are unable to participate in small-group discussions will not benefit from the opportunity to provide and receive explanations. Examples like these depict the numerous ways in which the social and academic dimensions of schooling are intertwined. As Green et al (1988) have observed, "The academic text [of a lesson] . . . can be viewed as embedded in and realized through a social text" (p. 13).

Second, research documents the power of the action structure to define the parameters of appropriate social behavior. It is important to remember, however, that *within* action structures teachers and students create unique academic and social events through a process of mutual engagement and influence (Mehan 1980; Green et al 1988). Thus, even as students and teachers jointly *enact* the IRE sequence of a traditional recitation (Mehan 1979), they jointly *construct* a conversation that is never entirely prescribed or predictable. The game of baseball provides a helpful metaphor: Although three strikes normally constitute an out, one can never predict exactly who will strike out when. Moreover, in the classroom the action structure of a segment can be modified. The interaction patterns in KEEP reading groups (Au 1980) and in reciprocal teaching (Palincsar & Brown 1985) are examples of deliberate alterations of the action structure that normally characterizes teacher-directed small groups.

Third, the research underscores the dominant-subordinate relationship of teacher to students. The teacher emerges as one who initiates, monitors, and evaluates, while the student waits, listens, and responds (Jackson 1968). The chapter's emphasis on classroom communication only serves to highlight the differences in their roles. In Cazden's (1988) words:

> In typical classrooms, the most important asymmetry in the rights and obligations of teachers and students is over control of the right to speak. To describe the difference in the bluntest terms, teachers have the right to speak at any time and to any person; they can fill any silence or interrupt any speaker; they can speak to a student anywhere in the room and in any volume or tone of voice. And no one has any right to object (p. 54).

From the ecological perspective of this chapter, however, this dominance of the teacher is viewed not as an attempt to socialize youngsters into conformity but as an adaptation to the demands of the classroom environment. In the compulsory, crowded, unpredictable world of the classroom, a major function of the teacher's role is to "solve the problem of order" (Doyle 1986)—to create group activities that allow students to move smoothly through time, space, and curricula. Teacher-dominated segments serve this function well (although their value in promoting learning is less clear), and as we have seen, it is not always easy for participants to learn the new roles required by segments such as peer-directed small groups. On the other hand, the research on reciprocal teaching and KEEP indicates that teachers can depart from teacher-centered action structures when the press of the large group is less immediate.

Finally, the research reviewed here demonstrates the powerful ways in which the formal social organization of the classroom can influence students' informal interactions. Children enter school with differential status based on socioeconomic background, gender, race, and ethnicity; reading achievement soon constitutes an additional status variable. Participation in the activity segments of the classroom can exaggerate or diminish these differences in status. If students spend most of the school day in recitation formats and ability-based small groups, the status hierarchy is reinforced, and friendship groups tend to be academically homogeneous. On the other hand, formats such as peer-directed cooperative groups can break down barriers between students and attenuate status differences. Given the increasing heterogeneity of our school population, it is crucial that we continue to investigate how the formal social organization of the classroom can counteract the tendency toward separation and stratification.

In sum, impressive progress has been made in understanding the classroom as a social environment; however, numerous issues remain to be explored. First, the literature review conducted for this chapter uncovered only a few studies at the secondary level; it is clear that we need to know more about the activity segments that comprise high-school classrooms. Similarly, we need to know more about the ways subject matter affects participation in various activity segments. For example, the differences in the social contexts of high- and low-achievement reading groups have been well documented. Do similar differences exist in mathematics groups? Research by Webb (1984) has indicated that females tend to be ignored in majority-male mathematics groups at the junior-high level. Would this same pattern exist in English, a more stereotypically female subject, or at the elementary level, where females are perceived as being more academically competent than males (Nelson-LeGall & DeCooke 1987)?

In addition, the issue of cultural discontinuity has received only sporadic, uneven attention across activity segments. Philips's (1972) work has revealed the difficulties that Native Americans experience during recitations. From KEEP (Au 1980), we have learned about the joint productions that Hawaiian children prefer to use during small reading groups. The studies conducted by Michaels and Cazden (Cazden 1988) have taught us about the different narrative styles used by black and white children during sharing time. As classrooms in the United States and some other countries become increasingly heterogeneous, we need to learn more about the culturally based patterns of language and interaction that children bring with them to school and about how these patterns mesh with the action structures of the classroom. Indeed, we need to expand this work by examining cultural patterns that *facilitate* participation in particular activity segments. The work by Kagan and his colleagues (Kagan et al 1985) on students' competitive-cooperative social orientations and competitive-cooperative classroom structures exemplifies this more inclusive approach.

We also need to know more about how participation in the action structures of classroom segments affects interpersonal relationships among students. For example, does ability to tell a good sharing-time story enhance a child's position in the classroom social hierarchy? Do white children react to the narratives of their black peers with the same confusion that a white teacher does, and does this affect friendship patterns? Do successful sharing times build affiliation among students? Similarly, is affiliation fostered by seatwork segments in which helping one another is not only legitimate but encouraged? Can cooperative learning formats help to integrate socially neglected "omega" children (Garnica 1981), who may lack the communication skills required for effective help-seeking?

In closing, it is useful to reflect on the theme expressed in the title of this chapter: "the classroom as a social context for learning." The studies reviewed in this chapter attest to the fact that the classroom is not simply a social context in which students learn academic lessons. It is a social context in which students also learn social lessons—lessons about appropriate behavior in various contexts, about one's self as a learner and one's position in a status hierarchy, about relationships with students from other ethnic and racial groups, about the relative value of competition and cooperation, and about friendship. Experiences in activity segments influence the content of these lessons. Thus, knowledge of activity segments enables us to generate opportunities for positive interaction and to create settings in which students can learn lessons of caring, justice, and self-worth.

ACKNOWLEDGMENTS

Preparation of this chapter was supported by a grant from the Rutgers Faculty Scholars Program. I am grateful to Paul Gump and Walter Doyle, who early in the preparation of this chapter discussed its possible scope and organization. Thanks are also due to Deborah Smith and Daniel Diamond, who carried out many aspects of the library research. I also wish to acknowledge the assistance of Neil Weinstein, Louise Cherry Wilkinson, and Anita Woolfolk, who reviewed earlier versions of this chapter. Finally, Paul Gump's support, encouragement, and gently-voiced but tough-minded critiques deserve a special note of gratitude.

Literature Cited

Allington, R. L. 1980. Teacher interruption behaviors during primary-grade oral reading. *J. Educ. Psychol.* 72:371–77

Allington, R. L. 1983. The reading instruction provided readers of differing reading abilities. *Elem. Sch. J.* 83:548–59

Amarel, M. 1983. Classrooms and computers as instructional settings. *Theor. Pract.* 22:260–70

Anderson, L. M. 1985. What are students doing when they do all that seatwork? In *Perspectives on Instructional Time*, ed. C. W. Fisher, D. C. Berliner, pp. 189–202. New York: Longman

Aronson, E., Blaney, N., Stephan, C., Sikes, J., Snapp, M. 1978. *The Jigsaw Classroom*. Beverly Hills, Calif: Sage

Au, K. H. 1980. Participation structures in a reading lesson with Hawaiian children: analysis of a culturally appropriate instructional event. *Anthropol. Educ. Q.* 11:91–115

Au, K. H., Mason, J. M. 1981. Social organizational factors in learning to read: the balance of rights hypothesis. *Read. Res. Q.* 17:115–52

Au, K. H., Tharp, R. G., Crowell, D. C., Jordan, C., Speidel, G. E., Calkins, R. 1985. The role of research in the development of a successful reading program. In *Reading Education: Foundations for a Literate America*, ed. J. Osborn, P. Wilson, R. Anderson, pp. 275–92. Lexington, MA: D. C. Heath

Barr, R. 1989. Social organization of reading instruction. In *Locating Learning: Ethnographic Perspectives on Classroom Research*, ed. C. Emihovich, pp. 57–86. Norwood, NJ: Ablex

Bellack, A. A., Davitz, R. J., Kliebard, H. M., Hyman, R. T. 1974. The classroom game. In *Teaching: Vantage Points for Study*, ed. R. T. Hyman, pp. 347–54. Philadelphia: J. B. Lippincott Co. 2nd ed.

Berliner, D. C. 1983. Developing conceptions of classroom environments: some light on the T in classroom studies of ATI. *Educ. Psychol.* 18:1–13

Bloome, D., Theodorou, E. 1988. Analyzing teacher-student and student-student discourse. In *Multiple Perspective Analyses of Classroom Discourse*, ed. J. L. Green, J. O. Harker, pp. 217–48. Norwood, NJ: Ablex

Blumenfeld, P. C., Pintrich, P. R., Meece, J., Wessels, K. 1982. The formation and role of self-perceptions of ability in elementary classrooms. *Elem. Sch. J.* 82:401–20

Borgh, K., Dickson, W. P. 1986. Two preschoolers sharing one microcomputer: creating prosocial behavior with hardware and software. In *Young Children and Microcomputers*, ed. P. F. Campbell, G. G. Fein, pp. 37–44. Englewood Cliffs, NJ: Prentice-Hall

Bossert, S. T. 1979. *Tasks and Social Relationships in Classrooms. A Study of Instructional Organization and Its Consequences*. Cambridge: Cambridge Univ. Press

Brattesani, K. A., Weinstein, R. S., Marshall, H. H. 1984. Student perceptions of differential teacher treatment as moderators of teacher expectation effects. *J. Educ. Psychol.* 76:236–47

Burns, R. B. 1984. How time is used in elementary schools: the activity structure of classrooms. In *Time and School Learning: Theory, Research and Practice*, ed. L. W. Anderson, pp. 91–127. London: Croom Helm

Cazden, C. B. 1985. Research currents: What is sharing time for? *Lang. Arts* 62:182–88

Cazden, C. B. 1986. Classroom discourse. In *The Handbook of Research on Teaching*, ed. M. C. Wittrock, pp. 432–63. New York: Macmillan. 3rd ed.

Cazden, C. B. 1988. *Classroom Discourse: The Language of Teaching and Learning*. Portsmouth, New Hampshire: Heinemann

Clements, D. H., Nastasi, B. K. 1988. Social and cognitive interactions in educational computer environments. *Am. Educ. Res. J.* 25:87–106

Cohen, D. K. 1988. *Teaching Practice: Plus ça change. . . .* Issue Paper 88-3. East Lansing, MI: Natl. Cent. Res. Teach. Educ., Michigan State Univ.

Cohen, E. G. 1984. Talking and working together: status, interaction, and learning. In *The Social Context of Instruction*, ed. P. L. Peterson, L. C. Wilkinson, M. Hallinan, pp. 171–88. New York: Academic

Cohen, E. G. 1986. *Designing Group Work: Strategies for the Heterogeneous Classroom*. New York: Teachers College Press

Collins, J. 1986. Differential instruction in reading groups. In *The Social Construction of Literacy*, ed. J. Cook-Gumperz, pp. 117–37. Cambridge: Cambridge Univ. Press

Cooper, C. R., Marquis, A., Ayers-Lopez, S. 1982. Peer learning in the classroom: tracing developmental patterns and consequences of children's spontaneous interactions. In *Communicating in the Classroom*, ed. L. C. Wilkinson, pp. 69–84. New York: Academic

Cuban, L. 1984. *How Teachers Taught: Constancy and Change in American Classrooms 1890–1980*. New York: Longman

Daiute, C. 1985. Issues in using computers to socialize the writing process. *Educ. Commun. Technol. J.* 33:41–50

Dembo, M. H., McAuliffe, T. J. 1987. Effects of perceived ability and grade status on social interaction and influence in cooperative groups. *J. Educ. Psychol.* 79:415–23

deVoss, G. G. 1979. The structure of major lessons and collective student activity. *Elem. Sch. J.* 80:8–18

Dickinson, D. K. 1986. Cooperation, collaboration, and a computer: integrating a computer into a first-second grade writing program. *Res. Teach. English* 20:357–78

Dillon, J. T. 1983. *Teaching and the Art of Questioning.* Fastback 194. Bloomington, IN: Phi Delta Kappa Educ. Found.

Doyle, W. 1981. Research on classroom contexts. *J. Teach. Educ.* 32:3–6

Doyle, W. 1986. Classroom organization and management. See Cazden 1986, pp. 392–431

Eder, D. 1981. Ability grouping as a self-fulfilling prophecy: a micro-analysis of teacher-student interaction. *Sociol. Educ.* 54:151–62

Eder, D. 1982. Differences in communicative styles across ability groups. See Cooper et al 1982, pp. 245–65

Eder, D. 1983. Ability grouping and students' academic self-concepts: a case study. *Elem. Sch. J.* 84:149–61

Eder, D., Felmlee, D. 1984. The development of attention norms in ability groups. See Cohen 1984, pp. 189–208

Emihovich, C. A. 1981. Social interaction in two integrated kindergartens. *Integrated Educ.* 19:72–78

Emihovich, C. A. 1989. Learning through sharing: peer collaboration in Logo instruction. In *Locating Learning: Ethnographic Perspectives on Classroom Research,* ed. C. Emihovich. Norwood, NJ: Ablex

Erickson, F. 1982. Classroom discourse as improvisation: relationships between academic task structure and social participation structure in lessons. See Cooper et al 1982, pp. 153–82

Erickson, F., Shultz, J. 1981. When is a context? Some issues and methods in the analysis of social competence. In *Ethnography & Language in Educational Settings,* ed. J. L. Green, C. Wallat. Norwood, New Jersey: Ablex

Evans, M. A. 1987. Discourse characteristics of reticent children. *Appl. Psycholinguist.* 8:171–84

Farrar, M. T. 1988. A sociolinguistic analysis of discussion. In *Questioning and Discussion—A Multidisciplinary Study,* ed. J. T. Dillon. Norwood, New Jersey: Ablex

Filby, N., Barnett, B. 1982. Student perceptions of "better readers" in elementary classrooms. *Elem. Sch. J.* 82:435–50

Fisher, C., Filby, N., Marliave, R., Cahen, L., Dishaw, M., et al. 1978. *Teaching Behaviors, Academic Learning Time, and Student Achievement. Final Report of Phase III-B, Beginning Teacher Evaluation Study.* San Francisco: Far West Lab. Educ. Res. Dev.

Fivush, R. 1984. Learning about school: the development of kindergartners' school scripts. *Child Dev.* 55:1697–1709

Florio-Ruane, S. 1989. Social organization of classes and schools. In *Knowledge Base for the Beginning Teacher: A Handbook,* ed. M. Reynolds. Oxford, United Kingdom: Pergamon

Gamoran, A. 1984. Egalitarian versus elitist use of ability grouping. Presented at Annu. Meet. Am. Educ. Res. Assoc., New Orleans. ERIC Document #ED 245 821

Garnica, O. K. 1981. Social dominance and conversational interaction—the omega child in the classroom. See Erickson & Schultz 1981, pp. 229–52

Genishi, C. 1988. Kindergartners and computers: a case study of six children. *Elem. Sch. J.* 89:185–201

Gerleman, S. L. 1987. An observational study of small-group instruction in fourth-grade mathematics classrooms. *Elem. Sch. J.* 88:3–28

Getzels, J. W., Thelen, H. A. 1960. The classroom as a unique social system. In *National Society for the Study of Education Yearbook,* ed. N. B. Henry, *Vol. 59.* Chicago: Univ. Chicago Press

Goodlad, J. I. 1984. *A Place Called School.* New York: McGraw-Hill

Grant, L., Rothenberg, J. 1986. The social enhancement of ability differences: interactions in first- and second-grade reading groups. *Elem. Sch. J.* 87:29–49

Graybeal, S. S., Stodolsky, S. S. 1985. Peer work groups in elementary schools. *Am. J. Educ.* 93:409–28

Green, J. L., Harker, J. 1982. Gaining access to learning: communicative, contextual, and academic demands. See Cooper et al 1982, pp. 183–222

Green, J. L., Wallat, C. 1981. Mapping instructional conversations—a sociolinguistic ethnography. See Erickson & Schultz 1981

Green, J. L., Weade, R., Graham, K. 1988. Lesson construction and student participation: a sociolinguistic analysis. See Bloom & Theodorou 1988, pp. 11–48

Gump, P. V. 1967. *The Classroom Behavior Setting: Its Nature and Relation to Student Behavior.* Final Report, Project No. 5-0334. Washington, DC: US Off. Educ. Coop. Res. Branch

Gump, P. V. 1980. The school as a social situation. *Annu. Rev. Psychol.* 31:553–82

Gump, P. V. 1982. School settings and their keeping. In *Helping Teachers Manage Classrooms,* ed. D. L. Duke. Alexandria, VA: Assoc. Supervision Curric. Dev.

Gump, P. V. 1987. School and classroom environments. In *Handbook of Environmental Psychology,* ed. D. Stokols, I. Altman. New York: John Wiley & Sons

Gumperz, J. J. 1976. Language, communication, and public negotiation. In *Anthropology and the Public Interest,* ed. P. R. Sanday. New York: Academic

Gumperz, J. J. 1981. Conversational inference and classroom learning. See Erickson & Schultz 1981, pp. 3–24

Hallinan, M. T., Sorensen, A. B. 1985. Ability grouping and student friendships. *Am. Educ. Res. J.* 22:485–99

Hallinan, M. T., Teixeira, R. A. 1987a. Students' interracial friendships: individual characteristics, structural effects, and racial differences. *Am. J. Educ.* 95:563–83

Hallinan, M. T., Teixeira, R. A. 1987b. Opportunities and constraints: black-white differences in the formation of interracial friendships. *Child Dev.* 58:1358–71

Hallinan, M. T., Tuma, N. B. 1978. Classroom effects on change in children's friendships. *Sociol. Educ.* 51:270–82

Hatch, J. A. 1986. Alone in a crowd: analysis of covert interactions in a kindergarten. Presented at the Annu. Meet. Am. Educ. Res. Assoc., San Francisco. ERIC Doc. Reprod. Serv. No. 272 278

Hawkins, J., Homolsky, M., Heide, P. 1984. *Paired Problem Solving in a Computer Context. Technical Report No. 33.* New York: Bank Street Coll. Educ., Cent. Child. Technol.

Hawkins, J., Sheingold, K., Gearhart, M., Berger, C. 1982. Microcomputers in schools: impact on the social life of elementary classrooms. *J. Appl. Dev. Psychol.* 3:361–73

Heap, J. L. 1989. Collaborative practices during word processing in a first grade classroom. In *Locating Learning: Ethnographic Perspectives on Classroom Research,* ed. C. Emihovich. Norwood, NJ: Ablex

Hoetker, J., Ahlbrand, W. P. Jr. 1969. The persistence of the recitation. *Am. Educ. Res. J.* 6:145–67

Hymes, D. 1974. *Foundations in Sociolinguistics.* Philadelphia: Univ. Penn. Press

Jackson, P. W. 1968. *Life in Classrooms.* New York: Holt, Rinehart and Winston

Johnson, D. W., Johnson, R. T. 1987. *Learning Together and Alone.* Englewood Cliffs, NJ: Prentice-Hall. 2nd ed.

Johnson, D. W., Johnson, R. T. 1981a. Effects of cooperative and individualistic

learning experiences on interethnic interaction. *J. Educ. Psychol.* 73:444–49

Johnson, R. T., Johnson, D. W. 1981b. Building friendships between handicapped and nonhandicapped students: effects of cooperative and individualistic instruction. *Am. Educ. Res. J.* 18:415–23

Johnson, D. W., Johnson, R., Maruyama, G. 1983. Interdependence and interpersonal attraction among heterogeneous and homogeneous individuals: a theoretical formulation and a meta-analysis of the research. *Rev. Educ. Res.* 53:5–54

Kagan, S. 1985. Dimensions of cooperative classroom structures. In *Learning to Cooperate, Cooperating to Learn,* ed. R. Slavin, S. Sharan, S. Kagan, R. Hertz Lazarowitz, C. Webb, R. Schmuck, pp. 67–96. New York: Plenum

Kagan, S., Zahn, G. L., Widaman, K. F., Schwarzwald, J., Tyrrell, G. 1985. Classroom structural bias: impact of cooperative and competitive classroom structures on cooperative and competitive individuals and groups. See Kagan 1985, pp. 277–312

Kounin, J. S. 1970. *Discipline and Group Management in Classrooms.* New York: Holt, Rinehart and Winston

Kounin, J. S., Friesen, W. V., Norton, A. E. 1966. Managing emotionally disturbed children in regular classrooms. *J. Educ. Psychol.* 2:129–35

Kounin, J. S., Sherman, L. 1979. School environments as behavior settings. *Theor. Pract.* 14:145–51

Lazarowitz, R., Baird, J. H., Hertz-Lazarowitz, R., Jenkins, J. 1985. The effects of modified jigsaw on achievement, classroom social climate, and self-esteem in high-school science classes. See Kagan 1985, pp. 231–248

Lazarus, P., Homer, S. L. 1980. Sharing time in kindergarten: a study of the relationship between structure and content. Presented at the Annu. Meet. Rocky Mountain Educ. Res. Assoc., Las Cruces, New Mexico. ERIC Doc. Reprod. No. ED 194 930

Lew, M., Mesch, D., Johnson, D. W., Johnson, R. 1986. Positive interdependence, academic and collaborative-skills group contingencies, and isolated students. *Am. Educ. Res. J.* 23:476–88

Lockheed, M. E., Harris, A. M. 1984. Cross-sex collaborative learning in elementary classrooms. *Am. Educ. Res. J.* 21:275–94

Lockheed, M. E., Harris, A. M., Nemceff, W. P. 1983. Sex and social influence: Does sex function as a status characteristic in mixed-sex groups of children? *J. Educ. Psychol.* 75:877–88

Madden, N. A., Slavin, R. E. 1983. Effects of cooperative learning on the social acceptance of mainstreamed academically handicapped students. *J. Spec. Educ.* 17:171–82

Marshall, H. H., Weinstein, R. S. 1984. Classroom factors affecting students' self-evaluations: an interactional model. *Rev. Educ. Res.* 54:301–25

Marshall, H. H., Weinstein, R. S. 1986. Classroom context of student-perceived differential teacher treatment. *J. Educ. Psychol.* 78:441–53

McDermott, R. P. 1977. Social relations as contexts for learning in school. *Harvard Educ. Rev.* 47:198–213

McHoul, A. 1978. The organization of turns at formal talk in the classroom. *Lang. Soc.* 7:183–213

Mehan, H. 1978. Structuring school structure. *Harvard Educ. Rev.* 48:32–64

Mehan, H. 1979. *Learning Lessons: Social Organization in a Classroom.* Cambridge, MA: Harvard Univ. Press

Mehan, H. 1980. The competent student. *Anthropol. Educ. Q.* 11:131–52

Merritt, M. 1982a. Distributing and directing attention in primary classrooms. See Cooper et al 1982, pp. 223–44

Merritt, M. 1982b. Repeats and reformulations in primary classrooms as windows of the nature of talk engagement. *Discourse Processes* 5:127–45

Michaels, S. 1981. "Sharing time": children's narrative styles and differential access to literacy. *Lang. Soc.* 10:423–42

Michaels, S. 1984. Listening and responding: hearing the logic in children's classroom narratives. *Theor. Pract.* 23:218–24

Michaels, S. 1986. Narrative presentations: an oral preparation for literacy with first graders. See Collins 1986, pp. 94–116

Michaels, S., Foster, M. 1985. Peer-peer learning: evidence from a student-run sharing time. In *Observing the Language Learner*, ed. A. Jaggar, M. T. Smith-Burke. Urbana, Illinois: Int. Reading Assoc. Natl. Council of Teachers of English

Mitman, A. L., Lash, A. A. 1988. Students' perceptions of their academic standing and classroom behavior. *Elem. Sch. J.* 89:55–68

Morine-Dershimer, G. 1983. Instructional strategy and the "creation" of classroom status. *Am. Educ. Res. J.* 20:45–661

Nelson-LeGall, S., DeCooke, P. A. 1987. Same-sex and cross-sex help exchanges in the classroom. *J. Educ. Psychol.* 79:67–71

Nelson-Le Gall, S., Glor-Scheib, S. 1986. Academic help-seeking and peer relations in school. *Contemp. Educ. Psychol.* 11:187–93

Olson, C. P. 1988. Computing environments in elementary classrooms. *Child. Environ. Q.* 5:39–50

Palincsar, A., Brown, A. 1985. Reciprocal

teaching: a means to a meaningful end. See Au et al 1985, pp. 299–310

Papert, S. 1980. *Mindstorms.* New York: Basic Books

Peterson, P. L., Janicki, T. C., Swing, S. R. 1981. Ability x treatment interaction effects on children's learning in large-group and small-group approaches. *Am. Educ. Res. J.* 18:453–73

Peterson, P. L., Wilkinson, L. C., Spinelli, F., Swing, S. R. 1984. Merging the process-product and the sociolinguistic paradigm: research on small-group processes. See Cohen 1984, pp. 126–52

Philips, S. 1972. Participant structures and communicative competence: Warm Springs children in community and classroom. In *Functions of Language in the Classroom*, ed. C. Cazden, V. John, D. Hymes. New York: Teachers College Press

Rizzo, T. A. 1989. *Friendship Development among Children in School.* Norwood, NJ: Ablex

Roby, T. W. 1988. Models of discussion. See Farrar 1988, pp. 163–91

Rosenbaum, J. E. 1984. The social organization of instructional grouping. See Cohen 1984, pp. 53–68

Rosenholtz, S. J., Simpson, C. 1984a. Classroom organization and student stratification. *Elem. Sch. J.* 85:21–37

Rosenholtz, S. J., Simpson, C. 1984b. The formation of ability conceptions: developmental trend or social construction? *Rev. Educ. Res.* 54:31–63

Rosenshine, B. V. 1980. How time is spent in elementary classrooms. In *Time to Learn*, ed. C. Denham, A. Lieberman. Washington, DC: Natl. Inst. Educ.

Ross, R. P. 1984. Classroom segments: the structuring of school time. See Burns 1984, pp. 69–87

Rothenberg, J. 1979. Ecological theory of teaching. Task structure analyses of three fourth grade classroom instructional social systems. Far West Lab. Educ. Res. Dev., San Francisco. ERIC Doc. Reprod. Serv. No. 186 398

Sharan, S. 1980. Cooperative learning in small groups: recent methods and effects on achievement, attitudes, and ethnic relations. *Rev. Educ. Res.* 50:241–71

Sharan, S., Kussell, P., Hertz-Lazarowitz, R., Bejarano, Y., Raviv, S., Sharan, Y. 1984. *Cooperative Learning in the Classroom: Research in Desegregated Schools.* Hillsdale, NJ: Erlbaum

Sharan, S., Sharan, Y. 1976. *Small-Group Teaching.* Englewood Cliffs, NJ: Educ. Technol. Publ.

Sharan, Y., Sharan, S. 1989–1990. Group investigation expands cooperative learning. *Educ. Leadership* 47:17–21

Sheingold, K., Hawkins, J., Char, C. 1984. "I'm the thinkist, you're the typist": the interaction of technology and the social life of classrooms. *J. Soc. Issues* 40:49–61

Shulman, L. S. 1986. Paradigms and research programs in the study of teaching: a contemporary perspective. See Cazden 1986, pp. 3–36

Shultz, J., Florio, S. 1979. Stop and freeze: the negotiation of social and physical space in a kindergarten/first grade classroom. *Anthropol. Educ. Q.* 10:166–81

Shuy, R. 1988. Identifying dimensions of classroom language. See Bloom & Theodorou 1988, pp. 113–34

Sieber, R. T. 1979. Classmates as workmates: informal peer activity in the elementary school. *Anthropol. Educ. Q.* 10:207–35

Simpson, C., Rosenholtz, S. J. 1986. Classroom structure and the social construction of ability. In *Handbook of Theory and Research for the Sociology of Education*, ed. J. G. Richardson, pp. 113–38. New York: Greenwood Press

Slavin, R. E. 1983. *Cooperative Learning*. New York: Longman

Slavin, R. E. 1985. An introduction to cooperative learning research. See Kagan 1985, pp. 5–15

Slavin, R. E. 1990. *Cooperative Learning: Theory, Research, and Practice*. Englewood Cliffs, NJ: Prentice Hall

Stodolsky, S. S. 1984. Frameworks for studying instructional processes in peer work groups. See Cohen 1984, pp. 107–124

Stodolsky, S. S. 1988. *The Subject Matters: Classroom Activity in Math and Social Studies*. Chicago: Univ. Chicago Press

Stodolsky, S. S., Ferguson, T. L., Wimpelberg, K. 1981. The recitation persists, but what does it look like? *J. Curric. Stud.* 13:121–30

Swing, S. R., Peterson, P. L. 1982. The relationship of student ability and small-group interaction to student achievement. *Am. Educ. Res. J.* 19:259–74

Warring, D., Johnson, D. W., Maruyama, G., Johnson, R. 1985. Impact of different types of cooperative learning on cross-ethnic and cross-sex relationships. *J. Educ. Psychol.* 77:53–59

Weade, R., Evertson, C. E. 1988. The construction of lessons in effective and less effective classrooms. *Teaching & Teacher Educ.* 4:189–213

Weade, R., Green, J. L. 1985. Talking to learn: social and academic requirements for classroom participation. *Peabody J. Educ.* 62:6–19

Webb, N. M. 1980. A process-outcome analysis of learning in group and individual settings. *Educ. Psychol.* 15:69–83

Webb, N. M. 1982a. Group composition, group interaction and achievement in cooperative small groups. *J. Educ. Psychol.* 74:475–84

Webb, N. M. 1982b. Peer interaction and learning in cooperative small groups. *J. Educ. Psychol.* 74:642–55

Webb, N. M. 1984. Sex differences in interaction and achievement in cooperative small groups. *J. Educ. Psychol.* 76:33–44

Webb, N. M. 1985. Student interaction and learning in small groups: a research summary. See Kagan 1985, pp. 147–172

Webb, N. M., Cullian, L. K. 1983. Group interaction and achievement in small groups: stability over time. *Am. Educ. Res. J.* 20:411–23

Webb, N. M., Kenderski, C. M. 1984. Student interaction and learning in small-group and whole-class settings. See Cohen 1984, pp. 153–170

Weinstein, C. S. 1979. The physical environment of the school: a review of the research. *Rev. Educ. Res.* 49:577–610

Weinstein, R. S. 1984. The teaching of reading and children's awareness of teacher expectations. In *The Contexts of School-Based Literacy*, ed. T. E. Raphael, pp. 233–52. New York: Random House

Weinstein, R. S., Marshall, H. H., Sharp, L., Botkin, M. 1987. Pygmalion and the student: age and classroom differences in children's awareness of teacher expectations. *Child Dev.* 58:1079–93

Wilkinson, L. C. 1982. Introduction: a sociolinguistic approach to communicating in the classroom. See Cooper et al, pp. 3–12

Wilkinson, L. C., Calculator, S. 1982a. Requests and responses in peer-directed reading groups. *Am. Educ. Res. J.* 19:107–20

Wilkinson, L. C., Calculator, S. 1982b. Effective speakers: students' use of language to request and obtain information and action in the classroom. See Cooper et al, pp. 85–100

Wilkinson, L. C., Spinelli, F. 1983. Using requests effectively in peer-directed instructional groups. *Am. Educ. Res. J.* 20:479–501

Wood, D., Wood, H. 1988. Questioning versus student initiative. See Farrar 1988, pp. 280–305

Wright, J. L., Samaras, A. S. 1986. Play worlds and microworlds. In *Young Children and Microcomputers*, ed. P. F. Campbell, G. G. Fein, pp. 73–86. Englewood Cliffs, NJ: Prentice-Hall

Ziegler, S. 1981. The effectiveness of cooperating learning teams for increasing cross-ethnic friendship: additional evidence. *Hum. Organ.* 40:264–68

Annu. Rev. Psychol. 1991. 42:527–61

SOCIAL COGNITION

David J. Schneider

Department of Psychology, Rice University, Houston, Texas 77251

KEY WORDS: Categorization, accuracy, person perception, attribution, trait

---

CONTENTS

INTRODUCTION

This is the fifth biennial review of the social cognition literature (with an additional two chapters devoted specifically to attribution) covering the last decade. It is time to think about where we have been and where we are going.

0066-4308/91/0201-0527$02.00

The State of the Field

Over the last decade social cognition has become a dominant, perhaps the dominant, perspective in social psychology. It occupies a major position in developmental, personality, industrial-organizational, and clinical areas as well. The published work in the area continues to be a blend of various issues and methodologies. I begin by briefly reviewing the state of the classic issues of the past decade. I then review more intensively some promising directions that may see us well into the 1990s.

ATTRIBUTION   Despite the field's age, attribution research continues to be undertaken in quantity. Theoretical advances and renewed attention to the behavior-trait link are examined below. Much recent attribution research has been oriented toward applications, including attempts to explain relationships (Bradbury & Fincham 1990), depression (Abramson et al 1989), and attribution of responsibility (Karlovac & Darley 1988; Alicke & Davis 1989), to name three traditional concerns.

MENTAL SIMULATION   While offerings from and membership in The-Bias-of-The-Month Club decreased substantially in the last part of the decade, there continues to be major interest in social judgment, reasoning, and heuristics as well as cognitive bias. Recently, investigators have paid particular attention to simulation of mental events and counterfactual reasoning in assessing the impact of real and imagined events (Dunning & Parpal 1989; Gavanski & Wells 1989; Wells & Gavanski 1989; Miller et al 1989).

MEMORY   Memory has been the central totem of modern social cognition. Lately less effort has been expended in testing a stream of new box-and-arrow memory models (see Watkins 1990 for criticisms of the proliferation of memory models) and more attention has been paid to explaining recognizable phenomena of the social world. Attempts have been made to explain how we represent conversations, for example (Holtgraves et al 1989, Wyer et al 1990), and how we remember the temporal order of events (Fuhrman & Wyer 1988). Research on how affect, mood, and emotion are represented in memory increased over the decade but may now be leveling off or decreasing (Johnson & Magaro 1987; Forgas et al 1988; Rholes et al 1987). Attention to the effects of goals and sets on memory has likewise increased (e.g. Carpenter 1988; Lassiter 1988; Lassiter et al 1988; Devine et al 1989 for recent versions). The last *Annual Review* chapter on this topic (Sherman et al 1989) reviews memory research in more illuminating detail.

STEREOTYPING   Stereotype research has continued along by now familiar lines. The effects of categorization on stereotyping have been a major concern, especially the attribution of characteristics and the distribution of characteristics to out-groups (Linville et al 1989). The steady stream of research on the illusory correlation approach suggests that salient traits are overascribed to salient groups. Factors such as mood incongruence (Mackie et al 1989) and arousal (Kim & Baron 1988) that might be expected to increase the use of knowledge structures also foster illusory correlation. Motivation effects induced by group membership (Schaller & Maass 1989) and self-reference (Sanbonmatsu et al 1987a) also can play a role along with purely cognitive factors. One important line of work suggests that while illusory correlation for groups tends to reflect differential association of salient (usually infrequent) stimuli with salient (often minority) groups, for individuals illusory correlations tend to reflect overassignment of frequent traits to salient individuals (Sanbonmatsu et al 1987a,b); this reflects differences in how information about individuals and groups is processed. Hamilton & Sherman (1989) and Mullen & Johnson (1990) have provided recent reviews of illusory correlation effects.

THE SELF   A striking growth industry during the past decade has been research on the self. One tradition in the 1980s conceived of the self as a knowledge structure, influential because it processed information about itself and others. However, during the past three or four years scholars have grown skeptical about the self's privileged status in the information processing domain (Higgins et al 1988; Greenwald & Banaji 1989; Klein & Loftus 1988; Klein et al 1989). Work on self-attribution and the basis of self-knowledge has clearly been declining. On the other hand, one issue honored by decades of research interest, the interaction of motivational and cognitive factors in the maintenance of the self concept through selective interaction and information processing, has continued to be a strong focus (Esses 1989; Kunda & Sanitioso 1989; Swann et al 1988, 1989; Tesser et al 1989; Wenzlaff & Prohaska 1989). One variation on the theme of self that has intuitive appeal and possibly extraordinary importance is work on autobiographical memories (Ross 1989).

MENTAL CONTROL   The extent to which our cognitive processes are automatic continues to be a major focus of social cognition research. It is now clear that degree of automaticity involves many dimensions; Bargh (1989), Logan (1989), and Uleman (1989) have reviewed this work. Thought suppression has also been studied—especially its effects on mental and physical health (Wegner 1989; Wegner & Schneider 1989; Pennebaker 1989). Will and will-power seem destined for a return engagement in social and personality psychology after an absence of a century.

Some Criticisms

EXTERNAL CRITICISMS   Some observers feel that social cognition's dominance of social psychology has been greedy. To some extent this criticism is
generic; whatever perspective is dominant in a field at a given time inevitably
skews that field, and there are bound to be those who feel abandoned on the
long tail of the distribution. Nonetheless, social cognition in its modern guise
has clearly led to a downplaying of traditional social psychological variables.
Modern social cognition tends to focus on intrapsychic cognitive processes
and places little emphasis on the social context or behavioral implications of
these processes. Until fairly recently few scholars have attempted to incorporate motivational variables into social cognition, although these variables have traditionally been at the heart of the social psychology enterprise.
Others object that research in social cognition today is often driven more by
model testing than by the traditional social psychological efforts to explain
intuitively interesting and immediately important social phenomena.

A strong case can be made that what such critics reproach is actually a set
of virtues. Social cognition breathed new life into a social psychology that had
lost direction in the early 1970s and was being battered by something then
called the "crisis" in social psychology. At its best, social cognition has given
us new insights into how people think about their social worlds, and it has
done so in a way that stresses the continuities with other areas of psychology.
But there is a cost: Social cognition can seem sterile and bloodless as much of
the richness of the everyday social world gets processed and abstracted out.

This is part of a broader problem. For example, Neisser (1978, 1988) has
been sharply critical of laboratory memory research for ignoring seemingly
important everyday memory phenomena. Critics of that position (e.g. Banaji
& Crowder 1989; Roediger 1990) argue that laboratory research provides a
perfectly adequate basis for understanding everyday memory, and that we
best find our way toward enlightenment by using integrated and well-tested
theory. Smith (1990) has made similar points with regard to social cognition
research. This isn't the place to lay out the rights and wrongs of each
perspective, but allow me to suggest the following. Let those who prefer
model testing try a little harder to fulfill the promise of their approach by
linking their efforts to the rich world just beyond their computer screens. And
let those who consider such models vacuous think back to the 1960s and
1970s when social psychology was badly infected with too-cute experiments
based on too-cute ideas with too-cute titles that ultimately produced little
insight and no theory. Can't we find a middle ground?

AN INTERNAL DEBATE   The criticisms from without have been accompanied by an internal tension about the definition and scope of social cognition. The tension is between what we might call hard and soft approaches to

social cognition.[1] Social cognition existed long before what we have come to call the cognitive revolution. Social psychologists have been studying the perception and cognition of people and social events at least since the 1920s and 1930s and were doing so when the rest of psychology hadn't yet rediscovered the mind. Social psychology has always had a strong cognitive flavor. In the early adolescence of modern social psychology during the 1950s person perception was a well-recognized specialty. The focus was on phenomenology (content of perceptions of others), normative questions of accuracy and adequacy, stimulus-driven processing, and the structure of impressions and attitudes. This traditional approach, however, had a rather soft focus and was really a set of vaguely related issues rather than a theory or approach. This soft social cognition tended to use structural explanations, had weak models, used limited methods, and often described conscious processing rather than examining underlying processes.

In the 1960s processing of information moved to center stage with the development of attribution models, although conceptualization of the processing mechanics was primitive by today's standards. In the 1970s a passionate mating of traditional person perception problems with the models and especially methodologies imported from cognitive psychology produced the hybrid hard approach to social cognition, which became less an area of focus than an approach or perspective (Sherman et al 1989; Wyer & Srull 1989). In extremely broad terms, traditional structural, content, and normative questions have evolved into concerns about processing. In hard social cognition, explanations tend to involve microprocessing. In its steady pursuit of underlying mechanism, hard social cognition has little interest in phenomenology and conscious experience. Indeed computer simulation is used increasingly as a way to test social cognition models (Ostrom 1988). To paraphrase William James, hard social cognition means business and not chivalry.

SOME ASSUMPTIONS: THE PROCESS MODEL   This newer, hard social cognition perspective works with several implicit but strong assumptions. While not all proponents of the newer social cognition endorse them all, these assumptions have collectively guided much research in the area.

Process is general   First, since process is general and fundamental it is detached from any particular content; indeed there is little to distinguish social cognition from other forms of cognition. While no one would argue that social and physical stimuli are exactly alike, in practice little attention has been paid to how people and their behavior differ from chairs, triangles, and other

[1]While the basic distinction is well recognized, there is little agreement on its precise nature. The present account falls far short of dealing with all the issues. Wyer & Srull (1989), Devine & Ostrom (1988) and Ostrom (1990) offer alternative perspectives.

physical stimuli. The generality of process also has some methodological implications. Because processing is assumed to be relatively context free, most research involves informationally impoverished and novel stimuli.

Information processing stages   Second, the processing of information follows a defined sequence, and in that sequence memory has pride of place. Indeed memory is such a fundamental part of the processing of information that memory measures are crucial means of accessing underlying processes and structure. The definition and measurement of distinct processes can also be addressed through reaction-time measures. Whether memory or reaction-time measures are used, ecological validity for such measures is not assumed. Such measures are used as probes into mental process and structure, though they are not necessarily important features of the everyday processing of information.

Knowledge structures are crucial   Third, the encoding and storage of information are affected by knowledge structures. Thus incoming information is transformed—perhaps as early in processing as the recognition stage, but certainly by the point at which the information gets plugged into a memory system. Information processing is fundamentally "top-down" or schema driven, in part because the human cognitive system, like computing machines, is resource limited. We cannot attend to or take in every detail of every piece of information that comes our way. We are cognitive misers (Fiske & Taylor 1984). Thus our minds prefer abstract representations of information, representations that presumably preserve important and ignore unimportant detail. There is little room in such models for the messy content of our mental lives.

Bias is crucial   Consequently our processing of information is error prone. In part this occurs because we compress information too much and lose important details. In addition, our minds are strongly biased toward preservation of existing cognitive structures, and hence we tend to interpret and remember information as consistent with what we already know. Finally, we tend to use cognitive shortcuts or heuristics that inhibit the full use of whatever knowledge we can bring to bear.

The Rest of the Chapter

While hard social cognition has sometimes been overbearing in its evangelical enthusiasm, we have simply learned too much and been too excited by what we have learned in the last decade to turn back. Nonetheless, some of the basic assumptions of the processing approach have been examined with a critical eye of late, and so the rest of this review focuses on selected reappraisals.

HOW ABSTRACT ARE KNOWLEDGE STRUCTURES?

Social cognition researchers have been heavily addicted to the study of knowledge structures (called variously schemata, scripts, frames, world knowledge, stereotypes) in information processing. Social psychologists have long posited abstract mental constructs, whether attitudes or schemata, that summarize past experience and guide subsequent behavior. It has been clear to social psychologists for 50 years and to cognitive psychologists for at least 25 that past experiences, needs, values, and goals affect the seeking and molding of incoming information.

Thus a major assumption of classic social cognition is that because our information processing apparatus is resource limited we develop highly abstract knowledge structures. However, in recent years it has become clearer that our information processing systems may be constrained less by resource limitations than by information limitations (Medin 1988). Neither the structure of what we know nor the processing of what we do not yet know can be determined by requirements of simplicity and abstractness.

At least four kinds of questions have been raised in this context: How abstract are our cognitive representations? Under what circumstances are knowledge structures overwhelmed by incoming data? Why are people and behaviors categorized one way as opposed to another? How abstract are process schemata such as attribution models?

How Are Categories Represented?

One of the major cognitive tasks humans face is that of placing things, events, and people into categories. Modern cognitive psychology strives to understand the nature of such categories (Medin 1989). Two kinds of category model have dominated social cognition.

PROTOTYPE MODELS   Traditional *prototype* models assume that for any given category (e.g. professor) the cognizer stores a single prototype representation that contains attributes (tweedy, politically liberal, otherworldly, etc). This prototype is assumed to be some average of instances so classified, and may or may not correspond closely to any existing member of the category. These prototypes are knowledge structures independent of—abstracted from—context. So, for example, the prototype of the professor does not easily allow for information about particular circumstances in which individual professors might be arrogant or helpful.

EXEMPLAR MODELS   *Exemplar* models (e.g. Hintzman 1986; Nosofsky 1986), on the other hand, assume that individuals store representations of instances, and that judgments about new stimuli are made by comparing them with these known exemplars. Some exemplar models (Hintzman 1986) specify that every instance is stored whereas others (Linville et al 1989) assume that somewhat abstracted types can also be used as exemplars. Attributes are stored at the individual exemplar level: Professor A is happy, tweedy, liberal, and kind; Professor B is tweedy, short, liberal, arrogant, etc. Exemplar models put no premium on cognitive efficiency, allowing that the same attributes are stored repeatedly with multiple exemplars.

Although exemplar models require a complex representation, the representations are concrete rather than abstract. According to this model, categorization is based on similarity to retrieved exemplars and not to the abstract prototype. Thus a person will be classified as extroverted if she behaves like other extroverted people the perceiver can retrieve from memory. In addition, even category parameters such as the mean and distribution of various category-relevant features can be computed from retrieval of stored representations (Linville et al 1989).

In a seminal paper on stereotypes, Rothbart & John (1985) argued that in making judgments about groups we give special weight to good exemplars. Therefore people who are not good exemplars (e.g. the academically motivated fraternity member) are doomed to having their behaviors count for little in judgments about their groups. Rothbart & Lewis (1988) have confirmed that stereotype-inconsistent behaviors have a greater impact in changing the stereotype when they are exhibited by otherwise good exemplars. So the tweedy, old-car-driving professor who espouses conservative causes will do more to change the stereotype of professors as liberal than will the conservative professor in an expensive Italian suit and sports car.

HAVING IT BOTH WAYS   Surely both prototypes and exemplars are used in social cognition at different times and in different ways. Smith (1990) has argued that exemplars should be favored when perceivers try to form impressions of individuals rather than groups, whereas attempts to summarize or remember groups should favor prototypes. Exemplars should also be favored when the perceiver approaches people without prior stereotypes (Smith & Zarate 1990) or thinks about in-group features rather than those of some out-group (Judd & Park 1988). People store information about both groups (close to a prototype) and the people (exemplars) comprising them (Park & Hastie 1987; Judd & Park 1988), a fact with important implications for stereotyping. Smith's (1990) discussion of these and other issues surrounding the prototype vs exemplar controversy is excellent.

THE STRUCTURE OF CATEGORIES   Social categorization operates at various levels. For example, in a social situation an individual may observe behaviors and comprehend them in terms of his schemata for behaviors: "Those are acts of kindness." In due course he may implicitly decide what sort of a person performed that behavior: "That's a kind, generous, optimistic woman." The behavior must be encoded in terms of specific traits (Srull & Wyer 1989), goals (Read & Miller 1989), or other dispositions. Under at least some circumstances these already abstracted behavioral representations or trait attributions will then be encoded in terms of some higher organizational principle and attached to persons or situations: "She is kind to those who are less fortunate than she because she is a deeply religious person." We may ultimately attribute this behavior to a group generating what we usually call a stereotype. Relevant groups and subgroups may be cognitively arranged in various ways.

Researchers have labored to find a single memory structure capable of storing all such categories, but it now seems probable that humans have multiple ways of storing information. Why does it matter whether information about others and their behaviors is represented as "behavior category" or in the form "type of person"? One reason is that a lot depends on how readily we can access various kinds of information. For example, if one has a favor to ask of Mr. Hoo and therefore seeks to determine whether Mr. Hoo is a kind person, does one check Mr. Hoo's characteristics against memory representations of kind behaviors, or does one access representations of kind persons? In addition, knowing how we encode and store information about the social world may enable us to determine how and where mistakes of processing are made.

How Is Category Relevant Information Processed?

Cognitive psychologists have long sought to establish whether cognitive processing is predominantly "top-down" or "bottom-up" ("theory-driven" or "data-driven"). While no one argues that theory dominates data in every situation and for every cognitive task, most social cognition research during the last decade or so has been designed to show the dominance of knowledge structures.

Debate on this issue during the 1980s was stimulated in part by Locksley's research (Locksley et al 1980), which seemed to show that at least for gender, stereotypes guided inferences only in the absence of individuating behavioral information. Two strong theoretical traditions met head-on at this issue. On the one hand, schema and stereotype theories assume that expectations based on knowledge structures dominate; on the other hand, abundant research (Borgida & Brekke 1981) shows that base-rate information (analogous to stereotype information) is often under-utilized in favor of even undiagnostic individuating information—i.e. gender stereotypes do not always greatly influence performance evaluations of men and women (Swim et al 1989). A variety of circumstances affect whether stereotypes or data predominate. For example, the relative diagnosticity of stereotype and attribute information affects their use (Krueger & Rothbart 1988), and information that is not diagnostic for the rating at hand may still be used if judges think it is generally diagnostic (Hilton & Fein 1989). The relative effects of abstract and individuating information may also differ depending on the type of judgment required (Glick et al 1988).

THE PROCESSING SEQUENCE   Some researchers have examined the whole information processing sequence in an attempt to determine the points where prior structures and incoming data play their different roles. Brewer (1988) and Fiske & Neuberg (1990) have argued for a sequence of stages. While the Brewer and Fiske models differ in important ways in terms of cognitive representations and the effects of motives and goals (see Fiske 1988), they agree broadly on the sequence of stages, the primacy of categorization, and the importance of category- (or stereotype-) based inferences. I outline the process from Fiske's perspective here.

When first we encounter the stimulus person we categorize him/her immediately and without reflection in terms of some gender, race, occupational, or other category. We disregard many people who come our way (Rodin 1987) and do not think about them further. However, for people who attract our attention, if available behavioral data match our initial categorization attributes we make category-based (or stereotypic) attributions and inferences—e.g. we assume a male we've categorized as a jock to be stupid. If these inferences are violated by data, however, we try to recategorize—e.g. place the stimulus person in a subcategory such as "smart jock" or "student athlete." If such alternative categorizations are belied by data, we try to fashion an impression piecemeal. Thus schemata and behavioral information interact in various ways, but schematic processing dominates unless clearly contradicted by behavioral data. This approach suggests how schema and behaviors may play different roles at different points in the process.

CATEGORY VS ATTRIBUTE PROCESSING   Several factors affect the interplay between category and attribute processing. Category information is likely to be most important when categories are salient, particularly early in the information processing sequence (Pavelchak 1989). When attributes are perceived to be inconsistent with the category, attention to and use of attributes increase (Fiske et al 1987). The goals of the perceiver also play a role. We process attributes to a greater extent for people on whom we depend, presumably because we seek to predict their behavior more accurately (Neuberg & Fiske 1987). When people are interdependent, whether in a competitive (Ruscher & Fiske 1990) or cooperative (Erber & Fiske 1984) relationship, they are highly motivated to attend to inconsistent attributes and thus are likely to encode inconsistent behaviors dispositionally.

Kruglanski (1989b) has argued that a great need for structure can lock a person into a preferred or existing way of looking at the world. Time pressures and task demands may also inhibit attribute-based processing, simply because such processing takes more time (Bodenhausen & Lichtenstein 1987). On the other hand, needs for accuracy promote attribute processing (Neuberg 1989). Tetlock's theory of accountability argues that when people have to justify their positions to others (high accountability) they will work harder at integrating information and rely less on existing cognitive structures (Tetlock & Kim 1987).

Task type is also important. For example, Zuroff (1989) exposed subjects to the conversation of a woman described as having either conventional or "liberated" gender attitudes. Subjects reported subsequently that they had heard more masculine traits in the "liberated" woman's conversation, a trend suggesting the operation of gender stereotypes. However, when subjects were asked to estimate the frequency of particular adjectives in the woman's discourse, their judgments were responsive to the actual frequencies and were not affected by stereotypes. Catrambone & Markus (1987) have argued that our self-schemata exert their greatest impact on the way we perceive others when we make inferences about them; by contrast, when we focus on the actual behaviors of others our perceptions are less affected by self-schemata.

MEMORY EFFECTS   Do people best remember information consistent or inconsistent with their schemata? Pure schema theories have trouble accounting for enhanced recall of schema-inconsistent material. The usual explanation of this phenomenon is that schema-inconsistent material receives special attention during encoding, which establishes stronger links to other material stored in memory (Srull & Wyer 1989). However, it has also been suggested (Ruble & Stangor 1986; Higgins & Bargh 1987) that enhanced recall for inconsistent information would not be found when people have strong expectancies and schemata, a prediction that has been confirmed (Stangor & Ruble 1989).

THEORY AND DATA REVISITED   The question of whether our perceptions are dictated primarily by stimuli or by our existing knowledge structures is unanswerable. Every stimulus is affected by basic knowledge, previous experiences, language, and so on. For their part, schemata require a push from the external world and are guided by incoming information. Surely whether "theory" or "data" drives social cognition depends on goals, situations, familiarity and salience of stimuli, and perhaps even the physical state of the perceiver.

Choice of Categories

A given behavior can be seen as helpful or condescending, hostile or kidding, depending upon circumstances. Persons, too, can be variously categorized. Consider the case of Pete Rose. Shall we classify him as a male, a white person, a white male, an athlete, a typical jock, a baseball player, a white baseball player, a liar, a gambler, a man with a bad haircut, a father, a jockish father, a divorced man, a remarried divorced man, a brash and cocky person, or a future Hall-of-Famer?

CUES FOR CLASSIFICATION   I discuss behavior classification below, but for now consider what determines how people are classified and categorized. Surprisingly few data have been reported that bear on what cues we use for classification. Readily perceptible and highly correlated cues tell us a person is a woman, for example, but which do we consider most diagnostic: hair length, facial conformation, body shape, gait, voice tone? How do we determine that a person is mentally ill, a professor, gay, likely to be helpful, retarded? Needless to say, these classifications have social significance, and all are prone to error.

AUTOMATIC CATEGORIZATION   It is probably useful to consider certain classification processes automatic. These occur without conscious effort and may be uninhibitable; they produce categorization based on immediately obvious cues, such as race, age, and gender (McArthur 1982; Brewer 1988). Such categorizations are usually well practiced, and their use is supported (indeed often demanded) by the larger culture. Each of us probably has additional categories used so often that they have become readily accessible (Bargh 1989; Higgins 1989) and are thus used fairly automatically.

METHODS FOR STUDYING IMPLICIT CATEGORIZATION   Several methods— e.g. clustering in recall (see Srull 1984), cued-recall (Uleman 1987), and release from proactive inhibition (Mills & Tyrrell 1983)—have been used to show various bases of classification. The most popular method is one pioneered by Taylor et al (1978) in which perceivers are asked to indicate which of several group members made a given remark. Errors within category (e.g. assigning a remark made by one man to another man) are compared with between-category errors (assigning a comment by a man to a woman). When people make an error of assignment *within* a category, they are assumed to have encoded the remark in terms of that category. (It is also possible, however, that other cues associated with the category—e.g. hair style with gender—actually provide the basis for encoding.) Gender, race (Taylor et al 1978), and physical attractiveness (Miller 1988) cue more preponderance of intracategory memory errors than expected by chance.

Another method uses reaction times in what is called a category verification task (Zarate & Smith 1990). Subjects are asked whether or not an image depicts a female (or a male, a black, a white, etc). Response speed for accurate responses can be used as an index of category accessibility, and this can be related to various perceiver variables. For example, Zarate & Smith found that female faces could be categorized as female faster by females than by males and that male faces could be correctly categorized faster by males than by females. Zarate & Smith also found that speed on the racial verification task correlated positively with a measure of racial stereotyping.

CATEGORY ACCESSIBILITY   The accessibility of categories can be increased (primed) by recent and frequent activation, controlled activation of goals, or situational demands. Such effects have been discussed often (Bargh 1989; Higgins 1989; Smith 1990; Wyer & Srull 1989), but interpretations vary substantially. They may be due to schema activation, with bin (Srull & Wyer 1989) and synapse (Higgins et al 1985) metaphors having been prominent. Higgins & Stangor (1988) argue that accessibility variations are examples of general context effects. Smith (1988) suggest that a category becomes more accessible through addition of exemplars to its representation, Smith & Branscombe (1988) discuss category accessibility in terms of implicit memory effects (see Roediger et al 1989), and Smith et al (1988) and Smith (1989a) argue that inference procedures rather than content schemata are primed. Clearly our theoretical cups run over in this area.

CAN WE CONTROL THE EFFECTS OF CATEGORIZATION?   Can we avoid categorizing and stereotyping each other? At present we understand neither the categorization processes that must be controlled nor how such control might be exerted, although Bargh (1989), Fiske (1989), and Uleman (1989) provide illuminating discussions of this issue's complexities.

At a minimum the issue involves two major questions. First, can we control how we categorize people? Categorizations such as gender and race are probably so well practiced that they cannot be inhibited, but other categorizations probably can be. In addition, given that persons can be put into multiple categories, perceivers may be able to "override" primary race and gender categories with others—e.g. one might make a successful conscious effort to think of this black woman as a lawyer instead of as a woman or as black.

Second, what happens to subsequent information processing once categorization has taken place? Categorization brings in its wake inferences and assumptions. Once a person is classified as a male, it may be all too easy to stereotype him as assertive. Fiske (1989) has argued that we can somewhat control the inferences we draw by trying to pay attention to a person's individual attributes.

Devine (1989) suggests that although inferences follow certain kinds of categorization fairly automatically, some individuals can more or less consciously use their own values and knowledge to break this cognitive connection thereby reducing prejudice. On the other hand, D. T. Gilbert and J. G. Hixon (unpublished) show that race stereotypes are not activated when perceivers are busy at other tasks, suggesting that such categorizations are far from automatic (i.e. they require significant cognitive resources); once a stereotype is activated, however, busy people are more likely than idle ones to make stereotypic inferences, presumably because they need to use cognitive shortcuts.

New and Different Attribution Models

THE CLASSIC MODEL   Although most work on schema-based processing deals with content schemata, various processing schemata have also received attention in the recent literature. The schema properties of balance theory are tested occasionally (Hummert et al 1990); but the most intensively studied of the processing schemata are attribution models, especially the classic one proposed by Kelley (1967). A trend toward more concrete attribution models is apparent.[2]

Kelley originally proposed that attributions follow Mill's (1872) method of logic. According to this model (which is formally similar to analysis of variance), we can answer the question "Why did Jon fail the test?" if we have consensus information (how many others also failed), distinctiveness information (how Jon performed on other tests), and consistency information (Jon's performance on the same test at several times). According to Kelley, people will make actor attributions (Jon is stupid or poorly motivated) when consensus and distinctiveness are low, and consistency is high (everyone else did well, Jon failed all tests and always failed this test), whereas they will make entity attributions (the test was hard) when all three are high (many others also failed, Jon did well on other tests, but he always failed this one). While earlier tests of the model seemed to support this basic logic, several inconsistencies in the data and the logic have given rise to reformulations of the model.

Criticisms   Hilton (1988) summarizes most of the criticisms of Kelley's model. One of its problems is that by positing only three highly abstract kinds of information (e.g. consensus) the model ignores an attributor's considerable

---

[2]In his unpublished paper, "Attribution theory and research: returning to Heider's conceptions," Eliot Smith discusses some of the issues in this section from the standpoint of recent processing models in social cognition.

schematic knowledge about particular situations and behavior (Read 1987). For example, most people know why parents help their crying infants without having to do an explicit attributional analysis.

Many theorists have criticized research based on the Kelley model for being unfaithful to the ANOVA metaphor in not providing sufficient data to subjects (Jaspers 1983; Försterling 1989). With three possible attributions—to person, entity, and circumstances—the full design should comprise person 1 vs person 2, entity 1 vs entity 2, and time 1 vs time 2; but in attribution model research subjects are typically given information about only three or four of the cells. In particular, perceivers are usually not told how the other actor(s) behaved with respect to other entities at other times. Kelley's model also ignores the ability of attributors to distinguish between necessary and sufficient causes.

Perhaps the most telling criticisms are that the underlying logic of the Kelley model is vague and unnecessarily complex (Jaspers 1983; Jaspers et al 1983; Hilton & Slugoski 1986; Hewstone & Jaspers 1987; Hilton 1990).

THE ABNORMAL CONDITIONS TEST   Informal models of causation face a major epistemological problem: The set of possible causes for any event is huge, if not infinite (see Hesslow 1988). Potential causes of Jon's failure on the test thus may be thought to include his having been born (and everything else that ever happened to him), the test having been given (and everything else connected with the test's existence), and so on. Since the time of Mill, but particularly for the last 25 years or so, philosophers have wrestled with how we sort through this causal jungle to identify The Cause.

According to the abnormal conditions model (Hilton & Slugoski 1986), attributions are made to those conditions that stand out. So when Jane fails the test and others do not (Kelley's low consensus), she stands out; conversely, when she performs just the way others do Jane seems normal. If Jane fails this test but not others, the test stands out as a cause, and if Jane fails this test once but not another time, circumstantial factors become prominent. If two or more causes stand out as abnormal, then both are used in making the attribution. So if Jane fails the test while others pass, and if Jane rarely fails tests, we might have explanatory recourse to some combination of Jane-causes and test-causes—Jane doesn't take this kind of test well. Classic attribution research shied away from such hybrid attributions, but they are probably common in everyday life. For example, having concluded that Sue loves him, Jack attributes her love not to his being especially lovable or to her being especially loving but to a particular chemistry (read: entity-actor attribution).

Thus a major advantage of the abnormal conditions model is that it requires perceivers to coordinate each source of information with one and only one type of attribution; it does not require the more complex pattern matching of the original Kelley version. Nor does this model restrict attributions to the usual actor-entity-circumstance trio of factors, since it assumes attributors to have many complex attribution possibilities at their disposal.

Another potential advantage of the abnormal conditions model is its explicit recognition that attributional processing is not context free. The perception of abnormality is a matter not only of information presented but also of presuppositions that perceivers bring to the task. So when we discover that June hated the juicy steak, we are predisposed to see something about June as the cause, given our assumption that most people like steak juicy. In particular for highly scripted activities, high consensus and low distinctiveness information is already assumed. People seek consensus information only when it cannot be presupposed from their store of cultural knowledge (Hilton et al 1988). For example, we're told Harry goes to the bar and has a drink. The information that everyone else at the bar also had a drink and that Harry also drinks when he goes to other bars does little to help us make attributions about Harry, since it is already part of our knowledge about bar going.

CONVERSATIONAL CONTEXTS   Turnbull & Slugoski (1988), Hilton (1990), and others argue that in forming attributions perceivers make assumptions based on context in much the way people in conversation do. For example, when one person asks another why Jim drove to the store, social context and voice inflections would indicate what the questioner already knew and what she wanted to know. For example, knowing that the store was only a block away the questioner might wonder why Jim *drove* instead of walked to the store. Alternatively, if there were many potential drivers, the questioner might want to know why *Jim* (and not someone else) did the driving, and so forth. It follows that the ways attributional questions are phrased affect the kinds of attributions. "Why did you, in particular, pick this major" elicits actor attributions whereas "Why did you you pick this major, in particular" yields more attributions to the major (McGill 1989). Thus attributional processing depends heavily on various contexts, most notably a social context that operates according to familiar Gricean principles of conversation. These newer models have moved toward the Jones & Davis (1965) emphasis on contrastive reasoning and information gain and away from the traditional Kelley approach based on abstract processing schemata.

THE BEHAVIOR-TRAIT CONNECTION

Some would argue that the central issue in social cognition is how and under what circumstances perceivers infer traits and other discrete attributes from behavior. Surprisingly little attention has been devoted to this issue over the years.

Attributional Approaches

Heider (1958) suggested that the attribution of dispositional properties (which includes traits) was a central feature of social cognition. Upon the formation of various attribution models, however, trait attribution somehow got lost in a welter of more global questions about internal and external causality. Correspondence Inference Theory (Jones & Davis 1965) spoke directly to issues of how we attribute specific qualities to others, but research oriented to that theory has tended to focus on attitude attribution and tests of what is now called correspondence bias. It might be claimed that internal or actor attributions are basically the same as trait attributions, but work by Bassili (1989a) suggests that such attributions are not always isomorphic and are differentially sensitive to various information conditions.

THE IDENTIFICATION OF BEHAVIOR   The behavior-to-trait link seems clear enough. A perceiver observes behavior and then does or does not infer a corresponding trait. There are bound to be several steps in the process. In the first step, which Trope (1986) calls the *identification phase,* the behavior must be categorized and labeled. Most behaviors can be labeled in various ways, at various levels of generality (Vallacher & Wegner 1985; Semin & Fiedler 1988). Behaviors are probably identified in terms of accessible categories, but relatively little research has been published on interpretation of behavior outside of laboratory settings.

SPONTANEOUS TRAIT ATTRIBUTIONS   Most accounts of trait inference (e.g. Jones & Davis 1965) follow the general approach of social cognition in postulating that once behavior has been labeled in some way there ensues a conscious, effortful inference process involving formal attributional reasoning; but inference from behavior to trait can also be spontaneous and nonconscious (Newman & Uleman 1989; Gilbert 1989; Lupfer et al 1990; Smith 1989b). Scholars debate how automatic such trait inferences are and whether inferred traits are summaries of behavior or are immediately assigned to persons (see Newman & Uleman 1989; Bassili 1989b).

Quick and cognitively effortless inferences may have a schematic basis but are more likely to be examples of procedural efficiency. Smith (1989b) has shown that practice at inferring traits from behavior leads to dramatic improvements in speed of processing. Some of the effect is specific to judging whether behaviors indicate specific traits, but practice also affects the general trait-inference process (Smith et al 1988; Smith 1989a).

DISPOSITIONAL INFERENCE   Trope (1986; Trope & Cohen 1989) holds that in the *dispositional-inference stage* a deliberate judgment is made that the observed person has a specific disposition, typically a trait. At both the behavior-identification and dispositional-inference stages situational and behavioral cues as well as prior expectations about the person play a role in the trait-attribution process. Trope and Srull & Wyer (1989) note that such prior expectations can be based on knowledge about people in general, on the categorization of people (i.e. stereotypes), or on acquaintance with the individual in question. Because most past attribution research has focused on perceptions about strangers, we know little about how such expectations affect our perceptions about people we know well; yet the latter may be not only more interesting theoretically but more important in our lives.

A CORRECTION STAGE   Gilbert (1989) has argued that there are two distinct processes in Trope's disposition-inference stage. In the first, which Gilbert calls the *characterization* stage, perceivers automatically attribute behaviors to a corresponding disposition. In the *correction* stage the perceiver may consciously take situational information into account to correct an already implicit dispositional inference. Thus when I see Jan performing what I consider to be a friendly behavior, I spontaneously characterize her as friendly. Subsequently, however, I may determine that the situation imposed friendliness and decide that Jan is not so amiably disposed after all.

The Trope and Gilbert models agree in many important ways, but Trope believes situational information is generally processed early, often, and consciously, whereas Gilbert believes such information is taken into account late if at all.

Several elegant experiments have tested Gilbert's model. Assume that those parts of the attribution process that require conscious attention should be more disrupted than the automatic parts by additional cognitive tasks. Cognitive busyness should thus affect Gilbert's correction stage (which requires conscious weighing of situational and behavioral information) more than it does the characterization stage (where traits are implied directly by behavior). Gilbert's studies demonstrate that people do take less account of situational reasons for behavior when cognitively busy than when idle (Gilbert et al 1988; Gilbert & Osborne 1989); owing presumably to interference with the correction stage, the "busy" subjects assign too much causality to dispositions and not enough to the situation. The initial characterization phase is not disrupted by cognitive overload, which suggests that inferring a trait from behavior is a more automatic process than the presumed subsequent correction (Lupfer et al 1990).

The Information in Stimuli: Social Ecology

Most social cognition theories assume that the stimuli of the social world (e.g. the behaviors of other people) are subject to cognitive distortion by schemata and other knowledge structures because behavior is inherently ambiguous

(Schneider et al 1979). In recent years this assumption has been challenged. Some scholars assert that social stimuli contain enough information to provide at least beginning levels of meaning without elaborate cognitive processing (McArthur & Baron 1983).

PERSONALITY INFERENCES FROM FACES   Those who insist on the informativeness of stimuli have tended to focus on personality inferences from facial displays. For example, Zebrowitz-McArthur and her students (e.g. Berry & McArthur 1986) have shown that baby-faced adults are perceived to be less dominant than more mature-appearing adults and to exhibit more childish personality attributes. Perhaps natural selection has left human adults particularly sensitive to the distinctive bodily and facial conformations of their young. In any event, adults evidently apply their perceptions about the young to other adults who resemble children.

POINT-LIGHT DISPLAYS   Perceivers asked to view a darkened human figure with points of light attached (such that only the lights are seen as the figure moves) easily glean information about gender, age, physical effort, and attributes such as power and happiness (Berry 1990a; Montepare & Zebrowitz-McArthur 1988). At a minimum these reports suggest that mere physical movement has considerable information value, but they do not tell us why or even how extensively our cognitive systems are involved in such activity. One interpretation is that after literally millions of encounters with faces and moving bodies, we have abstracted essential and fairly primitive features that we more or less automatically associate with certain age, gender, and trait variables.

DO BEHAVIOR AND APPEARANCE CONVEY PERSONALITY?   Evidence is available that links some personality traits to superficial behavior and appearance. Albright et al (1988), Watson (1989), and Berry (1990b) asked previously unacquainted subjects to rate one another almost immediately after meeting. Some inter-rater agreement was found with respect to certain personality traits. Moreover, these "naive" ratings significantly predicted the targets' self ratings along these dimensions. Berry (1990b) showed that trait ratings based on photographs of people predicted ratings by other perceivers not only after a brief acquaintanceship but also after a longer one. Consider an explanation of such results based on cultural stereotypes: If our culture teaches us that furrowed brows connote responsibility, and Joe's brow is furrowed more than Harriet's, Joe will be seen as more responsible by everyone. It is a bit harder to explain how Joe and Harriet come to join in this stereotype game, given that neither is likely to spend much time monitoring the furrows in their brows. An alternative explanation is that the cares and woes of acting responsibly lead naturally to certain facial expressions.

Regardless of the interpretation, such research suggests that at least some trait inferences are not driven by high-level cognitive processes such as those postulated by various attribution models.

THE BEHAVIOR STREAM   Newtson et al (1987) have provided an extensive and thought-provoking summary of Newtson's work on segmenting the behavior stream. Following Asch (1952), Newtson and his colleagues have argued that behavior is organized into natural patterns readily and naturally perceived by normal perceivers without much overlay from higher cognitive processes.

Combining Multiple Behaviors

VARIOUS MODELS   Wright & Mischel (1987) propose a non-attributional view of the inference of traits from behaviors. Their model, heavily influenced by continuing debates over personality assessment, holds that perceivers have multiple, situation-contingent means of assigning traits. First, for example, perceivers might assign traits after calculating rates of behavior: A person who performs many helpful behaviors over a defined period and across many situations will be seen as helpful. Second, the perceiver might find certain situations particularly diagnostic of helpfulness: A woman who helps when most people don't will be seen as particularly helpful. Third, perceivers might carry personality prototypes in memory: A helpful person is one who does X and Y when such and such conditions obtain. The contingency aspect of this model jibes closely with Heider's conceptions of dispositional qualities. After all, a vase with a disposition to fragility only breaks when sufficient force of the proper sort is applied.

THE ROLE OF SITUATIONAL CONTINGENCIES   Several experiments have shown that people do take situational contingencies into account when assigning traits (Wright & Mischel 1988; Shoda et al 1989). A situational-contingency model has several advantages. First, it does not claim that situational and personal influences are mutually exclusive; it holds that both kinds of information are useful for trait attributions, and that no trade-off between the two is necessary. Second, it agrees with the findings discussed above suggesting that people use exemplar information and base social judgments on concrete information rather than abstract summaries. Third, this model implies that expertise affects social judgments. Obviously the person who has more experience with particular trait domains will have a clearer sense of those behaviors for which situational contingencies are especially relevant (Dawson et al 1989).

Not All Traits Are Created Equal

Some behaviors lend themselves better than others to trait inference. Put another way, somewhat different attribution rules seem to apply for different trait categories. In the pioneering work of Heider there were strong hints that this should be so, but early suggestions and demonstrations of different attributional outcomes for different types of dispositions (McArthur 1972) went largely unnoticed.

THE LINGUISTIC MODEL   Early work by Brown & Fish (1983) showed that some verbs (e.g. in "John hit Mary") bias perceivers toward making John (actor) attributions whereas others ("Mary astonishes John") tend to lead to Mary (the stimulus or entity) attributions. These two kinds of verb have been called action and experience verbs, respectively; they can be distinguished on the basis of a variety of linguistic criteria (Miller & Johnson-Laird 1976). Roger Brown has preferred to term the first kind actor-patient verbs ("John [actor] hits Mary [patient]"), the second kind either experiencer-stimulus ("John [experiencer] admires Mary [stimulus]") or stimulus-experiencer verbs ("Mary [stimulus] astonishes John [experiencer]"). (The latter two sub-kinds do not differ in attributionally fundamental ways.) Note that the distinctions we're considering here have nothing to do with the grammatical status of subject and object; indeed the verbs imply causality in either the grammatically active or passive voice.

Experience verbs   Research confirms that the experience verbs (whether experiencer-stimulus or stimulus-experiencer) tend to be understood as assigning causality to the stimulus: John admires Mary because (we tend to assume) she is admirable and not because John is generally admiring; and when told that Mary astonishes John, we are disposed to think it's because she is an astonishing person, not because he is routinely astonishable. Such results have frequently been confirmed with American samples and also occur in a variety of other languages (Au 1986; Van Kleeck et al 1988; Brown & Van Kleeck 1989).

Note that these verbs do not declare a causal direction; they only dispose us to a certain attribution. John may indeed be an indiscriminately astonishable or admiring sort of guy. The dispositional force of such verbs can be tempered by traditional consensus and distinctiveness information (Van Kleeck et al 1988).

Action verbs   Most action verbs tend to assign causality to the actor (the person doing the hitting, yelling, helping), but there are many exceptions (Au 1986); for example, when John praises Mary, Mary is given more causal weight than John.

Why the differences?   Why do verbs produce the effects discussed above? Brown and his colleagues suggest that language usage simply reflects real and fundamental differences among types of behaviors and reactions, but another way to think about the process is in terms of commonness and distinctiveness. In the case of experience verbs, we impute to all people the capacities to love, be astonished, hate, and admire—i.e. to be experiencers—but we impute to fewer people the capacities to stimulate these experiences; thus the stimuli seem rarer, draw more cognitive attention, and seem more causal. Similarly in the case of action verbs, all people can be hit or helped (i.e. be patients), but fewer people are hitters or helpers (agents); thus a statement with an action verb draws our attention to the agent.

Fiedler & Semin (1988) argue that people base causal inferences about sentences on the behavioral context in which they occur. "To help", for example, implies a different sort of prior relationship between people than does "to like," and such context may guide reaction to the two verbs.

A continuum of verbs   The differences among verbs run deeper than a mere linguistic difference between two categories. Semin & Fiedler (1988) argue that language exhibits a continuum of abstractness ranging from *descriptive action verbs* (call, lift, visit), to *interpretative action verbs* (command, hurt, manipulate) to *state verbs* (admire, understand) to *adjectives* (brutal, fair). Thus the same behavior might be described in various ways: "Jim hit Sam," "Jim hurt Sam," "Jim hates Sam," and "Jim was hostile." Such statements vary in how much they reveal about the actor; how enduring, verifiable, and disputable the action or state is; and how much they tell us about the situation. Linguistic abstractness varies across contexts in interesting ways. For example, more abstract descriptors are preferred for positive in-group and negative out-group characteristics than for the reverse (Maass et al 1989).

STRUCTURAL DIFFERENCES AMONG TRAITS   The structural and psychological properties of traits vary a good deal.

Confirmability of traits   Rothbart & Park (1986) suggest that ease of confirmability varies among traits. Negatively evaluated traits, for example, were seen as easy to confirm (in the sense of requiring few confirming behaviors before the attribution is made) and difficult to disconfirm (in the sense of requiring many disconfirming behaviors before the attribution is changed). Positively evaluated traits, on the other hand, are hard to acquire and easy to lose. So subjects reported that it would take few disagreeable behaviors to lead them to decide that a person is offensive and many agreeable ones to decide that a person is kind or nice. Funder & Dobroth (1987) generally confirmed the patterns of correlation found by Rothbart & Park, although they did not find as strong an inverse relationship between confirmability and disconfirmability.

Dispositional nature of traits   Traits differ in stability, causality, duration, situational scope (Chaplin et al 1988), breadth (Hampson et al 1986), and relevance (Paunonen 1988). Following up on earlier work by Gifford (1975), Schneider & Fazio (unpublished) examined correlations among the Rothbart & Park measures as well as other measures such as perceived centrality to personality, perceived stability, and the like. A factor analysis produced five interpretable factors: social desirability, openness to observation, pervasiveness, deep-seatedness, and situation-boundness. It remains to be seen, of course, whether such differences among traits make a major difference in the ways traits are used by naive perceivers.

Asymmetrical attributions   Reeder & Brewer (1979) suggested a complementary analysis of two classes of traits. For *partially restrictive* traits, both confirming and disconfirming behaviors are possible though not equally likely. We expect a person we consider stubborn to behave stubbornly much of the time but are not surprised by his occasional flexible response. *Hierarchically restrictive* traits, on the other hand, allow less leeway. For example, most perceivers assume that honest people are not likely to display dishonest behaviors; a person who behaves dishonestly even once or twice tends to be labeled as dishonest. On the other hand, we assume that a dishonest person may perform both honest and dishonest behaviors. This model suggests that honest behaviors are not especially diagnostic since both honest and dishonest people can display them, whereas dishonest behaviors are diagnostic because they can only be displayed by the dishonest person. Thus there can be a more direct link between dishonest behaviors and the corresponding trait than between honest, stubborn, or flexible behaviors and their dispositions.

Reeder & Brewer suggested that hierarchically restrictive traits tend to concern morality and ability. Immoral and high-ability behaviors should produce stronger trait inferences than moral and low-ability behaviors. That this is the case has been confirmed by subsequent research (Reeder 1985; Reeder & Coovert 1986). D. Trafimow and D. J. Schneider (unpublished) show that behavior led to stronger trait inferences for hierarchically restrictive traits than for partially restrictive ones; situational pressures and person expectancies had less impact on inferences about hierarchically restrictive than on those about partially restrictive traits. Skowronski & Carlston (1987) show that immoral, high-ability, and extreme behaviors are seen as especially diagnostic; such behaviors are weighted heavily in impressions (Skowronski & Carlston 1989).

IS BIAS INEVITABLE OR CAN PEOPLE JUDGE OTHERS ACCURATELY?

Modern theories of social cognition tend to emphasize bias and error in cognitive activities. To some extent the fascination with error and bias seems natural or is at least a close relation of the interest most people seem to have with the abnormal and the negative. In any event social psychologists over the years have exhibited a certain amount of glee in showing all the ways our cognitive systems can play us wrong.

Nonetheless a renewed interest in accuracy has become apparent in recent years.[3] The two approaches are complementary, since people may extract information from their environment accurately and then, given certain processing goals, fail to make optimal use of it.

Problems

FOCUS ON INDIVIDUAL DIFFERENCES   Empirical work before the 1960s tended to focus on individual differences in accuracy, even though such differences account for vanishing small proportions of variance of judgments. This practice has probably retarded the study of accuracy.

THE CRITERION PROBLEM   In order to assess the accuracy with which perceivers judge the characteristics of others we must know what the judged person is actually like: We require a criterion of accuracy (see Schneider et al 1979). Most research on accuracy (Kenny & Albright 1987) has used one of the major content criteria: self-report, third-person judgments, objective (often behavioral) measurement, mean judge ratings, and operational criteria (e.g. targets are told to lie and the issue is whether this can be detected).

Process-oriented approaches to accuracy have their own perspectives on the criteria of accuracy. Hastie & Rasinski (1988) suggest that if some cue (e.g. higher voice pitch) is known to be objectively correlated with some criterion to be predicted (e.g. honesty), then judges' failures to use the cue constitutes an error. Similarly if some cue (e.g. failure to maintain eye contact) that is known to be uncorrelated with the criterion is used by the judge in making judgments, this also counts as process error. Much of the work of the past decade on error and bias uses one or both of these criteria to assert that people often err.

MEASUREMENT   Measurement of accuracy is tricky. One reason accuracy research died out for 25 years or so was the well-known fact that differences

---

[3]Industrial-organizational psychologists have retained a lively interest in rating accuracy over the years and have made advances in the arts of measuring it (see Sulsky & Balzer 1988 for a recent discussion). I am indebted to Bob Dipboye for reminding me of this literature.

between judges' ratings and criterion scores have several components (Cronbach 1954). A recent reanalysis of the Cronbach components and a redefinition of some in terms of dyadic interaction are available (Kenny & Albright 1987).

In Defense of Accuracy

People process social information ineffectively and inelegantly at times, and we are cognitively better equipped for some tasks than for others. However, over the years there have been several attempts to defend the epistemological integrity of the lay perceiver. Swann (1984) argued that although perceivers may be globally inaccurate about a person (incorrectly believing that Joe is generally hostile, for example) they may know more accurately how Joe will behave in specific situations (Joe is generally hostile when inebriated). Swann noted that at least some of this circumscribed accuracy results from the fact that perceptions of Joe as hostile may (owing to various self-confirming prophecy mechanisms), make Joe hostile around the perceiver. Of course a particular perceiver may also be *more* accurate about Joe's general tendencies than about his more circumscribed ones.

Swann (1984), McArthur & Baron (1983), Funder (1987), and others have also charged that the laboratory (where most tendencies to err are demonstrated) is an environment that places the average subject at a disadvantage. In the lab subjects are cut off from a rich ecology of cues that may promote greater accuracy. In addition, a kind of pragmatic accuracy may ultimately be more significant than accuracy based on correspondence to some criterion (Swann 1984; Kruglanski 1989a). For example, while Joe may not score high on a well-defined test of extroversion, those who know Joe may have more satisfactory interactions with him by assuming he is extroverted. Whether Joe is really extroverted may matter less than whether he is defined as such in some cultural or social sense.

In the laboratory we may try to measure a degree of accuracy inappropriate to everyday life. The gross judgment that Barb is introverted may suffice to facilitate casual social interactions. Just as playing an old record on a high-fidelity sound system can obscure the music by emphasizing surface noise and substandard recording techniques, so the laboratory technologies we use to measure accuracy may magnify low attribution fidelities that are irrelevant to normal social interaction.

Research

TRAITS AND STIMULUS PERSONS   Rhetoric has outstripped research about accuracy issues in recent years, but a few empirical studies have been published. Perhaps the most surprising finding has been that of a nontrivial agreement among perceivers about target-person traits, even after the briefest of acquaintanceships. Such "stranger" ratings predict targets' self-ratings, and perceivers' predictions of targets' self-ratings improve when the perceiver and target are better acquainted (Funder & Colvin 1988; Park & Judd 1989; Watson 1989). Traits or dimensions that are rated as being highly visible and "objective" (e.g. extroversion) are more accurately judged by others than those rated less visible (e.g. emotional stability) (Park & Judd 1989; Funder & Colvin 1989; Watson 1989).

OTHER DETERMINANTS   Situational and motivational factors ought to affect accuracy, but this turns out to be a complex issue. Consider motivational factors. If inaccurate attributions result from simple inattention or careless-ness, then a desire to be accurate might improve accuracy; but it is not clear that people can will themselves to avoid bias and be rational, let alone accurate (Kruglanski 1989a,b). Similarly, many of our inaccuracies stem not from too little information but from too little sense of how to cope with what information we have. For example, Tetlock & Boettger (1989) have shown that accountability to others (which generally reduces bias) can increase a perceiver's attention to task-irrelevant as well as task-relevant details and can actually decrease the accuracy of predictions.

Global accuracy of attribution may be less important to social life than knowledge of various interactions between persons and situations. I may gain more from my social environment by knowing in what sorts of situations particular friends are angry or nice than by knowing which friends are globally angry or nice. Wright & Dawson (1988) have examined how sensi-tive perceivers are to the relationship between situation and behavior. They made use of extensive observations of boys' behavior in a variety of settings at a summer camp for boys considered to have behavioral problems. Camp counselors who knew the children and their situations well were asked to rate them for a variety of traits. Counselor ratings of aggression correlated highly (.75) with observed aggression aggregated across several situations and occa-sions. Ratings of other traits, such as withdrawal, were not as accurate, presumably because this trait was not as directly relevant to the activities of the camp. Observers were also fairly accurate in predicting the variability of the children's aggression, but not their withdrawal, across situations.

Conclusions

There seems little point in arguing global issues of accuracy, because in making judgments people depend on a variety of experiential and situational variables.

Processing models also bring a subtle bias with them. When we compare human performance on cognitive tasks against precisely defined and cali-brated models of *processing,* errors stand out. By contrast, when we think about accuracy and bias in terms of *content* we may be less inclined to expect high-fidelty cognition, the content of the world being fluid and ill defined. In the everyday world, if not always in the laboratory, people often make judgments about others that are accurate by the broad criteria culture provides.

WHERE, OH WHERE, IS THE SOCIAL IN SOCIAL COGNITION?

During the last decade social cognition researchers have relied increasingly on the models and methods of general cognitive psychology. Social psychology has always been a borrower in just this way. During the heyday of behaviorism, many theories in social psychology were heavily dependent on learning and associated motivation theories. Recall, as an example, how much emphasis Festinger placed on the language of drives in his theories of social comparison and cognitive dissonance.

However, social psychologists have returned at least as much as they have borrowed. At its best social psychology is an integrative discipline,[4] applying ideas from other fields to issues of everyday thought and behavior in all their macroscopic glory. At less than its best, however, social cognition research can be more concerned with the latest fashions from cognitive psychology than with social phenomena.

Social and Nonsocial Stimuli

What distinguishes social cognition from other kinds? Similarities in the ways physical, verbal, and social stimuli are processed may have blinded social cognition theorists to the possibility that social and nonsocial stimuli differ fundamentally. For pathways into the literature on this issue see Zajonc (1980), Schneider et al (1979), Lingle et al (1984), Ostrom (1984), Brewer (1988), and Feldman (1988).

Social Effects on Cognition

Soft social cognition tended to argue that social cognition is an area of inquiry, a set of problems that require cognitive answers. We lose this focus on issues at our peril. Maintaining this focus might encourage us to ask about the effects of social variables on cognitive processes. However, the effect of social and cultural variables upon cognitive processes has not proved a popular topic among psychologists, in part because no one is sure what the problems, paradigms, and methods of such a research enterprise might be. I

---

[4] I am indebted to the participants at the informal seminar, "Social Psychology: Past, Present, and Future," in honor of Al Hastorf at Stanford University in December, 1989, for forcibly but agreeably reminding me of these and other points.

see two approaches one might take. The first is to examine the cognitive implications of a social variable. For example, Mullen (1990) has recently summarized several meta-analytic studies in which proportionate size of in- and out-groups is shown to affect (among other variables) self-focused attention, social projection, in-group bias, and binocular resolution effects.

SOCIAL MEMORY   In a second approach, one would assess how social variables affect a single cognitive process. Given the centrality of person memory over the last decade, let's consider a social memory model.

Social factors can affect memory in many ways. [Wegner (1987) provides an illuminating discussion in a provocative paper on transactive memory, and Ostrom (1989) briefly discusses social memory.] First, our knowledge structures are to some degree cultural products. How Americans understand a Tom Clancy thriller, for example, depends on socially acquired knowledge about war, espionage, and violence. Second, groups often assign memory roles to members (Wegner 1987)—e.g. an organization is built of people charged with remembering various subsets of the informational whole. Third, our sometimes feeble attempts at remembering often take place in a social context. A husband and wife, for example, may try to fashion a mutual "memory" from their disparate recollections of a vacation trip.

Clark & Stephenson (1989) summarized data showing that group remembering is more accurate than individual. Is this because group members stimulate one another with better retrieval cues? Does the context of the group itself help in terms of encoding specificity mechanisms? How do groups as opposed to individuals handle the processing of schema-incongruent information? What might a structural model of group memory look like?

All macro cognitive processes are likely subject to social influence. In formal organizations there are those who specialize in attention, recognition, labeling, encoding, and retrieval. In a typical husband and wife team, one partner recognizes problems the other does not, one labels their child's misbehavior naughty while the other sees it as normal, and each recalls different aspects of their joint lives.

Such distributions of cognitive processes and information have consequences (Resnick et al 1991). For example, Stasser and his colleagues (Stasser & Titus 1987; Stasser et al 1989) have begun to explore the effects of shared and unshared information on group performance.

COMMUNICATION   Social psychology devotes too little attention to communication, an obviously important social mechanism that links cognitive processes and social behavior. One line of research (e.g. Zajonc 1960; Higgins et al 1982; Fussell & Krauss 1989; Sedikides 1990) shows that when we communicate to others and when we think "to ourselves" we organize our thoughts in different ways, surely a fundamental point. The demands of communication are among the most primitive and important ways cognition is affected by social variables.

IN CONCLUSION

Whether a field or an approach, whether hard or soft, social cognition is alive and well and feeling strong. Its successes are obvious, its message seductive. Yet, traditional hard social cognition has dominated social cognition in ways that have not been altogether happy. Few would wish to return to the issues and methods of the 1970s, but perhaps we can now have the best of both approaches—the rigor of hard social cognition and the focused attention to the social world fostered by the older, soft approach.

ACKNOWLEDGMENTS

I thank John Bargh, Susan Fiske, Dave Hamilton, Dan Gilbert, Brain Mullen, Tom Ostrom, Bernadette Park, Glenn Reeder, Eliot Smith, Chuck Stangor, Jim Uleman, and Dan Wegner for their comments on an earlier draft of this paper.

Literature Cited

Abramson, L. Y., Metalsky, G. I., Alloy, L. B. 1989. Hopelessness depression: a theory-based subtype of depression. *Psychol. Rev.* 96:358–72

Albright, L., Kenny, D. A., Malloy, T. E. 1988. Consensus in personality judgments at zero acquaintance. *J. Pers. Soc. Psychol.* 55:387–95

Alicke, M. D., Davis, T. L. 1989. The role of a posteriori victim information in judgments of blame and sanction. *J. Exp. Soc. Psychol.* 25:362–77

Asch, S. 1952. *Social Psychology.* Englewood Cliffs, NJ: Prentice-Hall

Au, T. K. 1986. A verb is worth a thousand words: the causes and consequences of interpersonal events implicit in language. *J. Mem. Lang.* 25:104–22

Banaji, M. R., Crowder, R. G. 1989. The bankruptcy of everyday memory. *Am. Psychol.* 44:1185–93

Bar-Tal, D., Kruglanski, A. W., eds. 1988. *The Social Psychology of Knowledge.* Cambridge: Cambridge Univ. Press

Bargh, J. A. 1989. Conditional automaticity: varieties of automatic influence in social perception and cognition. See Uleman & Bargh 1989, pp. 3–51

Bassili, J. N. 1989a. Trait encoding in behavior identification and dispositional in-ference. *Pers. Soc. Psychol. Bull.* 15:285–96

Bassili, J. N. 1989b. Traits as action categories versus traits as person attributes in social cognition. See Bassili 1989c, pp. 61–90

Bassili, J. N., ed. 1989c. *On-Line Cognition in Person Perception.* Hillsdale, NJ: Erlbaum

Berry, D. S., McArthur, L. Z. 1986. Perceiving character in faces: the impact of age-related craniofacial changes on social perception. *Psychol. Bull.* 100:3–18

Berry, D. S. 1990a. What can a moving face tell us?. *J. Pers. Soc. Psychol.* 58:1004–14

Berry, D. S. 1990b. Taking people at face value: evidence for the kernel of truth hypothesis. *Soc. Cognit.* In press

Bodenhausen, G. V., Lichtenstein, M. 1987. Social stereotypes and information-processing strategies: the impact of task complexity. *J. Pers. Soc. Psychol.* 52:871–80

Borgida, E., Brekke, N. 1981. The base rate fallacy in attribution and prediction. In *New Directions in Attribution Research,* ed. J. H. Harvey, W. Ickes, R. F. Kidd, 3:63–95. Hillsdale, NJ: Erlbaum

Bradbury, T. N., Fincham, F. D. 1990. Attributions in marriage: review and critique. *Psychol. Bull.* 107:3–33

Brewer, M. B. 1988. A dual process model of impression formation. *Adv. Soc. Cognit.* 1:1–36

Brown, R., Fish, D. 1983. The psychological causality implicit in language. *Cognition* 14:237–73

Brown, R., Van Kleeck, M. H. 1989. Enough said: three principles of explanation. *J. Pers. Soc. Psychol.* 57:590–604

Carpenter, S. L. 1988. Self-relevance and goal-directed processing in the recall and weighting of information about others. *J. Exp. Soc. Psychol.* 24:310–32

Catrambone, R., Markus, H. 1987. The role of self-schemas in going beyond the information given. *Soc. Cognit.* 5:349–68

Chaplin, W. F., John, O. P., Goldberg, L. R. 1988. Conceptions of states and traits: dimensional attributes with ideals as prototypes. *J. Pers. Soc. Psychol.* 54:541–57

Cronbach, L. J. 1954. Processes affecting scores on "understanding of others" and "assumed similarity". *Psychol. Bull.* 52:177–93

Clark, N. K., Stephenson, G. M. 1989. Group remembering. In *Psychology of Group Influence*, ed. P. B. Paulus, pp. 357–91. Hillsdale, NJ: Erlbaum

Dawson, V. L., Zeitz, C. M., Wright, J. C. 1989. Expert-novice differences in person perception: evidence of experts' sensitivities to the organization of behavior. *Soc. Cognit.* 7:1–30

Devine, P. G. 1989. Stereotypes and prejudice: their automatic and controlled components. *J. Pers. Soc. Psychol.* 56:5–18

Devine, P. G., Ostrom, T. M. 1988. Dimensional versus information-processing approaches to social knowledge: the case of inconsistency management. See Bar-Tal & Kruglanski 1988, pp. 231–61

Devine, P. G., Sedikides, C., Fuhrman, R. W. 1989. Goals in social information processing: the case of anticipated interaction. *J. Pers. Soc. Psychol.* 56:680–90

Dunning, D., Parpal, M. 1989. Mental addition versus subtraction in counterfactual reasoning: on assessing the impact of personal actions and life events. *J. Pers. Soc. Psychol.* 57:5–15

Erber, R., Fiske, S. T. 1984. Outcome dependency and attention to inconsistent information. *J. Pers. Soc. Psychol.* 47:709–26

Esses, V. M. 1989. Mood as a moderator of acceptance of interpersonal feedback. *J. Pers. Soc. Psychol.* 57:769–81

Feldman, J. 1988. Objects in categories and objects as categories. *Adv. Soc. Cognit.* 1:53–64

Fiedler, K., Semin, G. 1988. On the causal information conveyed by different interpersonal verbs: the role of implicit sentence context. *Soc. Cognit.* 6:21–39

Fiske, S. T. 1988. Compare and contrast: Brewer's dual process model and Fiske et al.'s continuum model. *Adv. Soc. Cognit.* 1:65–76

Fiske, S. T. 1989. Examining the role of intent: toward understanding its role in stereotyping and prejudice. See Uleman & Bargh 1989, pp. 253–86

Fiske, S. T., Neuberg, S. L. 1990. A continuum of impression formation, from category-based to individuating processes: influences of information and motivation on attention and interpretation. *Adv. Exp. Soc. Psychol.* 23:1–74

Fiske, S. T., Neuberg, S. L., Beattie, A. E., Milberg, S. J. 1987. Category-based and attribute-based reactions to others: some informational conditions of stereotyping and individuating processes. *J. Exp. Soc. Psychol.* 23:399–407

Fiske, S. T., Taylor, S. E. 1984. *Social Cognition*. Reading, MA: Addison-Wesley

Forgas, J. P., Burnham, D. K., Trimboli, C. 1988. Mood, memory, and social judgments in children. *J. Pers. Soc. Psychol.* 54:697–703

Försterling, F. 1989. Models of covariation and attribution: How do they relate to the analogy of analysis of variance? *J. Pers. Soc. Psychol.* 57:615–25

Fuhrman, R. W., Wyer, R. S. Jr. 1988. Event memory: temporal-order judgments of personal life expectancies. *J. Pers. Soc. Psychol.* 54:365–84

Funder, D. C. 1987. Errors and mistakes: evaluating the accuracy of social judgment. *Psychol. Bull.* 101:75–90

Funder, D. C., Colvin, C. R. 1988. Friends and strangers: acquaintanceship, agreement, and the accuracy of personality judgment. *J. Pers. Soc. Psychol.* 55:149–158

Funder, D. C., Dobroth, K. M. 1987. Differences between traits: properties associated with interjudge agreement. *J. Pers. Soc. Psychol.* 52:409–18

Fussell, S. R., Krauss, R. M. 1989. The effects of intended audience on message production and comprehension: reference in a common ground framework. *J. Exp. Soc. Psychol.* 25:203–19

Gavanski, I., Wells, G. L. 1989. Counterfactual processing of normal and exceptional events. *J. Exp. Soc. Psychol.* 25:314–25

Gifford, R. K. 1975. Information properties of descriptive words. *J. Pers. Soc. Psychol.* 31:727–34

Gilbert, D. T. 1989. Thinking lightly about others: automatic components of the social inference process. See Uleman & Bargh 1989, pp. 189–211

Gilbert, D. T., Krull, D. S., Pelham, B. W. 1988. Of thoughts unspoken: social inference and the self-regulation of behavior. *J. Pers. Soc. Psychol.* 55:685–94

Gilbert, D. T., Osborne, R. E. 1989. Thinking backward: some curable and incurable consequences of cognitive busyness. *J. Pers. Soc. Psychol.* 57:940–49

Glick, P., Zion, C., Nelson, C. 1988. What mediates sex discrimination in hiring decisions?. *J. Pers. Soc. Psychol.* 55:178–86

Greenwald, A. G., Banaji, M. R. 1989. The self as a memory system: powerful but ordinary. *J. Pers. Soc. Psychol.* 57:41–54

Hamilton, D. L., Sherman, S. J. 1989. Illusory correlations: implications for stereotype theory and research. In *Stereotyping and Prejudice: Changing Conceptions*, ed. D. Bar-Tal, C. F. Graumann, A. W. Kruglanski, W. Stroebe, pp. 59–82. NY: Springer-Verlag

Hampson, S. E., John, O. P., Goldberg, L. R. 1986. Category breadth and hierarchical structure in personality: studies of asymmetricalities in judgments of trait implications. *J. Pers. Soc. Psychol.* 51:37–54

Hastie, R., Rasinski, K. A. 1988. The concept of accuracy in social judgment. See Bar-Tal & Kruglanski 1988, pp. 193–208

Heider, F. 1958. *The Psychology of Interpersonal Relations.* NY: Wiley

Hesslow, G. 1988. The problem of causal selection. See Hilton 1988, pp. 11–32

Hewstone, M., Jaspers, J. 1987. Covariation and causal attribution: a logical model of the intuitive analysis of variance. *J. Pers. Soc. Psychol.* 53:663–72

Higgins, E. T. 1989. Knowledge accessibility and activation: subjectivity and suffering from unconscious sources. See Uleman & Bargh 1989, pp. 75–123

Higgins, E. T., Bargh, J. A. 1987. Social cognition and social perception. *Annu. Rev. Psychol.* 38:369–425

Higgins, E. T., Bargh, J. A., Lombardi, W. 1985. The nature of priming effects on categorization. *J. Exp. Psychol.: Learn., Mem. Cogn.* 11:59–69

Higgins, E. T., McCann, C. D., Fondacaro, R. 1982. The "communication game": goal-directed encoding and cognitive consequences. *Soc. Cognit.* 1:21–37

Higgins, E. T., Stangor, C. 1988. Context-driven social judgment and memory when "behavior engulfs the field" in reconstructive memory. See Bar-Tal & Kruglanski 1988, pp. 262–98

Higgins, E. T., Van Hook, E., Dorfman, D. 1988. Do self-attributes form a cognitive structure? *Soc. Cognit.* 6:177–207

Hilton, D. J. 1988. Logic and causal attribution. See Hilton 1988, pp. 33–65

Hilton, D. J., ed. 1988 *Contemporary Science and Natural Explanation: Commonsense Perceptions of Causality.* Brighton, England: The Harvester Press

Hilton, D. J. 1990. Conversational processes and causal explanation. *Psychol. Bull.* 107:65–81

Hilton, D. J., Slugoski, B. R. 1986. Knowledge-based causal attribution: the abnormal conditions focus model. *Psychol. Rev.* 93:75–88

Hilton, D. J., Smith, R. H., Alicke, M. D. 1988. Knowledge-based information acquisition: norms and the functions of consensus information. *J. Pers. Soc. Psychol.* 55:530–40

Hilton, J. L., Fein, S. 1989. The role of typical diagnosticity in stereotype-based judgments. *J. Pers. Soc. Psychol.* 57:201–11

Hintzman, D. L. 1986. "Schema abstraction" in a multiple-trace memory model. *Psychol. Rev.* 93:411–28

Holtgraves, T., Srull, T. K., Socall, D. 1989. Conversation memory: the effects of speaker status on memory for the assertiveness of conversation remarks. *J. Pers. Soc. Psychol.* 56:149–60

Hummert, M. L., Crockett, W. H., Kemper, S. 1990. Processing mechanisms underlying use of the balance schema. *J. Pers. Soc. Psychol.* 58:5–21

Ickes, W., Robertson, E., Tooke, W., Teng, G. 1986. Naturalistic social cognition: methodology, assessment, and validation. *J. Pers. Soc. Psychol.* 51:66–82

Jaspers, J. M. F. 1983. The process of attribution in common sense. In *Attribution Theory: Social and Functional Extensions*, ed. M. R. C. Hewstone, pp. 28–44. Oxford: Basil Blackwell

Jaspers, J. M. F., Hewstone, M. R. C., Fincham, F. D. 1983. Attribution theory and research: the state of the art. In *Attribution Theory: Conceptual, Developmental, and Social Dimensions*, ed. J. M. F. Jaspers, F. D. Fincham, M. R. C. Hewstone, pp. 3–36. London: Academic

Johnson, M. H., Magaro, P. A. 1987. Effects of mood and severity on memory processes in depression and mania. *Psychol. Bull.* 101:28–40

Jones, E. E., Davis, K. E. 1965. From acts to dispositions: the attribution process in person perception. *Adv. Exp. Soc. Psychol.* 2:219–76

Judd, C. M., Park, B. 1988. Out-group homogeneity: judgments of variability at the individual and group levels. *J. Pers. Soc. Psychol.* 54:778–88

Karlovac, M., Darley, J. M. 1988. Attribution of responsibility for accidents: a negligence law analogy. *Soc. Cognit.* 6:287–318

Kelley, H. H. 1967. Attribution theory in social psychology. In *Nebraska Symposium on Motivation*, ed. D. Levine, pp. 192–238. Lincoln: Univ. Nebraska Press

Kenny, D. A., Albright, L. 1987. Accuracy in interpersonal perception: a social relations analysis. *Psychol. Bull.* 102:390–402

Kim, H., Baron, R. S. 1988. Exercise and the illusory correlation: Does arousal heighten stereotypic processing. *J. Exp. Soc. Psychol.* 24:366–80

Klein, S. B., Loftus, J. 1988. The nature of self-referent encoding: the contributions of elaborative and organizational processes. *J. Pers. Soc. Psychol.* 55:5–11

Klein, S. B., Loftus, J., Burton, H. A. 1989. Two self-reference effects: the importance of distinguishing between self-descriptiveness judgments and autobiographical retrieval in self-referent encoding. *J. Pers. Soc. Psychol.* 56:853–65

Krueger, J., Rothbart, M. 1988. Use of categorical and individuating information in making inferences about personality. *J. Pers. Soc. Psychol.* 55:187–95

Kruglanski, A. W. 1989a. The psychology of being "right": the problem of accuracy in social perception and cognition. *Psychol. Bull.* 106:395–409

Kruglanski, A. W. 1989b. *Lay Epistemics and Human Knowledge: Cognitive and Motivational Bases.* NY: Plenum

Kunda, Z., Sanitioso, R. 1989. Motivated changes in the self-concept. *J. Exp. Soc. Psychol.* 25:272–85

Lassiter, G. D. 1988. Behavior perception, affect, and memory. *Soc. Cognit.* 6:150–76

Lassiter, G. D., Stone, J. I., Rogers, S. L. 1988. Memorial consequences of variation in behavior perception. *J. Exp. Soc. Psychol.* 24:222–39

Lingle, J. H., Altom, M. W., Medin, D. L. 1984. Of cabbages and kings: assessing the extendability of natural concept models to social things. See Wyer & Srull 1984, 1:71–117

Linville, P. W., Fischer, G. W., Salovey, P. 1989. Perceived distributions of the characteristics of in-group and out-group members: empirical evidence and a computer simulation. *J. Pers. Soc. Psychol.* 57:165–88

Locksley, A., Borgida, E., Brekke, N., Hepburn, C. 1980. Sex stereotypes and social judgment. *J. Pers. Soc. Psychol.* 39:821–31

Logan, G. A. 1989. Automaticity and cognitive control. See Uleman & Bargh 1989, pp. 52–74

Lupfer, M. B., Clark, L. F., Hutcherson, H. W. 1990. Impact of context on spontaneous trait and situational attributions. *J. Pers. Soc. Psychol.* 58:239–49

Maass, A., Salvi, D., Arcuri, L., Semin, G. 1989. Language use in intergroup contexts: the linguistic intergroup bias. *J. Pers. Soc. Psychol.* 57:981–93

Mackie, D. M., Hamilton, D. L., Schroth, H. A., Carlisle, C. J., Gersho, B. F., et al. 1989. The effects of induced mood on expectancy-based illusory correlations. *J. Exp. Soc. Psychol.* 25:524–44

McArthur, L. 1972. The how and what of why: some determinants and consequences of causal attribution. *J. Pers. Soc. Psychol.* 22:171–93

McArthur, L. Z. 1982. Judging a book by its cover: a cognitive analysis of the relationship between physical appearance and stereotyping. In *Cognitive Social Psychology*, ed. A. Hastorf, A. Isen, pp. 149–211. NY: Elsevier North-Holland

McArthur, L. Z., Baron, R. M. 1983. Toward an ecological theory of social perception. *Psychol. Rev.* 90:215–38

McGill, A. L. 1989. Context effects in judgments of causality. *J. Pers. Soc. Psychol.* 57:189–200

Medin, D. L. 1988. Social categorization: structures, processes, and purposes. *Adv. Soc. Cognit.* 1:119–26

Medin, D. L. 1989. Concepts and conceptual structure. *Am. Psychol.* 44:1469–81

Mill, J. S. 1973 [1872]. System of logic. In *Collected Works of John Stuart Mill*, ed. J. M. Robson. Toronto: Univ. Toronto Press. 8th ed.

Miller, C. T. 1988. Categorization and the physical attractiveness stereotype. *Soc. Cognit.* 6:231–51

Miller, D. T., Turnbull, W., McFarland, C. 1989. When a coincidence is suspicious: the role of mental simulation. *J. Pers. Soc. Psychol.* 57:581–89

Miller, G. A., Johnson-Laird, P. N. 1976. *Language and Perception.* Cambridge, MA: Harvard Univ. Press

Mills, C. J., Tyrrell, D. J. 1983. Sex-stereotypic encoding and release from proactive interference. *J. Pers. Soc. Psychol.* 45:772–81

Montepare, J. M., Zebrowitz-McArthur, L. 1988. Impressions of people created by age-related qualities of their gaits. *J. Pers. Soc. Psychol.* 55:547–56

Mullen, B. 1990. Group composition, salience, and cognitive representations: the phenomenology of being in a group. *J. Exp. Soc. Psychol.* In press

Mullen, B., Johnson, C. 1990. Distinctiveness-based illusory correlations and stereotyping: a meta-analytic integration. *Brit. J. Soc. Psychol.* 29:11–28

Neisser, U. 1978. Memory: What are the important questions? In *Practical Aspects of Memory*, ed. M. M. Gruneberg, P. E. Morris, R. N. Sykes, pp. 3–24. London: Academic

Neisser, U. 1988. What is ordinary memory the memory of? In *Remembering Reconsidered: Ecological and Traditional Approaches to the Study of Memory*, ed. U. Neisser, E. Winograd, pp. 356–373. Cambridge: Cambridge Univ. Press

Neuberg, S. L. 1989. The goal of forming accurate impressions during social interactions: attenuating the impact of negative expectancies. *J. Pers. Soc. Psychol.* 56:374–86

Neuberg, S. L., Fiske, S. T. 1987. Motivational influences on impression formation: outcome dependency, accuracy-driven attention, and individuating processes. *J. Pers. Soc. Psychol.* 53:431–44

Newman, L. S., Uleman, J. S. 1989. Spontaneous trait inference. See Uleman & Bargh 1989, pp. 155–88

Newtson, D., Hairfield, J., Bloomingdale, J., Cutino, S. 1987. The structure of action and interaction. *Soc. Cognit.* 5:191–237

Nosofsky, R. M. 1986. Attention, similarity, and the identification-categorization relationship. *J. Exp. Psychol.: Gen.* 115:39–57

Ostrom, T. M. 1984. The sovereignty of social cognition. See Wyer & Srull 1984, Vol. 1, pp. 1–38

Ostrom, T. M. 1988. Computer simulation: the third symbol system. *J. Exp. Soc. Psychol.* 24:381–92

Ostrom, T. M. 1989. Three catechisms for social memory. In *Memory: Interdisciplinary Approaches*, ed. P. R. Solomon, G. R. Goethals, C. M. Kelley, B. R. Stephens, pp. 201–20. NY: Springer-Verlag

Ostrom, T. M. 1990. The maturing of social cognition. *Adv. Soc. Cognit.* 3:153–63

Park, B., Hastie, R. 1987. Perception of variability in category development: instance-versus abstraction-based stereotypes. *J. Pers. Soc. Psychol.* 53:621–35

Park, B., Judd, C. M. 1989. Agreement on initial impressions: differences due to perceivers, trait dimensions, and target behaviors. *J. Pers. Soc. Psychol.* 56:493–505

Paunonen, S. V. 1988. Trait relevance and the differential predictability of behavior. *J. Pers.* 56:599–619

Pavelchak, M. 1989. Piece-meal and category-based evaluation: an idiographic analysis. *J. Pers. Soc. Psychol.* 56:354–63

Pennebaker, J. W. 1989. Stream of consciousness and stress: levels of thinking. See Uleman & Bargh 1989, pp. 327–50

Read, S. J. 1987. Constructing causal scenarios: a knowledge structure approach to causal reasoning. *J. Pers. Soc. Psychol.* 52:288–302

Read, S. J., Miller, L. C. 1989. Interpersonalism: toward a goal-based theory of persons in relationships. In *Goal Concepts in Personality and Social Psychology*, ed. L. Pervin, pp. 413–72. Hillsdale, NJ: Erlbaum

Reeder, G. D. 1985. Implicit relations between dispositions and behaviors: effects on dispositional attribution. In *Attribution: Basic Issues and Applications*, ed. J. H. Harvey, G. Weary, pp. 87–116. NY: Academic

Reeder, G. D., Brewer, M. B. 1979. A schematic model of dispositional attribution in interpersonal perception. *Psychol. Rev.* 86:61–79

Reeder, G. D., Coovert, M. D. 1986. Revising an impression of morality. *Soc. Cognit.* 4:1–17

Resnick, L., Levine, J., Behrend, S., eds. 1991. *Perspectives on Socially Shared Cognition*. Washington, DC: Am. Psychol. Assoc. In press

Rholes, W. S., Riskind, J. H., Lane, J. W. 1987. Emotional states and memory biases: effects of cognitive priming and mood. *J. Pers. Soc. Psychol.* 52:91–99

Rodin, M. 1987. Who is memorable to whom: a study of cognitive disregard. *Soc. Cognit.* 5:144–65

Roediger, H. L. 1990. Review of "Remembering Reconsidered: Ecological and Traditional Approaches to the Study of Memory." *Am. J. Psychol.* 103:403–9

Roediger, H. L., Weldon, M. S., Challis, B. H. 1989. Explaining dissociations between implicit and explicit measures of retention: a processing account. In *Varieties of Memory and Consciousness: Essays in Honor of Endel Tulving*, ed. H. L. Roediger, F. I. M. Craik, pp. 3–41. Hillsdale, NJ: Erlbaum

Ross, M. 1989. Relation of implicit theories to the construction of personal histories. *Psychol. Rev.* 96:341–57

Rothbart, M., John, O. P. 1985. Social categorization and behavioral episodes: a cognitive analysis of the effects of intergroup contact. *J. Soc. Issues* 41:81–104

Rothbart, M., Lewis, S. 1988. Inferring category attributes from exemplar attributes: geometric shapes and social categories. *J. Pers. Soc. Psychol.* 55:861–72

Rothbart, M., Park, B. 1986. On the confirmability and disconfirmability of trait concepts. *J. Pers. Soc. Psychol.* 50:131–42

Ruble, D. N., Stangor, C. 1986. Stalking the elusive schema: insights from developmental and social-psychological analyses of gender schemas. *Soc. Cognit.* 4:227–61

Ruscher, J. B., Fiske, S. T. 1990. Interpersonal competition can cause individuating processes. *J. Pers. Soc. Psychol.* 58:832–43

Sanbonmatsu, D. M., Shavitt, S., Sherman, S. J., Roskos-Ewoldsen, D. R. 1987a.

Illusory correlation in the perception of performance by self or a salient other. *J. Exp. Soc. Psychol.* 23:518–43

Sanbonmatsu, D. M., Sherman, J. J., Hamilton, D. L. 1987b. Illusory correlation in the perception of individuals and groups. *Soc. Cognit.* 5:1–25

Schaller, M., Maass, A. 1989. Illusory correlation and social categorization: toward an integration of motivational and cognitive factors in stereotype formation. *J. Pers. Soc. Psychol.* 56:709–21

Schneider, D. J., Hastorf, A. H., Ellsworth, P. C. 1979. *Person Perception.* Reading, MA: Addison-Wesley. 2nd ed

Sedikides, C. 1990. Effects of fortuitously activated constructs versus activated communication goals. *J. Pers. Soc. Psychol.* 58:397–408

Semin, G. R., Fiedler, K. 1988. The cognitive functions of linguistic categories in describing persons: social cognition and language. *J. Pers. Soc. Psychol.* 54:558–68

Sherman, S. J., Judd, C. M., Park, B. 1989. Social cognition. *Annu. Rev. Psychol.* 40:281–326

Shoda, Y., Mischel, W., Wright, J. C. 1989. Intuitive interactionism in person perception: effects of situation-behavior relations on dispositional judgments. *J. Pers. Soc. Psychol.* 56:41–53

Skowronski, J. J., Carlston, D. E. 1987. Social judgment and social memory: the role of cue diagnosticity in negativity, positivity, and extremity bias. *J. Pers. Soc. Psychol.* 52:689–99

Skowronski, J. J., Carlston, D. E. 1989. Negativity and extremity biases in impression formation: a review of explanations. *Psychol. Bull.* 105:131–42

Smith, E. R. 1988. Category accessibility effects in a simulated exemplar-based memory. *J. Exp. Soc. Psychol.* 24:448–63

Smith, E. R. 1989a. Procedural efficiency: general and specific components and effects on social judgment. *J. Exp. Soc. Psychol.* 25:500–23

Smith, E. R. 1989b. Procedural efficiency and on-line social judgments. See Bassili 1989, pp. 19–38

Smith, E. R. 1990. Content and process specificity in the effects of prior experiences. *Adv. Soc. Cognit.* 3:1–91

Smith, E. R., Branscombe, N. R. 1988. Category accessibility as implicit memory. *J. Exp. Soc. Psychol.* 24:490–504

Smith, E. R., Branscombe, N. R., Bormann, C. 1988. Generality of the effects of practice on social judgment tasks. *J. Pers. Soc. Psychol.* 54:385–95

Smith, E. R., Zarate, M. A. 1990. Exemplar and prototype use in social categorization. *Soc. Cognit.* In press

Srull, T. K. 1984. Methodological techniques for the study of person memory and social cognition. See Wyer & Srull 1984, Vol. 2, pp. 1–72

Srull, T. K., Wyer, R. S. Jr. 1989. Person memory and judgment. *Psychol. Rev.* 96:58–83

Stangor, C., Ruble, D. N. 1989. Strength of expectancies and memory for social information: What we remember depends on how much we know. *J. Exp. Soc. Psychol.* 25:18–35

Stasser, G., Taylor, L. A., Hanna, C. 1989. Information sampling in structured and unstructured discussions of three- and six-person groups. *J. Pers. Soc. Psychol.* 57:67–78

Stasser, G., Titus, W. 1987. Effects of information load and percentage of shared information on the dissemination of unshared information during group discussion. *J. Pers. Soc. Psychol.* 53:81–93

Sulsky, L. M., Balzer, W. K. 1988. Meaning and measurement of performance rating accuracy: some methodological and theoretical concerns. *J. Appl. Psychol.* 73:497–506

Swann, W. B. Jr. 1984. Quest for accuracy in person perception: a matter of pragmatics. *Psychol. Rev.* 91:457–77

Swann, W. B. Jr., Pelham, B. W., Chidester, T. R. 1988. Change through paradox: using self-verification to alter beliefs. *J. Pers. Soc. Psychol.* 54:268–73

Swann, W. B. Jr., Pelham, B. W., Krull, D. S. 1989. Agreeable fancy or disagreeable truth? Reconciling self-enhancement and self-verification. *J. Pers. Soc. Psychol.* 57:782–91

Swim, J., Borgida, E., Maruyama, G., Myers, D. G. 1989. Joan McKay versus John McKay: Do gender stereotypes bias evaluations? *Psychol. Bull.* 105:409–29

Taylor, S. E., Fiske, S. T., Etcoff, N. L., Ruderman, A. J. 1978. Categorical and contextual bases of person memory and stereotyping. *J. Pers. Soc. Psychol.* 36:778–93

Tesser, A., Pilkington, C. J., McIntosh, W. D. 1989. Self-evaluation maintenance and the mediational role of emotion: the perception of friends and strangers. *J. Pers. Soc. Psychol.* 57:442–56

Tetlock, P. E., Boettger, R. 1989. Accountability: a social magnifier of the dilution effect. *J. Pers. Soc. Psychol.* 57:388–98

Tetlock, P. E., Kim, J. I. 1987. Accountability and judgment processes in a personality prediction task. *J. Pers. Soc. Psychol.* 52:700–9

Trope, Y. 1986. Identification and inferential

processes in dispositional attribution. *Psychol. Rev.* 93:239–57

Trope, Y. 1989. Levels of inference in dispositional judgment. *Soc. Cognit.* 7:296–314

Trope, Y., Cohen, O. 1989. Perceptual and inferential determinants of behavior-correspondent attributions. *J. Exp. Soc. Psychol.* 25:142–58

Turnbull, W., Slugoski, B. R. 1988. Conversational and linguistic processes in causal attribution. See Hilton 1988, pp. 66–93

Uleman, J. S. 1987. Consciousness and control: the case of spontaneous trait inferences. *Pers. Soc. Psychol. Bull.* 13:337–54

Uleman, J. S. 1989. The self-control of thoughts: a framework for thinking about unintended thought. See Uleman & Bargh 1989, pp. 425–49

Uleman, J. S., Bargh, J. A., eds. 1989. *Unintended Thought.* NY: Guilford

Vallacher, R. R., Wegner, D. M. 1985. *A Theory of Action Identification.* Hillsdale, NJ: Erlbaum

Van Kleeck, M., Hillger, L., Brown, R. 1988. Pitting verbal schemas against information variables in attribution. *Soc. Cognit.* 6:89–106

Watkins, M. J. 1990. Mediationism and the obfuscation of memory. *Am. Psychol.* 45:328–35

Watson, D. 1989. Strangers' ratings of the five robust personality factors: evidence of a surprising convergence with self-report. *J. Pers. Soc. Psychol.* 57:120–28

Wegner, D. M. 1987. Transactive memory: a contemporary analysis of the group mind. In *Theories of Group Behavior,* ed. B. Mullen, G. R. Goethals, pp. 185–208. NY: Springer-Verlag

Wegner, D. M. 1989. *White Bears and Other Unwanted Thoughts.* NY: Viking

Wegner, D. M., Schneider, D. J. 1989. Mental control: the war of the ghosts in the machine. See Uleman & Bargh 1989, pp. 287–305

Wells, G. L., Gavanski, I. 1989. Mental simulation of causality. *J. Pers. Soc. Psychol.* 56:161–69

Wenzlaff, R. M., Prohaska, M. L. 1989. When misery prefers company: depression, attributions, and responses to others' moods. *J. Exp. Soc. Psychol.* 25:220–33

Wright, J. C., Dawson, V. L. 1988. Person perception and the bounded rationality of social judgment. *J. Pers. Soc. Psychol.* 55:780–94

Wright, J. C., Mischel, W. 1987. A conditional approach to dispositional constructs: the local predictability of social behavior. *J. Pers. Soc. Psychol.* 53:1159–77

Wright, J. C., Mischel, W. 1988. Conditional hedges and the intuitive psychology of traits. *J. Pers. Soc. Psychol.* 55:454–69

Wyer, R. S. Jr., Budesheim, T. L., Lambert, A. J. 1990. Cognitive representation of conversations about persons. *J. Pers. Soc. Psychol.* 58:218–38

Wyer, R. S. Jr., Srull, T. K., eds. 1984. *Handbook of Social Cognition,* Vols. 1–3. Hillsdale, NJ: Erlbaum

Wyer, R. S. Jr., Srull, T. K. 1989. *Memory and Cognition in Its Social Context.* Hillsdale, NJ: Erlbaum

Zajonc, R. B. 1960. The process of cognitive tuning in communication. *J. Abnorm. Soc. Psychol.* 61:159–67

Zajonc, R. B. 1980. Cognition and social cognition: a historical perspective. In *Retrospectives on Social Psychology,* ed. L. Festinger, pp. 180–204. NY: Oxford Univ. Press

Zarate, M. A., Smith, E. R. 1990. Person categorization and stereotyping. *Soc. Cognit.* 8:161–85

Zuroff, D. C. 1989. Judgments of frequency of social stimuli: How schematic is person memory? *J. Pers. Soc. Psychol.* 56:890–98

AUTHOR INDEX

563

SUBJECT INDEX

CUMULATIVE INDEXES

CONTRIBUTING AUTHORS, VOLUMES 35–42

CHAPTER TITLES, VOLUMES 35–42

595